GIAMBATTISTA VICO

GIAMBATTISTA
VICO

AN INTERNATIONAL
SYMPOSIUM

Giorgio Tagliacozzo, Editor
Hayden V. White, Co-editor

Consulting Editors:

Isaiah Berlin

Max H. Fisch

Elio Gianturco

1969

The Johns Hopkins Press
Baltimore

THIS BOOK HAS BEEN BROUGHT TO PUBLICATION
WITH THE GENEROUS ASSISTANCE OF THE
EDGAR J. KAUFMANN CHARITABLE FOUNDATION.

The frontispiece is a reproduction of the plate facing page 3
of Giambattista Vico's *Scienza nuova* (Naples, 1744) and
was supplied by the University of Chicago Library.
The jacket illustration is taken from the editor's copy of
Vico's *Principi di scienza nuova . . .* (Naples, 1811).

Giorgio Tagliacozzo   PREFACE

I

The tercentenary year of Giambattista Vico's birth is particularly significant in that today a widespread diffusion of authentic Vichian thought is
possible for the first time.   As a consequence of cultural developments that
have taken place over the past several decades, the authentic Vico is being
discovered and is at last receiving the attention he deserves.   Without fault-
ing the enthusiasm for Vico evinced by so many thinkers in the time since
his death, the ideas and suggestions drawn from his work, its influences, and
the superior interpretive labors of scholars like Fausto Nicolini, it should be
said that the current return to Vico is largely a natural occurrence, a product
of many recent and interdependent circumstances.   Among those circumstances the following should be stressed: first, the emergence in the most
diverse fields of knowledge of viewpoints similar to those which occupied
Vico's mind (I refer to philosophical pragmatism, linguistic philosophy,
Gestalt psychology and the innumerable applications of the Gestalt concept,
phenomenology, organismic biology, genetic and social psychology,
cultural, philosophical, and structural anthropology, certain trends of
sociology and of the philosophy of history, the widespread anti-Cartesian
attitude, new pedagogic trends, the emergent biologico-genetic Weltanschauung, and so on); second, a more widely diffused awareness of the above-
mentioned analogies and parallels and hence of the possible usefulness of
knowing the fundamental principles of Vico's thought in order to discover
the roots of contemporary points of view and the concepts with which certain
problems might be solved; third, the existence of a cultural climate favorable
to a truly *objective* interpretation of Vico's thought.   By this I mean that the
current return to Vico is to a considerable extent a general and not infrequently unconscious collective activity, and that the new interpretation of
him, when it comes, will be a consequence of the necessary blending, combination, and possible synthesis of concepts from the most widely divergent
fields.   Until a short time ago, the interpretation of Vico's thought was
almost exclusively the work of individual scholars who stamped it with their
own particular characteristics; the Vichian ideas introduced into their works
were often uprooted from their natural context and forced into structures
which served to distort Vico's thought rather than to give a true account of it.

My stressing the necessity of this collective analysis of Vico is not meant to obscure the value of the several studies of Vico carried out in recent years, particularly in Italy, which have discredited old myths, shed light on many technical points, and opened up new prospects for study in the future.[1] One must, however, distinguish between the tide of the times and the work of a few individuals. The importance of that tide is an indisputable fact and an essential premise of the present return to Vico.

II

This international symposium bears witness to the return to the great Neapolitan philosopher. The following pages of introduction are intended to give the reader an idea of the presuppositions on which the symposium is based, the way it was put together, and the material that comprises it. In this connection, certain general aspects of the return to Vico and of the collective activity mentioned above should be stressed.

First, it should be noted that one of the most fertile fields for an authentic Vichian revival is the social sciences, taken in their broadest sense, that is, psychology, anthropology, sociology, economics, politics, history, geography, psychiatry, and law[2]—all disciplines to which Vico contributed or whose principles he anticipated. During the past few decades, the social sciences have advanced sensationally, particularly in the Anglo-Saxon countries, but up to twenty years ago no English translation of the *Scienza nuova* existed. In 1944 Max H. Fisch and Thomas Bergin published an English version of Vico's *Autobiografia*, prefaced by a long and very informative introduction by Fisch. But only in 1948 did the excellent translation of the *Scienza nuova*, by Bergin and Fisch, finally appear. This translation rendered Vico's major work accessible to thousands of scholars whose training had endowed them with a particular capacity to understand it, thereby giving a decisive impetus to that recovery of Vico mentioned above. Elio Gianturco's English translation of the *De nostri temporis studiorum ratione*, which appeared in 1965, continued the work begun by Bergin and Fisch, and was received with interest in American pedagogic circles.

Second, from a certain point of view the significance of the current return to Vico is quite different from any possible similar return to Plato, Thomas Aquinas, or Descartes.[3] In fact, even though there is always something new

[1] For a review of Vichian studies in Italy after Croce, see Paolo Rossi, "Lineamenti di storia della critica vichiana," in W. Binni, *I classici italiani nella storia della critica* (Florence, 1961), II, 38–41.

[2] See Editor's Introduction, *International Encyclopedia of the Social Sciences* (New York: Macmillan, 1968).

[3] Cf. my "Vico, oggi," a lecture delivered on May 15, 1968, at the Accademia dei

to discover in the work of great thinkers, or some new interpretation to place on their thought, it is also true that the thinkers mentioned above have "had their day"—in the sense that much of what they had to offer has already been absorbed. Each of them has served as a dominant authority for some era in the past in which his thought has permeated the whole of culture, so that, by the historical process itself, they have now been partly left behind in the general mainstream of Western culture. Vico, however, has not "had his day" in this sense. No interpretation of his thought has held out for long or permeated broad sectors of culture; and his influence—even though it has penetrated one field or another almost at random, quietly, as if by osmosis—has not so far made itself felt as a pervasive cultural accent. This is probably because Vico's thought embraced too many different aspects of too many cultural epochs, presupposed the simultaneous dissolution of too many traditions and commonplaces, and represented too original a synthesis to gain a hold at the time of its formulation or immediately thereafter. Certain isolated ideas of Vico's have struck later thinkers like flashes of light, but his thought as a whole has been neither understood completely nor utilized fully. Today, however, the time seems ripe for him, in the sense that the peaks Vico reached in one bound have gradually been conquered one by one over a long period, and his moment appears to have arrived.

Third, since Vico's authentic thought and its relationship with contemporary culture are still waiting to be discovered, and since no adequate or dominant interpretation of Vico's thought as a whole exists at present, the principal aims toward which Vichian research is inevitably directed are twofold: (1) a direct aim is to lay the groundwork for a future over-all reinterpretation based on investigations in all the innumerable fields which, because of the polyhedral nature of Vichian thought, such a reinterpretation will have to cover; and (2) an indirect aim is to glimpse a possible scheme for such a reinterpretation in the results of current Vichian studies.

III

The above-mentioned general view of the present-day return to Vico came to me as a result of particular circumstances in my life, and those circumstances have influenced the presuppositions of this symposium and the criteria for its constitution. A few explanations may be in order here. I first encountered Vichian thought thirty years ago,[4] and for the past twenty-

---

Lincei in Rome, on the occasion of the Convegno Internazionale "Campanella e Vico" held there May 12–15, 1968. All the lectures delivered at the Convegno will soon be published in a special volume of the *Atti* of the Accademia.

[4] During the preparation of the volume *Economisti napoletani dei secoli XVII e XVIII* (Bologna: Cappelli, 1937).

five years, as a lecturer on the history of ideas[5] and as editor of an international cultural radio program,[6] I have had to deal in considerable depth with the most divergent fields of culture, their origins and their historical vicissitudes. This has provided me with an opportunity to discover analogies to, or parallels with, Vichian thought (which I have borne in mind since that first encounter) in fields that I would not perhaps otherwise have considered. It also led me to reflect on the history of the problem of the unity of knowledge, the study of which is, in my opinion, essential to a full and profound understanding of the significance of Vico's thought.[7] Thus, when I later conceived the idea of editing an international symposium for the tercentenary of Vico's birth, I was inevitably inclined to consult with, and to invite the collaboration of, scholars in the most divergent disciplines as well as philosophers from the most varied schools.

At the beginning of 1965, reflecting on the possible significance of a re-examination of Vico's thought in the light of modern culture, particularly in view of its current importance in fields that had previously disregarded it, I was struck by the scant knowledge or distorted notion of it that generally prevailed and by the lack of an adequate interpretation of the whole. The idea came to me that the tercentenary celebrations presented an opportunity for the publication of an extensive international symposium volume which would, so to speak, focus on "Vico today," and which would also pave the way for any scholar who might in the future undertake the enormous task of preparing a comprehensive and unified work on Vico. I began by surveying the field, consulting with not only the few experts on Vico and authoritative exponents of disciplines which (as in the philosophy of history) have traditionally paid some attention to Vico's thought, but also, and mainly, the large number of scholars and scientists in fields which, unjustifiably but out of inveterate habit, have so far disregarded Vico: psychology, cultural anthropology, sociology, biology, pedagogy, and so on. In other words, initially my main task was to discuss with experts from the most varied fields those Vichian ideas which seemed to have a relationship—of derivation or by analogy—with some aspect of their fields, and, whenever an interesting point emerged from those discussions, to invite the expert concerned to submit an essay on that point for the proposed symposium.

During the next two years (from the spring of 1965 to the spring of 1967) I visited, telephoned, or wrote to a multitude of scholars all over the United States and made three trips to Europe to consult with anyone interested in Vico. From the very first (I remember particularly a long and illuminating

---

[5] At the New School for Social Research, New York.

[6] The program entitled *Università Internazionale Guglielmo Marconi da Nuova York*, prepared by me since 1945 for Radiotelevisione Italiana (RAI) in collaboration with the Voice of America and broadcast over the Italian Third Program.

[7] In this connection see the Epilogue to the present volume.

discussion in Washington with Isaiah Berlin in April, 1965) I was amazed at the interest and enthusiasm which the mention of Vico frequently evoked, even though it was not rare to find the enthusiasm tempered by a feeling of regret over an inadequate knowledge of, or familiarity with, him. This confirmed my notion that the incipient return to Vico that I had perceived was no mere chimera. This interest in Vico was all the more significant in that many of the scholars consulted were exponents of disciplines from which the name of Vico has so far been absent. This number included Margaret Mead and Claude Lévi-Strauss (anthropology); Michael Polanyi and Rudolph Arnheim (Gestalt psychology); Erich Fromm and Silvano Arieti (psychoanalysis); Edward Shils, Talcott Parsons, and Pitirim Sorokin (sociology); Ludwig von Bertalanffy, Theodosius Dobzhansky, René Dubos, and George Gaylord Simpson (biology); Jerome Bruner (psychology and pedagogy); Leo Strauss (political science); Stephen Toulmin (history of science), and so on. With regard to the attitude of the contributors, I like to recall the late Herbert Read's reply to my invitation: "It is really a question of my being well enough, but I am making good progress and although I must not make a definite promise I will place this commitment among my first priorities."

My contacts with over three hundred scholars on both sides of the Atlantic finally yielded the forty-one essays collected in this volume and provided a broad spectrum of data and opinions. Forty-one is a small number in comparison with the number of subjects that were or should have been discussed, but not so small when one considers that scholars are always overburdened by many commitments. Nonetheless, despite the inevitable imperfections and gaps, these essays are, I believe, sufficiently representative and, I hope, significantly indicative of the Vichian problems that are most pressing today and of the climate of opinion which is at present forming around Vico throughout the world.

IV

The subdivision of the symposium into four parts—*Comparative Historical Studies*; *Vico's Influence on Western Thought and Letters*; *Vico and Contemporary Social and Humanistic Thinking*; *Vico and Modern Philosophy, Pedagogy, and Aesthetics*—obviously has no more than an empirical significance. Nevertheless, a few brief comments on each part may be useful.

There is certainly no need to stress the importance for Vichian studies of the historical comparisons between Vico and certain thinkers or currents of thought both prior and subsequent to him; these comparisons obviously constitute *one* of the basic premises of any rethinking of Vico. For a number of easily understandable reasons the Italian scholars, beginning with Eugenio

Garin, are at present in the forefront of this research.   In his *Storia della filosofia italiana*,[8] Garin has probed profoundly the crucial problem at the root of the most vital historical comparisons with Vico, the problem which might be called "Vico and the Renaissance."   I look back with pleasure on more than one illuminating conversation with Garin on this and other Vichian topics, and should like to take the opportunity here to express the hope that he will elaborate further on the subject.   This would be, in my opinion, the most valuable service that a scholar of his talents could render toward a simultaneous understanding of the significance of the Renaissance, of Vico's thought, and of the most authentic stream of the Italian philosophical tradi-tion, not only in their individuality, universality, and affinity with modern thought, but also in their capacity as vital forces of contemporary culture.

I have stressed the fact that comparative historical studies relating to Vico constitute only *one* of the basic premises of any rethinking of that philosopher because at least one other basic premise exists: the need for the student of the past to feed and quicken his historical curiosity with a full awareness of present culture and a feeling for present problems.   Above all, I wanted to draw the attention of those Italian scholars who are in the forefront of com-parative studies relating to Vico (as demonstrated in the first part of this volume) to the kind of Vichian studies that prevail outside Italy and partic-ularly in the Anglo-Saxon countries (studies of the type included in the third and fourth parts of this volume), as well as introduce to non-Italian scholars the profound and indispensable contributions of a historico-comparative nature originating mainly in Italy.   In sum, it is possible to distinguish two foci in contemporary Vichian research: one whose point of departure and sphere of action are in the past, but which does not forget the present; and one which is immersed in the present but seeks its roots, relation-ships, and justifications in the past.   In my opinion, these two foci must exercise a reciprocal influence on each other, must converge and unite, if the current return to Vico is to yield all its potential fruits.   In short, in these days when an over-all reinterpretation is called for, the detailed "micro-scopic" studies of Vico and the broader "macroscopic" studies are equally important.

It is easy to appreciate the substantial difference between the above-mentioned comparative historical studies and those (which are exemplified in the second part) whose aim it is to clarify Vico's influence on Western thought and letters.   To appreciate these differences it is sufficient to reflect on the broad and extremely varied panorama of trends, fields, and authors which these studies encompass and on the necessity for them to lead to over-all judgments of such complicated material.   These, too, are important studies, since they may be able to dispel long-standing prejudices and to open up new historical avenues.

[8] (Turin: Einaudi, 1966), vol. II, chap. 5, pp. 920–54.

The studies on Vico and contemporary social and humanistic thinking and those on Vico and contemporary philosophy, pedagogy, and aesthetics—represented, respectively, in the third and fourth parts of this symposium—are those which reflect most specifically the collective activity repeatedly referred to above.   This activity is, as the symposium evinces, international and spontaneous; that is, it seems to be a product of the times rather than the result of the choice of a few scholars.   Its center of interest is the present (while searching for the roots of that present in the past), and its predominantly macroscopic approach represents the second of the two foci of the present-day return to Vico—that is, it takes its departure largely from the social sciences, linguistics, and those trends in contemporary philosophy, pedagogy, and aesthetics which are related to, or bound up with, the social sciences and linguistics.   It is noteworthy that the essays included in the third and fourth parts of this symposium bring to light "recourses" of ideas similar to Vico's, or *parallel* ideas, more frequently than *influences*.   But these are very significant "recourses" or parallels, which not infrequently lead to the discovery of historical gaps, unknown links, common sources, and even unsuspected indirect influences.   During my discussion of Vico and Dilthey with Garin, he indicated that it was not unlikely that the two thinkers had some Renaissance sources in common.

V

I said at the beginning that the collective Vichian activity now in progress has a second natural aim: to glimpse a possible scheme for a general reinterpretation of Vico's thought based on the results of current Vichian studies.   I shall not elaborate on this aim here since any conjectures that might be made on the subject presuppose a certain familiarity with the contents of the present volume.   I shall, however, indicate my viewpoint in this regard—which is that the future over-all reinterpretation of Vico's thought will hinge on the problem of the unity of knowledge—and shall expand upon it in the Epilogue to this volume, and I trust that in so doing I will succeed in further clarifying the reasons for the exceptional importance of Vico's thought today.

ACKNOWLEDGMENTS

This symposium was made possible by the participation of many distinguished scholars from several countries, to whom I wish to express my deepest gratitude, and also by a series of fortunate encounters with generous persons who gave me a helping hand precisely when I most needed it at every stage of the project.

My first and deepest thanks go to Professor Max H. Fisch, who has helped me in countless ways since we began corresponding in 1961 in connection with a course I was conducting at the New School for Social Research, in which Vico's thought was discussed as a premise to the analysis of contemporary cultural trends. Throughout the preparation of this volume Professor Fisch has been unstinting in his advice and assistance.

In the spring of 1965 I had the good fortune to discuss my ideas for an international symposium on Giambattista Vico with Sir Isaiah Berlin, on the occasion of his visit to Washington to deliver the Mellon lectures at the National Gallery of Art. His enthusiasm for Vico, his encouragement of my project, and his suggestions regarding possible European contributors were of immense help at that crucial stage.

The problem of obtaining financial assistance for this undertaking, involving overseas trips and translations from several foreign languages, was solved, thanks to the lively interest taken in the project by Mr. Edgar J. Kaufmann, Jr., President of the Edgar J. Kaufmann Charitable Foundation of Pittsburgh. Without this aid, the symposium might never have seen completion.

There are no words to express my gratitude to Professor Hayden V. White for generously accepting my invitation in August, 1967, to contribute his editorial skills, his Vichian scholarship, and his command of the English language to the symposium as its co-editor. From that moment on, Professor White has practically had full responsibility for editing the manuscripts and translations, in collaboration with Penny James of The Johns Hopkins Press, whose assistance has been invaluable. Professor White has also taken part in all decisions concerning the organization of the volume.

The problem of translations was solved when Professor Elio Gianturco, one of the consulting editors and an outstanding Vichian scholar, agreed to translate many of the foreign-language essays. He has also been helpful to me on many other occasions. I also wish to thank Professors Hayden V. White, James M. Edie, A. William Salomone, and Himilce Novás for their translations.

Finally, I want to remember with love and gratitude Barbara B.W., whose constructive criticism in the early 1950's immeasurably broadened my horizons in philosophy and social science.

GIORGIO TAGLIACOZZO

TABLE OF CONTENTS

CONTRIBUTORS

NICOLA BADALONI. Professor of History of Philosophy at the Facoltà di Lettere of the University of Pisa. Author of *La filosofia di Giordano Bruno* (1955), *Introduzione a G. B. Vico* (1961), *Marxismo come storicismo* (1962), the chapters on Giordano Bruno and Tommaso Campanella in volume V of the *Storia della letteratura italiana* (Milan: Garzanti), and of essays in various periodicals.

YVON BELAVAL. Professor of Philosophy at the Sorbonne and Vice-President of the Leibniz-Gesellschaft of Hanover. Author of *Leibnitz critique de Descartes* (1960), *Leibnitz: Introduction à sa philosophie* (1961), and of several articles on Leibniz and the history of Leibnizianism.

ISAIAH BERLIN. President, Wolfson College, Oxford. Author of *Karl Marx: His Life and Environment*, *Historical Inevitability*, *The Hedgehog and the Fox* (*A Study of Tolstoy's historical Scepticism*), and *Two Concepts of Liberty*.

DAVID BIDNEY. Professor of Anthropology and Philosophy at the University of Indiana. Author of *Theoretical Anthropology* and *Psychology and Ethics of Spinoza*.

GLAUCO CAMBON. Professor of Romance Languages and Comparative Literature at Rutgers University.

SANTINO CARAMELLA. Professor of Philosophy at the University of Palermo. Editor of *Antologia Vichiana* (1959). Author of *L'Estetica di Vico* (1959), *Metafisica Vichiana* (1961), *Conoscenza e Metafisica* (1966), *Introduzione a Kant* (1966), and *G. B. Vico* (1967).

RAMÓN CEÑAL, S.J. A member of the Instituto de Filosofía "Luis Vives" of Madrid. Author of several books and articles on the history of Spanish thought.

ANTONIO CORSANO. Professor of Philosophy at the Facoltà di Lettere e Filosofia of the University of Bari. Author of *Tommaso Campanella* (1944; 2d ed. 1961), *Ugo Grozio* (1948), and *G. B. Vico* (1956).

GIROLAMO COTRONEO. Assistente Ordinario to the Chair of Theoretical Philosophy of the Facoltà di Lettere e Filosofia of the University of Messina. Author of *Jean Bodin teorico della storia* (1966).

ENRICO DE MAS. Professor at the Istituto Superiore di Magistero in Pisa. Author of *Bacone e Vico* (1959) and *Francesco Bacone da Verulamio: La filosofia dell'uomo* (1964).

TULLIO DE MAURO. Professor of General Linguistics at the University of Rome. Author of *Storia linguistica dell'Italia unita* (1963), *Introduzione alla semantica* (1965), *Il linguaggio della critica d'arte* (1965), *Ludwig Wittgenstein: His Place in the Development of Semantics* (Dordrecht, 1967), and an introduction to F. de Saussure's *Corso di linguistica generale* (1967).

GILLO DORFLES. Professor of Aesthetics at the University of Milan. Author of many books, including *Il disegno industriale e la sua estetica* (1963), *Simbolo, comunicazione, consumo* (1962), and *Nuovi riti, nuovi miti* (1965).

JAMES M. EDIE. Associate Professor of Philosophy, Northwestern University. Editor of *What is Phenomenology?*, *Invitation to Phenomenology*, and *Phenomenology in America*. Coeditor of *Russian Philosophy* and *Christianity and Existentialism*.

DARIO FAUCCI. Libero Docente of Moral Philosophy at the University of Florence. Author of books on Italian neo-idealism, ethics in Plato and Aristotle, and aesthetics. Has made special studies in Holland on Grotius in preparation for the Italian edition of the *De jure belli ac pacis*.

MAX H. FISCH. Professor of Philosophy at the University of Illinois. His publications have been largely in the fields of history of science and philosophy. His Vichian works and translations are listed in the Bibliography of this volume.

RAFFAELLO FRANCHINI. Professor of Philosophy at the University of Messina. Author of *Esperienza dello storicismo* (1953), *Metafisica e storia* (1958), *Teoria della previsione* (1964), and *La teoria della storia di B. Croce* (1966).

ELIO GIANTURCO. Professor of Italian and Comparative Literature in the Department of Romance Languages at Hunter College. His Vichian works and translations are listed in the Bibliography of this volume.

MARIA GORETTI. Professor of History and Philosophy at the Liceo classico "M. Minghetti" in Bologna. Author of *Il paradosso Mandeville* (1958), *La scuola e il fanciullo* (1966), and other pedagogic books, and editor of an Italian edition of Vico's *De nostri temporis studiorum ratione* (1958).

ERNESTO GRASSI. Professor of Philosophy at the University of Munich. Editor of *Rowohlts deutsche Enzyklopädie* and of *Rowohlts Klassiker*. Author of *Il problema della metafisica platonica* (1933), *Vom Vorrang des Logos* (1946), *Verteidigung des individuellen Lebens* (1947), *Vom Ursprung der Geistes und Naturwissenschaften* (1950), *Kunst und Mythos* (1957), and *Die Theorie des Schönen in der Antike* (1962).

STUART HAMPSHIRE. Professor of Philosophy at Princeton University. Author of *Spinoza* (1951), *Thought and Action* (1959), *Freedom of the Individual* (1965), *Philosophy of Mind* (1966), and of articles in philosophical journals.

H. A. HODGES. Professor of Philosophy at the University of Reading, England. Author of *Wilhelm Dilthey: An Introduction* (1944) and *The Philosophy of Wilhelm Dilthey* (1952).

H. STUART HUGHES. Professor of History at Harvard University. Author of several books, notably *Consciousness and Society* (1958), *History as Art and as Science* (1964), and *The Obstructed Path* (1968).

EUGENE KAMENKA. Professorial Fellow in the History of Ideas in the Institute of Advanced Studies, Australian National University, and Professorial and Senior Fellow in the Research Institute on Communist Affairs, Columbia University. His books include *The Ethical Foundations of Marxism* (1962), *Marxist Ethics* (1967), and *The Philosophy of Ludwig Feuerbach* (in press).

GEORGE L. KLINE. Professor of Philosophy at Bryn Mawr College. Author of *Spinoza in Soviet Philosophy* (1952), translator of V. V. Zenkovsky's *History of Russian Philosophy* (1953), and co-editor of, and contributor to, *Russian Philosophy* (1953).

EDMUND LEACH. Provost of King's College, Cambridge, and University Reader in Social Anthropology. Author of several books and of numerous articles in anthropological journals. Editor of, and contributor to, various anthropological symposia.

A. WALTON LITZ. Associate Professor, Department of English, Princeton University. Author of *The Art of James Joyce* (1961) and editor of *Modern American Fiction: Essays in Criticism* (1963). Has published a number of studies on Joyce in learned journals.

ENZO PACI. Professor of Theoretical Philosophy at the University of Milan. Author of *Ingens Sylva: Saggio su Vico* (1957), *Tempo e relazione* (2d ed., 1966), *Funzione delle scienze e significato dell'uomo* (3d ed., 1966), *Relazioni e significati*, 3 vols. (1965–66), and editor of the philosophical journal *Aut-Aut*.

PIETRO PIOVANI. Professor of Moral Philosophy at the Facoltà di Lettere e Filosofia of the University of Naples. Author of *Per un'interpretazione unitaria del Critone* (1947), *Normatività e creatività* (1949), *La teodicea sociale di Rosmini* (1957), *Giusnaturalismo e etica moderna* (1961), *Filosofia e storia delle idee* (1965), and *Conoscenza storica e conoscenza morale* (1966).

ALAIN PONS. Assistant de Philosophie at the Faculté des Lettres et Sciences humaines de Paris-Nanterre. Author of "Nature et histoire chez G. B. Vico" (in *Les études philosophiques*, 1961). Now working on a book entitled *Histoire et philosophie chez Vico*.

HERBERT READ. Former Charles Eliot Norton Professor of Poetry, Harvard University, 1953–54, and Andrew W. Mellon Lecturer in Fine Arts at the National Gallery of Art, Washington, D.C., 1954. His publications include *Collected Essays in Literary Criticism* (1938), *Education through Art* (1943), *The Philosophy of Modern Art* (1952), *Icon and Idea: The Function of Art in the Development of Human Consciousness* (1955), *The Forms of Things Unknown* (1960), *The Contrary Experience* (1963), *The Origins of Forms in Art* (1965), and *Collected Poems* (1966). Sir Herbert died in June, 1968.

H. P. RICKMAN. Reader in Philosophy at the City University, London. Author of *Meaning in History: Dilthey's Thoughts on History and Society* (1961), *Preface to Philosophy* (1967), *Living with Technology* (1967), *Understanding and the Human Studies* (1967), and of numerous articles.

A. WILLIAM SALOMONE. Wilson Professor of European History, University of Rochester. Author of *Italian Democracy in the Making* (1945), *Readings in Twentieth Century European History* (1950), *Italy in the Giolittian Era* (1960), and of articles for professional journals.

ELIZABETH SEWELL. Chairman of the Experimental College at Fordham University. Author of *The Orphic Voice: Poetry and Natural History* (1960), *The Human Metaphor* (1964), and other books.

WERNER STARK. Professor of Sociology, Fordham University. Author of *The Sociology of Knowledge* (1958), *Montesquieu: Pioneer of the Sociology of Knowledge* (1960), *The Fundamental Forms of Social Thought* (1962), and *The Sociology of Religion* (1966).

GIORGIO TAGLIACOZZO. Former Libero Docente at the University of Rome (1935–38) and Lecturer at the New School for Social Research (1946–61). Editor of the Voice of America–RAI *Università Internazionale Guglielmo Marconi* since 1945. Author of *Economia e massimo edonistico collettivo* (1933), and *Economisti napoletani dei secoli XVII and XVIII* (1937). Has published a number of studies on the history of economics and on the unity of knowledge in American and Italian learned journals.

RENÉ WELLEK. Sterling Professor of Comparative Literature at Yale University. His publications include *Immanuel Kant in England* (1931), *The Rise of English Literary History* (1941, 1966) (with Austin Warren), *Theory of Literature* (1949, 1956), *History of Modern Criticism* (1955, 1965), *Dostoevsky: A Collection of Critical Essays* (1962), *Concepts of Criticism* (1963), *Essays on Czech Literature* (1963), *Confrontations: Studies in the Intellectual and Literary Relations between Germany, England and the United States during the Nineteenth Century* (1965).

GEORGE A. WELLS. Reader in German in the German Department at University College, London. Author of *Herder and After* (1959).

GEORGE WHALLEY. Professor of English at Queen's University, Kingston, Ontario. Author of *Poetic Process, Coleridge and Sara Hutchinson*

(1955), and *The Legend of John Hornby*. Has contributed to Miss Kathleen Coburn's edition of the Coleridge *Notebooks* and is preparing editions of Coleridge's *Marginalia* and *Poetical Works* for the *Collected Coleridge*.

HAYDEN V. WHITE. Professor of History, University of California at Los Angeles. Author (with Willson Coates) of *The Emergence of Liberal Humanism* and of the article on Vico in the *International Encyclopedia of the Social Sciences*.

BIOGRAPHICAL NOTE

Giambattista Vico was born in Naples on June 23, 1668, and died there—seventy-six years later—on the night of January 22–23, 1744. In an age that prided itself on the recognition of genius in all fields, he lived a singularly obscure life and one marked by poverty, marital tragedy, and betrayal by those he believed to be his patrons. Trained in law at the University of Naples, he was appointed professor of rhetoric at that university in 1699, a position he filled until 1741. He never attained to the chair of civil law to which he aspired all his life, and so he turned to history, to the study of literature, society, and philosophy—and to the relations between them. The main product of his studies in these fields was the *New Science* (the first edition of which was published in 1725), a work which was at once a challenge to Cartesian rationalism, to the natural-law tradition, and to the antiquarianism of latter-day Renaissance Humanists. Above all, however, the *New Science* was a new approach to history, a synthesis of Vico's critical reading of Plato, Tacitus, Grotius, and Sir Francis Bacon, and an anticipation of much that would subsequently serve as the basis of modern social science. This great work, which remained unrecognized throughout the eighteenth century, was augmented and emended in two subsequent editions, in 1730 and 1744, so different in conception and tone as to constitute a new creation; and it is these revisions that are referred to collectively as the *Second New Science (La scienza nuova seconda)* in Vichian scholarship.

The originality and intellectual fecundity of the *New Science* were recognized only in the nineteenth century, when thinkers as diverse as Goethe, Michelet, Mazzini, Coleridge, Thomas Arnold, Marx, Engels, and a host of others appealed to him as an anticipation of their own extensions of, and deviations from, the tradition of Enlightenment humanism. In the twentieth century, thinkers and writers as different as Croce, Gentile, and Collingwood in philosophy; Joyce and Yeats in literature; Toynbee and Trotsky in historiography; Pareto, Sorel, and Sorokin in social thought; and Edmund Wilson and Erich Auerbach in literary criticism, have recurred to Vico for inspiration and guidance in their attempts to make sense of history and to probe the deeper recesses of human consciousness.

Yet the *New Science* was not the only evidence of Vico's genius. Works like *On the Study Methods of Our Time* (*De nostri temporis studiorum ratione*, 1709); *The Most Ancient Wisdom of the Italians* (*De antiquissima Italorum sapientia*, 1710); *Universal Law* (*Diritto universale*, comprised of three parts: *The One Principle of Universal Law* [*De uno universi iuris principio et fine uno*, 1720], *The Consistency of the Jurisprudent* [*De constantia iurisprudentis*, 1721], and the *Notes* [*Notae*, 1722]); the *Heroic Mind* (*De mente heroica*, 1732); and the *Autobiography* (*Vita di Giambattista Vico scritta da se medesimo*, 1725, with additions in 1728 and 1731)—all these display the richness and range of Vico's fertile mind. It is not surprising that Vico has had to wait for the three hundredth anniversary of his birth for proper recognition. His thought was too complex, his prose too labored, to inspire the foundation of a school. And European society required the agony of the French Revolution before it could come to an awareness of the complexity of history necessary for a proper appreciation of Vico's profundity as a social philosopher. It is perhaps fitting that in an age that faces a barbarism more virulent than anything he could have imagined, this theorist of myth and unreason should finally come into his own as a culture-hero. Perhaps only the twentieth century has suffered sufficiently to match sensibility with the great Neapolitan thinker; he is certainly one of the few "ancients" able to serve as a guide to our own uncertain future.

HAYDEN V. WHITE

Part I   COMPARATIVE
                  HISTORICAL STUDIES

Enrico De Mas   VICO'S FOUR AUTHORS

From the very first pages, the reader of Vico's *Autobiography* cannot fail to
be struck powerfully by the mythical and prophetic tone that animates the
narrative; it is as if, instead of recounting the humdrum events of the life of
a humble man of letters, the author were reporting to us on the great deeds
of a famous army leader, or those of a messianic redeemer, whose existence
must tally, point by point, with the "signs" of the times, with the most
important tokens of the hoped-for renovation, following a precise astro-
logical graph.   There is no detail which is not introduced at the proper
moment, so as to be utilized in the course of the narration with an obvious
demonstrative intent, even if it infringes upon the real sequel of events and
the outspoken will to "narrate plainly with the candor proper to an historian" the course of Vico's studies, since through the narration itself the
author proposes to bring out the erroneousness of the Cartesian method,
which he opposes.   From his infancy, when a nasty fall brought about a
deep change in his psychological makeup, in order to mold him into the form
intended by Providence, assigning him to the category of men who are
endowed with both genius and sagacity, capable of taking pleasure in flashes
of acute wit but intolerant of captious jests and specious quibblings, a superior
destiny takes hold of Vico's life and alters his original vitality, impatient of
rest, in order to confer upon it a new structure, to turn it into a melancholy
and irritable disposition.   This disposition is an indication of nobler and
higher plans.   Another "sign" was given, when, as a youth, he gladly submitted to the harshest self-inflicted discipline, studying, at times, the whole
night long, because he felt such a strong inclination toward a literary career;
and there were "signs" again when he assiduously engaged in detecting, in
the way a philosopher should, the motives of equity implicit in positive law-
enactments and simultaneously strove to interpret, as a historian should, the
technical terms of juridical texts, gaining an acquaintance with that kind of
study which the legal experts of his time called *de verborum significatione*.   He
was thus able to discriminate between the two aspects, the philosophical and
the philological, of the *New Science of Nations*.   Not last in importance, as a
premonitory sign of Vico's inward ripening, was his repudiation of the
baroque "turns of wit," of those queer and gaudy conceits which had created

such a stir in Neapolitan poetry at the time of Giambattista Marino (1569–1625) and his followers, and which Vico asserts to have used himself "as an exercise of the mind, which affords pleasure only through falsehood so eccentrically presented as to catch by surprise the expectation of its hearers." It was, in his opinion, an exercise that chills and represses the intellectual power of young men, as he demonstrates in his *On the Study Methods of Our Time* (*De nostri temporis studiorum ratione*), the pedagogic essay whose results are summarized in the *Autobiography*. Thus the whole process of his own spiritual formation is made to converge on the novennial solitude of Vatolla, which was destined to cap his labors by causing him to submerge and bury himself in the study of both civil and canon law and by leading him to discover the correct median position in the vexatious theological controversy of his epoch, that is, the conflict between freedom and grace, doggedly fought over by Jesuits and Jansenists. At Vatolla, Vico seemed to go into seclusion, but in reality he achieved a better adjustment to the coeval milieu by assimilating and utilizing those elements available to him which he found good and helpful, in order to recast all the scholarship he had absorbed into a marvelous and powerful synthesis. This synthesis was transfused, in a concrete form, into his mature works. It was then, after attaining ripeness, that he undertook to set down in writing the events of his earlier life, with a new and curious retrospective attitude, which Croce characterizes in these words: "the history of the work which Providence ordered him to do, which it led him to carry out through various and different vicissitudes which appeared to be adversities and were, instead, opportunities." [1]

The grandiose plan of Providence, which guides nations in their historical coursings and recurrences, finds a full and coherent realization in the *Autobiography* as well. Writing this book, Vico proposed to arrange the recital of the events of his life in such a way as to "demonstrate that it was absolutely necessary for him, on the basis of such events, to develop into such a man of letters" as he was, so that it would be impossible to think that he might have developed into a different kind of intellectual personality. Vico intends to do exactly the opposite of what was done by René Descartes in the biographical section of his *Discourse on Method*, where "he craftily feigned as to the method of his studies, simply in order to exalt his own philosophy and mathematics and downgrade all other studies included in divine and human erudition." [2]

The studies of F. Nicolini and of Mario Fubini (both of whom have published their own editions of the Italian text of the *Autobiography*) show how inexact and lacking in rigor is Vico's narrative, especially insofar as his youthful years are concerned. That narrative, in reality, is patterned after

[1] B. Croce, *Theory and History of Historiography* (Bari: Laterza, 1954), p. 262.

[2] Max H. Fisch and Thomas G. Bergin, trans., *The Autobiography of Giambattista Vico* (Ithaca, N.Y.: Cornell University Press, 1963), p. 113.

and framed upon the Cartesian account that Vico had denounced as pur- posely figmental. "The solitude of Vatolla" corresponds punctually to the voluntary exile in a foreign land which Descartes chose in order to escape the commitments that hampered him at home and in order to devote himself wholly to speculative research, after clearing his mind of any preconceived opinions. Vico, too, if we credit what he says, made himself "a stranger in his own land" and became "self-taught," "*autodidactic*," in order to empha- size by his isolation the originality of his ideas and his anti-Cartesianism in selecting those who became his "authors." To these authors, he asserts, he owes a great part of himself, and he frames them mythically within his intellectual biography. He has no intention of freeing himself from the principle of authority. Instead, he carefully selects his authors in order to utilize them—symbolically idealized—in support of his own philosophy, which he has already brought to completion.

The authors who at first appear in his *Autobiography* as exemplary models, "to have ever before his eyes in meditation and writing," are only three: Plato, Tacitus, and Francis Bacon.

With an incomparable metaphysical mind, Tacitus contemplates man as he is, Plato as he should be. And as Plato with his universal knowledge explores the parts of nobility which constitute the man of intellectual wisdom, so Tacitus descends into all the counsels of utility whereby, among the infinite irregular chances of malice and fortune, the man of practical wisdom brings things to good issue.[3]

The admiration that Vico says he always felt for these two authors derives from an evident idealization, which will remain with him always. Those two writers represent for him the antithesis between philosophy and philol- ogy. Plato (and, undoubtedly, the Humanists' Neo-Platonism as well) represents the Greek spirit, contemplative and constantly directed toward the concept of "oughtness." This spirit draws strength from moral teachings that endow man with intellectual wisdom and cause him to become im- pervious to sensual allurements. Tacitus (or rather the "Tacitism" of Vico's epoch) represents the spirit of the old Romans, the conquerors of the world wholly bent upon practical utility and set on learning the art of maneuvering among the dangerous, uncertain events of life, events that are not subject to "fixed" rules but that remain entrusted to personal cunning and fortune, the only forces that enable us to manage them profitably. These two ideals, that of Plato and that of Tacitus, seemed to be made to supply each other's lack and to be undisjoinable. Vico repudiates the separation between moralism and utilitarianism and adopts them both in that ideal synthesis which characterizes the modern age, an age that is the inheritor of Greek culture as well as of the Roman conquest and that is conceptually and ideally represented by Francis Bacon. As Vico says in the *Autobiography*: "And

[3] *Ibid.*, p. 138.

now at length Vico's attention was drawn to Francis Bacon, Lord Verulam, a man of incomparable wisdom both common and esoteric, at one and the same time a universal man in theory and in practice, a rare philosopher and a great English Minister of State." [4]

Vico's attention was signally drawn by the particular structure of the great Baconian encyclopedia, the treatise *De dignitate et augmentis scientiarum*, which is made up of two parts, distinct but mutually mediating: the one devoted to a re-examination of the knowledge of his epoch, the other intended to bring new sciences into existence or to amend those already existing. The new sciences constitute the desiderata of universal knowledge and point out its gaps; the list of these sciences, at the end of the volume, bears the title *Novus orbis scientiarum*. Furthermore, Bacon had indicated in scientific objectivity the criterion to be followed in order to amend and renovate the sciences, requiring every scientist to rid himself of prejudices (*idola*) insofar as these prejudices stem from the nature of man, not from the nature of things (*ex analogia hominis, non ex analogia rerum*). In this way, the learned British chancellor, who had been a statesman under James I, seemed to incarnate that synthesis which Vico hoped would evolve in the modern epoch, since he had shown at the same time, in his encyclopedia, both the present status of the sciences and the desirability of their future integrations, expansions, and corrections. Bacon's life seemed to have transformed into reality the union of the two wisdoms: the "vulgar" wisdom of the statesman and the "recondite" wisdom of a supreme philosopher. In Bacon, Vico at length perceives that he has found his path, the "ideal" model to follow, the guideline that was to lead him to the attempt to found a new science, the science of civilization. The *Autobiography* relates it thus:

Leaving aside his other works, on whose subjects there were perhaps writers as good or better, from his *De augmentis scientiarum* Vico concluded that, as Plato is the prince of Greek wisdom, and the Greeks have no Tacitus, so Romans and Greeks alike have no Bacon. He marveled that one sole man could see in the world of letters what studies remained to be discovered and developed, and how many and what kinds of defects must be corrected in those it already contained; and that without professional and sectarian bias. . . .[5]

From the four categories of *idola* which Bacon had discriminated, Vico, with the words just quoted, singles out the *idola specus* and the *idola theatri*. They derive from those mental habits which are the results, respectively, of professional deformation and of ideological sectarianism. Both of these types of *idola* can be found in the culture of antiquity. Stripping the scientists of their prejudices, Bacon does justice to all sciences. For each of them he seeks the right place, to which each is assigned, so that all of them

[4] *Ibid.*, p. 139.
[5] *Ibid.*

may profitably contribute to the common progress.   This seemed to him modern culture's claim to glory: its longing to become European, to overstep the by now too narrow bounds of the Mediterranean Basin.   In Bacon's pages Vico found, many times repeated, the motif that the progress of the intellectual world ought to correspond to that of the material world, the knowledge of which had been opened by the oceanic navigations beyond the pillars of Hercules, through the great transatlantic seas.   In Bacon he rightly saw the prophet of the new time when the universality of knowledge was to be actualized, not according to a rigid norm, but according to a pliable one, like the Lesbian masons' rule, bending to fit itself to the sinuosities of bodies in order to measure them in each flexure, so that true science should not be considered in the Platonic fashion, as "a lark soaring aloft and delighting in song, unable to do anything else . . . but should be viewed as a hawk flying through the upper regions of the air, capable, however, of pouncing down to earth in order to grab his prey." [6]

Bacon saw that theory and practice had a common origin and wanted his works to be the clearest demonstration of the soundness of his theories. His strictures were intended to discredit ancient science on the ground of its sterility.   In order to render it productive, no help could be derived from the Cartesian method, wholly centered upon mathematical abstractions, unfit for topical research, and powerless to detect those arguments which are necessary to make truth accessible to all, ascertaining the validity of universal concepts by the particular test of facts, according to the approved "method of study of our time" which Vico found in Bacon.   In the *De augmentis*, in fact, we not only come upon the delineation of the inventive method, made up of *tabulae*, *instantiae*, and *topica particularia*, but we also meet with a recognition of the necessity of eloquence, to which philosophy should resort in order to be handed on and to be justified.   Thus the universality of philology stems from the universality of philosophy, while both are embraced in the great encyclopedia of the sciences.   This encyclopedia is not only a collection of concepts but also an accurate assemblage of facts, expressly chosen in order to make up a web of cogent argumentations indispensably required for the purpose of transforming science into common persuasion and hence into a civilizing force.   The Baconian doctrines made a great impression on the mind of the still-young professor of eloquence at the University of Naples.   Vico perceived in them the great impact that his academic teachings could exert on his public, if he were to emphasize their necessity, their pertinence, in regard to the total aggregate of the sciences. In order to extol that necessity, that pertinence, he wrote in 1708 his seventh inaugural oration, which he presented "as an argument that should bring some new and profitable discovery to the world of letters, a desideratum

[6] *De augmentis* VIII. 2.

worthy to be numbered among those listed by Bacon in his *New World of Sciences*." [7]

The text of the *Autobiography*, in this as well as in a number of other points, is corrupt. The emendation suggested by Villarosa must be rejected. The authentic reading should be *New World of Sciences*, not *New Organ of the Sciences*, since Bacon's *Novum organum* is not a list of desiderata; rather, it is itself one of the desiderata listed in the *Novus orbis scientiarum*. The latter is added as an appendix to the *De augmentis* in order to mirror the idea of constructing and describing the great geographical map of the sciences, with its explored and unexplored zones, according to an image that had struck the fancy of many writers of the time.

The oration *On the Study Methods of Our Time*, delivered in 1708, is full of the importance of Bacon, in whose range it moves even when Vico dissents from him on some particular point, such as the famous image of Time, which, like a river, submerges the heavier objects (that is, the best authors) while it carries toward us, on its surface, the lighter ones (the superficial writers). Bacon's antitraditionalism displeases Vico, who feels implicit in it a rejection of the heritage of that humanism which is so dear to his heart. He tries, however, to correct Bacon with Bacon when he attributes to the transcription of codices, done by hand, the merit of having handed on to us the productions of the great leaders of *antiquity*, chosen because of their renown. Book I of the *De augmentis* is devoted to the extolment of the dignity of the sciences in the persons of their most authoritative representatives. The preamble to Book II serves the same purpose. In that preamble, Bacon deplores the separation of the inventive from the mnemonic power in academic practice and petitions the king for a greater use of rhetoric. Vico appropriates Bacon's request, developing it in an anti-Cartesian sense.

As for Vico's repudiation of another work by Bacon, *De sapientia veterum*, it should be considered from this viewpoint: Vico, in the first stage of his intellectual growth, took pleasure in the recondite, esoteric wisdom contained in it and felt impelled to repeat Bacon's attempt in a work of his own. This was the *De antiquissima Italorum sapientia* (*On the Most Ancient Wisdom of the Italians*), published in 1710. In Vico's *De antiquissima*, the etymological problem replaces the mythological. In the preamble of the *De antiquissima*, Vico states that his only aim was to fulfill one of Bacon's desiderata. Bacon had expressed the same intention and had introduced into the *De augmentis* his discussion of the "sapiential" content of some ancient myths as examples of a *philosophia secundum fabulas antiquas*.

At a later time, when Vico wrote the first part of his *Autobiography* (1725), he had already changed his opinion. The esoteric wisdom contained in the ancient myths is now explained by him in terms of the inflated self-esteem of

[7] Fisch and Bergin, *Autobiography*, p. 146.

the learned (*boria dei dotti*); the heroes of ancient myths become, in Vico's interpretation, "poetical characters" (symbols of collective representations). By this exegetic transformation, Vico felt that he had paid the debt he had incurred toward his favorite author; that he had, in other words, gone beyond him intellectually. He allowed people to believe that he owed to Bacon the initial impulse only, and that subsequently he had been able to proceed on his own. In reality, Vico learned from Bacon a considerable amount of linguistics and everything that pertains to non-literate means of expression. All this Vico found in Book VI of the *De augmentis* and in the *De sapientia veterum*.

The existence of a language without sound, expressed through signs, used by persons speaking different languages or by individuals deprived of the power of speech, and therefore the existence of a linguistic vehicle that acts as a means of universal communication, preceding the formation and diffusion of national languages, the persistence of hieroglyphs and characters representing physical objects in the writing of the most ancient peoples, like the Chinese, the anteriority of a fabulistic literature to rational argumentation, the independence of the history of the Hebrews, a people privileged by God, whose national events are to be viewed as standing entirely apart from the ordinary vicissitudes of mankind—these and similar notions are common to both Bacon and Vico. Such notions undoubtedly derive from the reports of travelers and missionaries sent back to their home bases from the countries opened up by the explorations of new continents. The reader must think, for instance, of the *Historia natural y moral de las Indias* (Seville, 1590) by the Spanish Jesuit José de Acosta (1539–1600), a whole chapter of which (Book VI, chapter V) is taken up by the illustration of the "ideographic writing" of the Chinese. And it is not a question of occasional or sporadic remarks, having no weight within Bacon's system and "introduced by way of light banter" (as F. Nicolini thinks); it is, instead, a question of solid points of doctrine broached at the outset; points that, fermenting and swelling, were later transfused into veritable, precise theories. One of these is the rejection of the attribution of the paternity of myths to poets, a rejection which is antithetical to the Stoic and Neo-Platonic allegorism stemming from the complex symbology of the alchemists. Bacon follows Cicero in judging such interpretations to be "not the judgment of philosophers, but the dreams of delirious men."[8] In *De sapientia veterum* and *De augmentis* Vico found several anticipations of his "poetical wisdom," including the anonymity of myth. And perhaps the theme of "historical recurrence" itself finds a presumable origin in Bacon's *rerum vicissitudo*, which presents some common modalities in regard to the concept of "reversion," to the postdiluvian repristination, to the second medieval barbarism, to the degeneration of philosophy into sophistry, to the relapse into original sin as a

---

[8] *De natura deorum* I. 42.

product of academic culture, to the anteriority of the birth of the arts in regard to sciences; all these are theories pertaining to the genesis of the grand Baconian program of the *Instauratio scientiarum*. Thus Francis Bacon is present in Vico's thought as more than an intellectual symbol. It seems plausible that Plato and Tacitus may have been "adopted" by him as "poetical characters" rather than as veritable authors (thereby substantiating the assumption of Guido Fassò); on the other hand, it is true that Bacon was adopted and judged on the basis of certain precise doctrines, such as are to be found in those works of his that Vico studied with admiration.

Nevertheless, it cannot be asserted that Bacon's program for the renovation of the sciences through the inductive method found complete endorsement and perfect understanding in Vico. That this was so is shown by the fact that the work destined to set forth the logico-practical precepts of that program, the *Novum organum*, was not viewed with particular consideration by Vico. There is, besides, the notable misconception owing to Vico's desire to present the inductive method as the synthesis of two logical aspects: the first, inherent in the *cogitare*, the second, in the *videre*. This misconception led Vico to state that, in connection with his *Organum*, Bacon elaborated another book, whose title is *Cogitata et visa*.[9] Vico is unaware of the fact that the two participles making up the title *Cogitata et visa de interpretatione naturae* (an incidental piece of writing by Bacon) should be understood in the meaning of "thoughts and conclusions," not in the sense of "things thought and things seen." *Visa*, in this case, derives from the verb *videor* (it seems to me), and not from *video* (I see), as is evident from the structure of the book, which is divided into nineteen *cogitationes*, each one of which opens with the words *cogitavit et illud* (Francis Bacon also thought that) and closes usually with *itaque visum est ei* (and therefore he drew this conclusion). Vico's miscomprehension would be unintelligible if it were ascertained that he had read this book; but it is more probable that he merely came across a reference to it in some listing of Bacon's *Opera omnia* and was struck by the coupling of the two participial forms turned into substantive nouns. In the expression *cogitata et visa* he glimpsed the emblem of that synthesis which he was striving to create, and deemed it to be identical with the Baconian induction. He hurriedly concluded that the *novum organum* of modern knowledge was a mere resumption of the Socratic induction, which he took pleasure in contrasting with the sorites of the Stoics. Later, for reasons of symmetry, he saw that this antagonism was being repeated in the divergence between the great scientific schools—the English one of Bacon and the French one of Descartes.

The anti-Cartesian argument, which began with the *De nostri* and became the constantly renascent motif of all of Vico's subsequent works, was vigorously fed by his familiarity with Bacon, who seemed to offer (so to

[9] Vico, *Vindiciae*, XVI, par. 551.

speak) a *cheval de bataille* for Vico's manner of polemizing. Vico's miso-gallicism corresponds to Bacon's aversion for the ancient Greeks and their sterile intellectualistic philosophy. And in this way Vico found his path smoothed out, it being sufficient for him to follow the track described by Bacon, by simply transferring the Baconian method from the study of physical facts to that of the phenomena of society. (This procedure was advocated by not a few of the minds of his epoch, especially those of the Enlightenment.)

Until then things had been going along peacefully insofar as the "three" authors were concerned. The unexpected popping up of the fourth, Grotius, seemed to produce a commotion; hence the disparity of judgments among scholars regarding this point. F. Nicolini states that the reading of the *De jure belli ac pacis* was for Vico like a *coup de foudre*, a bolt of lightning, which caused, in Vico's mind, a surfacing of observations and considerations previously encountered by him, to which he had attached no weight or authentic prestige. Guido Fassò, who examines the whole problem from a juridical viewpoint, finds only in the "author" Grotius (a true jurist) that synthesis of truth and certitude, of philosophy and legal expertise, for which Vico would have sought vainly in his "author" Bacon. Bacon had been very successful as a philosopher but rather unsuccessful as a jurist. He had been incapable of supplying Vico with that synthesis, that "intimate union" which was closer by far than "a simple connection."

In fact, the page of the *Autobiography* which introduces the "fourth author," Grotius, does not differentiate the latter from Bacon, except on the ground of the universality of laws, which, according to Vico, the British chancellor was unable to perceive, because of the diversity of the English legal system from the Roman, which is the only one capable of rising to a really universal plane. Indeed, a great difference marks the two thinkers in regard to their respective training in the field of legislation. Vico had paid particular attention to the historical aspect of European law, tracing its precise derivation from the *jus romanum* through Alciati's nomenclature and method, whereas Bacon, a professional law-practitioner, had been interested in judiciary casuistry and the pragmatic standards governing the interpretation and application of legal rules. The new perspective illuminating the relationships among the "four authors" becomes synthesized as follows: "And here he found a fourth author to add to the three he had set before himself. For Plato adorns, rather than confirms, his esoteric wisdom with the common wisdom of Homer. Tacitus intersperses his metaphysics, ethics and politics with the facts, as they have come down to him from the times, scattered and confused and without system." [10]

Plato—the "divine philosopher" as the Humanists called him—kept his gaze constantly fixed on truth and did not seek for a confirmation of his

[10] Fisch and Bergin, *Autobiography*, p. 154.

views in Homer's fables, the knowledge of which he ostentatiously displays in his *Dialogues*, but to which he claims to be opposed. There is in Plato no synthesis of philosophy and philology. As for Tacitus, the astute political thinker of the "Tacitists," his historical works are thickly studded with maxims of civil prudence; but he failed to weave such maxims into a full-fledged juridical-political system. He was incapable of raising legal knowledge to the level of universal law. And what about Bacon? The *Autobiography* tells us: "Bacon sees that the sum of human and divine knowledge of his time needs supplementing and amending (in what it has and in what it has not), but as far as laws are concerned he does not succeed, with his canons, in compassing the universe of cities and the course of all times, or the extent of all nations."[11]

Bacon knew how to unite the advantages of philosophy with those of civil prudence, but he did not succeed in universalizing law, as can be seen in that specimen of a *tractatus de justitia universali, sive de fontibus juris* (contained in chapter III of Book VIII of the *De augmentis*) which boils down to an aggregate of technical precepts on the manner of interpreting legal enactments and of applying them in forensic practice. Bacon's attempt to formulate the "laws of laws" (as he terms them) could not be carried out successfully, since it is hard for an English jurist to master the science of Roman law (Roman law having had only secondary influence in Britain, where its reception was belated and limited). To sum up: Bacon was unable to give us a valid example of how to put his method into effect, how to transfer it from the scientific domain to that of social phenomena. That valuable deed was found to have been performed by Grotius. Thus, the *Autobiography* notes: "Grotius, however, embraces in a system of universal law the whole of philosophy and philology, including both parts of the latter, i.e., the history (on the one hand) of facts and events, both fabulous and real, and (on the other) that of the three languages, Hebrew, Greek and Latin."[12]

In Grotius, Vico saw (or thought that he saw) an admirable realization of that principle of method which he had already assimilated by reading Bacon. The principle had been stated in the *De augmentis*. In order to effect a real renovation of current knowledge it was necessary to hark back to the genesis of the sciences that were desiderata, by rediscovering the common wellspring of ancient languages and of non-literate means of expression, and by setting up an incontrovertible link between the actual reality—the "issues" of law—and the idealistic conception—the "oughtness" of human nature. The reading of Grotius was for Vico the circumstance that led him to fasten onto his new, nascent science the unsuitable jusnaturalistic designation "universal law," or the "natural law of nations." The apparition of

[11] *Ibid.*, p. 155.
[12] *Ibid.*

Grotius does not invalidate (on the contrary, it confirms) our remarks concerning the role played by Vico's three favorite "authors" in the formation of his thought. That role is not impaired or changed in the least by the intervention of a "fourth" author. To Vico's mind, Grotius must have appeared as the European "stand-in" of the British chancellor. Nor does it matter that Vico had his own reservations concerning the religious faith of that "heretical" author, since he had already made such allowances in regard to Bacon. The difference in religious affiliation was, for Vico, a ground for an imperfect speculative adherence, and it is not by chance that, of the "four authors," two are pagans and two are thinkers of the Reformation. We know that one of Vico's ambitions was to be considered as the anti-Descartes of modern philosophy, as the most European among the modern philosophers of the Catholic persuasion.

Bibliographical Note

The history of our problem concerning Vico's four authors is recent. Prior to F. Nicolini's studies, when the literature on Vico had not yet broadened so as to embrace the philologic field, only rare hints of the problem can be found, like those contained in C. Cattaneo's *Saggio su la scienza nuova*. There we read: "Later, Vico added Bacon to Tacitus and Plato. From Bacon, he derived encouragement for his plan to establish a new science, and suggestions as to the method of drawing philosophical abstractions from the sources of experience, i.e., of history. Finally, Vico set up, as the fourth author, Grotius, who, for him, was the outstanding representative of the modern science of abstract justice, the thinker who had carried out the Platonic idea [in the field of legal relations]" (C. Cattaneo, *Opere* [Florence: Sansoni, 1957], I, 45). Croce, in his monograph on Vico (published in 1911) and in the pages he devotes to him in his *History of Aesthetics*, points out Vico's kinship to Bacon, manifested in their common aversion to the syllogism and to scholastic philosophy, but rapidly concludes that "the Bacon of whom Vico speaks is mostly a product of his imagination, and is somewhat Platonized" (B. Croce, *La filosofia di Giambattista Vico* [Bari: Laterza, 1953], p. 53). In reality, however, Vico's Platonism is a fable, believed in only by the most traditionalist interpreters, like G. Gentile. A more serious listing of the affinities between Bacon and Vico is to be found in S. Casellato's *F. Bacone* (Padua, 1941). Nicolini, in his edition of the *Autobiografia* (Milan: Bompiani, 1947), lingers with particular pleasure on Book VI of the *De augmentis*, which he judges to be "one of the most important sources of Vico's linguistics," in evident contrast to the Crocean thesis of a pre-Romantic Vico, "first discoverer of the science of aesthetics." Guido Fassò, in his book *I " quattro auttori" del Vico* (Milan: Giuffrè, 1949), has reconstructed with a great wealth of detail the formation of Vico's thought, portraying the "authors" as genuine "poetical characters" and not as actual sources. This judgment, which is, perhaps, valid for the pagan authors, does not apply to Bacon, since some broad zones of agreement and evident coincidences of views exist between Vico's works and Bacon's thought. Those zones of agreement and those coincidences are predicated upon a long and mature assimilation and meditation. Concerning this topic, I may take the liberty to refer the reader to my *Bacone e Vico* (Turin: Filosofia, 1959). Useful pointers may be found also in P. Rossi's *Francesco Bacone: Dalla magia alla scienza* (Bari: Laterza, 1957) and in A. Corsano's *G. B. Vico* (Bari: Laterza, 1956), pp. 196–200, which takes up the clues set forth by Rossi in one of his prior publications. There remains open the other problem of Vico's relationship to Grotius, on which some light is shed by D. Faucci's surmise stated in his "Vico: Editore di Grozio?" (*Giornale storico della letteratura italiana* [1959], pp. 97–105). The importance of the role played by Bacon in Vico's formation is emphasized by Professor Fisch in his introduction to the Fisch and Bergin translation of the *Autobiography* (Ithaca, N.Y.: Cornell University Press, 1963), to which all the quotations contained in the present paper refer. That importance is underscored also by Professor Elio Gianturco, author of the first English translation of Vico's oration *De nostri temporis studiorum ratione* (*On the Study Methods of Our Time* [Indianapolis, Ind.: Bobbs-Merrill, 1965]). Gianturco's edition supplies also an extended bibliographical survey of Vichian studies (pp. 85–98).

Translated by Elio Gianturco

Glauco Cambon   VICO AND DANTE

There would be reasons to bring Dante Alighieri and Giambattista Vico together, across the intervening gulf of six centuries, even if Vico's pronouncements on Dante[1] were not there to elicit such a linkage. The linkage, in fact, has implicitly or explicitly occurred a few times during the last one hundred and fifty years. Not accidentally, in the two founders of modern Italian criticism—the liberal patriots Ugo Foscolo[2] and Francesco

While this symposium was going to press, I was finally privileged to see a short essay, "Dante et Vico," by the French scholar J. Chaix-Ruy, originally read at the 1965 International Convention of Dante Studies in Florence. The address is now published in Atti del Congresso Internazionale di Studi Danteschi *(Florence: Sansoni, 1966), pp. 131–42. It is of a more general nature than mine, but it does discuss the letter to Gherardo degli Angioli and the* Giudizio sopra Dante *in the light of Vico's propensity for Homer.—G. C.*

[1] As Fausto Nicolini shows in his note on p. 953 of a substantial selection of Vico's works edited by him (*Giambattista Vico: Opere*, 1 vol. ed. [Milan-Naples, 1953]), references to Dante are scattered throughout Vico's writings, from the *Fourth Academic Oration*, dating from the year 1703, down to the third edition of the *New Science* (1744). Of particular importance are the references contained in the *Autobiography* (1728–29) and in the three editions of the *New Science* (1725, 1730, 1744). Two sustained statements on Dante which have the importance of independent essays are the letter to Gherardo degli Angioli of December 26, 1725, and the review article "Discoverta del Vero Dante" ("Discovery of the True Dante"), written between 1728 and 1730. The latter essay has been translated by Irma Brandeis in *Discussions of the Divine Comedy* (Boston, 1961).

[2] Though Foscolo's greatest achievement is his poetry, his vigorous criticism bears consideration as a fruitful contribution, especially to Dantesque studies, in the early nineteenth-century context of Italian and English culture. René Wellek throws generous light on Foscolo as critic in vol. II of *A History of Modern Criticism, 1750–1950* (New Haven, Conn., 1955), but fails to mention the connection with Vico's thought. Foscolo's "Parallel between Dante and Petrarch" (which Irma Brandeis reprints in *Discussions of the Divine Comedy*), from his *Essays on Petrarch* (London, 1823), in part develops Vico's ideas, as the following excerpt may show: "Dante, like all primitive poets, is the historian of the manners of his age, the prophet of his country, and the painter of mankind. . . ." Vichian ideas, colored by his own sense of personal self-assertion and patriotic engagement, likewise inform his academic address of 1809, held at Pavia University, "On the Origins and Function of Literature." Even more strikingly, the *New Science*'s epic sense of human history suffuses Foscolo's best known poem, *Of Sepulchers* (1807):
> Since nuptial ceremonies, tribunals and altars
> Managed to civilize the human beasts. . . .

De Sanctis[3]—zest for Dante's poetry went hand in hand with a pervasive affinity for Vico, and the same was true of S. T. Coleridge in England. Later on in the nineteenth century, Karl Werner, an Austrian scholar of more conservative views in politics and religion, had this to say:

> Vico was a thoroughly national thinker, and he reflects in his creative activity the spirit and mentality of his own people just as characteristically as the Frenchman comes through in Descartes, the Englishman in Locke, the German in Kant. As against Descartes' spiritual rationalism, or Locke's empirically realist intellectualism, it is in the artistically formative mind that Vico recognizes the source of all true insight and the immediate shaper of man himself in the totality of his being. . . . The world encompassed by Vico's thought is that of historical man, in which, as in Dante's great poem, all spheres of cosmic reality find their center; Dante is to him the prince of poets, Homer, returned in the Christian era and as such also the interpreter of his own vision; the Virgil whom Dante chose for his guide corresponds, as a representative of the purposively shaping human reason, exactly to the idea that Vico himself has of that faculty's essence. . . .[4]

In 1963 the Swiss scholar Theophil Spoerri, in what promises to remain an enduring contribution to the study of Dante's poetry and thought,[5] said that Dante's Dark Wood image is of a piece with Vico's idea of a primordial wood from which the beastlike giants constituting the degenerated remnants of gentile mankind long after the Flood would have started their arduous evolution toward civilization under the hidden guidance of an immanent Providence. It is from the Dark Wood of error, we may remember, that Dante's bewildered pilgrim persona finds his circuitous way to salvation and

---

With classical polish the Vichian epic of civilization makes itself heard also in Foscolo's last verse composition, *The Graces*. Dante and Vico were both supreme exemplars of moral and intellectual achievement to Foscolo, whose poetic persona, in the *Sepulchers*, carries strong connotations of a Dante-like exile, and rightly so, because Foscolo did prefer exile to political compromise.

[3] De Sanctis' memorable studies on Dante appeared in 1866 in a collection of critical essays and in 1870 when his *History of Italian Literature* was published. They are accessible in Joseph Rossi and Alfred Galpin's *De Sanctis on Dante* (Madison, Wis., 1957). Though his philosophical approach (based on Hegel) differs from Foscolo's, De Sanctis resembled his older compatriot in many respects. Like him, he was politically engaged on the liberal side and suffered exile, and like him he joined a love for Dante with a love for Vico, whose thought has always appealed to Italian Hegelians. De Sanctis' stature as a critic has been vindicated by René Wellek in vol. IV of his *History of Modern Criticism*. Useful outlines of Vico's fortune are to be found in the Preface to Max H. Fisch and Thomas Bergin's translation of Vico's *Autobiography* (Ithaca, N.Y., 1944), now reprinted in a paperback edition, and in Nicolini's Introduction to *Opere*.

[4] Quoted from Karl Werner, *Giambattista Vico als Philosoph und gelehrter Forscher* (Giambattista Vico as Philosopher and Erudite Researcher) (Vienna, 1879), pp. 301–2; translation mine.

[5] Theophil Spoerri, *Dante und die europaeische Literatur—Das Bild des Menschen in der Struktur der Sprache* (Dante and European Literature—The Image of Man in the Structure of Language) (Stuttgart, 1963).

enlightenment, with some supernatural assistance. Unquestionably, I would add, both myths are historical re-enactments of the Fortunate Fall—one in the guise of personal allegory, the other in the shape of that collective archetype or "imaginative universal" (*universale fantastico*) which Vico posits as the organ of expression and knowledge for the "heroic" (or prerational) ages of mankind. For he was himself very much a poet, capable of re-attaining in his own passionate meditation those bygone phases of turbulent imagining which, in his view, had fostered the greatest poetry; and, no matter how trenchantly he may affirm, in the *New Science* (Book I, section II, paragraph 219), that philosophy and poetry are as good as mutually irreducible, an epic power of vision seethed at the center of his thinking. This power, to be sure, he shared with Dante, as Mario Fubini has recognized since 1946 in the only systematic investigation of Vico's relationship to Dante made so far.[6]

Fubini's essay in turn took its cue from Croce's study of Vico's philosophy,[7] especially where Croce remarks that for all its sketchiness Vico's interpretation of Dante's poetry had been a revolutionary step into modern criticism because, in Croce's opinion, before Vico no one had ever looked at the *Divine Comedy* in that poignant way. Since Fubini's departure is more specifically literary, his chapter on Dante's relevance to Vico, no less than his entire approach to Vico's style as a writer, amounts to a landmark in Vichian studies. Accordingly, before developing further aspects of the problem, I shall try to summarize Fubini's main points.

Briefly, Fubini holds that, through his frequent references to Dante (in one of the *Orations*, in the *De uno universi iuris principio et fine uno*, in the *New Science*, in the *Autobiography*, in the letter to Gherardo degli Angioli, and in the book review called "Discoverta del vero Dante" or "Discovery of the True Dante"[8]), Vico evinces a predominantly historico-philosophical interest in the medieval poet, whom he sees as a new Homer, as the singer of Italy's "barbarous age," to illustrate his theory of recourses and of barbaric or "heroic" ages as the prime seedbed of great poetry. The literary aspect of the *Divine Comedy* remains subordinated, in Vico's vision, to this bird's-eye view of history, which involves certain distortions of fact such as the unqualified description of Dante's Italy as barbarous, ferocious, and so on. It also entails a reduction of Dante's poetry to another piece of evidence for

[6] Mario Fubini, *Stile e umanità di Giambattista Vico* (Style and Humanity of Giambattista Vico) (Bari, 1946). The relevant chapter is called "Il mito della poesia primitiva e la critica dantesca di G. B. Vico" (The Myth of Primitive Poetry and G. B. Vico's Dantesque Criticism), pp. 173–205. Another chapter of the same book which has some bearing on our subject is "La lingua del Vico" (Vico's Language), pp. 97–158, formerly published as an independent work in 1943.

[7] Benedetto Croce, *La filosofia di Giambattista Vico* (Bari, 1911), trans. R. G. Collingwood, *The Philosophy of Giambattista Vico* (London, 1913).

[8] Translated by Irma Brandeis, in *Discussions of the Divine Comedy*, pp. 11–12.

Vico's aesthetics of the primitive sublime, which is supposed to have found in Homer an unequaled embodiment; in general, Vico makes it very clear that his Dante must be read in the light of his non-Augustan Homer—the less civil and urbane, the greater.

Yet it is this very reduction, this radical rejection of Dante's doctrinal superstructures in favor of the naïve, unfettered element in his imagination, that marks Vico as the ancestor of Romantic aesthetics and, by the same token, of nineteenth-century Dantesque criticism, in sharp contrast to the overrefined Arcadian taste of his own age, which set polish above power and thus could not stomach Dante's rugged greatness. And when, in the letter to Gherardo degli Angioli, he says that Dante's wrath in the *Divine Comedy* is like Achilles' wrath in the *Iliad*, Vico is throwing vivid light on what certainly forms a seminal nucleus of Dante's poetry, even though he fails to solve the problem aroused by his identification of poetry with myth as such and with the barbarous, unintellectual ages of mankind.

Does civilization necessarily kill poetry? Vico (unlike Hegel) would not have answered this question in the affirmative, says Fubini, and the proof comes from the otherwise misplaced faith Vico expressed in the poetical powers of his young friend Gherardo degli Angioli, whose craving for Dante's strong fare and its likes in the midst of an effete Arcadian-intellectualist epoch, he assumed, bespoke the austere taste that promises fresh creativity. In Gherardo, Fubini rightly observes, Vico was projecting his own self-portrait, and, when we read in the *Autobiography* how solitary, melancholy, and choleric Vico was, we recognize in the eighteenth-century Neapolitan thinker a very Dantesque type: proud, at loggerheads with his age, absorbed by an encompassing vision which his own time failed to share or understand, and possessed by an epic sense of the past. Dante certainly nurtured Vico through an elective affinity, and even similarities of style are to be noticed, for example, in Vico's predilection for the graphic idiom to seal a sweeping utterance. Vico's conception of a providential pattern in human history also would have linked him to Dante. The primacy of poetic imagination cannot be denied in Vico, and thus his penchant for Dante comes into proper focus as the meeting of a poet-philosopher with a philosopher-poet.

The fact that in the "Discovery of the True Dante" Vico was evolving toward a less generically historical and more literary appraisal of his congenial author is not lost on Fubini, and Fubini's assessment of Vico's limitations versus Vico's pioneering originality in the whole matter of Dantesque studies can hardly be contested. Hopefully, however, there is room for further considerations. For instance, a reading of the "Discovery of the True Dante" in sequential perspective makes one wonder why Vico should have failed to develop its full implications as an internal critique of some overly systematic claims of the *New Science*. While reasserting his Homeric analogy and Dante's consequent dependence on the barbarous ages of medieval Italy, Vico now speaks of an "expiring," rather than rampant, "barbarism" in Dante's time, thus shading his earlier statement. From the historical viewpoint he passes on to a linguistic one to correct the thesis (likewise set forth in the letter to Gherardo) of a Dante gleaning idioms from all the Italian dialects—a thesis possibly derived, directly or indirectly, from Dante's own treatise *De vulgari eloquentia*. Dante is now firmly moored to the Tuscan speech, which in Vico's estimate must have shared a number of current locutions with other Italian dialects anyway. Finally, in terms of aesthetic value, Dante appears unique and original: sublime poetry like Dante's "cannot be learned by skill or craft"; it has priority over all rules. Dante's sublimity, elsewhere described as verging on the primitive and the grotesque, is now connected with a "loftiness of mind" which, instead of accruing from the temper of the age, sets the poet apart in his contempt for whatever "greedy . . . soft, effeminate men commonly admire."[9] This loftiness of mind shown in the exclusive concern for glory and immortality (of the humanistic type) and in a soul "informed by great and public virtues—and above all by magnanimity and justice," as witness the Spartan education (despite its lack of emphasis on literature)—seems to Vico to have been fostered once in people "whose daily expressions . . . would adorn the work of the most illustrious tragic and heroic poets."

Clearly, Vico has moved beyond the conception of a "barbarous" Dante, whose only title to poetic greatness would have been the awesome portrayal of his age's cruelest passions, to bring him a step closer to full civilization. Indeed, the "Discovery of the True Dante" was written in the years (1728?, 1729?, 1730?) immediately preceding the academic address *De mente heroica* (*Of the Heroic Mind*, 1732), in which, partly owing to its pedagogic aim, the idea of heroism has shed its barbaric implications to denote a consuming passion for knowledge as the mainspring of civil virtue. There is thus a heroism of the philosopher, the civilizer of late ages, and a heroism of the representative poet, the civilizer of early ages; they share such basic traits, if we take for our texts the "Discovery of the True Dante" and the oration *Of the Heroic Mind*, that one wonders whether the shaping spirit of imagination and the piercing spirit of speculation are not about to become one in Vico's mind. They do, of course, in the poem he wrote in 1730 for Clement XII's accession to the papal throne,[10] where our thinker takes advantage of the official occasion to sing his own flight from the dejection of an aggravating earthly scene to the "inaccessible light" beyond the sky. This transcendental zone "girds and envelops the world," to figure for the astral pilgrim's eye the vicissitudes of time-bound empires in timeless fashion: it is

[9] *Ibid.*, p. 12.
[10] This poem is to be found on pp. 352–55 of Vico's *L'autobiografia, il carteggio e le poesie varie* (Autobiography, Letters, and Sundry Poems), ed. Benedetto Croce and Fausto Nicolini (Bari, 1929).

obviously the "ideal eternal history" Vico descries as a recurrent pattern governing human history in the *New Science*. In this poem, though, the exercise of timeless contemplation counts above all as a personal deliverance for the time-ridden, grief-burdened persona who, while "down there in the low world," could not make rhyme or reason of human wrongs, because his outraged intellect vainly sought truth in things human seen each by itself in disjointed isolation (*"tutte scevere e sole"*); now a total perspective has superseded the partial one to reveal the essential goodness of an over-all design which ceaselessly redeems the corruptions of history. Vico is telling us of the cathartic value of the *New Science* for its author; but in so doing he is unmistakably echoing certain climactic moments of Dante's *Paradiso*, many of whose lines will come to mind as we read of Vico's persona soaring "from sphere to heavenly sphere, from planet to planet and from star to star" (stanza 1), while the constellations of Argo, Perseus, and Hercules dwindle below him and vanish (stanza 1). In stanza 2, lines 18–20 ("Oh quanto corto, oh quanto/ col suo lungo aguzzar l'occhio ne' vetri/ è quel che ne le stelle Urania osserva!" ["Oh how short-sighted indeed is Urania's observation of the stars, despite her intent peering through the 'telescope's' glasses!"]) take their stylistic cue from *Paradiso* XXXIII. 121–23:

> Oh quanto è corto il dire e come fioco
> al mio concetto! e questo, a quel ch'i'vidi,
> è tanto, che non basta a dicer "poco."

> (Oh how my words fall short of my concept,
> and how they dim it! and it in turn, compared
> to what I saw, is not even enough to
> say "little.")

Again, lines 50–51 (stanza 3) have an unmistakable Dantesque ring:

> Oh mio pur troppo infermo occhio mortale!
> che là nel basso mondo,
> etc. etc.

> (Oh my so sadly feeble mortal eye!
> which down there in the low world. . . .)

One cannot help but recall Dante's turning back to look on the *"aiola che ci fa tanto feroci"* (the patch of land which makes us so ferocious) from the starry heights of paradise. For Vico has earned the right to conjure Dante's style, not only episodically, but as a matter of "heroic frenzy," as another poet-thinker would have said; and here the heroism of the philosophical mind does incorporate the heroism of a poetical mind likewise committed to the experience of a total cosmic perspective. At this threshold, they become one.

To return to the "Discovery of the True Dante," we must also see that, no matter how Vico may occasionally soar toward that supreme identification, he is by no means surrendering his central idea that spontaneity, *Zeitgeist*, and *Volksgeist* are essential to poetry:

... What was most peculiar to Dante's sublimity resulted from his having been born with the gift of genius in the era of Italy's expiring barbarism. For human talents are like those of the earth, which, if brought under cultivation after fallow centuries, produces at the outset fruits marvelous for their perfection, size, and abundance; but which, once tired from overmuch cultivation, yields only few, wizened, and small. And this is why, at the end of the barbarian period, there arose a Dante in sublime poetry, a Petrarch in delicate poetry, a Boccaccio in light and graceful prose: all three incomparable examples which we must by all means follow, but which we can by no means overtake. Whereas in our own highly cultivated era, such fair works of art as are being created may well raise in others the hope not merely of overtaking, but of surpassing them.[11]

At the same time, Vico no longer discounts the doctrinal-allegorical layers of Dante's work, but makes them contingent on the alert reader's response; his conception of a merely "Homeric," that is, primitive, Dante is now significantly qualified to take into account Dante's uniqueness and individual reality, as against Homer's composite, collective, anonymous, reality in the *New Science*. If so, the recourse to barbarism in medieval history can be seen as a new phase with poignant analogies rather than as a literal repetition of the earlier cycle; the image of Sisyphus, implicit in the pattern of "ideal eternal history," must yield to that of a progressive spiral, and the poet becomes more a Carlylian hero than a deterministic function of his time. Besides, the allowance made for Petrarch's "delicate" poetry is revolutionary within Vico's system if we consider how "delicacy" generally recurs in his vocabulary as a term of disparagement. Vico is averting or at least undermining a possible mechanization of his own grandiose system.

The qualities he sees in Dante, with due respect to historical juncture, are those he thought he saw at the potential stage in Gherardo degli Angioli but actually harbored in himself. Even more importantly, they are the very qualities that would appear in the new poets of an Italy Vico was never to see: aristocratic, choleric, liberty-minded Alfieri; rebellious, public-spirited, Vichian Foscolo; melancholy, austere Leopardi; earnest, historically minded Manzoni.[12] The letter to Gherardo thus amounts to a prophecy of things to come, of the rebirth of Italian literature from the renewed experience of those "virtues" which Vico saw little trace of around him. Arcadian frills

[11] From Brandeis, *Discussions of the Divine Comedy*, p. 12.

[12] With the exception of Alfieri, these writers were all variously affected by Vico. While Foscolo and Leopardi responded to Vico's ideas on myth and history in a starkly irreligious way, Manzoni was drawn as a liberal Catholic to Vico's conception of Providence, which operates, with certain modifications, in the world of *The Betrothed* and of the tragedy *Adelchi*.

would not do. And the problem of the compatibility of strong poetry with humane civilization was the same as Schiller one day would see, and solve in his way, in the *Briefe über aesthetische Erziehung* (Letters on Aesthetic Education) and in *Über naive und sentimentalische Dichtung* (On Naïve and Sentimental Poetry). If civilization is just a passive consumption of the past, it is "soft," effeminate, barren; if it is a shaping spirit, then mankind does not have to relapse into barbarism in order to renew itself (though perhaps Vico conceivably would have seen a return to barbarism in the violent outbursts of the French and Russian revolutions).

The very fact that even a glance at one aspect of Vico's work calls into question so much of the culture of his time and of the times to come is symptomatic of his exceptional stature, which enabled him to meet Dante as an equal. There are striking parallels between Dante's intellectual development and that of Vico. In a letter to Father Giacco (October 12, 1720) [13] he confesses to his resentment of those fellow citizens who remember only the "weaknesses and errors" of his youth, as if subsequent progress were not of decisive import; and this brings to mind the solitary years from 1686 to 1695, which he spent in the rural isolation of Vatolla sul Cilento as a tutor to the Rocca children, the years from which Vico's early acquaintance with meditation and anguish date, the years so laconically covered in the *Autobiography*, though from them sprang the *canzone* "Affetti d'un disperato" (Emotions of a Despondent Soul). This *canzone*, which happens to be Vico's best verse composition, according to Fausto Nicolini,[14] expresses a despondency out of tune with Catholic orthodoxy; and Professor Fisch[15] adds that the years of intellectual torment at Vatolla must also have witnessed Vico's contacts with the free-thinkers of Naples, some of whom were to get into trouble with the Inquisition. The heresy in question was connected with the Gassendian atomism[16] that found so much favor in Neapolitan circles at the time; indeed, Lucretius, the poet of Democritean atomism, was one of Vico's favorite authors and main sources, so that, as

---

[13] *L'autobiografia*, pp. 154–56.

[14] *Ibid.*, p. 367: "The somber pessimism of this poem is perhaps to be related to the religious 'weaknesses and errors' that worried Vico's youth, and also to his poor health. . . ." The poem was written in 1692, published in 1693, and, while it harks back to Petrarch, it has a strength of its own, surprisingly anticipating Leopardi. Toward the end, it envisages the Vatolla groves as a Dantesque "harsh wood." The despondent mood reappears in much of Vico's verse, but the sonnet to Filippo Pirelli counteracts it with the prophecy of glory to come after death to the thinker who was led by Providence to discover the purposive order of human history and thereby to overcome his own misery (*L'autobiografia*, p. 363; *Opere*, p. 164).

[15] See the Introduction to Fisch and Bergin's translation of Vico's *Autobiography*.

[16] For Vico's connections with this school as well as with other contemporary and earlier philosophical sects, see also Nicola Badaloni, *Introduzione a G. B. Vico* (Milan, 1961), a work, however, that limits our philosopher's originality to make Vico sound more time-bound than he actually was.

Fisch remarks, *De rerum natura*'s Book V affords quite a repertory of thematic cues for the *New Science*.

That being so, the "errors" of Vico's pensive youth are comparable to Dante's straying from the "right path" during the years between *Vita nuova* and *Convivio* (possibly under the influence of Cavalcanti's Averroism), while the overcoming of doubts and "errors" in the universal vision of the *New Science*, which reaffirms the relentlessly purposive action of a historical Providence over any "Stoic," i.e., Spinozan, conception of fate, on the one hand, and any "Epicurean," that is, Hobbesian-Machiavellian-Gassendian, conception of mere chance in human affairs, on the other, parallels Dante's spiritual trajectory from the gropings of his youth and early virility to the encompassing synthesis of the *Divine Comedy*. Through the obvious differences, we can descry a common pattern of intellectual development and singular integrity in the inner careers of these two solitary writers who quarreled so much with their respective times because they were in search of a universal truth. This truth they gained by personal suffering, one remaining a factual exile to the last, the other a spiritual exile in his own city. The note of estrangement rings out more than once in Vico's *Autobiography*: "With this learning and erudition Vico returned to Naples a stranger in his own land. . . ." [17] "For these reasons Vico lived in his native city not only a stranger but quite unknown. . . ." [18] Both were men of fiery temper, and each felt the singularity of his life as a spur to conquer a vision so much larger than himself, a vision by which his entire progress would be tested and his singularity vindicated yet transcended. Hence Vico's application of the providential concept to his autobiography, which becomes a pilgrimage toward intellectual truth. The ordeals and intercessions through which Dante the pilgrim progresses toward his kind of truth reflect a comparable design.

Of course, Vico's dialectic is not Dante's. Vico's idea of Providence is only a metaphor by comparison to Dante's Augustinian view of history, since the post-Renaissance Humanist conceives of Providence as an immanent force—indeed, as man's collective mind operating beyond the conscious motives of man's actions toward a rational order of society in *this* world—whereas Dante's conception involves a divine force intervening in human affairs from above and, on occasion, through miracles. Dante would have found it impossible to accept Vico's revolutionary statement that man makes his own world in history, indeed makes himself in the

---

[17] Fisch and Bergin, *Autobiography*, p. 132.

[18] *Ibid.*, p. 134. To these statements add the remarks in the concluding paragraph of the book, where Vico tells how many fellow citizens shunned or mocked him as a lunatic, and how he took advantage of these aggravations to withdraw to his desk, where, as in a "high, unbreachable fortress," he would meditate further works, thus eventually achieving his masterpiece.

process, and can therefore know the relevant laws from the "modifications" of his own mind.   Dante is immersed in the mythology Vico tests by his critical solvents; Vico's proto-Marxist reduction of all myths to the merely human and social element is the reverse of Dante's transcendent faith.   Yet Vico, the dismantler of myth, was a mythmaker of sorts, for he could not help fashioning his own myths in the process of describing the epos of aboriginal history.   No wonder, then, that he should warm up to mythographer Dante, with whom he shared a dramatic sense of the mind's workings, an epic sense of human action, and a keen power of sensuous perception to embody his ideas.   Vico's philosophy, unlike Kant's, never hovers for long in the spheres of logical abstraction, but takes the characteristic form of vivid axiomatic insights, with corollaries of rushing eloquence, all things seen and action felt, which stand to their generating axioms as the movements of a Beethoven symphony stand to the sharp initial statement of their themes.   Vico, like Dante, thinks in concrete terms, and the physical world is never far from his focus; we are never allowed to forget that Sir Francis Bacon, the philosopher of experience, is among his cardinal authors.   Vico does not just *talk* about the origins, development, and crisis of civilization: he makes us *see* the crucial scenes and imaginatively participate in the choral action, even while taking his bearings in the vastest perspective he can afford.

"Men at first feel without perceiving, then they perceive with a troubled and agitated spirit, finally they reflect with a clear mind" (axiom LIII, paragraph 218, *New Science*).   The ternary rhythm of existential growth is the rhythm of knowledge, and it governs the cycles of human history—the *storia ideale eterna*.   One could point out its affinity to the Aristotelian rhythm of tragedy from passion to epiphany, as reinterpreted by Francis Fergusson and by him applied to the structure of Dante's poem.[19]   For these three archetypal phases of consciousness and existence are the secularized versions of hell (unthinking passion), purgatory (the suffering that enlightens), and paradise (pure vision of being).   A common dynamic pattern underlies the philosophical dialectic of the mature Vico and the poetico-theological dialectic of the mature Dante.   Vico, the secularist, is far from irreverent; he has the piety of humanity, whose unfolding through recurrent conflict is the drama of all dramas, the crowning essence of all poetry.   He calls his critique of history a "reasoned civil theology," and, though he still sets the history of the Chosen People apart from gentile history, it is but a step from his conception to Hegel's final dictum that "all history is sacred history." He is moved, and moves us, by the imagined spectacle of fallen mankind, a lawless herd of "big beasts all stupor and ferocity," wandering aimlessly through the huge postdiluvial forest, eventually to be stricken with numinous fear by the thunderbolts a sky saturated with moisture finally flings at them

[19] Francis Fergusson, *The Idea of a Theater* (Princeton, 1949); *idem, Dante's Drama of the Mind* (Princeton, 1953); *idem, Dante* (New York, 1966).

as if it were an angry Zeus. With the dawning of religion from fear in the naïve mind of the bestial giants, the long journey toward civilization begins, and the inarticulate "cyclops" are on the way to becoming human, social, rational. We move from the infernal to the purgatorial phase, from the Dark Wood of error and violence, from the City of Dis and Malebolge, toward a glimpsed order.

> And oh! how hard it is to describe
> This savage forest, harsh and impervious.
> So bitter is it, that death is scarcely more.
> But to deal with the good I found therein
> I shall speak of the other things I saw in that very place.

The providential pattern, ontologically externalized by Dante in accordance with his faith and epistemologically reduced by Vico to an indwelling force of the collective mind, operates from the start, turning to account the worst predicament in order to make a virtue out of necessity. To say it with Hölderlin, "Wo aber Gefahr ist, waechst/ Das Rettende auch" (But where danger is, there grows/ Salvation also).[20]

If it is possible to use Dante as an illustration of Vico, and Vico in turn as a commentary on Dante's authenticity, it is because each writer, in terms of his cultural framework, grasps archetypes of human experience. The poem of salvation can be read as an allegory of civilization; conversely, the *New Science* is itself such a poem, divested of the supernatural aspects that had to go into the making of the *Divine Comedy*. Accordingly, the more recent of these two structures of vision incorporates a number of elements from the older one and transmutes them into its own fabric. The forest and the city, opposed yet interchangeable, appear as fundamental images throughout the *Divine Comedy*, as well as in the *New Science* and in Vico's letter to Gherardo. Farinata, Capaneus, Ulysses, Ugolino, with the enormity of their passions, correspond to the "atheist giants" in the *New Science*, whom Jupiter's thunderbolts—a self-projected fiction of the susceptible primitive mind— will eventually humble into submission to the rudiments of law. The similarity of images is counterpoised by the antithesis in philosophical conception, since here Vico's social redemption in history supersedes Dante's theological condemnation of his unredeemable rebels in the beyond, and we could expect no less from the philosopher who revalued myth in the very act of applying to it his anthropological reduction because he could both see through it and feel it as something alive. Again, mythical giants appear in the *Inferno*, and one of them, Nimrod, has to do with the Tower of Babel and the bewildering multiplication of languages—a theme of the utmost interest to Vico, as seen in section II of the *New Science* ("Poetic Logic"), especially paragraph 445.

[20] From Hölderlin's "Patmos," ll. 3–4.

In Vico's own mythology it is one of the traits of primitive giants that they are mute, as the demons are in Dante's *De vulgari eloquentia*, which makes speech the absolute privilege of man. Whether Vico ever read the *De vulgari eloquentia* is a matter of surmise, but the Giants' Canto in *Inferno*, which is directly related to that treatise, was not lost on him, for it fed his imaginative hypothesis on the origins of mankind. Both writers—the philosophical poet and the poetical philosopher—were focally interested in the theme of language, for Dante gave us in the *De vulgari eloquentia* the first historical treatise on linguistics and infused the poetical action of the *Divine Comedy* with a unique linguistic awareness,[21] while Vico, in the section of the *New Science* called "Poetic Logic," practically founded modern language theory, anticipating Ernst Cassirer's *Philosophy of Symbolic Forms*. Concern with language actually informs most of Dante's treatises from *Vita nuova* to *Convivio* and *De vulgari eloquentia*, to come to a head in the writing of his major poem; with Vico the same concern asserts itself in the *De antiquissima Italorum sapientia*, of 1710, which uses a factitious linguistic archaeology to convey the author's metaphysics and theory of knowledge at this stage.

In this connection we can hardly forget how Dante and Vico likewise debated with themselves for a time whether to use the Italian vernacular or the time-honored Latin of scholars, finally to decide in favor of Italian in their respective crowning works. Here, too, Vico seems to rehearse his great predecessor's career. See his *Autobiography* for the resolve to leave "Tuscan" and Greek and to concentrate on Latin at a certain point of his life,[22] and remember that, just as after the Latin works of Dante—*De vulgari eloquentia*, *Epistles*, and *Monarchia*—came the vernacular *Divina Commedia*, so the *New Science* came after a long series of books which Vico wrote in Latin: the six academic *Orations*, the *De antiquissima*, and the *De uno universi iuris principio et fine uno*, of 1720, which may be considered the first version of the *New Science* itself. In addition, Vico's Italian is not unlike Dante's in its grafting of Latinisms onto a strongly idiomatic stock, as well as in its pre-dilection for energetic expressions focusing on verbs that at times verge on the peculiar. Style and vision, in both writers, evolve from a relative initial abstractness to the rich concreteness of the final works, the *Divine Comedy* and the *New Science*, into which they gathered the full fruits of their ripening.

It involves no injustice to the necessary distinctions between the medieval poem of salvation and the early modern philosophical epic of civilization to see Dante and Vico as mutually illuminating. Their relationship is dialectical. Dante's imagination builds on the very hypostases that Vico's genetic theory unmasks, but, because Vico is no thin-blooded rationalist, he interprets without devitalizing and leaves us with the life of pulsing experience, not just

---

[21] See my "Dante and the Drama of Language," in *The World of Dante: Six Essays in Language and Thought*, ed. S. B. Chandler and J. A. Molinaro (Toronto, 1966).
[22] Fisch and Bergin, *Autobiography*, pp. 133–34.

with abstract schemata. The *New Science* absorbs in its imaginative and rational economy that *Inferno* which, during the Enlightenment, was repelling bloodlessly fastidious tastes *à la Voltaire*. Cannibalism, immoderate lust, the "infamous promiscuity of things and of women," [23] untold violence, down to fecal sordidness (see "Malebolge" in the *Inferno* along with paragraph 369, Book II, "On Poetic Wisdom," of the *New Science*)—these are the archaic experiences of the human race, since the human builds on the brutal and social chaos is the matrix of social order. Dante must pass through hell to get to see the stars again. Historical Providence is forever at work, transforming, not punishing or suppressing, the amoral forces of instinct, and myth, poetry, religion—these necessary fictions of childlike giants—are the agents of that providential sublimation. Thus we see that the *New Science* closely parallels Dante's poem by celebrating in its choral way the perennial *purging process* of mankind, which in the *Divine Comedy* focuses on the pilgrim persona. Dante's beyond has become Vico's here and now; heaven and hell, as Blake was to say in unconsciously Vichian style, reappear as psychological realities dialectically related: the pole of energy, namely, live instinctual matter, and the pole of reason, or form, to shape that inner substance of wild instinct.

In the process, what Vico calls "the grossness of heroic minds" [24] sharpens itself by expressing its mythic fictions in the very first kind of cognitive experience there can ever be. If we discount the inevitable differences, such purification finds its counterpart in Dante's ascent from world to world. When he rises into the heady ether of Paradise in his earthly shape, he lacks terms to decipher the new experience, so that Beatrice tells him:

> Tu stesso ti fai grosso
> col falso imaginar. . . .[25]
>
> (You embroil yourself in grossness
> through false imaginings. . . .)

Beatrice, here in *Paradiso*, canto I, has taken over Virgil's function as provi-

[23] Thomas Bergin and Max H. Fisch, trans., *The New Science of Giambattista Vico* (Ithaca, N.Y., 1948; Garden City, N.Y., 1961), sec. VII, par. 688; Conclusion, par. 1099. In the unabridged 1948 edition see par. 369 of bk. II, "Of Poetic Wisdom," where the unattended children of fallen mankind roaming the world-wide forest after the Flood are left to their own devices to roll in their excrement, which is supposed to bring about an abnormal growth of the body, thus making them giants. This is one of the strongest passages, stylistically speaking. On a different level, take par. 1108 from the Conclusion of the work, for a masterly treatment of the idea of historical Providence as mankind's propelling mind working against and beyond each particular purpose of human action to bring about courses and recourses of civilization. Cogency of thought is here allied to poetical strength of style, with a concision worthy of Dante.

[24] Bergin and Fisch, *New Science*, par. 457, p. 111.

[25] *Paradiso* I. 88–89.

dential guide to direct the pilgrim's growth; Vico's indwelling providence performs the same function for the collective pilgrim, mankind, which must forever rise from its own volcanic abysses to the purgatory of humanization, and on to full self-knowledge. It is no accident that language here, as elsewhere, should clinch the point with sharp analogy, perhaps even an intentional echo on Vico's part. For it is precisely the "false imaginings" which start the deliverance of primitive mankind from brutish "grossness." Vico left several lyrics that intermittently reveal his poetical gift, but he was never so much the poet as when he wrote the charged prose of the *New Science*. What an irony, that right there (axiom LIII, paragraph 218) he should have declared poetry and philosophy mutually incompatible; for it was this very polarity which tensed the sinews of his writing and enabled him to relive Dante's vision on his own terms.[26]

[26] I like to stress the problematic versus the systematic aspect of Vico's thought because it brings him closer to our own difficult age. But already Leopardi's dilemma of fiction and truth could be said to resume certain emphases of Vico's. In any case, Vico's revaluation of Dante was a prophecy of Romanticism, and the two writers were to have a revival in Romantic times.

Santino Caramella   VICO, TACITUS,
                         AND
                         REASON OF STATE

Cornelius Tacitus was one of the "four authors" favored by G. B. Vico
for his meditations; indeed, Vico placed Tacitus with Plato as a fundamental
text for his philosophical studies before he added Bacon and Grotius to their
company. "For with an incomparable metaphysical mind Tacitus contemplates man as he is, Plato as he should be; and as Plato with his universal
knowledge explores the parts of nobility which constitute the man of
intellectual wisdom, so Tacitus descends into all the counsels of utility
whereby, among the infinite irregular chances of malice and fortune, the
man of practical wisdom brings things to good issue."[1]
    In fact, Vico devoted to the study of Tacitus such care and attention as to
deserve a high place among students of *tacitismo* (Tacitism).[2]   Not only did
he use this author as a classic text in his public and private lessons and comment upon him for his philological characteristics as well as for his own
literary and historical theories, praising Tacitus for his wisdom and educative
gifts,[3] but he continually drew from him illustrations and maxims fundamental to the elaboration of systematic doctrines expounded in the *Diritto
universale* and the *Scienza nuova* and to the interpretation of the ancient world
contained in the latter work.[4]
    However, the way Tacitus "descends into all counsels of utility" was not
interpreted by Vico in the tendentiously Stoic or theological manner that
had prevailed among the Tacitists.   Particularly after the discovery of the
first six books of the *Annales* in the Medicean Codex,[5] the Tacitists had
interpreted the criticism of the tortuous and tyrannical policy of Tiberius as

[1] Vico, *L'autobiografia*, in *Opere*, ed. F. Nicolini (Naples, 1953), pp. 31–32, 48, 49.   On
the relation between Vico and Tacitus see G. Fassò, *I "quattro auttori" del Vico* (Milan,1949).
[2] G. Toffanin, *Machiavelli e il Tacitismo* (Padua, 1921), p. 220.
[3] See the sketch for a historical commentary (after 1730) on "Gli 'Annali' di Tacito al
lume della 'Scienza nuova,'" published by Nicolini in the *Scritti storici di G. B. Vico*,
vol. VI (1939) of Nicolini's *Opere*, 8 vols. (Bari, 1914–40), pp. 401–13.   On the judgment
and use of Tacitus' works by Vico's school see vol. V of the *Opere* (Bari), pp. 959, 965.
[4] Citations of Tacitus, with exegeses and critical inductions, in the *De uno universi iuris
principio et fine uno* and in the *De constantia philologiae* number some fifty; in the *Scienza
nuova* (of 1744) there are at least sixty.
[5] Filippo Cavriana, *Discorsi sopra i primi cinque libri di C. Tacito* (Florence, 1597);
Curzio Pichena, *Ad C. Taciti opera notae* (Florence, 1600).

the exaltation of the ethical integrity of the republican conscience. Vico, on
the other hand, contraposed to the ideal of the incorruptible prince—even in
his own times proclaimed by Paolo Mattia Doria in *Della educazione del
principe* (Naples, 1710)—"that prince whom Cornelius Tacitus and Nicolò
Machiavelli endowed with every evil art of government."[6] Both great
historians agreed, therefore, in studying and describing the insidious arts of
government in the real figure of a head of state, for perhaps they believed, as
Vico did, that with their impositions tyrants demand or forgo the certainty
of facts, however painful, thereby arousing by contrast, through the sense of
the "certain," the "consciousness that does not doubt the state."[7] They
were thus in accord in maintaining that in the tests which men must face
through extreme cases of fortune, *id aequius quod validius*, the greatest merit,
insofar as justice is concerned, belongs to valor, to heroic strength.[8]

The reason for this parallel between Tacitus and Machiavelli lies in that
contemplation (according to the consciousness of the state) of man "as he is"
which the *Scienza nuova*, in one of its celebrated *degnità*, defines as the true
purpose of legislation: "Legislation considers man as he is in order to turn
him to good uses in human society. Out of ferocity, avarice, and ambition,
the three vices which run throughout the human race, it creates the military,
merchant, and governing classes, and thus the strength, riches, and wisdom
of commonwealths. Out of these three great vices, which could certainly
destroy all mankind on the face of the earth, it makes civil happiness."[9]
With the intention of furnishing the legislative work of states and statesmen
with a body of facts objectively appraised, Vico, through this conception,
accounted for the narrative and psychological crudities in Tacitus; he linked
a realistic consideration of utilitarian and passional motives—in which
Machiavelli had seen the nourishing elements of the forms and mutations of
political life—with the principle of the "heterogenesis of ends," which his
philosophy of history would place in the forefront.[10]

[6] Vico, *De antiquissima Italorum sapientia: Liber primus seu metaphysicus* (1710), in *Opere* (Naples), I, 246.

[7] Vico, *Sinossi del diritto universale*, in *Opere* (Bari), II, 5.

[8] Vico, Prologue, *De uno universi iuris principio*, in *Opere* (Bari), II, 32.

[9] Thomas G. Bergin and Max H. Fisch, trans., *New Science* (Garden City, N.Y., 1961), bk. II, sec. II, par. 7; cf. Nicolini's critical edition of the text in *Opere* (Bari), IV, 437.

[10] Nicolini has proved the derivation of *degnità* no. VII from bk. I, chap. 3, of Machiavelli's *Discorsi sopra la prima deca di Tito Livio*, which Vico cites as *Lectiones livianae*. Cf. *Opere* (Naples), pp. 562, and *Opere* (Bari), IV, 1472; cf. also other *degnità* (e.g., nos. XXX–XXXI, LXXIV, LXXXVIII, and XCIII) with *Discorsi*, bk. I, pp. 11, 2, and 37, respectively. Nicolini deals with the problem in greater detail in his *Commento storico . . .* (Rome, 1949), pp. 11ff., and in his essay "Su taluni rapporti ideali tra il Vico e Hobbes, con qualche riferimento a Machiavelli," *English Miscellany* (Rome, 1950). Still, Vico never retracted the negative sentence contained in the *De constantia philologiae*, which held that "Macchiavellus genus romanae re reipublicae non assecutus" (*Opere* [Bari], II, 562).

At this very point the convergence between Tacitus and Machiavelli ceased, "for the skeptics Epicurus, Machiavelli, Hobbes, Spinoza, Bayle, and others claimed that man is social through utility, having been made so by need and fear, but they did not notice that the reason for things is one thing and the occasions another: utility changes but equality is eternal."[11]   Vico attributed this utilitarianism as a theory of contingency and occasionalism to almost all rationalist political thinkers, down to those of his own day.   He himself was the thinker who at long last attained the moment of legitimation of utilitarian activity through an understanding of the origins of civilization and of the formation of the human personality.   For him, the useful consists of the positive and efficient initial guidance exerted upon the senses and their efforts by fantasy and passions, through which they are eventually made dependent upon the purposive justification of reason.   But to circumscribe the development of utility in the realm of law and of political life only within the first phases of the senses and of the passions behind action, by maintaining, as Machiavelli and Hobbes did, that reason was subordinate and instrumental, was like continually reverting civilization to its primitive substratum and tended to despoil man of what he had made of himself over and above nature in order to re-present him with those primordial tendencies which he believed he had surpassed and forgotten.[12]

Other great political thinkers, such as Bodin, had in part avoided this error by studying at closer range the practice and theory of the Romans,[13] but they had not succeeded in resisting the suggestiveness of the mythico-heroic moment and had attributed to it a fundamental value that it did not have. In fact, Bodin had believed that at the beginning of the Roman Republic the aristocracy, once it came to power, had laid the foundations for the democratic state, whereas, before its evolution, it was incapable of establishing anything more than an aristocratic state.[14]   In the same manner, Bodin had seen the monarchy—according to the legend of Rome as a model of the origins of the history of every State—as being capable of determining the popular forms, and then the aristocratic, as the most perfect.   For Vico it was not a question of the monarchy but of the general principle of the state,

[11] Nicolini, *Opere* (Bari), II, 4.   The same arguments can be found in the *Diritto universale*, in *ibid.*, pp. 32, 301, and in the *Scienza nuova*, par. 1109.

[12] In "the Cyclopes . . . Plato recognizes the first family fathers of the world.   This tradition, misunderstood, gave rise to that common error of all political theorists, that the first form of civil government in the world was monarchic.   They are thus given over to those false principles of evil politics: that civil governments were born either of open violence or of fraud which later broke out into violence" (Bergin and Fisch, *New Science*, par. 522).   Cf. the text in Nicolini's edition of the *Opere* (Bari), IV, pt. 1, p. 230.

[13] *Scienza nuova prima*, in *Opere* (Bari), III, 225; *Scienza nuova seconda*, in *Opere* (Bari), IV, 320, 71.

[14] *Scienza nuova seconda*, in *Opere* (Bari), IV, par. 952.

that is, of that "eternal natural royal law by which the free power of a state, just because it is free, must be actualized."[15] Roman historians like Tacitus had exalted the part played by the monarchy during the period of origins and they began again the periodization of the Empire from the principate of Augustus in order to assert their political preferences.[16]

But, even for the theorists of pure natural reason, that function of myth had been decisive. When Spinoza "speaks of the commonwealth as if it were a society of hucksters,"[17] he is referring, according to Vico, to a commercial social system in transition from the utilitarian medieval economy to modern juridical institutions; it was, therefore, partly a barbaric tradition founded on the myth of hoarded money, which in due time was to be submitted to laws of rational necessity. And Locke, who based his appeal for a rational order upon free will, founded his theory of civil society on the passions of ambitious interest.[18] At any rate, not even in the formulations of absolutist theories of modern politics had it yet been possible to leave out consideration of the resolutive mythical moment, like that of the God of Hobbes, who intervenes in order to impose the authority of the monarch as His representative, capable of realizing a geometric order of justice and a principle of autonomy through the equally mythical claim of everyman to everything.[19] The question of the mythical moment was one of those connections of ideas through which Vico derived many of his problems from those same rationalists whose adversary he was.

Other relationships in the field of political problems were established by Vico through his knowledge and analysis of absolutist politics.[20] The War of Spanish Succession aroused in him profound reflection and grave historical meditation.[21] In that war he saw the delineation of the conflict between different conceptions of traditional feudal law which continued to signify the persistence of medieval civilization: he thus discerned the opening of the first great crisis that was to lead to the revolutionary dissolution of that civilization. He was able to compare the equal assertion of a new absolute regime

[15] *Ibid.*, par. 1084.

[16] *Ibid.*, pars. 1009–19.

[17] *Ibid.*, par. 335; cf. Spinoza's *Tractatus theologico-politicus* (Amsterdam, 1670), chap. XVI.

[18] Vico, "Riprensione delle metafisiche di Renato delle Carte, di Benedetto Spinoza e di Giovanni Locke," in Nicolini's *Opere* (Bari), vol. IV, pt. 2, pp. 198–99.

[19] See F. Meinecke, *Die Idee der Staatsräson* (Munich, 1925), pp. 259–78; H. J. Krüger, *Theologie und Aufklärung* (Stuttgart, 1966), pp. 24–33.

[20] The principal relevant text, from the standpoint of the study of the facts, is the *De rebus gestis Antoni Caraphaei* (1716). Nicolini has stressed the text (of bk. I, chap. II) in which the superiority of men endowed with practical sensibility rather than with "secret wisdom" is asserted (*Opere* [Naples], pp. 975–77).

[21] In the oration "In morte di Anna Aspermont d'Althann" (*Opere* [Naples], pp. 987–93) and in the "Principum neapolitanorum coniurationis anni MDCCI historia" (*Opere* [Naples], pp. 993–1009).

over the kingdom of Naples through the establishment of the monarchy of Philip V of Bourbon in 1702 and through that of Charles III of Bourbon in 1734, and thus to determine the order of royal traditions of the latter dynasty.[22] In the meantime, his active participation in the life of the University of Naples under four successive authoritarian regimes was directed toward the interpretation of their presence according to the principles of culture and law. The entire experience of Neapolitan culture, in its fortunate or adverse alternatives for Vico, was considered by him to be a political experience of the contrast between the rationalistic tendencies (Epicurean and Cartesian) and the traditional tendencies (of the "Romanists" and the jurisdictionalists)[23] which was still resolved in favor of myth.

The mythical moment of history did not, however, have meaning for Vico only as a base of, or as an immediate solution to, political life (such as, for instance, the utilitarian development of barbaric energies, the assertion of heroism, the generation of law from force). For him the mythical moment had also a mediating and teleological function, and in this lies the secret motivating idea of his philosophy of history. Now, when he celebrates the merit of Tacitus by saying that the latter "strews his metaphysics, moral and political, through facts, as the times strew them before him, confused and without system,"[24] to which metaphysics does he aim to refer: to the poetical metaphysics of the primitive and heroic world, or to the rational metaphysics of law? There is no doubt that the reference is to the first of these two meanings, for, considering as a definition of "a true property of human mind" the maxim of Tacitus "*mobiles ad superstitionem perculsae semel mentes*" (*Annales* I. 28), Vico interprets *superstitio* as a center of forced interest for all sense activities. And he believes that through this type of *superstitio* primitive men "whatever they saw, imagined, or did themselves they believed to be Jove,"[25] that is, that they formed the first "fantastic universal" —myth par excellence. Because—again according to a formula from Tacitus (*Annales* V. 10), which Vico rendered proverbial—"*fingebant simul credebantque*": for it is this act of believing in one's own fiction that in the minds of the people gives authority to poetry and allows it to form and transmit with its myths the "*metaphysica gentium*," traditional ideas on religion, immortality, morality. However, even the metaphysics of Epicurus is founded on atomic images that mythically fly through the spaces and times of the world, and it is therefore in unjustified contrast with the wisdom of a

[22] Vico read, for the University of Naples, the *Panegyricus* for the visit of King Philip V in 1702 (*Opere* [Bari], VII, 118–32) and the allocution for the accession of King Charles III (*ibid.*, pp. 179–80), whose consecutive number he claimed he had established. Cf. *ibid.*, VI, 423–24.

[23] S. Mastellone, *Pensiero politico e vita culturale a Napoli nella seconda metà del Seicento* (Messina, 1965).

[24] *L'autobiografia*, p. 48.

[25] Bergin and Fisch, *New Science*, pp. 29, 76–77.

primitive and fanciful era.[26]   Now, the metaphysics of Epicurus, through the Humanists, was the foundation of the utilitarianism of Machiavelli, and here, indeed, one may find the reason for the different evaluations of Tacitus and Machiavelli made by Vico.   For Tacitus evidently uses the metaphysics of the legendary epoch and of the "ancient roman law," which was "a serious poem" ("*serioso poema*"),[27] in order to comprehend and judge the mythical elements of historical facts, while Machiavelli reduces these elements to a rational system all his own.

Even in the interpretation of the course of events, Cornelius Tacitus represented for Vico a vaster and more profound conception of history.   His *Annales* begin with the characteristic proposition (I. 1): "*Urbem Romam a principio reges habuere.*"   Why *habuere*, and not a verb that might point to domination, power?   *Habuere* "is the weakest of the three degrees of possessions distinguished by jurisconsults: *habere, tenere, possidere*, in order to signify the uncertainty of heroic kingdoms, which are preserved through the physical possession of the edifices of the city."[28]   The age of the kings of Rome did not have to be defined according to a finished form of early monarchy, but rather as the primitive appearance of a weak royal power, against which the work of Tiberius as Augustus' successor (in the narration of the first book of the *Annales*) reveals the arts of a reform of the republic into a monarchy.[29]

The probing search of the thought of Tacitus in relation to the new historical concept of myth is demonstrated in other Vichian propositions. Thus we read that, "in the long course that rumor has run from the beginning of the world, it has been the perennial source of all the exaggerated opinions which have hitherto been held concerning remote antiquities unknown to us, by virtue of that property noted by Tacitus in the *Life of Agricola* (chapter 20), where he says that everything unknown is taken for something great (*omne ignotum pro magnifico est*)."[30]   There is no tradition without myth; but the initial alogicality of this implies the objective projection of ignorance, according to the relativity of the human mind.

It is therefore understandable how Vico's interest in Tacitus and in Tacitism was converted from the start into the study of the "just reason of state" as the most advisable form of political science.   It had to consider the general principle of power in the state on the basis of the reality of jurisprudence and thus to identify itself with "civil equity."   "*Aequitas civilis* is the same as *aequitas naturalis* but spans a still wider compass, since it is not dependent on the utilitarian motive of the promotion of the interests of

[26] *Ibid.*, p. 75; cf. *De uno universi iuris principio*, sec. 185, in *Opere* (Naples), p. 212.

[27] Nicolini, *Opere* (Naples), p. 343.

[28] *Ibid.*, p. 200; and "Gli 'Annali' di Tacito," *Opere* (Bari), VI, 401.

[29] *De uno universi iuris principio*, sec. 160, *Opere* (Bari), II, 169; cf. *Ragionamento secondo*, par. 1456, in *Opere* (Naples), pp. 899–900.

[30] Bergin and Fisch, *New Science*, p. 120.

private individuals but its major concern is the public weal."³¹   Understood in this manner, "*ragion di Stato*" encompassed three moments: excellent counsels, which united civil equity with natural equity; counsels that with some damage to private individuals produce much greater public utility; and counsels of private utility which are not contrary to the interests of the state.   Excluded as acts of rebellion were those counsels in favor of the utility of single individuals but contrary to the state; and, as tyrannical acts, those which were injurious to both the single individual and the state.

In the Vichian "reason of state," collective interest therefore represented the first necessary indication of the moralization of individual utility.   Its basis lay in natural law, which Hugo Grotius, citizen of a popular republic, had first succeeded in interpreting in this sense, a sense which nevertheless remained concealed from the ingenuous and egocentric realism of the masses.³²   Furthermore, the unity of civil justice and the justice of nature was not just a criterion nor merely a scientific rule.   That unity required the correlation between "reason of state" and Providence because it is this that disposes the general plan of history ("*storia ideale eterna*") upon which human actions develop in time, even as it attracts and directs human actions toward its ends of perfection and the good.   "Reason of state" functions as a mediator between the providential order of institutions and of political events and the common understanding of the natural order as it manifests itself in social relations.   It maneuvers the activities of legislation and jurisprudence in such a way as to lead men toward the ultimate and religiously ascertained purposes of social life.   The mediating term that it employs is the very same as that of civil equity, of which "golden is the definition" as "a kind of probable judgment, not naturally known to all men" (as natural equity is) but "to those few who, being eminently endowed with prudence, experience, or learning, have come to know what things are necessary for the conservation of human society.   This is what is nowadays called 'reason of state.' "³³

But how is the scientific and democratic exigency implicit in "reason of state" reconciled with its character as a science proper to men of government and therefore still aristocratic and unknown to the majority of citizens?   In resolving this decisive problem Vico parts ways even with Tacitean doctrine: he considers "reason of state" itself (in a political sense) as a mediating moment between theocratic and democratic polity.   Three "kinds of reason" ("*spezie delle ragioni*") must be distinguished in the process of development of states:

The first is divine and understood only by God; men know of it what has been revealed

───────

³¹ Elio Gianturco, trans., *On the Study Methods of Our Time* (Indianapolis, Ind., 1965), p. 66.

³² Nicolini, *Opere* (Bari), VII, 27.

³³ Bergin and Fisch, *New Science*, p. 50.   Vico arbitrarily attributes to Ulpian this classical formula of the juristic *maximarium*.

to them. . . . This by the eternal property that when men fail to see reason in human institutions, and much more if they see it opposed, they take refuge in the inscrutable counsels hidden in the abyss of divine providence. The second was reason of state, called by the Romans *civilis aequitas*, which Ulpian defined for us as not naturally known to all men but only to the few experts in government who are able to discern what is necessary for the preservation of mankind.[34]

It was in this oligarchic rationale of a ruling class that the Roman Senate excelled both in the aristocratic and in the popular phases of the Republic, but the way in which it succeeded demonstrates its limitations. The political wisdom of the Romans consisted in asserting literally and scrupulously the forms of civil equity (of the collective interest) achieved by political consciousness through the forces of heroism, which had introduced and constituted its original experience. It is therefore necessary to think of a third kind of reason in political life: that which considers the identification of equity with the good, the *aequum bonum* or "natural reason" of full justice, and which will indeed be the "true" reason of state. This is proper to the modern world because it is realized "in the human times, in which free popular states or monarchies develop. In the former the citizens have command of the public wealth . . . [while] in the second the subjects are commanded to look after their own private interests and leave the care of the public interest to the sovereign."[35] The reserve of a strict science, with which reason of state in popular monarchic governments was privileged, was therefore admissible only as a consequence of the entrusting of political authority to the prince; however, the morality of the democratic conscience was its condition.[36]

For "in the purely free republic everything is conducted openly and generously." For Vico, Tacitus' highest merit lay in his having criticized the importance assigned by Aristotle (and again by the treatise-writers of the Renaissance) to the "mixed forms" of states in contrast with the three "pure" ("mere") forms of aristocracy, democracy, and monarchy, which represent the natural order given by Providence to history. "For others besides these three [forms] mixed by human providence, since the nature of nations does not support them, are defined by Tacitus . . . as 'more praiseworthy than capable of being attained, and, if by chance there are others, they are not at

[34] *Ibid.*, pp. 299–300.

[35] *Ibid.*, p. 301.

[36] Also with respect to the practice of reason of state by ministers, Vico would have preferred that it be developed in terms of friends and private counselors of the prince, rather than of authorized governors. Thus he praised the example given by Sallustius Crispus, nephew of the famous historians. Cf. Tacitus *Annales* III. 30; Gianturco, *On the Study Methods of Our Time*, pp. 53, 78. In this Vico agreed with the Tacitist Anton Giulio Brignole Sale, *Tacito abburattato* (Genoa, 1643), reprinted in B. Croce and S. Caramella, eds., *Politici e moralisti del Seicento* (Bari, 1930); cf. especially Machiavelli, *Discorsi*, bk. VIII, pp. 219–31.

all durable.' " [37]   The possibility of the conception of a pure democracy, as a perfect political form and basis for all others, was truly the principle in which Vico most decidedly anticipated and prophesied the development of eighteenth-century thought, which closed with the most rigorous affirmation of exactly such a principle.   Through this prospect Vico seems to have interested Montesquieu, who admits no other political forms than those distinguished by him as republican (democratic and aristocratic), monarchic and despotic.[38]   And in this same sense the thought of Vico reappears in its full efficacy in the doctrines of the Neapolitan Jacobins Francesco Mario Pagano and Vincenzo Cuoco.

It was above all in its prophetic aspect that Vico's political thought anticipated his century—in the glance that, in the last pages of the *Scienza nuova*, he cast upon the "modern world of nations."   He already saw "a complete humanity spread abroad through all nations" through the absolute prevalence of great unitary (monarchic) states on all continents.   Even if some of these retained forms of aristocratic administration, they all evolved toward a synthesis between democracy and monarchy and, especially in Europe, they contained a great number of free cities, the fruit of greater progress in scientific culture.   The union of a great number of sovereign powers in leagues of nations not only was the modern political form destined to resolve within itself aristocratic tendencies that were suspicious of progress but it also led toward the formation of a new and truer aristocracy—that of confederated democratic states, in which the perfection of civilization is achieved.[39]

Translated by A. William Salomone

---

[37] Tacitus *Annales* IV. 33; cf. Vico, *Scienza nuova seconda*, in *Opere* (Naples), pp. 387, 812, and the *De uno universi iuris principio*, sec. 151, *Opere* (Bari), II, 151–52.

[38] Montesquieu, *De l'esprit des lois* (Geneva, 1748), II, 1–2.

[39] Bergin and Fisch, *New Science*, pp. 370–72.

Ernesto Grassi   CRITICAL PHILOSOPHY
OR TOPICAL PHILOSOPHY?
Meditations on the
De nostri temporis studiorum ratione

Today we are so far-removed from the terminology of Vico that the question contained in the title of this essay must appear meaningless. It is true that Vico constantly set in opposition to critical philosophy—the most important representative of which for him was Descartes—what he called *ars topica*, which might be rendered "topical philosophy." But this opposition seems to us today to be linked to a set of problems having for the most part only a historical interest; it certainly has little contemporary relevance. For who today knows what significance the term "topics" (so dear to Vico) might have as an antithesis to Cartesian, or critical, philosophy? The very terminology has been superseded; at least, so it will seem to the greater part of today's readers.

I

From the beginning, the Western philosophical tradition has made a basic distinction between rhetorical-pathetic and logico-rational discourse. Rhetorical discourse seeks to move souls, to act upon the "pathos"; it achieves its end by using patterns that act on our instincts, on our passions, which generally become aroused by images (which hold sway over the imagination), and does not seek to justify itself rationally. Rational discourse, however, is based on the human capacity to make deductions and thereby to link conclusions to premises. Rational discourse achieves its demonstrative effect and its compulsion by means of logical demonstration. The deductive process is completely closed within itself and as such cannot admit other forms of persuasion which do not derive from the logical process.
    Thus it is that rhetorical discourse—inasmuch as it is pathetic discourse— cannot make claims or command respect in the sphere of rational discourse, which is the form proper to the sciences. At the very beginning of modern philosophy, Descartes consciously excluded rhetoric—and other subjects proper to humanistic education—from philosophy conceived as pure search for truth. In Descartes' view, philosophy does not seek to express truth in a "beautiful" or rhetorically "convincing" way; the sole scientifically valid

assertion is that which arises from demonstration, that is, by the adduction of the reasons for one's own assertions, by "showing" them, "explaining" them, to the auditor.   Thus, rhetoric appears as an imperfect, imprecise, even destructive way of speaking; acting on the passions, it can only disturb the clarity of logical thought.

From this dualism of *pathos* and *logos*, of rhetorical and rational discourse, arise consequences of profound importance for subsequent pedagogy and practical affairs.   First of all, since the rational process is deductive and should be achievable by everyone according to logical rules, independent of the individual subjective disposition, rational (or scientific) discourse will appear to be characterized by its anonymity (*anonimicità*).   That is to say, every subject can and should be replaceable in the reasoning process.   Moreover, inasmuch as the conclusions of the rational process are not and cannot be limited to a given time or place, and are deduced by universal and necessary stringency, their *ahistoricity* is manifest.   The only things that change according to time and place are problems.

The characteristics of rhetorical discourse are radically different; every pathetic moment—precisely insofar as it is irrational and therefore not universally valid—appears as subjective, relative, bound to a single personality, to a given place and time.   In his *Rhetoric*, Aristotle says that rhetorical discourse must be born from the vision of the particular, that is, of the conditions in which each one speaks, through recognition of the situation and the state of mind of one's auditor.   Because of these, its particularities, rhetorical discourse will never be anonymous, or ahistorical, since neither the orator nor the situation is replaceable.

In spite of the arguments here listed, arguments which lead to the thesis of the superiority of rational discourse, it is obvious that in the history of the relationship between rational and pathetic discourse, the problem of their relationship has not been definitively resolved by the postulated dualism, for the following reasons: rational discourse arises from reason and is determined by it; the passions, the pathetic element in the human mind, cannot be reached by reason, for only sensible schemata, visual or auditory schemata, have influence over them.   Hence the importance of images, gestures, the rhythm of the discourse, which have no rational value whatsoever.   From this it follows that, if man is distinguished from other living beings above all by reason, it is also true that he is a feeling, pathetic being.   And from this, again, it has always been held that to rhetorical methods belongs chiefly a pedagogical function, and that in the scientific sphere rhetoric will serve primarily to "soften" the severity, the aridity of reasoning, thereby rendering it more easily accessible.   Thus the effect of science would be strengthened and science itself would be more widespread.   Images, metaphors, would facilitate the acceptance of rational truths.

Similar is the widely diffused thesis that art has a rhetorical function, inasmuch as it sweetens truth with its nectar, or better, sweetens the bitter rim of the jar of wisdom; inasmuch as art makes use of images and schemata that act on the pathetic life of man, artistic exposition of rational truth is revealed as an important factor in truth's dissemination. The pathetic-artistic aspect becomes the "formal" element in the exposition of truth, an element which remains distinct from the rational content. It is obvious, however, that, in spite of these attempts to throw a bridge between pathetic "form" and rational "content," the original dualism remains untouched. The scientist, in order to speak pathetically, draws upon certain capacities that are essentially extraneous to rational, truly scientific activity. And in turn the orator, when he places himself at the service of science, has in the first place to familiarize himself with rational contents not strictly linked to his pathetic capabilities. From this dualism derive those hybrid products used so widely in the so-called popularization of science in the contemporary world, products that constitute one of the principal aims in the cultural programs of socialist states, which are particularly concerned to interest the masses in the discoveries of science.

The separation of pathetic from rational discourse implies other con-clusions. Men become themselves only within the context of a community, since man is essentially a political animal. And a political "community" never simply "is"; it constantly "becomes," in order to realize itself in response to changing and incessantly recurring historical conditions, which men must learn to dominate or succumb to. The individual as a single element of the political community must possess the capacity to recognize and assess the particular situations in which he finds himself; this faculty was called *phronesis* by the Greeks and *prudentia* by the Romans. As Vico him-self observes, confronted by the particular case, the general rules for an act dictated by reason appear as either too many or too few; too many because before the concrete case it is difficult to separate them and to divine which to apply, or too few because the single cases are infinite, always novel. In the light of these difficulties, the dualism of pathetic and rational discourse appears woefully inadequate; the political attitude (characterized by the vision of the particular) is not rationally deducible (that is, from the uni-versal), and, at the same time, it has to function pathetically. Yet the purely rational orator will never gain the palm of victory in debate or succeed in winning over the community. But, if the pathetic and rational spheres remain totally separated, who will ever dedicate himself to politics with any hope of achieving victory?

II

The thinker who tried, at the end of the humanistic tradition, to overcome the dualism of *pathos* and *logos*—an aim which had been pursued by Giovanni and Gianfrancesco Pico, Valla, and Nizolio—was Vico; and the basis of his effort was a discussion of the pre-eminence of topical versus critical philosophy. In order to understand the lively currency of Vico's problematic proposition (a currency which, with respect to this point, was obscured if not simply ignored by the Italian idealism of Croce and Gentile, to which otherwise we owe the revaluation and rediscovery of Vico), it is necessary to recall his peculiar—and to us today at times strange—terminology. The expression "critical philosophy" does not offer many difficulties, but the expression "topical philosophy" is quite obscure.

In chapter III of the *De nostri temporis studiorum ratione* (1709) Vico stresses the fact that, in his time, "the critical attitude" prevailed in philosophy, by which he meant a method that claimed to give a new basis to the edifice of science. The reference to Descartes is evident. "To begin with the instruments of the sciences, nowadays we begin our studies with [philosophical] criticism." Vico sees this procedure as the basis of Cartesian philosophy, inasmuch as Cartesianism claims to be undogmatic, critical insofar as it admits nothing not rationally demonstrated, from which derives the inevitability of methodical doubt. Consistent with this method, Descartes proposes to revise the entire philosophical tradition from which he derives, in order to find a new and indubitable basis for philosophizing and for overcoming all doubt.

The preceding formulation of Vico's is not complete; it is necessary to remember his next assertion, with which he claims to exhaust completely the essence of the Cartesian method and philosophy. Speaking of the new critical method, Vico continues: "Now, such speculative criticism, the main purpose of which is to cleanse its fundamental truths not only of all falsity, but also of the mere suspicion of error, places upon the same plane of falsity not only false thinking, but also those secondary verities and ideas which are based on probability alone...."[1] According to this assertion, there are three fundamental moments characteristic of the Cartesian method.

1. First of all, it claims that it starts from a fundamental truth ("primo vero"), and in order to find it, as we know, it applies the technique of methodical doubt; such a fundamental truth must necessarily have a necessary and universal character, which is Descartes' principle of obviousness. With the discovery of the "fundamental truth," philosophy assumes a clearly rational character; once the first, obvious, and undeducible truth is found, the aim of "critical philosophy" will be to draw—by means of the rational process of deduction—all the consequences implicit in it. This process will consist—the Vichian interpretation continues—of the construction of a science in which varying opinions will have no place.

2. In the second place, if the *primum verum* is posited as the basis of philos-

[1] Elio Gianturco, trans., *On the Study Methods of Our Time* (Indianapolis, Ind., 1965), p. 13.

ophy, the exclusion of all the "secondary verities" follows necessarily. By "secondary verities" Vico means principles that form the foundation of the various sciences; the principles, the axioms, of mathematics are valid only as their existence is considered under the aspect of quantity, that is, being *as* number; the axioms of geometry refer only to being *as* magnitude; the axioms of physics, only to being *as* movement, and so on. It is already evident from these formulations that the principles of the individual sciences cannot be identified with the first principles, which deal with *being as such* (the "*on he on*" of the Greeks, according to Aristotle's terminology). Insofar as the principles of the various sciences are not primary, they can be replaced. Depending upon the geometrical principles with which one starts, one will have either a Euclidean geometry or a kind which cannot be identified with three-dimensional geometry. And the same can be said for physics: the constructions of the physical world change according to the principles from which one starts.

It could be argued that the sphere of principles and of "secondary verities" corresponds to that which the Greeks called *techne*. As a matter of fact, by *technai* the Greeks meant the individual sciences, which arrived at individual findings (*conoscenze*) and practical results on the basis of particular principles. We do not intend to clarify here by which criteria the first principles and the "secondary verities" were chosen: certainly not on the basis of theoretical interests, but rather on the basis of practical, productive, or rather "poietic" interests—and primarily in order to subject nature to human needs. It should be borne in mind that, from Descartes' standpoint (that is, starting from a "fundamental truth" and excluding the "secondary verities") a philosophical justification is indispensable for every science. This notion will be expanded in modern thought, which, with the idealism of Fichte and Hegel, will return to Descartes in a desperate attempt to deduce the individual sciences philosophically, in order to assure them of a theoretical basis. Such was the purpose of Fichte's *Wissenschaftslehre* and of Hegel's attempt to deduce the natural sciences a priori.

In passing it might be pointed out that the search for a philosophical fundament—for a first truth on which to construct the entire "system" of the natural sciences—stands in absolute contrast to the humanistic tradition, which has its origin in the *De nobilitate legum et medicinae* of Coluccio Salutati, is expanded in the notes of Leonardo da Vinci, and culminates in the thought of Galileo. In this tradition a practical value, not a cognitive significance, is attributed to the natural sciences. For Leonardo, nature in itself remains unknowable, since it responds only to the questions that are put to it (and this will be the first presupposition of the experiment), questions that man poses in order to realize his particular ends.

3. Finally, what does Vico mean when he says that Descartes, as a result of the thesis of the "first truth," excludes not only every "secondary verity"

but also every *probable* truth? What does Vico mean by *probable*? In order to answer this question, we must return briefly to Aristotle's *Rhetoric*, where it is stated that science is possible only where the phenomena have a necessary and universal character. That which constantly changes, which manifests itself sometimes this way, sometimes that way, can be the object of individual ascertainments, but never of a general theory. To this sphere belong, for example, those human actions which, arising from many different situations, call forth reactions that are always different and new. Rhetoric, Aristotle says, has a similar character, since pathetic language must be developed adequately to the situation in which one finds oneself, by considering the state of mind of the auditor; it is a mode of discourse which will always and necessarily manifest itself in different forms, without the support of fixed rules. Rhetoric is the seizure by consciousness of the essence of historical human speech, mutable, proper to the here and now.

It is evident that, if the chief aim of Descartes was the discovery of a "first truth" from which to deduce the metaphysical consequences, rhetoric was necessarily excluded from his research, for he explicitly defined it as not belonging to philosophy and as therefore to be excluded from instruction. His point of view lives on today, so that rhetoric is no longer a subject of instruction and perdures only as a historical memory. Vico, justifying the sphere of the "probable" which could not be replaced by the "true," not only recognizes and affirms the importance of rhetoric, but points out the dangers that derive from any obscuring of it. Continuing the preceding quotation, he writes: ". . . common sense arises from perceptions based on verisimilitude. . . . I may add that common sense, besides being the criterion of practical judgment, is also the guiding standard of eloquence. It frequently occurs, in fact, that orators in a law court have greater difficulty with a case which is based on truth, but does not seem so, than with a case that is false but plausible." [2] By the exclusion of rhetoric and politics from philosophy—since politics also arises from the vision of the particular—the critical method obscures two of the most important aspects of human activity. And Vico deplores the one-sidedness produced by this exclusion. In chapter VII of the *De studiorum ratione*, he writes: "Our young men, because of their training, which is focused on these studies, are unable to engage in the life of the community, to conduct themselves with sufficient wisdom and prudence; nor can they infuse into their speech a familiarity with human psychology or permeate their utterances with passion." [3]

Vico stresses the fact that the critical method obscures as well the significance of the image, of fantasy, which is essential to man.

Our modern advocates of advanced criticism rank the unadulterated essence of "pure" primary truth before, outside, above the gross semblances of physical

---

[2] *Ibid.*
[3] *Ibid.*, pp. 33–34.

bodies. . . . Just as old age is powerful in reason, so is adolescence in imagination. . . . Furthermore, the teacher should give the greatest care to the cultivation of the pupil's memory, which, though not exactly the same as imagination, is almost identical with it. In adolescence, memory outstrips in vigor all other faculties, and should be intensely trained. Youth's natural inclination to the arts in which imagination or memory (or a combination of both) is prevalent (such as painting, poetry, oratory, jurisprudence) should by no means be blunted.[4]

At this point it can be asked, "What is the relation between the problem that we have raised and the Vichian rejection of 'critical' philosophizing?" It arises precisely in this context with the appearance of the term "topical philosophy," which Vico sets against "critical philosophy": "For just as the invention of arguments is by nature prior to the judgment of their validity, so topical philosophy (Lat.: *doctrina*) should be given precedence over critical."[5] Thus *inventio* precedes *demonstratio*, discovery precedes proof.

What is the relation between *invention* and *topics*? We have noted that, once a first truth is discovered, the scientific process necessarily consists of the rigorous application of deduction. But for Vico the idea that the essence of philosophy might be found exclusively in the rational deductive process was unacceptable, above all because he presupposed the necessity of another activity, that of invention, which preceded deduction. In fact, Vico identifies *the doctrine of invention with topical philosophy*.

III

If we go back to the early theoretical reflections of Aristotle on topics, they do not seem to clarify the problem of the relation of topics to philosophy. Aristotle's *Topics* begins in the following way: "Our treatise proposes to find a line of inquiry whereby we shall be able to reason from opinions that are generally accepted about every problem propounded by us, and also shall ourselves, when standing up to an argument, avoid saying anything that will obstruct us."[6] Aristotle proceeds to distinguish between syllogisms based on "true and primary" premises and those based on simple opinion. This provides him with a way of stressing the utility of topics in the exercise of reason, for, if one possesses a method, it will be much easier to discuss any theme raised; the utility of such a method will appear in the art of disputation because, if one knows the opinions of many, it will be easier to enter into discussion; and finally, with regard to the sciences connected with philosophy, topics will aid in the recognition of difficulties relative to the solution that has

[4] *Ibid.*, pp. 13–14.
[5] *Ibid.*
[6] *Topics* 100a. 18, trans. W. A. Pickard-Cambridge, in *The Basic Works of Aristotle*, ed. R. McKeon (New York, 1941).

been given to a problem.[7]   In fact, as Aristotle exemplifies it, topics recognizes what actually happens in dialectics and medicine: nothing is obscured, all the relevant arguments are borne in mind so that they can be retrieved and applied at the appropriate moment. Topics, therefore, has the task of determining "how many, and what kind of, things arguments will refer to, with what materials they will start, and how we are to become well supplied with these. . . ."[8]

From the above passages it is perhaps possible to glimpse, although it is not yet evident, how Vico might attribute to topics a philosophical function. Moreover, we could turn for help to another task that Aristotle consigns to topics: to it is given the task—in an essential way—of "finding" the arguments necessary for both rational and rhetorical discourse. Topics is thus revealed as a doctrine of invention (*inventio*).

In order to understand this concept, it will be helpful to turn to Cicero and Quintilian, for the formulations they give us clarify the philosophical character of topics.   In Cicero's *De oratore* we find the following significant passage: "Sed Aristoteles, is quem maxime admiror, posuit quosdam locos e quibus omnis argumenti via non modo ad philosophorum disputationem sed etiam ad hanc orationem qua in casis utimur *inveniretur*."[9]

Two elements of this passage should be stressed.   First, there is the translation of the word *topoi* as *loci*.   In another passage Cicero translates the term as *sedes* or *nota*; Quintilian uses the phrase "*sedes argomentorum*."   Similarly, Tacitus in his dialogue on the orator uses the following phrase: ". . . a Peripateticis aptos et in omnem disputationem paratos jam locos" (". . . from the Peripatetics their stock arguments, suited and ready in advance for either side of any discussion").[10]   In the second place, it should be noted that, for a profitable debate, the orator must have present in his mind all the arguments, that is, the "common places," in order to be able to retrieve them and present them.   In the passage from Cicero we find the term *invenire*, as well as that of *locus*; he points to that invention which profits from the grouping of arguments under the *loci* or the *notae* corresponding to them.   "It is easy to find things that are hidden if the hiding place is pointed out and marked; similarly if we wish to track down some argument we ought to know the places or topics: for that is the name given by Aristotle to the 'regions,' as it were, from which arguments are drawn.   Accordingly we may define a topic as the region of an argument."[11]

In order to understand the Vichian problematic proposition and terminology, another passage from Cicero will be cited; this passage is of fundamental

[7] *Topics* 101a. 29.
[8] *Topics* 101b. 13, Pickard-Cambridge trans. [emended to accord with Grassi's translation].
[9] II. 33. 152.
[10] *Dialogus* . . . , trans. William Peterson, Loeb Classical Library (1914), XXXII. 97.
[11] Cicero *Topics* II. 7, trans. H. M. Hubbell, Loeb Classical Library.

importance inasmuch as it is evidently the source of Vico's distinction between topical and critical philosophy. "Every systematic treatment of argumentation has two branches, one concerned with invention of arguments and the other with judgment of their validity; ... The Stoics have worked in only one of the two fields. That is to say, they have followed diligently the ways of judgment by means of the science which they call διαλεκτική (dialectics), but they have totally neglected the art of invention, which is called τοπική (topics)."[12] In another passage of the *De oratore* Cicero refers to the art of judging (which Vico calls criticism), and he stresses that it has nothing in common with invention, that it is, in fact, "opposed to invention."[13] The art of judging has the task of deriving determinate consequences from given premises, while topics is the art of invention. Indeed, during the Middle Ages, Boethius, in his *De differentiis topicis*, attributed an inventive character to topics inasmuch as it helped in *trahere argumenta*. Thus, he writes: "*Locus* is the region (*sedes*) of the argument, or that from which one draws the argument appropriate to the question raised."[14]

In order to show the philosophical importance that invention (and topics) has for Vico, one might recall the traditional division of rhetoric. It consists of matter and form, of *what* is said and the *way* it is said: "Omnis autem oratio constat aut ex iis *quae significantur* aut ex iis *quae significant*, id est *rebus et verbis*."[15] Every kind of discourse (the tradition distinguishes three basic kinds: juridical, political, encomiastic) consists of five parts, of which the first is "invention."[16] In order for the rational process to be terminated or for the consequences to be rhetorically derived, it is always necessary to "find" the premises; and it is invention which furnishes the arguments that permit the consummation of a logically and rhetorically effective discourse.

In the light of all this, we may ask how Vico conceives the philosophical function of topics.

IV

In the *De studiorum ratione* Vico laments the fact that moderns have no interest in topics because they have been conditioned to accept the critical method, so that it is sufficient, they believe, merely to be taught a certain thing, in order for them to discern immediately whether there is any truth in it or not ("nam satis est, inquiunt ... rem doceri, ut quid in ea veri inest

[12] *Ibid.*, II. 6; cf. *De oratore* II. 32. 115.
[13] *De oratore* II. 38. 157.
[14] Boethius, *Opera* (Basel, 1570), p. 827.
[15] Quintilian *Institutio oratoria* II. 5. 1.
[16] Cf. Cicero *De oratore* I. 31. 142; Quintilian *Institutio oratoria* III. 3. 1.

inveniant").[17]   The "probable," which borders on the "true," is to be recognized by the application of rules of logic, without special instruction and without any knowledge of topics.   Against the defenders of the critical method, Vico raises an objection in the form of a question: "But how can they be sure that they have considered *every* aspect of a question?"[18]   That is, how can one be sure that the premises from which the critical process begins do not reflect only a single aspect of reality, and, as a consequence, limit the conclusions that derive from those premises?   Has not the critical method neglected rhetoric, politics, the imagination, showing thereby its rationalistic bias?   Not only that: the "finding," the "inventing" (as it appears in purely rational philosophical processes), is identified solely with that which is "found" by means of the deductive process and can never escape this identification.   The heart of the problem resides in the "invention" of all the premises necessary for creating a discourse that is not only "subtle" but also rich, as Vico describes it; it resides in the primitive, rationally undeducible, "vision" of the relations between the primitive and undeducible premises.   In other words, the key to the Vichian rejection of the critical method and its related rationalism consists of the realization that the original premises themselves, since they underlie the logical processes, are as such undeducible, by virtue of which the rational process will never be able to discover them; or, since the rational process is essentially deductive, it will never be applicable to the premises, the axioms, or principles of the rational process itself.

While the critical method begins with *one* original premise and draws deductions that, however acute and complex, will always be limited to the sphere designated by the premise from which it moves, only the aim of discovering *all* the premises proper to the human world—and to them belong those of prudence, of imagination, of practical life, and so on—will render discourse fertile and inventive: "From that derives that supreme and rare epithet of oratory called 'comprehensive,' which leaves nothing untouched, nothing omitted, nothing which the listeners might have desired."[19]

It would be wrong, then, to consider topics as a mere "instrument" of arguments retrievable by recourse to certain "signs" and certain "places." Topics, for Vico, is the theory (*dottrina*) of invention.   Quite apart from the historical problem—which does not concern us here—of whether similar thoughts with regard to the philosophical conception of topics are to be found in Aristotle, it is legitimate to ask oneself if topical activity in its original meaning might be rooted in the "nous," in genius or talent, inasmuch as the first requirement for the finding of an argument adequate to one's circumstances is a rationally undeducible, inventive capability, or, as

---

[17] *De nostri temporis studiorum ratione*, chap. III.
[18] *Ibid.*
[19] *Ibid.*

the Latins called it, a native (*ingegnosa*) talent. In addition, it is certain that, for Vico, criticism is only logically coherent assertion, while topics is the art of rich, creative, copious assertion: "Critica est ars verae orationis, topica autem copiosae."[20]

In an article published in the *Giornale dei letterati*, one of Vico's critics summarized and commented on the individual chapters of the *De antiquissima Italorum sapientia* and wrote: "[The author] considers the three famous operations of the mind, perception, judgment, and reasoning, which he divides into topics, criticism, and method; so that topics appears as the faculty or the art of apprehending, criticism as that of judging, and method as that of reasoning. He brings under investigation the geometrical method and in some sciences and arts finds nothing useful, and in others finds rather more that is harmful than not."[21]

Topics corresponds to the doctrine of the original vision from which proceed those forms of instruction and learning rooted in a primitive vision and discovery (one might call this vision "archaic," not in the temporal sense of the term but in the sense in which it refers to the "archai" or origins), an ingenious, that is, rationally undeducible, faculty. "Topics finds and arrays; criticism divides and removes from the array; and therefore topical minds are more copious and less true, critical ones more true but also more dry."[22]

Vico always gives topics precedence over criticism and its corresponding rational activity by appeal to the argument that it is first of all necessary to know how to "find" the premises. "Providence did well by human things by promoting topics over criticism in human minds, since it is first necessary to know things before judging them. For topics is the faculty which renders minds ingenious, just as criticism renders them precise; and in these early times it was necessary to find all of the things necessary to human life, and the discovery of those things is the task of genius (*ingegno*)."[23]

Genius is the faculty that is turned toward the primitive, the "archaic." "The particular faculty of knowing (*sapere*), I call genius (*ingegno*), because with this faculty man brings together things which, to those lacking this faculty, seemed to have no relationship to one another at all."[24] Genius is the "comprehending" faculty, not the deductive one; and comprehension comes before deduction insofar as it is only by comprehension that one is able to deduce consequences. "Genius is the faculty of unifying separated

[20] *Ibid.*
[21] *Opere*, ed. F. Nicolini, I (Bari, 1914), 201.
[22] *Ibid.*, p. 271.
[23] Vico, *Scienza nuova*, bk. II, chap. 498, in Nicolini's *Opere*, vol. IV (Bari, 1928), pt. I, p. 213.
[24] Vico, *Giornale dei letterati d'Italia* (1711), in Nicolini's *Opere*, I, 213.

things, of correlating things moving in diverse directions" ("Ingenium facultas est in unum dissita, diversa coniungendi").[25]

Conclusions

Critical philosophy or topical philosophy? This was the question with which we began. Above all, it should be observed that the distinction between the two kinds of philosophizing made by Vico can no longer be considered a closed issue, solely of historical interest, but must be seen as a problem with much current relevance. Today we glory in science and in cybernetic instruments, entrusting our future to them, forgetting that we still have the problem of finding "data," of "inventing them," since the cybernetic process can only elaborate them and draw consequences from them. The problem of the essence of the human genius and of its creativity cannot be reduced to that of rational deduction, which modern technology is developing to improbable depths.

The second conclusion we may be permitted is the realization that the Vichian theories of topical philosophy are rooted in the Latin humanistic tradition, for which rhetoric had a function and an importance that have been totally forgotten. Humanistic thought was constantly concerned with the unity of *res* and *verba*, content and form, which once disjoined could never be reunited. If the rational element be admitted as the sole possible content of our speech, it will no longer be possible to give to it a "form" capable of moving souls; and, increasingly, philosophy will be consigned to the forgotten regions of history.

The re-evaluation of Vico begun by Italian idealism—which was based on the identity of the *verum* with the *factum* (the true with the created) propounded by Vico—saw in Vico above all the defender of the thesis of the creativity of human thought, and thus, in spite of everything, of the "cogito ergo sum." This was a misrepresentation of Vico's central idea and impeded understanding of his humanistic problematic position, which had nothing in common with the idealistic tradition or with Hegelianism in particular.

The humanistic distinction between the true and the probable rendered possible all the reflection on the essence of political action and the growth of the juridical tradition. Finally, the distinction between "first truth" and "secondary verities" has prevented the philosophical, aprioristic deduction of the natural sciences which is proper to idealism. But the true history of the humanistic tradition in its anti-Cartesian role has yet to be written.

Translated by Hayden V. White

[25] Vico, *De antiquissima Italorum sapientia*, bk. I, chap. 4, in Nicolini's *Opere*, vol. IV, pt. I, p. 179.

Girolamo Cotroneo

A RENAISSANCE
SOURCE OF
THE *SCIENZA NUOVA*:
Jean Bodin's *Methodus*

Introduction

One of the principal Vichian sources was without doubt *Les six livres de la République*, which Jean Bodin had first published in 1576 and which had had such great success and caused such a great stir in the field of political thought. Vico himself was to honor Bodin by defining him as an "equally most erudite jurisconsult and political thinker" and by dedicating to him, in a unique case of Vichian homage, an entire chapter in the *Scienza nuova*, in which he engaged himself in the "Confutation of the Principles of the Political Doctrine According to the System of Jean Bodin."[1]   On the influence which the great treatise of Bodin had upon Vico, some of the most attentive students of Vichian thought, such as Fausto Nicolini and E. Gianturco, have written very interesting pages.[2]   Nevertheless, in order to conduct a more exhaustive examination of the influence which the thought of Jean Bodin may have had upon that of Vico, it is necessary that one not limit one's attention to the *République* but consider also another important work by Bodin, the *Methodus ad facilem historiarum cognitionem*, published in Paris in 1566, in which the Angevin philosopher formulated his theories and his conception of history.   It is exactly in this work, as has been noted (even if only in the most general way) by some students of Bodin,[3] that numerous points of contact between the two authors are to be found.

Now, it is difficult, if not altogether impossible, to assert whether or not Vico knew this work of Bodin's to which he never made reference.   However, a comparative examination of the two texts reveals a series of co-incidences of thought, and at times of language itself, such as to give the clear impression not only that Vico may have known Bodin's work but that he may have drawn from it—naturally, through a re-elaboration in an altogether original cast—some of the basic ideas of his own work, such as the use of myths as instruments of historical research, theories on the origins of human

[1] G. B. Vico, *Scienza nuova seconda*, ed. Fausto Nicolini, 4th ed. (Bari, 1953), pp. 492 ff.
[2] F. Nicolini, *Commento storico alla seconda scienza nuova*, 2 vols. (Rome, 1949–50); E. Gianturco, "Bodin and Vico," in *Revue de littératures comparées*, 1948, pp. 272–90.
[3] Above all see H. Baudrillart, *Jean Bodin et son temps* (Paris, 1853), pp. 159–60; also J. L. Brown, *The Methodus ad facilem historiarum cognitionem of Jean Bodin: A Critical Study* (Washington, D.C., 1939), pp. 104ff.

society, the use of philology in historical inquiry, the critique upon the golden age, and so on. This group of problems, which we shall presently examine through a comparative collation of the two texts, joins the two works in a truly extraordinary manner. We shall re-evaluate Bodin's *Methodus*, which anticipated some of Vico's most important ideas by two centuries, even if, perhaps through the immaturity of the times, these ideas remained mere intuitions in the mind of their author, a *flatus vocis* from which he did not succeed in drawing significant consequences, whereas the re-elaboration—conscious or unconscious as it may have been—made by the author of the *Scienza nuova* has broken new paths in philosophical research.

The Origins of Human Society

The idea that the first form of social life was marriage is the first of the motifs which Bodin and Vico have in common. In fact, Vico writes that the first form of "human society" "was that of marriages" and that "from this nature of human things withstood this eternal property: that the true natural friendship is marriage, in which the three ends of good come together, that is, the honest, the useful, and the pleasurable; whence husband and wife experience by nature the same fate through the prosperity and adversities of life." And Bodin had written: "Nam prima societas quae est viri et uxoris, omnium antiquissima putatur; propterea quod animi corporis, omniumque fortunarum communitas quaedam est."[4]   But apart from this, which is a very common motif in the literature on origins, a passage where the similarity is truly extraordinary is that in which it is said that families united and founded the first villages in the proximity of fountains. Vico writes: "However, above everything else, on account of the perennial fountains [springs] it was said by political writers that the community of water was the occasion for the union of families in its vicinity, and that therefore the first communities were called *fratrai* by the Greeks, just as the first lands were called *pagi* by the Latins, and the fountain *paga* by the Dorian Greeks." On his part Bodin had maintained as follows: ". . . Tum vicinorum, qui propagate sobole, in plures vicinias coniunctis aedificiis coalescunt: hinc phratriae et pagi, quod ex *eautou freatos*, id est, puteo, vel *pagas*, id est, fonte biberent."[5]

To this concept another must be added, which is that the first societies became organized by virtue of friendship. In this connection Vico wrote: "Wherein it is also worthy of reflection that because the first men came to human society spurred by religion and by the natural instinct to propagate the

[4] Vico, *Scienza nuova*, p. 251; J. Bodin, *Methodus ad facilem historiarum cognitionem*, in *Oeuvres philosophiques de Jean Bodin*, ed. Pierre Mesnard (Paris, 1951), pp. 190b–91a.

[5] *Scienza nuova*, p. 283; *Methodus*, p. 191a.

generation of men . . . [they] gave beginning to a noble and aristocratic friendship." And, according to Bodin: "Cum vero ab affinitatis conjunctione
discesseris, proxima est amicorum virtute parta societas. . . . Sic paulatim
amicitia, societatis humanae vinculum, ab una domo in plures divisa familias,
vicos, urbes, civitates, nationes, eousque propagata est."[6] Another new and
no less important similitude may be found (always in relation to the origins
of society) in an idea for which Vico is justly famous, but for which it is
necessary to give credit for a first intuition to Bodin: the idea of the "conceit
of nations" (*"boria delle nazioni"*). Vico had observed, taking up again an
assertion by Diodorus Siculus, that among all the nations "whether Greek or
barbarian" each "has had the same conceit . . . that its remembered history
goes back to the very beginning of the world." Now it happened that
Bodin had expressed an analogous concept when he had discovered that
every people, through pride of race, had always felt itself superior to other
peoples: "Cum alii opibus, aut scelere, aut majorum virtutibus parta
nobilitate, seipsos ab aliis sponte divellerent, et eorum affinitatem repu-
diarent; extremum fuit arrogantiae genus eorum qui, humanae conditionis
obliti, se a diis ortos esse praedicarent."[7]

We have already maintained and pointed out above how difficult it is,
with such passages as these before us, to claim with certainty whether it is a
question of simple coincidences or of an attentive and sustained reading of the
Methodus on the part of Vico. Certain it is, however, that, even with all the
reservations that can and must be expressed on the idea of a forerunning,
the thesis that Bodin was a precursor of Vico is not easily rejected.

The Golden Age

Even greater affinities are discovered when we watch both authors confront
the problem of the customs of ancient peoples and arrive at practically the
same conclusion, that is, the refutation of the legend of the "golden age."
In this connection it is well to keep in mind that between the time of Bodin
and that of Vico there occurred the famous "*querelle des anciens et des
modernes*,"[8] which reopened a problem on which Bodin had passed judgment
a century before, thus showing that he possessed a secure sense of history
through the elaboration upon an idea of progress—and he was the first to do
so—which was truly modern by dint of its confutation of the prophecy of
Daniel concerning the four monarchies and the succession of the ages of gold,
silver, copper, and iron.[9]

---

[6] *Scienza nuova*, p. 251; *Methodus*, p. 191a.

[7] *Scienza nuova*, p. 43; *Methodus*, p. 241a.

[8] See R. Franchini, *Il Progresso: Storia di un'idea* (Milan, 1960), pp. 45ff.

[9] This is the thesis of chap. VII of the *Methodus*, the famous "Confutatio eorum qui
quatuor monarchias aureaque secula statuunt," discussed by almost all of the political

Is it possible that Vico did not know that the scheme of the four monarchies and that of the "golden ages" which he so eagerly rejected had been repudiated for the first time by Bodin? Henri Baudrillart maintains that to read the seventh chapter of the *Methodus* it seems "*presque à s'y méprendre,*" as if one were reading the pages of the *Scienza nuova,*[10] so remarkable are the similarities. In fact, Bodin denied the existence of an original "golden age." After analyzing the ancient myths in which violence, incest, plunder, gratuitous savagery, and the like were constantly recurring, Bodin exclaimed: "Haec igitur est illa aurea aetas quae talia monstra nobis educavit!"[11] And Vico, recalling the "most inhuman humanity" of the ancients, commented: "All these were those things which were called by Plautus '*Saturni hostiae,*' during the time which [certain] authors insist was the golden age of Latium. So mild, benign, discreet, tolerant, and dutiful it was!"[12] Exactly here, as we have said, the affinities are not merely of ideas but also of language, and they are considerable. Still referring to the ancients, Bodin asserted how, by them, "jus in armis fuisse positum," as did Vico, for whom "the heroic law" was that of Achilles, "who places all reason in the force of his spear."[13] Again, following Thucydides, Vico confirms that in ancient times the cities were "wall-less" ("*smurate*") and that "given their proud and violent nature, heroes repeatedly dethroned one another," while Bodin reminds us that "cum vero nullis adhuc moenibus cingeretur . . . veteresque colonos subinde a novis de possesione dejectos."[14]

One of the reasons for these recurring similarities, we think, is the fact that very often both authors used the same sources, as may be noted easily from the examples we have given. Both Bodin and Vico assert that brigandage was a frequent activity and not at all disreputable among the ancients, and they both bring evidence to the support of their thesis. "What is most to be wondered at," writes Vico, "is that Plato and Aristotle placed robbery among the kinds of hunting." And Bodin says: "Utetiam Aristoteles latrocinium . . . posuit inter genera venationis."[15] For the same reason, we find Thucydides cited: "Is testatum reliquit paulo ante sua tempora tantam fuisse hominum in ipsa Graecia barbariem ac ferinitatem, ut terra marique latrocinia palam exercerentur, et sine ulla contumelia quaeri a praetereuntibus consueverit utrum latrones utrum piratae essent necne." And likewise Vico

---

theorists following Bodin, as both Baudrillart, *Jean Bodin et son temps,* p. 158, and A. Garosci, *Jean Bodin: Politica e diritto nel Rinascimento francese* (Milan, 1934), pp. 167ff., have shown. See also my own *Jean Bodin teorico della storia* (Naples, 1966), pp. 196ff.

[10] Baudrillart, *Jean Bodin,* p. 160, n. 1.

[11] *Methodus,* p. 226b.

[12] *Scienza nuova,* p. 227.

[13] *Methodus,* p. 226b; *Scienza nuova,* p. 437.

[14] *Scienza nuova,* p. 311; *Methodus,* p. 226b.

[15] *Scienza nuova,* p. 305; *Methodus,* p. 226a.

writes: "And there is a golden place in Thucydides: that, until his own time, wherever wayfarers met on land or travelers by sea, they would ask one another among themselves whether they might be thieves." [16]   Even more evident, to the point of paradoxically appearing to be a translation, is a passage dealing with Caesar's writings on the Germans.   Let us cite Bodin first: "Latrocinia, inquit, nullam habent apud Germanos infamia, . . . atque ea juventutis exercendae, ac desidiae minuendae causa fieri praedicant"; and in the same manner Vico writes that among the Germans, "according to Caesar, robbery not only was not regarded as infamous but was reckoned among the exercises of valor by which those who were not brought up to the practice of any art escaped from idleness." [17]

The rejection, therefore, of the "golden age," of the beautiful harmony, and of the virtues of primitive peoples is another of the basic ideas that the two authors have in common and upon which they rested their concept of historical development.

Philological Research

The attempt to retrace the origins of peoples is among the most characteristic coincidences of interests between the two works.   This can be accounted for not so much by the subject, which, after all, is common to a great number of writers (one need think only of Lucretius, Ovid, and the Cato of the books on *Origins*), as by the similarity of the instruments that Bodin and Vico used in their research.   Thus we see Bodin—in an extraordinary coincidence with Vico—singling out in "*linguae vestigiis*" a potent means for the reconstruction of the origins of peoples.   Bodin reproaches historians for not having adopted this means: "Illud tantum quod nostri originum scriptores non satis aperuerunt, scilicet linguarum vestigia in quibus praecipuum est originis argumentum." [18]   There seems to be an echo here of Vico's famous reproach of the philosophers "for their not having ascertained their reasons through the authority of the philologists." [19]   However, it is important to note, despite the similarity of concept, how the two authors thereafter move in opposite directions.   The idea, which is so luminous in Vico, that the secret of ancient civilizations may be understood through languages, does not even skim Bodin's mind.   His philological interest consists only of finding again the most ancient languages whence "*primas origines omnium gentium illis, a quibus idiomata fluxerunt, tribuendas esse docent*"; [20] beyond this he cannot

[16] *Methodus*, p. 226b; *Scienza nuova*, p. 306.

[17] Thomas G. Bergin and Max H. Fisch, trans., *The New Science of Giambattista Vico* (New York, 1961), p. 194.

[18] *Methodus*, p. 242b.

[19] *Scienza nuova*, p. 77.

[20] *Methodus*, p. 243b.

go. In Vico we see this interest expand until it becomes an instrument of knowledge insofar as "the etymology of native languages . . . narrates the things which these voices signify," so that, for him, the philological instrument becomes a means fit to explain "the mental vocabulary of the things of human society, with the same substances felt by all nations and with diverse modifications explained differently through languages."[21] Nevertheless, even if he does not succeed in reaching such heights, it is not rare that the author of the *Methodus* seeks, through etymologies, to give a coherent explanation of the genesis of some words in a language which sometimes is incredibly similar to that of Vico.

Take, for example, the explanation of the term *urbs*. ". . . Deinde moenibus oppida sepserunt," writes Bodin, "quae propterea urbes a Latinis dictae sunt, vel ab urbo ut tradit Festus, vel ab orbe, ut Varro: quia interiore sulco fiebat orbis ad murorum descriptionem."[22] Vico depicts ". . . the first walls, which even philologists say were described by the founders of cities with the plough, whose curvature . . . was originally called '*urbs*,' whence the ancient '*urbum*,' which means 'curved.' "[23] Similarly apropos is the word *hostis*, where Bodin asserts that "hostes olim a Romani appellati peregrini" and Vico analogously concludes that " '*hostis*' meant 'guest and stranger' and 'enemy.' "[24] Other examples could be adduced to show that even Bodin, while lacking the fullness and systematic vigor of Vico, confusedly perceived (and was the first to use the awareness in such a sense) that the linguistic instrument could serve not only toward the discovery of the origins of peoples but also toward the comprehension of their spirit and customs.

Myths

The use of mythology as an instrument of historical inquiry is part of that group of common ideas in the two works which we are examining. It should be made clear, however, that the use which the two authors make of myth as a means of historical explanation and the standard of interpretation of myth itself are completely different. Nevertheless, both agree upon an essential point; that is, Vico believed that "such fables were all true and severe and worthy of the founders of nations, and that then, through the long passage of time, while on the one hand meanings became obscure, on the other, with the changing of customs . . . they were transformed into the filthy meanings with which they have come down to us";[25] and Bodin

[21] *Scienza nuova*, p. 130.
[22] *Methodus*, p. 191a.
[23] *Scienza nuova*, p. 248.
[24] *Methodus*, p. 241b; *Scienza nuova*, p. 289.
[25] *Scienza nuova*, p. 55.

stated that "veteres Poëtae rei veritatem a majoribus acceptam ad fabulas inanes transtulerunt."[26] At this point, the discussion becomes very complicated and delicate, and the solutions differ completely. What are these ancient truths and where are they to be found in their authentic forms, before their transformation into fables? Bodin does not hesitate to answer that the true history of the world is that which is narrated by the Bible, and he dedicates part of the seventh chapter of the *Methodus* to a demonstration of the idea that pagan mythology is nothing more than an imperfect representation of the same events narrated in the Bible.[27] Vico, too, asserts that "the Hebrews were the first people of the world," and that "they have with truth conserved their memories," and he adds that they "lived unknown to all the gentile nations."[28] It is known, however, that with these expressions Vico sought above all to avoid the problem of the authority of Holy Scriptures, which his Catholic conscience did not want to oppose. Croce has rightly shown how the Vichian interpretation of myths is neither allegorical nor—as it seems to have been for Bodin—euhemeristic, insofar as, for the author of the *Scienza nuova*, myths are "intrinsically histories, and their alleged alteration lies exactly in their truth as it appeared to primitive minds."[29]

This is not the place to engage in a long discourse on the subject of myths. Insofar as our argument is concerned, it is sufficient to note how, beyond the interpretative differences between them, Bodin had had an insight, even before Vico, into the manner in which myths could be used as instruments of historical inquiry, despite the fact that he failed to perceive the intimate significance which Vico, in due time, attributed to them.

Conclusion

As may be seen from the textual parallels we have presented above, the idea that the *Methodus* might have been a source of the *Scienza nuova* possesses a consistency which perhaps goes beyond that of a simple hypothesis, despite the fact that it is equally evident that Vico accomplished altogether original re-elaborations of those illuminating intuitions which are strewn throughout Bodin's work. For the latter reason, the conclusion that it may have been a matter of simple and fortuitous coincidence need not be dismissed. Nevertheless, the affinities—which redound completely to the advantage of Bodin —persist, and others can be discovered. Even without the triadic divisions of Vico (though the periodizations made by Bodin are always on the basis of

[26] *Methodus*, p. 236a.
[27] *Methodus*, pp. 226a–b and 236a.
[28] *Scienza nuova*, p. 44.
[29] B. Croce, *La filosofia di Giambattista Vico* (Bari, 1965), p. 65.

the number three) into "three kinds of customs," of "governments," of "languages," of "jurisprudences," and so on, the "courses that the nations follow" in the *Scienza nuova* correspond even terminologically to the *"conversiones Rerumpublicarum"* of the *Methodus*, and the "recurrence of human things" is the *"humanos casos qui velut in orbem sui similes aliquando recurrunt."* [30]

Yet, apart from these last passages, which belong to a tradition already old by the time of Bodin, we find a further motive binding these two works that ideally are already so close to each other.   At the conclusion of the *Scienza nuova* Vico speaks of an "eternal natural republic, excellent in all of its kinds, ordered by divine providence."   In the Bodin text this corresponds to the idea of the *"Respublica mundana."* [31]   From a parallel reading of the two works, one may see the community of a fundamental concept—that of the unity of mankind.   The study of the vicissitudes through which man's journey has occurred led Vico to the conclusion that "it certainly could be said that this is the great city of nations founded and governed by God." [32] A similar reflection on historical vicissitudes led Bodin to conclude that "ex quo sequitur, hunc mundum veluti civitatem aliquam esse, et omnes homines eodem jure quodammodo confusos, quod intelligunt se esse consanguineos, et subjectos omnes sub unam eandemque rationis tutelam." [33]   It has been observed a number of times by the most attentive students of Vico that this concept of the unity of mankind was derived by him from the theorists of natural law and in particular from Grotius, of whom Vico was a careful reader.   Grotius in his turn was a profound student of Bodin and of his *Methodus*, to whose rather unattractive Latin he called attention (*"Latinitate utentem haud plane nitidam"*), and he recognized that book to be a *"librum legi degnissimum,"* insofar as in it Bodin had revealed himself to be *"hominem rerum quam verborum studiosiorem."* [34]   There is no opportunity here to engage in an inquiry in this direction, but it is certain that the attention which Grotius devoted to Bodin was not altogether disinterested, since many of the concepts contained in the *Methodus* were of great importance to the recognized initiator of the modern doctrines of natural law (*giusnaturalismo*).

In conclusion, it seems to us, on the basis of the examination we have conducted here of the problem of the relations between Bodin and Vico, that those relations should be pursued beyond the traditional ones, even in such directions as we have attempted.   This brief analysis of a few points of contact between the *Methodus* and the *Scienza nuova* has revealed how,

---

[30] *Scienza nuova*, pp. 431ff. and 503ff.; *Methodus*, pp. 190b ff. and 115b.

[31] *Scienza nuova*, p. 539.   On the concept of *Respublica mundana* in Bodin see Brown, *The Methodus*, pp. 89ff.   We also recall our own *Jean Bodin*, pp. 219ff.

[32] *Scienza nuova*, p. 545.

[33] *Methodus*, p. 173a.

[34] U. Grotius, *Epistolae* (Amsterdam, 1687), p. 127.

beyond some singular terminological coincidences and expressions, a number of genial flashes of intuition render the work of Bodin perhaps the closest antecedent of the *Scienza nuova*. Undoubtedly, those "Vichian" concepts which we have discovered in Bodin are in a potential state, devoid of coherent application or improperly applied. Nevertheless, without in the least detracting from the greatness of Vico, we believe that they are a necessary step toward an understanding of the unfolding of historical reason.

Translated by A. William Salomone

Dario Faucci   VICO AND GROTIUS:
                            Jurisconsults of Mankind

Vico and Grotius were very different personalities, as unlike as the era and
the historical environment in which they grew up. Grotius was a great
lawyer and diplomat; he belonged to the elite of the Netherlands and of
international society. His boundless historical and literary scholarship and,
above all, his juridical competence, for which he was called "Holland's
miracle," gave him tremendous prestige. As a youth, he was sent on
diplomatic missions and was appointed to an important political position.
    Quite different is the picture in which Vico appears. Devoid of ambition
and of forensic success, endowed with such scanty prestige as to be unsuccessful in his attempt to achieve a professorship of civil law in the university, where all his life he remained as a teacher of rhetoric, appreciated
and sought after only as a paid inditer of funeral encomiums, inscriptions,
and dedications, in contact with, but at a distance from, and not as an equal
of, the powerful grandees of his town, Vico exerted absolutely no influence
on the public affairs of Naples, was neither in favor of, nor in opposition to,
the existing government. [It was perhaps this apolitical attitude which kept
him aloof from Giannone, who, in those years, under the stimulus of urgent
modern problems, was writing his *Civil History of the Kingdom of Naples*
(1723), as a result of which he was forced into exile and imprisonment.]
    On the other hand, Vico, like Grotius, was a jurist and a humanist. This
was the ground on which they met: the domain of the grand juridical and
literary monuments of the ancient world, the records of the ancient folkways
in war and peace, in public and private concerns. The modern reader who
opens the Dutchman's *De jure belli ac pacis* and the Neapolitan's *Scienza
nuova* is confronted with the same archaic atmosphere. But the construal—
that is, the reconstruction and interpretation—of the same world is quite
different.
    It is doubtful whether we should accept as true the information contained
in Vico's *Autobiography* (1725), according to which he read the *De jure belli ac
pacis* (first published in Paris in 1625) when he was preparing to write the *Life
of Marshall Antonio Carafa*, published in 1716.[1] The *Inaugural Orations*,

[1] Vico, *L'autobiografia, il carteggio e le poesie varie*, in vol. V of *Opere*, ed. B. Croce
and F. Nicolini, 2d ed. (Bari: Laterza, 1929), pp. 38, 39.

delivered by Vico between 1699 and 1708, contain, in the opinion of some
critics, concepts and expressions that are reminiscent of Grotius.[2] It is
nevertheless beyond doubt that, unlike Grotius, who, from the viewpoint of
reason, frequently criticizes Roman *jural science*, Vico attaches great value to
Rome's juridical-political history. Complete evidence substantiating this
statement may be found in the last of Vico's inaugural orations, *On the Study
Methods of Our Time*, delivered in 1708. Vico remarks that, whereas among
the Greeks the science of law was to be found in and identified with general
philosophy, and was distinct, on the one hand, from the task of the *pragmatici*
(which was that of collecting and making available the texts of positive law)
and, on the other, from the task of the judicial pleaders (or lawyers: *rhetorici*),
"In Rome, the philosophers themselves were jurists. In the Romans' view,
the whole range and compass of knowledge was involved in legal expertise.
The Roman jurists thus became the chief instruments for the preservation of
the unadulterated 'Sapientia' of the 'heroic epoch.'"[3] Quoting Horace as
his authority, Vico writes: "The Romans attached to the word *jurisprudentia*
the same meaning as the Greeks attached to the word 'wisdom' (*sapientia*).
For the Romans, *jurisprudentia* was the knowledge (*scientia*) of all things
religious and secular. And, since the whole of *sapientia* consists in justice
and civil wisdom, they learned the arts of government and that of justice in
a much more efficient and correct way than did the Greeks. The Romans
did not engage in discussions about these arts; they practiced them through
the positive experience of public affairs."[4]

The significance of the history of Roman law for Vico is luminously
brought out by Giuseppe Ferrari: "Together with the philosophic ideas in
Vico's mind, the history of Rome, traced in the succession of its laws, had
been shaping up. In his oration *On the Study Methods of Our Time* he
epitomized, combined, and simultaneously abridged all of that which the
divining intuition of his predecessors had discovered in the history of Roman
legal science. The spectacle of the Roman laws was marshaled before him,
endowed with the unity of a drama performed by a people of giants."[5]

All in all, the appreciation of Grotius expressed by Vico in his *Autobiography*

[2] Among rather recent publications see N. Badaloni, *Introduzione allo studio di G. B.
Vico* (Milan, 1961), pp. 310ff.

[3] Vico, *Le orazioni inaugurali, il de Italorum sapientia, le polemiche*, in vol. I of *Opere*,
ed. G. Gentile and F. Nicolini (Bari, 1914), p. 101. The passage quoted is from Elio
Gianturco's translation of the *De nostri temporis studiorum ratione* (*On the Study Methods of
Our Time* [Indianapolis, Ind.: Bobbs-Merrill, 1965], p. 49).

[4] *Ibid.*; cf. Horace's *Ars poetica*, ll. 396–99:
In this did pristine wisdom consist:
in the separation of public from private rights, of sacred from profane matters,
in the prevention of vagrant unions, in fixing the rights of husbands,
establishing urban communities, carving laws on wooden tablets.

[5] G. Ferrari, "La mente di G. B. Vico," in *Tavola analitica delle dottrine di G. B. Vico*,
in *Opere di G. B. Vico*, ed. G. Ferrari (Milan: *Classici Italiani*, I, 1837), p. 108.

is highly positive. In Grotius "Vico saw the fourth author, to be added to the other three whom he had set up as models," [6] that is, Plato, Tacitus, and Bacon. Vico added Grotius because he considered him to be superior to the other three. Whereas Plato, Vico remarks, "adorns, rather than firmly establishes, his esoteric wisdom with the vulgar wisdom of Homer," Grotius "firmly grounds his wisdom on natural law, bolstering it up with the attestations of Homer and of the poets." Whereas Tacitus fails to organize his factual materials into a system, so that they remain scattered and incoherent, and whereas Bacon, despite his idea of a grandiose reform of the whole religious and secular cosmos of knowledge, "insofar as laws are concerned, failed to rise, in any perceptible degree, to the universal viewpoint, to the ensemble of all existing states and nations, at all epochs and everywhere," Grotius, instead, "combines into a system of universal law the whole of philosophy and the whole of philology. Concerning philology, for instance, he takes into account both of its parts, that is, the history of events, either fabulous or certain, and the history of the three languages, Hebrew, Greek, and Latin, these languages being the three major tools of scholarship handed down to us by the Christian religion."

Vico adds that "he went deeper and deeper into this work of Grotius (that is, *Jus belli ac pacis*) when, on the occasion of its reprinting, he was asked to write some annotations to it. He began to write them, more to criticize the notes that Gronovius had composed upon Grotius' text than to comment upon Grotius (Gronovius had appended his notes more as an act of flattery to free governments than in homage to justice). Vico had already run over Grotius' first book and half of the second when he interrupted his task, being stopped by the consideration that it was unbecoming to a Catholic to undertake to enhance by annotations the work of a heretical author."

Nothing is known concerning these footnotes, which apparently have been lost. From what has just been cited, it may be conjectured that they were either statements endorsing the opinions of Grotius or expressions of praise "adorning" the book.

Formerly, Vico scholars knew nothing about the particular edition of the *De jure belli ac pacis* to which Vico refers. Now we know that this work of Grotius actually appeared (with no mention of place or publisher) with the date of 1719, and with Gronovius' footnotes, in punctual correspondence with the information given in the *Autobiography*.[7] But the most important thing is that this edition is preceded by a dedication to Prince Eugene of Savoy, a

[6] Vico, *Opere*, V.

[7] *Ibid.*, p. 117. Concerning the discovery of this edition and the attribution of the dedicatory letter, the reader is referred to D. Faucci, "Vico editore di Grozio?" *Giornale storico della letteratura italiana*, 136, no. 413 (1959): 97–104. As for the confirmation of the identification of the work and of the letter see F. Nicolini, "Vico e Grozio," *Biblion*, 1, no. 2 (1959); see also D. Faucci, "Ancora su Vico e Grozio," *Annali della scuola normale superiore di Pisa*, series II, vol. XXXI, fascs. I–II (1962), p. 103.

dedication whose concepts and style unmistakably point to Vico as the author, and in which he gives us, not a retrospective judgment of Grotius, but a judgment coeval to the commentary. Vico writes:

Rightly, O most Serene Prince Eugene, the volumes being published today, that is, the books of Hugo Grotius, a man of imperishable fame, concerning the law of war and peace, books in which he thoroughly discusses the 'sacred law of nations' (*fas gentium*), the rights originating from a divine source (*jura a deis orta*), and the laws issued to mankind (*leges humano generi positae*), are inscribed to you, who are the greatest and most invincible of all army commanders. In these volumes, the most learned master of alliances and of covenants between monarchs and commonwealths introduces us to that science to which you give attestation, not indoors, but in the open fields, among armies and battles. Grotius' books do not treat of the laws enacted by either the Athenians or the Romans, but of that law which God's providence established among all men and which has been preserved by all nations, the law according to which you defend from the onslaught of foreign nations the kingdoms entrusted to your military power, and guard their existence.

The most characteristic feature of this introduction is the fact that the content of Grotius' work, that is, the *Law of War and Peace*, is denoted, not by expressions typical of its author, but by an interlacing of expressions drawn from Roman legal science, which will be repeated, almost as if they were sacramental formulas, in Vico's future writings, for the purpose of designating his "universal law" or "natural law of nations." In particular, Vico employs the definition of the *jus gentium* given by Gaius (quoted in Justinian's *Corpus juris civilis*). Vico, however, replaces the words "natural law" with the expression "God's providence."[8] By doing so, he departs from Grotius' terminology. Grotius, as we know, distinguishes "natural law," which is rational and immutable, from the "law of nations," which he views as voluntary law.[9]

In general this typical presentation of Grotius' juridical ideas enables us to perceive the limits of Grotius' influence upon Vico.

Vico sees in the work of Grotius a "universal system" of law. This system derives from rationally valid principles, concerns all nations (Grotius

[8] See Justinian's *Institutes* 1. 2. 1 for the definition of *jus gentium* which Vico applies to the law treated by Grotius, and for the words "divine providence," substituted for "natural reason." The substitution is practically and theoretically significant: the religious phrasing made the thought that the author introduced more acceptable, and, for that matter, the expression is the one that Vico uses in order to indicate the key to his future conception of law and of history.

[9] "Natural law is an ensemble of rules dictated by right reason, by which it teaches us that a certain action is honest or dishonest" (Grotius, *De jure belli ac pacis*, 1646 ed., bk. I, chap. I, p. x). As for *jus gentium* see *ibid.*, p. xiv; see also *The Classics of International Law* (Washington, D.C.: The Carnegie Institution, 1913). It should be noted that the meaning of the expression *jus gentium* is still different in Pufendorf (*De jure naturae et gentium*, 1672). By *jus gentium* Pufendorf means that part of natural, rational law which deals with international relations.

adduces philological evidence of this), and attests, against the Cartesians, that reason could be applied not only to physical nature but to the world of societies as well.   Shortly thereafter, however, Vico felt entitled, by Grotius' idea of the universality of law, to extend the truths discovered by him in the field of Roman law to the history of other nations as well.   Grotius, the anti-Romanist, thus suggested to Vico, and supplied him with proofs, that Roman *sapientia* had its counterpart in the wisdom contained in the folk-ways, customs, and laws of that world of antiquity whose vestiges, docu-ments, and monuments Grotius masterfully knew how to trace in the writings of theologians, historians, and poets.

Under the enthusiastic impact of this encounter, from the union of the idea of a juridico-political, still empirical, realism with the idea of the rationality of law, there took shape in Vico's mind the ideal diagram of a peculiar jusnaturalistic doctrine whose outlines, contained in the dedicatory letter, persist basically unchanged in Vico's subsequent writings.

Let us emphasize that this diagram was purely ideal, since it did not correspond to Grotius' thought.   Yet it was under the guise of the diagram that Vico presented Grotius' masterpiece.   Correspondingly, we may say, he coined a highly eulogistic title for the author of that "ideal" system, i.e., "jurisconsult of mankind." However, when for the first time we find that title used in the preamble (*Proloquium*) of Part I of the *Diritto universale*, we find it attributed to Grotius himself.[10]

Was Vico, then, still unaware of the basic diversity between Grotius' thought and his own?

In fact, the conformity with that "ideal" diagram is still present in the "Idea of the Work," prefixed to the *Scienza nuova* of 1725, where Vico uses, as mottoes for Books II, III, and IV, the expressions *jura a deis posita, fas gentium*, and *leges aeternae*.   Essentially, such expressions are the same as

---

[10] "Iurisconsultus generis humani."   See Vico, *Sinopsi del diritto universale* and *De uno universi iuris principio et fine uno*, in *Opere*, II (Bari, 1936).   This confirms the validity of Nicolini's judgment: "Vico makes a present to Grotius of what he later accomplishes in the *De universi iuris uno principio* and in the *Scienza nuova*" (see Vico, *Opere*, ed. F. Nicolini [Naples: Ricciardi, 1953], p. 48).   Gentile's judgment in *Studi vichiani*, 2d ed. (Florence: Le Monnier, 1927), p. 183, is analogous to Nicolini's.

The appellation "jurisconsult of mankind" is given particular emphasis by W. Y. M. van Eysinga; he considers it to be "la meilleure caractéristique de l'auteur du *De jure belli ac pacis*, parce que, mieux que celle plus commune de 'père du droit international,' elle relève que c'est le droit de l'humanité entière, pas des Etats seulement, mais en premier lieu des individus, que déploie l'oeuvre de Grotius" ("Grotius resurgens," *Nederlands tijdschrift voor internationaal recht*, October, 1953).

This remark of Van Eysinga's constitutes the starting point of A. Droetto's article entitled "Hugo de Groot in de Italiaanse interpretatie van G. B. Vico," published in *Italiaans Cultureel Bulletin*, nos. 12–13 (1955), and later, in Italian, in *Annali della scuola normale superiore di Pisa*, series II, vol. XXX, fascs. I–II (1961), under the title "Ugo Grozio nell' interpretazione di G. B. Vico."

those to be found in the dedicatory letter.[11]   Vico employs them again in a further rhetorical writing of 1731, addressed to Ernest von Harrach, son of the Viceroy of Naples.

The legal scholarship that in the past was called *fas deorum*, whose enactments were extolled as *leges generis humani* (laws of mankind), *leges aeternae, foedera humanae societatis* (covenants of human society), and whose specialist can rightly be called the jurisconsult of mankind, is a study well worthy of your great soul.   This is a jural competence by far more excellent than the mere knowledge of the laws of Athens, Sparta, or Rome. . . . the particular legal enactments of these states were but small fractions of the universal and eternal law system.   It is a wisdom worthy of the Roman people.   Without any trace of flattery, Virgil grants to the Greeks all the fine arts of genius, the esoteric sciences . . . the glory of eloquence; but he reserves this kind of legal expertise to the Romans.[12]

Here, too, in connection with the "ideal" figure of the jurisconsult of mankind, we find Grotius' name.   "Hugo Grotius was the first to treat of this universal and eternal law; and, thanks to his incomparable scholarship and learning (which were required for that treatment), he became the topmost leader in such a field of studies."

Notice that Vico says that Grotius was the first, that is, the path-breaker, in these studies (Vico completely overlooks all of Grotius' scholastic predecessors), and became the foremost leader of the jusnaturalism of his time. But to what an extent does this encomium of Grotius mean, for Vico, the acceptance of Grotius' thought as fully valid?

The answer is contained in the sequel of the *Autobiography* where, immediately after the eulogy that explains Vico's adoption of Grotius as his fourth author, the clear statement is made:

As a result of these studies, of the knowledge he had acquired, of his adoption of these four authors whom he admired above all others, as a result of his wish to use them in the service of the Catholic religion, Vico finally understood that the cultural world did not yet possess a system capable of harmonizing the best philosophy (that is, Platonic philosophy subordinated to Christian religion) with a philology scientifically organized in both of its aspects, that is, the history of language and the history of events.   The philology he had in mind would make it possible to bestow objective certitude on the history of language by co-ordinating it with the evidence supplied by historical facts.   The system Vico would have liked to devise would bring into friendly relationship both the maxims of academic scholars and the practices of the political sages.   This train of thought definitely gave rise, in the mind of Vico, to the plan that

---

[11] Vico, *La scienza nuova prima, con la polemica contro gli atti degli eruditi di Lipsia*, in vol. III of *Opere*, ed. F. Nicolini (Bari, 1931), p. 5.

[12] "Dedicatoria al D'Arrach, scritta in nome del traduttore e premessa alla '*Sifilide*' di Girolamo Fracastoro volta in italiano da Pietro Belli; a proposito della presentazione della seconda 'Scienza Nuova' a Monsignor d'Harrach."   Quoted from Vico, *Scritti vari e pagine sparse*, in vol. VIII of *Opere*, ed. F. Nicolini (Bari, 1940), pp. 25–27, with the editor's notes.

had been outlining itself in the *Inaugural Orations* and that he had roughly blocked out in his discourse *On the Study Methods of Our Time.* . . .[13]

This statement, in our view, corresponds to the actual mental process of Vico. His problem was the search for a system, or for a philosophical conception, that would enable him to achieve a deeper understanding of Roman history and of Roman legal institutions, so as to allow him to translate them into a universal law. Evidence of this may be found in the *De nostri temporis studiorum ratione.* Grotius suggested this problem but did not give the solution of it. This is why, in Vico's treatise on universal law, the praiseful appellation of "jurisconsult of mankind" is at once followed by a reservation: "If we weigh the principles of Grotius on the scales of criticism, they all turn out to be probable and verisimilar, rather than necessary and irrefutable."[14]

In reality, apart from this indecisive evidence, Vico's scientific work (from 1719 on) may be construed as a progressive attempt to differentiate his thought from that of Grotius in point of natural or "universal" law, in order to replace Grotius' solution with his own. The adoption of Grotius as principal author develops into a critical and polemical, explicit and precise, elaboration that extends far beyond single juridical concepts. Vico bases the superiority of his position upon the philosophical vision which he, not Grotius, has achieved. Part I of Vico's treatise on universal law is entitled *On the Single Principle and the Single Aim of Universal Law.* This principle is justice, according to the Platonic-Augustinian concept of the good, that is, according to the recollection of God, whom men were privileged to contemplate in the Garden of Eden. The cause of civilization, the "mother of law and of human society," is *honestas*, morality, the love of justice. Utility and necessity constitute merely occasions for the rise of society and law. Grotius was unable to distinguish between *honestas* and *utilitas*. Consequently, he envisaged self-advantage, calculated by reason, as the cause, not the occasion, of law.

On the one hand, Grotius failed to illustrate the relationship between reason and authority, which is an aspect of the relationship between certitude and truth (*certum* and *verum*). The distinction between reason and authority does not mean, however, mutual exclusion. Authority, even when it be-

[13] Vico, *Opere*, V, 39–40.
[14] Vico, *Il diritto universale*, in vol. II of *Opere*, bk. I, p. 32. It should be observed, on the other hand, that such appellation is given him even though Vico emphasizes that he failed to consider Roman civil law: Grotius is the jurisconsult of mankind, just as Cujas (and perhaps, Antonio de Goveano) is the foremost interpreter of Roman law. This is the essential meaning of pars. 19 and 20 of the Prologue to the *De uno universi iuris principio*. It is not to be excluded that the expression in quotes may have been borrowed from another author (also in reference to Grotius). But, as Van Eysinga's remark shows, no one among the Grotius or Vico scholars knows about this.

comes force and violence, may contain a principle of reason.[15]   On the other hand, the uncompromising purism and the Stoic rationalism of Grotius, who ignores the condition of man, fallen and weak, but assisted by God, may lead, through skeptical despair, to utilitarian solutions and to a totally unprincipled political realism (as in the case of Hobbes and Bayle).

In 1724 Vico prepared a treatise which has been lost and which is usually called *The New Science in Negative Form*.   In Part I of this work, Vico, through a continuous polemical refutation of the jusnaturalists (Grotius, Selden, Pufendorf, and their followers) and of ancient and modern utilitarians, explored the origins of civilization.[16]

The year of publication of the *Principles of a New Science Concerning the Nature of Nations, wherein the Principles of Another System of Jusnaturalism are Discovered* was 1725.   This work was thus officially introduced to the scholarly world as a scientific, philosophical, and philological method aimed at the construction of a natural-law system different from, even though not contrary to, the already existing ones formulated by Grotius and his followers.[17]   The new system was to be set beside its compeers, although Vico failed to mention the scholastic systems of Suarez and Vitoria.

It should be pointed out that in these *Principles*, next to the distinction between the newly discovered "science" and the "system" of natural law, the connection that closely links the one to the other is already present.   In one of its aspects, this first version of the *Scienza nuova* is a real methodology of historical research, born under the concrete influence of the Baconian method,[18] and has its precedent in Part II, Book II of the *Diritto universale* (*De constantia philologiae*, chapter I, "*Nova scientia tentatur*").[19]

The other aspect of the *Scienza nuova prima* is that, like the *Diritto universale*, and to no less an extent, it constitutes a search for the formative principle of a

[15] As for the first concept, see particularly proposition XLVI of the *De uno universi iuris principio*; the second remark can be found in the Prologue to the same work.   See Vico, *Opere*, vol. II, bk. I, pp. 54ff. and p. 32, respectively.

[16] Vico, *Opere*, III, Nicolini's *Nota* to the *Scienza nuova prima* (1725), 327.

[17] Such a purpose is explicitly stated in the volume's dedication to the universities of Europe, "whose professional lectures are intended to illustrate the 'natural law of nations,' of which the Spartan, Athenian, Roman, law orders are merely partial aspects, just as Sparta, Athens, Rome, are merely small parts of the big wide world."   To these universities of Europe Vico inscribes his "principles of a different" jusnaturalistic system, elaborated by him "jointly with a new science concerning the nature of nations."   The principles stand in close causal connection with that nature, "since undoubtedly they have sprung from it."   It is Vico's hope that the European universities in which the discipline of *jus naturae* is taught may, through their scholarship and wisdom, integrate, improve, and promote the principles he has discovered.   In a 1728 catalogue, the title of the *Scienza nuova prima* is given as follows: *Principi di una scienza nuova d'intorno alla natura delle nazioni per li quali si trovano altri principi del diritto naturale delle genti che li tre ne meditarono Grozio, Seldeno e Pufendorfio*.

[18] See E. De Mas, *Bacone e Vico* (Turin: Edizioni di Filosofia, 1959).

[19] Vico, *Opere*, II, 308.

civilized society. The problem has grown more complicated because the nature of nations has now revealed itself to be the development, in stages, of an "ideal" historical pattern, but it has remained identical. The problem consists in discovering how "justice is evaluated" [20] and carried out in the life of a nation, enabling it to live in a civilized fashion. In this way the task of the *New Science* (the discovery of the nature of nations) coincides with that of the discovery of that "natural law of nations" which is the foundation of their existence. If such a law were neglected, "ideal" history would be nothing but a naturalistic description of human stages, whereas ideal history arises, to no less an extent than does Grotius' legal science, from the problem concerning the reason and justice which rule human collectivities.

This is a science dealing with "certain beginnings, or initial stages, of the development of civilization among nations." It is a science connected with the growth of nations toward a state of perfection which they can attain, and from which they decline. Correspondingly (*Idea of a Science of the Legal Institutions of Mankind*) we read: "The science of the institutions of the natural law of nations may be envisaged as a science of man's modes of thinking. Man is [naturally] inclined to his own preservation from destruction." [21]

And law is the "evaluation of justice," which preserves human nature from destruction. The exemplary model remains the legal science of the Romans, that is (for the ancient period), "a science of how the mind of the Decemvirs envisaged the utilitarian values of civil life during the epoch when Rome's moral standards still bore a character of great severity," a character which became milder with the passage of time, but which constantly aimed at the supreme goal of public welfare, at the preservation of the Roman polity.

In Book II of the *Scienza nuova prima* we come across a treatment of the "Natural Order of Ideas Concerning the Concept of Eternal Justice" (chapter IV) and "Concerning Universal Justice" (chapter V). In the preamble to Book III, we find this statement: "The principles hitherto discussed give us the key to the philosophy and history of mankind. In order to bring to a termination the other section of this *jurisprudence of the natural law of nations*[22] we shall, through the other principles just set forth, proceed to discover the science of a common language of such a law, a language shared by the whole of the human species" (paragraph 248).

In Vico the expression "natural law" embraces the total aggregate of the natural laws of an "eternal commonwealth," but this constantly varies in accordance with epochs and places. The discovery of this "eternal" political

---

[20] The expression recurs several times. See, for instance, *Scienza nuova* (1744 ed.), par. 938.

[21] Vico, *Opere*, III, 30.

[22] Italics mine.

pattern is the second "general discovery" after that of the "ideal" timeless pattern of history (*"storia ideale eterna"*) (paragraphs 521 and 520).

Vico's discoveries, far from being taken up and promoted by the academies of Europe, were the object of a contemptuous note in the August, 1727, issue of the *Acta Eruditorum* of Leipzig.   Otherwise they were ignored, or found no understanding.   This result shattered Vico's hopes of being ranked among the great jusnaturalists such as Grotius and others.[23]   It was useless for him to enter into competition with the masters and advocates of the science of *jus naturae*.

Evidence of this changed psychological and practical attitude is given in the title of the *Scienza nuova* of 1730, which fails to mention "natural law": "Five books of a new science concerning the common nature of nations, evolved in a more pertinent fashion in this edition, and with additions."[24]

Actually, the last and long labor of Vico's, which culminates in the posthumous edition of 1744, consists in digging down and bringing up "evidence" of the "eternal ideal history," particularly in relation to the epoch when man's soul "adverts to external phenomena, and is perturbed and stirred by them" (axiom LIII).   As a consequence, the bulk of the 1744 edition is made up of Book II, "On Poetical Wisdom," of which Book III, the "Discovery of the True Homer," is an illustration.

On the other hand, the human world is seen in its entirety, and the perspective of its "civil" aspects is unchanged: natural law still occupies (undoubtedly without any practical purpose) the center of the stage.   It is enough to mention, among the axioms, axiom VII, concerning legislation, which "transmutes vices into civil happiness," and concerning "Providence, a divine legislative mind"; axiom IX, which terms "human needs and utilitarian interests" according to the "common sense of men," the two

---

[23] It is thus understandable that, in his fiery *Vindiciae* in reply to the Leipzig *Acta Eruditorum*, Vico should write, in order to emphasize the original feature of his discovery of the genesis of associated life: "The chief point, therefore, is not the natural law of nations, but the common nature of the whole aggregate of nations.   It is from this common nature that there springs, flows into, and diffuses itself through all peoples [of the earth] in a manner thoroughly identical, a constant and universal mode of envisaging things religious and secular.   It is from this mode of envisaging, then, that a new system of natural law can be derived.   This new system constitutes, so to speak, the principal corollary of that science [of the common nature of nations]."   Vico's statements are clear enough: the diversity of his universal law from that of Grotius is predicated upon a different conception of human reality and history.   The chief point of the discovery was, undoubtedly, the "eternal ideal history" (the conceptual pattern underlying the history of "facts").   But this does not mean that the problem was not that of justice, i.e., that of the "eternal, ideally perfect commonwealth," viewed against the background of historical concreteness.   As for the book notice in the *Acta*, and Vico's review, see Vico, *Vici vindiciae*, in vol. III of *Opere*, pp. 291ff.

[24] Among the additional items, however, we find: *Ragionamenti intorno alle XII Tavole;* and *Ragionamenti intorno alla Lex Regia*.

"chief sources of the natural law of nations" (this point being re-emphasized in axiom XIII);[25] and, finally, the last axioms, grouped under the title "Providence is the enacter of the natural law of nations" (paragraph 328), which close with a renewed expression of disapproval of the system of the three major jusnaturalists, Grotius, Selden, and Pufendorf, "whose mistake consists in assuming that the 'ideal' pattern of natural equity could have been grasped by the heathen nations at the time of their primal beginnings."

This is the problem which remained of basic importance in the *Scienza nuova*. The treatment of "poetical wisdom," even though it seemed to engage the author's entire attention, for he was fascinated by the picture of the most interesting period of man's history (with this, one might justify Vico's title-deed of honor as "progenitor of aesthetics"), is, above all, concerned with examining the way in which the primitive epoch "assessed" justice. It is this assessment, this evaluation, which constitutes the basis of society. In that primordial epoch, the manner of living by which nations are preserved, and by which they progress, was proposed and imposed by poets and legislators, not by academic, purely theoretical philosophers. At the beginning of Book IV we read that in the previous book "the discovery has been made that the poems of Homer are two treasure-troves of the natural law of the nations of Greece, just as the Roman law of the Twelve Tables has been found by us to represent a most weighty testimonial of the natural law of the nations of Latium" (paragraph 915).

In Book IV, which deals with "The Historical Course of Nations," in rhythmical consonance with the three stages of the history of mankind, the term "jurisprudence" is equivalent to "wisdom." In Vico's mind, the coincidence (which he asserts in the *De nostri temporis studiorum ratione*) between the Greek definition of philosophy and the Roman one of juris-prudence,[26] is still valid. The factor of justice, truly human and divine, is the most important for society; jurisprudence, the science of justice, is "the wisdom by which man achieves perfection"; the jurisconsult is he whose judgment specializes in the "estimation of what is just." In the political philosopher the figures of the sage and the jurisconsult coincide.

This happens in all eras; there are, actually, three kinds of jurisprudence (paragraphs 937ff.). But what should be the characteristics of jurisprudence

[25] Here is one of the most characteristic of the axioms: "The criterion imparted to the nations by the providence of God, in order that they might achieve [a feeling of] certitude in regard to [matters pertaining to] the natural law of nations, is the common consensus of all peoples." This axiom constitutes the kernel, in the *Scienza nuova*, of Vico's polemical argument against Grotius, who, Vico claims, talks about "the natural law of nations" without taking into account the common consensus of all peoples in regard to human needs and utilitarian interests.

[26] Jurisprudence is "the knowledge of all things divine and human; the science of what is just or unjust" (Justinian's *Institutes* I. 2. I).

in the epoch of reason's fullest development, that is, the epoch in which Vico lived? When, in the "Conclusion of the Work," he emphasizes again that the result of his research in the historical development of the human mind is "the discovery of an eternal natural form of human association conforming to a prototype, an ideal pattern, established by the providence of God" (paragraph 1097), he presents, essentially, his own *Scienza nuova* (which has finally succeeded in achieving the intellection of the "natural law of nations") as "the jurisprudence of mankind" and himself as "the jurisconsult of the whole human species."[27]

Van Eysinga, however, is of the opinion that the title of "jurisconsult of mankind" should more rightfully be given to Grotius, who extols the rights of all individual men beyond the distinction of race and religion.[28] Van Eysinga thus connects Grotius with the ideal, recurring in our time, of a more rational organization of society. It was to this aim that Grotius' activity for peace in many fields (the religious as well as the political) was directed. In fact, in Grotius' view, Christianity as a norm of life is (as it is for his inspirer, Erasmus) identical with the humanistic ideal of irenic ecumenicalism. Anticipating Spinoza, Grotius derives from that ideal whatever is nobly useful and reasonable for human coexistence, above and beyond all factional and sectarian conflicts. Hence, Grotius' strong leaning toward Arminius and the Remonstrants; hence his resistance to Calvinism's uncompromising advocacy of the dogma of grace, which gave rise to the charge of Socinianism; hence the spirit of toleration, which caused him to be favorably inclined even toward the Church of Rome, that is, toward a "catholic" universal communion of the faithful.

Vico does not tread the same path. That modern commitment to the moral progress of mankind which, after Grotius, other thinkers (especially Kant, *A Plan for Perpetual Peace*) were to engage in, remains almost completely outside the visual compass of Vico.[29]

---

[27] Ferrari's statement (contained in *Tavola analitica delle dottrine di G. B. Vico*, cited in n. 5 above) is therefore quite appropriate and correct: "The jurisprudence of the natural law of nations is the science of the mind of man directed to the preservation of the individuals and that of society" (I, 303). The meaning of F. Nicolini's words seems to be identical when, in connection with one of Vico's researches (the *Canoni mitologici* in the *Nota* to the *Diritto universale*), he asserts that this research was closely bound up with the quest for a new system of the natural law of nations. (In modern terminology we would phrase it thus: "the quest for a new way of configuring the development of the history of civilization." See Vico, *Opere*, III, 326.

[28] See n. 10 above.

[29] Did Vico, as a political thinker, consider the realization of this end to be impossible? Does the following consideration by Manzoni correspond to a personal persuasion of Vico's? "Society is a mystery of contradictions in which the human intellect is lost unless it views it as a state of trial, of preparation for another existence" (see Manzoni's essay *Sopra alcuni punti della storia longobardica in Italia*). The statement quoted is to be found in close proximity to the famous parallel between Vico and Muratori (see Man-

For Vico the religion and the politics of his time were institutional conditions almost fatally given. From theology he borrowed two concepts,
which are embedded in his *New Science*. One is that of man fallen and weak
(contrasted with the dull-witted "simpletons" of the "Socinian" Grotius); the
other is the idea of "eternal justice as the basis of Society." These concepts,
however, are more apt to further our understanding of what happened in
history than to constitute direct principles and norms for our action and
conduct.

Thus, in the *Scienza nuova*, beside the ethico-religious component (the
feeling of pudency as the beginning of civilized behavior) there appears, and
by chance predominates, the vitalistic component: the preservation of associated life through the work of Providence and through that of the legislators
of the earth. Through that work, vices are made to contribute to the advantage of society, are transmuted into the strength, wealth, and wisdom
of political collectivities (paragraph 132). As the reader can see, this idea is
closely akin to B. Mandeville's thesis set forth in his *Fable of the Bees:
Private Vices, Public Benefits* (1714).

In other respects Vico, apart from (or perhaps precisely because of) his
flaunted and scrupulous declarations of orthodoxy, appears to be linked to
Catholicism as to an institutional force, upon which he leans for protection
and support for his scientific labors. He intends to *place* these labors under
the aegis of Catholic culture, in order to present them as an adornment of,
and as a signal credit to, that culture. This is significant as a point of contrast
to Grotius. While Vico extols the most outstanding jurisconsult among the
Reformers, he constantly portrays himself, in his writings, as the Catholic
anti-Grotius.

Carlo Cattaneo synthesizes the historical position of Vico's thought in
the following fashion (and in so doing he is not far removed from the Italian
neo-idealistic interpretation): "Vico fuses the doctrine of self-interest,
which is predominant in Machiavelli, with the doctrine of reason, emphasized
by Grotius. He thus does away with the contradiction that splits history
from philosophy."[30]

In effect, as we saw, the two components thus identified met and were
interwoven in Vico in various ways. Are we to understand the meeting of
Machiavelli with Grotius as a resolving synthesis which eliminated the
previous positions, especially that of Grotius, as superfluous?

Insofar as modern problematics is concerned, it is more useful to view
Vico and Grotius as representatives of two perspectives. They do not

---

zoni's *Tutte le opere* [Florence: Barbera, 1928], p. 345). The conception of society as a
"state of trial" does not seem to be a part of the organic tissue of Vico's work.

[30] C. Cattaneo, "Su la 'Scienza Nova' del Vico," in *Scritti filosofici, letterari, e vari,*
ed. F. Alessio (Florence: Sansoni, 1957), p. 53.

mutually exclude each other, nor does one "surpass" (in the Hegelian sense) the other. It is best to remember them as "jurisconsults of mankind" who are entitled to this honorable appellation for two different reasons: Vico, because he induces in us a fuller understanding, without prejudice, of human reality as incessant activity, "poetical reason,"[31] i.e., as inventive genius, evolving out of itself the forms that are apt to satisfy the needs and requirements of associated life; Grotius, because he represents in his own way (the way permitted to him by his historical conditions) the unshakable faith (or "religion," in Kant's sense) in human reasonableness, the purpose of which is to carry into reality a type of social organization designed for the utter prevention of a recurrence of barbarism.

Bibliographical Note

There does not yet exist a study wholly devoted to the relationships between Vico and Grotius. These relationships become all the more interesting, the greater the acknowledgment that the juridico-political problem constitutes the foundation of the *Scienza nuova*. The scholar who, more than others, has undertaken the investigation of both problems is A. Corsano. See his: *Ugo Grozio: L'umanista–Il teologo–Il giurista* (Bari, 1948); and *G. B. Vico* (Bari, 1956). A considerable portion of G. Fassò's *I " quattro auttori" del Vico* (Milan: Giuffrè, 1949), an essay on the genesis of the *Scienza nuova*, is devoted to Grotius.

Judgments concerning the impact of Grotius' thought on that of Vico, Vico's appreciation of the Dutch jusnaturalist, and hence of the relative weight Grotius had with him vis-à-vis Vico's other "authors" (Plato, Tacitus, Bacon) evince, if not essential antithesis, dissimilar emphases on chief aspects.

To a greater extent than all other scholars, A. Droetto (see his *U. Grozio nell' interpretazione di G. B. Vico* and other writings) perceives in Grotius' *De jure* an almost rounded-out model of the *Scienza nuova*. According to Droetto, the synthesis of realism-rationalism, mediated through Tacitean-Machiavellian influence, is already to be found in Grotius. Droetto, therefore, judges Vico's strictures, insistently leveled at the "jurisconsult of mankind," to be unauthentic and uttered only in deference to ecclesiastical authorities.

F. Nicolini (see his *Opere di G. B. Vico*, edited and annotated, in the Ricciardi Collection [Milan-Naples, 1953], as well as the *Bibliografia vichiana*,

---

[31] I am borrowing this expression (conceptually quite appropriate) from a Florentine professor of philosophy, G. Chiavacci, author of *La ragione poetica* (Florence: Le Monnier, 1949).

published under the joint editorship of Croce and Nicolini, but augmented and recast by Nicolini [Naples: Ricciardi, 1947–48], asserts that Vico's *De uno universi iuris principio et fine uno* and the *Scienza nuova* were inspired by Grotius. Nicolini views the two works as different versions (redactions) of a single *opus*. According to Nicolini, it was Grotius who enabled Vico really to profit from the perusal of the other "authors."

Guido Fassò sees in Grotius, no less than in Bacon, the one who taught Vico the method that the latter employed in the *Scienza nuova*, i.e., the combination of *verum* and *certum*. As a matter of fact (according to Fassò), that combination was much more than a mere connection; it was an intimate union. The model of that intimate union of *verum* and *certum* appeared in Grotius.

E. De Mas (*Bacone e Vico* [Turin, 1959]) thinks, instead, that Vico's master in methodology basically was Bacon, and that Grotius' work represents for him a "practical exemplification" of the Baconian method.

Within the framework of general studies on Vico, precise judgments on the Vico-Grotius relationship are to be found, as we saw, in Ferrari and Cattaneo, and, in the nineteenth century as well, in N. Tommaseo's *Vico e il suo secolo* (Turin: Utet, 1930), app. II, p. 103. Tommaseo's work appeared in 1843.

In his basic volume *La filosofia di Giambattista Vico* (Bari: Laterza, 1911), Croce collects Vico's critical statements on Grotius, translating them, in terms of his *Filosofia della pratica*, into the [general] reproach "of having forgotten the aspect of force, in order to focus entirely on those of justice, equity, and morality" (3d ed., 1933, p. 103).

G. Gentile interprets Vico's interruption of his commentary on Grotius as being caused by the intuition of the new system that was taking definite shape in his mind, and not as the result of religious scruples (see *Studi vichiani*, 2d ed. [Florence: Le Monnier, 1927], p. 183).

The relationships between law and philosophy have received only slight emphasis in the interpretation of Vico by Italian idealism. Croce, viewing the concept of natural law as a totally ahistorical abstraction, observes that "Vico, without seeming to do so, gets rid of the ideal code of eternal values," while Gentile asserts that for Vico (contrary to what Vico says about the studies of his youthful period) "jurisprudence became an occasion to find, or a collection of indifferent materials apt to reveal, in the determinations of the human spirit, the basic principles and concepts" (*Studi vichiani*, p. 27) of the philosophy of the mind.

Relationships between law and philosophy are, instead, a favorite point with legal philosophers. We limit ourselves to mentioning G. Solari, *La scuola del diritto naturale nella dottrina etico guiridica dei secoli XVII e XVIII* (Turin: Bocca, 1904). Solari particularly emphasizes the fact that Grotius and Vico coincide in their ideas of justice as the foundation of historical rights.

Important are the researches of B. Donati entitled *Nuovi studi sulla filosofia civile del Vico* (Florence: Le Monnier, 1936), which contain a piercing analysis of Vico's and Grotius' legal concepts. A remarkable contribution, acute and scintillating, is that of Pietro Piovani, "Ex legislatione philosophia," in his *Filosofia del diritto come scienza filosofica* (Milan: Giuffrè, 1963), pp. 137–256.

On Vico's religion, opinions vary. He was attacked by the Catholic critics of his time (see G. F. Finetti, *Difesa dell' autorità della S. Scrittura contro G. B. Vico*, ed. B. Croce [Bari: Laterza, 1936]), considered with favor by the Catholic liberals of the nineteenth century, and judged to be unimpeachably orthodox in our time. See *G. B. Vico*, a memorial volume, ed. A. Gemelli; and F. Amerio, *Introduzione allo studio di Vico* (Turin: SEL, 1947), controverting Croce's "immanentist" interpretation, which views Vico as a precursor of Croce's own "religion of freedom" (Croce: "Vico sought for God in the heart of man." *La filosofia di Giambattista Vico*, p. 96). In regard to Vico's declared loyalty to the Church, Croce thinks that this was not due to a clever political calculation. Vico, not wishing to make this point clear to himself, went so far as to "idolize himself in the guise of a *defensor ecclesiae*, at the very moment when he was supplanting the religion of the Church with that of 'humanity' " (*ibid.*). On the religious theme see also A. Corsano, *Umanesimo e religione in Vico* (Bari, 1935), later recast in his *G. B. Vico*. As for the secular and biblical components of Vico's thought, mention should be made of E. Paci's *Ingens sylva* (Milan: Mondadori, 1949), which emphasizes the importance of Lucretius' influence.

N. Badaloni's volume *Introduzione allo studio di G. B. Vico* (Milan: Feltrinelli, 1961) throws into relief the influence of Grotius on Vico's *Orazioni inaugurali*, as well as his effect on that sector of Neapolitan culture to which the "free-thinking" friends of Vico's youth belonged and on Pietro Giannone's *Storia civile del regno di Napoli*.

Translated by Elio Gianturco

Yvon Belaval   VICO AND
                              ANTI-CARTESIANISM

If we are to trust Vico's autobiographical notice,[1] in 1685 the people of
Naples (at that time a Spanish possession) still clung to Jesuitic teaching
(Suarez, Alvarez, Ricci, and others), thought that metaphysics should be a
prerogative of cathedral schools (76), read Marsilio Ficino's Christianized
Plato (76), and had hardly begun to get acquainted with Epicurus' theories
as they are embodied in Gassendi's system (64). In 1695, when Vico returns
to Naples after nine years of seclusion in the forests of Vatolla, where,
"guided by his good genius, without giving preference to any particular
trend of traditional ideas, he had almost brought to an end the course of his
studies" (72), the most distinguished Neapolitan intellectuals are engaged in
extolling Descartes' *Physics*, and Vico finds himself "a stranger in his native
town" (70).

  Undoubtedly, Vico feels resentment against Descartes. The latter has
slipped some fictions into his *Discours* (51); he does not acknowledge his
readings (169); in his "greed for glory" he has planned, in opposition to the
Metaphysics of Aristotle, to establish "his empire in the cathedral schools"
(68); he has hidden himself behind Regius[2] in order to launch his own
system (67); he has become the leader of a sect (168–69); his method is sterile
(167); some of his followers are quacks (166); the final result of his philosophy
is fatalism (67), and so on. Even disregarding his grudge, Vico could not
help but feel out of his own element in Cartesianism. For him the four
great men were (or were going to be) Plato, Tacitus, Bacon, and Grotius,
and "he strove to interpret them in the spirit of the Catholic religion" (94);
he never went beyond Euclid's fifth proposition (60); for him, universal
knowledge was summed up in legal science (186–87). How, then, could he
feel at home in a doctrine which secularizes philosophy, which takes physics

---

[1] Quoted in the volume of Jules Michelet's *Oeuvres complètes de J. Michelet* (Paris, n.d.)
devoted to Vico; throughout this paper, numbers in parentheses refer to the pagination
of this volume.

[2] *Henrici Regii ultrajectini* (i.e., Henri de Roy, 1598–1679, professor of medicine at the
University of Utrecht) *Philosophia naturalis, in qua tota rerum universitas per clara et facilia
Principia explanatur* (Amsterdam, 1661). Vico repudiates the claim expressed by this
title. In particular, he seems to have read bk. I (*De natura*) and bk. V (*De homine*) of this
work.

as its center and mathematics as a model of *mathesis universalis*? How could he have read Descartes with an unprejudiced mind?

Did he read him? He quotes the titles of the *Discours*, the *Méditations*, the *Principes*, the *Traité des passions de l'âme*. On the other hand, since he consistently "refused to learn French" (70), in what language did he read the *Discours*?[3] He believes the *Discours* to be later in date than the *Méditations* (76) and most often associates it with the *Logique* of Arnauld. He happens to speak of the *Méditations* in such terms that one is left wondering whether he may instead be referring to the *Principes* (77). Did he borrow what he says about refraction and the parallelogram of forces from Descartes' *Dioptrics*, *Principes*, or from Regius? Does his knowledge of the hypothesis of the pineal gland (which he once objected to) derive from the *Traité des passions de l'âme*, which, Vico says, "may be linked rather with medicine than with ethics" (69)? In this connection Vico refers to "the Cartesians" rather than precisely to Descartes (259). Ultimately, Vico's statements seem constantly to be the products of second-hand information. He admits that his initiation into Cartesian physics took place by way of Regius' *Philosophie naturelle*, that is, through the work of an author whom Descartes had repudiated in 1647. He refers to Arnauld, Pascal (69), Spinoza (183, 640), and Malebranche (69, 262).[4] We may ask once again, "To what extent did Vico's acquaintance with these authors stem from a direct reading?" Vico's references are merely that. Nevertheless, Vichian criticism is of twofold interest: it informs us about Vico himself, and it strikes upon some of Descartes' weak points.

The humanist nurtured on Greek, Latin, and Tuscan poets, the philologist who seeks in philology for the method par excellence of the *Scienza nuova*, is shocked at hearing Descartes, in Part I of the *Discours*, affirm that he has failed to find in literature "all that is useful in life"; show his contempt for languages or for the "gracefulness of fables," which are only too likely to cause us to "imagine as possible a number of events which are not so"; see in the legal and medical expertise nothing but pursuits productive of honors and wealth, etc. Vico protests against the barbarians, "true Scythians, true Arabs," who, in the name of method, outlaw the ancients and abhor philology (104); who, whereas instruction should begin with language-teaching [languages being "the most powerful tool for stabilizing human society" (163)], consider the study of language, and consequently the study of poets, to be useless (167), alleging as a pretext for the latter judgment that poets "set

[3] "If it is true that minds are shaped by languages, rather than languages by mind," we shall have to admit that "the new method is better fitted for the minds of Frenchmen than for those of Italians," since by its abstract substantive nouns, so appropriate for the expression of generalities, the French language is that which suits philosophy best (153–54).

[4] Jules Chaix-Ruy, *La formation de la pensée philosophique de G. B. Vico* (Gap, 1943), chap. VI, perhaps overemphasizes Pascal's influence.

forth nothing but fables." The study of "the orators and historians and of the Greek and Latin language is equally neglected" (174, 175); and, as if "young men, leaving the schools of higher learning, were going to meet a world made up entirely of geometrical and algebraic signs, they are lectured to in terms of self-evident axioms, of demonstrated truths, while any consideration of the viewpoints of probability is strictly excluded (175)."

What Vico finds objectionable in Descartes is his attempt to reduce method to a search for that kind of certitude which results from a geometrical demonstration founded on evidence. Vico's criticism means that, far from considering (as does the first of the *Regulae ad directionem ingenii*) that human wisdom is everywhere unitary and identical, irrespective of the diversity of the objects to which it applies, such wisdom should change according to the object upon which it is brought to bear. "What the Cartesians generally call method is only one species of it, that is, the method of geometry. It behooves us to emphasize, instead, that there are as many methods as there are subject matters to be dealt with" (164). Vico remains faithful to the traditional conception of method. The consequence is that, whenever applied to a non-mathematical subject matter, the Cartesian method, which is peculiar to mathematics, becomes abstract and generates a confusion of *truth* with *certitude*. The long chains of reasons which mathematicians generally use permitted Descartes to imagine that "all things which fall under human knowledge are subject to the same consecutiveness," whereas, for Vico, such an order precludes the attainment of the reality of physics (150), of philosophy (166), and of politics, because mathematical certitude has nothing in common with that of political matters (173). Since prudence is not regulated by a table of precepts, like an art, to wish to introduce the geometrical method into practical life "is equivalent to reasoning falsely by means of national rules" (269). It is tantamount to "disregarding the nature of man, which is uncertain because of man's freedom" (152). The geometrical method develops a taste for order (174), but philosophizing *more geometrico* (Vico probably thinks of Spinoza) is an affectation (165–66) which destroys the sacred respect owed to truth (167). Against the deductiveness that contrives the fabrication of a false world, Vico therefore advocates the rights of induction and congratulates the English on having prohibited the teaching of the Cartesian method (275). To the author of the *Principes* (Descartes), he prefers Bacon (78, 433), who shows us the usefulness of Aristotle's *Topics* by the application of the topical method to the drawing up of scientific research tables (271). Against the geometrical method, Vico proposes to re-establish the dignity of the sciences of man. Against a method which deals with the true and the false, he reiterates that "philosophers should be satisfied with the probable" (166); that the statesman, the general, the orator, the judge, the medical practitioner, the casuist, are most often in the right when they do not depart from the probable. The

Cartesian method not only leads us astray when it assigns the same truth to different objects, but it ignores the variety of human thought and the interest inherent in its genesis. If the Cartesian method is barren (the Cartesians borrow their facts from the experimentalists [167]), and if, as is characteristic of the followers of that method, the mind seems "struck with sterility and impotence," the cause is the insistence, promoted by that method, that the same kind of certitude should be exacted in any and every domain of knowledge. The Cartesian procedure disjoins and disperses, so to speak, the forces of understanding, a faculty destined by nature to grasp the whole, the ensemble, of every topic or object (172). Cartesianism forgets that methodological reasoning emerges—in the life of the individual as well as in that of mankind—*after* perception (a faculty which is connected with topics, which Arnauld slights) and judgment, which is bound up with criticism (268, 431).

Pedagogical order demands that instruction begin by developing the memory and the imagination. Instead of teaching children how to master the excessively difficult *Logique* of Port Royal, one should shape the faculties through different exercises: "memory, by the study of languages; imagination, by the readings of poets, historians, and orators; judgment, by linear geometry, which is a kind of painting whose numerous elements strengthen memory, whose delicate figures give an aesthetic turn to imagination, and which, finally, trains judgment, since geometry forces it to run over all those lines and to select out of them only those which are necessary to express the dimensions desired." Vico believes that, in teaching, algebraic geometry should be discarded. For him, linear geometry alone has educational value, first of all, because it involves and stimulates imagination and memory, and, then, because it creates the habit of judging, without allowing that habit to extend automatically to domains other than the representation of lines.

Why does Vico emphasize imagination and memory? Because in these faculties there dwells the secret of the genius for invention. "Imagination is the eye of the natural genius, just as judgment is the eye of intelligence" (275). Being peculiar to youth, to the individual man's youth, as well as to that of mankind, imagination is the source of poetical invention. No longer is imagination—for Vico any more than for Descartes—a simple auxiliary of the intellect, which the union of soul and body renders useful. We should, instead, envisage it as the primal, positive power of seizing analogies and similarities; without that power, chance would never result in creation (272). It is in imagination that the secret of that *ingenium* (273) resides, of which Descartes speaks to Burmann, without, however, linking it with its true origin. Furthermore, the method of the *Discours*, barren because of its abstractions, is pedagogically sterilizing because, in its critical spirit, it harasses the imagination.

This barrenness, moreover, is connected with the preponderance, in the

Cartesian method, of the analytical over the synthetic aspect. For Vico, to synthesize is to compose, to analyze is to decompose, that is, to resolve into constituent elements. Synthesis proceeds from the simple to the complex, from the singular to the general; and, starting from the point or unit (64, 237), it does so as far as the infinite. Analysis, by contrast, proceeds from the complex to the simple, from the general to the singular, from the infinite to the finite. Thus Aristotle's *Analytics* starts from the universal, and its syllogistics progress by decompoundings such as algebra or chemistry (220, 433). No one will deny that the *operations* of synthesis and analysis are endowed with an equal amount of certitude, and Vico never expressed any doubt concerning the certitude of the Cartesian method, except that this certitude is not present in physics, where it is not a question of *defining* words but *objects*, where every axiom is likely to be contradicted, and where, finally, one cannot enter into any agreement with Nature nor compel Nature to accept any postulate (165, 221). Hence in the sciences of nature a synthetical deduction makes no sense, except in cases where, having isolated certain phenomena, one can explain them by experimentation, as Galileo and the English experimentalists do. Synthetical deduction has no meaning if we wish to construct the world by taking its primary elements as points of departure, since a start from the infinite is possible to God alone (247). By its nature incapable of resolving the infinite into its constitutive elements, the human mind is no less incapable of analyzing the world. "Let us conclude, then, that what we must introduce into physics is not the geometrical method, but demonstration itself" (274). In mathematics the method par excellence is, in Vico's eyes, the synthesis of the ancients, linear geometry, which Descartes has outstripped with his algebraic geometry. Vico admires that synthesis because it demonstrates in the process of constructing (275), excites imagination and memory, stimulates intelligence and teaches it how to invent, whereas algebraic analysis, to which we should resort in a complementary way and for want of something better (63), enervates the mind, freezes the imagination, tires the strength of memory, slows judgment (62, 150), and turns the art of drawing conjectural inferences into a sort of mechanical process (151). To sum up: if we translate synthesis as composition, and analysis as resolution (decomposition), the Cartesian synthesis is abstract when it claims to reconstruct the world, and it is thrown into the shade by a blind analysis in mathematics. Irrespective of whether the Cartesian method is viewed as analysis or synthesis, Vico, without disputing the validity, the certitude, of those "long concatenations of reasons," does not think that reality, however capable it may be of supplying us with the coherent aggregate of an encyclopedia (186, 187), can be surveyed with that unbroken movement of thought which Descartes prescribes to himself as a rule, and which, from Vico's viewpoint, merely evokes the sterilizing sorites of Zeno (273, 433)—"that procedure which compels us to pass from one idea to the nearest one, without skipping any intermediary link, and which therefore incapacitates us for perceiving the connections which exist between things far apart and different" (150).

Vico does not accept, and cannot accept, the criterion of *evidence*. Contrasting this criterion with common sense supported by erudition, he sees in the Cartesian standard nothing but the assertion of individual opinion, of subjective sense (167, 168). "Let us be grateful to Descartes," Vico says, "for having established that criterion which frees us from the mortifying thralldom of the authority of the Schoolmen" (168), but let us not forget the subjectivist nature of that standard, since "among the Cartesians themselves, what is a *clear and distinct* idea in the eyes of one of them, is, in those of another, obscure and muddled" (177, 271).[5] Should we unqualifiedly adopt this criterion, we would run the risk of turning into sect leaders (168); we would fancy that we hold in our possession, without having toiled for it, "an equivalent of all the libraries in the world" (170); we would disregard the point of view of verisimilitude, without which moral sciences are an impossibility (175); and finally, "that excessive trust in individual evidence, which any of our passions can elicit, may easily lead us into skepticism" (175-76).

Furthermore, outside the domain of mathematics, where, starting with elements such as the point and the unit, we are able to construct objects and truths, the criterion of clear and distinct ideas is inapplicable (168). Indeed, how could our minds apply it, since the mind is unable to see the totality of aspects, the attributes, of an object or a concept (270)?

This Vichian criticism is twofold. On one hand, Vico opposes the Cartesian criterion with his own: "he is sure of a truth, who has *made* that truth himself" (227). "We are able to demonstrate geometrical propositions because we are capable of making, of creating, them ourselves; if we could demonstrate the principles of physical nature, it would mean that we would be capable of creating that nature" (236, 250, 265, 276). In this opposition, the antithesis between *definitio realis* and *definitio nominalis* is recognizable. Vico may have come across it in the texts of many thinkers. His critics have mentioned Torricelli, Galileo, Sanchez, and some of them have gone back as far as Aristotle;[6] we might as well quote Hobbes, Spinoza, and the Port-Royal *Logique*. A philologist may find some interest in tracing the history of this distinction. It was a topic brought into vogue by the debates aroused by Cartesianism, and it did suggest, in 1763, the question

[5] Vico also charges Gassendi with "having set up individual sense as the standard of truth" (177). Chaix-Ruy, *op. cit.*, p. 28, n., quoted this sentence from a letter of Arnauld (1691): "I am not astounded at the news I have received from Naples that some crazy-headed young men have become atheists and epicureans as a result of having read the works of Gassendi."

[6] B. Croce, *The Philosophy of Giambattista Vico*, trans. R. G. Collingwood (New York, 1913), pp. 332-34.

propounded by the Academy of Berlin. It may be recalled that it was precisely in connection with this question that Kant set forth his views on definition as envisaged by the mathematician, the experimentalist, and the metaphysicist. For Vico, the clear and distinct objects that the human mind constructs are abstractions; the mathematician, or the physicist, powerless to grasp the ultimate nature of things (221, 236), defines names only, whereas the objects of reality, which are works of God, can be known clearly and distinctly only by his infinite mind. Consequently, Cartesian evidence does not apply to reality, which, in our eyes, always involves something indistinct and obscure.

A further consequence is that knowledge as clear and distinct ideas is an attestation to our finitude and insufficiency, inasmuch as every reality involves an infinite which is accessible only to God. As Vico says, "the human mind perceives the object, which it cognizes distinctly, just as we see at night by the light of a lantern; so [it is] that, in seeing the object, our mind loses sight of all that surrounds it." This metaphysical brightness (here Vico undoubtedly remembers a traditional comparison to be found particularly among the mystics) "resembles the brilliance that we see environed by opaque bodies" (248, 236–37), which is contrary to Descartes' affirmation that clarity is perceptible only because it is in contrast to the solid surrounding darkness of bodies.

On the other hand, it should be pointed out that Vico's criticism is directed against Cartesian innatism. If, for Descartes, evidence is not a matter of subjectivity, it is because the components of the distinct idea are simple natures that God, who is capable of creating eternal truths, has freely implanted in us, and that, owing to this supreme goodness, are conformable to the world itself, which is also the product of a free creation. The ultimate elements of knowledge are accessible to us because the idea, which originally was transcendent, has become immanent in our minds; thus, in order to cognize the world, we have but to consult ourselves. For Vico, this dogmatism, destructive of a long tradition, shocking to faith as well as to common sense, is reminiscent of the arrogant claims of Stoicism. The Stoics, "like our moderns, set up man's intellect as the standard of truth" (148), but that will not do. "We should model human knowledge on the pattern of the science possessed by God, and then corroborate our knowledge of God by means of the human science which is ours" (245–46).

By his refusal to set up the human intellect as the standard of truth, Vico refuses to identify truth with certainty (*verum* with *certum*) as Descartes does. Truth, whose contrary is falsity, indicates thought's conformity with the reality of the objects created by the eternal reason of God; certainty, whose contrary is dubiousness, designates a human belief unassailable by doubt (185–86, 365). How does one escape doubt? By the *cogito*, replies

Descartes.[7]   But Vico, as his critique of the criterion of evidence has just shown, requires the presence of an opaqueness of bodies in order to set off, to render visible, the light of metaphysics; he therefore discards the Cartesian doctrine of *intuitus*. The *certum* must be bolstered by the authority of attestations and personal experience; significantly, the Greek word αὐτοψία, which indicates that experience (186), is defined in the *Scienza nuova* as "sensory evidence" (432).

The *cogito* would be powerless to convince a skeptic because "the skeptic does not doubt that he thinks; he even grants so fully the certitude of what appears to him that he defends it by chicanery and pleasantries; he does not doubt that he exists," but "he affirms that his knowledge of the world is but an awareness of it, not a science of it." Science being the cognition of the "form," or cause, according to which an object is created, certitude is not identical with truth. The skeptic, therefore, will deny that "the awareness of oneself as a thinking substance can give us the knowledge of being" (225–27). The criterion of evidence cannot be given in reply to the skeptic; but, once Vico's criterion is adopted ("he is sure of a truth, who has made that truth himself"), we are compelled to grant that appearance has a cause, and that the knowledge of a cause refers us to the Cause of causes, that is, in the final analysis, to our belief in God (227–28). Drawing close to Malebranche, Vico is amazed to find that such a penetrating intellect as Malebranche's is in agreement with Descartes concerning the primary truth ("I think, therefore I am"), because, according to the dogma that it is God who creates the ideas that are in man, he should say: "Something thinks in me, therefore that something exists. In my thought I do not perceive anything corporeal; consequently, that which thinks in me is the purest spirit, namely, God." In short, Malebranche should have taught that the human mind receives from God the knowledge of itself (262).

Vichian criticism constantly reverts to the same theme: the human mind should not have been set up as the criterion of truth. By doing so, Descartes has cut himself off from reality. Hence the Cartesians, "with the exception of that primal truth which they derive from self-awareness—'*I think, therefore I am*'—borrow the truths that govern them as rules solely from arithmetic and geometry, that is, from the [intellectual] truths that we create," and by the same token condemn themselves to the impossible task of "creating" physics (275–76). Furthermore, the self-awareness that is their starting point is not a science. Arising from doubt, the *cogito*, together with the criterion of evidence which it involves, is killed by doubt. The evidences of our passions deceive us (176); the great *meditator* has forged "a skepticism

---

[7] It should be noted that Vico quotes only the formula "*I think, therefore I am*," even when referring to the *Méditations*, where that formula is not to be found. (We find, instead, "*I think, therefore I exist.*")

rouged with truth" (168), a "metaphysical critique whose starting point is also its terminal one, that is, skepticism" (173).

After this twofold onslaught against evidence and the *cogito* the ontological argument, as presented by Descartes, loses its value. Just as we could demonstrate physics *only* if we were able to create it, so too the ontological argument demonstrates the existence of God only if the clear and distinct idea is taken as the point of departure. "We must therefore stigmatize as guilty of a rash and impious curiosity those thinkers who attempt to prove a priori the existence of God, the Lord of all goodness and greatness. That attempt denounces the mad arrogance of setting ourselves up as gods of God, and denying the God whom we are seeking. The splendor of metaphysical truth is like that of light, which we perceive only as a contrast to darkness; it is in the objects, and not by pure intuition, that we see this brightness" (236–37).

The rejection of the ontological argument is best understood on the basis of the metaphysics (and its relationship to physics) for which Vico pleads. Against Descartes' geometrical physics, he emphasizes that in God alone (and not in the ideas immanent in our minds) "are to be found the veritable *forms* of the objects to which the nature of such objects refers" (150). The superiority of metaphysics to physics results from the fact that metaphysics deals with virtual potentialities and with the infinite (246). What virtual potentialities? Let us proceed synthetically from God to the world. God is real, infinite, unextended, and consequently is motionless in himself; the world has a created reality, is made up of space and motion, and as such is the object of physics (237). We do not know how the infinite can descend into the finite: we are unable to apprehend it and can merely conceive it with our thought (247).[8] We can at least conceive some intermediaries [existing] between God's rest and the world's motion, between the immobile activity of the Creator and the change of place of mobile beings, between the unextendedness of the Primal Cause and the extension of nature. Those intermediaries may be reduced to conation and the power of extension (237). Vico associates conation with rest because conation involves the potential of engendering (and actually engenders) motion and because its essence is the *becoming* (244); but in itself conation is motionless, and such a rest is in God. Contrary to Descartes' doctrine, "rest is a metaphysical, not a physical, thing" (253).

As for the power of extension, if we start synthetically from an unextended God, we are compelled to assert that God contains in an *eminent* manner the potential of extension (242). Conation and the power of extension being inseparable, Vico—beguiled by his reading of Pascal's famous *chiquenaude* (finger-snapping) and undoubtedly by his reading of Malebranche as

8 On this problem see Jean Laporte, *Le rationalisme de Descartes*, rev. ed. (Paris, 1950), pp. 291–93.

well [9]—draws from that inseparability an argument for disproving Descartes' thesis (a thesis unworthy of the Creator), which maintains that God produced matter and movement by *two* distinct operations (243); moreover, he infers that the power of indefinite divisibility of extension is a dependence of metaphysics (242), and that, therefore, the indefinite is not quantitative (243) and cannot designate the *qualitas*, the proper and essential nature of the world. The site of the application of the power of extension resides in the Zenonian point, which, while metaphysically real, is unextended, indivisible (238), in the same way that the Pythagorean unity (which, likewise, is metaphysically real) is not a number but generates the number (90). Thus, the imaginary point of the geometrician (243), or the unit of the arithmetician (220), has a real metaphysical foundation; and it is easy for us to understand (since there are "points and conations by and through which objects begin to emerge from their nothingness") that "geometry's truth stems from metaphysics" and can, conversely, reflect its own truth on metaphysics.

Metaphysics, as we pointed out, "shapes human science after the pattern of God's science, and later corroborates the latter by means of the former" (245–46). Descartes fails to see this "because, by an analytical method, he first posits matter as created and then divides it" (246). It is no longer God, but Descartes, who first divides, then tries to "compose," to reassemble, the world; but the Cartesian syntheses are abstract and, taken together, are but an empty account because they do not start from the metaphysical point, but from the imaginary point of the geometricians. The proof thereof is that Descartes allows himself to be led astray by Aristotle, who, having failed to understand that the Zenonian point is an indivisible point of conation, and not a particle which has no parts (243), objects that, if we cut a rectangular isosceles triangle with lines parallel to one of its sides, we can show that unequal lengths (that is, one side and the hypotenuse) are endowed with the same number of points. We can escape this paradox only by resorting to the hypothesis of "an unextended substance which is equally contained in bodies of unequal magnitude" (90), that is, we can avoid the difficulty only by postulating a potential of extension, of a spiritual character, which is anterior to extension (239). Consequently, divisibility of matter ad infinitum cannot be explained (as Descartes and Aristotle do) by a mathematician's reasoning, which abstracts geometry from matter (239), but only by a metaphysical virtuality. In effect, striving to be a geometer-mechanician,

---

[9] Chaix-Ruy, *La formation de la pensée philosophique de G. B. Vico*, p. 138, cites Vico's fragment 1301: "René Descartes, by taking as a starting point of his *Physics* the initial motion of bodies, begins his treatment of that science as a poet." This can hardly be viewed as a eulogy, unless it be considered praiseworthy to have written, not a treatise on *Physics*, but a fairy tale, a fine "novel on physics." It is well known, in regard to that "initial *motion of bodies*" (the *chiquenaude*, or finger flick, of which Pascal speaks), that this theory is to be found, not in Descartes, but in Malebranche.

Descartes "directly introduces physics into metaphysics, and speaks of meta-physics as a physicist, in terms of *actus* and *formae*" (247). Thus he commits an error which is the converse of that of Aristotle. The latter, speaking of physical nature in terms of potencies and faculties, "directly introduces metaphysics into physics" (246).

Although Descartes atones for his blunder through his explanations of particular phenomena (Vico has in mind Descartes' laws of optics [244] and his theory of heat and cold [88–89]), the principles of his mechanicism are no less defective. "There are no figures in the immaterial, and there is nothing mechanical in the indefinite" (241, 251). Undoubtedly, in the physical world everything can be reduced to motion and space. But rest, except relative rest (246), does not exist in this world; and extension (space) is not the essence of matter, as the dualists claim. This matter is divided, but it is its *division*, not its *divisibility*, which is conditioned by physics (242); divisi-bility ad infinitum does not have the same meaning for Vico that it has for Descartes. On the other hand, action derives from metaphysical points; and this is a thesis which, in the final analysis, would establish a certain kinship between Vico and Malebranche (262–63). The consequence is that *extensa non conantur* (249), a principle of which Descartes (for whom matter does not move, but is moved) would approve; however, for Descartes, the com-munication of motion starts with the divine initial impelling act, as if the world were self-sufficient (the preservation of the same quantity of motion renders it nearly autonomous), whereas, for Vico—anxious to reserve to God, through metaphysical *formae* and points, a mode of actual operation down to the smallest detail—motion is not communicable (255, 263). Contrary to what Descartes asserts, motion is progressive, even the motion of light. In other respects, Vico deplores that it should be so; the instantaneity of light, for instance, would prove, by a physical fact, the metaphysical reality of the points of conation, since the instant—which is a division of the indivisible eternity—is a point of conation (246, 249).

When Descartes "posits, as a basis of his fine ideas on the reflection and refraction of movements, that motion differs from that which determines it" (244), and when he conceives oblique motion as being the resultant of two forces, horizontal and vertical, he clearly understands "this truth, that under the same mode of determination there can be a greater or smaller amount of motion"; whereas, being led astray by Aristotle's opinion, which is antag-onistic to that of Zeno, Descartes pretends not to see the fact that, "just as there is an equal virtuality of extension in the case of the diagonal and lateral lines, so also is there an equal kinetic force in the case of a perpendicular motion or of a motion oblique in respect to the horizon" (245). For that matter, since, in the universal plenum (241), all motions are composed (not simple), there cannot be any straight motion. "The straight stands above nature, in order to serve as a norm for the irregular" (252); "there is no straight, except in metaphysics" (253). Hence we have here a twofold consequence. Geometry is justified by metaphysics, when it resolves a curve into indivisibles; thus it becomes "the only legitimate intermediary enabling us to pass from metaphysics to physics. This justification, however, is not the one to which Descartes would have resorted. Moreover, the second part of the principle of inertia also has a metaphysical value: it, too, depends on points of conation. Nevertheless, there does not exist in nature a non-resisting milieu where a moving object left to itself would describe a straight line ad infinitum (252). Like the straight, the identical does not exist in space; for instance, "I fancy myself to be always the *same*; whereas, increasing and waning at every instant, receiving new particles, and losing some, I am different at every moment of time" (252). Since everything is in motion, everything changes, and since the life "of all beings is like a river, which seems to be always identical, but rolls ever-new waters" (254), this means that there is not really any homogeneous extension, that there are no identical instants (Vico seems almost to be about to enunciate the principle of the indiscernibles). This means, furthermore (as the theory of the points of conation teaches), that it is impossible to uphold physical mechanicism, unless this mechanicism is propped up by a metaphysical dynamism. Devoid of the metaphysical support of the *formae*, Cartesian mechanicism deals only with the modifications of the substances (69); it leaves the universe to itself, as it were, and ends by joining Epicurus, the sole difference being that, instead of letting it run by chance, it places the universe under the rule of necessity (177). Here, Vico seems to hold Descartes responsible for Spinozism.

Vico admits the dualistic position, "since, in our religion, we profess the separation of the soul of man from any corporeality" (226); he even admits, at least in appearance, the doctrine of the animal-machines, since the brutes have no inner principle of motion (258). In Cartesian dualism, however, Vico points out a logical shortcoming. Descartes' physics, according to which the variety of bodies cannot be explained by substantial "forms," and which deals with nothing but the modifications of substance, "would require a metaphysics admitting only *one* kind of substance, that is, a bodily substance, acting by necessity" (168). Although Vico refers to Epicurus in this passage, does he not also have Spinoza in mind? We must remark, however, that Vico views Descartes' dualism as "the sketch of a metaphysical system of the Platonic kind," a system which subordinates matter to a spiritual agent (68); and he hastens to add that such systems are as common as a baker's dozen (77).

A further grievance of Vico's against Descartes is that the latter fails to hold to the traditional distinction between *animus*, which is immortal, being the site of ideas, that is, *mens*, and *anima*, the principle of life. Descartes, keeping abreast of the latest discoveries of anatomy, thought that the seat of the soul was in the pineal gland;[10] nevertheless, persons on whom the surgical operation of trepanning has been performed, do not cease to think, and it is quite unlikely that the soul dwells in that part of the body where there is more mucus than blood, and thus is the most inert and slothful of all (259). Descartes speaks of animal spirits; the Schoolmen drew a sharper distinction between "vital" spirits, connected with the blood and the heart, in charge of our volitional activities, and "animal" spirits, connected with our nerves, their "humors," our fibers, and performing autonomous functions (257).

In regard to the description of the human soul as a spider sitting in the center of its web, there is this to be said: Descartes was forced to resort to such a device *ex machina* because, being ignorant of the cause that produces thought, he found it impossible to explain the relationships between body and soul (226). Undoubtedly, Vico does not criticize his predecessor for having failed to harmonize our free will with God's foreknowledge (263); but such a mystery becomes dangerous in a system in which the pretended communication of motion and the giving up of "substantial forms" run the risk of becoming locked up in monism and necessitarianism. Hence, just as the Cartesian method failed to bring forth a radically new logic, so, too, Cartesian metaphysics has been useless to medicine, "since anatomy was unable to discover in physical nature the man of Descartes." It should be added that the Cartesian method has failed to give rise to any system of morality favorable to the Christian religion (69).

Religion! Here, undoubtedly, is the domain where Vico's opposition to Descartes has, if not its origin, at least one of its deepest springs. One of the seventeenth-century themes was that the Cartesian system was a threat to religion. This theme appeared more and more frequently after the divulgence of Spinoza's *Ethics*; and it was exploited particularly by the conservative circles of Naples. At all times and places, religion has opposed that philosophical dogmatism which, to the detriment of faith's humility, assigns too high a rank to reason. It was felt, whether rightly or wrongly, that "the great *meditator*" (224), like the Stoics before him, had set up the human mind as the standard of truth. Vico reacts in Huet's way; and he is no more a mathematician than Huet is. This ignorance of mathematics prevents him from understanding the treatises appended by Descartes to his *Discours*, or at least Book II of the Cartesian *Principes*. When Vico recalls that in Naples it was a eulogy for a philosopher to hear it said of himself that he was able to understand Descartes, when he states that the Port-Royal *Logique* contains examples that are too difficult for a young reader, it is

[10] Chaix-Ruy (*ibid.*) quotes Vico's fragment 1213: "The location of the pineal gland, placed at the top of the human brain, which is the seat of the soul, according to Descartes, seems to me (with all due respect to him) to be the invention of a man who is entirely ignorant of metaphysics."

evident that he voices his own perplexities. Moreover, because he is a historian and a philologian, history teaches him to discriminate between what is true and what is evident, to accept, in antithesis to subjective evidence, the authority of criticized attestations, to trust in common sense, to restore the prestige of verisimilitude or probability, against the dubious and the certain. In this matter, Vico the scholar reacts like Bayle, when, in the *Prospectus* of his *Dictionnaire*, the latter pleads for the certitude of historical *facts* against the certitude of mathematical *abstractions*. At the very source of Vico's opposition to Descartes there are "typological" reactions which go beyond Vico, Descartes, and their epoch, and which are constant phenomena in the history of philosophy, that is, the mistrust of faith in the presence of dogmatic reason, the disinclination of the literary mentality toward the mathematical mode of reasoning, the hostility of the metaphysician or the Humanist against what today goes by the name of scientism.

Let us revert to Vico. By examining his milieu and his epoch, we are able to "spot" a number of events that gave the initial stimulus to Vico's opposition to Descartes: the intellectual evolution of Naples, the actions of Gregorio Caloprese (1653–1715) and of Paolo Mattia Doria (1661–1743), the publication or circulation of certain works, of certain periodicals, the reading, after Plato and Tacitus, of Bacon, Grotius, Hobbes, and so on. It should be observed, in this connection, that Vico, who, in unison with his whole epoch, views Descartes' philosophy as pivoting on the *Discours* and the *Principes*, does not impress us as having read his author with close attention. He has heard Descartes spoken of, has leafed through his books, but has never actually studied him. He would doubtless have been incapable of doing so. Hence, it is really not Descartes whom he attacks, but Cartesianism (Pascal, Malebranche, Spinoza, etc.); and we should discriminate between Neapolitan Cartesianism and anti-Cartesianism. His arguments are often those which could be heard everywhere.

Should we infer that they are valueless, and are not stamped with his originality? Not in the least. Curiously, Vico bears a certain likeness to Leibniz, although the latter was a great mathematician and a true reader of Descartes; but, like Vico, he was quite fond of the ancients, striving to preserve something of scholasticism, and, as a scholar, philologian, historian, he was anxious to be active in the field of religion and in that of the sciences of man.[11] Like Leibniz, Vico congratulates himself on being self-taught, "without preference for any school," and criticizes Descartes and Cartesianism for their sectarian trend, for the concealment of sources, the sterility of their method, the contempt shown toward languages, law, and history. Furthermore, he charges Descartes and his followers with the subjective character of their "evidence," the uselessness of their methodic doubt, the equivocalness

[11] On this question, we would refer the reader to Yvon Belaval's *Leibniz critique de Descartes* (Paris, 1960).

of their concept of "being," the unqualified abandonment of the *formae*, the reduction of physics to space and motion without basing them on the dynamism of nature, the slighting of the experimental viewpoint. In Vico's view, we should make an effort to assemble, in all arts, the elements of a cyclopedia and the information needed for enriching the *loci* of *Topics* or for constructing the Baconian tables. Vico blames Descartes for having advocated a necessitarianism that abandons the world to all the combinations of which it is capable, without resorting to providentialist finalism. He objects to an abstract doctrine incapable of acknowledging the principle of indiscernibles; to a metaphysics unfavorable to religion; to a mechanicism unconcerned with the task of preparing a world of minds which would constitute "a natural commonwealth where God, enthroned like a monarch, would preside over the good of all" (278). This multitude of coincidences does not simply underscore the importance of Stoicism during the seventeenth century (Vico's "points of conation" seem to have something in common with the Leibnizian monads); it also prompts us to wonder about Leibniz's possible influence upon Vico. Leibniz knew one of Vico's admirers, the Abbé Antonio Conti, who exchanged letters with the philosopher of Hanover, polemicized against Christian Thomasius, and was a reader of Bayle. Both Leibniz and Vico drew from a common fund of anti-Cartesianism.

Were we to issue a judgment on Vico's critique of Descartes, we could state that it appears rather weak when compared with the Cartesian texts; but we could also assign to it a twofold value. The critique expresses a permanent, typical aspect of philosophical reflection,[12] but it also offers an original synthesis of anti-Cartesianism in its combination of a theory of conation, of the virtualities of "space," a concept of "rest" in the domain of physics, and new views in the fields of language, philosophy of history, aesthetics (doctrine of the "poetical genius"), and humanistic scholarship. Vico acknowledges that humanistic learning does not constitute the only path to wisdom (173); and there is, in his synthesis, a pre-Rousseauan premonition of the "sciences of man."

Translated by Elio Gianturco

---

[12] J. Michelet writes of Vico: "His system appears to us . . . as an admirable protest of that part of the human mind which pleads for the wisdom of the past, preserved in religion, language, and history: for that 'vulgar wisdom' which is the mother of philosophy, and too often ignored by it" (10–11).

George A. Wells   VICO AND HERDER

Although Herder's attention was drawn to Vico's work as early as 1777, he does not mention it in any of his publications until 1797—well after his own peak—and even then does not discuss it in detail.[1] That the two writers had much in common is obvious enough. Vico set out to apply to history the method Bacon had used in science, namely, "to think and to see," to meditate on ideas, and to study facts. Thus he called his *New Science* a combination of philosophy (the meditation) and philology (the textual and other evidence constituting the facts).[2] This combination was precisely what Herder sought to achieve in his *Ideen zur Philosophie der Geschichte der Menschheit*, where he marshaled evidence from geography, ethnology, and history in order to base a judgment on facts and not merely on philosophical theory. Both writers were determinists at a time when it was fashionable to believe that a civilization's progress was entirely arbitrary.[3] And both strove to reconcile their determinism with some conception of the providential control of human affairs, positing a providence that functions by general laws, not by particular interpositions.[4] Furthermore, their speculations on human society took much the same form. They were not so much concerned with the practical problem—well to the fore in Locke and Rousseau— as to which type of constitution is to be recommended at the present time.

All references to Vico's New Science *are to the Anchor ed.* (New York, 1961) *unless otherwise stated. Numbers in parentheses indicate the paragraphs as numbered by Nicolini. Herder is quoted from B. Suphan's ed. of his works,* Sämtliche Werke (Berlin, 1877–1913).

[1] For details see B. Croce, *The Philosophy of Giambattista Vico*, trans. R. G. Collingwood (London, 1913), p. 271; Max H. Fisch, Introduction, *The Autobiography of Giambattista Vico*, trans. Max H. Fisch and Thomas G. Bergin (New York, 1944), pp. 67–68.

[2] *New Science* (138, 140, 359), pp. 21, 26, 65.

[3] Vico says: "Whenever the time and guise are thus and so, such and not otherwise are the institutions that come into being" (*New Science*, p. 22 [147]). Herder declares: "No occurrence in human affairs stands alone: arising from anterior causes, the spirit of the times and the disposition of nations, it is to be considered only as the dial, the hand of which is moved by internal springs" (*Ideen*, XIV, 448). Vico contrives to combine this standpoint with belief in individual free will. Herder follows Spinoza (of whom Vico did not have a high opinion) on the question of free will (*Vom Erkennen*, VIII, 201–2).

[4] For details see my book *Herder and After* (The Hague, 1959), p. 104.

Rather, they inquired into the historical facts and sought to explain the varying courses of development of civilized institutions. Because they were pioneers in such an inquiry, both inevitably oversimplified the facts to some extent in order to reach coherent generalizations, and both resorted to conjecture where facts were not available. Vico, on his own admission, attempted to "fill in the beginnings of universal history, purely by understanding" (that is, by conjecture). Croce went so far as to accuse him of a kind of "drunkenness; confusing categories with facts, he felt absolutely certain a priori of what the facts would say." The same charge has been leveled at Herder, often in a similarly provocative formulation. But it ought to be realized that premature generalization and speculation are necessarily the lot of pioneers. Honest seekers after more comprehensive theories have valued the work of both Vico and Herder, in spite of their limitations. Of this, H. T. Buckle is a signal example.[5]

For the purpose of their inquiries into the evolution of civilized institutions, Vico and Herder had to construct some idea of the primitive stage from which modern civilization grew. On this matter they differ radically, there being no trace in Vico of Herder's idea of the essential nobility of primitive man.[6] This difference between them obviously resulted in part from the fact that Rousseau's ideas were available to Herder but not to Vico; but it is also to be attributed to differences in their source materials. Vico was primarily a student of ancient history and ancient legend, and so he was acutely conscious of the barbarous rituals of primitive peoples, the torture and the human sacrifice. He made surprisingly little use of modern travelers' accounts.[7] Herder, however, found in these accounts ample evidence of the degradation of savage peoples under the influence of civilization, and consequently was led to believe in a primitive state of innocence. Furthermore, his view of human nature in general is thoroughly optimistic. Here again he is quite opposed to Vico, although what both say on this topic is colored, not to say dictated, by their religious standpoints. For Vico, man is a brutal egoist who needs to be tamed by religion, while, for Herder, man is kind and gentle because he was created in the image of divine goodness.[8]

[5] For Vico's admission see *New Science* (Ithaca, N.Y., 1948), pp. 252f. (738). For Croce's charge see his *The Philosophy of Vico*, p. 152. For details concerning the same criticism of Herder by other authors see *Herder and After*, pp. 155f. For Buckle's indebtedness to Herder see *ibid.*, pp. 245f. His references to Vico show equal warmth; see Fisch, Introduction, *Autobiography*, p. 93.

[6] This difference between Vico and Herder is stressed by E. Auerbach, "Vico and Herder," *Deutsche Viertel Jahrschrift*, 10 (1932): 681–82.

[7] C. E. Vaughan (*Studies in the History of Political Philosophy* [Manchester, 1925], I, 228n.) chides him for the paucity of his references to Red Indians, Patagonians, Japanese, and Chinese.

[8] For Herder's views see *Herder and After*, pp. 64–66. He expresses strong feelings about the way modern Europeans have ruined savages with brandy and dragooned them from economic motives (*Auch eine Philosophie*, V, 546, 550).

Vico and Herder do agree, however, that primitive man was a simple creature, incapable of the sophisticated theorizing that some philosophers appeared ready to ascribe to him. They both complain repeatedly of predecessors who interpreted savage myths as profound allegories,[9] and the whole burden of Herder's *Archäologie des Morgenlandes*, written in 1769, is that it is futile to seek philosophemes in a myth such as the biblical Creation story. Their agreement on the simplicity of primitive man is strikingly illustrated by their remarks on Egyptian hieroglyphics (then still undeciphered). Vico, anticipating Warburton, denounced "the false opinion . . . that the hieroglyphs were invented by philosophers to conceal in them their mysteries of lofty esoteric wisdom." For, he adds, "it was by a common natural necessity that all the first nations spoke in hieroglyphs." He means that, before the origin of conventional oral language, men could "express themselves [only] by means of gestures or physical objects which had natural relations with the ideas; for example, three ears of grain, or acting as if swinging a scythe three times, to signify three years." Herder (acknowledging his debt to Warburton) says the same. We shall, he declares, look in vain for secret treasures of wisdom among the hieroglyphics of the pyramids, for hieroglyphics are man's first crude attempt at explaining his ideas in signs.[10]

It is appropriate at this point to discuss the views of Vico and Herder on the origin of language. Both rejected a divine origin, although Herder later recanted[11] and Vico exempted the Hebrews from his theory of naturalistic origins. Eighteenth-century philosophers were often anxious not to openly contradict *Genesis*, and so Vico, Condillac, and Monboddo all resorted to a fiction which, while ostensibly leaving *Genesis* intact, posits a postdiluvian state of affairs in which man, having by one means or another lost the art of speech, is compelled to reinvent it.[12] Thus Vico supposed that after the Flood the children of Noah were dispersed over the world and ran wild, forgetting all the arts of civilization and even the use of speech, so that out of this stage of "bestiality" they were to emerge only by their own efforts. Herder did not share all of Vico's religious scruples and frequently showed a remarkable readiness to treat Jewish history and Jewish sacred texts exactly

[9] Vico, *New Science*, p. 19 (128); Herder *Fragmente*, I, 434, 448.

[10] Vico, *New Science*, pp. 98, 100 (431, 435); Warburton, *The Divine Legation of Moses* (London, 1765), vol. III, bk. IV, sec. 4, pp. 70, 106–13; Herder, *Älteste Urkunde*, VI, 387, 391–92, and *Ideen*, XIV, 79. If the hieroglyphics were deciphered, he adds, they would be found to contain nothing more than chronicles or adulation of the man on whose monument they are inscribed.

[11] For details see *Herder and After*, p. 43.

[12] Thus J. B. Monboddo says that, if "the gift of speech was once bestowed by God, it may well have been lost . . . after the fall," and "we have no warrant to believe that another miracle would be wrought" (*Origin and Progress of Language*, 2d ed. [Edinburgh, 1774], I, 212–13).

as he treated pagan history or Homer. Vico surely would have been horrified by his statement that the story of the Flood (on which a good deal of Vico's theorizing about early man depends) is shown by fossil remains (which prove that the earth was submerged for centuries) to be a Jewish "national myth." [13] Nevertheless, Herder did waver over this question of the origin of language.

Herder gives a naturalistic account of the origin and development of language as early as 1766, arguing in the first volume of his *Fragmente* that primeval man was like a child, gaping at everything with terror and then with bewildered admiration as his fear receded; and that the language proper to such emotions consists of gestures and simple unarticulated cries—sounds that are high-pitched and that may be said to be sung rather than spoken. Later in this work he writes of a primitive "natural" language of gestures, expressions, and cries. He obviously is thinking, for example, of facial expressions, which betray immediately whether a man is feeling angry, affectionate, or bored. Such expressions and cries of joy or pain are "natural" in that an understanding of them does not depend on knowledge of any conventions. Next, as man became more familiar with his environment, his emotional reactions to it were weakened, and instead of expressing himself with passionate cries he began calmly to name objects on the basis of onomatopoeia. The next stage was the formation of words to express abstract ideas. This was effected by making use of words already available to denote concrete things. (An example would be the expression "moss-colored" to denote the quality "green.") A necessary consequence was profusion of metaphor.

At this stage sounds were still high-pitched and sung rather than spoken, since they were used primarily to express emotions. In respect both of its metaphors and of its songlike quality, the language of this day was akin to poetry. But in time people ceased to be conscious that the word for an abstraction implied comparison with a concrete. Metaphor became dead metaphor and finally was lost altogether, with the result that, although the word continued to denote the idea, it came to do so in a completely colorless way. Herder infers from all this that language is poetic when it is relatively primitive, but merely correct at later stages.[14] In his essay on the origin of language, written in 1770, he adds a further reason for the primitive profusion

[13] *Ideen*, XIII, 436–37. Herder's rejection of flood stories as a basis for historical reconstruction is illustrated by his sharp criticism of Boulanger, who had used them to illustrate his thesis that the history of the globe in antiquity had been a series of catastrophes, and that religion was born of the terror they generated in man. See Herder's remarks in *Archäologie des Morgenlandes*, VI, 113, and *Vom Geist der hebräischen Poesie*, XI, 249. According to Fisch (Introduction, *Autobiography*, p. 73), some thought that Boulanger had taken his views (without acknowledgment) from Vico. But, if Vico's opinions reached Herder in this indirect way, he was not impressed by them.

[14] *Fragmente*, I, 152ff., 386.

of metaphor—namely, the animism of early man. Even for the modern savage, he says, "everything that moves is alive, everything that makes a noise speaks." And in inventing language "man referred everything to himself . . . and represented everything to himself in a human manner. . . . In this regard, the language of those ancient savages is a study in the extravagancies of human phantasy." [15] For this reason, he adds, active verbs were used to denote objects that move. What he had in mind was restated a few years later by Thomas Reid (who himself followed the Abbé Raynal), namely, that "in all languages we find active verbs applied to those objects in which savages suppose a soul," that is, all objects which puzzle them by moving. "Thus we say that the sun rises and sets . . . the sea ebbs and flows, the winds blow. Languages were formed by men who believed these objects to have life and active power in themselves." [16] It is clear, then, that for Herder early language not only is poetic but also provides evidence of its inventors' way of thinking. Some sentiments, such as animism, being common to all early languages, must have been characteristic of the whole human species at the time; others, less widely distributed, will be represented in some languages but not in others. Thus it was that Herder in 1785 called for "a general physiognomy of the nations from their languages." [17]

We have seen already that Vico anticipated Herder by positing a primitive language of gestures which is not based on conventions. He, too, held that the next stage was the development of "articulate language" (as against mere unarticulated cries) "by way of onomatopoeia." He anticipated Herder's insistence that early language was akin to song because it was pronounced "under the impulse of most violent passions, even as we still observe men sing when moved by great passions, extreme happiness or grief." He held that it was full of metaphor because early man's tendency to personify objects led him to speak of heaven smiling, the wind whistling, and so on. Furthermore, he stated that, as language develops, it loses a good deal of this metaphor and so declines in beauty. Finally, he declared that "the vulgar tongues should be the most weighty witnesses concerning . . . ancient customs of the peoples that were in use at the time the languages were formed." [18]

[15] *Ibid.*, V, 53. Cf. *Zerstreute Blätter*, XV, 539–40, for the express statement that man imagines other things by analogy with himself. It is because of this natural tendency to personify things that man, says Herder, is essentially a religious animal, no nation, not even the most primitive, being wholly without religion (*Ideen*, XIII, 162). Vico had also denied that there are or have been religionless peoples; and he had given religion a similar basis, saying: "The physics of the ignorant is a vulgar metaphysics by which they refer the causes of the things they do not know to the will of God." *New Science* (182), pp. 28–29.

[16] Thomas Reid, *Essays on the Active Powers of Man* (Edinburgh, 1788), essay IV, chap. 3, pp. 281–82.

[17] *Ideen*, XIII, 364–65; cf. *Fragmente*, I, 148.

[18] *New Science* (151, 405, 445, 447, 821), pp. 23, 88, 105, 107, 261. Isaiah Berlin recently has noted the marked similarity between Vico's views concerning the "common

Such parallels do not prove influence, since the same ideas were available to Herder from other sources. Mandeville, followed by Condillac, Warburton, Monboddo, and Reid, had posited a stage at which language was restricted to natural cries and gestures. Condillac also held that "style was originally poetical, since it began by portraying ideas with the aid of the most graphic images." [19] And in 1764 Reid stressed that, as language progressed from natural signs to artificial ones, it became colorlessly correct. [20] Furthermore, as H. B. Nisbet has recently pointed out, Herder's view that language reflects national character can be traced to Bacon; [21] that this idea was in the air at the time Herder wrote is suggested by the fact that Reid stated it in 1788. [22] Finally, Herder diverges from Vico, as well as from other predecessors, in some of his views on early language. What he says about inversions and the relation between the verb and the noun is the opposite of what Vico said. [23]

In his essay on the origin of language, surprisingly enough Herder objects to all attempts to derive language as it is today from natural cries and gestures (although he still argues for its natural origin). It is perfectly natural, he says, to make some cry when in pain, despair, or love; but to make a noise in order to inform others of what one's emotions are is something very different. He does not see how there can be any transition from one to the other, and he criticizes philosophers (in particular, Condillac) who attempted to bridge the gap. Thus one of the strongest affinities between his views on the origin of language and those of his predecessors is soon obliterated. His essay of 1770 anticipates the standpoint of nineteenth-century writers who supposed that clear thinking is impossible without words and that language as we know it was therefore not developed for

---

sense" of each nation and Herder's doctrine of the "Volksgeist." See his "The Philosophical Ideas of Vico," in *Art and Ideas in Eighteenth-Century Italy* (Rome, 1960), pp. 199, 218.

[19] Bernard Mandeville, *The Fable of the Bees*, ed. F. B. Kaye, from the 1729 ed. (Oxford, 1924), II, 284–88; É. B. de Condillac, *Essai sur l'origine des connoissances humaines* (1746), in *Oeuvres* (Paris, 1798), I, 260ff., 349; Thomas Reid, *An Inquiry into the Human Mind on the Principles of Common Sense* (Edinburgh, 1764), pp. 102ff.; Monboddo, *Origin and Progress of Language*, I, 461ff.

[20] "Artificial signs signify, but they do not express; they speak to the understanding as algebraical characters may do, but the passions, the affections and the will hear them not; these continue dormant and inactive, till we speak to them in the language of nature, to which they are all attention and obedience" (Reid, *Inquiry into the Human Mind*, p. 108).

[21] "Herder and Francis Bacon," *Modern Language Review*, 62 (1967): 268.

[22] "There is no surer way of tracing the sentiments of nations before they have records than by the structure of their language, which, notwithstanding the changes produced in it by time, will always retain some signatures of the thoughts of those by whom it was invented" (Reid, *Active Powers of Man*, p. 282).

[23] Vico, *New Science* (452, 458), pp. 109, 111; Herder, *Fragmente*, I, 192, and *Auch eine Philosophie*, V, 83, 108.

purposes of more sophisticated communication from a primitive method of communicating by signs and gestures.

It is clear that for both Vico and Herder poetry is older than prose and is "the mother tongue of the human race." Herder found this view in many eighteenth-century writers, and its basis is obvious enough, namely, that the oldest pieces of language available to them were poetic compositions. The real reason for this is not, of course, that primitive man spoke poetry. It may simply be that he arranged what he considered important (for example, religious ideas) in meters, with rhyme or alliteration, so that it could be memorized readily; and that, while such important matters were transmitted orally and then (with the invention of writing) recorded, the ordinary ephemeral speech of the day has not survived. But this line of reasoning was not possible so long as the origin of man and the development of language were believed to reach back only a few thousand years. To Herder and his contemporaries, Old Testament Hebrew and Homeric Greek appeared so near in time to the very beginnings of language that they naturally were taken as a guide to the characteristics of primitive speech. Nevertheless, Herder does occasionally suggest that some of the characteristics of poetry may be mnemonic in origin.[24]

Is it necessary to assume that Herder knew Vico's work and was influenced by it? J. G. Robertson believed that "the whole wonderful conception of Herder's *Ideen zur Philosophie der Geschichte der Menschheit* is unthinkable without a knowledge of the *Scienza nuova*."[25] But, as we have seen, Herder makes no mention of Vico in this book, and judgments like Robertson's blur the fundamental differences between the *New Science* and the *Ideen*. First, Herder's scope is much wider; he gives a survey of universal history up to the Crusades, while Vico knew only the history of Rome and of modern Italy, and even despised the Egyptians and the Chinese for no other reason than that he wished (on religious grounds) to belittle their pretensions to antiquity.[26] Furthermore, as R. T. Clark has noted recently, "Vico . . .

---

[24] Thus he says that the biblical Creation story is an "oriental poem," a "mnemonic song" to fix in the mind the seven days of the week. In the same essay he derives the rhythm of poetry from that of the dance to which it was sung (*Archäologie des Morgenlandes*, VI, 32, 40, 42, 44).

[25] J. C. Robertson, *Studies in the Genesis of Romantic Theory in the Eighteenth Century* (Cambridge, 1929), pp. 288–89.

[26] Vico, *New Science* (126), p. 19. He argues that the states of culture represented by the Roman or Greek city-states or by the Chaldean, Egyptian, or Chinese nations were preceded by a patriarchal state in which the largest social unit was the family. Sacred history is, for him, "more ancient than all the profane histories that have come down to us," since the latter tell us nothing of the family stage of political evolution, whereas sacred history "narrates in great detail . . . the state of nature under the patriarchs" ([165], p. 26). So he has to suppose that evolution from family to state occurred everywhere independently at approximately the same time. For otherwise it could be held

neglected such matters as climate,"[27] whereas Herder's account of the geographical determinants of culture forms one of his major contributions to sociology. Indeed, the emphasis he placed on geography led some of his nineteenth-century critics to compare him unfavorably with Vico, on the ground that, while Vico studied social determinants, Herder was a gross materialist. This was the standpoint of Michelet in 1831 and of Jouffroy in 1838, and I have tried to show elsewhere that it rests on a misunderstanding of Herder.[28]

A fundamental difference between Vico and Herder is the latter's insistence on how often a civilization has advanced by assimilating and transmuting the ideas of another. Herder, for instance (in criticism of Shaftesbury and Winckelmann), shows how much the Greeks learned from the Egyptians and the medieval Europeans from the Arabs.[29] Vico, however, would allow few such cases of genuine cultural contact. And he did not attribute uniform ideas among different peoples to diffusion; rather, he supposed that, because of the human nature common to all men, all nations must have had essentially similar histories and have passed through the same stages.[30]

Vico and Herder also differ in their assessment of the efficacy of Christianity as a civilizing force. Vico attributes all that is noble in modern Europe to "the Christian religion," whereas Herder (in the *Ideen*) argues that Europe has become civilized despite, rather than because of, Christianity.[31]

Finally, Herder's attitude to myth is quite different from Vico's. Because

---

that Egypt and other gentile countries have no records of this condition because they passed through it long before the Hebrews.

[27] R. T. Clark, "Herder, Cesarotti and Vico," *Studies in Philology*, 44 (1947): 656.

[28] *Herder and After*, p. 255.

[29] *Fragmente*, II, 125. Shaftesbury had alleged that "Greece, though she exported arts to other nations, had properly for her share no import of the kind" (*Characteristics of Men, Manners, Opinions, Times*, ed. J. M. Robertson [London, 1900], II, 242). Winckelmann had reiterated this in his *History of Ancient Art*, trans. G. H. Lodge (Boston, 1880), I, 134, 136. Herder's views on the efficacy of foreign stimulation developed remarkably. In the *Fragmente* he held that great literature is dependent on fidelity to indigenous tradition (I, 363, 367). In *Von der Ähnlichkeit der mittleren englischen und deutschen Dichtkunst* (1777) he accounts for the literary efflorescence in Elizabethan England by supposing that the poets were inspired by the national folklore and made themselves the spokesmen of national prejudices. He argues that German literature will not surpass Elizabethan literature until it becomes similarly insular in outlook. In the *Ideen*, however—and this is his principal work—he no longer urges his countrymen to develop their own ideas from purely national traditions, but shows how often cultural advance had depended on foreign contact. Cf. *Herder and After*, pp. 58–59, 74, 89–93. Writers who represent Herder as a nationalist are obliged to quote his early works at the expense of his mature ones.

[30] *New Science* (144), p. 22. One of the exceptions he makes is the adoption by the Greeks of the Phoenician alphabet ([440–42], p. 103). This is one of many examples stressed by Herder, *Ideen*, XIV, 146.

[31] *New Science* (1094), p. 372; *Herder and After*, pp. 123ff.

Vico was sure that historical facts can be extracted from myth, he (as Vaughan complained) tortured all myths into a political meaning. That this approach did not appeal to Herder is clear from his complaint that Bacon "regarded mythology as a political portrait gallery because his eye was adjusted to seeing what is political." [32]

Clark has argued that, although Herder probably did not read Vico, the affinities between the two are "too important to be the result of mere chance." Some of the parallels that Clark mentions under this head (for example, Herder's opposition to "Hobbes's contractualism," and the conception that primitive man's animism made him a polytheist) can, however, be attributed to Herder's reading of Shaftesbury or Hume; and in other cases Clark himself notes sources independent of Vico. If there was actual influence, how were Vico's ideas transmitted to Herder? It was Hamann who first mentioned Vico to him in 1777, but Clark has plausibly argued that Hamann himself "knew nothing of Vico's philosophy and most certainly did not transmit any of it to Herder." Clark also shows that there is no reason to suppose (with Konrad Burdach) that Vico's ideas reached Herder via Blackwell or Montesquieu. His own explanation is that Herder read Melchiorre Cesarotti's notes to *Ossian* (rendered in Denis' German translation of Macpherson's work), notes which reproduce some of Vico's ideas and refer expressly to him. Herder undoubtedly did know these notes, although it is not certain that they influenced him decisively. Clark quotes a passage from them which, he claims, contains the germ of all that Herder wrote on the subject of the superiority of primitive language to philosophical language as a vehicle for poetry. But, according to Clark's own account, Herder did not receive the book containing Cesarotti's notes until 1768, when his own views on this topic already had been fully argued in the *Fragmente*.

It seems, then, futile to attribute much in Herder's thinking even to indirect Vichian influence. But Clark does show that Herder (through Cesarotti) must have had some acquaintance with Vico's opinions at an early date, and that, if he long failed to mention Vico (while warmly recommending Cesarotti), this was because, for him, "Vico was an unknown Italian authority whom Cesarotti, but few others had read," while "Cesarotti, the scholar who had seen the value of *Ossian*, was an ally in the struggle for general approval of 'natural' poetry." [33]

In the same year as that which saw the publication of Clark's paper, F. Nicolini drew attention to Herder's statement (in a letter to Heyne of May 13, 1795) that F. A. Wolf's *Prolegomena*, which had just appeared, contained nothing of importance that had not already been argued by Blackwell

---

[32] Vaughan, *History of Political Philosophy*, I, 231; Herder, *Fragmente*, I, 448.
[33] Clark, "Herder, Cesarotti and Vico," pp. 650, 669.

and Wood.[34]   Since Herder's purpose was to stress Wolf's lack of originality, he would hardly have failed to mention Vico's *Discovery of the True Homer* had it been known to him.   It seems, then, that he did not supplement his reading of Cesarotti's few quotations from Vico by turning to the original.

[34] F. Nicolini, in *Bibliografia vichiana* . . . , ed. B. Croce and F. Nicolini, 2 vols. (Naples, 1947–48), I, 368.

Pietro Piovani   VICO WITHOUT HEGEL

I

Contemporary philosophy delays recognition of its new characteristics by its reluctance to review, completely and drastically, its history. Yet, many established historical interpretations fall in the face of a new seizure of consciousness by philosophers, of philosophy's methods and its justifications. The same slowness with which reflections on the mathematico-physical sciences or the philosophies of the experimental natural sciences themselves achieve stable results from radical reassessment proceeds from the incapacity of men endowed with mathematico-physical mentalities to present their world view within the context of a general historical revision, which might correlate it in a new way, not only with the present and the future, but also with the past. And it is a fact that, from the eighteenth century on, new philosophies have required not so much an image of nature as an image of history; they have had to justify themselves historically. The world proposed by any conception differs according to the interpretation that it has of its own development, the result being the inevitable historicization that appears even in the most overtly and programmatically antihistorical positions.

Every philosophy must present its historical credentials. Contemporary philosophy will be better able to recognize its own unitary aspiration toward concreteness, its profound vocation in contact with experience, when it has better learned to make distinctions in its tradition between that which is truly favorable and that which is essentially hostile to such an aspiration. To be sure, individual, monographic historical excavations, offering new materials of documentation and criticism, aid this work of revision. Yet, by their very nature, when they are faithful to their principles, they proceed with a dutiful prudence and, even with their great merits, they are forced to excavate from the margins, exposed to continual erosions and to frequent collapses, requiring patient renewals and an interminable series of damming operations. While these exceedingly useful works are in progress, it is necessary to probe, however crudely, the wider issues, and to propose new interpretations on the broad plane, interpretations which might serve as provisional hypotheses, to be revised subsequently in their particulars.

II

Among the conventional historiographical schemes which have contributed little to the new developments in philosophy is that which links Vico with Hegel in a unity that presupposes not only a kind of "ideal" collaboration but even an essential, spontaneous, if indirect, sharing of speculative presuppositions.   In our view, no clarification of the differences between their incompatible forms of "historicism" is possible until such conventional couplings become objects of revision capable of establishing, in separation, the autonomy of their different, and in some respects essentially opposed, positions.

To be sure, the criticism of traditional historical constructions, even when it accepts the risk of a certain subversive rudeness, must guard against the dullness of obtuse overturning and negation, in the interests of *parti pris*. No tendentious argument can really convince the critical intelligence by substituting one subjective interpretation for another.   Anyone seeking to deny the debts that Vico's nineteenth-century fame owed to Hegel and Hegelianism would only fall into error and give evidence of an intrinsic bad taste.

That Vico was better appreciated and more widely studied because of the suggestion of the consonance of his thought with Hegelianism is undeniable. Even the general ignorance of the fundamental importance of Victor Cousin in the history of philosophical historiography has not always succeeded in obscuring how, even today, many of our most honored judgments derive from Cousinian suggestions.   Indeed, it was Cousin who, willy-nilly, habituated a multitude of both eager and reluctant readers of Vico to interpret him with a Hegelian key.   Cousin's remarks on Vico in chapter 11 of the *Cours de l'histoire de la philosophie*, held at the Sorbonne in 1828,[1] put his authority behind the already more or less "Cousinian" judgments of Edgar Quinet and Jules Michelet.   It is no exaggeration to say that, because of that authority, Cousin's remarks signaled a turning in the history of the European reading of Vico.   Not to take account of the significance of Cousin's words, to place them on the same plane as those of his direct and indirect followers, is to reveal an ignorance of that which successive schemes for organizing the history of philosophy owed to Cousin, in both a positive and a negative sense.[2]   It was Cousin who, by ratifying the intuitions of Michelet, established the convention of relating Vico to German Romantic

---

[1] V. Cousin, *Cours de l'histoire de la philosophie: Introduction à l'histoire de la philosophie*, *11ᵉ Leçon*, 2d ed. (Paris, 1841), pp. 341–45.

[2] Nicolini, concerned to disprove Cousin's views on Vico, missed the opportunity to pay tribute to the debt Vichian studies owed to Cousin's recognition of Vico's work; he did not see, therefore, the impact that Cousin's authority had in spreading Vichianism throughout Europe and Italy.   Cf. B. Croce and F. Nicolini, *Bibliografia vichiana . . .* , 2 vols. (Naples, 1947–48), II, 539–42.

philosophy; it was Cousin who, already exercising an influence on the Italian culture of the *Risorgimento*, made welcome in Paris Giuseppe Ferrari, "l'editeur de Vico";[3] it was "the eloquent Cousin" who inspired the Hegelian seizures of the shrewd Cattaneo in the essay "On the *New Science* of Vico," published in the *Politecnico* in 1839;[4] and it was Cousin who, around 1830, through the mediation of Galluppi, taught the Neapolitan scholars to manipulate history and theory in a conscious program intended to bring the cultural impulses of the Revolution and Restoration to fruition in a post-Enlightenment and Romantic inheritance, destined to have varied results in the rethinking of the Italian national tradition, now Europeanized, cosmopolitanized, and universalized, now vindicated in its claims to autonomous purities: similar and opposed moments of the tortured search for a new national-cultural framework. One can lament that the ambitions of the new historical and parahistorical frameworks compromised the development of the most original native current of Vichianism, that arising from Cuoco;[5] but it is impossible to obscure the borrowings which that current had already received from French culture of the pre-Napoleonic and Napoleonic periods or the fruitful graftings of that current onto a Lombardic culture sensitized to the philosophy of the ideologues and the eclectics.

In short, the "Hegelianization" of Vico, aided or prepared by Cousinian influences that filtered into the South, may appear as an alteration or even a deformation; however, it is undeniable that this questionable interpretation probed critically for the first time the connections between Vico and European philosophy, raising thereby the problem of a correlation. Admittedly, the correlation on broad lines suggested by Francesco De Sanctis[6] is more convincing and more critically subtle than that set forth in the impetuous speculations of Bertrando Spaventa;[7] but it should be remembered that both derived from a common matrix; and it must be conceded that the interest in idealism aided in arousing interest in Vico in Italy,[8] since the popularity of

---

[3] See S. Mastellone, *Victor Cousin e il Risorgimento italiano* (Florence, 1955), p. 65.

[4] Cattaneo, *Scritti filosofici*, vol. I: *Saggio*, ed. N. Bobbio (Florence, 1960), pp. 126–29 *passim*.

[5] Arnaldo Momigliano has recently commented on the difficulty of specifying, precisely, the debt that Cuoco owed to Vico. Cf. Momigliano, "La nuova storia romana di G. B. Vico," *Rivista storica italiana* (1965), p. 789, and "Vico's Scienza Nuova: Roman 'Bestioni' and Roman 'Eroi,' " *History and Theory* (1966). Presumably, Momigliano's intention was to signal the lack of a study dedicated to the problem of their relationship rather than to deny the relationship between them.

[6] "La Nuova scienza," in *Storia della letteratura italiana*, ed. Gallo and Sapegno (Turin, 1958), II, 815ff.

[7] Spaventa's interpretation, presented in his *Prolusione e introduzione alle lezioni di filosofia nella Università di Napoli, 23 novembre–23 dicembre 1861*, had already taken shape in the author's mind as early as 1847. Cf. G. Gentile, Preface to B. Spaventa, *La filosofia italiana nelle sue relazioni con la filosofia europea* (Bari, 1908), p. xi.

[8] See Oldrini, *Gli hegeliani di Napoli* . . . (Milan, 1964), p. 35, n. 41.

German idealism, imported along with Cousinian eclecticism, contributed
to the modernization of antiquated formulas and to the promotion of the
historicization of Vichianism and then turned the attention of Italian scholars
back toward more positive and more rigorously documented historical investigations.   In the next period it was the inadequacy of these positive
investigations, attired in abstractly positivistic and generically sociologizing
formulations, which, if anything, gave life to the revival of Spaventian
theoretico-historical propositions, which aimed to deepen the European
character of Vichian thought, though solely within the limits admitted by a
neo-Spaventian polemic.   During the early years of the twentieth century,
the neo-Spaventian vindication of the correctness of the interpretative theses
of B. Spaventa[9] fixed, seemingly once and for all, the genealogy of Vico as
"precursor" of Kant and Hegel,[10] seeing Vico as a participant in Kantian-
Fichtean Hegelianism, a "Kantian before Kant,"[11] as a column, therefore, of
idealistic and neo-idealistic thought.   Thus, in the development of Croce's
thought, Vico represented the first of the "four ages" of historicism, the age
of "absolute historicism," which anticipated the successive ages: those
dominated by Kant, Hegel, and Croce, respectively.[12]   This new schema
was more than a final development; it was the exhaustion of the older
nineteenth-century ferment caused by the linking of Vico with Hegel.
Still, to judge this movement by the stagnancy of its concluding statement
would be unjust.   It is more useful to stress that the linking of the two
thinkers, especially in terms which allowed for it without undue distortion,
contributed to the revelation of affinities and agreements worthy of great
interest in and of themselves, to be distinguished from the general evaluations
that can be drawn from them for specific polemical purposes.   This can be
done fairly by anyone desiring to take note of how the insistence on certain
consonances leads to the understanding of the indispensable distinction
between that which is, and that which is not, consistent with the ends of an
open and problematical historicism.

III

Obviously, any investigation of the possible relations between Hegel and
Vico, however intent it is on limiting itself to precise arguments, must rest
ultimately on nothing but conjectures.   Certainly Nicolini is justified in
holding that Hegel probably heard the name of Vico mentioned and praised

[9] B. Croce, *La filosofia di G. B. Vico*, 4th ed. (Bari, 1947), p. 329.
[10] Spaventa, *La filosofia italiana*, p. 138.
[11] Gentile, *Studi vichiani*, 2d ed. (Florence, 1927), p. 54, n. 2, and p. 137.
[12] See especially Croce's discourse "Il concetto moderno della storia," delivered in
1947 and published in B. Croce, *Filosofia e storiografia* (Bari, 1949), pp. 354–60; and
M. Ciardo, *Le quattro epoche dello storicismo* (Bari, 1947), esp. pp. 231ff.

—by virtue of a famous passage in Jacobi, or thanks to Cousin himself, through the translation of Weber, or better, Michelet, or as a result of French comparisons (such as those of Lerminier) of the Hegelian and Vichian positions.[13]   But a set of hypotheses, however well elaborated, still is not a proof. Against every hypothesis stands, for example, the fact that Karl Rosenkranz's classic *Hegels Leben* contains no mention of Vico at all.

In such a situation, the intellectual game of conjecture must yield to the construction of a catalogue of resemblances, either real or presumed. Thanks to these chance resemblances, Hegel can be placed in relation to Vico, right up to the point of converting Vichian positions into Hegelian ones.

Of course, the inventory of resemblances appears, in general, longer and more detailed the more closely the interpretations of the compared ideas are bound to the imperatives of a given exegetic system, a system closed in its certainties.   By contrast, the most persuasive interpretation is that which merely *suggests* without trying to *prove* too much.   Even Croce and Gentile, the thinkers who have given most to the establishment of the Hegelian-Vichian analogy, have had greatest success where they have limited themselves to the softest formulations.

Few would deny the exaggeration and heaviness of the figure that Croce uses, of a kind of Vichian metempsychosis in Hegel.   Croce finds in Vico "the very concepts, the metaphors and turns of phrase of Hegel" and notes their singularity, "inasmuch as the German philosopher did not know the earlier *phenomenology*, conceived a century earlier in Naples under the title of the *New Science*."   Then Croce concludes: "It almost seems as if the soul of the Italian and Catholic philosopher had transmigrated into the German, to reappear, at the distance of a century, more mature, more conscious."[14] Even the philosophical critic has a right to his moments of enthusiasm—to be sure, moments in which excessive feeling can serve to color his judgment too strongly.   More dangerous than a too-brightly-colored figure, however, is the general assertion that seems to rest on a point-by-point comparison. Statements such as the following, for example, might have dangerous consequences because of the assertive generalizations they contain:

The reality of the *New Science* is not only mind, but mind as self-consciousness; not abstract universality, which appears to itself as mind considered as object of itself (idea, intelligible world, transcendent God), but that concrete universality which is the subject that poses itself for itself and that actualizes itself by grasping itself in knowledge of itself.   It is, in sum, mind realizing itself in history.   In fact, the nature of things is nothing other than the manner in which they come into being . . .; and mind becomes by manifesting, thereby constituting, itself through the historical process. This is the concept of the spirit and of the absolute idea, as Hegel will try to think it.[15]

---

13 Croce and Nicolini, *Bibliografia vichiana*, I, 497–500.
14 B. Croce, *Saggio sullo Hegel*, 4th ed. (Bari, 1948), p. 52.
15 Gentile, *Studi vichiani*, 140.

When it is all summed up, the merit of Vico and Hegel, according to this passage, is reduced to their common capacity, appraised with a rather indulgent generosity, to find a place in the front ranks of the school led by Fichte, B. Spaventa, Croce, and, above all, Gentile.

However, writers like Croce, in particular, when confronted by the necessity of having to provide concrete instances of resemblance, know how to avoid generalizations that seek to prove too much and how to limit themselves to less heavy and more convincing suggestions. The list of resemblances adduced by Croce, and in part by Gentile, is questionable, but it certainly contains points that can be accepted by adherents of any position, even if the manner in which the list is presented often raises irrepressible feelings of doubt.

Examples of what I have in mind are easily enumerated. For example, it is undeniable that Vico and Hegel share a form of "dialectical thinking," [16] which, in both thinkers, has a place in an elaborate methodology appearing as a "dialectic of things," and, as such, is turned against the abstractness of non-historicized philosophies, anything not conforming to or confirmed by the appreciation of historical becoming, anything born of solitary, monastically isolated minds given to pure ratiocination, incapable of that direct contact with reality which is characteristic of the "political philosophers." [17] Certainly this aversion for the traditional philosophy of the abstract mind makes possible in the two thinkers a similar tendency to contrive a logic different from the traditional one, a more or less Aristotelian or Scholastic logic, a "logic of the certain" and a "logic of the imagination." [18] From this aversion arises the conviction, sometimes reasoned, sometimes intuited, (in Hegel, a conviction to be examined rigorously through the Schellingian mediations), that art must be counted among the forms of the spirit, [19] or, by another path, that religion, examined in its essential meanings, contains its own implicit philosophy, [20] in the same way that law might contain its own objectified social will, superior and antecedent to the encounter of the subjective volitions flowing together in the social contract. [21]

This set of coincidences, set forth without excessive insistence and formulated in short, can serve as a rough summary of established unexceptional affinities. Yet, even while we are praising them, doubts arise. In the matter of the dialectical method common to the two philosophers, it is well to be on guard, for example, in the presence of that love

[16] B. Croce, *Saggio sullo Hegel*, pp. 30, 49; cf. Croce's views in *Indagini su Hegel e schiarimenti filosofici* (Bari, 1952), pp. 18, 39.

[17] Croce, *Saggio sullo Hegel*, p. 50.

[18] *Ibid.*, p. 30.

[19] Croce, *La filosofia di G. B. Vico*, p. 252.

[20] Croce, *Saggio sullo Hegel*, p. 49.

[21] Croce, *La filosofia di G. B. Vico*, p. 253.

for the triad by which, as it is said, both Vico and Hegel reason. The Vichian triad, which can be shortened into a diad or translated into equal measures, often probed only timidly and rarely taken to its ultimate consequences, is born of the ascertainment of this or that rhythm of things. One is inclined to illustrate it and then to yield to the temptation to move from the illustration of a historical case to the formation of a triadic law that is at least as remote from Hegel as it is from Comte. The Hegelian triad incessantly presses the whole of reality into the antinomian mechanism of thesis and antithesis, valid less in themselves than in the victorious synthesis they necessarily generate. Again, in the case of the recognition of the potential speculative value of religion, it is not enough to point to the differences between the involuntary anti-Catholicism of Vico and the dubious Protestant fervor of Hegel, as Croce does.[22] It must be asked if the Vichian recognition of the objectively logical force, proper to religious experience, might not contain views that are irreconcilable with Hegel's evaluation of religion as the final, or penultimate, stage of the spirit's process. Finally, with respect to the historicity of law, obviously in many of its aspects contemplated in a similar manner by Vico and Hegel, it is well to guard against the facile adduction of coincidences. For in this field Hegel's encounters with the various determinate features of institutions and particular situations never impede the notoriously apologetic movement toward the resolutive and absorbing reality of the state, actualized in its concluded and perfected, its affirmed, ethicality—an entity of whose autonomous advent Vico, absorbed in grasping the secret of the innumerable succeeding peoples and societies, had no suspicion. For this oversight Vico was regarded with distaste by a contemporary, Giannone, who had clearly specified and foreseen the imminent strength of the state and its potently innovative power against outmoded institutions with their anachronistic defenses.

We have listed here three of the more convincing and least controversial examples; yet the necessary reservations already have opened the way to differences that are not minor, that touch the center of the major problems, revealing possible developments that are not only distinct but even opposed.

It is not surprising, then, that the presumed coincidences, viewed in their complex problematical aspects, can be converted into insuperable antitheses, if the discussion is broadened to vaster and less certain questions. By reason of these same difficulties, the interpreters who seek in Vico the precursor of Hegel, Hegelianism, and neo-Hegelianism are forced to become rigid and to devote their energies to exegetical commitments directly bound up with determined theses. For example, the Vichian and more or less Hegelian "ideal eternal history" is placed in the service of the Crocian dialectic of discrete entities (*distinzioni*).[23] Similarly, the Vichian conversion of the true

[22] Croce, *Saggio sullo Hegel*, p. 49.
[23] *Ibid.*, p. 58; cf. Gentile, *Studi vichiani*, p. 115.

(*vero*) and the created (*fatto*) is presented, without any second thoughts, as precursor of the "speculative movement that leads from Kant to Hegel and that culminates in the thesis of the identity of the true with the factual, of thought with being."[24]   Here, apart from the usual, questionable Hegelian-ization of Kant, the purpose is to stress the presence of the entire Hegelian interpretation of the historicity of the real—which is destined to encounter difficulties[25] every time it runs into the famous explanations given by the German philosopher to clarify how conceptually selected and selecting must be the *real* that is worthy of being rational[26]—in a selection in which the memory of Plato, never absent in Hegel, is so apparent as to please those critics most disposed to insist on the Platonic inclinations of Vico.   Yet a third example (still in the sphere of possible macroscopic disagreements) is to be found in the case of the assimilation of the Vichian *divine providence* to the Hegelian *cunning of reason*, by which it seems permissible to hold that "Vico, no less than Hegel, had the concept of the *cunning of reason*, and he called it *divine providence.*"[27]   This assertion, even in those who might be ready to accept it in large part, must raise doubts regarding a difference that cannot be reduced to a simple semantic problem: the difference that lies in the use of the term "providence" rather than "reason."   Simple lexical respect for a traditional binding word must in fact imply a series of distinc-tions which has to be investigated.

The truth is that the catalogue of coincidences, especially if based on the comparison of their widest conceptualizations, is worth only as much as the different supporting interpretations, which are not only comments on Vico or Hegel but conceptions of the whole of the history of philosophy, or of all philosophy.

IV

The presumed coincidences resist correlation, in particular and in general, even when one begins from the standpoint of the presumed ideal passage of Vico and Hegel along a single road, viewed as a unique historico-idealistic way.   But what happens if the doubt arises that the two philosophers are not traveling down the same street, but two divergent highways?   This hypothesis can be advanced with renewed confidence today, in the context

---

[24] Croce, *La filosofia di G. B. Vico*, p. 251.

[25] Croce, *Saggio sullo Hegel*, p. 158; idem, *Ultimi saggi*, 3d ed. (Bari, 1963), pp. 242–44; idem, *Discorsi di vari filosofia*, 2d ed. (Bari, 1959), II, 127.

[26] Cf. Hegel, *Enciclopedia delle scienze filosofiche in compendio*, trans. B. Croce, 3d ed. (Bari, 1951), sec. 6, pp. 7–8, and idem, *Lineamenti di filosofia del diritto*, trans. Messineo-Plebe, new ed. (Bari, 1950), p. 15.

[27] Croce, *Saggio sullo Hegel*, p. 50; see also his "La Provvidenza o l'astuzia della ragione" in *Discorsi di vari filosofia*, III, 124ff.

of contemporary philosophy, since in such philosophy it has become conventional to distinguish between one historicism and another, to deny that
historicism is a monolith launched in a predestined trajectory. In the
moment in which one begins clearly to discern the multiplicity of the forms
of historicism, and to combat the monopolistic claims of one form (not
casually "absolute") over the others, doubt concerning the essential affinity
that might bind Vico to Hegel acquires particular value.

The Hegelian criticism of the philosophy of reflection,[28] its desire to re-
conquer the entirety of thought by immersing philosophizing in the solid
sense of the religious life and of the life of the state, its desire to construct a
"phenomenology of the spirit" through contact with determinate reality
and a particular new consciousness of morality and *culture*,[29] indeed appears
at first glance, to be an indirect apology for Vichianism. And, for the rest, the
whole itinerary of Hegel's unconscious Vichianism seems to culminate in
phrases in the *Philosophy of History* which, without meaning to, evoke direct
passages of Vico. Who can read the following without thinking of Vico:
"The history of the world shows only how the spirit arrives little by little at
knowledge of and desire for the truth; first there is in it a crepuscular light,
then it divides into periods, and finally it arrives at full consciousness."[30]
The Vichian echo seems to resonate here in a truly striking manner. Yet
one could take precisely this sentence, a singular specimen of Vichianism in
Hegel, dissect it analytically, and use it as evidence of Hegel's anti-Vichianism.
Space does not permit such a dissection here, but it can be noted that the
crepuscular light which Hegel looks for is, in fact, that of sunset, while to
Vico it is the light of the dawn. The symbol of Vichian philosophy is not
the nocturnal owl of Minerva, but specifically the morning eagle, the supposed searcher for the waters of the sources, near which were established the
first settlements of men issued from the state of feral wandering. To continue in an imagistic mode, using terms of the Vichian and Hegelian type,
one could find, so to speak, in that acorn evoked in the *Phenomenology* the
nut of the potential disagreement dividing Hegel from Vico: "The first development is initially an immediacy, it is, in other words, the concept of this
new world. To the same extent that a building is incompleted when its
foundations are laid, so little is the concept of the whole which has been

---

[28] On this subject the fundamental work is the paragraph entitled "La critica della
filosofia della riflessione" in the chapter on Hegel in E. Cassirer's *Storia della filosofia
moderna*, trans. Arnaud from the German *Das Erkenntnisproblem in der Philosophie und
Wissenschaft der neueren Zeit* (Turin, 1955), III, 374ff. See also Cassirer, *Filosofia delle
forme simboliche*, trans. Arnaud (Florence, 1961), I, 16–17.

[29] The distance between Hegel and Vico could not be greater than it is in their
respective conceptions of the philosophy of culture. See, for example, Hegel, *Fenomenologia dello spirito*, trans. De Negri, 2d ed. (Florence, 1960), II, 46.

[30] Hegel, *Lezioni sulla filosofia della storia*, trans. Calogero and Fatta (Florence, 1941),
I, 62.

achieved the whole itself. When we desire to see an oak in the robustness of its trunk, in the intricacy of its branches, and in the luxuriance of its leaves, we are not satisfied if in its place we are shown an acorn; and, similarly, science, the crown of the spirit of the world, is not completed in its beginning."[31] This intimately revealing passage could not be more anti-Vichian. Confronting a perfect oak in its full maturity, Vico is not concerned with its achieved perfection; he is more interested in understanding its effectual nature by reconstructing it in its developmental process, departing precisely from the acorn. Hegel, however, values the *completion*, the perfection of the concept in which knowledge is realized in its authentic ideality.

All of Hegel's philosophy is a philosophy of becoming, a philosophy which looks at the becoming that unfolds only to arrive at the completed form, which is reality because it is conceptuality complete in its absoluteness. The parallel criticism of Aristotle and Hegel offered by G. Mure in his *An Introduction to Hegel* is convincing only on rare points;[32] but it is possible to see in Hegel, if not a revised and corrected continuation of the *Scala naturae*, a new form of that "system of development" which Windelband believes began with Aristotle. Unlike that of Vico, the Hegelian aversion for traditional formal logic measures itself with the determinate contradictions of the real solely in order to see how they contradict one another by annulling themselves in their antinomicity, which can only find its law in the self-consciousness of being in and for itself,[33] which must, in turn, find its logical normative criterion in that "absolute knowledge" where all *contingency* is overcome.[34] It is significant that, already in the *Phenomenology*, history, in which every synthesis is celebrated, is "history conceptually understood," which on the "Calvary of absolute spirit" finds "its realization, its truth, the certainty of its throne," because through its sacrifice it has redeemed all of the determinate individuations by overcoming them.[35] A titanic savior, Hegel knows that he has to smash all determinations in the total embrace with which he claims to save them; without the overcoming, which might perfect them by negating them, they cannot be saved. Their salvation lies in that "science" which elevates them to the level of the concept, which raises them to the summit of the idea.

For Hegel, only reflection is true civilization, and he does not fear a possible intellectualized "barbarism," for only a conceptualized science can, by systematization, liberate the individual from the contingency of being-in-

[31] Hegel, *Fenomenologia*, Preface, I, 9; this passage should be compared with another, in a similar vein, in the *Lezioni sulla storia di filosofia*, trans. Codignola and Sanna (Florence, 1930), I, 32.

[32] G. Mure, *Introduzione a Hegel*, trans. R. Franchini (Milan-Naples, 1954), chap. III.

[33] Hegel, *Fenomenologia*, I, 358.

[34] *Ibid.*, II, 287ff.

[35] *Ibid.*, p. 305; cf. the extremely subtle analysis offered by De Negri, *Interpretazioni di Hegel* (Florence, 1943), pp. 449–50.

itself, by universalizing it. The study of the determinations is only a methodical passage; what counts is the concluding reflection. Already in the *Philosophische Propädeutik* (the dense programmatic value of which should not be forgotten), the true "life is the idea in its immediate determinate being, by means of which it enters into the phenomenal field";[36] that is, it enters therein in order to issue from it as a confirmed and tested idea.[37] Already, "to reflect in general is to pass through the determinations of an object and therefore to gather them into a unity."[38] This *union* is Hegel's main concern because, for him, there is no true reality without a conceptually complete unification. The entire Hegelian theory of *Wirklichkeit* appears as conceptualizing realization. Therefore, Hegel often called attention to the importance of the section in the *Science of Logic* dedicated to *Wirklichkeit*:

Reality is the unity of essence and existence. . . . Existence is also immediacy emerged from the base, but lacking form. Insofar as it is determined and has form, it is appearance; and, insofar as this subsisting, determined only as reflection in the other, perfects itself to the point of becoming reflection in itself, it comes to constitute two worlds, two totalities of contents, of which the one is determined as reflection in itself and the other as reflection in the other. The essential relation represents, then, their realization of form, the completion of which is the relation of the internal and external, so that the content of the two is only a single identical base and equally only a single identity of form. . . . Such a unity of the internal and external is reality or absolute actuality. . . . Reality (actuality), possibility, and necessity constitute the formal moments of the absolute as relation to itself, or its reflection. . . . The unity of the absolute and its reflection is the absolute relation, or better, the absolute as relation to itself, substance.[39]

Nothing could be more formalized than this logic, which is meant to be a criticism of traditional formal logic. In the light of such logic, truly *scientific* in its systematization, one can see how the entire Hegelian dialectic is a kind of torture of the *logos*, which is degraded in its contact with the contingency of reality (an incomplete reality, not really real) only in order to be better exalted in its final conceptual apotheosis. Strictly speaking, its humiliation is its historicization, since the latter serves only to "eliminate the accidental," a process of selection which is valuable inasmuch as it guarantees the final purity of the absolute idea, which is the sole "absolute liberation."[40] The whole process is a catharsis which halts the dialectical process and concludes philosophy, purifying in its supreme being all subjectivity and all objectivity; it is self-contemplation of the *logos* because it is the conceptualization of the world.

---

36 Hegel, *Propedeutica filosofica*, trans. Radetti (Florence, 1951), sec. 68, p. 151; *idem, Enciclopedia*, sec. 216, p. 185.

37 Hegel, *Enciclopedia*, sec. 224, p. 189.

38 Hegel, *Propedeutica filosofica*, sec. 25, p. 137.

39 Hegel, *La scienza della logica*, trans. Moni (Bari, 1925), I, 186–87.

40 *Ibid.*, III, 360.

The whole of Hegel's philosophy is a phenomenology as a soteriology of the individuated; this, however, is redeemed only by means of the final logicalization, which deindividualizes it by freeing it from any taint of contingency. But his universal history must be, in the perfection of its own achieved realization, the logic of God, realized and discovered in the cleansed reality. History is valued by Hegel precisely because it is "theodicy," that is, because it is revelation of the occult "plan of God," [41] because it is, in the inevitable *Weltgeschichte*, [42] the universalization which gives new force and a new foundation to the universality of the concept; thanks to it, history, by being sublimated, becomes itself completely. It is natural, then, that at the apex of historical comprehension stands the history of philosophy conceived as history of the spirit which knows itself as itself. In fact, "That which is important in history is precisely the relation with a universal, its union with it, [for] the idea is thought in its totality and its determinateness." [43] That history is most persuasive which, in philosophy, makes ultimate testimony to the absoluteness of the spirit, emptying itself into the real in order to verify it: in this way "philosophy, completely explicated, reposes on itself." [44] Here the Hegelian philosophization of history reveals what it really is: the opposite of the historicization of philosophy. It is the idealization of history as logicalization of history. In Hegel it is not *logos* which is historicized, but history which is logicalized.

By virtue of all this, Hegel is not really the enemy of Descartes, but continues his work, attempting to perfect it by by-passing the insurmountable difficulties that Descartes encountered. Like Descartes, Hegel wanted a philosophy that could reduce the dispersed plurality of the real to a *science*, but, unlike Descartes, he wanted a science that encompassed history; as a good post-Cartesian he knew that, because of the eighteenth-century interest in the concrete reality of the historical world, Cartesianism had been shown to be inadequate in its program of scientifically rationalizing, or geometrizing, reality. [45] The reduction of reality to a *science*, not accomplished by the geometrizing rationalism of Descartes, had, Hegel knew, to yield to a more refined rationalism, which could enter into an alliance with history by

---

[41] Hegel, *Filosofia della storia*, I, 65, 66.

[42] This thesis has been fully developed in my own *Filosofia e storia delle idee* (Bari, 1965), pp. 103–6, 142–48, 253.

[43] Hegel, *Storia della filosofia*, I, 14, 30.

[44] *Ibid.*, p. 39.

[45] In his *Die Philosophie der Aufklärung* (Tübingen, 1932), Cassirer has shown how, in the Cartesian P. Bayle, and after him, the negative attitude of pure doubt of the Cartesians with respect to history diminished and even opened the way to a new comprehension of the value of the *facts* as belonging to a type of certitude different from mathematical facts and furnished with a new cognitive scientific attitude, autonomous and not reducible to Cartesian "science." Cf. Cassirer, *La filosofia dell'Illuminismo*, trans. Pocar, 2d ed. (Florence, 1952), pp. 282–94.

reducing history itself to a more circumspectly conceptualizing *logic*, to a knowledge that had been, so to speak, perfected in its universality because it had placed at its pinnacle the conceptualization that, instead of ignoring history, used it by incorporating it into a panlogistic world system.

Hegel's *science*, sensitive to the lessons of the *sciences* of Fichte and Schelling, contains a wider doctrine because it offers a new comprehension of history. But it comprehends history by purging it of the individuated and the individual, that is to say, of living and true historicity. The grandeur of Hegel's conception lies precisely in this profound attempt to insert history into philosophy, not by grasping the profound meanings of historicity, but by turning history to the service of a more expert and wider metaphysics, based on a subtler knowledge, dialectically, instrumentally, and provisionally immersed in the multiplicity of the real—not in order to understand the real in itself, but to rationalize it as a function of a new absolute.

V

Hegel, like Descartes but more than Descartes, returns in the end to traditional philosophy conceived as cosmology. His *Welt* is a perfected cosmos, the monism of which has been amplified by the insertion within it of a scientific knowledge of new contents, which, however, are always reduced, or elevated, to the status of cognitive concepts. Like Descartes, Hegel harbors a cosmologic-monistic vision of philosophy, but, perceiving the disintegration of it, he seeks to reconstitute it on completely new bases. His *world* is not, therefore, the "human world." It is a world that must coincide with a renewed conception of the universe which contains history within it, along with nature, in an improved cosmologic unity. In the last analysis, the multifold and dispersed "world of men," made up of irreducible individualities seeking to participate in the drama of universal process, is a humanistic obsession which disturbs Hegel as much as it did Descartes. Both were dominated by the concern to create a new metaphysical system capable of reducing that irreducibility to logical standards which were no longer traditional, but were heirs of the now-destroyed traditional logic.

Vico, a true anti-Cartesian, has no similar concern. Precisely because he was more of a "humanist" than a philosopher in the strict sense,[46] he was more familiar with the "civil world" than with the metaphysical universe. Even his Plato did not introduce him to the metaphysical universe, because his was a Plato who had been filtered through the many contradictory

[46] See Corsano, *Umanesimo e religione in G. B. Vico* (Bari, 1935).

cultural experiences of the Renaissance,[47] further filtered through a youthful, confused, but robust reading, which, in external obedience to scholastic suggestions, fundamentally free in their asystematic, personal tones, readied him to see in Platonism hints of a knowledge turned to the individual aspects of existence. Thanks to the freedom of his formative Platonic meditations, Vico could, without any internal inconsistencies, maintain and husband his curiosity about the ultimate properties of individual entities, distancing himself from his original Platonism,[48] not by rejecting it, but rather by bringing it to fruit in ever more pregnant contacts with historical existence.

The humanist who is an erudite, a historian, a literatus (in both the good and the bad sense of the word), is not bored or irritated by the irreducible multiplicity of the historical world; he does not aspire to a philosophical system that will reduce this multiplicity; he gives himself to the study of the inner meanings of individualities. He takes account of the new value that knowledge of such irreducible individual existences can assume in a new system of knowledge; he does not transform it through a logico-dialectical transcendence, but respects it by calling it by the *nomen* that is proper to it: "philology."[49] In this sense, philology, conceived as recognition of an individuated reality, viewed for itself within a wide system of forms of knowledge, not only can be listed among the major "discoveries" of Vico but also can be hailed as a deepening of a new epistemological dimension, which has not yet been utilized in all of its speculative implications. This epistemological dimension was inadmissible to Hegelianism, in which a point-by-point philological investigation had no meaning by itself. Hegelianism examined entities, not in their existential dimensions, but in their dialectical transcendence, to the point where they could be logically placed in a frame of authentic "self-realization," finding in the sphere of universal history the niche reserved for them.

Desirous of knowing the individuated entity in its critically penetrable philological manifestation, the philosophy of Vico centered on the investigation of the origins and maturations of real entities, not their conclusive logical perfections. In fact, Vico's philosophy, unlike Hegel's, is a philos-

[47] Concerning the quality of Vico's inherited "Platonism" and his processing of it for his own purposes, see N. Badaloni, *Introduzione a G. B. Vico* (Milan, 1961), esp. pp. 289–91; cf. E. Garin, *Storia della filosofia italiana*, new ed. (Turin, 1966), on the history of Platonism in Italian thought during the late Middle Ages and the Renaissance.

[48] On the contrasting opinions of Gentile, Nicolini, and Corsano see the balanced judgment of Garin, *Filosofia italiana*, p. 929, with which we obviously agree, even in the necessity of retaining the still persuasive reading of *Le orazioni inaugurali*, ed. Gentile and Nicolini (Bari, 1936).

[49] On Vico's conception of the place of philology in a new science see Pagliaro, "Lingua e poesia secondo G. B. Vico," in *Altri saggi di critica semantica* (Messina-Florence, 1961), pp. 345–46.

ophy of becoming—a philosophy not of the logically *developed*, but rather of the historically *self-developing*.

There is one Vichian theme which alone could clarify the difference: the theme of the *ingenium*. More than anything else, Vico valued this power because it is the class name of inventive force, and to him it stands at the heart of the primary capacity of the man who knows and who knows how to act, showing by this action the creative capacity of his thought in the raw concreteness of the *facere*. "Ingenii virtus est invenire, ut est rationis perficere," says the *De constantia*.[50] Hegel also views thought in its determinate concreteness, but he never loses sight of it as thought; as thought that is reflected in things, that is reflected between things and on things. In his dialectic, the essential moment is that of the *perficere*, which in Vichian terms equals *ratio*; for Vico, however, the most important moment is the *ingenium*, inasmuch as it is equivalent to *inventio*. The *ingenium*, in fact, is intimately bound to that imaginative faculty (*phantasia*) which, being proper to youth,[51] is found in the origins, in the adolescence of the world, which is the constitution of the world. The true Vichian rationality of history is imagination (*fantasia*), not reason; the decisive history, for Vico, is the "prima rerum historia," which is "mythology."[52] It is not by chance that even Roman law, genetically reconstructed in its various articulations and stratifications, becomes a "serious poem."[53]

One could say that, strictly speaking, Vico did not so much rationalize myth as mythologize history. Yet, he "demythologizes it," since, by returning to the obscurity of myth (in order to seek illumination of it), he grasps the fact of its authentic nature, which is its origin. The famous passage in which Vico asserts that "the nature of things is nothing but their coming into being,"[54] is a renunciation of the *perficere* for the *facere*, that is, the abandonment of the theory of nature as perfection of reality and the revolutionary proposal of the opposed theory, turned to the grasping of being, not in its completeness but in its genesis. Nature comes to be viewed in terms of the germinal *natures* of its various individualities: "We call *natures* the proper manners in which human things are born."[55] Here Vico stands at the antipodes of Hegel; in order to rationalize history, Hegel will wish only to see the unity achieved synthetically in the completion, in that divine *thought* (*pensato*) which is the historical development that has been perfected in

---

[50] Vico, *De constantia iurisprudentis: Pars posterior*, sec. XII; cf. *idem, Il diritto universale*, ed. Nicolini (Bari, 1936), p. 364.

[51] "... Ut senectus ratione, ita adolescentia phantasia pollet." Vico, *De nostri temporis studiorum ratione*, sec. III, in Gentile and Nicolini, *Le orazioni inaugurali*, p. 81.

[52] Vico, *De uno universi iuris principio et fine uno*, sec. CXXIV, and *De constantia iurisprudentis*, sec. I (*Il diritto universale*, pp. 114, 312).

[53] Vico, *La scienza nuova seconda*, ed. Nicolini (Bari, 1942), II, 123.

[54] *Ibid.*, I, 78.

[55] *Ibid., Correzioni, miglioramenti e aggiunte quarte*, app., II, 313.

absolute knowledge.   By contrast, Vico wishes to observe the *fatto*, seeking in its primitive *farsi* (self-making) its essence.   For Vico the essence is literally in the beginning; for Hegel it is in the conclusion, where history and logic meet and become identified one with the other.   The roads could not diverge more sharply.   Vico is concerned principally with the initial term of the development; Hegel dwells upon the developed process, perfect in its sententious self-reflecting.   For Vico, rationality opens history inventively; for Hegel, it closes history conceptually.   For Vico the new science is the science of the beginning of things "philologically," "etymologically" comprehended in their birth processes; for Hegel the new science is the science of triumphal fulfillments philosophically comprehended in their perfect self-manifestations.

For Vico, unfolding is contained in the process of self-forming and self-development; for Hegel the real unfolding is the unfolded, in the absence of which the real is mutilated, incomplete, not truly real, because it is not unifiable in the conceptual systematization of the absolute, which alone can really know it and make it known.

Moreover, Vico perhaps would not have the means to elevate history to the level of a new logic capable of making it into a new *logos*.   His original Platonism is—as we have noted—undoubtedly important as an attempt at an unprejudiced reconsideration of tradition,[56] as a tendency toward anti-Aristotelianism, and thus as the potential rejection of metaphysical physics and of physical metaphysics; however, his philosophical powers did not contain the technical means to direct the effort of a complete rethinking capable of reforming the philosophy of the spirit.   After the first attempts Vico left the field: the *New Science* is, precisely, evidence of a decision to move in the other direction, which is not that of the reform of the philosophy of the spirit, but the negation of every philosophy of the spirit which might seek to present itself as a science.   It is the inauguration of a different philosophy, a "philosophy of man."[57]   Such a philosophy had to pass from the explorations of the *"ratio civilis"*[58] to the foundation of a science which establishes its own primary novelty in an unpretentious pride in observing *"cose civili"* by securing the autonomous consciousness of a world different from that "order of natural things" which "up to the present the philosophers have studied"; Vico studies "the world of human souls, which is the civil world, or the world of nations."[59]   Having left the "philosophers" to their traditional contemplations, Vico foresees another philosophy, allied

---

[56] It is not by chance that Vico offers his own philosophy as a reconciliation of Platonism with history.   See Vico, *L'autobiografia*, ed. Croce and Nicolini (Bari, 1929), p. 39.

[57] *Ibid.*, p. 17.

[58] Vico, *De uno universi iuris principio*, sec. LXXXIII (*Il diritto universale*, p. 83).

[59] Vico, *Scienza nuova seconda*, I, 5.

not to physics but to philology, a different kind of contemplation, philosophically more reasonable by virtue of its capacity to provide tested proofs
of its experience-based historical interpretations.

It is rather difficult to say whether this distinction between nature and
history accords, even in its militant anti-Cartesianism, with a thesis of
Descartes,[60] or derives from Lucretian hints.[61] It is certain that the distinction excludes, against Descartes, any possible methodical reunification in
an all-reducing unitary science, for the only method it recognizes is that of
historico-genetic research. The *New Science* is philosophy inasmuch as it
provides a methodology for historico-genetic studies. The future, perfected
attempt of Hegel's to forge a more complete science, to reduce history to a
logic, is excluded because, for Vico, history is in itself epistemology. It is
the epistemology of the work of man, to be conceived as philological-
historical investigation. Vichian philologism and geneticism mean nothing
if they are not seen in the context of history as a new logic of the concrete,
jealous of its own concreteness and indisposed to turn to the forms—even
modernized and revised forms—of a conceptualizing logic, in a reconstituted
philosophy of the spirit.

By his programmatic adherence to the concrete, Vico's speculation tightens
the knots[62] between "ideas" and "things," drawing its new "universals"
ex rebus ipsis,[63] following patiently the course of man in the conquest of his
sovereignty over the civil world that is his, in the conscious acquisition of a
rationality uniquely his own: "Et uti Deus, summa libertate qua fruitur,
suae aeternae rationi immutabiliter haeret, quare poetae Iovem Fato
subiectum fingunt; ita civilis potestas, per summam ab omni coactione et vi
libertatem, suae ipsius rationi, nempe legi a se latae, paret."[64]

History, as "*temporum testis*," as "*vita generis humani*,"[65] has its own order;
it is an order peculiar to itself, different from the naturalized-metaphysic
order of tradition. It is, according to the celebrated principle, the world that
has "certainly been made by men."[66] In this respect, Vico has no need to
make secular history sacred and sacred history secular, for he emancipates
all history,[67] vindicating its autonomy, assured by that revivifying know-

[60] Löwith, *Vorträge und Abhandlungen: Zur Kritik der christlichen Überlieferung* (Stuttgart, 1966), p. 131.

[61] Nicolini, *La giovinezza di G. B. Vico* (Bari, 1932), p. 122.

[62] Vico, *L'autobiografia*, p. 13.

[63] Vico, *De uno universi iuris principio*, sec. CLXX (*Il diritto universale*, p. 184).

[64] *Ibid.*, sec. CXIII (p. 106).

[65] *Ibid.*, sec. C (p. 90); Vico, *De constantia iurisprudentis*, sec. I (*Il diritto universale*, p. 312).

[66] Vico, *Scienza nuova seconda*, I, 117.

[67] In this sense one could say with Löwith that: "Voltaire and Vico emancipated earthly history from celestial history, inserting the history of religion into that of civilization and subordinating it to the history of civilization" (*Significato e fine della storia*, trans. Tedeschi Negri [Milan, 1963] from *Meaning in History* [Chicago, 1949], p. 185).

ledge which is the logic of the concrete. Similarly, inasmuch as the investigation of the origins—an essential moment in such a logic of effective development—must continually recur to the *mythical* and the *sacred*, Vico only places sacred history at the service of civil history, illuminating one with the other. The adherence to the concrete has the effect of making Vichian history, inasmuch as it is an "ideal eternal history," able to hold that "*ex rerum publicarum natura disseruimus,*"[68] thus drawing from the nature of civil things their "eternal properties."[69]

In sum, the discovery of the historical dimension is a genuine discovery only if it leads to a *science* which is a new form of knowledge, a logic responsive to the many-sidedness of the concrete; if it is not concerned, therefore, to dissolve complexity in an overriding, absolutizing *unification*; and if thus it is free of any uneasiness in the face of the raw determinateness of reality. The familiarity of the erudite and philologian Vico with "things" permitted him to glimpse the truth that Dilthey, against Hegel, will point out as a characteristic of every true historism: the sciences of the spirit, as human and historical sciences, attempt to arrive at knowledge of the individual, thereby contradicting Spinoza's principle "omnis determinatio est negatio."[70]

For Hegel, as for Spinoza, determinateness signals an insufficiency of reality, to be comprehended, in Hegel's view, only dialectically, within the context of a hypostatized, sanctioning global being. For Vico, as for Dilthey, *determinatio* is not negation but enrichment, a precious, irreplaceable, and essential witness of a possible fullness of being, knowable only in the determinations in which it is individuated. Vico already perceives the individualities as the only plausible documentations for promoting a human approach to an unattainable being.

To be sure, Vico only glimpsed all this and did not really grasp it. The exegetic distortions of the Hegelianized reading of Vico warn us against any repetition of its errors, even in the opposite direction. Vico's history remained suspended between a love for philologically individuated determinateness and the "idealities" ready to be expanded into generalizations and historical cycles, potentially productive of new metaphysical speculations more or less "fantasized." Too often Vico's "civil theology" is turned to the service of theology; and even though his theology is a historicized one, it is still dangerously capable of being converted into a prototype of a theological history.[71]

[68] Vico, *De uno universi iuris principio*, sec. CCIV (*Il diritto universale*, p. 237).

[69] Vico, *L'autobiografia*, p. 26.

[70] W. Dilthey, *Einleitung in die Geisteswissenschaften*, vol. I of *Gesammelte Schriften* (Berlin, 1923), p. 26, cited from the Italian translation of Bianca, *Introduzione alle scienze dello spirito* (Turin, 1949), p. 38.

[71] But, by virtue of this ambivalence, Vico participates in a characteristic manner in a problem which is perhaps the central problem of historicism, exposed as it is to the

We know that there operated in Vico a kind of epistemological collectivism which seems to block the way to progress in the investigation of
individuated determinations in their philological minuteness. This same
collectivism leads to macroscopic reasoning—by entities and by heroic
"types," by "nations" and by "peoples," rather than by individuals—in a
continual effort to translate into characterizing symbolizations not only the
uncertain personal physiognomy of a Homer but even the certain historicity
of an Alexander or a Caesar. However, this appears to be a larger question
requiring its own investigation. Here it is sufficient to say that we would
accept completely neither De Sanctis' [72] acute observations on the matter nor
Croce's claim that Vico's problem was "the search for generic characteristics
or uniformities," [73] a view repeated by Meinecke, with important qualifications.[74] Fubini has wisely resisted these interpretations, stressing the lively
participation of Vico in the stories of justified men, so that the rationality of
the overly justifying general justification is, in him, almost halted—sometimes potentially and happily contradicted—by a feeling for the particulars
that, whether he wished it or not, formed a part of his historical knowledge.[75]

However it may be, such a question—which for us remains open—is
secondary to that of the character of the theorized interventions of Vichian
Providence, sometimes truly astute, now undeniably naïve, in their pro-
videntialistic explications. When all has been said, the Vichian Providence,
however much it is explained in history and with history, retains its
traditional function, by which its rationality, while being of a "legislative
mind," remains inscrutable.[76] Undoubtedly, the *New Science*, as a demonstration of Providence is, before all else, a bold and unprejudiced scrutiny of
the inscrutable; however, between the ordering divinity and human actions,
voluntary and involuntary, conscious and unconscious, there remains, in
Vico, a gap which is filled, now by the traditional workings of the all-seeing
Providence, now by the work of the responsible men of history. It might
be said that a providential optimism is not sufficient to cancel out Vico's
pessimism, which is shot through with awareness of the subsidences of the
historical world before every inadequacy of the human efforts of men, who
are buried in the epochs of time whenever humanity, in itself, is unable to
maintain its own level. Its vaunted continuities notwithstanding, the cloth
of Providence is not exempt from rents and tears; in the night of the times

---

danger of being converted into a theology of history, as the critical tradition arising from
Dilthey has taken pains to point out.

[72] De Sanctis, *Storia della letteratura italiana*, p. 828.

[73] Croce, *La filosofia di G. B. Vico*, p. 224.

[74] F. Meinecke, *Le origine dello storicismo*, trans. Biscione, Gundolf, and Zamboni
(Florence, 1954), pp. 46–48; see also Meinecke's *Aforismi e schizzi sulla storia*, trans.
Cassandro (Naples, 1962), p. 16.

[75] Fubini, *Stile e umanità di Giambattista Vico* (Bari, 1946), p. 220.

[76] Vico, *Scienza nuova seconda*, II, 67.

before history, it can be mended, sometimes well, sometimes poorly, like the cloth of Penelope, thus testifying to the rationality of *homo faber*, but not otherwise validly testifying to its own rationality.

In sum, divided between the providentialism of human historical action and traditional Providence, Vico cannot assure to his theory of Providence those characteristics which Hegel will guarantee to his, by conclusively identifying Providence with absolute reason, conceptualizing, in a closed system, the course of a history completely rationalized. Vico's history, less rationalistically ordered than is the logic of the universe because it possesses its own internal logic, cannot be wholly saved from traditional Providence without interventions that might conserve the simplicity of external influences and appear extrinsic to that human world which ought to regulate them from within. The rents in the providential cloth are certainly a function of the inadequacies and uncertainties, often detected by critics, of Vico's theory; but there are also residual free zones in which history, imperfectly subordinated by providential universality, remains open to the investigation of philology. In this way, in Vico, at the margins of a providentially universalized history, there remain zones of darkness still illuminable by "philological" history alone, by the historical science of origins. In Vico the world of man has lands still undisclosed to the universalizing work of providential reason, not because the philosopher had failed to initiate a reform of traditional Providence, but because he had not succeeded in carrying it to its finite completion and thus had conserved rich preserves for future philological discovery.

The harmonies of Vichian history possess something of the traditionally mechanical, like the harmonies found in the metaphysics, physics, and history of Leibniz. By virtue of their residual mechanism, of the classical type, both harmonies, though in different ways and different measure, are not established, but pre-established; yet, with the homage rendered to tradition, by their theoretical incompleteness they are liberated from the dangers of a more refined and more oppressing mechanism because they are now rationalized in a less naïvely traditional and more astutely conceived universalization. The harmonies of the Vichian and Leibnizian worlds thus concede to men disharmonic freedoms, worthy of autonomous analysis, not complying with the inevitably rigidifying uniformities of the reconstituted Hegelian future cosmos.

Beyond Hegel's neorationalistic providentialism, Vico, like Leibniz, has the possibility of conserving in his history fields of research reserved for the analysis of individual activities in and of themselves.[77] Precisely by virtue of his limitations and, thanks to his philology, Vico, like Leibniz but better

[77] Our alternation of Vico with Hegel coincides with suggestions offered by Meinecke in his *Le origini dello storicismo*, pp. 50ff., in which, in the first part, both Vico and Hegel are set among the "precursors" of the historicist movement.

than Leibniz, succeeds in partially grasping a historical knowledge which is an authentically individualizing historical knowing: an autonomous human science, fertile with "invidious" novelties, but a prelude to a new systematization of knowledge.

Obviously it would be absurd to reprove Vico (or Leibniz) for having failed to see that the individual has no need of being *universalized* in a pre-established harmony. For the individual contains in itself the freedom of the creative conscientious rule of stable and autonomous harmonies, for which universalization is nothing other than the capacity to universalize all the forms open to contents which can be assumed by humanity, which are universal models, in the rigor of an unrepeatable ethical tension. One cannot reprove Vico (or Leibniz) for not knowing the later, decisive suggestions of Kant, which opened up the most creative line for historicism, from Humboldt to Droysen, from Dilthey to Heidegger, and beyond. It is permissible, however, to stress how, in his fundamental teachings, Vico might have been open to such a course and might have moved along the same line, perhaps even anticipating successive, progressive steps. And it is legitimate to maintain that this course led in a critical and problematical direction, rather than toward the neometaphysical and absolute idealism of Hegel and his followers.

Perhaps it is historiographically correct to insist on the opposition of Vico and Hegel only within certain limits; and undoubtedly these limits have to be measured carefully and minutely. In any case, the hypothesis advanced in this essay serves to detach Vico from any necessary reference to Hegel, a reference which, from having been habitual, has become dangerously reflexive. Any discourse that, even in modest and inadequate terms, again brings their relationship under discussion will contribute to useful clarifications, perhaps useful even to the entire re-examination of the history of modern philosophy.

Translated by Hayden V. White

Elizabeth Sewell   BACON, VICO,
                                    COLERIDGE, AND
                                    THE POETIC METHOD

It is a strange thing, but one word keeps recurring in connection with these three great men.   Critics, editors, commentators, use it about them, and directly or by implication they use it of themselves.   Yet it is unexpected and, we might think, inappropriate.   It is the word "hero."

I mean to use that word as a key to the task which binds Bacon and Vico and Coleridge together.   Meantime, of course, there are factual connections between them that we may look at, though briefly, since these are mostly common knowledge.   They have all been called poets.   They share a remarkable universality of interest and knowledge, a deep concern with language, myth, philosophy, science, history, the body politic, education, thinking, and the mind of man.   Most of all, however, the last two in this line recognize and affirm their affinity with the first, constituting themselves one of those particular genealogies which occur from time to time within the wider family tree of genius.

One works backward with a family tree, so it is with Coleridge that we will begin.   References to Bacon abound in Coleridge's work: in *The Statesman's Manual, Philosophical Lectures, On the Constitution of Church and State*, the correspondence.   Beyond mere reference, however, lies the part played by Bacon's thought in Coleridge's writings on method, which he regarded as his own most important work—the *Essay on Method* contributed to the *Encyclopaedia Metropolitana*, of 1817, and the sections on method in *The Friend*, published shortly thereafter.   Bacon's work on method, that is to say, on thinking, is central to Coleridge's thought, and here we have the essence of the connection between these three men.   Poets they all may have been, methodologists they certainly were.   Here is the interest, the idea, that they hold in common, the very principle of their line of descent, for, as Coleridge finely says in *The Statesman's Manual*, "Every idea is living, productive, partaketh of infinity, and (as Bacon has sublimely observed) containeth an endless power of semination."   So, when Coleridge discovered Vico,[1] he recognized him at once as kin, and we find him proposing an edition of Bacon's *Novum organum* with parallel passages from the *Scienza*

[1] For an account of this, see Max H. Fisch and Thomas Goddard Bergin, trans., *The Autobiography of Giambattista Vico* (Ithaca, N.Y., 1963), pp. 83ff.

nuova, a project which, like so many from this marvelous and infuriating mind, never came to anything.

If Coleridge recognized his two forebears as being of the same lineage as himself, Vico certainly recognized Bacon, in his turn, in the same way. "And now at length," as we read in his *Autobiography*, "Vico's attention was drawn to Francis Bacon, Lord Verulam, a man of incomparable wisdom." [2] An even greater tribute to him appears in Vico's *Il metodo degli studi del tempo nostro*, of 1708, but here, too, the essential tribute lies in the constant use Vico makes of Bacon's thought throughout the whole of his own work, [3] particularly of the *De augmentis scientiarum*, *Novum organum*, *De sapientia veterum*, and *Cogitata et visa*. It is arguable, indeed, that Vico is Bacon's first real son in this methodological line, as Coleridge is his second. And so we come to the end of tracing the family tree, since one can hardly expect the founding father to look forward prophetically to his own spiritual progeny, although it seems as if Bacon does just that in the touching inscription in his own hand which heads his brief essay *Filum labyrinthi*: "AD FILIOS." He certainly knew that much time would elapse before he would begin to come into his own.[4] How true this is of Vico, we all know; and it holds, I believe, for Coleridge as well. These are three men, and a method, of the future.

So among themselves they establish their lineage and the nature of their affinity. But . . . as "heroes"? To most people, who do not write books, there is nothing heroic about being a writer, or even a thinker, however speculative and original, nor do the lives of these three men exhibit anything of the heroic as we ordinarily conceive of it; rather, we see in each case a melancholy human spectacle of disappointment, weakness, even failure. "Hero" is an odd word to find here.

Yet it occurs continually. I first really noticed it when I came upon Coleridge applying the term to Vico, as he does in a passage cited in *Inquiring Spirit*, which gives, incidentally, details of another of those unfulfilled projects of his: "Among my countless intentional Works, one was Biographical Memorials of Revolutionary Minds, in Philosophy, Religion, and Politics . . . with one or two supplementary volumes for the Heroes of Germany (Luther and his Company) and of Italy (Vico)." [5] Then Nicolini, in his introduction to the one-volume Italian edition of Vico's works, uses the word too, calling Vico a hero of the moral world and the world of thought,[6]

---

[2] *Ibid.*, p. 139.

[3] See the detailed and excellent study by Enrico De Mas, *Bacone e Vico* (Turin, 1959).

[4] "My words require an age; a whole age perhaps to prove them, and many ages to perfect them," Bacon says in the last section of *De augmentis scientiarum*.

[5] Kathleen Coburn, ed., *Inquiring Spirit* (London, 1951), p. 183. Bacon also turns up in a similar list of "revolutionary minds." See letter to William Godwin, March 26, 1811, in Earl Leslie Griggs, ed., *Collected Letters of S. T. Coleridge*, III (Oxford, 1959), 314.

[6] Giambattista Vico, *Opere*, ed. Fausto Nicolini (Milan, 1953), p. viii.

adding that this is a term Vico particularly delighted in.   And here is Vico himself, writing to Fr. Bernardo Maria Giacco in 1725: "I no longer bewail my hard lot and . . . denounce the corruption of letters that has caused that lot; for this corruption and this lot have strengthened me and enabled me to perfect this work.   Moreover (if it be not true, I like to think it is) this work has filled me with a certain heroic spirit, so that I am no longer troubled by any fear of death, nor have I any mind to speak of rivals."[7]

This makes an interesting beginning, and there is more to come.   Robertson, in his introduction to the standard English edition of Bacon's philosophical works, remarks: "Like Columbus, he was the hero of an Idea: and like so many heroes of fabulous quests, he bore a magic sword, to wit, his unrivalled power of speech."[8]   The image used here is not in the least a fanciful one.   The great contemporary image of voyage and discovery runs through Bacon's work, only he shifts it to an extended meaning—the exploration of what he calls "the intellectual globe," which is his own calling.   The latter phrase occurs in *Valerius terminus, Novum organum*, gives its name to *Descriptio globi intellectualis*, is the key image of *New Atlantis*, and occurs in the final sections of both *The Advancement of Learning* and the *De augmentis scientiarum*.   And, lest we should think it just a casual employment of an image current in those days, we come upon Bacon comparing himself explicitly to Columbus in *Novum organum*, Book I, section XCII: "And therefore it is fit that I publish and set forth those conjectures of mine which make hope in this matter reasonable; just as Columbus did, before that wonderful voyage of his across the Atlantic, when he gave the reasons for his conviction that new lands and continents might be discovered besides those which were known before. . . ." Curiously, when Coleridge much later wants to image his own task, he does so in similar terms.   He was haunted all his life by an epic poem he was always going to write and never did, an epic which changes shape confusingly from time to time, becoming now a scheme for the reform of philosophy and metaphysics, now a plan for education.   But, when he puts his quest, or life work, into an image, it takes the form of a march across country to the seashore,[9] at which point Coleridge, in the figure, warns his young companion to accompany him no farther unless prepared to risk all; for now ensues the "voyage of discovery," and the goal is described in this fashion: "You are going not indeed in search of the New World, like Columbus and his adventurers, nor yet an *other* World,

[7] Fisch and Bergin, *Autobiography*, p. 16.
[8] John M. Robertson, ed., *Philosophical Works of Francis Bacon* (London, 1905), p. xvi.
[9] It is this aspect, or figure, of the heroic which is accorded to Coleridge by his fellow explorer in the inner universe, who also saw his quest in terms of the heroic—Wordsworth.   *The Prelude* (1805 ed., bk. VI, l. 325) reads: ". . . But thou hast trod, /In watchful meditation thou hast trod/ A march of glory."   The thinking has constituted the heroic march, one observes.

that is to come, but in search of the other World that *now is*, and ever has been though undreamt-of by the Many, and by the greater part even of the Few, who have found it marked down in ancient charts or have had it reported to them by pretended re-discoverers of their own times, discredited as a dream." [10]

By way of final instance and summary, we may turn to Vico's fine address to students at the University of Naples in 1732, *Della mente eroica*, where he commends to them the intellectual life, as he saw it, in explicitly heroic terms. (Indeed, heroes and gods are both here, for Vico speaks to the students of a divinity in the mind, and this was no accidental dithyrambic burst of eloquence, for he quotes in the *Autobiography* a similar address of his, given in 1699, in which the phrase occurs, "cultivating a kind of divinity in our mind.") [11]   In the later oration, Vico recommends the heroic figures that students should keep before them: Alexander the Great pushing eastward, the sublime Galileo, Descartes, and Christopher Columbus, "who felt blowing upon his face a wind from off the Atlantic Ocean." In this context stands also the recommendation to study Bacon because he indicates how much of the universe is yet to be settled and taken over, even to be discovered. "The world," as we find Vico saying at the end of this passage, "is still young."

A heroic framework, then, is given these three, Bacon, Vico, Coleridge, with suggestions of voyaging and quest, of conquering marches, of the gods. What can they nevertheless be doing that would justify to their use this noblest, most ancient, bravest, loneliest, of human metaphors?

As we have seen, the factual answer to this question is that all three were investigating and extending a method, a way of thinking which, following in Vico's footsteps, we call the Poetic Method. Bacon, the beginner of it all, saw his efforts as directed toward "a kind of logic," as he says in the "Plan of the Work" that precedes *The Great Instauration*. He would have had qualms about calling it poetic, although it already has, in its first founder, the external characteristics of a method properly so-called, in the preoccupation with myth and language, for instance, which Bacon so clearly evinces. Nonetheless he would think of it as a scientific instrument first and foremost, and he intended it to be applied to what we should now call science and technology, and what he calls, in a marvelously grandiloquent phrase, "the power and dominion of the human race over the universe" (*Novum organum*, Book I, section CXXIX).

For Vico also, the method partakes of the nature of logic—poetic logic is part of his prolonged inquiry into poetic wisdom in the crucial second book of the *Scienza nuova*—and is applicable to the new science, while his interest

[10] Quoted in Alice D. Snyder, *Coleridge on Logic and Learning* (New Haven, 1929), p. 154.
[11] Fisch and Bergin, *Autobiography*, p. 141.

in language, philology, and myth is too well known to require emphasis. He affirms in part the method of his great predecessor, but turns it in a different direction, "carrying it over from the things of nature to the civil institutions of mankind." [12]   As is also well known, his key idea is that history is made by man, but made by poets, since early man thought as a poet, this being the point at which civil history and institutions began; so it is that a science that wants to understand these must go back to where they began, in history and in method. [13]   With Coleridge the pattern is similar. His work on method takes the intermittent form of a logic common to science and poetry.   Language and its ways play a central part in this method which he envisages, and he is of course a great poet and mythmaker in his own right.   Where Bacon applies the method to science and Vico applies it to history, Coleridge's principal concern, over and above the two already mentioned (for he shares both), is psychology. [14]   (One might remark here, although there will be no time to deal with this, that all three men are deeply interested in education, this also being part, as it seems, of the Poetic Method.)

So much for what can be said, at the top level, about the Poetic Method and these seekers after it.   Yet we still have not arrived at any explanation of the image of the hero, nor, I believe, at the real heart of the method.   It lies deeper down, within the mind, in those elemental times and places which, as Vico knew, are not simply the dwelling places of humanity in earlier times but the sources of our own mental powers in their primary form.   We will now adopt the Vichian or Poetic Method and go back to such beginnings.

We have before us an image of the hero, poetry, and a return to earlier times or forms.   If combined, they provide a clue to what we need, for together they coalesce into epic poetry.   The epic is, after all, one of the forms of what has long been called "heroic poetry," and it belongs with beginnings.   As we turn to it for guidance, we need only see, with Vico, that it is not simply a primeval phenomenon but a figure of some elemental working place, making place, in the mind, poetic, since all making is poetic, and possibly heroic as well. [15]

One of the best comments on epic poetry which I know of distinguishes three principal types: the struggle for creation, that is to say, the ordering

[12] *The New Science*, trans. Thomas G. Bergin and Max H. Fisch (New York, 1961), sec. 163.

[13] *Ibid.*, secs. 34, 314, 331, 376.

[14] See, for instance, the discussion of botany and the Linnaean System in *The Friend*, sec. 2, essay 6, or "Hints Towards the Formation of a More Comprehensive Theory of Life," written in 1816 but not published until 1848, in which Coleridge's first quotation from Vico occurs (see Fisch and Bergin, *Autobiography*, Introduction, p. 83, for details). Dr. Joseph Needham is an interesting commentator on Coleridge's scientifico-philosophical thought, in *Time the Refreshing River* and elsewhere.

[15] A Vichian point, of course—"they were called 'poets' which is Greek for 'creators'" (Bergin and Fisch, *New Science*, sec. 376).

and making of the world out of some primeval chaos; the discovery or quest
for the lost; and military conquest and the wars of migration.[16] It looks as
if the first two will be our main concern here, though the third may put in
an appearance from time to time.[17] So we shall take from epic poetry two
forms of heroism, as ways of understanding how the respective tasks of
Bacon, Vico, and Coleridge can be called heroic. The first image is that of
making a world, pulling it together into order and beauty out of chaos and
monstrosity. The second is that of quest, discovery, and retrieval of the
lost. Making something and discovering something seem at first encounter
to be two different activities; yet, as we consider them, they tend to come
together, as the meaning of the Latin *invenire* suggests, and as Bacon says in
the *Novum organum* (Book I, CXXIX): "Again, discoveries are as it were new
creations, and imitations of God's works." There appears to be a certain
primacy to making, however, in the Poetic Method, and it is with making,
as a part of the Poetic Method, that we shall begin.[18] If you have in your
head at this point anything approaching the horrid modern phrase "the
nature of creativity," please expunge it straightaway. This making is of
another order altogether. This is where worlds are made, worlds which
may include—if one can use that word—the universe of nature as we perceive
and control it, the history and institutions of man, and the thinking self.
Furthermore, it is not just a question of making. Here the imagery of
creation epics may help us if, as Rachel Levy says, such narratives never
assume creation out of nothing but rather assume it out of some primal chaos
which must then be ordered and subdued into a world. Thus Coleridge
remarks about poets: "They are the Bridlers by Delight, the Purifiers, they
that combine with *reason* and order, the true Protoplasts, Gods of Love who
tame the Chaos."[19] Chaos may have to be recognized as already existing
in the mind, or it may have to be reconstituted; the mind, and its frame of
things, may have to be unmade before it can be made. We begin to see now
why this is perhaps a heroic vocation. The danger and fear inherent in such
a task will be plain enough to those who have ever come near to trying it.
If one has not tried it, it is best not to judge.

[16] Rachel Levy, *The Sword from the Rock* (London, 1953), pp. 85–86.

[17] As in various remarks of Coleridge's: "the increase of consciousness in such wise
that whatever part of the *terra incognita* of our nature the increased consciousness discovers, our will may conquer and bring into subjection to itself under the sovereignty of
reason" (*Statesman's Manual*, app. B [1816]); "Dante . . . speaks of poets as guardians of
the vast armory of language, which is the intermediate something between matter and
spirit" (T. M. Raysor, ed., *Coleridge's Miscellaneous Criticism* [London, 1936], p. 151);
"Words not interpreters but fellow-combatants" (Kathleen Coburn, ed., *Notebooks*,
vol. II [London, 1962], entry 2356).

[18] Thus we find Coleridge saying (Coburn, *Notebooks*, vol. I [London, 1957], entry
950): "Into a *discoverer* I have sunk from an *inventor*."

[19] *Ibid.*, vol. II, entry 2355.

The method appears now first as an unmaking, then as a making anew, and this holds good for each of our three thinkers. In Bacon this takes the form of recognition of the need for "the expurgation of the intellect" as it stands in the "Plan of the Work" already mentioned, reaching perhaps its plainest form in his doctrine of the casting out of idols, that the true and living ideas may take over from them. He saw his task as the restoring of the mind to its original condition (both native and, in a curious but recurrent image, paradisal), when it would again be possible to establish a relation, so close that he uses for it the metaphor of marriage, between "the things of the mind and the things of nature." At its best (and Bacon is liable to slip back into thinking, as we also tend to do, that logic is an instrument or engine rather than an "organum," and it distorts his thought as it does ours) this is a marriage between two activities—the mind an activity of methodical relations directed toward operation, not contemplation, and nature an activity with "deeds and works" (*De augmentis* II. 2) whose inner forms are laws of action which the mind by its own analogous activity must discover.

In Vico the unmaking takes the form of an appeal to humility, an appeal that we rid ourselves of what he calls the conceit of scholars and of nations— their belief that the origins of our social and political world were either magnificent or intellectual—and that instead we go back to the first men, "wild and savage natures," which we recognize as being within ourselves, as being, indeed, that same poetic method by which our history and institutions are made, and by which alone they can be comprehended in depth: "for the world of civil society has certainly been made by men, and . . . its principles are therefore to be found within the modifications of our human mind" (*New Science*, secs. 331, 338, 779). We shall make, on this basis, the history, the method, and our own minds, at one and the same time: "Indeed we make bold to affirm that he who meditates this Science narrates to himself this ideal eternal history so far as he himself makes it for himself . . ." (*New Science*, sec. 349).

When we move on to Coleridge, he too invites us, by way of unmaking, to recognize the nullity of those habitual processes which we call thinking— "it is by a negation and voluntary act of no thinking that we think"[20]—and suggests that poetry is one of the ways of waking ourselves out of this torpor. Indeed he goes further, suggesting elsewhere in a daring passage that it is the poet's task to reconstitute chaos for us all, to call us back into potential so that the making and remaking can begin again, saying of the poet in this connection: "All other men's worlds (κόσμοι) are his chaos."[21] When we turn from unmaking to making, we find him saying that method "is employed in the *formation* of the understanding, and in the *constructions* of

[20] Note dated November 13, 1809, quoted from *Omniana*, in Stephen Potter, ed., *Coleridge: Select Poetry and Prose* (London, 1962), p. 198.
[21] Note on Barry Cornwall, in Raysor, *Coleridge's Miscellaneous Criticism*, p. 343.

science and literature," [22] the writer using "making" words in each case for what is going on. And, as in Bacon and Vico, we have the insight that the Poetic Method resides in, or is identical with, the deepest workings and activities of the human mind. Whereas in the "Plan of the Work" Bacon speaks of "the true powers of the mind," these to be applied to the interpretation and control of nature, and Vico identifies method with the modifications of our own human minds, by which we have created and alone can understand our history and institutions, Coleridge says: "If we would discover an *universal Method*, by which every step in our progress through the whole circle of Art and Science should be directed, it is absolutely necessary that we should seek it in the very interior and central essence of the Human Intellect." [23]

We seem to be moving toward our other epic image, that of discovery. Yet before we do this we must glance at Coleridge's Vichian or post-Vichian insight about what is being made. For Bacon it was correspondence between mind and nature; for Vico it was history and the way to understand it; for Coleridge, what is in the making, as part of the method, is the mind itself. Or, to expand that a little, what he sees is that the whole human organism, up to and including its thought processes, is constructing itself, starting at the level of sense perception and continuing through that process of self-construction which, for him, thinking *is*. The idea of the self making itself at every level appears frequently in his writing:

for sensation itself is but vision nascent, not the cause of intelligence, but intelligence itself revealed as an earlier power in the process of self-construction;

Quisque sui faber;

a state of mind analogous to mine own when I am at once waiting for, watching, and organically constructing and inwardly constructed by the Ideas;

In the *Paradise Lost* the sublimest parts are the revelation of Milton's own mind, producing itself and evolving its own greatness;

the subjective pole of the Dynamic Philosophy: the rudiments of Self-Construction.[24]

---

[22] *The Friend*, sec. 2, essay 4; italics added.

[23] "Essay on Method," sec. I, head 3; cf. also "the rules of the Imagination are themselves the very powers of growth and production" (*Biographia literaria*, chap. XVIII).

[24] Taking them in order, these extracts come from Coburn, *Notebooks*, vol. II, entry 2349; *idem, Inquiring Spirit*, p. 214; Raysor, *Coleridge's Miscellaneous Criticism*, p. 164; Griggs, *Collected Letters*, IV (Oxford, 1959), 767—the letter is addressed to C. A. Tulk and is dated September, 1817. The objective pole of the dynamic (or Coleridgean) philosophy is here stated to be the "Science of the Construction of Nature," giving a Coleridgean or Vichian turn to the Baconian work of the interpreter. Throughout the excellent third chapter of *Coleridge on Imagination*, 3d ed. (London, 1962), I. A. Richards speaks of this constructive aspect of Coleridge's method, e.g., of "his conception of the mind as an active self-forming, self-realizing system" (p. 69) or of "a technique for making certain assumptions—living them in order thereby to discover what it is we are

Putting the three visions or vocations together, we now can see more clearly the nature of the task and its immensity: it is a continual, profound, and lonely struggle to unmake and remake the deeps of the human mind (one's own first, then the minds of others—hence, in part at least, the concern with education), moving away from the null and dead habit, besetting distortions, and native disorder, and toward a creative order, out of which grow the human self and our own lives and thoughts, our civic institutions in their (and our) ongoing history, and our discoveries in science.

Discoveries—the word has been dogging us for a paragraph or two, reminding us of that second key which epic poetry offers us, the other aspect of the heroic life of thought in men such as those we are dealing with. This, we remember, was the voyage, the discovery, the quest for the lost.

So we come, though briefly, to the second aspect of the Poetic Method which these three men shared. Here we must be clear: this aspect of the heroic task is not, in itself, the making of discoveries; it is the fostering of the power that human thought possesses to think itself forward, its dimension to the future, to feel out and prophesy its own path toward its dimly perceived and due end. Poetry is traditionally linked with prophecy, so it is right that the Poetic Method should have this quality or power within itself. As Coleridge says, "All true insight is foresight." [25] The task of making that dark journey into the future of a thought, in search of something unclear and yet desired, and making it in consciousness so that it can in some measure at least be described, and so that others can be encouraged to pursue it along their own paths—this task belongs to men such as these, and once again the heroic dimension seems in no way out of place. All discovering speculative thought, in whatever discipline (for the term "poetic" in Poetic Method is to be taken very broadly, as indeed it always should be), is, if it is not to be mere empty fantasy, of this order.

The one who has most to say about this, and properly, since he is the psychologist in the trio, is Coleridge; in fact he has more to say on it than we can compass here. Bacon saw this property of the Poetic Method only as a shadow, I believe, expressing it mostly in metaphors such as that of the labyrinth, or of the reading of oracles. In a remarkable passage of his own, however, Coleridge reads more into Bacon than this: "Lord Bacon equally with myself demands what I have ventured to call the intellectual or mental initiative, as the motive and guide of every philosophical experiment; some well-grounded purpose, some distinct impression of the probable results,

---

making. . . . Coleridge's theory of knowing treats knowing as a kind of making . . ." (p. 49). Richards has previously remarked—whether with a conscious Vichian reference or not I do not know—that the possibilities in Coleridge's method could be carried forward "to become a new science" (p. 43).

[25] "On the Constitution of Church and State according to the Idea of Each," edited from the author's corrected copies with notes, by H. N. Coleridge (London, 1839).

some self-consistent anticipation as the ground of the *prudens quaestio*, the forethoughtful query, which he [Bacon] affirms to be the prior half of the knowledge sought, *dimidium scientiae. . . .*"[26] Coleridge gives this forward-thinking power of the mind a variety of names in his work. Indeed, even in the above passage one is aware that his mind is groping for expressions, using one after another, to realize this dark and central power of thought. Elsewhere he calls it intuition, precogitation, predesigning consciousness; but in two parallel passages, one from *The Friend* (section 2, essay 6) and one from the "Essay on Method" (section 1, heading 11) he himself uses the image of the quest, and very fascinatingly, the quest for the lost:

This instinct, again, is itself but the form, in which the idea, the mental correlative of the law, first announces its incipient germination in his own mind: and hence proceeds the striving after unity of principle through all the diversity of forms, with a feeling resembling that which accompanies our endeavours to recollect a forgotten name; when we seem at once to have it and not to have it; which the memory feels but cannot find.

The Idea may exist in a clear, distinct, definite form . . . or it may be a mere *Instinct*, a vague appetency towards something which the Mind incessantly hunts for, but cannot find, like a name which has escaped our recollection, or the impulse which fills the young Poet's eye with tears, he knows not why.

For a last look at this power of speculative thought within the Poetic Method, its forward-directed dimension, we turn or return to Vico. Vico calls it divination, relates it to godhead, and expresses it as prophetic self-discovery in the first place: "the full meaning of applying to providence the term 'divinity' from *divinari*, to divine, which is to understand what is hidden *from* men—the future—or what is hidden *in* them—their consciousness" (*New Science*, section 342). Divining is, from the beginning, the task of poets,[27] that is, part of the Poetic Method, a process, Vico says, "not rational . . . but felt and imagined," to which he will add a little later the astonishing and marvelous insight: "as rational metaphysics teaches that man becomes all things by understanding them (*homo intelligendo fit omnia*), this imaginative metaphysics shows that man becomes all things by *not* understanding them (*homo non intelligendo fit omnia*); and perhaps the latter proposition is truer than the former, for when man understands he extends his mind and takes in the things, but when he does not understand he makes the things out of himself and becomes them by transforming himself into them."[28] Here, too, as in the former epic image we discussed, the Poetic Method will work only

[26] *The Friend*, sec. 2, essay 9.
[27] ". . . Poets or sages who understood the language of the gods expressed in the auspices of Jove; and were properly called divine in the sense of diviners . . ." (Bergin and Fisch, *New Science*, sec. 381).
[28] *Ibid.*, sec. 405.

on terms of the full commitment of the self to it[29] (this is, in part, what gives it its mythological character). In thinking it takes the form of commitment to one's own proper quest, or question, the pursuit of what Vico calls—and he says that this is what poetry aims at—"the credible impossibility."[30] In living, which is also a speculative discipline if the life to be lived is in any way a life of thought as well as of action, it takes the form of the quest for the future forms of the self perhaps. In each case it is profoundly mythological as well as logical, and is as yet only partially revealed and understood. None of our three thinkers, Bacon, Vico, Coleridge, left completed or finished work, and perhaps we should see this not as evidence of human weakness but as a further clue to the nature of the method itself, and to our relation to it.

The heroic image, then, which these three use of themselves and which we have asked epic poetry to unfold for us, relates to this: they unmade and remade their own minds, as universe and activity, and set out, each on a dark voyage of quest and discovery. This is what it is to think. As is fitting for heroes, they go in shadow ahead of us. It may have been something of this sort that Michelet glimpsed when he wrote of the year in which he encountered the work of Vico and found himself transformed by that experience: "1824. Vico, infernal shades, grandeur, the golden bough."

For Giambattista Vico and the Others with Him

Can he himself make new
    Move into darkness
    Slough off the mortal image, re-emerge
    In starlight only—
    This, like mating,
    No work for the day—
        Without invitation or return to chaos
        Voluntary anarchy
        Which is for weaklings and the sophisticated-obtuse
Can he himself make new
    Sleek as a snake
    Glossed black and silver
A hero forces the very gods to change

---

[29] There have been a number of examples of partial commitment to it, attempting to combine with the Poetic Method a more conventionally "logical" or "scientific" set of operations at the same time, just as Bacon did—for instance, in the work of Freud, Lévy-Bruhl, or Cassirer. It seems as if outright scientists, as well as poets, may have a greater chance of grasping the Poetic Method. It is the method of discovery in science as well as elsewhere.

[30] Bergin and Fisch, *New Science*, sec. 383.

Then shall he hear
The great ranks go by,
Hosts of the air
Shifting in measure
    Not for them the agony, cold sweats, abandonments
    Of our thinking substance
Shall the hero see
Dull glint of swords
Slope high down the darkness,
Our archangelic powers, mail on thigh,
    And beyond, the changeless bright geometry of the stars
    Which need not think and alter

Scion, and rare, in this line
    Frustrate, ailing, misconstered
    At peril, darkly glorious
Set out
    Coolly possessed of faculties
    In full attention
Set out, hero-making-other, to divine.

Eugene Kamenka   VICO AND MARXISM

I

"Vico remains to this day a curiously intractable author," Patrick Gardiner writes in the *Encyclopedia of Philosophy*.[1] "His style is often obscure and scholastic, and his pronouncements tend to be dark and suggestive rather than sharp-edged and clear; nor was his mode of presenting and arranging his thought conducive to easy understanding." More than a century earlier Savigny had made virtually the same point:

> Vico, with his profound genius, stood alone among his contemporaries, a stranger in his own country, overlooked or derided. . . . Among such unfavourable circumstances his spirit could not come to full fruition. It is true that one finds in him scattered thoughts on Roman history resembling Niebuhr's. But these ideas are like flashes of lightning in a dark night by which the traveller is led further astray rather than brought back to his path. No one could profit from them who had not already found the truth in his own way.[2]

Savigny was writing before the second great Vichian revival associated with the names of Sorel and Croce, and even for his time he no doubt put the matter a little strongly. Nevertheless, Vico—like Heraclitus—has been celebrated more as a pregnant and suggestive forerunner than as a systematic founder; he has been "interpreted" and admired for particular phrases or general attitudes much more frequently than he has been studied with care and devotion. Until the end of the nineteenth century, at least, he was cited for confirmation above all by men whose interest in him arose from the fact that they had reached similar conclusions or attitudes by themselves. Whatever exceptions there may be to this, they are not to be found among orthodox Marxists.

"It is in authors like Vico, Ferguson, and Mandeville that Marx seems to have found, in diverse and contradictory forms, the constituent elements of a Promethean vision of history," a careful and informed scholar writes in his intellectual biography of Karl Marx.[3] Maximilien Rubel's opinion com-

[1] Paul Edwards, ed., *The Encyclopedia of Philosophy* (New York–London, 1967), VIII, 248.
[2] Savigny, *Vermischte Schriften*, IV, 217, as cited in Max H. Fisch and Thomas G. Bergin, trans., *The Autobiography of Giambattista Vico* (Ithaca, 1944), p. 70.
[3] Maximilien Rubel, *Karl Marx: Essai de biographie intellectuelle* (Paris, 1957), p. 315.

mands respect, but it is difficult to find any concrete evidence for the inclusion of Vico among the many direct influences on Marx's thought. Vico, no doubt—as Eduard Gans recognized in his introduction to the posthumous edition of Hegel's *Lectures on the Philosophy of History*—was the great fore-runner of the whole conception of a philosophy of history; but there is no reason whatever to suppose that Marx got his conception and most of the concrete details that went into its early formulation from anyone but Hegel himself. The materialist conception of history which Marx, we are told, "discovered" between the summer of 1844 and the spring of 1845 could certainly be treated as an extension of one aspect of Vico's methodology and of the well-known Vichian statement that "the course of ideas is determined by the course of things." But it is much more plausible, biographically, I think, to treat this materialist conception of history as an extension of the Feuerbachian analytical critique of religion.[4] Neither is there any particular reason to suppose that the "truth is praxis" line taken by Marx in his *Theses on Feuerbach* owes anything to Vico's *verum-factum*; it is rather a logical critique of Feuerbach's views using conceptions drawn from Feuerbach's own work and from French materialism. The insistence that men make their own history, which is found in the *German Ideology* and repeated, many years later, in Marx's *Eighteenth Brumaire*, has, of course, a Vichian ring, but there is no evidence whatsoever to show that Marx or Engels actually got it directly from either Vico or Michelet. Certainly, throughout the 1840's and 1850's we find no reference to Vico or any of his works in any of Marx's published writings, manuscripts, or notes. Yet, when Marx found anything that interested him, he tended to use it over and over again.

It is in 1862 that Marx seems to have come across Vico or to have been suddenly reminded of him, and he reacts in a characteristic manner, that is, by making a fair noise about it. On April 28, 1862, he writes to Lassalle that he has read Lassalle's book *The System of Acquired Rights* carefully and notes that Lassalle seems not to have read Vico or his *New Science*. He would not have found in the *New Science*, Marx writes, anything bearing on Lassalle's conceptions directly, but he would have got a *philosophical* treatment of the spirit of Roman law and not a Philistine one. He advises Lassalle to use Princess Belgioioso's French translation (of 1844), since the Italian is in com-plicated Neapolitan idiom, and he cites a few passages "to whet [Lassalle's] appetite." "Vico," Marx writes, "contains the seeds of Wolf (on Homer), Niebuhr (*History of the Roman Caesars*), the foundations of comparative philology (even if capriciously), and much more that is original. So far I have never been able to lay my hands on his purely legal writings." On the

---

[4] I have endeavored to show in detail the way in which Marx's view of the relationship between Civil Society and the Political State develops under the impetus of logical requirements and approaches the materialist conception of history in Eugene Kamenka, *The Ethical Foundations of Marxism* (London–New York, 1962), pp. 51–69.

same day, in a letter to Engels, Marx jokingly referred to Vico's conception
that only Germany had a heroic language left.   And at some stage between
1862 and 1867 he wrote the footnote to *Kapital*—his only reference to Vico
in a published work—in which he says that someone should write a critical
history of human technology and continues:

> Since, as Vico says, the essence of the distinction between human history and natural
> history is that the former is made by man and the latter is not, would not the history
> of human technology be easier to write than the history of natural technology?   By
> disclosing man's dealings with nature, the productive activities by which his life is
> sustained, technology lays bare his social relations and the mental conceptions that
> flow from them.[5]

This, we should note, is the sum total of Marx's references to Vico.   They
suggest that something happened in 1862 to introduce him to Vico or to
remind him of Vico but that his attention was caught only in passing.   It is
possible, of course, that Marx had heard of Vico in Paris in 1844 when
Princess Belgioioso published her translation, or that he had come across the
Michelet book or Weber's 1822 German translation of the *New Science* even
earlier.   The Wolf and Niebuhr references in the letter to Lassalle hint that
Marx may have been aware of the discussion of the relationship between
Wolf's and Vico's criticism of Homer and between Niebuhr's and Vico's
views on Roman history which appeared in the German periodical literature
of the first three decades of the nineteenth century.

Perhaps "men make their own history" *is* an echo of Vico.   But, while
Marx had the sort of unpedestrian mind that would be quick to appreciate
Vico's greatness, it seems clear that he never found occasion to grapple with
Vico or to use him in plotting out the Marxian system.   The reason is
probably simple.   As a philosopher of history Vico would have seemed to
Marx, as he did to Gans, to have been absorbed and transcended by Hegel;
as a social scientist or materialist, Vico would have seemed to him a herald
rather than a performer.   The most plausible view, then, is that Marx read
some (or all) of Vico's *New Science* in Princess Belgioioso's translation early
in 1862, and there is no reason to suppose that he had assimilated anything
more than vague "echoes" of Vico before that or that Vico aroused in him
more than a passing interest and admiration.   Benedetto Croce, opening a
congress of philosophers in Rome on October 25, 1920, in his capacity as
Minister of Public Instruction, said that the working classes, although indirectly and somewhat remotely, had gone through the historical school of
Marx and, *through him*, had encountered that of Hegel and Vico; but in our
present state of knowledge there is no ground for taking that statement as a
justified affirmation of Vico's direct influence on Marx.   Let us say rather—
and this is probably what Croce meant—that Marxian thought leads us, in

---

[5] Karl Marx, *Das Kapital*, bk. I, pt. IV, chap. 13, n. 89.

many respects, to positions and concerns that were also Vico's, and that it reinforces some of Vico's most interesting points.

II

In his introduction to the English translation of Vico's *Autobiography*, Fisch refers to the sympathetic interest in Vico of such Marxists as Antonio Labriola and Paul Lafargue. "It is no accident," he writes, ". . . that Vico enjoys high repute in present-day Russia as the progenitor of the theory of the class struggle; or that Trotsky quoted Vico on the first page of his *History of the Russian Revolution*; or that Edmund Wilson started *To the Finland Station* from Michelet's discovery of Vico."[6] Apart from the reference to Vico's standing in Russia (which is completely misleading), these statements are all true, but they can easily give a false impression.[7] Naturally, Marxists have praised those aspects of Vico's thought that fit in with their own line: notably the emphasis in Vico on class struggles in antiquity; his recognition that law is not imposed on society from outside but arises out of social conflicts; his belief that the sciences are not exercises of abstract reason but arise out of social needs; his recognition that the course of ideas is determined by the course of things; his general belief in development, historicity, and laws of social development; and his treatment of Providence in a manner analogous to Hegel's cunning of reason. But it is very striking that no orthodox Marxists have produced serious work on Vico; Vico excited those people—like Sorel and Croce—who were seeking a supplementation of Marxism, who were using Vico to depart from and/or transcend Marx, and not those who remained within classical Marxism or who founded the ideology of Bolshevism. There are no references to Vico—so far as I know —in the work of Engels and Lenin, and the references by Antonio Labriola, Kautsky, and Plekhanov are quite perfunctory. For them, Vico is (with Montesquieu and Herder) a significant forerunner of Marxism, lending it a sort of historical respectability and serving as an illustration of the inadequacy

[6] Fisch and Bergin, *Autobiography*, p. 107.

[7] The only significant Soviet Vichian literature I have been able to find is the following (the list includes and transcends the bibliography of Soviet literature on Vico given in the Soviet *Philosophical Encyclopedia*): Giambattista Vico, *Osnovanniya novoi nauki ob obshchoi prirode natsii*, trans. A. Guber, with commentary (Moscow, 1940); V. N. Maksimovskii, "Vico and His Theory of Social Cycles," *Arkhiv K. Marksa i F. Engel'sa* (1929), bk. 4; *idem*, "The Aesthetic Views of Giambattista Vico," *Literaturny kritik*, no. 11 (1935); M. Lifshits, "Giambattista Vico," *Literaturny kritik*, no. 2 (1939); L. German, "Giambattista Vico," *Pod znamenem marksizma*, no. 12 (1940); G. F. Aleksandrov et al., eds., *Istoriya filosofii*, II (Moscow, 1941), 273–78; M. A. Dynnik et al., eds., *Istoriya filosofii*, I (Moscow, 1957), 461–63; F. V. Konstantinov et al., eds., *Filosofskaya Entsiklopedia*, I (Moscow, 1960), 259.

of the eighteenth-century Enlightenment; even more frequently he is used as a scholarly adornment, as a source for an impressive or incisive phrase. Lafargue, it is true, devotes a chapter of his *Le déterminisme économique de Karl Marx* to the historical laws of Vico, but he adds nothing to a serious understanding of Vico.

The case of the founder of the Italian Communist party, Antonio Gramsci (1891–1937), is special. Gramsci could be regarded as the only *Marxist* thinker to continue calling himself a Marxist and yet be significantly influenced by Vico. Concerned to combine the practicality of communist revolutionary work and theory with the ideal of genuinely making the proletariat heir to the whole of Western cultural development, Gramsci rejected the Stalinist dogmatization of Marxism and the view that dialectical and historical materialism could be regarded as the "culmination" of philosophy. A particular school might reach a culmination or an apogee, Gramsci argued, but culture and philosophy as such do not "culminate." In his attempt to work out a synthesis of Lenin and Croce, as in his acceptance of a spiral theory of culture, the influence of Vico is quite marked. But the conditions of Gramsci's life (his philosophical writings are collections and selections of short fragments found in the thirty-two notebooks he wrote during the eleven years he spent in Mussolini's prisons, edited after his death) prevented him from undertaking sustained critical philosophical work, from contributing a genuine work to Vichian literature, for instance. At the same time, the place which Gramsci will occupy in the history of Marxist thought and the extent to which he may help to produce or shape a critical neo-Marxism of the future are still to be determined. At present, Gramsci's work is still poorly known and comparatively uninfluential outside Italy.

Among Bolshevik writers the interest in Vico has been decidedly lukewarm. V. N. Maksimovskii wrote popular articles on him (in 1929 and 1935). In 1940, it is true, a Russian translation of Vico's *New Science* by A. Guber (Huber) (based on the third edition, but citing passages from the first in an appendix and including in the notes some passages from the second) was published in Moscow by the state publishers specializing in belles-lettres, with an introduction by M. A. Lifshits. The introduction praises Vico for his historical approach, his enmity to Cartesian rationalism, his "profound dialectical understanding of the history of spiritual culture," and his emphasis on social structure; it insists, however, that the main feature of Vico's philosophy—his acceptance of reality—has reactionary as well as progressive features. A review of the book by L. German in the philosophical journal *Under the Banner of Marxism* praises the translation and much of the introduction, but denies that Vico can be called "profoundly" dialectical or that he can be presented as a completely uncompromising enemy of Cartesian rationalism, since his thought retained much that was itself rationalistic. While the discussion shows that Lifshits and German obviously have an acquaintance with Vico's work, the points at issue are drearily ideological or verbal and provide no insight for the general reader, let alone the scholar.

Even more significant is the fact that this publication was handled by a belles-lettres publishing house and not by one of the political or philosophical publishers. The name of Vico does not figure in any of the Soviet single-volume textbooks on the history of philosophy or on the history of legal and political thought. (This omission is very striking; it is the result of the very formal plans, approved by the Ministry of Education, which such textbooks follow.) It hardly ever appears in monographs.[8] It is only in substantial reference works—in the three-volume *History of Philosophy* edited by G. F. Aleksandrov in 1941, in the first volume of the Soviet *Philosophical Encyclopedia*, which appeared in 1960, and in the six-volume *History of Philosophy* published between 1957 and 1965—that Vico rates a mention. While emphases vary slightly, the general line is to praise him for seeing society as developing through definite stages subject to laws independent of the desires of men, but to emphasize that he was as yet far from a scientific grasp of the question, that he was incompletely emancipated from religion, and that his cyclical theory gave aid and comfort to subsequent bourgeois reactionaries. Thus N. Novikov, in the *Philosophical Encyclopedia*, describes Vico's system as "an inconsistent, objective idealist system in which God and the world are identical and in which Divine Providence is merely another name for empirical laws within reality itself" and finds a neat expression of this contradiction between idealism and materialism in the fact that Vico's favorite philosophers were Plato and Bacon. The "material cause" of this contradiction, according to Novikov, lies in the contradictions of Italian society in Vico's time. Vico's views express the position of the Italian bourgeoisie at the end of the seventeenth and the beginning of the eighteenth century, on the one hand demanding the development of capitalist relations and a socio-political transformation, and on the other hand inclined toward an alliance with Catholicism and feudalism. In the six-volume *History of Philosophy* there is an interesting attack on Vico (interesting politically, in the Soviet context, rather than intellectually) for exempting *the Jews* from the laws of history. The possibility that Vico's conception of "sacred history"

---

[8] There are passing references to Vico in various Soviet publications, such as S. F. Oduev, *Reaktsionnaya sushchnost' nitssheanstva* (Moscow, 1959), p. 101; A. V. Gulyga, *Gerder* (Herder) (Moscow, 1963), pp. 79, 93, 169—the usual passing references to Vico's influence on Herder; P. Togliatti, "Development and Crisis of Italian Thought in the Nineteenth Century," *Voprosy filosofii*, no. 5 (1955), pp. 57ff.; and the Russian translation of Michele Abbate's *La filosofia di Benedetto Croce e la crisi della società italiana*, published in Moscow in 1959 with a very critical introduction by Z. N. Meleshchenko. More than twenty single-volume histories of philosophy, introductions to the history of philosophy, histories of political thought, and even G. F. Aleksandrov's *History of Western European Philosophy*, published between 1936 and 1966, make no reference to Vico.

was a device to escape religious condemnation, a possibility at least considered by most Western authors, is neither mentioned nor examined. In the *History* and the *Encyclopedia* there are references to Vico's social theory of language and of art and to his recognition of the importance of social struggles; the *History* adds that, although Vico was opposed to the working-class and peasant movements of his time, he was influenced by popular movements in his youth and that his work *On the Most Ancient Wisdom of the Italians* played a role in the formation of the ideology of the people's struggle. It is striking, however, not only that Soviet writers have not sought to make any significant contribution to the study of Vico but that their references to him are formal and decidedly lukewarm.

Part II   VICO'S INFLUENCE
                           ON WESTERN THOUGHT
                                  AND LETTERS

Enrico De Mas

VICO AND
ITALIAN THOUGHT

Let us state at once that the title of this paper is somewhat fictitious because it is justified only by a requirement of symmetry with analogous papers inspired by the principle of nationality. The title is misleading also inasmuch as it may cause the reader to believe that in Italy, Vico's home country, there was and still is a philosophical trend capable of assimilating, and of assessing at their right value, the profound doctrines that he passed on to posterity. The fact of the matter is different. Vico has been much talked about in Italy and by many, and (as is natural) at an earlier date than in other nations. But this has been done mainly in order to exploit the authority of his name and the success of his universally known work. There have been very few attempts to penetrate adequately the meaning of that work or to carry on the message of his thought.

Vico's complex personality, his difficult philosophy, his boundless erudition, his wide competence in almost all fields of learning, were first discussed in Naples, then in the north of Italy and in foreign countries, where the Neapolitan exiles had found a refuge from political persecution. What should at once be underscored is that, aside from a few reservations of out-and-out traditionalists, Vico did not encounter any opponents, but found, instead, scholars inclined to appreciate him, even to proclaim their discipleship to him. Yet, until Croce's monograph of 1911, there were, in Italy, no interpretations equal to those of the Romantic era by Michelet and Coleridge, which had a truly European resonance.

During the more than two centuries which have elapsed since the death of Vico (1744), Italian thought has been dominated by some of his ideas and, in general, has engaged in the search for a historico-speculative connection between these ideas and later trends. Thus the many-sided and powerful personality of the Neapolitan philosopher has become an object of study and a source of inspiration for the most disparate philosophical, scientific, and political conceptions, from the Jacobinism of the Enlightenment to *Risorgimento* nationalism; from historicism to neo-idealism, from positivism to fascism, from Neo-Platonism to Catholic neoscholasticism; from Marxism to existentialism, from neohumanism to cultural anthropology, and so on. Never well-understood, and often misjudged, Vico had, however, the good fortune (which few thinkers have ever had) not to be repudiated by any cultural trend. It is a mark of the greatness of his genius, but also of the insufficiency of partial and particular interpretations.

What accounts for the benevolent reception accorded to him is the fact that his philosophy, oriented as it is toward historical research rather than toward dogmatically precise statements, consents to being aimed at, to being reduced to, different goals. Vico's philosophy, explicitly, is neither so decidedly traditionalistic as to disavow numerous innovations (the paternity of which is attributed to him on undisputed grounds, particularly in humanistic studies), nor so innovational as to destroy the links with tradition. (A proof of this can be seen in the assumption of the existence of a *feral* state, which is but the philosophical version of the *Christian dogma of the fall of man*, of man destined to rise again by his own efforts, but with the help of Providence.) Vico's major work, the *Scienza nuova*, recast and developed several times, presents (though not in organic form) an encyclopedic synthesis of the knowledge of his time in its most characteristic features, inclusive of the traditional as well as of the original aspects. The *Scienza nuova*, which offers a multiform and polyhedral view of history, is both retrospective and anticipative. It should properly be placed between Bacon's treatise *De dignitate et augmentis scientiarum* and the great *Encyclopédie* of the French thinkers of the Enlightenment.

Of the Baconian pattern of revision and renovation of the sciences, the *Scienza nuova* preserves the general proceeding by introducing (side by side with traditional sciences after their amendments) not one (as the title would have us believe), but several, new sciences. These sciences are born from a new genetic articulation of the whole of knowledge, in lieu of the systematic method currently established. The result is an unusually rich and various cultural panorama, hard to grasp at first sight, but full of brilliant and vivid lights, so as to justify the judgment of Vincenzo Monti, who compares the *Scienza nuova* to the mountain of Golconda, bristling with crags and pregnant with diamonds. A writer who, because of certain obscurities and imprecisions, was far from popular in Italy or abroad, Vico failed to give rise to a school. Instead, he has exerted a series of sporadic impacts, which have been all the stronger and more binding in proportion to the significance of the author who underwent the impact (Cousin, Michelet, Coleridge, Sorel, Croce), and who was bent on making of Vico, in some way, his own precursor.

It is therefore easy to understand the origin of the myth (lasting until our days) of Vico as the "isolated thinker," "misunderstood by his epoch" because he was "forging ahead toward a subsequent and better time." In the recent past this myth has become so binding that some writers of textbooks of literary history have felt compelled to break the chronological sequence in order to find a place for Vico's original personality, assigning it, well beyond the epoch in which he lived, to the heyday of nineteenth-century romanticism; to such an extent has Croce's distorting interpretation of Vico acted negatively and in utter disregard of that historicity which Croce proclaimed as the universal canon of right judgment. (The partiality of Croce's interpretation is now fully recognized in Italy, with no detraction, however, from the merits it otherwise possesses.)

For some years now, on the initiative of Nicola Abbagnano and through scholars like Fausto Nicolini, Eugenio Garin, Paolo Rossi, Pietro Rossi, Franco Venturi, Nicola Badaloni, and Pietro Piovani, assiduous attempts have been made to describe and define the historical milieu, the environmental eighteenth-century framework, within which Vico's work is to be fitted. There has been a detailed investigation into the cultural atmosphere of his native city, Naples, an atmosphere from which Vico drew the greater part of his intellectual nurture (admirably outlined by him in his *Autobiography*), and from which emerged his earliest and best direct disciples.

A glory of Naples he undoubtedly was, before he became an Italian or European one, because, in spite of the powerful afflatus of his scholarship, which spellbinds in a dialogue on the international level the major protagonists of culture of all epochs and countries, Vico is a typical expression (and certainly one of the best expressions) of the milieu and the mentality of Naples, a milieu and a mentality which were provincial, but not in a strictly parochial sense. They were provincial, not as the synthesis of a province, but of the whole kingdom of the *Italia meridionale*, rich with vivid intuitions and thrilling discoveries, full of sparkling and penetrating judgments, exuberant and prolific like the sky and the sea of southern Italy.

In regard to Vico's thought, and to its presence and absence in Italy (in the sense illustrated above), it behooves us to keep the work of the eighteenth century separate from that of the nineteenth. It is a fact that the evaluation of Vico in Italy took different directives as it passed from cosmopolitanism to nationalism. Truth to tell, neither the former nor the latter historico-speculative trend contributed to an adequate apprehension and penetration of Vico's philosophy. This result could be achieved only through a diffused knowledge of Vico's historical milieu, a knowledge which the historical scholarship of that epoch lacked. It is also a fact that, in the eighteenth century, the figure of the Neapolitan thinker became the standard-bearer of that politico-cultural movement which tended to insert the Italian South into the framework of European reformism. In this sense (but in this sense alone) it is permissible to speak of a Neapolitan Vichian school, a school which, because of the presence in it of Antonio Genovesi (1713–69), another authoritative master of southern thought, inferior to Vico in conceptual depth but not in local reputation, is also called Genovesi's school.[1]

[1] See B. Croce and F. Nicolini, eds., *Bibliografia vichiana . . .* , 2 vols. (Naples, 1947–48), I, 256, where the following judgment by Vincenzo Cuoco is cited: "In Italy, the school of

The following account, schematized down to the essentials, endeavors to place due emphasis on the main figures of this school, drawing each of them close to the aspect, or aspects, of Vico's thought within which each figure was most active. None, however, was able to embrace and dominate the whole of Vico's work in the wealth and complexity of its motivations.

A preliminary remark seems indispensable, and it is that Vico had no academic succession. It is true that his son Gennaro, whom Vico wanted first as an assistant and then as his successor in the professorship of rhetoric at the University of Naples, represents the continuity of his academic presence, but he does so merely as a teacher of eloquence and by no means as author of the *Scienza nuova* or as thinker. Fossilized in the science of grammatical and stylistic rules belonging to the *ars dicendi*, Gennaro Vico was incapable of penetrating deeply into, or of moving with self-assurance through, the at times gloomy or sunlit forests of his father's masterpiece. He knew, however, how to keep his memory alive: by directing attention to him privately and by paying perennial homage to his achievements. For this tribute of affectionate love to his father, Gennaro received a supreme reward when he played host, in his house (the house where his father had lived), to Vincenzo Cuoco, who had come to discuss with Gennaro the possibility of publishing the *Opera omnia* of Vico. The eighteenth century did not, however, produce an edition of Vico's complete works; two such editions appeared in the nineteenth century, under the editorship, respectively, of Giuseppe Ferrari and a lawyer by the name of Pomodoro.[2]

The absence of a Vichian academic tradition is not without significance; it indicates a certain faithfulness to the spirit of the philosopher, who had not entrusted to his university classes the best part of his message, but had diffused that message through private channels, either through epistolary correspondence or through personal contacts. Some acknowledgment came to him from remote regions, not from the "official" culture of his time.

Vico's presence in the work of Antonio Genovesi is constant, even if partial and scattered. We find traces of it as early as in Genovesi's celebrated *Ars logico-critica*, which appeared in 1745 but which was composed while Vico was still alive and Genovesi was a habitual visitor to his home. In the *Prolegomena* of that work, where, under Walchius' guidance he sketches the outlines of a history of logic and bars the possibility of an "Adamitic logic" referrable to the mentality of primitive peoples (such a primitive logic is an obvious product of the culture of the Enlightenment), Genovesi refers to the Vichian "conceit of the learned" (*boria dei dotti*), borrowing the quotation

Genovesi, who was Vico's disciple, held him always in greatest esteem; and in proportion as the influence of Genovesi's school spread through the other regions of Italy, Vico's reputation has grown. This indicates two things: (1) the fact that the school of Genovesi coincides with that of Vico; (2) the intellectual continuity between Vico and Genovesi."

[2] For these two editions, see *ibid.*, pp. 140–46.

from the 1730 edition of the *Scienza nuova seconda* in order to prove the absurdity of the very concept of primitive men capable of philosophizing and arguing according to the rules of logic.[3]

Although it may be true that Genovesi "did not draw essential nurture" from the *Scienza nuova*, as Franco Venturi authoritatively asserts, it is, however, indubitable that he never forgot his early reading of Vico. That reading was undertaken as early as 1737; twenty years later (apart from the admiring statements to be found in all the works of Genovesi), in his *Logic for Young People (Logica per i giovanetti)* (1766), Genovesi mentions the "conceit of the antiquaries, which prompts them to put into the mouths of the ancients all those things which none but present-day youth thinks, in order to congratulate themselves on their knowledge." And he continues, with a characteristic application of Vichian standards of interpretation: "When Homer says that Dawn and Sun are born in the morning from the Ocean, and at sunset they both plunge into it, what else does he mean but what he actually says? The literal meaning of such passages must be clung to; we should not seek for recondite significations, which are alien to the mentality of primitive times." One of Genovesi's problems is still that of antique myths, in the deciphering of which great philosophers like Bacon and Vico (not to speak of a notable number of mythologists, emblematographers, fabulists, and others) wore out their minds.

In the second edition of his *Logica italiana* also, Genovesi adopts the Vichian version of primitive mentality. Referring to fantasy, he states: ". . . it has often been said that the fantasy of ignorant nations is naturally poetical. It bestows on all the facts of men, on all the phenomena of nature, an expression, an aspect, a certain refracted light, which transmutes them; like lenses, which enlarge and distort the objects that are seen through them."

In the history of nations the place of fantasy is assigned by Genovesi (on the basis of Varro's partition) to three ages: the dark, the fabulous, and the historical. God, heroes, and men, therefore, find their speculative utilization in the intellectual world of Genovesi, who ascribes to the fabulous epoch not only the consolidation but also the deformation of religion, the most ancient of social institutions: "In every nation, the oldest institution is religion. Consequently, nothing has undergone more forcefully the impact of fantasy. Consider the great number of Egyptian, Greek, and Roman fables pertaining to deities, oracles, and miracles. When facts were lacking, impostors, in order to give foundations to those fables, invented them, and nations, whose fantasy was rough and coarse, magnified them."

[3] A. Genovesi, *Elementorum artis logico-criticae libri V* (Bassano, 1779), *Prolegomena,* sec. 13: "It is the practice of the *literati*, when seeking for the origins of some particular art, to start from Adam. This practice is scored by our Vico with an expressive turn of phrase: he calls it "scholarly presumptuousness." Genovesi's reference is to *Scienza nuova* (1730 ed.), bk. I.

It is obvious that the assessment of poetry is now profoundly changed. From the Vichian force, generative of uniform beliefs, apt to bolster the compactness of society, and capable of keeping it unaltered, poetry, under the influence of the Enlightenment, has turned into a power which disintegrates and corrupts the most genuine beliefs, and, consequently, even the society that created them. It is a shift of perspective to which attention should be drawn because it is indicative of the whole cultural climate of the Neapolitan school. In this school, the anticurialistic and masonic spirit is very strong and constant. It expresses itself, in the first place, through a vigorous and cogent critique of the traditions of folk religion, a critique which aims at discriminating between the credible and the incredible, at separating the necessary from the superfluous.

It seems clear that Genovesi, in order to carry out this critique, utilizes some elements of Vico's philosophy. Ancient fables, with their incongruities, become superstitions added to the original nucleus of beliefs; the fantasy of "coarse, uncouth nations," with their myths, becomes a power for the corruption and deformation of truth. Hercules, Prometheus, and Hermes Trismegistus are no longer the founders of primitive religions, but are now unmasked as contemptible quacks. Within this general framework some of the characteristic interests of Vico still put in an appearance: his concern for the etymological derivation of "poetical" terms, for the Homeric question, for the primitive and mythical world, for the lawless conditions of life. But the tone is changed; it takes on, now, a more precise political and social configuration, even though it does not decidedly overstep the bounds of orthodoxy.

The point of the Vichian doctrine which had stirred up the greatest perplexity among Catholic believers was the theory of the "feral roaming" (*erramento ferino*) of primitive mankind, with its natural corollary of the "poetical characters," which seemed to demand a revision of biblical hermeneutics and even to imply the denial of the historical existence of the great personalities of scriptural history. Even if Vico, by an act of prudence, had warned that his canons, valid for heathen mankind, did not hold for the Hebrews (a people beloved by God and therefore exempt from bestial degeneration), in reality the first image of Vico formed by his coevals and the men of the generation following his was that of a scholar bent on the exegesis of sacred and secular antiquity and on the demolition of established "*fulcra*," of traditional certainties of history, like the Law of the Twelve Tables. The controversy that arose from Vico's assumption of the *feral roaming* was opened by Lami and Damiano Romano; it reached its apex during the last years of Genovesi's life, between 1764 and 1768, when, in reply to the Vichian Duni, Finetti printed in Venice his famous *Apology for Mankind Accused of Having Once Been Bestial*. Under the Hellenized name of Filandro Misoterio (that is, lover of men and hater of beasts), Finetti impugned, on the basis of Scripture, the tenability of the thesis of feral roaming, even if limited to gentiles alone, and implicated in charges of heresy Vico's whole procedure: "... said manner of philosophizing by Vico is very handy for those who wish to utilize it in order to assail, or cast doubt upon, Sacred Scripture and Revelation. I am not making this charge without a foundation. Monsieur de Boulanger, one of the unbelievers of our time, who has made use of that hypothesis, backs up my indictment."

The preface of Finetti's *Apology*, entitled "Character of G. B. Vico," closes with a minute comparison of Vico's doctrines with those of Nicolas Boulanger, the French *libertin*. In that comparison, frequent references are made to Boulanger's *Researches on the Origin of Eastern Despotism* and to his biblical dissertation *On Elias and Enoch*.

These parallels are important because they allow us to perceive the true reasons behind the anti-Vichian controversy which took place in those years. When Franco Venturi writes that interest in Vico revived in Naples two decades after his death,[4] he hints at a renewed interest in the *feral roaming* affair, that is, at the formation of parties of *pro-ferals* and *anti-ferals*. Quite apart from any reference to the original Vichian texts, affiliation with the former party was equivalent to sharing the antireligious intellectual position of Boulanger. The thesis of the "primitive bestial monsters, naked in body and mind," became the battle flag of "erudite libertinism" simply because it was connected (in Boulanger, not in Vico) with the so-called theory of historical catastrophes. It was possible to see in it a "scientific" explanation of the rise and death of religions, the causes of which Boulanger, who was a geologist, sought in great terrestrial cataclysms, whereas Vico had traced the origins of religions to primitive man, to man conditioned by the Flood, by vegetation, by lightning, by caves, by wild beasts, but nevertheless to man spiritually active, capable of instincts, passions, feelings, volitions. Boulanger's impiety consisted, instead, in reducing man and his faculties to physical products, and religion to a cosmico-geological fact ascribable to the physical changes of the earth rather than to man's vicissitudes on earth.

The difference is essential. But the affinities were noticed more readily than the differences, so that Finetti, foreshadowing Galiani's charge, says that Boulanger could have plagiarized Vico: "it seems hard not to posit that the former may have profited from the latter, although their systems are quite different, and their goals still farther apart."[5]

---

[4] F. Venturi, ed., *Illuministi italiani: riformatori napoletani* (Ricciardi, 1962), in the collection *Storia e testi della letteratura italiana*. The assertion is repeated by Venturi at several points in his valuable introductions to the authors he presents. See also his "Boulanger e Vico," *L'antichità svelata e l'idea del progresso in N. A. Boulanger* (Bari, 1947), pp. 124–40.

[5] G. F. Finetti, *Difesa dell'autorità della sacra Scrittura*, ed. B. Croce (Bari: Laterza, 1936), p. 22.

The affinities between Boulanger and Vico are discovered by Finetti (and later by Mario Pagano) in the cyclical trend of historico-cosmic events, constellated and subdivided by great revolutions, which cause the human species to decline and nature to revert to its primordial waste. The last survivors of mankind take shelter in mountain caves from the threat of the ravenous wild beasts set into motion by earthquakes, fires, and other catastrophes. It was thus that the patriarchs of the surviving families chose a god as protector and sovereign ruler and traced directly to him their power to govern other men (*theocracy*). From the theocratic state two peoples arose, heroes and serfs (Vico calls them heroes and *famuli*); the former were descendants of the early sacerdotal leaders, the others, of the original plebeians (this is the name that Boulanger gives to them). The whole of civilization, and religion simultaneously, was born in this "lawless state." In the absence of law, injustice unchecked and supreme was everywhere rampant. The strongest oppressed the weak and forced them to accept their "civil" customs (that is, marriage in lieu of promiscuity, public administration of penalties instead of private revenge and retaliation; fear of the gods instead of blasphemous beastliness; burial of corpses instead of their abandonment to the ravages of wild beasts).

Mindful of the Vichian-rationalistic instruction imparted to him in Padua by his teacher Melchiorre Cesarotti, Foscolo sings, in *Sepolcri*:

> From the day when nuptials, law-courts, and altars
> caused the wild, bestial men of
> primeval times to feel compassion for themselves
> and their kin. . . .

An instrument of social erosion in the hands of the thinkers of the Enlightenment (had he not shown that civilization, so proudly vaunted, had originated in oppression and violence ?), Vico was naturally opposed by the anti-Rationalists and, in general, by all those who had been warned of the danger of overstepping the bounds of orthodoxy. Among the latter is Genovesi, who in his *Theology* (one of his writings that were submitted to ecclesiastical censorship),[6] and later in his *Diceosina* (Book II, chapter 1, sections 3–6), expressly rejects the thesis of the feral roaming, for the additional reason that he found it in an atheist like Lamettrie. The thesis, however, involved the whole "rationalistic" interpretation of Vico. It made use not only of the argument of the "monstrous primeval beings" but also of the theory of the spontaneous origin of language, of the barbaric recurrence of feudalism, of the cruelty of medieval institutions, of the "natural" origin of

---

[6] A. Genovesi, *Universae christianae theologiae elementa dogmatica-historica-critica*, bk. IV, chap. IV, of the posthumous edition published in Venice in 1771. This work, written in 1748, aroused a veritable storm of controversy against the author and wrecked his career as a theologian.

pagan religions, of the mythical meaning of monarchic theocracy, etc. Driv-
ing the discoveries of the *Scienza nuova* well beyond the intentions of Vico
(his indecision in regard to large ethico-social problems is well known),[7] the
thinkers of the Enlightenment subjected the *Scienza nuova* to a process of dis-
memberment, disengaging and developing those parts of the work which
best fitted their aims and disregarding the others. They were helped in
doing this (we should add) by the insufficient organicity of Vico's work.
The boldest ones went to the length of seeking in his work some support for
the principle of the natural equality of all men (a principle dear to the new
believers) and found it in the "poetical characters," who had redimensioned
and leveled in a popular way the great figures of secular history, and who
could be increased to include the best-known biblical figures. Boulanger
had shown what could be done by utilizing Vico's method. Under his
criticism, patriarchs and prophets, Hebrew judges and kings, were reduced
to astronomical symbols, or to metaphoric characters. As a result of this
treatment, the grandiose historico-mythological panorama of the *Scienza
nuova*, eroded and undermined by the new criticism, which remained something extraneous to it, was shattered and distorted into a multiplicity of
particular theses, each with its own polemical intent, which no longer
allowed an ensemble view, a synoptic glance. The best portion of Vico's
work, the speculative depth of some of its assertions, the poetic beauty of
some of its figurations and the typically Neapolitan vigor that animates
them—all this was gradually being disfigured under the disintegrating and
polemicizing action of writers who nevertheless (and rightly) are considered
to be the most outstanding Vichians of the post-Genovesi Neapolitan school:
Duni, Galiani, Pagano, Cuoco. It is unnecessary to use more than a few
words to illustrate their labors. In a treatment as schematic as the present
one, it will be enough to point them out as concisely as possible.

    1. Emanuele Duni, a jurist of Matera and professor at the Sapienza in
Rome, elaborated an *Essay on Universal Jurisprudence*, where, endeavoring to
investigate the common features of the "customs constantly practiced by the
most civilized nations," he utilizes, in a cosmopolitan sense, the connection
established by Vico between philosophy and philology, and ends by
emphatically reasserting the concept of Providence. It is Providence, in
Duni's view, which, starting at the deepest core of historical development,

---

[7] For such an evaluation, see Paolo Rossi's preface to his edition of *Opere di Vico*
(Milan: Rizzoli, 1961), although he places greater emphasis upon the traditionalist (or,
as he says, the "conservative and reactionary") aspect of Vico's culture. See, by Rossi
also, the preface to his anthology of Vico's writings entitled *Il pensiero di G. B. Vico*
(Turin, 1959), pp. xvi ff. Rossi's judgments have been vigorously called into question
by Nicola Badaloni at the end of his substantial volume *Introduzione al Vico* (Milan,
1959), which instead underscores Vico's aspects as an innovator. This duality of interpretation confirms the essential incertitude of Vico's thought in regard to the serious
problems of social ethics.

takes care of translating into the universal terms of "natural" law all those "barbaric legal practices, springing from coarse, rough, materialistic ideas, which, as time went on, gradually became less gross, and drew closer to the refinements of "natural equity."

From this viewpoint, which is obviously dominated by the Enlightenment's myth of a constant, unarrestable progress toward a goal of indefinite perfection, Duni utilizes the hypothesis of the "feral state" (which he strongly champions against Finetti) in order to bolster up his intention of showing how notable is the gap between the initial and the terminal point of progress, between the primitive, brutish stage of mankind and the civilization of "cultivated" nations. Duni's devotion to Vico was great. Vico had been his teacher in Naples, as is evinced by a letter from Duni to Bernardo Tanucci; Max Fisch quotes an excerpt from it.[8]

2. Ferdinando Galiani, somewhat skeptical as a philosopher, but a brilliant conversationalist in the intellectual salons of Paris, a strikingly gifted writer, is classed among the economists because of his *Treatise on Money*. In this work he shows the absurdity of assigning to economic value a conventional assessment rationally agreed upon by men. Appropriating Vico's argumentation against the social-contract theory, Galiani asks: Where was the agreement stipulated whereby it was decided that, from among all metals, gold and silver were to be held highest in value and hence to be coined into currency?

The barbarians who destroyed the Empire, and the Romans who were defending it, while they were stubborn enemies and antagonists in all other respects, were agreed on this point alone: that gold and silver should be rated as wealth. It is therefore obvious that whenever all men are agreed on a single opinion, and continue to agree on it for many centuries, we are not confronted with the deliberation of a conference held at the foot of the Tower of Babel or at the exit of Noah's ark. That agreement tells us that we are dealing with the perennial propensities of our intelligence and the intrinsic structures of physical reality. These are always identical, and they have been so in every age.

Here, Galiani paraphrases two of Vico's *degnità*: the one stating that "uniform ideas must have a common motive of truth," and the other, that "the nature of things is their *nascence* (their genesis) at certain times and in certain ways," as F. Nicolini and Giorgio Tagliacozzo have pointed out.[9]

---

[8] *The Autobiography of G. B. Vico*, translated from the Italian by Max H. Fisch and Thomas G. Bergin (Ithaca, N.Y.: Cornell University Press, 1948), contains a remarkable Introduction which features an account of *Vico's reputation and influence*. This rich and scholarly section has been amply utilized in Croce and Nicolini's *Bibliografia vichiana*, and constitutes the best contribution, in English, to our topic; for the dedicatory letter to Tanucci, see p. 63.

[9] F. Nicolini, *G. B. Vico e F. Galiani*, p. 159, cited by Giorgio Tagliacozzo in his *Economisti napoletani dei sec. XVII e XVIII* (Bologna, 1937), pp. xli and 126.

Galiani admits both Providence and the hypothesis of "feral roaming," but broadens both of these assumptions according to the world view of the Enlightenment:

Since, by the efforts of these ineffectual bodies of ours, we have, not without many hardships, managed to exchange that feral kind of existence in which we devoured one another, with this civilized tenor of life in which we live in peace and with normal intercourse, let us not allow them now, by an uncompromisingly rigorous exercise of pure intellect, to plunge us back into that barbarism from which, thanks to the benignity of Providence, we have happily escaped.[10]

Here Galiani seems to pray: "From the feral state deliver us, O Lord"; Vico's "reason fully unfolded" apparently is appealed to as if it were a synonym for the old transcendent God.

3. The *Political Essays* of Mario Pagano (1748–99), the outstanding jurist from Basilicata, are pragmatically Vichian inasmuch as they aim at "illustrating the philosophical history of nations and the mythology of poets." Next to Vico, Mario Pagano points out, one of his spiritual guides is Boulanger: "These researches, which are intended to make up a complete treatise of philosophical philology . . . will endeavor to carry to the furthest point of philosophical speculation the ideas of the immortal G. B. Vico, and will, moreover, rectify those of Pluche and Boulanger, while avoiding Boulanger's exaggerations."

The years between 1770 and 1780 in Naples witnessed the renewed favor of the Parisian engineer Boulanger, whose views had been so hotly debated in the circles of the *Encyclopédie*, and whose *L'antiquité dévoilée* (1766), published in a posthumous edition, had contributed to spreading the knowledge of his ideas among a wider readership.

The most outstanding minds of the time, such as Gaetano Filangieri, Francescantonio Grimaldi, Mario Pagano, and many others, strove to achieve some clarity in regard to a problem which had become the fashionable topic: Does the march of history follow a uniform, progressive course, or is such a course a pliant and cyclical one? An acquaintance with Boulanger caused some writers to lean toward the latter possibility, leading them to rediscover, through the idea of catastrophes, the cyclical view peculiar to ancient Platonism, a view which, to minds trained in the classical tradition, could not be altogether alien.

In Pagano, the cyclic view appears not *qua* pure idea but in all its terrifying material reality. The recollection of the tragic earthquake that devastated *Calabria ulteriore* (1783) (the first of Pagano's *Political Essays*, published in the ill-omened year of 1783, opens with an extended reference to that disaster)

[10] F. Galiani, *Della moneta*, chap. II, cited by Tagliacozzo in *Economisti napoletani*, p. 104. The invocation to be found in the text is addressed to the "clever" despisers of the "natural" tendencies of men; i.e., it assails the conceited attitude of the thinkers of the Enlightenment.

is still, in the Vichian mode, portrayed as the product of a universal uniformity of feelings and judgment vis-à-vis the repetition, in that land, of events so charged with alarms and fears. The Calabrian earthquake, on the other hand, is openly assessed, in Boulanger's fashion, as one of those "memorable physical catastrophes of the earth" which perpetuate in the hearts of men the fear of divine wrath: "While men, transfixed by terror, saw whole cities collapsing, the earth writhing and shaking, mountains coming down in ruins, the soil cracking into horrendous crevices, no idea was uppermost in their perturbed minds but that of universal doom. They could not help thinking of a catastrophe in which the whole of nature was being dissolved, and a wrathful and vengeful God was exacting penalties for sins committed by mortal creatures."[11]

Reverting to the problem of the fables (myths) of antiquity, Pagano explains them as "popular errors of the ancients" (precisely as the young Leopardi did later), brought about by a "moral perturbation of the human soul." The assumption derives from Boulanger. Fables are "physical phenomena, altered by the human mind when a veil of terror or of ignorance darkens it."

Terror and ignorance are now coupled. The emotional perturbation is accounted for by the ineptitude of the mind. Nothing more is needed for the transformation of Vico into a Rationalist viewing fables as the contaminated products of sheer "mental penury" and of cultural obscurantism. Ignorant savages, foolish enough to worship the forces of nature, are now being superimposed on Vico's "huge brutes" (*bestioni*), grossly sensual, but endowed with generous impulses and noble passions. Those foolish savages do not even deserve the appellative of "men," "inasmuch as the name of man cannot be given to that repulsive, beastlike being, who, naked and alone, covered only by his shaggy hair, armed with a sturdy club, roams through the forests, horridly bellowing, and showing in his witless, insentient face, the profound torpor of his soul."

We can therefore understand Pagano's rejection of the "feral roaming" (a rejection attributable, perhaps, to Pagano's contacts with Francescantonio Grimaldi), and his liking, instead, of Saturn's mythical epoch, when all men were equal and equally enjoyed the products of the earth. At the end of his description of the earthquake of 1783, he remarks that the Calabrians, rich and poor, noble and lowborn, found themselves all united and equal in the face of that disaster, and were forced to begin their lives again from a zero point, according to the iron law of cyclical alternation, by which a concentrative force forthwith replaces a diffusive one in a ceaseless consecutive relay. Undoubtedly Pagano had found such an explanation in his second master, Antonio Genovesi.[12]

[11] See the pages devoted to Pagano in Franco Venturi's *Illuministi italiani*.

[12] This concept underwent a notable development in Genovesi's last works, i.e., in his

4. From the quasi-Jacobin Vico of Pagano to the nationalist Vico of Vincenzo Cuoco, there is a rather longish step; but that step is taken within a few years, under the immediate influence of the tragic failure of the Neapolitan revolution of 1799. The differences are clear. Cuoco drew from Vico those elements which distinguish the national *Risorgimento* from the French Revolution, which the Neapolitan patriots had taken as a model. He began that exclusion of transalpine philosophers which characterizes nineteenth-century Italian philosophy, bent on an autonomous elaboration of a concept of revolution that would not implicate or threaten traditional institutions. For Cuoco, Vico is the originator of that historicism which Croce and Gentile will theorize later, and from the viewpoint of which it is said so often that the constitution given to the Parthenopean Republic by the Neapolitan Jacobins was fundamentally wrong, because it had been patterned on the French constitutional order, while the particular requirements of the *Mezzogiorno* were thoroughly disregarded. Cuoco's Vico is, pre-eminently, the author of the sociology of the two peoples, a thinker for whom history is never the creation of the lowest stratum of the population (the plebeians), but, instead, is the work of a minority. It is this minority, according to Cuoco, which, under any form of government, heads that government and exercises the leadership of the nation. It is the minority of the intellectually and economically strong, of those most capable, by training and preparation, to play the role of leader. In the *Scienza nuova* this minority is called *famiglie dei figliuoli* (the clan of legitimate descendants), in order to distinguish it from the class of the *famuli* (serfs). It is this minority, finally, which had the power to determine throughout the centuries the destiny of Naples. It was this class which had been hopelessly disregarded by the leaders responsible for drafting the Parthenopean constitution. These men had sought a political structure valid for all *mankind*, with no distinction between nations; they were, therefore, guilty of the rationalistic fallacy, and had fallen victims to a utopia which had soon turned into a tragedy.

After his *Essay on the Parthenopean Revolution of 1799* (published in 1801), Cuoco wrote *Plato in Italy* (1803–6), where Neapolitan events are portrayed as if they had already happened in the cities of *Magna Graecia*, and where Jacobin theories are put in the mouths of the ringleaders of that time. More

---

Logica, Diceosina, and *Lezioni di commercio.* Here is an excerpt from his *Logica italiana* (1766), par. XXIII:

There are two mutually antithetical forces in the human heart. The physicists call them *centripetal* and *centrifugal*: I shall call them *concentrative* and *diffusive*. The concentrative force (i.e., self-love) causes us to strive to gather everything to ourselves; the diffusive, instead, impels us to give everything to others. Each of these two forces, whenever it operates in separation from the other, destroys man. The concentrative force, acting alone, detaches man from the species and isolates him, whereas man is an animal incapable of living in solitude, Diffusive force, acting alone, detaches him from himself, bringing about his annihilation. Man's happiness, therefore, lies in the harmonization of those two forces.

than elsewhere, in this work Vico is merely a pretext for expounding anti-democratic theories, as was the case with Joseph de Maistre, the French reactionary whom Cuoco had taken as guide in his studies of Vico's works.

Cuoco must also be charged with the paternity of, and the responsibility for, that Vichian interpretation which makes of him the forerunner of theories subsequent to him, particularly those of romanticism. I am referring to the image of Vico as the discoverer of modern aesthetics and the "initiator of nineteenth-century philosophical historiography," as Croce describes him. This interpretation reached Croce (as well as Nicolini, Croce's follower) through Bertrando Spaventa. Spaventa gave it firm status by underpropping it with his theory of the circulation of Italian thought within nineteenth-century European thought. In order to place him in spiritual communication and material contact with literary men like Francesco de Sanctis, historians like Niebuhr and Mommsen, jurists like Savigny, and philosophers like Fichte and Hegel, Vico was catapulted into the century subsequent to the one in which he lived, and was in this way made to appear utterly "antihistorical." The "guiding thread" of this interpretation is to be found in anti-Jacobinism and nationalism, two political and philosophical currents which, from Cuoco, through the *Risorgimento* and the period of Italian unity, reach as close to us as Croce's and Gentile's time. Insofar as Vichian studies are concerned, this interpretation, after the decline of idealism in Italy, was unmasked as being evidently and substantially baseless. Such an interpretation not only failed to lead Vichian studies back into their right channel (this channel being the endeavor to "situate" Vico's work within the framework of the Neapolitan culture of the eighteenth century) but also made a notable contribution to deflecting such studies from that line of research, by setting up Vico as a sort of collective emblem, or patriotic banner, uncollapsible through the changes of centuries and the vicissitudes of the nation. Thus Vico became the symbol of the best spiritual characteristics of the Italian people, the testimonial of its imperishable genius. This conclusion, where the premonitory signs of Gioberti's *Primato* are already present, was ultimately to result in the praise of fascism and to crash in ruins after its downfall.

A notable thrust in this direction was given to Vichian studies by the French, who, following in the footsteps of Michelet, included Vico in the ranks of the Romantic philosophers of history, together with Herder (although in antagonism to him). The most salient characteristics of that interpretation (which reached its apex in Flint's famous monograph) and the historical reasons accounting for it have been studied by Alain Pons. In Pons' essay (see pp. 165–85) the readers of this volume will find the basic "leads" enabling them to follow the growth of Vico's influence in the Italo-French nineteenth century, starting with the diaspora of the Neapolitan patriots fleeing the Bourbon political reaction in southern Italy, and tracing, in separate lines, the vicissitudes of the "Cisalpine" Vichians after Marengo (1800). These Cisalpine Vichians were the transmission channels of Vico's thought to Milan and northern Italy (at the beginning of the nineteenth century there was published in Milan an edition of Vico's works in three volumes), and, subsequently, from these regions to foreign countries. An exile, Gioacchino de' Prati, acted as an intermediary between the Cisalpine Vichians and Coleridge and other non-Italian Romanticists. A similar role was performed by another exile, Pietro de Angelis, in regard to Michelet and Cousin.

The insertion of Vico's name among the "philosophers of history" gave rise to a misinterpretation of his philosophy which has lasted until the present. Because of this misinterpretation, Vico was believed to have concentrated his attention mainly on the investigation of the causes and the trends of progress, according to the fashion introduced by the Anglo-Scottish sociologists and historians, such as Ferguson, Priestley, Robertson, and Hume, for whom a study of the topic of progress constituted a necessary prelude to any treatise on historiography. In reality, however, Vico's *Scienza nuova* is something more than, and something substantially different from, a speculative introduction to historiography, and it is strongly doubted that a theory of progress is to be found there.[13]

The intermediary agent between Vico and the Scottish philosophical school was a work by the Marquis de Chastellux entitled *On Public Happiness, or Considerations on the Lot of Men in the Different Historical Epochs* (1772). A translation of this book, published in Naples ten years later, caused Cuoco to state, with evident exaggeration: "Chastellux has understood the theories of Vico better than anyone else."

David Hume introduced Chastellux and his crypto-Vichianism into Scotland. From then on it seemed as if the vogue of Vico would keep step with that of the Scottish writers. Michelet, at the time when he was working on his translation (which bears the title of *Principles of the Philosophy of History*), read Ferguson's and Priestley's works. Some passages of the former's *Essay on the History of Civil Society* (1767) have been profitably compared by Professor Max Fisch with some ideas of Vico's. Fisch would like to place Ferguson among the *animae naturaliter vicianae*.[14]

Italians found Michelet's translation more easily comprehensible than the original, and the label, tacked onto Vico, of "philosopher of progress and history," circulated successfully throughout the nineteenth century. This

[13] See the luminous and acute discussion by Nicola Abbagnano, prefixed to his edition of the *Scienza nuova e opere scelte di Vico* (Turin: UTET, 1952, 1962), based on the rightful conviction of the necessity of retrieving the whole of Vico beyond any partial interpretation. The unity of Vico's thought is seen to consist in the vindication of human freedom; this excludes the inevitability of "progress" in the idealistic-romantic sense. Abbagnano's Introduction is followed by an extensive bibliographical note by Paolo Rossi.

[14] Fisch and Bergin, *Autobiography*, p. 82.

took place thanks to what we may call a process of rebounding, by which Vichianism sprang back to Italy through the action of the great *Risorgimento* patriots, who had lived for many years in foreign countries most deeply saturated with Romantic culture. The Vico whom these men reintroduced into their home country, prior to and after unity, had been stripped of all Neapolitan elements, but had acquired a great many European features, at a time when "European" was synonymous with "Romantic." The fact of having among their greatest writers a "Romanticist" like Vico, whom some even considered as one of "patriarchs" of romanticism, was naturally a ground of pride for those patriots, who, during their stay abroad, had not failed to assert the "parity" of their national culture vis-à-vis the foreign ones.

The formula of Vico, the "glory of our nation," which had originated outside of Italy, was adopted with favor by the *Risorgimento* writers. Through Claude Fauriel, that formula reached Manzoni, who made use of it in a parallel between Vico and Muratori, which can be read in his *Longobardic History in Italy.*[15] It was, furthermore, taken over by Mazzini, Tommaseo, and Pasquale Stanislao Mancini.[16] It was, more than by any other writer, exploited by Gioberti, who gave currency to the image of Vico as investigator of the most ancient linguistic and poetic Italian wisdom, to be linked with the uninterrupted tradition of a "pious philosophy" harking back to the humanistic-Platonic trend. Gioberti thus becomes the immediate source of an ontological exegesis of Vico's thought which has its own history, made up of reiterated appearances, and which is advocated by Carabellese, Giusso, and, recently, by Augusto del Noce.[17]

This exegesis emphasizes the religious, Catholic (but not in a Thomistic sense) character of Vico's thought and relates, in a way, to the other Catholic interpretation, that is, to the official Scholastic one, typified by names like Emilio Chiocchetti and Franco Amerio.

Nor does Carlo Cattaneo (1801–69), author of a wonderful essay *Sulla Scienza nuova di Vico* (written at first as a critical notice of Giuseppe Ferrari's edition), escape the Romantic suggestion, which by this time had become universally accepted. In Vico's work he sees nothing less than "a science of all histories, thanks to which we are exempted from the obligation of keeping strict tab on epochs and places." The *Scienza nuova* is "an analysis of the growth of the human mind in historical perspective." It shows, taking its

[15] A. Manzoni, *Opere varie* (Milan, 1845), chap. II, pp. 168–71.

[16] For all these writers, see Croce and Nicolini, *Bibliografia vichiana, s.v.* their respective names. In regard to P. S. Mancini, see his *Saggi sulla nazionalità*, ed. Flavio Lopez de Oñate (Rome: Sestante, 1944), pp. 18–21.

[17] For Gioberti, see Croce and Nicolini, *Bibliografia vichiana*. For the Neo-Platonic interpretation, see Lorenzo Giusso, *La tradizione ermetica nella filosofia italiana* (Rome: Bocca, n.d.), pp. 141–79. Giusso is also the author of a much criticized volume, *La filosofia di G. B. Vico e l'età barocca* (Rome: Perrella, 1943).

point of departure from the beastlike state postulated by the jusnaturalists, how mankind has finally reached a stage "where mutual help is possible, and humans are able, through civilized institutions, to foil the aims of reciprocal egoism."[18] We perceive in these words the echo of Romagnosi and Beccaria (both of whom were conversant with Vico) and, in general, the dominating presence of that problem of human civilization which had perplexed the English utilitarians: how to reconcile the enjoyment of the maximum happiness possible for the greatest number with the guarantee of the maximum social security possible for all. From Hobbes to Locke, and from Beccaria to Bentham and the two Mills, this problem had a long history; but Vico failed to tackle it, because the political state was envisaged by him as the outcome of selfish drives curbed not by human reason but by the providence of God. That difficulty (on which the utilitarians found themselves stranded) of discovering a way whereby private utility could be transmuted into public advantage must have seemed to Vico to have been solved at the very outset by his system. Cattaneo, however, trained in the climate of the northern Enlightenment, and being very sensitive to the problem of public welfare, is aware of that difficulty and transfers it to Vico: "Thus Vico fused the doctrine of personal advantage, which stands out in Machiavelli, with the doctrine of reason, emphasized by Grotius, and eliminated the contradiction which separated history from philosophy," by causing truth to coincide with fact, and by developing the formula of the *verum ipsum factum* in a positivistic sense.

The "philosophy of history" of the Positivists (to which Cantoni and Siciliani contributed, mainly with their Vichian studies)[19] is distinguished from the Romantic and idealistic trend by this feature: it is more intensely attuned to rationality and to antimetaphysical scientism. Positivism accepts history to the extent that, enlightened by science and washed clean of superstition, history becomes indicative of true civilization, placing public welfare ahead of selfish private interest. Positivistic theory assumes that history brought about this result through the intrinsic power of better institutions, and by no means through the agency of a hypothetical Providence or in the name of religion. There is nothing Vichian, as the reader can see, about this conclusion.

It was Croce's task to do away with the philosophy of history *qua* idealistic-positivistic pseudoscience. He denied that the grandiose pattern of the *Scienza nuova* may be viewed as "a universal history philosophically narrated," that "the *provident* deity may be raised to the status of a *progredient* deity," that the *corsi e ricorsi* may be conceived of as "the internal rhythm of progress." He opposed this opinion by setting against it the religiosity of Vico, who asserts the freedom of fallen man together with the presence

---

[18] For Cattaneo, see Croce and Nicolini, *Bibliografia vichiana.*
[19] For these, too, *ibid.*

of God's grace. Furthermore, Croce was firmly convinced that the representation of the *Scienza nuova* as a philosophy of history is sharply disavowed
by the apologetic purpose of the work. It was Vico's intent to settle the
strife between Hebrew and gentile history, between scriptural and secular
narrative, by showing to what extent sacred history could be attested to by
its secular antitype. Whether such critical objections are part and parcel of
"what is alive" or "what is dead" in Croce's thoughts concerning Vico, I
shall leave to another contributor to decide.

A conspectus of post-Crocean studies on Vico has been skillfully and
serviceably compiled by Paolo Rossi.[20] But I should like to close by noting
that, if one can discern positions analogous to those of Vico in pragmatism,
German historicism, the philosophy of symbolic forms, Marxism, and phenomenology, and in other currents that did not really originate in the main
line of Vichianism,[21] clearer and more obvious analogies are to be seen in a
tendency in current Italian philosophy which, on the contrary, has inherited
the best aspects of the Vichian tradition and which is, in a certain sense, the
finest fruit of the recent, most authoritative Vichian criticism, of the criticism
of Crocean thought, and of some fundamental aspects of modern philosophy.
I refer to the concept of "philosophy as historical knowledge" (or "neo-
Vichianism") which has been distilled in the many distinguished works of
Eugenio Garin on the Renaissance and the Enlightenment,[22] articulated in
a volume carrying this title,[23] and which has influenced the work of other
Italian thinkers profoundly.[24] In Garin's hands, Vichianism has been treated
as what it should have always remained, namely, a canon of historico-critical
interpretation, which (outside any preconceived and rigid metaphysical
schema) serves to identify (as Garin has done in a masterful way) the continuity and the imperishable potentialities of the rhetorical-juridical tradition
so typical of Italian thought.[25]

Translated by Elio Gianturco

[20] See *I classici italiani nella storia della critica*, ed. Walter Binni (Florence, 1961), II.
Paolo Rossi's *Lineamenti di storia della critica vichiana* is a much more objective and
impartial work than the repeatedly quoted *Bibliografia vichiana* by Croce and Nicolini,
whose judgments are wholly conditioned by the "classical" Crocean exegesis.

[21] On these currents, see Part IV of this symposium.

[22] A synthesis of these studies can be found in Garin's *Storia della filosofia italiana*, new
ed. (Turin: Einaudi, 1966).

[23] See Garin's *La filosofia come sapere storico* (Bari: Laterza, 1959).

[24] P. Piovani, "Il pensiero filosofico meridionale tra la nuova scienza e la 'Scienza
nuova,'" *Atti della Accademia di Scienze Morali e Politiche della Società Nazionale di Scienze,
Lettere, e Arti in Napoli*, 70 (1959): 66–95; *Filosofia e storia delle idee* (Bari: Laterza,
1965); and "Totalismo, idealismo, conoscere storico," *De Homine*, nos. 11–12, pp.
99–118.

[25] On this aspect of Italian thought, see the essay by Grassi in this symposium and an
important German study, not cited by Grassi, by Theodor Viehweg, *Topik und Jurisprudenz*, 2d ed. (Munich: J. C. Beck, 1963), Italian trans. *Topica e giurisprudenza* (Milan:
Giuffré, 1962), the first chapter of which is inspired by Vico.

Alain Pons   VICO AND
                                   FRENCH THOUGHT

Let me at once dispel the ambiguities that the rather vague title of the
present essay may occasion: it is not my purpose to inquire into the French
sources of Vico's thought; I merely intend to deal with the reception of
Vico's *work* in France, with the contribution that France has made to a better
knowledge of it, and with the influence which that work may have exerted
on French thought. Even thus limited, the topic is too big to be treated
with the amplitude desirable within the framework that is available to me
here, while, on the other hand, the history of Vico's reputation in France has
already been studied as a whole by Croce and Nicolini, in their indispensable
Bibliografia vichiana, and by Paul Hazard.[1] I will therefore endeavor
primarily to trace the main stages of the diffusion of Vico's thought in
France, and to raise some questions concerning the causes which may have
favored or hindered that diffusion. It will be my task to underline some
particularly significant aspects and to lay stress upon some writers for whom
the reading of Vico had a real importance and who have contributed new
and momentous interpretations of his theories. Hence I will refrain from
any attempt at establishing a check list of all those writers who may have
quoted the name of the Neapolitan philosopher.[2]

A further preliminary remark is in order. It was long ago remarked that
Vico's status in the history of thought is that of an unacknowledged pioneer
whose genius-like anticipations have been picked up again and developed at
a much later time and in a thoroughly independent fashion. Hence there
exist some "ideal" comparisons with other thinkers, some parallels which
have actually been set up, or remain to be set up, and which are often

[1] Paul Hazard, "La pensée de Vico," pt. III: "Son influence sur la pensée française,"
Revue des cours et conférences, December, 1931. On the same problem, see the more
succinct but stimulating remarks by Max H. Fisch in the Introduction to his and Bergin's
translation of Vico's *Autobiography* (Ithaca, N.Y.: Cornell University Press, 1944) and
those of Isaiah Berlin in his "The Philosophical Ideas of G. B. Vico," offprint from *Art
and Ideas in 18th Century Italy* (Rome: Edizioni di Storia e Letteratura, 1960), IV.

[2] For a complete bibliography on this topic, I refer the reader to B. Croce and F.
Nicolini's *Bibliografia vichiana . . .* , 2 vols. (Naples, 1947–48). I shall give only a few
bibliographical pointers on the major studies that I have used, and particularly on those
not mentioned by Croce and Nicolini because of their recent publication date.

justified and fertile. In contrast, I prefer to take here a strictly historical viewpoint. In the balance sheet which I am about to draw up, I will take into account only authors whose works attest beyond the shadow of a doubt that they actually read Vico and, in one way or another, were affected by that reading.

Why should I insist on this seemingly obvious precaution? Because the study of Vico's reputation in eighteenth-century France involves vexing problems. If, in point of fact, one adheres to the restrictive viewpoint which I have just specified, he is compelled to admit that Vico remains almost totally unknown in France as late as the last years of that century. During Vico's lifetime, if we except the notice devoted to the *De universi iuris uno principio* and the book review of the *De constantia philologiae* published in 1722 at Amsterdam by Jean Leclerc (1657–1736) in his *Bibliothèque ancienne et moderne*, we can point out only a short allusion to the *Scienza nuova prima*, in the *Memoires de Trevoux* of 1727, and a quotation by P. N. Bonamy in his dissertation *Sur l'origine de la Loi des XII Tables* (1735). We must wait until 1772 in order to find in Chastellux's *De la félicité publique* a reference to Vico, who is spoken of as the author of a "paradoxical" thesis on the origins of Rome. Let us add Court de Gébelin (1725–84) and his *Monde primitif* (1774), which ranges Vico among the "allegoristic interpreters" of mythology, and the list of explicit citations is at an end. One could stick to this meager balance sheet and at once attempt to summarize the reasons for the almost total ignorance of eighteenth-century France in regard to the Neapolitan philosopher, who, in the rare texts where he is spoken of, appears only as a learned jurisconsult, responsible for certain bold theories concerning the initial period of Roman history. It is, however, impossible not to tackle a question which was posited long ago: Did eighteenth-century French philosophers plagiarize, plunder, or, at least, extensively borrow from Vico's works without acknowledging their debt? This charge, in fact, has often been brought forth, particularly in Italy, and, above all, in the first half of the nineteenth century. Montesquieu, it seems, was the first to be accused; but Predari, in the Introduction to his edition of the *Scienza nuova* (1835), ranks beside him, among Vico's plagiarists, President de Brosses, D'Alembert, and Rousseau (besides Hume, Reid, Bentham, and Jacobi). Gennaro Rocco, in his *Elogio del Vico* (1844), adds to this list the names of the materialists D'Holbach and Helvétius. Condillac, Turgot, Condorcet, are not exempt from the same suspicion, nor is, in particular, Boulanger, who is supposed to have "stolen" from Vico, if we trust a letter sent by Galiani to Tanucci in 1766. The whole of eighteenth-century French philosophy is thus obviously accused of having found in Vico a source of unacknowledged inspiration.

Set forth in such extreme form, the thesis is indefensible. Even in an epoch when the sense of copyright was less developed than it is today, it was impossible (unless one is willing to admit the existence of a vast conspiracy whose reasons are not perceptible) that some writers, otherwise quite scrupulous in the mention of their sources, should have swerved from their honesty to the detriment of Vico alone.   In fact, in the allegations of Predari and Rocco one should make allowance for a certain spirit of national re-vindication, and, moreover, for the irresistible tendency that drives all admirers of Vico to find his ideas everywhere, and to atone for the injustice of posterity in regard to his great unrecognized genius.   On the other hand, if certain comparisons are unjustifiable, others seem defensible; and, without attempting to discover out-and-out plagiarisms, it seems worthwhile to inquire whether some traces of Vico's influence may be found in certain eighteenth-century French works, without hiding from oneself the hazardous character of such an undertaking.   Indeed, how are we to produce proof substantiating the assumption of an influence, when such influence is unadmitted or is not authenticated by irrefutable textual coincidences? Most of the incriminated authors may have heard Vico spoken of, since relationships between France and Italy were close enough, and Vico's renown was sufficiently widespread in Italy (Montesquieu, Condillac, De Brosses, and Rousseau traveled through Italy; and it is generally admitted that Galiani was the ambassador [an unfortunate one, as we will shortly see] of Vico's thought).   Nevertheless, the fact that an influence is possible does not prove that it is real.   In order to proceed further we must resort to internal criteria, bring out profound similarities in the problem treated, in the method employed, in the general spirit of the works.   But how, in that case, do we avoid subjective and unverifiable appreciations and risky con-jectures?

The case of Montesquieu is characteristic.   Montesquieu traveled through Italy, spent some time in Naples, and, according to Paul Hazard,[3] owned a copy of the 1725 *Scienza nuova*.   Did he read it, or did some Vichian ideas reach him through the intermediation of Paolo Mattia Doria, as Chaix-Ruy assumes?[4]   The reading of Montesquieu's works does not force an affirmative answer.   The comparison between Montesquieu and Vico, whose minds were nurtured by the same authors, but nevertheless reveal a different inspiration, is of the greatest interest; but it is undoubtedly fruitless to attempt to find, come what may, traces of the influence of the *Scienza nuova* in the *Esprit des lois*.

The same thing holds for the alleged impact of Vico's linguistic theory on Condillac.   The *Essai sur l'origine des connaissances humaines* presents some detailed similarities to Vichian theses, particularly in regard to the origin of language, writing, and poetry, but the philosophical presuppositions of the

[3] "La pensée de Vico," p. 130.
[4] J. Chaix-Ruy, "Montesquieu et J. B. Vico," *Revue philosophique de la France et de l'étranger*, 1947.

two writers have nothing in common. As Folkierski has shown,[5] we must go back to Warburton and to his *Essay on Hieroglyphics* in order to find the source of Condillac.

It is furthermore to Warburton and to Condillac, not to Vico, that the primary inspiration of Charles de Brosses' *Traité de la formation mécanique des langues et des principes physiques de l'étymologie* (1765), as well as that of Rousseau's *Essai sur l'origine des langues* (1770), must be referred. As for the *Discours sur l'origine de l'inégalité* and the *Contrat social*, F. Nicolini excludes (after first having admitted it) that Rousseau may have come into contact, in Venice, with Vico's work, during 1743-44, when he was secretary to the French ambassador Montaigu. Is it necessary, on the other hand, to insist on the radically different conceptions of Rousseau and Vico in regard to the origin and evolution of society, to mankind's primitive conditions, to the idea of a social contract?[6]   Did Vico have an influence on French materialists, and particularly on the D'Holbach circle? Here it is not a question of knowing that a certain naturalism, even materialism, may not be the "veritable message" of Vichianism; from Finetti to Badaloni, there is no lack of interpretations in this sense, but that is a problem of a different kind.

The reading of D'Holbach's texts allows us to pick out some very superficial analogies to Vico; and these analogies can be explained through sources common to both, that is, through Epicurus and Hobbes.[7]   The case of N. A. Boulanger is more perplexing. Boulanger's *Despotisme oriental* (1761) and his *L'antiquité dévoilée* cause us to think irresistibly of certain passages of the *Scienza nuova*.   Vico and Boulanger possess the same dramatic sense of the obscure origins of mankind; and Boulanger, who was a geologist, gives ample space to the theme of natural cataclysms that cause the emergence of religions. However, as Frank E. Manuel says, "while for Vico the creation of a religious idea became the guiding force in man's self-humanization, for Boulanger the birth of false terrors of the next world and the wasteful devotion of the whole of life to a contemplation of doom was the great pall which had descended upon mankind."[8]   Galiani claims that Boulanger "stole" from Vico, but, in fact, there is no evidence that he read him, or that he even knew his name.[9]   F. Nicolini and J. Chaix-Ruy nevertheless

[5] W. Folkierski, *Entre le classicisme et le romantisme* (Krakow-Paris, 1925). Did Warburton feel Vico's influence? *Bibliografia vichiana* leans toward a negative answer.

[6] F. Nicolini, "Vico et Rousseau," *Revue de littérature comparée*, 10 (1930). On Rousseau's sources see R. Derathé, *J. J. Rousseau et la science politique de son temps* (Paris, 1950).

[7] Frank E. Manuel, *The Eighteenth Century Confronts the Gods* (Cambridge: Harvard University Press, 1959).

[8] *Ibid.*, p. 221.

[9] J. Chaix-Ruy, in his study "Un disciple heterodoxe de Jean-Baptiste Vico: Nicolas Boulanger," *Revue de littérature comparée*, 21 (1947), asserts that Boulanger must certainly have known the ideas of Vico through Abbé Galiani. But Galiani did not

affirm that there was a direct influence.[10]   Personally, I lean toward the contrary opinion, like F. Venturi,[11] J. Hampton,[12] and F. E. Manuel,[13] who emphasize the totally different inspirations which actuate the two works.

And here we must speak of what may well be called "the myth of Galiani" as a Vichian propagandist in France.   As a young man, Galiani knew Vico; and, although he almost never refers to him in his works, Vico's spirit permanently impregnates them.   Thus it has often been assumed that, during his stay in France, Galiani fervently pleaded the cause of his great compatriot in the philosophical *salons* of which he was a guest (that of Madame d'Epinay, for instance, and that of Madame Geoffrin) and that he frequently spoke of Vico to his friends Diderot, D'Holbach, and Helvétius. The assumption is likely to be correct, but the results of such propaganda are (we must admit) hard to discern.   One point seems to be well established, and it is that Galiani's ideas on economics (ideas which evince Vichian inspiration) strongly influenced those of Turgot, as G. Tagliacozzo has shown.[14]   On the other hand, Condorcet's philosophy of history, as well as Turgot's, seems to owe nothing to Vico.   Characterized as they are by the idea of uninterrupted progress, these intellectualistic and optimistic philosophies are less concerned with the problem of the origin than with the problem of the future of human institutions.   As we shall see, during the Romantic epoch this typically French conception of history, taken up again and elaborated by Saint-Simon and Auguste Comte, was compared with, and even opposed to, that of Vico; but nothing indicates that, at the outset, it owed anything to Vico's thought.[15]

While not excluding the possibility that new documents may be discovered, we can venture to affirm, then, that the assumption maintaining that eighteenth-century France drew unacknowledged inspiration from Vico does not survive serious scrutiny.   It should be added that this assumption is paradoxical, since it stems from critics who depict Vico as an enemy of the Enlightenment *avant la lettre*, representing him as an antirationalist too deeply imbued with historism to be understood by a century devoid of historical

---

arrive in Paris before the beginning of 1759, barely a few months before Boulanger's death; Boulanger had written his *L'antiquité dévoilée* several years earlier.

[10] Croce and Nicolini, *Bibliografia vichiana*.

[11] Franco Venturi, *L'antichità svelata e l'idea del progresso in N. A. Boulanger* (Bari, 1947).

[12] John Hampton, *N. A. Boulanger et la science de son temps* (Geneva-Lille, 1955).

[13] Manuel, *The Eighteenth Century*.

[14] Giorgio Tagliacozzo, *Economisti napoletani dei sec. XVII e XVIII* (Bologna, 1937); see also Umberto Segre, "Il pensiero economico nell' illuminismo italiano," in *La cultura illuministica in Italia*, ed. Mario Fubini (Edizioni Radio Italiana, 1964).

[15] On this French philosophy of history see particularly Frank E. Manuel, *The Prophets of Paris* (Cambridge: Harvard University Press, 1962).

sense.   Is it not contradictory to claim that the French philosophy of the Enlightenment was incapable of understanding Vico, while contending, at the same time, that it derived its inspiration from him?

In order to answer this question, we must undoubtedly revise our long-prevailing traditional conception of the eighteenth century.   This century, as we are beginning to see, was not as ignorant of history as the succeeding century claimed it to be.   On the contrary, the eighteenth century, especially its second half, was haunted by the problem of the historical origins of societies, of social institutions, religions, laws, languages, and it strove to un-tangle these phenomena by means of the interpretation of myths.   We know that it is in the *Scienza nuova* that this problem of origins is posited for the first time, no longer out of a pure concern for erudition, but in the frame-work of a global perspective, historical and philosophical at the same time. From this viewpoint the numerous comparisons that have been made be-tween Vico's work and the productions of eighteenth-century French philosophers become perfectly understandable.   On the other hand, how could these philosophers have failed to acknowledge Vico as one of their own, have failed to quote him or even to read him?   Let us admit a quota of chance, a factual ignorance caused by the relative geographic and intellectual distance of Naples.   It is nevertheless striking to find that those who heard Vico mentioned, and even those rarer ones who read him, did not realize his importance, and saw in him only the representative of a long progeny of Neapolitan jurisconsults.   We must, then, in spite of all, revert to the image so often evoked, from Cuoco to Croce, of Vico as a thinker born "out of his time," as a misfit in his century, both belated and precursory, alien to the spirit which became that of the century of the Enlightenment.   I stated that such an image is grossly inadequate because it underrates a whole aspect of eighteenth-century thought.   The century of the Enlightenment was not un-aware of history nor of the irrational powers hidden in man's soul; but it is nevertheless a fact that the eighteenth century did not see (and, without a doubt, could not see) in Vico the philosopher, in the deepest meaning of this term, one who established an essential link between history and philosophy and opened up a new epistemological domain.   Vico has a very strong sense of the necessity and positivity of each historical moment viewed as a stage in the development of man *qua* totality, that is, union of body and mind.   The past, therefore, is not for him the place where errors and illusions originate, as it is for the Cartesian and intellectualistic tradition, which is essentially critical, pre-eminently committed to the present, and oriented toward the future.   Neither is the past, for him, the depository of absolute truth or of sacred tradition, as religious orthodoxy and social and political conservatism claim it to be.   The past does not crystallize, for Vico, the dreams of a lost innocence, as it does for Rousseau.   Opposing the main currents of thought which dominate the eighteenth century, Vico upholds, between the utopia

of the future and the utopia of the past, the unity and indivisibility of the
reality of history.

More or less unknown in eighteenth-century France, Vico has his requital
in the first half of the following century.   It is actually between 1825 and
1850 that the great and only period of veritable fame, the genuine influence
of Vico's work in France, occurs.
   This success was made possible by the consolidation and expansion of his
reputation in Italy itself.[16]   During the last third of the eighteenth century,
with Filangieri, Duni, Pagano, Stellini, Cataldo Jannelli, and finally Cuoco,
a real Vichian school is established, and it contributes to the knowledge of
Vico abroad, particularly in France.   Joseph de Maistre quotes him in his
Considérations sur la France (1796).   Within the ranks of the *idéologues*, De
Gérando and, above all, Fauriel, Manzoni's friend, study him, but they speak
of him only later, when Michelet had already made him famous.[17]   The
year 1799—with the Revolution of Naples, the scattering of the Neapolitan
patriots, the battle of Marengo, which opens to them the gates of Milan—is
an important date for the propagation of Vico's work.   The effects of these
events are felt in France at a slightly later time.   In 1819–20, F. S. Salfi, a
Neapolitan who took refuge in France after 1815, deals with Vico in a set of
articles in the *Revue encyclopédique*.   Subsequently, in 1824 and 1825, things
develop rapidly.   Ballanche travels through Italy with Madame Récamier
and discovers the greatness of Vico's work.   A lawyer, Allier, and a still
little-known young historian, Michelet, simultaneously begin translating the
Scienza nuova.   Another Neapolitan exile, Pietro de Angelis, puts these men
in touch with his friends in Naples.   In 1827 Ballanche publishes the first
section of his *Palingénésie sociale*, Michelet, his own translation of Vico under
the title of *Principes de la philosophie de l'histoire*, and Jouffroy, an article on
"Bossuet, Vico et Herder" in the *Globe*.   In 1828 Victor Cousin again takes
up the comparison between these three authors in lesson XI of his course at
the Sorbonne.   Thus Vico achieves glory.
   Before speaking at greater length of the craftsmen of this glory, I should like
to inquire into the reasons for this success which follows so much obscurity.
One should not attempt to explain everything, since many imponderables go
into the success of a writer or of an artist, but it is certain that historical or ideo-

[16] See Eugenio Garin, *Storia della filosofia italiana* (Turin, 1966), vol. III, pt. V,
"Eredità vichiana e indagini etiche."
[17] Among the manuscripts of Claude Fauriel, preserved in the Bibliothèque de
l'Institut in Paris, there are about ten pages of excerpts from the *Scienza nuova*, selected
from the "Metafisica poetica" and in particular from the "Logica poetica."   Fauriel
was struck, chiefly, by Vico's remarks on Dante, and traces of them are to be found in
his own book on Dante.

logical circumstances favored the response which Vico met at that time, and these consequently allow us to understand the way in which he was interpreted.

Romanticism, in the broadest sense of the term, is characterized by the taste for history or, more exactly, by the taste for the past. A powerful movement of interest, which is first manifested in Germany and England at the end of the eighteenth century and then spreads to France, impels not only historians but literary men as well to turn toward their natural past in order to recapture it in its freshness, in its primal reality, in order to bring about its "resurrection," as Michelet phrases it. The chronicle, which relates the succession of realms, battles, and treaties, the history of great men, is replaced by the history of nations. In his *Essai sur les moeurs* Voltaire had already tried this reversal of perspectives, but he remained a prisoner of the critical and militant rationalism of his century. With the advent of romanticism we witness the rehabilitation of the powers of feeling, of the imagination, of irrationalism in general. Historical and literary sensibilities turn toward folk traditions, legends, and epics, which are viewed as spontaneous emanations, anonymous expressions of the "national spirit." Homer and Dante are freed from the timelessness of the literary pantheon where they had been relegated by humanistic and classical criticism, and are assigned a major place among primeval and national poets, side by side with bards and epical songsters. Religion itself, so roughly treated by the century of the Enlightenment, receives a justification. Hence the apologists of Roman Catholicism, like Chateaubriand and the more or less heterodox mystics of the school of Lyon, which had such a deep influence on De Maistre and Ballanche, emphasize the revealed and transcendental character of religious truth less than its immanent historical role. For them, religion has, above all, the value of an interpersonal bond, the value of an expression of mankind's needs which is not pure reason, but, to an equal and even greater extent, is feeling, and which is founded on an awareness of being pledged to a destiny which surpasses reason.

Such a historical sense not only finds its expression in literature, criticism, and erudition but leads, moreover, to a reflection on the global meaning of the movement of history. This reflection crystallizes around a "privileged" event: the French Revolution of 1789. The contemporaries, as well as the generations immediately following them, were deeply perplexed by the radical upheavals brought about by the Revolution in France and Europe. These upheavals raised problems which could be answered only by a philosophical meditation upon history. To what extent were those tragic happenings necessary? Could they have been avoided? What were their deep-lying causes? Who was responsible for them? What future do they open to mankind? What light do they shed on the mystery of human fate? These are the questions in which the wish to understand is often tinged with religious and even mystic anxiety; they are the questions which stir the minds of Joseph de Maistre, Bonald, Madame de Staël, Chateaubriand,

Saint-Simon, and, subsequently, of Ballanche, Victor Cousin, and Michelet. According to Cousin, the ill-defined discipline which, under the name of philosophy of history, triumphs in France from 1820 to 1850, has no other origin. "As for us," he writes,

whom the perpetual storm of revolutions has, turn by turn, plunged into so many and so different situations; as for us who have witnessed the fall of so many empires, sects, and opinions . . . we are tired, we moderns, of the ceaselessly changing face of the world. . . . It was natural that we should end by wondering whether these games which hurt us so much had any meaning at all, whether human fate remains the same, whether mankind gains or loses, advances or retrogresses, in the midst of these revolutions which upset it; why there are revolutions, what they take away or bring in; whether they have an aim, whether there is something serious in these turmoils and in the general lot of mankind. All of these questions, more or less unknown to antiquity, begin to perplex our souls and secretly to disquiet our most serious intellectuals.[18]

Vico's work, then, had the historic chance of finding the ground prepared, and we can now better understand the aspect of the great precursor, founder, and inspirer which his figure takes on in the eyes of historians and philosophers at the beginning of the nineteenth century.

He appears, in the first place, as the father of modern historical criticism, and Michelet does not hesitate to write, in the Preface of his *Histoire de la république romaine*:

In the vast system of the founder of the metaphysics of history, there exist already, at least germinally, all the works of modern scholarship. Like Wolf, Vico said that the *Iliad* is the collective product of a nation. . . . like Creuzer and Goerres, he pointed out the conceptual and symbolic aspects of the heroic or divine figures of primitive history. Before Montesquieu, before Gans, he showed how legal institutions spring from the depths of nations and faithfully mirror the stages of their history. What Niebuhr was to find through his vast researches, Vico divined; he raised up again the structure of patrician Rome, resurrected its *curiae* and its *gentes*. . . . All the giants of criticism are already contained by, and comfortably lodged in, the small pandemonium of the *Scienza nuova*.

At the more specifically philosophical level of what Michelet calls "the metaphysics of history," Vico takes on reference value, to the extent that his inspiration is in accord with the great ideological currents of the epoch. The philosophy of the Enlightenment is discredited, the optimism of its theory of progress is proved to have been tragically wrong, and the "Goddess Reason" is held responsible for the blood that was shed. The Enlightenment is accused of having an unfeeling, negative, cosmopolitan spirit; it is charged with having undermined the very bases of the political, social, moral, and religious structure; with having failed to size up the dangers of

18 This is a note of V. Cousin's concerning the *Histoire abrégée des sciences métaphysiques et politiques de D. Stewart*, published in the supplement to that work in vol. III. The text is quoted by P. Viallaneix, *La voie royale: Essai sur l'idée du peuple dans l'oeuvre de Michelet* (Paris, 1959).

such an operation; and with having precipitously "scorched" along the highways of history with utter disregard for the slow maturation of its stages. The *idéologues*, who were the Enlightenment's inheritors, quickly lost their influence. Through Royer-Collard, Jouffroy, and Cousin, that eclectic spiritualism which dominated French philosophy during the Romantic period was formed.[19]   These authors, it should be noted, make reference to Reid and Stewart; the rehabilitation of "common sense," brought about by the Scottish philosophers, can be used to justify the new conception of history; there is, therefore, a convergence between the data of psychology and those of historical criticism.   And in regard to this, too, Vico, with his anti-Cartesianism, his anti-individualism, his deprecation of what he terms "scholarly conceit" (*boria dei dotti*), appears as a precursor.

The Christian concept of history, as Bossuet formulated it, continues to enlist the preference of the strict advocates of Roman orthodoxy, but is no longer satisfactory to most minds. A tributary to the old-fashioned chronicle, it assumes a mode of activity of Providence which is far too impenetrable for man's intelligence, too transcendental in relation to the course of events—in a word, too unhistoric.   Instead, Vico is given credit for having sought after the immanent law of history's movement, even if his conceptual pattern is too rigid and his theory of the cyclic recurrences (*corsi e ricorsi*) too pessimistic.

Here, then, are some of the reasons which enable us to understand why Vico was chosen to sponsor romanticism's theory of history.[20]   Undoubtedly Hegel could have supplied a more modern and rigorous inspiration, but, despite the efforts of Cousin and Gans, Hegelianism failed to take root in France.   The only rival of Vico was Herder, who was translated by Edgar Quinet at the same time that Michelet was publishing his version of the *Scienza nuova*.   The scrutiny of the respective merits of Vico and Herder became a commonplace.   Jouffroy, for instance, in an article published in the *Globe* (to which I have already referred), sets Vico's spiritualism against Herder's materialism.   For Vico, Jouffroy says, man's development has no other principle than the absolute laws of his thought, whereas Herder places that development under the dependence of external nature.   The former disregards the role of nature, the latter, the role of man.   Victor Cousin, in lesson XI of his course on the history of philosophy (1828), after expressing his self-congratulation for "having encouraged two young men" (Michelet

[19] See George Boas, *French Philosophies of the Romantic Period* (Baltimore, 1925).

[20] Robert Flint, *History of the Philosophy of History* (London, 1893); Henri Tronchon, "Les études historiques et la philosophie de l'histoire aux alentours de 1830," *Revue de synthèse historique*, 34 (1922); *idem, Romantisme et préromantisme* (Paris, 1930); *idem, Fortune intellectuelle de Herder en France* (Paris, 1935); *idem, Études: France, Allemagne, Italie, Hongrie, Pays Baltiques* (Paris, 1935); Pierre Moreau, *L'histoire en France au XIX siècle: État présent des travaux et esquisse d'un plan d'études* (Paris, 1935).

and Quinet) to make Vico and Herder known to France, credits Vico with having introduced the human point of view into history, but thinks that "Herder's is still the greatest monument that has been raised to the history of mankind."[21]

The two men particularly responsible for the diffusion of Vico's thought in France during the Romantic period are Ballanche and, above all, Michelet. These are the only two authors who studied Vico closely and who were deeply under his influence.

Ballanche is little known, even in France itself. The work of this "discreet" writer has remained in near-shadow, and his name evokes more often the image of the faithful friend of Madame Récamier than that of the author of *La palingénésie sociale*. This latter work, however, deserves our interest to the extent that, by its unclassifiable character, it is a document of the incertitudes, the confused aspirations, and the ideological disturbances which are typical of French thought during the Restoration. Ballanche's *Palingénésie* constitutes, as it were, an epico-lyric meditation upon the destinies of mankind and foreshadows both Vigny's *Destinées* and Hugo's *Légende des siècles*. Bordering, at times, on religious heresy, because he admits a kind of metempsychosis, Ballanche arranges the history of mankind around the ideas of decadence, expiation, and rehabilitation, which alone can justify, in the plans of Providence, the crimes of the Revolution and the royal blood shed on the scaffold. Although close to De Maistre and De Bonald, he rejects their absolute historical pessimism, and dreams of reconciling tradition and progress, royalty and liberalism.[22]

Ballanche's conception of history may already be glimpsed in his *Essai sur les institutions sociales* (1818); but it takes final form thanks to his reading of Vico, which he undertook during his stay in Naples and Rome from 1823 to 1825. The ample ensemble that he planned under the title of *Palingénésie sociale* was never completed, but he published its main parts under different titles: *Prolégomènes* (1827); *Orphée*, accompanied by a translation of Vico's *De antiquissima Italorum sapientia* (1829); "La formule générale de tous les

[21] Around 1840 the thought of Cousin enjoyed a boundless prestige in Italy, and especially in Naples. Francesco Zerella, *L'eclettismo francese e la cultura filosofica meridionale nella prima metà del secolo XIX* (Rome, 1952), points out that the vogue of eclecticism was particularly favored by Vico, who, by his deep analysis of the convertibility of *verum* and *certum*, had attempted to reconcile the absoluteness and universality of the "oughtness" with the concreteness of experience. Some of the great Neapolitan admirers of Cousin are Vichians, such as A. Fazzini and particularly Luigi Blanch, who strives to unite the inspiration of Reid and the Scottish school with that of Royer-Collard and Cousin and with that of Vico. It should be noted that it is Cousin who is accountable for Hegel's penetration into Naples. In this sense we may hold him remotely responsible for the Hegelianized Vico of Spaventa and Croce. See Garin, *Storia della filosofia italiana*, vol. III, pt. VI, "Il pensiero meridionale e Pasquale Galluppi."

[22] See G. Frainnet, *Essai sur la philosophie de Ballanche* (Paris, 1903); Albert J. George, *P. S. Ballanche* (Syracuse, N.Y.: Syracuse University Press, 1945).

peuples appliquée à l'histoire du peuple romain" and "La première sécession plébeienne" (*Revue de Paris*, 1829); *La vision d'Hébal* (1831); "La ville des expiations" (*La France littéraire*, 1832–35).[23]

In his *Prolégomènes* and in his "La formule," Ballanche speaks at length about Vico's thought, which he contrasts with the revolutionary ideology. This anti-Jacobin interpretation of Vico had already been sketched by Joseph de Maistre and by Vincenzo Cuoco. De Maistre, in his *Considérations sur la France* (1796), quotes Vico's idea, stating that a nation in which the members of the nobility have lost the sense of their duties is a nation doomed to ruin. The reference is a brief one, but E. Gianturco has shown in a convincing fashion that De Maistre's whole work presupposes that of the Neapolitan philosopher.[24] As for Cuoco, he writes, for instance, in his *Saggio storico* (1801): "Whoever had his mind permeated with the ideas of Machiavelli, Gravina, and Vico, could not trust the promises, or applaud the actions, of the revolutionaries of France."[25] In Ballanche's view, if Vico, whose ideas "are antithetical to all those of the eighteenth century," had been more widely known, Voltaire would not have attempted to subvert all the religious beliefs of all places and times, and he would have become aware that society is a product of religion, while Rousseau would not have brought up his "brilliant absurdities" concerning man's primitive estate, the authentic bases of the social contract would have been respected, and "the frightful storm" of 1789 could have been prevented. "A somnambulist of genius . . . he came a century ahead of his time, and thus could not witness the revolution which at the present moment is being carried out in the science of history. . . . the bright light which Vico shed at the inception of the last century could only be noticed at the beginning of our own. Profoundly intuitive, he could have no effect on the assimilative men who were the sole rulers of the eighteenth century."

Ballanche borrows from Vico a certain number of essential themes, and, to start with, we will consider that of *the origins*. History, for him, is like a *palimpsest*, a parchment which has been written upon twice, the first writing having been erased. The study of the origins alone will enable us to decipher the primitive text. It is a question, Ballanche states elsewhere, of "plunging a geological sounding-line into the entrails of history." The sounding-line is the study of language, to the extent that ideas are embodied

[23] Oscar A. Haac has published, under the title of *La théodicée et la Virginie romaine* (Geneva-Paris, 1959), a previously unprinted piece by Ballanche devoted to "La seconde sécession plébeienne" (the "Première sécession" appeared in 1829 in the *Revue de Paris*). In his interesting introduction, Professor Haac expatiates on the relationships between Ballanche and Vico.

[24] Elio Gianturco, *Joseph de Maistre and Giambattista Vico: Italian Roots of De Maistre's Political Culture* (New York: Columbia University Press, 1937).

[25] V. Cuoco, *Saggio storico sulla rivoluzione napoletana del 1799: Seguito dal rapporto al Cittadino Carnot*, ed. F. Nicolini (Bari, 1929), p. 40.

in language. "A language, at its origins, attests not to the wisdom of those who spoke it at that time, but to the cosmogonic and synthetic power which inheres in all languages." Ballanche adds: "Words are destiny." He borrows from Vico the latter's theory of myth as "*vera narratio*." ("History illustrates myth, and myth, better known, in its turn illustrates history.") Like Vico, Ballanche affirms the unity and identity of the traditions that unroll in time the convolved and unchanging forms of the human mind.

To the extent that "all the histories of human events are alike or analogous, the course of human societies is always alike and analogous at all times and places." Consequently, for Ballanche, "Roman history is paradigmatic and prototypical of all possible histories." He attributes to the struggle between patricians and plebeians a symbolic significance and views it as the manifestation of the principle of antagonism which causes history to progress. The patricians represent the particularistic forces of conservatism, and the plebeians, those of the whole of mankind on its march toward freedom and conscience. Ballanche, therefore, rightly envisaged the dialectical character of history, the importance of interhuman antagonisms, and, in this sense, he learned Vico's lesson better than did Michelet, for whom the history of freedom, in the last analysis, is a confrontation between man and nature.

Ballanche, however, departs from Vico in regard to the mystical and initiatory role that he assigns to history. He goes beyond Vico's providentialism in order to attempt the construction of a "theodicy of history" ruled by the themes of decadence, expiation, and rehabilitation: a theodicy which appears in the final utopia of the *Ville des expiations*. Vico, for him, is wrong in admitting a human spontaneity independent of Revelation, and in reserving Revelation for the Jewish people alone. It is a question of recapturing, thanks to the "golden bough of initiation," a lost truth. This idea of Ballanche's savors of hermeticism, of Saint-Martin, of De Maistre, and of Bonald; we are very far from Vico.

Ballanche, in spite of a certain "plebeianism," more mystical than political, presents a traditionalist, even reactionary, reading of Vico. In Michelet, who claims Jacobin ancestry, we are confronted with a democratic, progressivist interpretation which reconciles Vico with eighteenth-century France, with the 1789 Revolution, and makes of him the bold discoverer (bold, but hardly aware of his audacity) of the grand Promethean principle "Humanity is its own creation."[26]

Much has been written on the relationship between Michelet and Vico.[27]

[26] This interpretation has been resumed and developed by Edmund Wilson, who places Vico at the origins of the humanistic-democratic-socialist-Marxist lineage, the terminal of which is the "Finland Station." See E. Wilson, *To the Finland Station* (New York, 1940).

[27] The most important writings tackling this task are: G. Lanson, "La formation de la méthode de Michelet," *Revue d'histoire moderne et contemporaine*, 7 (1905–6); G.

I do not claim any ability to add a great deal, within the framework of such a general essay as the present one, to previous contributions. I shall remark at the outset that between the two authors, separated by more than a century, there is an exchange of services which is astonishing enough. Michelet has not "invented" Vico; but Michelet's translation (or rather, adaptation), published in 1827, gave to the Neapolitan philosopher, in France as well as in other countries of Europe, a renown which he had failed to enjoy up to that date and which he never enjoyed afterward. Whereas the translation, complete and more literal, made by Princess Cristina Belgioioso (1808–71) and published in 1844, drew little or no notice, the translation by Michelet, which rode on the crest of the wave of the author's prestige, remained for a number of years the only vehicle of access to Vico's work outside of Italy. However, if Vico's reputation owes much to Michelet, the latter never ceased to proclaim his total indebtedness to Vico, nay, his spiritual descent from him. Quotations on this point are readily at hand: "My Vico, my July, my heroic principle." "Since 1824 a furious infatuation for Vico [has taken possession of me], an unbelievable intoxication with his great historical principle has seized hold of my mind." "I had no other master than Vico. To his principle of the living force, of mankind's self-creation, my book and my teaching owe their very existence."

Michelet undoubtedly modified Vico's texts to a certain extent. With his prodigious faculty for assimilation he pulled Vico to his side so that there was no endeavor on his part to understand his author objectively. But no purpose is served by reproaching Michelet, the visionary historian, for failing to submit to the strict methods of interpretation which we demand today.

It is, instead, more profitable and interesting to ask in what kind of intellectual climate it was possible for a young professor, between 1820 and 1830, to discover the work of Vico, to identify himself with it, to set it up as a sort of catalyzer, of unifying principle, pulling together those interests, those multiple exigencies, which dominated his mind.

The deep affinity that existed *ab initio* between Michelet and Vico is shown by Michelet's "Address on the Awarding of Prizes," a speech delivered at the Collège Sainte-Barbe on August 17, 1825. In this address, Michelet, at the dawn of his career, extols the unity of knowledge and emphasizes the necessary union, in the education of the young, of all sciences, particularly of

---

Monod, "Michelet et l'Italie," in *Jules Michelet: études sur sa vie et ses oeuvres, avec des fragments inédits* (Paris, 1905); see also G. Monod, *La vie et la pensée de Jules Michelet,* 2 vols. (Paris, 1923); B. Donati, *Nuovi studi sulla filosofia civile di G. B. Vico* (Florence, 1936); G. Fassò, "Il Vico nel pensiero del suo primo traduttore francese," *Memorie Reale Accademia delle Scienze dell'Istituto di Bologna,* 1947; O. A. Haac, *Les principes inspirateurs de Michelet* (Paris–New Haven, Conn., 1951); J. L. Cornuz, *Jules Michelet: Un aspect de la pensée religieuse au XIX⁰ siècle* (Geneva-Lille, 1955); P. Viallaneix, *La voie royale: Essai sur l'idée de peuple dans l'oeuvre de Michelet* (Paris, 1959).

the sciences of history and language.   It is impossible to read this address without thinking of Vico's *De mente heroica*, although Michelet was not acquainted with it at that date.   At a much later time he underscores the revelatory coincidence himself: "Vico wrote a discourse, *De mente heroica*, dealing with intellectual heroism, with that bold aptitude on the part of a young scholar to embrace all sciences and all epochs, with the impossibility of being a specialist in any field without being a universalist [as well]. Several years before reading Vico's admirable *Discourse*, I had, myself, composed a weak and mediocre speech on the same topic.   What Vico recommends I had already felt instinctively in myself." [28]

The search for the principle that determines the unity of thought prepares Michelet for his reception of Vico.   He explains this point, himself, in a note to his *Introduction to Universal History* (1831): "The obligation under which I was to teach in succession (and, not seldom, simultaneously) philosophy, history, and languages, drove me to become keenly aware of the ever-present and intimate union between intellectual and factual studies, of the links between the ideal and the real."   In fact, Michelet construes as a professional duty an impulse which corresponds to a need of his mind and of his sensitivity.   We shall presently see how Vico was, for him, the meeting point of the influences he underwent and of the demands of his own genius, and how he came across Vico's thought while he was following the spontaneous proclivity of his own mind and scholarship.

Schematically, we may say that Michelet went to Vico along three different yet converging paths, or (in an alternative phrasing) that Michelet discovered him under three distinct aspects, corresponding to the themes of his own meditation, that is, to his reflections on languages, on history, and on the nature of man.

The first path followed by Michelet is the "historical philosophy of languages."   The first Vico he encountered was the author of the *De antiquissima*, the "etymologist."   He later describes Vico as one who "showed that the heroic or divine characters of primitive history are ideas, symbols."   As early as 1819 Michelet dreams of writing a book on the "Characters of Nations Discovered in the Vocabulary of their Languages" or a "History of Civilization Derived from a Study of Languages." [29]

The earliest quotation of Vico by Michelet is to be found in the latter's *Journal des idées* and is dated December, 1823.[30]   Michelet quotes Vico alongside Plato (the Plato of the *Kratilos*), Gibbon, Herder, Madame de Staël, Joseph de Maistre, and Gérando.   And when our historian reads the German scholars Wolf, Creuzer, Niebuhr, Humboldt—always with a view

---

[28] Note of 1868 (MS in the files of the Bibliothèque Historique de la Ville de Paris, cited by P. Viallaneix in his *J. Michelet: Écrits de jeunesse* (Paris, 1959).
[29] On Michelet's years of preparation see particularly Viallaneix, *La voie royale*.
[30] See Viallaneix, *J. Michelet*.

to preparing the book which he will never publish—he cannot help feeling that Vico is their precursor.

The second path by which Michelet approaches Vico is that of the philosophy of history. It was Victor Cousin who introduced this expression and this concept, in January, 1824 (in a supplement to Volume III of Dugald Stewart's *History of the Moral and Political Sciences,* translated by Buchon).[31] Michelet was strongly impressed by Cousin's article, insofar as it gave to his own reflections on history the philosophical framework which they lacked. He began reading Kant's minor works and undertook a "comparative study of Vico, Condorcet, Turgot, and Ancillon."

He now meets Vico again, but in reference to the "philosophy of history" (let us not forget that Michelet's 1827 translation is entitled *Principles of the Philosophy of History*), and when, in April, 1824, he submits his plans to Cousin—plans for the "comparative study" quoted above and a translation from Vico—we understand why Cousin exhorts him to go ahead and offers him his sponsorship. Viewed from this angle Vico supplies Michelet with the guideline that makes it possible for him to understand the historical process. Bossuet "narrows universal history down to small dimensions"; Voltaire "scatters it like dust in the wind, delivering it up to blind chance." Vico, instead, "causes Providence, the God of all centuries and nations, to shed its light, for the first time, over universal history." "He is even superior to Herder. Mankind appears to Vico, not under the aspect of a plant which, through a process of organic growth, rises from the earth under the dew of heaven, but as an organic system of the world of societies. In order to study man, Herder takes his stand in nature, whereas Vico installs himself in man [in human nature]. He shows us man becoming humanized by social forces."[32]

The third path of access to Vico is opened by Scottish philosophy, which, as we saw, was the object of a general infatuation at that time. It was Reid who, in the eyes of Michelet, dominated the history of eighteenth-century thought. Reid demonstrated that man is "peculiarly a social" being, while his theory of "common sense" liberated historical truth from the grip of Cartesian doubt. Like all men of his generation, Michelet is convinced that

[31] In the same volume there is to be found a short note of Buchon's on Vico, inspired by Salfi. It was thought for a long time that Michelet had discovered Vico by reading that note. In fact, Michelet quotes Vico in his *Journal des idées* (December, 1823), whereas vol. III of the abridgment of Dugald Stewart's *History of Moral and Political Ideas* was not published until later, in January, 1824. As for Cousin's role in Michelet's acquaintance with Vico, it was quite modest. "Cousin had imparted to me no directions, had given me only the vaguest indications. He had no notion of the scope of the *Scienza nuova.*" These words, written by Michelet in 1869, are undoubtedly correct, but they are tokens of a slight ingratitude since the encouragement and support of Cousin were, even in the absence of concrete advice, precious for the young beginner.

[32] The final note of Michelet's *Introduction à l'histoire universelle* (1831).

collective rather than individual consciousness is the repository of certitude. "Historical traditions are the voice of mankind," Michelet asserts in his course of lectures delivered in 1827–28 at the École Normale. It is impossible not to recognize in those lectures the impact of Lamennais' *Essai sur l'indifférence*. However, whereas both De Maistre and Lamennais draw conservative and even reactionary conclusions from that principle, Michelet finds therein the promise of a humanity which is its own creation and is on its way to freedom. The construction that Michelet puts upon Vico can be explained only by this constellation of themes which the French historian, to his astonishment, finds already indicated by Vico and, above all, integrated into a unitary perspective by the grand principle "which constitutes the true light of the modern age" —"Humanity is its own creation."

It should be noted that we must await the appearance of the Preface to Michelet's *Histoire de la république romaine* (1831) in order to find this explicit formulation of the "major slogan of the *Scienza nuova*." The *Discours* that precedes the 1827 translation is a still timidly respectful, objective setting forth of Vico's ideas. We are therefore entitled to think that, in keeping with a process of intellectual self-assertion, Michelet gradually enucleated those which he viewed as the fundamental implications of Vico's system. Michelet's interpretation is predicated upon a bold utilization of the theory of the *verum-factum*, whose ontological and epistemological meaning he, rather than trying to define, enshrines as the "key motto" of a conception of history. In this conception, man is "his own Prometheus." Such an interpretation implies some obvious distortions insofar as the letter and spirit of the Vichian texts are concerned. The role of Providence, although not denied, is reduced to that of a mere guarantee of the significance of history. The function of Providence is that of assuring us that man is bound up with God and that the "battle for freedom" may result in a victory. The theory of the *corsi* and *ricorsi* is judged to be fatalistic; it is therefore at first modified into a "spiral development," then abandoned. Above all, Michelet identifies mankind with the people, i.e., with the anonymous mass of simple, innocent beings, women, and children. History, without "first names and heroes," becomes a narrative having but one character, one and only one hero, the people. This word is to be understood in terms of the Romantic definition, whereas in Vico we find a vigorously dialectical conception of the conflict between social classes as a propulsive factor of history.

Michelet's historical view, with its ambition to unite and to reconcile all contrasts, is, in the final analysis, much more pronouncedly moral, much more mystical, than that of the author of the *Scienza nuova*.

The "Promethean" interpretation of Vichian principles becomes more precise and radical as Michelet goes through the evolution that detaches him more and more from Christianity and ends in a violent break with it. After thinking that Christianity should be "transposed," Michelet deems it imperative, now, to destroy it, and at the same time he ever more resolutely pulls Vico in a non-Christian, even anti-Christian, direction.

This is a point which has not been sufficiently emphasized previously, and which is aptly illustrated by a note made by Michelet at Nervi (Italy) in May, 1854:

Vico shows how gods are made and unmade; he teaches us the art whereby gods are created, the living process which weaves the twofold fabric of human destiny: religion and legislation, faith and law. It is man who is the creator of them. He ceaselessly molds his own self, he manufactures his earth and his heaven. This revelation is so bold and shocking that Vico is himself afraid of it and endeavors to convince himself that he is still a believer. Christianity, the "true creed," remains in utter isolation as the only exception to the perishable nature of all religions; to Christianity the rash thinker bows in humble respectfulness, swearing that it has nothing whatever to fear from that sudden disclosure. Vergil and Vico are non-Christians, perhaps super-Christians. Vergil represents the plaintive melody sung for the death of the gods; Vico, the process whereby the gods are created again. Translating Vico, I hoped to be still able to reconcile science and religion; after 1833, however, I laid it down that Christianity was temporarily dead; and in 1848, I asserted the death of all religions. Through Italy, I have had a very free, non-Christian education. My masters were Vergil, Vico, and [Roman] law. I spent ten years (1830-40) in reconstructing the tradition of the Middle Ages. I showed how empty that tradition is. It took me ten years more (1840-50) to reconstruct the anti-Christian, anti-messianic tradition.[33]

Here the mystery is lifted: Michelet has just read Feuerbach. Some days after the above-quoted entry, he writes in his *Journal* under the date of June 4, 1854: "The great eighteenth-century message was heralded (in Italy) by a solitary giant who surpasses everything and who contains not only Feuerbach but Feuerbach's successors. However, Vico was unaware of his own achievement, while this achievement was ignored by others."[34] From the Vico viewed as the precursor of Wolf and Niebuhr to the Vico as precursor of Feuerbach, the stretch may seem more than considerable; yet, no less a distance than this was spanned by the spiritual itinerary of Michelet.

Side by side with Ballanche and Michelet we must place, among those who propagated Vico's renown, Lerminier, a professor of legal philosophy at the Collège de France. In fact, around 1830, legal philosophy in France had a success which is, in a way, parallel and concurrent with that of the philosophy of history; and Vico, whom Lerminier salutes together with his masters Niebuhr, Savigny, Gans, and Hegel, profits from this vogue.[35]

[33] Unpublished note (in the files of the Bibliothèque Historique de la Ville de Paris), partially quoted by Monod ("Michelet et l'Italie") and by Viallaneix (*La voie royale*).

[34] Michelet, *Journal*, II (Paris, 1962).

[35] See Henri Tronchon, "Une concurrence à la Philosophie de l'Histoire en France: La Philosophie du Droit," *Mélanges Charles Andler* (Strasbourg and Paris, 1924).

It would be tedious to multiply the proofs of Vico's fashion during the 1830–50 period. Philologists, literary critics, novelists, preachers, and philosophers, quote him, praise, and at times attack him. In Balzac's novel the "celebrated Gaudissart," a salesman, is made to say: "Vico sells well." Nevertheless, it must be granted, all this is very superficial; Vico remains a name, the symbol of that philosophy of history which is in vogue, and his work is not studied in a truly profound way. The only exceptions, perhaps, are the chapter of Francisque Bouillier's *Histoire de la philosophie cartésienne* (1854) devoted to Vico as an opponent of Descartes, and Ferrari's *Vico et l'Italie* (1839). But Ferrari, although he settled for a while in France, really belongs to Italian philosophy.

Before leaving this period, I should like to note the almost total absence of contacts between Vico's thought and the conception of history inspired by Saint-Simon. Neither Saint-Simon, nor Bazard, nor Enfantin refers to it; Pierre Leroux and Buchez accuse it of disregarding human perfectibility and set against it the essentially French theory of progress championed by Turgot, Condorcet, and Saint-Simon. (Michelet, too, on the other hand, criticizes Vico's cyclic conception of the *corsi e ricorsi* and tries to reconcile it with the idea of progress, by suggesting the image of the "spiral.") [36]   As for Auguste Comte, he writes to John Stuart Mill, on October 21, 1844, that he has just read Vico's work and that he does not regret that he failed to read it earlier. "Had I come across it twenty years ago, it would not have been instrumental in facilitating my mental advance, and perhaps it would even have hindered or sidetracked it." The Saint-Simonians' attitude of reservation toward Vico may appear surprising. Did not the *Journal de l'instruction publique* of 1836 remark, in connection with the infatuation stirred up by the translations of Vico's and Herder's work, that this infatuation constituted a "lucky strike" for Saint-Simonianism? [37]   In fact, the Saint-Simonian school could have derived great profit from Vico, especially from his dialectical interpretation of history, his theory of the antagonism of social classes, and his anticipations in regard to the sociology of knowledge. However, the Saint-Simonians had but a scanty acquaintance with Vico, they knew him through exaggeratedly Romantic interpretations, and they attached too much importance to scientific, technical, and economic progress not to see in him an archaic, antiquated thinker.

With the end of the movement that had carried him forward, with the discredit that, beginning in 1860, overtakes the great philosophies, the great "religions," of history of the Romantic period, Vico, in France, goes back into the semi-obscurity from which he has never emerged completely. The historians lock themselves within a narrow positivism, and history becomes

[36] Cf. P. J. Buchez, *Introduction à la science de l'histoire*, 2d ed. (Paris, 1842), vol. I, chap. 5, and Pierre Leroux, *Doctrine de la perfectibilité*, vol. II of *Oeuvres* (Paris, 1851), p. 55*n*.
[37] See Tronchon, "Les études historiques. . . ."

a science utterly unwilling to borrow anything whatever from philosophy. (Did Fustel de Coulanges read our author? Does he show traces of this reading? Probably so, but Fustel fails to acknowledge the fact.) French philosophers take the path of the reflective philosophy of the mind, inherited from Descartes and Kant, or their interest turns to the methodology of the natural sciences. They remain impenetrable (with the exception of Cournot) to the historical dimension of man. Even reactions against the tyranny of intellectualism are waged in the name of life (as in the case of Bergson), not in the name of history. Consequently, in France the intellectual climate is hardly favorable to a growth of Vico's influence. In order to be read, Vico needs mediators. Hegel, Marx, Dilthey, Nietzsche, may act as middlemen; it is through Hegel, for instance, that Italy rediscovers Vico, with Spaventa, and later with Croce. But these authors find readers in France late, and with difficulty, only after World War I.

The only notable exception is Georges Sorel. Perhaps, in order to love and understand Vico, an isolated thinker, another isolated thinker was needed. Independent Marxist, theoretician of revolutionary syndicalism, Sorel is, in fact, claimed by fascism as one of its own; and the hard path that he chose, between what he calls the utopianism of the left and the utopianism of the right, is naturally likely to cause misunderstandings. Sorel becomes acquainted with Vico by way of Labriola and Croce and devotes to him a long essay, published in the September, October, and November, 1896, issues of the *Devenir social*. The meeting is decisive because it is in the light of Vico's thought that, as G. Goriely, the most recent of Sorel's interpreters, points out, some basic themes of Sorel's thought should be construed.[38]

In a footnote to his *Kapital*, Marx states that it would be easier to construct a history of human technology than it would be to write a history of the natural organs of plants and animals, since, as Vico says, man's history differs from the history of nature because men have created the former, but not the latter. This Vichian idea, to which Marx refers only incidentally, is emphasized by Sorel, who makes it the fundamental theme of his work. Man knows only what he himself has done (Sorel repeats after Vico), and the human creation par excellence is history. There is a "natural nature" and an "artificial nature," which is history. Through Vico the sense of history is introduced into the analysis of human institutions: language, religion, law, and science evolve and express the different stages of society. In the eyes of Sorel, this "ideogenetic" law of Vico's foreshadows Marx.

Sorel's irrationalism—with its onslaughts against the Cartesian spirit, against the ideology of progress and positivism, against the "intellectuals," who want to settle everything through "reason"—finds its justification in Vico, as well as in Bergson, William James, Nietzsche, or Freud. "Man cannot become a purely intellectual being," Sorel asserts, trying to capture

[38] G. Goriely, *Le pluralisme dramatique de Georges Sorel* (Paris, 1962).

in the deep life of emotions the origins of historical actions. Reason is never completely triumphant; it only stands out against the ever-present background of emotional forces. Thus, violence stands at the very heart of history, and the proletariat will win its freedom, not by means of intellectual enlightenment alone, but by its heroism and just violence.

Sorel reproaches Vico for having doubled empirical history with an ideal, Platonic history and for having hypostasized, in the idea of Providence, the rationality that we postulate from history. It is this rationality which Sorel disputes; in the last analysis, beyond the aspects of his own history which man is capable of understanding, there exists no truth of the eternal order of things known by God and established by his will: there are only freedom and myth. The cyclic theory of the recurrences (*corsi e ricorsi*) does not, then, express the fatal law governing the life of societies; it symbolizes, instead, the never-resolved tension in man between the emotions and reason, between poetry and prose, myth and science, barbarism and civilization, war and law. None of these aspects achieves its own realization by suppressing the others at specific historical stages; instead, they coexist at every moment, like permanent possibilities.

After Sorel, Croce's influence affects the rare French author who concerns himself with Vico, and we can mention only Paul Hazard[39] and Jules Chaix-Ruy.[40] What perspectives can be opened up by a prudent conclusion? The faint signs of a revival of attention seem to become manifest. With the new historical school founded by Lucien Febvre and Marc Bloch, with the interest in language evinced by linguists and philosophers, with the ethnological researches of Lévi-Strauss, certain conditions are perhaps present and may occasion a renewed reading of Vico.[41] The "philosophy of history," the problem of historical periodization, "catastrophic" romanticism, of the Fascist or Marxist brand, which was fashionable in the immediate prewar era—these seem to be less topical today. An interpretation of Vico *à la* Spengler or *à la* Malraux is no longer possible. Attention is reverting to the eighteenth century. Will Vico, or, rather, will French culture, again come across the chance that was missed by both over two centuries ago?

Translated by Elio Gianturco

[39] Hazard, "La pensée de Vico."
[40] J. Chaix-Ruy, *La formation de la pensée de G. B. Vico* (Gap, 1943).
[41] H. Stuart Hughes, *History as Art and Science* (New York: Harper & Row, 1964).

Ramón Ceñal, S.J.
VICO AND
NINETEENTH-CENTURY
SPANISH THOUGHT

In this study of Vico's influence on nineteenth-century Spain, I focus my attention on two thinkers of considerable significance in the Spanish culture of the past century: Juan Donoso Cortés (1809–53) and Jaime Balmes (1810–48). The influence of Vico's thought on their writings should, I believe, interest the students of the Neapolitan philosopher.[1]

Donoso was an impassioned student of history. He always searched for the profound meaning that lies beneath the mere chronological succession of events. He became interested in history at an early age: "The study of history is the study of the progress of the human spirit, and this study cannot be engaged in without [one's] first having perused the philosophical history of the different societies, from their birth right up to the state of perfection where we find them."[2] For Donoso, history is a complex plot, very difficult to understand and requiring much study; it demands a broad outlook which does not stop at minute details, but rather embraces the full range of societies and epochs.[3]

Donoso's predilection for the philosophy of history is most apparent in his admiration for Vico's ideas. In his *Lecciones sobre derecho político* (1837) (*Lessons on Public Law*), he exhibits clearly his high esteem for Vico and his interpretation of history:

Since the fifteenth century, when arts and letters were reborn in Europe, scholars have

---

[1] Among the men of Spain influenced by Vico, the rhetorician Ignacio Luzán (1702–54) should be remembered. During his stay in Naples (1715–33) he must have known Vico, and it seems possible that he was his disciple. Menéndez Pelayo believes that Luzán's writings reflect Vico's marvelous intuition concerning the epos and the nature of primitive poetry. See Menéndez Pelayo, *Historia de las ideas estéticas en España*, III (Madrid, 1940), 116. And, simply as an anecdote, let me recount that Angel Saavedra, Duque de Rivas (1791–1865), the famous Spanish Romantic writer, was urged to read Vico's works during his stay in Naples. He wrote to the man who had recommended the reading to him: "I have read Vico and I am annoyed with him." See Juan Valera, *Obras completas*, 3d ed. (Madrid: Aguilar, 1961), II, 734.

[2] Juan Donoso Cortés to Jacinto Hurtado, August 18, 1829; cf. Juan Donoso Cortés, *Obras completas: Recopiladas y anotadas, con la aportación de nuevos escritos*, ed. Juan Juretschke, 2 vols. (Madrid: Biblioteca de Autores Cristianos, 1946), I, 20. Our references to Donoso refer to the volumes and pages of this edition.

[3] See Donoso Cortés, *Obras completas*, I, 154–55.

studied the internal organization of the Roman Republic.   In subsequent times, some had, if not the awareness, at least a vague intuition that Roman historians had cast light on the dark origins of their city with brilliant but somewhat mythological remarks.   That intuition soon gave way to a profound skepticism with regard to the history of the origins of Rome.   And the criticism went from skepticism to dogmatic denial to the dogmatic affirmation of facts.   Louis de Beaufort was the sower of destruction; Vico was the reaper of reform.   The former's criticism was negative and therefore sterile.   The latter's was affirmative and fecund.   Beaufort demonstrated that the early Roman people had had no historians.   Vico gave us their history.

Although I shall discuss Vico later in greater detail, I shall now briefly point out that his *Scienza nuova* not only revived the interest in historical studies in our epoch and laid the foundations for the reformist school of the Rhine, but was the work where the daring Neapolitan philosopher most thoroughly canvassed the obscure symbolism of past ages.   The reform that he started was completed by Niebuhr, the greatest historian of modern times.[4]

Donoso kept the promise he made in his *Lecciones de derecho político* with an extensive essay called "Filosofía de la Historia: Juan Bautista Vico."[5]   This essay was published in the newspaper *Correo nacional* in September and October of 1838.   It is made up of eleven articles with the following titles: (1) Spain and the New Historiography; (2) Historiography and Philosophy of History; (3) A Biographical Sketch of Vico; (4) The Doctrine of the Three Ages; (5) The Origins of Religious Concepts; (6) Historical Symbols; (7) Family and Property; (8) Society and Government; (9) Patricians and Plebeians; (10) The Eternal Cycles of Recurrence and Their Characteristics; (11) Vico's Theory and European History.

These articles had not been collected in any of the editions of the works of Donoso prior to that of Juan Juretschke's.   No Spanish encyclopedia mentions Donoso's articles on Vico.   Not even Schramm, a laudable critic of Donoso's ideas, utilizes these articles in his analysis of Vico.   Because of the way in which Nicomedes Pastor Díaz refers to them, Schramm un-

---

[4] *Ibid.*, p. 291.   We suppose that Donoso is making reference to Louis Beaufort's first work, *Dissertations sur l'incertitude des cinq premiers siècles de l'histoire romaine* (Utrecht, 1738).   The destructive and skeptical criticism of this first book is continued with more restraint in his second work, *La république romaine: Ou plan général de l'ancien gouvernement de Rome* (The Hague, 1766).

[5] Donoso Cortés, *Obras completas*, I, 531–72.   Fausto Nicolini's observations are interesting.   He states that Donoso's articles on Vico first appeared in the *Diario de la Tarde* of Buenos Aires in January and February, 1838; see Vico, *Opere*, ed. Fausto Nicolini (Naples: Ricciardi, 1953), p. xxv.   This fact is undoubtedly connected with the great interest in Vico that was brought to the Argentine capital via the Neapolitan Pietro de Angelis, who arrived in Buenos Aires in 1827 and who, before that time, in Paris had initiated Jules Michelet into the world of Vichian thought.   Cf. Nicolini, *ibid.*, and J. Michelet, *Oeuvres complètes: Oeuvres choisies de Vico, contenant ses Mémoires écrits par lui-même, La Science Nouvelle, les Opuscules, Lettres, etc., précédées d'une Introduction sur sa vie et ses ouvrages* (Paris: E. Flammarion, n.d.), pp. 284–85.

doubtedly must have thought of them as brief newspaper sketches.[6] Juretschke believes that these articles alone justify his own edition of the works of Donoso.   He writes: "The historical thought of Donoso constantly revolves around the renowned Italian, with occasional assent or dissent, but always, of course, in continuous dialogue.   Westemeyer brilliantly sets forth this phenomenon in his excellent work, in spite of the fact that he, as well as Schramm, was not acquainted with Donoso's essay."[7]

As I proceed to bring out the contents of Donoso's articles on Vico, I do not mean to underestimate Juretschke's great contribution.   These articles were, in fact, responsible for revealing Vico's importance as a founder of the philosophy of history to Spain at a time when the Neapolitan was still relatively unknown, even in the most progressive cultural circles.

Donoso quotes Jules Michelet and Simon-Pierre Ballanche among the "disciples and fervent imitators of Vico" in France.[8]   One can perhaps assert that Ballanche was an imitator of Vico, but I do not believe that one could rightfully call Michelet an imitator.   He was, rather, a well-informed herald and a well-intentioned translator of the Neapolitan philosopher. However, having recognized its merits, one must indeed add that Donoso's essay is to a great extent an imitation of Michelet.   The comparison of Donoso's text and Michelet's *Discours sur le système et la vie de Vico* demonstrates clearly that the former's article is largely a rearrangement and in several passages a literal translation or paraphrase of the *Discours*.   But let Donoso's excuse be the fact that newspaper articles at that time did not provide a medium for great scholarly disquisitions.   It is also correct to acknowledge that not all of Donoso's essay is a sheer rearrangement of Michelet's *Discours*.   The Spanish writer gives his own judgments, expounds the contents of the *Scienza nuova* with greater thematic distinction, and adds references to Vico's work which Michelet fails to indicate in his *Discours*. I suspect, however, that Donoso must have used the abridged edition of the *Scienza nuova* (1744 edition), which Michelet published under the title of *Principes de la philosophie de l'histoire*.[9]

---

[6] See N. Pastor Díaz, *Galería de españoles célebres contemporáneos*, IV (Madrid, 1845), 205, cited by Juretschke in *Obras completas*, I, 531; Edmund Schramm, *Donoso Cortés: Leben und Werk eines spanischen Antiliberalen* (Hamburg, 1935), p. 98.

[7] See *Obras completas*, I, xiii; Dietmar Westemeyer, *Donoso Cortés: Staatsmann und Theologe* (Münster, 1941), p. 98.

[8] I cannot determine precisely which of Michelet's works Donoso used, whether the first, *Principes de la philosophie de l'histoire* (1827), or the second, *Oeuvres choisies de Vico* (1835), in which we find reprinted the *Discours sur le système et la vie de Vico* (originally published in the first work).   For our study we have consulted Michelet's *Oeuvres complètes*.

[9] The abridged translation of the *Scienza nuova* which Michelet presents in *Oeuvres choisies de Vico* (1835), reproduces the text of *Principes de la philosophie de l'histoire* (*traduits de la Scienza nuova*) of 1827; cf. Michelet, *Oeuvres complètes*, p. 283.   About Michelet's

Donoso, in the introduction to his essay, posits the problem of the philosophy of history and of its possible existence and purpose:

Just as there is a philosophy of economics, a political philosophy, a social philosophy, why can there not be a philosophy of history? In other words, do the different peoples scattered over the earth partake of an independent and complete life, or do they lead an interrelated existence? Do their particular histories constitute a complete unity, or are they different pages of the same book in which the history of the human race is recorded? If the human race has a history, of which the particular histories are fragments, are the revolutions, the catastrophes, and the progressive movements that we find in it the work of Chance, or are they necessary effects brought about by necessary principles and by providential and eternal laws? If mankind has a life unto itself and if there are certain unalterable laws that it must, perforce, obey, then those laws could be catalogued. He who sets them down will be a philosopher, and that catalogue, systematically arranged, will constitute the philosophy of history.[10]

The problem, Donoso asserts, "was resolved practically in the seventeenth century by Bossuet, the last father of the Church, and in the eighteenth century by Giambattista Vico, enlightened reformer of historical studies, unhappy during his lifetime and forgotten after his death until the nineteenth century, when, along with those of other great men, his ideas were revived."[11]

Donoso believed that two thoughts were basic for the creation of a philosophy of history: (1) "that history had already existed for many centuries." Only thus, knowing the great historical evolutions, could one compare them and discover the general law, or laws, which preceded their rise and development; (2) "that the notion of moral sameness among men already existed in the world, for philosophy could not exist without historical unity, nor historical unity without moral identity among men." And this notion "did not exist in the world until Christianity tore down the barriers that separated nations and peoples, and the unity of the human race was proclaimed all over the earth. The philosophy of history, therefore, could only exist in modern societies."[12]

The fifteenth and sixteenth centuries belong to historiographers. Only in the seventeenth century, the century of reason, does historical knowledge

---

translation, Nicolini says, too critically perhaps, that "considerata da un osservatorio rigorosamente scientifico, . . . è da qualificare piuttosto travestimento, per non dire vero e proprio tradimento"; see Nicolini, *Opere*, p. xxiii. Nicolini also reproaches Michelet for having made a great mistake with his title *Principes de la philosophie de l'histoire*: "non ultima, forse, tra le ragioni per cui il precursore dello storicismo assoluto è stato considerato, a lungo, nient'altro che un filosofo della storia, nel senso vulgato e deteriore dell'espressione" (*ibid.*). Naturally, this censure can be justified only if one contends that an absolute historicism—at least an incipient one—is to be found in the *Scienza nuova*.

[10] Donoso Cortés, *Obras completas*, I, 541.

[11] *Ibid.*

[12] *Ibid.*, p. 542.

reach a reasoned, fecund synthesis. The philosophy of history is born, according to Donoso, with Bossuet's *Discours sur l'histoire universelle* (1681). "But, since this philosophy was intuitively glimpsed rather than logically demonstrated, it took a later philosopher to cause it to penetrate the minds of the people by explaining it in a scientific fashion." [13] This was Vico's accomplishment in the eighteenth century—a century that was not favorable to the diffusion of a philosophy of history, because of its fanatic irreligiosity and its skepticism. "The philosophy of history is impossible without God because history is chaos if God does not set its web of events in order." [14] Yet, in the century of the Enlightenment, irreligious and skeptical, "an ardent young man of melancholic moods thought about the whole wide range of the sciences in his solitary meditations and, enriched with all the knowledge of times past and present, laid the foundations for the philosophy of history. That young man was Giambattista Vico." [15]

According to Donoso, the *Scienza nuova* is a "prodigious work." It covers the entire course of history, deciphers its most remote origins, traces the parallel developments of its evolution, and discovers that, underneath the individual histories, there is an "ideal" and eternal history.

Such was the vast task that Vico's genius accomplished in the work that he called the *Scienza nuova*. Even if some Germans, in our time, have reformed some of that magnificent history, it is still the most complete of all the works of its kind. Its foundations are so firm and solid that it still stands, supporting the vast edifice placed

---

[13] *Ibid.*, p. 543.

[14] *Ibid.*, p. 544.

[15] *Ibid.* Describing the cultural period in which Vico developed, Donoso picks out two names: Voltaire, prince of history, and Descartes, prince of philosophy. The former, writes Donoso, concentrates all his attention on facts, without considering their reason or lawfulness. The latter, disregarding facts, concentrates on his own thought as the sole source of all knowledge. "Vico could not accept this divorce between ideas and facts, between the providential laws and the contingent local phenomena, between truth and reality, between philosophy and history. Philosophy and history, according to Vico's dogma, are sisters" (*ibid.*). In the third article, "Portrait of Vico," the paragraph which begins "When he returned to Naples . . ." (*ibid.*, p. 545) is almost a literal translation of Michelet's *Discours* (*Oeuvres complètes*, pp. 12–13), where the latter, in his turn, includes an abridged piece of Vico's *Autobiography* ("La vie de Vico, écrite par lui même," *ibid.*, pp. 70–72). Cf. Nicolini, *Opere*, pp. 25–26; J. B. Vico, *Autobiografía*, Spanish ed. by F. Gonzalez Vicen (Buenos Aires: Espasa-Calpe, 1948), pp. 38–39. Donoso's thoughts on Vico's anti-Cartesianism are also clearly inspired by Michelet. From Michelet he transcribes the text "We owe much to Descartes . . ." (pp. 545–46); cf. Michelet, *Discours* (*Oeuvres complètes*, p. 14). This text is found in *Risposta di Vico all'articolo X del tomo VIII del Giornale de' Letterati d'Italia* (1712), in which Vico's *De antiquissima Italorum sapientia* was unfavorably reviewed (cf. Nicolini, *Opere*, p. 362). Michelet (*Oeuvres complètes*, pp. 164–69) translates a fragment of the *Risposta*, in which the passage alluding to Descartes is to be found. As to Vico's anti-Cartesianism, I believe that it is still worthwhile to read Francisque Bouillier, *Histoire de la philosophie cartésienne*, 3d ed. (Paris, 1868), II, 536–45.

over it, in spite of the revolutions in scientific philosophy, history, and politics which took place during the last century and are continuing in this one. Nowadays, Vico still has disciples and enthusiastic imitators in France. Among them, the most eminent are M. Michelet and M. Ballanche, who fruitfully and fervently cultivate history, philosophy, and literature.[16]

Since it is addressed to the readers of a daily newspaper, Donoso's exposition of the *Scienza nuova* is, perforce, schematic and unscholarly. It is, without doubt, objective, but it is tinged with an excessively dithyrambic tone, which gives the impression that the author has little critical insight.

The *Scienza nuova*, Donoso affirms, is held together by the concept of religion, and it rests on two foundations: philosophy and philology. That is to say, its bases are, on the one hand, the science of reason or of abstract truths, and, on the other, the science of events preserved in traditions and languages. Vico's entire method consists in deducing certitude from the concordance between that which reason dictates and that which history teaches.[17] After enumerating what Donoso calls Vico's "three philosophical dogmas" (divine providence, the moderation of passions, and the immortality of the soul), founded, in turn, on three universal historical institutions (religion, marriage, and burial), Donoso briefly sets forth Vico's doctrine of the three ages. The discovery of the historical value of fables or myths is for Donoso "a true revolution accomplished in the domain of history."[18] He finds equal merit in Vico's ideas on the origins of religion.[19] Vico's doctrine of historical symbols, while not totally convincing for Donoso, does have great value: "Even if we may not adopt on all counts the theory that Homer is an ideal character, it will always be Vico's glory to have demonstrated that the majority of heroes and gods mentioned in the various histories are symbols of certain social epochs and personifications of

---

[16] Pierre Simon Ballanche (1776–1847) is the author of *Antigone* (1814) and of the *Essais de palingenèse sociale* (1827). His doctrine regarding the value of "expiation" in the development of history is mentioned by Donoso in lesson IX of his *Lecciones sobre derecho político* (Donoso Cortés, *Obras completas*, I, 318), where he writes: "Ballanche, melancholy, pious, and yet free; Ballanche is a harmonious lyre whose soft vibrations are the softened, sweet, plaintive, and melodious echo of the unfortunate Vico." Regarding Ballanche, Nicolini writes: "Ammiratore così fanatico della *Scienza nuova*, da scrivere che, se questa fosse stata apprezzata sin dal suo apparire, la foga distruggitrice del secolo decimottavo avrebbe trovato un freno; gli studi, oltre che penetrare molto più nell'intimo delle cose, avrebbero assunto quel carattere religioso che in quel secolo fece loro difetto; il Voltaire, il Rousseau e altri scrittori si sarebbero tenuti lontani dai loro errori perniciosi; e 'le terrible orage de 1789 aurait peut-être été évité (!)'" (*Opere*, p. xxiii).

[17] Cf. Donoso Cortés, *Obras completas*, I, 548. Donoso's philosophy is constantly inspired by this philosophy. He repeats literally, or with similar words: "Reason dictates and history confirms. . . ."

[18] *Ibid.*, p. 550.

[19] *Ibid.*, p. 553.

nations."[20] In subsequent articles, Donoso presents Vico's ideas on the origin of family and property, society and government, and the class struggle between patricians and plebeians. His dislike for liberalism makes him emphasize the mistake of those who claim that the seeds of modern democracies are to be found in the historical epochs of Greece and Rome. The words "fatherland," "people," "liberty," and "king" all have, as Vico demonstrates, meanings that in no way resemble those which they possess in the language of doctrinal liberalism.[21]

Donoso also readily accepts Vico's doctrine regarding the eternal recurrence of historical stages. And, in order to prove it, he applies Vico's theory of the three ages of antiquity to European medieval history. Donoso believes that Vico's doctrine proves that "the march of civilization is the same in every century and among all peoples and nations, and that certain analogous phenomena are always present in the three social stages that mankind traverses in its progressive development. The identity of these phenomena and of these epochs is a clear testimony of the fact that humanity is ruled by certain providential laws whose charting constitutes the philosophy of history."[22]

Donoso refers to Vico once more in his "Paris Letters" (Cartas de Paris) of 1842. In reference to Guizot's History of European Civilization, he writes:

Should you desire to find out what the role of Providence is in human events, do not go to Guizot; he does not write with his eyes gazing at the heavens; go to St. Augustine or Bossuet, and they will show you the solemn finger of God pointing at the circles that he writes in history. If you want to find out what ways the human race follows, what laws govern its childhood, manhood, and old age, do not go to M. Guizot, for his eyes embrace neither the full scope of the different ages nor the full rondure of

[20] Ibid., p. 556. In his articles about the Antecedentes de la cuestión de Oriente (Antecedents of the Eastern Question) (1839), Donoso writes: "What is the lion-fighting Hercules but the personification of man struggling against nature? . . . Hercules is a character whom all peoples of the world claim as their own . . . [and] this is the proof . . . that it is a universal symbol and the personification of an epoch common to all nations" (ibid., p. 593). In his essay on Catholicism, Liberalism, and Socialism (Ensayo Sobre el Catolicismo, el Liberalismo y el Socialismo) (1851), Donoso formulates Vico's doctrine of historical symbols (caratteri poetici) in the following way: "This law whereby all that exists in the masses exists more perfectly in the aristocracy, and in a manner even more incomparably perfect in a person, is so universal that it can rightly be considered as the law of history" (ibid., II, 538–39).

[21] See ibid., pp. 565–66. Vico, Scienza nuova (bk. II, sec. V, chap. VII, par. 663), writes: "Questa voce 'popolo,' presa de' tempi primi del mondo delle città nella significazione de' tempi ultimi (perché non poterono né filosofi né filologi immaginare tali spezie di severissime aristocrazie), portò di seguito due altri errori in queste due altre voci: 're' e 'libertà'; onde tutti han creduto il regno romano essere stato monarchico, e la ordinata da Giunio Bruto essere stata libertà popolare. . . ." Concerning Donoso's position with regard to doctrinal liberalism, cf. Luis Díez del Corral, El Liberalismo Doctrinario (Madrid, 1945), pp. 505ff.

[22] Donoso Cortés, Obras completas, I, 572.

the earth. Go to Vico, and he will show you the peaceful, immense course of the river of humanity and lead you to explore its mysterious wellsprings, more deeply hidden than the uncertain dawn of history and the deceitful fulgurations of myths and fables.[23]

In his criticism of Fermín González Morón's *Curso de historia de la civilización en España* (1843), Donoso refers to Vico together with St. Augustine and Bossuet, whom he calls "princes" among historians: "After Bossuet comes Vico, born in the land of Pythagoras, and heir to his melancholy and profound genius of research. He died unknown to scholars, but today even the ignoramuses speak of him, and his work has become an inspiration to Germany and has reformed the study of history in Europe."[24]

But Donoso's thought, influenced as it was by the traditionalist French school of De Bonald and De Maistre, caused him to concentrate his attention more and more on an interpretation of history revolving around Christian revelation, with the dogma of redemption as its axis. Thus Donoso looks at St. Augustine and Bossuet, hoping to find the key to the laws of history. The stimulation of Vico's thought constantly remains with him, and, above all, the desire for a rational explanation of history, even within a predominantly theological, rather than philosophical, framework of interpretation. In later times, however, the enthusiasm of the 1838 essay yielded to a more critical attitude and to a certain dissatisfaction with Vico's historical schematic patterns. In *Bosquejos históricos* (Historical Sketches) (1847), Donoso writes: "According to some, humanity's progress cannot be defined, since it travels in a perpetually straight line; according to others, humanity is doomed to weave and unweave the fabric of time, marching in perpetually circular lines. . . ."[25] Undoubtedly, these words allude to Vico's doctrine of the *corsi e ricorsi*. Regarding this and other nineteenth-century doctrines, Donoso says that they constitute "vain speculations and sterile debates." When Donoso reached maturity of thought, he concluded that history is kept in motion by a single principle, that of the evil of sin and the good of Christ's redeeming grace. To him this principle means two things: "The natural triumph of good over evil, and the supernatural triumph of God over evil by a direct, personal, and pre-eminent action."

[23] *Ibid.*, p. 792.

[24] Donoso adds (*ibid.*): "After Vico, who held history to be ruled by laws, comes Montesquieu, who explains everything through history, Voltaire, who falsifies it, Rousseau, who scorns it, Robertson, an elegant compiler of the Voltairian school, Hume, the greatest historiographer of England, and Gibbon, a man of formidable and choice erudition. . . ." He then mentions Hegel and his disciple Gans, Niebuhr and Savigny, Guizot, "who believes that politics springs from history, history from philosophy, and philosophy from good sense; and, finally, Chateaubriand, the last and the greatest of all, who, closing this immense cycle, opens his arms in all directions and converses familiarly and simultaneously with philosophical historiographers, with poet-historiographers, with the German scholars, with Moses, Herodotus, and Homer."

[25] *Ibid.*, II, 110–11.

These words are followed by a commentary which contains the last explicit reference to Vico in Donoso's writings and which clearly conveys his position in regard to Vico's thought:

This, for me, is philosophy, all the philosophy of history. Vico was on the brink of seeing the truth, and if he had seen it, he would have expounded it better than I. But soon he lost the well-lighted path and found himself surrounded by darkness. He always thought he had discovered a certain limited number of political and social forms in the infinite variety of human events. In order to demonstrate that he was wrong, one need look only at the United States, which does not comply with any of those forms. Had he fathomed the Catholic mysteries more deeply, he would have realized that, if he had only inverted his proposition, he would have come across the historical truth. Truth lies in the substantial sameness of events, cloaked by, and hidden beneath, the infinite variety of forms.[26]

Balmes dedicated two chapters of his *Philosofía fundamental* (Fundamental Philosophy)[27] to Vico's epistemology, that is, to his principle "*verum ipsum factum.*" Balmes' work was published in 1847. This fact, it seems to me, is of unusual significance. Vico's philosophy of history drew attention to itself in the first decades of the nineteenth century. However, the most strictly philosophical principles of his philosophy—his epistemology and metaphysics—apparently were the subjects of later studies. It has been stated that it was Bertrando Spaventa who, toward 1860, discovered Vico's metaphysical philosophy.[28] And, as we know, it was Croce and Gentile, the Neo-Hegelians, who bestowed renewed currency on Vico's thought, contending that the seed of that philosophy of the "spirit" which actualist idealism claims to set up lies in Vico's *verum-factum.* Balmes, as I stated, became interested in Vico's axiom as early as 1847. It is true, nevertheless, that Balmes' judgment concerns Vico's epistemology only; Balmes is far from discovering in that Vichian axiom a principle of the philosophy of the spirit. It is also true that Balmes examines only the presentation of the *verum-factum* in the *De antiquissima Italorum sapientia* and makes no reference to the final development of that principle in the *Scienza nuova.*[29]   But this

26 Donoso to Montalembert, March 22, 1849 (*ibid.*, p. 209).

27 Balmes, *Filosofía fundamental*, I, chaps. XXX and XXXI; see Jaime Balmes, *Obras completas*, ed. I. Casanovas, XVI (Barcelona, 1925), 287–313. All references to Balmes are to this edition.

28 See George Uscatescu, *J. B. Vico y el mundo histórico* (Madrid, 1956), p. 16. In speaking about Vico's influence in Spain, Uscatescu refers to Donoso but utterly ignores Balmes.

29 With regard to *De antiquissima Italorum sapientia*, Michelet remarks: "Cet ouvrage est le seul dont Vico n'ait point transporté les idées dans *La Science nouvelle*" (see *Oeuvres complètes*, p. 15). In regard to the main point with which we are concerned here—that is, *verum ipsum factum*—F. Nicolini also recognizes, as we shall see later, that the meaning and value of this principle in *De antiquissima Italorum sapientia* is radically different from the meaning and value that it has in the *Scienza nuova.*

does not make Balmes' criticism less valid or less interesting.   If his exclusively epistemological interpretation of the *verum-factum* does not enucleate
its full value, it certainly points out Vico's initial intention in setting up that
axiom.   To give it a Neo-Hegelian interpretation may also be somewhat
justified, but, on the other hand, this may falsify Vico's principle by mixing
it up with ideas entirely alien to it.

Balmes examines the criterion *"verum ipsum factum"* within the general
framework of the problematic judgment of truth.

This philosopher [Vico] believes that on the basis of such a criterion we only know the
truth of an object if we have been active in its creation; that our knowledge is endowed
with complete certitude when such a circumstance is present; but that our knowledge
loses its certainty whenever our intelligence loses its causal power in relation to
external objects.   God, who is the cause of everything, knows everything perfectly.
Man, who is capable of being a cause only in a narrow sense, has limited knowledge.
And, if in any sphere the human mind can resemble the infinite, it is only within the
confines of the ideal world that it creates for itself and that it can enlarge at will, without being hampered by a single barrier which could not be removed.[30]

In order to confirm what he has set forth, Balmes quotes and translates a
long passage from *De antiquissima Italorum sapientia*,[31] where Vico, having
established the principle of *verum ipsum factum*, proceeds to classify the
sciences according to their degree of certainty.[32]   Balmes quotes the following words from Vico: "Since human science is based entirely on abstraction,
the sciences grow less certain as they approach corporal matter."[33]   According to Balmes' interpretation, Vico's judgment attributes the greatest
certainty to mathematics, while "in the moral sciences" certainty is minimal
"because they are not concerned with the movements of bodies, which
stem from a certain and constant origin (that is, physical nature), but with
the movements of souls, which are born in great depths and quite often without cause."[34]   One cannot deny that Balmes' preoccupation with criticism
hides from him the main value of Vico's principle and of its application to

---

[30] Balmes, *Filosofía fundamental*, chap. XXX, n. 294, in *Obras completas*, XVI, 287.

[31] Balmes is quoting from *De antiquissima Italorum sapientia*, bk. I, chap. 1.   By the
way in which he quotes and, above all, owing to the style of the text, we think it certain
that Balmes used Michelet's translation of *De antiquissima*, which he published in his
Oeuvres complètes, pp. 211ff.

[32] Balmes, *Filosofía fundamental*, chap. XXX, n. 295, in *Obras completas*, XVI, 290.

[33] *Ibid.*, p. 291.   Balmes quotes: *De la ant. sab. de la Italia (ibid.*, p. 1); cf. Michelet,
Oeuvres complètes, p. 222.

[34] Balmes, *Obras completas*, XVI, 290.   This passage, more than a mere interpretation
of Balmes', actually reproduces Vico's text with a few paraphrases.   Cf. Michelet,
Oeuvres complètes, p. 223: "... La morale est moins certaine encore que la physique,
parce que celle-ci considère les mouvements internes des corps, qui ont leur origine dans
la nature, laquelle est certaine et constante, tandis que la morale scrute les mouvements
des âmes, qui se passent à des grandes profondeurs, et qui proviennent le plus souvent du
caprice, lequel est infini."

the cultural sciences. However, in spite of these limitations, his criticism, in view of the times in which he wrote, deserves attention.[35]

"It cannot be denied," says Balmes,

that Vico's theory reveals a profound thinker who has carefully meditated on the problems of the mind. The dividing line regarding the certainty of the sciences is most interesting. At first glance, there is nothing more deceptive than the difference between the mathematical sciences and the moral and natural sciences. Mathematics is absolutely certain because it is the work of the intellect; mathematical certitude is as reason sees it, because it is the intellect that constructs it. The natural and moral sciences, on the other hand, concern themselves with objects that are independent of reason and that have an autonomous existence. Thus the intellect knows very little about them and is very easily misled when it enters a sphere where its constructive powers do not apply. I have called this theory misleading because, upon examining it in depth, one finds that it lacks a solid foundation. I do, nonetheless, acknowledge the author's deep insight in treating the sciences the way he does.[36]

Balmes begins his criticism by affirming that causality is not the sole origin of all possible knowledge.[37] "To understand something is not to cause it. There can exist—and indeed there does exist—a creative intellect, but, in general, the act of understanding and that of creation should be differentiated. Intelligence implies activity, for without activity one cannot conceive of the inner life that characterizes the intelligent person. But this productive

[35] In my opinion, Balmes' interpretation of Vico's concept of the relative certainty of the sciences, with regard exclusively to *De antiquissima Italorum sapientia*, is not erroneous. Nicolini, in the passage cited above, makes the following commentary: "Tesi opposta a quella sostenuta nella *Scienza nuova*, nella quale alle scienze morali e politiche verrà assegnata certezza maggiore che non alla stessa geometria. Cf. [*Scienza nuova*] . . . il capov. 349, tanto più importante in quanto, in esso appunto, la teoria del *verum-factum*, dal mondo astratto dei numeri e delle grandezze, verrà estesa al mondo concreto della storia; o, ch'è lo stesso, forma certissima di conoscenza verrà affermata precisamente quella storica (storicismo assoluto)" (*Opere*, 255). Consult *Scienza nuova*, bk. I, sec. IV, par. 349: "Così questa Scienza procede appunto come la geometria, che, mentre sopra i suoi elementi il costruisce o 'l contempla, essa stessa si faccia il mondo delle grandezze; ma con tanto più di realtà, quanto più ne hanno gli ordini d'intorno alle faccende degli uomini, che non ne hanno punti, linee, superficie e figure. E questo istesso è argomento che tali pruove sieno d'una spezie divina, e che debbano, o leggitore, arrecarti un divin piacere, perocché in Dio il conoscer e 'l fare è una medesima cosa" (*ibid.*, pp. 489–90). Another problem—which we cannot discuss here—is whether Vico's text lays the foundations of that absolute historicism of which Nicolini speaks.

[36] Balmes, *Filosofía fundamental*, chap. XXX, n. 296, in *Obras completas*, XVI, 291–92.

[37] Before, in chap. XIII ("Representación de causalidad y de idealidad"), n. 134 (*ibid.*, p. 136), Balmes, referring to the knowledge of God with regard to things created, writes: "Inasmuch as the knowledge which the First Being has of objects distinct from himself is inseparably connected with the fact that he is their cause, we gather that the representation of ideality is joined with that of causality. Thus the principle of a profound Neapolitan thinker, Vico, 'The intellect knows only what it itself does,' receives partial confirmation."

activity of known objects is exerted in an immanent fashion on such objects as are assumed to be already in union with the intellect, in a meditated or unmeditated fashion." [38]   And he argues:

If intelligence were destined to know only what it does itself, it would not be easy to conceive how the act of understanding could start.   Placing ourselves at the instant when it begins, we would not know how to explain the development of this activity, because, since the mind can only understand what it does, what will it understand at the initial moment, when it has not yet done anything?   In the theory that we are discussing, the mind acts only upon that which it creates itself.   On the other hand, understanding without an object to be understood is a contradiction.   Thus, at the initial moment, since nothing has yet been produced, nothing can be understood, and intellection is therefore inexplicable.   It is not correct to assume that activity takes place blindly.   There is nothing blind about a matter of mental representation, and productive activity refers essentially to the things represented insofar as they are expressed.   The fact that these things are produced outwardly, and possess an existence distinct from their expression, is irrelevant to the question of understanding.   Thus, as Vico himself explains, human reason knows what it creates in a purely ideal world, and God knows the Word that he generates, even if this Word is not external to the divine essence but coessential with it. [39]

Balmes criticizes the theological applications that Vico makes of his principle with the laudable purpose of reconciling his theory with Catholic doctrine.   Speaking about the eternal generation of the Word of God, Vico writes: "In this Word, truth is the understanding of all the elements of this universe, which could form infinite worlds.   From these known elements which are contained in the divine omnipotence, the true, absolute Word is *formed*, known by the Father from eternity and engendered by him since all eternity." [40]   Balmes comments: "If the author means that the Word is conceived by that which is contained in divine omnipotence, his assertion is false.   If he does not mean this, his wording is incorrect." [41]   And he appeals to the authority of St. Thomas, for whom the Word also expresses the creatures of the earth, but is conceived by the intellective power of these and, primarily, by means of the knowledge of the divine essence. [42]   Vico attempts to reconcile his theory and principle of the *verum-factum* with the theological process of the engendering of the world, while he maintains that

[38] *Ibid.*, chap. XXX, n. 298 (p. 292).

[39] *Ibid.*, n. 299 (p. 293).

[40] *Ibid.*, n. 300 (pp. 294–95).   Balmes quotes from Vico's *De antiquissima*, bk. I, chap. I; the emphasis is Balmes'.   Cf. Michelet, *Oeuvres complètes*, p. 217: "Dans ce Verbe, le vrai est la compréhension même de tous les éléments de cet univers, laquelle pourrait former des mondes infinis; c'est de ces éléments connus et contenus dans la toute-puissance divine que se forme le Verbe réel, absolu, connu de toute éternité par le Père, et engendré par lui de toute éternité."

[41] Balmes, *Obras completas*, XVI, 295.

[42] *Ibid.*; Balmes quotes St. Thomas *Summa theol.* I. 34. 3c and m.

the referent of that engendering is not the divine essence insofar as it is known, but insofar as it is engendered. Balmes counters Vico with the doctrine of St. Thomas according to which every intellection (including that which is peculiar to the divine essence), the process of intellection itself, and the concept of the object grasped in that process are anterior to any possible relationship of generation or production sustained by the known object.[43] "It is evident," adds Balmes, "that in order to produce in the intellectual domain it is necessary to have previous understanding. Therefore, we should place intuition, and not creative action, at the initial moment of every process of intellection."[44] One finds the same logic with regard to the creation of the Word in God. Balmes does not want to charge Vico with a grave theological error: "I have only wanted to point out the inaccuracy of his words; I am quite fair to him, on the other hand, by believing that he understood everything in the fashion in which I have explained, even if he was not altogether successful in rendering his thought clearly."[45]

Balmes exposes other inconsistencies deriving from Vico's axiom. "The soul," writes Vico, "knowing itself, does not 'make' itself, and therefore does not know the fashion in which it knows itself."[46] Vico, argues Balmes, denies in these words that our soul is endowed with any criterion of truth by which it can gauge the value of its self-awareness. But this is inadmissible. The identity of the knower with the known is for Balmes a fundamental standard of truth. If Vico's axiom were the only criterion of truth, no one could have self-knowledge, for nothing "makes" itself. And one would even have to say that God cannot know himself, for God does not create himself either. "Nor is it enough to say that we gain knowledge in the Word, for, if one does not presuppose intellection, the Word is impossible."[47]

If *verum ipsum factum* were the only criterion of truth, human understanding would be deprived of all true knowledge of the realities of the external world. Vico's doctrine, according to Balmes, paves the way for the most unadulterated skepticism. "The only method of destroying skepticism is to adopt as a criterion of truth the principle that each one of us is certain about the verity of what he has created himself."[48] Vico's endeavor to refute skepticism by considering causality the only source of truthful knowledge, even if resorting to the Primal Cause (as Vico has done), is thoroughly in-

[43] Balmes, *Filosofía fundamental*, chap. XXX, n. 301, in *Obras completas*, XVI, 297 (Balmes quotes Thomas *Summa theol.* I. 27. 1c).
[44] *Ibid.*
[45] *Ibid.*, n. 302 (p. 298).
[46] *Ibid.*
[47] *Ibid.*
[48] *Ibid.*, p. 299. Balmes quotes from *De antiquissima*, bk. I, chaps. I and III; cf. Michelet, *Oeuvres complètes*, p. 227.

effective. "If there is no other criterion than causality, understanding is isolated, powerless to advance further than the point reached by the effects that it itself has produced. In the realm of cause, on the other hand, the human mind cannot rise any higher than its own self, for, if it rises, then it already knows things which it has not made, that is, the cause which produced the human mind itself." [49]

Balmes' criticism of the principle of *verum ipsum factum* is not, however, entirely negative. He recognizes that this principle possesses, even if with some limitations, a certain validity in the domain of ideal truths. Especially is this true in the field of geometric knowledge, where reason constructs its own science and generates its rational progression, beginning with definitions or postulates that it imposes upon itself. Balmes agrees that in pure mathematics "the intellect constructs in a purely ideal world" and that, in this case, "it knows what it is doing, for its operation is present to it." [50] But he also emphasizes that the intellect "knows more than what it does; there are truths that cannot be its works, for they are the foundation of all its works—for example, the principle of contradiction." [51] "Even in regard to things which are purely intellectual creations," Balmes adds, "the intellect knows what it is doing, but it does not act entirely at its will. Were it otherwise, one could say that the sciences are absolutely arbitrary." [52] But this is inadmissible; reason, even in its purely ideal constructions, is subject to laws that cannot be the result of the free constructive ability of reason itself. And even in the progress of its ideal constructions, reason always discovers truths that the intellect has not made, but is capable of grasping by cognition." [53]

Balmes recognizes Vico's merit in "having indicated one of the reasons for the certitude of mathematics and of other purely ideal sciences," but he also exposes Vico's mistake of exaggerating the value of that fundamental criterion: "There is no doubt that the human intellect in some way creates the 'ideal sciences,' but in what way? Only by taking postulations and combining data in different ways. The creative force of the intellect ends here, for, in those postulations and combinations, the mind of man discovers necessary truths not posited by it." [54] On the other hand, while in the purely "ideal" sciences reason obeys no laws but its own, in the sciences that deal with physical objects, reason "cannot disregard the objects which it studies, cannot dispense with considering them in themselves, suffering all

---

[49] Balmes, *Obras completas*, XVI, 309. It is interesting to note that Francisco Sánchez ("*el tudelano*," not to be confused with "*el Brocense*," whom Vico quotes more than once), in his *De multum nobili et prima universali scientia: quod nihil scitur* (1581), formulates his skepticism in a fashion similar to that of Vico: "No one can know what he does not create or make. Only God knows all things perfectly." Cf. Marcial Solana, *Historia de la filosofía española: Epoca del Renacimiento*, I (Madrid, 1941), 398.

[50] Balmes, *Filosofía fundamental*, chap. XXXI, n. 306, in *Obras completas*, XVI, 304.

[51] *Ibid.*, n. 307 (p. 305).

[52] *Ibid.*, n. 308 (pp. 305–6).   [53] *Ibid.*, n. 310 (p. 307).   [54] *Ibid.*

the disadvantages under which those objects labor because of their very nature."[55]   Balmes concludes: "That is why Vico says, and quite correctly, that our knowledge loses certitude proportionally as it moves farther and farther away from the 'ideal' order and becomes engulfed in reality."[56]

Translated by Himilce Novás

[55] *Ibid.*
[56] *Ibid.*   Balmes (*ibid.*, n. 311 [pp. 309–10]) writes: "Dugald-Stewart probably took advantage of this doctrine of Vico's in order to explain the cause for the greater certitude of the mathematical sciences," and he remarks (n. 312) that the Schoolmen had already said the same thing when they pointed out "that there is no science of the contingent or the particular; and that sciences deal only with the necessary and universal."   Balmes mentions Vico in *Curso de filosofía elemental* (1848), III, n. 217 (see *Obras completas*, XXIII, 160), in reference to his doctrine of metaphysical points and in n. 291 (*ibid.*, pp. 218–19), where he draws a pen portrait of Vico and briefly epitomizes the interpretation and criticism given in his *Filosofía fundamental.*

George L. Kline   VICO IN
                        PRE-REVOLUTIONARY
                                   RUSSIA

Interest in the thought of Giambattista Vico in pre-revolutionary Russia focuses on two periods: (1) the late 1860's and early 1870's, a time when Russian intellectuals were turning from the natural sciences to the historical disciplines; and (2) the late 1890's and early 1900's, when the Marxist theory of history and social change was generating new interest in the thinker whom many Russians considered the "father of the philosophy of history." This interest is expressed in half a dozen works, ranging in length from seven to nearly a hundred pages, as well as in an encyclopedia article (see bibliography). No separate monograph or book on Vico was published in pre-revolutionary Russia, although the chapter devoted to Vico in Stasyulevich's 1866 study is of monographic length.

Vico's rejection of the Cartesian emphasis on physics to the neglect of history is curiously echoed in Russia in the rejection by the "men of the seventies" of the views of the "men of the sixties." But the men of the seventies succeeded for a time in dominating Russian intellectual life, whereas Vico's critique of Descartes remained largely without influence in his own century.

The change in the Russian cultural and intellectual climate of the period can be dated quite precisely by the publication of two extraordinarily influential works: P. L. Lavrov's book *Historical Letters*, of 1868–69, and N. K. Mikhailovski's long essay "What is Progress?" of 1869. These two works marked a shift from the one-sided emphasis placed on the natural sciences by Chernyshevski and Pisarev. The men of the seventies had lost faith in the "magical" power of Bazarov's microscope (see Turgenev's *Fathers and Sons*); they no longer believed, with Pisarev, that "the salvation of Russia [lay] . . . in the frog [as a symbol of experimental physiology and applied medicine]."

The shift in Russian thought around 1869—from science to history, from the study of nature and of man as biological organism to the study of society and of man as historical agent—would have been congenial to Vico. Whether he himself had some part in bringing it about is an open question. Vico was first discussed by Stasyulevich in 1866,[1] just two years before the

[1] M. M. Stasyulevich, *Opyt istoricheskovo obzora glavnykh sistem filosofii istorii* (St. Petersburg, 1866), pp. 52–147.

publication of the first installments of Lavrov's *Historical Letters*.[2] It is likely that both Lavrov[3] and Mikhailovski read Stasyulevich's book soon after it appeared. Mikhailovski refers to it in his own essay on Vico in 1872. Lavrov, who discussed Vico explicitly as early as 1868, is very likely to have read anything published in his native St. Petersburg which dealt *in extenso* with Hegel's philosophy of history. (Stasyulevich devotes more than a hundred pages to Hegel.)

Whether Vico's ideas were only loosely parallel to those of the "men of the seventies," or were related to them as (partial) cause to effect, is a question which we must leave unanswered. I shall briefly review the Russian studies of Vico, taking them in chronological order: Stasyulevich (1866), Lavrov (1868), Mikhailovski (1872), Chicherin (1872), Dzhivelegov (1896), and Vipper (1900). First, however, a word about Alexander Herzen's relation to Vico.

Although the Soviet *Philosophical Encyclopedia* solemnly includes listings of several pages from the works of Herzen in its Vichian bibliography,[4] Herzen's references to Vico fall into two equally insubstantial classes: (1) early letters to his friend Ogaryov (dating from July and August, 1833, when Herzen was twenty-one years old) stating his intention to read Vico—along with Michelet, Montesquieu, Herder, *et al.* (whether Herzen ever studied Vico's own works is an open question); (2) a scattering of references in his *From the Other Shore* (1850) to the *corsi e ricorsi* of history, sometimes with mention of Vico's name, sometimes without.[5] In any event, Herzen can scarcely be considered a serious student of Vico.

Stasyulevich's ninety-six-page essay is largely expository and contains

[2] Stasyulevich first read Vico when he was preparing to write a prize essay on Homer set by classics professor Grefe of St. Petersburg University in 1846 (cf. *ibid.*, p. 109*n*). In 1863 Stasyulevich included a brief Russian translation from Vico in his anthology of texts, *Istoriya srednikh vekov* (A History of the Middle Ages) (St. Petersburg), I, 65–69, and a note on Vico, pp. 69–70. The translation is from the *New Science*, bk. I, axioms 64–68, and the opening paragraphs of bks. IV and V. In the note, Stasyulevich calls the *New Science* a "work of genius" and its author "the father of the philosophy of history," adding that Vico has at last gained the fame due "the genius of this remarkable reformer of the method of science" (*ibid.*, pp. 69, 70).

[3] The first complete English translation of the *Historical Letters*, by James P. Scanlan, was published in 1967 by the University of California Press. Excerpts from this translation had appeared earlier in *Russian Philosophy*, ed. James M. Edie, James P. Scanlan, Mary-Barbara Zeldin, and George L. Kline (Chicago, 1965), II, 123–69.

[4] *Filosofskaya entsiklopediya*, I (Moscow, 1960), 259.

[5] In the nine-volume edition of Herzen's works recently published in Moscow the first group of references falls in vol. IX, pp. 242, 244, and 246; the second, in vol. III, pp. 259, 339. (An English translation of the latter appears in *From the Other Shore*, ed. I. Berlin [London–New York, 1956], pp. 34, 147.)

many extended quotations from Vico's *New Science*.[6]   In fact, the author anticipates that he will be criticized for expounding Vico's position so fully and for quoting him so extensively.[7]   But he justifies this procedure on the ground that Vico is almost entirely unknown to Russian readers.   Stasyulevich himself translates from Vico's Italian text (unlike Mikhailovski and Chicherin, who used Michelet's very free French "translation"), and in general is accurate.[8]   Stasyulevich's own interpretive and critical comments, although brief, strike me as being generally balanced and fair.

Stasyulevich makes it clear from the beginning that he considers Vico a thinker of genius, the father of the discipline of philosophy of history, and "one of the most remarkable heroes of thought of the last century."[9]   He sees dangers in Vico's comparative method (comparing the political and social systems of Venice and Athens, etc.), but finds it sound in its essentials. Stasyulevich adds that nineteenth-century comparative history, comparative philology, and comparative law all owe their existence to Vico.[10]   He agrees with Vico that language and law (*pravo = diritto = jus*) are the two chief products of the human mind and spirit.

Stasyulevich, like other Russian commentators on Vico, dutifully catalogues the three constant factors in the life of all peoples (religion, marriage rites, funeral rites), the three ages of history, the corresponding forms of language, and so on.   But he notes acidly that Vico failed to recognize the legend of the three ages (Egyptian in origin) as itself a myth or hieroglyph, a bit of poetic metaphysics.[11]   What Stasyulevich finds of value in the theory of the "three ages" is the stress on the continuity of social development, and the recognition of the need to discover its laws.[12]   But he insists that Vico's three ages are all simultaneously present in a given period: the masses live in the age of the gods, some individuals have advanced to the age of heroes, and a very few exceptional individuals have reached the age of men.   He refers to "those three historical strata of society which are fated to lead a single common historical life" and to the hostility of those still living in the age of heroes toward those who would bring society, through

---

[6] For example, axioms 1–4, 10, 13, 14, 17–19, 21–22, 28–30, 32–36, 52–53, 57–62, 64–69, 92, 95–96; see Stasyulevich, *Opyt istoricheskovo obzora*, pp. 60–76.

[7] *Ibid.*, p. 133.

[8] Mikhailovski's strictures on Stasyulevich's translation do not seem quite fair.   He points out that Stasyulevich uses "wonderful" or "miraculous" (*chudesnoye*) for "wonder" or "astonishment."   (Michelet's term is *admiration*, Vico's is *maraviglia*.) And he claims, without specifying, that Stasyulevich makes other errors, a fact which, he says, undermines confidence in the entire translation.   See N. K. Mikhailovski, "Ocherki iz istorii politicheskoi literatury: Viko i yevo 'Novaya nauka,'" *Otechestvennyie zapiski*, no. 11 (1872): 90n.

[9] Stasyulevich, *Opyt istoricheskovo obzora*, p. 54.

[10] *Ibid.*, p. 53.   [11] *Ibid.*, p. 137.   [12] *Ibid.*, p. 139.

reform, into the age of men—"in the name of the idea of humaneness [*chelovechnost*]."[13] (This formulation may well have suggested to Lavrov his doctrine of the "critically thinking individuals" whose critical thought helps lift the masses out of their animal existence.)

Stasyulevich notes that for Vico every society is a kind of phoenix, reborn from the ashes of previous societies: "*L'humanité est morte! Vive l'humanité!*" And he adds: "One may delight in such a poetic idea of the immortality of mankind, but it can scarcely serve as a firm scientific foundation for historical truth." In fact, he insists, "the death of a society is not like the death of an individual. . . ."[14]

Stasyulevich sees Vico's central contribution in the conviction that, if there is not a universal and eternal (hence repetitive) course of events, history cannot be a science, "since a science [*nauka*] can have as its object only what is eternal, that is, what is subject once and for all to general and unchangeable laws."[15] Stasyulevich adds that the "direction taken by Vico places history for the first time on a scientific basis, although the general laws [for instance, those of funeral rites] which he adduced are arbitrarily selected. . . ."[16]

As for Vico's *filologia*, many of his etymologies are absurd, but the trail which he blazed is "astonishing in its correctness and in the results to which it will undoubtedly lead with further advances in philology."[17]

Lavrov in 1868 notes that "the profundity and power of this lonely eighteenth-century thinker" was not appreciated until half a century after his death.[18] He himself stresses Vico's contemporaneousness, maintaining that, if Vico's works had been discovered in manuscript at mid-nineteenth century, they would have been judged to be of much later origin than they in fact were, mainly because of their "general methods of thought." But Lavrov sees Vico as, in other respects, out of touch with, and behind, his own age—praising Plato and polemicizing with Descartes at a time when Newton reigned in physics and Locke in philosophy.

According to Lavrov, the pious Vico did not realize that his axiom 35,

---

[13] *Ibid.*, pp. 140f.

[14] *Ibid.*, pp. 142, 143.

[15] *Ibid.*, p. 77. Lavrov, who defined history as the "science of progress" (*nauka o progresse*), would have rejected the Vichian stress on the ideal and eternal nature of historical patterns. Mikhailovski would have done so even more vehemently.

[16] *Ibid.*, p. 136.

[17] *Ibid.*

[18] P. L. Lavrov, "Razvitiye ucheniya o mificheskikh verovaniyakh" (The Development of the Theory of Mythical Beliefs), *Sovremennoye obozreniye*, no. 3 (1868): 393–425 and no. 4 (1868): 67–107; quoted from the reprinting in Lavrov, *Sobraniye sochineni* (Collected Works), series V: Essays on the History of Religion, pt. 1 (Petrograd, 1917), p. 48.

"Wonder is the child of ignorance," offered a powerful weapon to the anti-religionist. The Vichian axioms 1 and 32, Lavrov declares, "lay at the basis of Feuerbach's anthropological theory of religion and the entire contemporary science of myths."[19]   Like Voltaire, Holbach, and Hume, Vico wanted to apply "scientific criticism" to all realms of human thought.   He regarded the laws of nature and of human activity as immune to all arbitrariness—including that of the divine will.   But, unlike eighteenth-century thinkers, who were concerned to *combat* the past, Vico (in this respect, we might add, like Hegel) was mainly concerned to *understand* the laws of past development.

Lavrov sees in Vico's theory of myths a parallel to Locke: Locke tried to show the genesis of "innate ideas" in the isolated individual; "one of Vico's chief merits was to have explained the genesis of the fundamental forms of the people's life in terms of the collective individual," for instance, in his theory of the "symbolically collective significance of Homer."[20]   "Vico," Lavrov concludes, "remained a lonely and premature, but at the same time great, phenomenon in the history of the theory of myths."[21]

Mikhailovski sees in Vico "one of the most original figures of the past century, . . . both in his works and in his fate.   Creator of a work of genius, he taught eloquence for forty years, composing epitaphs, epithalamia, words of greeting and of praise for various dukes, marquis, and electors. . . . A remarkable thinker, who in many ways set the direction for his age, he . . . was unknown to his contemporaries and almost useless to his posterity."[22] In a long life, all that this "great thinker" managed to win was "some dozens of people who confessed themselves his disciples, and the title of founder of the philosophy of history."[23]

Vico's "new science" is our "philosophy of history or [*sic*] social dynamics," Mikhailovski declares, using a fashionable Spencerian term.[24]   But, he adds, the *New Science* is a repetitive, awkward, strangely organized, sometimes overly concise book.   It is also a chaotic work; Vico's ideas are scattered through the first four books in "unimaginable disorder."   The work is filled with "sometimes witty and profound, sometimes amusing, historical and philological comparisons."[25]

As I have already suggested, it was the stress on the humane and historical disciplines, as against the physical sciences, that Mikhailovski and other

[19] *Ibid.*, p. 52.
[20] *Ibid.*, pp. 51, 53.
[21] *Ibid.*, p. 53.
[22] Mikhailovski, "Ocherki iz istorii politicheskoi literatury: Viko i yevo 'Novaya nauka,' " pp. 74f.
[23] *Ibid.*, p. 86.   [24] *Ibid.*, p. 88.   [25] *Ibid.*, pp. 87, 90.

"men of the seventies" found most congenial in Vico. Mikhailovski applauds Vico's critique of the Cartesian neglect of the "moral" (including "political") disciplines.[26] And he adds: "This obliviousness to moral-political questions must have offended Vico's organic intellect—as a gap, a one-sidedness, an inequable, unharmonious distribution of the component parts of the new world view." [27]

Mikhailovski emphasizes the antisocial character of Descartes' criterion of truth.[28] He even considers Cartesianism an "anarchic" doctrine, taking *anarchy* in the broad sense as an "absence of all general (*obshchiye*) or, more precisely, social (*obshchestvennyie*) guiding principles." [29]

According to Mikhailovski, Vico clearly grasped the possibility, necessity, and "great importance" of the philosophy of history. This alone guarantees him "one of the most prominent places" in the history of political theory of "all times." [30]

Mikhailovski sees Vico's primary insight in the idea that social development is governed by definite laws. Vico's related historical critique, Mikhailovski adds, is without precedent: his philosophical proofs (based on the generic traits of human nature) and his philological proofs (based on the historical facts) are intended to show that a given phenomenon could not have existed at a given time in the form in which it is reported to have existed.[31]

Vico, Mikhailovski complains, combined "theological" and "scientific" explanation in a purely mechanical way. But, as a reformer of historiography, he anticipated and surpassed Voltaire, who is usually given the credit for such reform. (1) He had a clearer idea of the "lawlike character" (*zakonosoobraznost*) of history than did Voltaire; (2) before Voltaire he recognized that history is not just a description of battles and reigns but "a study of the development of ideas, mores, and the social situation of peoples"; (3) before Voltaire he "dispersed the fables and legends that enveloped gray-haired antiquity in a thick cloud," and he did this more profoundly and completely than Voltaire did. However, Mikhailovski adds, Voltaire turned his own researches into "deadly machine guns [of social criticism], whereas Vico offered to a critical age a historical justification of obsolete and obsolescent principles. This accounts for the success of the one and the lack of success of the other." [32]

Mikhailovski finds in Vico's axiom 32 (about men attributing their own nature to things of which they are ignorant) the basic idea of both Hume's and Feuerbach's account of religion. This point had already been made by Lavrov in his 1868 article.

According to Mikhailovski, Vico's theory of historical cycles (*ricorsi*)

[26] *Ibid.*, p. 76.　　　[27] *Ibid.*, p. 85.　　　[28] *Ibid.*, pp. 78, 81.
[29] *Ibid.*, p. 102.　　　[30] *Ibid.*, p. 88.　　　[31] *Ibid.*, p. 95.
[32] *Ibid.*, p. 96.

places him between the majority of eighteenth-century believers in steady, rectilinear progress, on the one hand, and Rousseau, the believer in steady, rectilinear retrogression, on the other. The theory of historical cycles remains descriptive rather than explanatory. Furthermore, its proponents like to stop the cycle at their own favored point, admitting only rectilinear development from there on. Vico is no exception; he sees in the contemporary period "the definitive triumph of humaneness (*chelovechnost*), and repudiates the thought that this triumph must be followed by a renewal of the barbarism of the age of the gods."[33]

What Vico and others have taken as a "law" of recurrent historical cycles is in fact a result of the struggle of opposed political, economic, and moral principles. When the same principle triumphs more than once, there is an apparent historical recurrence. "Political phenomena recur," Mikhailovski concludes, "that is a fact; societies die—that is also a fact. Upon these two facts Vico constructed his theory of historical cycles."[34] Its later proponents have added nothing essential to it.

Chicherin's chapter on Vico, in his general *History of Political Theories*, published in the same year as Mikhailovski's article, has little to say about Vico's theory of history, focusing instead on his theories of law and political organization. Chicherin devotes more space (23 pages) to Vico as political theorist than to Grotius (16 pages), Leibniz (20 pages), or Hobbes (21 pages). (He devotes 31 pages to Locke and 33 pages, each, to Spinoza and Montesquieu.)

Chicherin is the only Russian commentator on Vico to discuss Vico's metaphysics. He notes that Vico borrowed certain Cartesian principles from Malebranche—for example, the occasionalist theory of causation, and the mind-body dualism—but that he understood the body in a Leibnizian sense, as a kind of monad. Chicherin also mentions Vico's debt to Grotius in natural-law theory and to Campanella in political theory, while duly noting his differences from both. "Vico," he declares, "was the true founder of the philosophy of history."[35]

[33] *Ibid.*, pp. 98, 99.

[34] *Ibid.*, pp. 101, 102.

[35] B. N. Chicherin, *Istoriya politicheskikh ucheni*, pt. 2 (Moscow, 1872), p. 303. This estimation, generally shared by Russian commentators, was sharply rejected by Kareyev, who denied Vico (and Montesquieu) the title of philosopher of history *tout court*. (See N. N. Kareyev, *Osnovnyie voprosy filosofii istorii* [Fundamental Problems of the Philosophy of History], 2d ed., I [Moscow, 1887], 6, 7.) However, in a later work Kareyev softened his judgment somewhat, admitting that Vico had been the first "to set before science a new task, that of investigating what were later to be called historical laws" ("Teoreticheskiye voprosy istoricheskoi nauki" [Theoretical Problems of Historical Science] [1890], reprinted in *Istoriko-filosofskiye i sotsiologicheskiye etyudy* [Studies in Sociology and the Philosophy of History], 2d ed. [St. Petersburg, 1899], p. 81).

Chicherin criticizes Vico's definition of justice as "an equalizing of utilities," commenting: "Justice equalizes things only with respect to people, not with respect to the things themselves."[36] He adds that Vico himself seemed to sense this when he placed his theory of society immediately following his theory of justice. Chicherin sees in Vico's derivation of the three basic rights of man ("defense, freedom, and property") from "power, desire, and reason" an idea that is "original and apt." But he rejects as "arbitrary" Vico's derivation of the forms of polity from these three basic rights, a derivation first stated in *De universi iuris uno principio et fine uno* (1720) but repeated in the *New Science*. Chicherin also rejects Vico's definition of freedom as that "quae in aequabili usu rerum consistit," preferring Vico's alternative definition (not compatible with the first), "libertas est jus vivendi ut velis."[37]

Chicherin adds that in the *New Science* Vico "corrected" his earlier view of the historical position of monarchy, but that, even there, both monarchy and democracy fall in the third of the three ages, "which ascribes an identical character to both."[38] Chicherin gives Vico credit for introducing the idea of "a principle of internal development in the history of mankind," but adds that Vico treated modern history superficially and was generally "weak" in his treatment of the historical facts. "Concerning the mythical and heroic periods, despite the paucity of critical resources, he offers many brilliant ideas; but what he says about later periods lacks value."[39]

Vico's theory of cyclic recurrence is an "abstract scheme" applied only to certain peoples or civilizations, not to mankind as a whole. Still, Vico's over-all achievement is "enormous." It was he who first put forward the idea that "peoples develop out of themselves, on the basis of inner laws that spring from human nature." Vico even "dimly anticipated" the historical dialectic of Hegel[40]—high praise indeed from Chicherin, a devout Hegelian in the philosophy of history.

Dzhivelegov traces his interest in Vico to the new "economic materialist" (that is, Marxist) philosophy of history. Though Vico was the founder of the discipline, he was not valued by his contemporaries, and in fact was harshly and unfairly criticized. In metaphysics he produced nothing noteworthy. His main debts were to Plato and Tacitus, Bacon and Grotius.

Dzhivelegov rejects Flint's view that Vico remained unrecognized because his work was "too Italian." Instead, he sees three related reasons for the neglect of Vico: (1) his unseasonable anti-Cartesianism; (2) the difficulty of the *New Science*—"written in a language which is a mixture of Neapolitan

---

[36] Chicherin, *Istoriya politicheskikh ucheni*, pt. 2, p. 308.
[37] *Ibid.*, pp. 311, 312.   [38] *Ibid.*, p. 322.   [39] *Ibid.*, pp. 318, 323.
[40] *Ibid.*, p. 324.

dialect and Latin, burdened with minute details . . . , frequently returning to problems already treated, disorderly despite its systematicality," the book demanded a close attention and effort that eighteenth-century readers were reluctant to give it; (3) the public wasn't ready for a thinker who could anticipate Wolf in Homer criticism, Savigny in philosophy of law, and Niebuhr in historical criticism.[41]

Dzhivelegov says that the *New Science* gives the impression of "a brilliant fundamental idea and the amassing of innumerable facts from all the fields of knowledge then current in order to prove this idea; on the whole—a powerful system."[42]

He finds Vico's views on the origin of religion among the most interesting in the *New Science*, though he makes some disparaging remarks about the "theological swaddling clothes" from which Vico had not yet managed to free himself.[43] He finds Vico's views on the origin of language "widely shared" today, although Vico's theory of primitive patriarchy is not. He praises Vico's interpretation of the decemvirs but warns against studying Roman history through Vico. He gently rebukes Vico for neglecting economic factors in history.

Dzhivelegov considers the theory of *ricorsi* one of the weakest parts of Vico's system and suggests that it should have been replaced by a theory of an "endlessly unwinding historical spiral." Setting it aside, along with other weak parts of the work—such as the historical inaccuracies, strange etymologies, and lack of rational criticism—Dzhivelegov says, "We have in Vico an original thinker, with whom one can agree or disagree while remaining at the level of our contemporary knowledge."

Dzhivelegov sums up Vico's main contributions as "the solution of the Homeric question, [and] the theory of the historical development of law, the state, and religion."[44]

For Vipper, writing in 1900 (although the substance of his book had been presented as university lectures in 1898–99), Vico was the "major scientific initiator" of the eighteenth century. His "new science," says Vipper, is our "historical science" (*istoricheskaya nauka*). The *New Science* is an "astonishing book,"[45] marked by "stunning force and originality." Vico had an exceptional imagination; he could "read the vanished whole from the parts

[41] A. K. Dzhivelegov, "Viko i yevo sistema filosofii istorii," *Voprosy filosofii i psikhologii*, 7, no. 34 (September–October, 1896): 399–401.

[42] *Ibid.*, p. 403.

[43] *Ibid.*, pp. 406, 407.

[44] *Ibid.*, p. 427.

[45] R. Yu. Vipper, *Obshchestvennyie ucheniya i istoricheskiye teorii XVIII i XIX vv.* (St. Petersburg, 1900), p. 7.

which had survived." Still, Vipper warns, "no one will ever read the *New Science* with pleasure, as a classic work; . . . it will always be known only in paraphrase from the words of others."[46] Vipper is especially impressed by Vico's "profound historical interpretation of religious concepts and language," by his account of the earliest stages of social development, and by the Vichian interpretation of great historical figures as ideal collective images, "symbols of customs and beliefs, types of social classes."[47]

According to Vipper, "Vico could never discriminate among the wealth of his own knowledge; he could not separate the clearly possible and probable from the veridical; his material was tangled, and his proofs were not clearly articulated." Vipper adds that we are shocked to find in so great a thinker "something awkward, clumsy, unsystematic; annoying repetitions and diffuseness, an inability to put forward and emphasize ideas. . . ."[48] But, he adds, it would be hard to find "in our science" a "more original, rich, creative mind."[49]

This seems to have been the last pre-revolutionary Russian word on Vico.[50] The use—and abuse—of Vico's ideas by Soviet Marxist-Leninists is quite another story. It is told elsewhere in this volume.

Bibliography

Chicherin, B. N. *Istoriya politicheskikh ucheni* (A History of Political Theories), pt. 2. Moscow, 1872. Vico: pp. 302–24.

Dzhivelegov, A. K. "Viko i yevo sistema filosofii istorii" (Vico and his System of the Philosophy of History). *Voprosy filosofii i psikhologii*, 7, no. 34 (September–October, 1896): 396–428.

Kareyev, N. I. *Osnovnyie voprosy filosofii istorii* (Fundamental Problems in the Philosophy of History). 2d ed. St. Petersburg, 1887. Vico: pt. I, pp. 5–7, 22–24; pt. II, p. 256.

———. "Viko" (Vico). In *Entsiklopedicheski Slovar Brokgausa-Efrona*, VI (i.e., XI). St. Petersburg, 1892. P. 289.

---

[46] *Ibid.*, p. 18.

[47] *Ibid.*, p. 16.

[48] *Ibid.*, p. 18.

[49] *Ibid.*, pp. 17–18.

[50] Among Russian-born scholars well known abroad, Pitirim Sorokin (1889–1968) has perhaps been most clearly influenced by Vico. However, his sociological writings published in Russia between 1911 and 1922 contain only the most casual and infrequent references to Vico. For example, in discussing Lavrov's view of the "mechanism of the historical process," Sorokin writes: "The idea of the rhythmic tempo of the historical process is not new. To say nothing of Vico, it was developed later in almost the same form by St.-Simon, Bazard, and Comte." (P. Sorokin, "Osnovnyie problemy sotsiologii P. L. Lavrova" [Fundamental Problems in P. L. Lavrov's Sociology], in *P. L. Lavrov: Stati, vospominaniya, materialy* [Petersburg: Kolos, 1922], p. 289.)

Lavrov, P. L. "Razvitiye ucheniya o mificheskikh verovaniyakh" (The Development of the Theory of Mythical Beliefs) (signed "P. L-ov"). *Sovremennoye obozreniye*, no. 3 (1868): 393–425; no. 4 (1868): 67–107. Reprinted in Lavrov, P. L. *Sobraniye sochineni* (Collected Works), series V: Essays on the History of Religion. Petrograd, 1917. Pt. I, pp. 26–123. Vico: pp. 47–53.

Mikhailovski, N. K. "Ocherki iz istorii politicheskoi literatury: Viko i yevo 'Novaya nauka' " (Essays from the History of Political Literature: Vico and His 'New Science'). *Otechestvennyie zapiski*, no. 11 (1872): 73–103. Reprinted in *Polnoye sobraniye sochineni N. K. Mikhailovskovo* (Complete Works of N. K. Mikhailovski). 4th ed. St. Petersburg, 1909. Vol. III, cols. 73–104.

Mishle: O sisteme i zhizni Viko. Istoriko-biograficheski etyud s prilozheniyem podrobnovo perechnya soderzhaniya "Novoi nauki" (Michelet: On Vico's System and Life. An Historical and Biographical Study, with the Addition of a Detailed Listing of the Contents of the "New Science"). Translated from the French by Nikolai Parokonny, student at the Imperial Kharkov University, under the editorship of Professor B. P. Buzeskul. Kharkov, 1896. Includes a preface by Parokonny.

Stasyulevich, M. M. *Opyt istoricheskovo obzora glavnykh sistem filosofii istorii* (Attempt at a Historical Survey of the Main Systems of Philosophy of History). St. Petersburg, 1866. Vico: pt. I, chap. 2, pp. 52–147. A second edition, entitled *Filosofiya istorii v glavneishikh yeyo sistemakh: Istoricheski ocherk* (Philosophy of History in Its Chief Systems: An Historical Essay), was published in St. Petersburg in 1902.

Vipper, R. Yu. *Obshchestvennyie ucheniya i istoricheskiye teorii XVIII i XIX vv.* (Social Doctrines and Historical Theories of the Eighteenth and Nineteenth Centuries). St. Petersburg, 1900. Vico: pp. 7–18. These lectures were delivered at Moscow University in 1898–99; a second edition (with A. K. Dzhivelegov) was published at Ivanovo-Voznesensk in 1925.

René Wellek   THE SUPPOSED INFLUENCE
OF VICO ON ENGLAND
AND SCOTLAND IN THE
EIGHTEENTH CENTURY

In the thirties I studied a neglected question, the history of literary histori-ography. I finally published what was to be the first installment of a pro-jected history of English literary historiography, *The Rise of English Literary History*.[1] There, in two places, I referred to Vico. I was struck by the attempts of several eighteenth-century critics to construe a deductive, speculative universal history of poetry modeled on schemes of the general history of mankind. "It came," I wrote incautiously, "obviously im-mediately from Montesquieu and Condillac and ultimately from Vico."[2] A little further on I discussed the parallel between theories of the rise of poetry and the origins of language, and pointed to the importance of the breakdown of the intellectualist concept of language and its replacement by an emotionalist conception. "The latter was, of course, not an entirely new idea. Already Epicurus had derived language from 'pathos', from feeling, dislike and like, and Lucretius stressed the desire for sensual ex-pression. The notion was elaborated by Vico, who, directly or indirectly, must have influenced the whole century with his emotionalist theory of language and its origin."[3] I went on to give an account of Mandeville's, Blackwell's, Warburton's, Harris', and Blair's views of the role of metaphor in early language and poetry.

Max H. Fisch, in the introduction sketching a history of "Vico's Reputa-tion and Influence" to his and Thomas G. Bergin's translation of *The Auto-biography of Giambattista Vico*,[4] referred to these passages and to my book in general in support of his view that "it is scarcely credible that the Vichian ideas scattered through the writings of Blackwell, Ferguson, Hume, Wol-laston, Warburton, Hurd, Monboddo, Wood, Blair, Duff, Mason, Brown, Lowth, Warton and Burke, are due solely to their having been in this or that respect *animae naturaliter Vicianae*, or to a gradual unfolding of Shaftesbury's seminal thoughts, or even to an indirect and diluted Vichian influence

---

[1] (Chapel Hill: University of North Carolina Press, 1941), reprinted with a new preface (New York: McGraw-Hill, 1966).

[2] *Ibid.*, p. 74.

[3] *Ibid.*, p. 86.

[4] (Ithaca, N.Y., Cornell University Press, 1944).

through Italian and French authors mentioned in previous sections."[5]   In a
review of Mr. Fisch's introduction[6] I examined this hypothesis of Vico's
direct influence on English and Scottish eighteenth-century critics and
historians and came to an entirely negative conclusion.   I can today merely
repeat my arguments, somewhat modified and amplified in the light of the
large literature devoted to Vico since 1944.

Mr. Fisch first reviews the channels through which a knowledge of Vico
may have reached England.   Gilbert Burnet was in Naples in 1685, and his
son William was there early in the eighteenth century.   Vico probably met
them both.   But there is no evidence of this and even less of any effect of
this conjectured meeting.   The third Earl of Shaftesbury, during his stay in
Naples (1711–13), knew some of Vico's friends, Giuseppe Valletta and Paolo-
Maria Doria, "on whose behalf he transmitted to Burnet and Newton 'some
small literary works' which probably included Vico's *Treatise on Method* and
Ancient Wisdom of the Italians."[7]   But no evidence can be produced for this
guess nor for Mr. Fisch's further conjecture that Vico "later introduced his
second *New Science* with an allegorical engraving and commentary thereon,
a procedure doubtless suggested by Shaftesbury in his *Second Characters."*[8]
But Shaftesbury's *Second Characters* were left unfinished at his death and
were not published until they were unearthed in 1914.[9]   It seems highly
unlikely that Vico would have had access to the English manuscripts of Lord
Shaftesbury or that he would have needed a knowledge even of the allegorical
frontispieces in the *Characteristics* for the device used in front of the second
New Science thirty years later.

The frontispiece of Hobbes's *Leviathan* (1651) is much more similar to
Vico's allegory than anything in Shaftesbury.[10]   In the 1963 reprint of the
Autobiography Mr. Fisch changed "doubtless" to "perhaps,"[11] but even that
probability seems extremely slim.   Nor can much be made out of the fact
that George Berkeley was in Naples in 1717–18 and knew the same Paolo-
Maria Doria.   The next item produced by Mr. Fisch, the report from
Francesco Lomonaco's life of Vico (1836) that "some Englishmen who were
in Naples bought up all the copies" of the first *New Science* (1725) they could
find and sent them to London,[12] is based on an oral tradition confusing
London with Venice.   In the "Continuation" of the *Autobiography* (1731)

[5] *Ibid.*, p. 82.
[6] In "English Literature: 1660–1800: A Current Bibliography," *Philological Quarterly*,
24 (1945): 166–68.
[7] Fisch and Bergin, *Autobiography*, p. 81.
[8] *Ibid.*, pp. 81–82.
[9] *Second Characters; or the Language of Forms*, ed. Benjamin Rand (Cambridge, 1914).
[10] This is pointed out by Fausto Nicolini, *Commento storico alla Scienza nuova*, 2 vols.
(Rome, 1949), I, 21.
[11] (Ithaca, N.Y.: Great Seal Books, 1963), p. 82.
[12] *Ibid.*, quoted from *Vite degli eccellenti Italiani* (Lugano, 1836), II, 296.

we hear from Vico himself that the "Venetian Resident in Naples had acquired all the copies left in the shop of Felice Mosca the printer,"[13] a passage which seems the source of the tradition set down more than a century later.   Nor does Mr. Fisch's last item yield much more.   "Vico himself sent a copy" of the first *New Science* "to Newton which may have reached him about a year before his death."[14]   But the elaborate account of this shipment through intermediaries leaves this a doubtful possibility, and there is no trace of the book in Newton's library.[15]   Mr. Fisch himself admits that "no one has so far reported any evidence of direct acquaintance with Vico's writings . . . or indeed as much as a passing allusion to him"[16] in eighteenth-century England.

Still, in spite of this negative evidence, Mr. Fisch lists many English authors in the passage quoted above and suggests, then, that "Hume's natural history of religion, for instance, is up to a point eminently Vichian.   So is Blair's view that the 'times which we call barbarous' were 'most favorable to the poetical spirit', and that 'imagination was most glowing and animated in the first ages of society.'   So is Monboddo's theory of the origin and progress of language.   So are many such passages in . . . Ferguson's *Essay on the History of Civil Society.*"[17]   Ferguson is then quoted as saying that "mankind have twice, within the compass of history, ascended from rude beginnings to very high degrees of refinement," that "no constitution is formed by concert, no government is copied from a plan," that "nations actually borrow from their neighbors . . . only what they are nearly in a condition to have invented themselves," and finally: "when we attend to the language which savages employ on any solemn occasion, it appears that man is a poet by nature."[18]

The only explanation Mr. Fisch suggests for the strange silence on Vico is that Addison's *Remarks on Italy* (1701) had given "prevalence to a low opinion of contemporary Italian culture . . . which effectively discharged borrowers from Vico of the obligation to acknowledge their debts."[19]   But this is surely unconvincing.   I know of no suppression of references to other contemporary Italian scholars such as Gravina, Crescimbeni, Muratori, Tiraboschi, Algarotti, and others whose names I have encountered in my

[13] Fisch and Bergin, *Autobiography*, p. 182.   The "Venetian Resident" was Giovanni Zuccato.   See Benedetto Croce, *Bibliografia vichiana*, augmented and revised by Fausto Nicolini, 2 vols. (Naples, 1947–48), I, 237.

[14] Fisch and Bergin, *Autobiography*, p. 82; cf. Vico, *Opere*, ed. F. Nicolini, V, 55*n.* Newton died on March 20, 1727.

[15] See Croce and Nicolini, *Bibliografia vichiana*, I, 237–38.

[16] Fisch and Bergin, *Autobiography*, p. 83.

[17] *Ibid.*, p. 82.   The quotations come from Hugh Blair's *Critical Dissertation on the Poems of Ossian* (London, 1763), pp. 3–5, cited in my *Rise of English Literary History*, p. 63.

[18] Mr. Fisch quotes from the 3d ed. of Ferguson's *Essay on the History of Civil Society* (1768), pp. 182, 204, 280, 286.

[19] Fisch and Bergin, *Autobiography*, p. 81.

systematic reading of English eighteenth-century scholarship. There is ample evidence that Vico was almost unknown in other European countries until very late in the century. The difficulties of his exposition and style, the whole aura of seventeenth-century erudition still untouched by the new critical spirit,[20] and probably also the situation of Neapolitan learning and publishing (rather than Italian in general) must have been effective barriers which even his genius could not surmount at that time.

Some solution other than unacknowledged or even deliberately suppressed borrowing must be found. The most reasonable is the assumption that the ideas Mr. Fisch considers as peculiarly Vichian were known before Vico and were developed by English writers from sources other than Vico. This is no reflection on Vico's originality, which consists frequently in the bold combination of scattered ideas, in the radical thinking out of their consequences, or in a final systematic coherence. Croce, in a study of the sources of Vico's theory of knowledge, argued that "the search for precedents does nothing to explain the new thought that followed them."[21] There, and in another paper on Vico's Homer criticism,[22] Croce showed how completely Vico transformed older suggestions and how different a meaning they assumed in their new context. A glance at Fausto Nicolini's immensely erudite annotations to the second *New Science*[23] should convince everyone that Vico refers to many Latin books on philosophy, history, jurisprudence, and archaeology by Englishmen—to Bacon, to Hobbes, to Lord Herbert of Cherbury, to Thomas Stanley, to John Selden, Thomas Dempster, John Marsham, and possibly others—and to many more Latin books by Frenchmen, Dutchmen, Spaniards, and Germans which were accessible to eighteenth-century Englishmen. Vico has usually been thought of as an isolated figure, an outsider and precursor, which is true enough if we think of his lack of influence in his own century, but false if we ignore his roots in the past. I cannot here enter into the controversy over his relation to Platonic, Scholastic, and Renaissance thought in general, but clearly the relations to Descartes (polemical as they were), Bacon, and Hobbes define his position in the history of thought. Recently, a monograph by Enrico de Mas, *Bacone e Vico*,[24] added greatly to earlier discussions of the congruencies between the two thinkers and has helped to define one of the common sources of Vico and English eighteenth-century thought.

[20] Cf. "Vico was isolated in his times partly because he was a great thinker but partly also because he was a worse scholar than his contemporaries" (Arnaldo Momigliano, *Contributo alla storia degli studi classici* [Rome, 1955], p. 93).

[21] "Le fonti della gnoseologia vichiana," in *Saggio sullo Hegel* (Bari, 1947), pp. 234–62 (quote on p. 249).

[22] "Il Vico e la critica omerica," *ibid.*, pp. 263–76.

[23] See n. 10 above.

[24] (Turin, 1959); there are references to older treatments of the relationship by Nicolini, Sante Casellato, Guido Fassò, and others.

I shall limit myself to a few examples from ideas relevant to aesthetics, poetics, linguistics, and historiography in order to show that isolated ideas occurring in British writers of the eighteenth century need not have come from Vico. Thus, the view that imagination was strongest in the earliest ages of history was a commonplace of Renaissance debates on nature versus art, of the comparisons between Homer and Virgil, and in discussions of the origins of poetry. To give an example which could not have been known to Vico nor have been derived from him, Fontenelle in his "Traité de la poésie en général"[25] hails the end of "*le règne des images fabuleuses et matérielles,*" the end of inspiration and talent, which he hopes will be replaced by the poetry of *esprit*. As a good Rationalist he values things differently than Vico, but he traces the same general scheme. The English and Scottish "primitivists" say the same, but they did not need Vico to say it.

The idea that language arose from the expression of emotion dates back to Epicurus and Lucretius. Vico refers to a passage in Origene's *Contra Celsum* for the Stoic doctrine of language and oddly enough identifies the metaphysics of Epicurus with that of the poets.[26] Warburton, who is on Mr. Fisch's suspect list, in the fourth volume of *The Divine Legation of Moses* (1741) refers to Diodorus Siculus and Vitruvius, to Gregory of Nyssa and the French Oratorian, Richard Simon, who was also known to Vico.[27] Mandeville's similar discussion of the origin of language dates from 1728.[28] Condillac, in *Essai sur l'origine des connaissances humaines* (1746), draws freely from Warburton, whose fourth volume had been translated into French in 1744.[29] Condillac, rather than Vico, was known to Rousseau, Monboddo, Hamann, Herder, and the many other expounders of an emotionalist theory of the origin of language. Nicolini considers an influence of Vico on Warburton a possibility, but concludes that Condillac had no knowledge of Vico and derived entirely from Warburton.[30] But we must assume also Warburton's ignorance of Vico because he quotes sources very freely and nowhere expounds a doctrine which is exclusively Vichian.

Nor is it true that Warburton's and Vico's view of hieroglyphics—that

[25] Written about 1678, first published in 1751; see his *Oeuvres* (Paris, 1790), II, 193.

[26] See Antonino Pagliaro, "La Dottrina linguistica di G. B. Vico," in *Accademia dei Lincei, Memorie, Scienze morali*, ser. VIII, vol. VIII, no. 6 (1957), p. 400; Vico, "Metaphysica Epicuri eadem ac poetarum," in *De uno universi iuris principio et fine uno* (1720), chap. CLXXXV, par. 10.

[27] See Warburton, *Works*, ed. Richard Hurd (London, 1811), IV, 116, 133, 137–38, 170; Richard Simon, *Histoire critique du vieux testament* (Amsterdam, 1685), pp. 85ff. For Vico and Simon see Nicolini, *Commento storico*, I, 145.

[28] See F. B. Kaye, "Mandeville on the Origin of Language," *MLN*, 39 (1924): 136–42.

[29] *Essai sur les hiéroglyphes des égyptiens*, trans. Marc-Antoine Léonard de Malpeines (Paris, 1744).

[30] Nicolini, *Commento storico*, I, 29, and Croce and Nicolini, *Bibliografia vichiana*, I, 279–80.

they do not contain esoteric wisdom but are rather an early form of picture-writing—is very original. Bacon, who calls hieroglyphics a "flying" form of gesture language, shared this view and connected—as Vico did later—myths and hieroglyphics.³¹ The Renaissance conception of Egyptian mysteries locked in hieroglyphics had been effectively destroyed by Isaac Casaubon's argument that the *Hermetica*, supposedly dating back to hoary antiquity, is actually a product of early Christian times. But Casaubon's proof, propounded in *De rebus sacris et ecclesiasticis exercitationes XVI* (London, 1614), either was rejected or was relatively unknown for a long time. Casaubon's arguments, however, were taken up by Ralph Cudworth, the Cambridge Platonist, in *The True Intellectual System of the Universe* (1678). Although he tried to establish the authenticity of some hermetic books, he discussed hieroglyphics in terms of "figures not answering to sounds of words but immediately representing the objects and conceptions of the mind" (page 537). Cudworth was known to Warburton and was used by him extensively in his *The Divine Legation of Moses Demonstrated*. Also, Bishop Wilkins, in the essay *Towards a Real Character and a Philosophy of Language* (1668), and M. F. D. Colberg, in *Platonisch-Hermetisches Christentum* (1690), have been cited as skeptics about the mysteries of hieroglyphs. Warburton knew Wilkins but almost certainly did not know Colberg.³²

Vico's view of Homer was undoubtedly highly original. His "discovery of the true Homer"—"an idea or a heroic character of Grecian men as they told their history in song"³³—cannot be paralleled before his time. But many presuppositions for Vico's conception were common knowledge before his writing. Vico himself refers to the passage in Josephus Flavius which defends the view that Homer "left his poems to the memory of his rhapsodes because in his time vulgar letters had not yet been discovered."³⁴ That Homer dates from preliterary times and that the poems were sung by illiterate strolling bards were the conclusions reached by Jakob Voorbroek (Perezonius) in his *Animadversiones historicae* (Amsterdam, 1685) and by Abbé d'Aubignac in his *Conjectures académiques sur l'Iliade* (1715).³⁵ These two

³¹ *De augmentis scientiarum* VI. 1, in *Works*, ed. J. Spedding, R. L. Leslie, and D. D. Heath, I (London, 1889), 652–53. "Ut sapientia literis, ita parabolae argumentis antiquiores" (Preface, *De sapientia veterum*).

³² On Casaubon see Frances A. Yates, *Giordano Bruno and the Hermetic Tradition* (London, 1964), pp. 398ff. A fuller treatment is given in Liselotte Dieckmann's forthcoming *Hieroglyphics: The History of a Literary Symbol* (London: Warburg Institute, 1969). I owe access to the manuscript to the kindness of Mrs. Dieckmann. On Wilkins see Wladyslaw Folkierski, *Entre le classicisme et le romantisme* (Krakow, 1925), pp. 130–31n. On Colberg see Liselotte Dieckmann, "Renaissance Hieroglyphics," *Comparative Literature*, 9 (1957): 320.

³³ See Nicolini, *Commento storico*, I, 29, 47; and II, 9–10. Cf. *Scienza nuova*, par. 873.

³⁴ *Contra Apionem* I. 2, referred to in the second *Scienza nuova*, par. 66; see Nicolini, *Commento storico*, I, 47.

³⁵ D'Aubignac's treatise dates from 1664 but was not published until 1715. It was

treatises seem not to have been known to Vico, but the general idea must have been widespread, because Richard Bentley and Henry Felton refer casually to Homer's "loose songs" and "strings of ballads" in 1713.[36] Even the idea of Homer as a collective name for the composers of the two great epics was adumbrated before Vico. Charles Perrault, in 1693, argued *"qu'il n'y a jamais eu au monde un homme nommé Homère"* and that there were dozens of such poets writing perhaps twenty or thirty short episodes every year.[37] These anticipations of Wolf's theory do not, I am well aware, describe Vico's theory exhaustively, but they are sufficient to account for the more or less primitivistic interpretations of Homer propounded by Blackwell, Wood, and other English writers of the eighteenth century.[38]

The general historiographical schemes of Vico also have their antecedents. Nicolini concludes that the similarity between Vico and Hume's *Natural History of Religion* is the result of their both having read and used Hobbes.[39] The idea of a cyclical progress was extremely widespread in the sixteenth and seventeenth centuries. A text from Velleius Paterculus was constantly appealed to.[40] Machiavelli, Campanella, Bodin, and Pascal adopted it in diverse contexts. A book by Louis Le Roy, *De la vicissitude ou variété des choses en l'univers* (1577), is devoted to an exposition of the scheme.[41]

Similar arguments could be worked out for Vico's ideas on early religion, Roman history, the theory of contract, and others—ideas the history of which is outside of my immediate field of competence. The one discovery made since Mr. Fisch's study of two references to Vico in the eighteenth century illustrates the whole matter excellently. John Gillies (1747–1836), a Scottish historian, now completely forgotten,[42] referred to Vico twice, as

---

almost unknown in its own time. See also Nicolini, "Sugli studi omerici di G. Vico," in *Accademia dei Lincei, Memorie, Scienze morali,* ser. VII, vol. V, no. 10 (1954), p. 470.

[36] Richard Bentley, *Remarks upon a Late Discourse of Free Thinking* (London, 1713), pp. 18–19; Henry Felton, *A Dissertation on the Reading of the Classics* (London, 1713), pp. 22–23.

[37] Charles Perrault, *Parallèle des anciens et des modernes* (Paris, 1693), II, 93.

[38] For a good account see Donald M. Foerster, *Homer in English Criticism: The Historical Approach of the Eighteenth Century* (New Haven, 1947). Foerster does not mention Vico.

[39] *Bibliografia vichiana,* I, 309–11.

[40] See Jan Kamerbeek, "Legatum Velleianum," in his *Creative Wedijver* (Amsterdam, 1962).

[41] Cf. E. Spranger, in *Sitzungsberichte der preussischen Akademie der Wissenschaften* (Berlin, 1926); F. J. Teggart, *Journal of the History of Ideas,* 1 (1940): 494–503; Clara Marburg, *Sir William Temple* (New Haven, 1932), pp. 43ff.

[42] Arnaldo Momigliano, in "George Grote and the Study of Greek History" (1952), claims priority for Gillies in the study of Greek politics (see his *Contributo alla storia degli studi classici* [Rome, 1955], pp. 214–16).

Mr. Duncan Forbes discovered in 1954.[43] The first—the very first in English—reference occurs in *A History of Ancient Greece* (1786) in a note to a passage in which Gillies rejects "the search for the mythological tenets of Greece in the opinions of other nations, a subject of inquiry upon which much learned conjecture and much laborious ingenuity have already been very laudably, but I fear not very successfully employed." The note lists "Bochart's *Geograph*, Bryant's *New Analysis*, Fourmant, Le Clerc, de la Pluche, etc.," and continues: "Their doctrine is opposed in the extraordinary work of Veco [*sic*] Neapolitano, entitled 'Principi di Scienza nuova d'intorno alla comune natura delle nazioni'. The third edition of this work was published at Naples in 1744."[44] The second reference appears in Gillies' *A View of the Reign of Frederick II of Prussia with a Parallel between that Prince and Philip II of Macedon* (1789). Gillies alludes to Frederick's *L'Antimachiavel* (1741) and his late attack on "the fashionable but absurd doctrine of Materialism: But the transactions of his whole life arraign the extravagance of that oeconomical system, invented by the false subtlety of Italy, that the state machine is capable of playing regularly, and producing the most salutary effects, without being directed by the skillful hand of the political artist." A note after "false subtlety of Italy" refers—this time correctly— to "Vico Neapolitano *Scienza Nuova*, and Count Verri *Oeconomia politica*."[45] Gillies obviously alludes to Vico's theory of the "heterogeneity of ends" or, as Vico says more simply, "things are brought into being far apart and some- times quite contrary to the proposals of men."[46] This is the passage re- sembling the quotation from Ferguson adduced by Mr. Fisch and it is the view against which Gillies is arguing: he admired the enlightened despots Philip of Macedon and Frederick of Prussia and, as a good eighteenth-century Rationalist, believed in the role of great men and the reforms imposed by them. Alluding to Vico and Pietro Verri, he was actually arguing against Ferguson and Adam Smith, who believed in the beneficent play of im- personal historical and economic forces.[47] In Vico, however, this view is part of his scheme of divine providence, for which it is hardly necessary to find a precedent in Campanella's *Città del sole*,[48] while in Ferguson and Adam Smith, whatever its ultimate religious motivation, it constitutes a much more secular view of the workings of social forces.

[43] "Scientific Whiggism: Adam Smith and John Millar," *Cambridge Journal*, 7 (1954): 643–70, noted by Max Fisch in the 1963 reprint of the *Autobiography*, p. 222A.

[44] John Gillies, *A History of Ancient Greece* (London, 1786), I, 42*n*.

[45] John Gillies, *A View of the Reign of Frederick II of Prussia with a Parallel between that Prince and Philip II of Macedon* (London, 1789), p. 30. I have seen the Dublin, 1789, reprint, where the passage appears on p. 26.

[46] The second *Scienza nuova*, par. 344; see the Bergin and Fisch translation (Ithaca, N.Y., 1948), p. 91.

[47] Duncan Forbes argues this well in the article cited in n. 43 above.

[48] Nicolini, *Commento storico*, I, 119.

There is, in addition, very strong supporting evidence for our argument in the parallel development of Vico's reputation and influence in France and Germany. Even Montesquieu's knowledge of Vico is highly doubtful. Montesquieu, while in Venice in 1728, entered in his journal his intention of acquiring the *New Science* in Naples, but there is no evidence that he did so or that he met Vico. There is no copy of the volume in the catalogue of Montesquieu's library nor is it among the books today preserved at La Brède.[49] No evidence of an acquaintance with Vico can be produced in the case of Condillac, Rousseau, Diderot, and others, although they frequently expound ideas as similar to Vico's as those of the British writers cited by Mr. Fisch.[50] In Germany, Hamann got hold of a copy of the *New Science* in 1777; he clearly did not know it before, although his aesthetic ideas were fully elaborated by 1762.[51] Croce's paper on Hamann and Vico lists some similarities between their teachings.[52] But Otto von Gemmingen assembled many more striking parallels.[53] Very similar ideas, we have to admit, can be arrived at independently, and, as a case in point, "Vichian" ideas were developed from their pre-Vichian forms in directions that often came close to the actual statements of Vico. But no one in the eighteenth century, least of all in Great Britain, absorbed or even discussed the totality of Vico's stupendous scheme of history. Vico, as a philosopher of history, as a sociologist *avant la lettre*, was, we must conclude, discovered early in the nineteenth century, and only Croce, in 1901, saw the full import of his ideas on aesthetics and poetics.

[49] Robert Shackleton, *Montesquieu: A Critical Biography* (Oxford, 1961), pp. 115–16. Croce and Nicolini's assertion that there is a copy at La Brède (*Bibliografia vichiana*, I, 292–93) is based on an unsubstantiated assertion made by E. Bouvy in *Bulletin Italien* (Bordeaux, 1904), p. 363.

[50] See Croce and Nicolini, *Bibliografia vichiana*, I, 279ff., 297ff., 352.

[51] Hamann's letters dated December 21 and 22, 1777; see Nora Imendörffer, *J. G. Hamann und seine Bücherei* (Königsberg, 1932).

[52] "Hamann e Vico," in *Saggio sullo Hegel*, pp. 309–15.

[53] *Vico, Hamann und Herder* (Munich, 1918).

George Whalley   COLERIDGE AND VICO

When Coleridge first opened the pages of Giambattista Vico's *Auto-biography* and the *Scienza nuova* on May 2, 1825, in his fifty-third year, his response was as quick, hospitable, and delicately incisive as one imagines it would have been twenty years earlier when he first discovered Giordano Bruno.   Coleridge's habit in reading, as we know well from the copious and nervous notes that for more than thirty years he wrote in the margins of his books, was not that of a suspicious and tendentious scholar quibbling with the *ipsissima verba* of the text, nor was his motive that of the intellectual prospector panning or digging for pay dirt—though he knew well how to gut a book for his own purposes if he needed to.   Whatever book commanded his sustained attention became the focus for the full play of his mind: it might, and often did, provide a valuable personal relationship with an author long ago dead.   Least peremptory and judicious, he would seek to establish an inner dialogue with his author, respecting—and often revering—the intention of the original, his comprehensive and skillful attention tendriling outward like the alert awareness of a solitary but gregarious person in the presence of a fascinating and reticent stranger.

The impression given by much traditional comment on Coleridge—particularly as a philosopher—is that he was an eclectic who patched together other people's leading thoughts into a plausible pattern of his own contriving. Something more human, and more germane to Vico, was in fact the case. "My memory, tenacious and systematizing" is a phrase he used in a letter to his brother in 1794, when he was twenty-four; such a mind led him along the *hodos chameleontos*.   What he read affectionately he digested and assimilated, and his intellectual color would be subtly modified or sharpened, as the diet of a transparent insect will declare itself to the observer; but what he took to himself seemed already to be his own.   His heuristic activity begins in recognition and ends in an enlarged self-knowledge.   He was fond of old books, not simply as living records of fine minds in action, but as evidence of the abiding principles of thought and feeling; his concern to restore neglected authors of stature to their rightful authority was an assault upon what was dangerous because novel, fashionable, or merely topical; he affiliated himself with what was radical and permanent wherever he could find it, in any period or culture accessible to him, in any of the languages he could use.   And when, pressing his own most original personal discoveries, he found that he had been feloniously anticipated by Plato, Bacon, Bruno, Spinoza, Kant, Schelling, he was encouraged rather than disappointed, finding assurance that the insistent pressure of his inquiry, in whatever field— and he inquired in many—would bring him again and again to recognize and discover to his satisfaction the continuity of "the shaping spirit," the abiding patterns of human thought.   Perception, imagination, reason, he saw as activities implicating the whole person, and all the infinitely various products of our faculties were evidence to him of man's integrative nature and a capacity for wholeness; for he conceived of the "faculties" as dynamic and concentric.   His sense of social responsibility was on the same pattern. With a large generosity that matched the physical exuberance of his youth, he seems to have considered that no thought was his own until he had given it away.   The reception of his prose writings encouraged him little enough, for he writes ruefully in the *Biographia literaria*, turning a favorite figure: "Prudence itself would command us to show . . . a due interest and qualified anxiety for the offspring and representatives of our nobler being.   I know it, alas! by woeful experience!   I have laid too many eggs in the hot sands of this wilderness, the world, with ostrich carelessness and ostrich oblivion. The greater part indeed have been trod under foot, and are forgotten; but yet no small number have crept forth into life, some to furnish feathers for the caps of others, and still more to plume the shafts in the quivers of my enemies, of them that unprovoked have laid in wait against my soul."[1] But his was a germinal mind, and he was a teacher by instinct.   In the case of Vico, as with other writers and auditors before and after him, Coleridge's admiration and his gift of faithful incisive comment were to be fertile, but the tradition does not clearly carry his name.

Always the poet, Coleridge returns again and again to the integrity of the word, to the fascinating self-containedness and self-shaping energy of words —a mystery that, as a writer of poetry, he was able at times to encompass with triumphant·success and that, as psychologist and philosopher, he observed and interpreted with exceptional subtlety and rigor.   His definition of *philosophy*, for example, starts from the word itself, and the definition reveals the man: "The term *philosophy* defines itself as an affectionate seeking after the truth; but Truth is the correlative of Being."[2]   He wrote this down in the *Biographia literaria* before September, 1815 (the book was not to be published until July, 1817).   But the habit of mind could be seen at an early date.   In the letter of March, 1794, to his brother, he had said: "I have little *Faith*, yet am wonderfully fond of speculating on mystical schemes— Wisdom may be gathered from the maddest flights of Imagination, as

---

[1] *Biographia literaria*, ed. George Watson (London, 1960), p. 27; hereafter cited as *BL*.
[2] *Ibid.*, p. 80.

medicines were stumbled upon in the wild processes of Alchemy—."[3]   This looks forward to his grouping of "Mystics" and "Revolutionary minds"; and, when we turn forward to the *Biographia literaria* again, we find the elements and axioms that were to vibrate sympathetically, at first touch, to Vico's central and hard-won principles.   "Truth is the correlative of Being. This . . . is no way conceivable but by assuming as a postulate that both are *ab initio* identical and co-inherent; that intelligence and being are reciprocally each other's substrate."[4]   The early study, he says, of Plato and Plotinus, of Proclus and Bacon, of Boehme and Bruno, "has all contributed to prepare my mind for the reception and welcoming of the *Cogito ergo sum, et sum quia cogito*; a philosophy of seeming hardihood, but certainly the most ancient and therefore presumptively the most natural."[5]   In his philosophical lectures of 1818–19 he was to treat the history of philosophy not as a chronological record of successive philosophical theories and conclusions but as a study of the development of the European mind as though it were one mind, in its growth, its digressions, its decline, its renaissance.   In a marginal note on Tetens's *Philosophische Versuche über die menschlichen Natur und ihre Entwicklung*, perhaps as early as 1806, he asked: "What are my motives [of action] but my impelling thoughts—and what is a Thought but another word for 'I think-ing'?"[6]   In tracing Coleridge's contact with Vico's work there is an opportunity to trace something of the activity of a great intellect at play; and Coleridge, in advance of twentieth-century psychology, was aware of some of the serious implications of play.

If we are to take a sufficiently comprehensive starting point for under-standing how Coleridge used his books, how he welcomed new ideas, how he recognized what Vico called "a common mental language" in the strange and exotic, the crabbed and fantastic, the self-preoccupied and even the self-deceived, and found there evidence for a conceivably single shapely activity radical to the human nature and condition, it is well to note a passage from Kathleen Coburn's introduction to *Inquiring Spirit* in which she discusses the psychological coherence that Coleridge could discern in details diverse, multitudinous, and even anomalous.

The strange and unfamiliar may have laws and significance if we but look.   Dreams are strange, if common, experience, but are they merely what they commonly appear to be?   Are they mere accidents?   Do they not indicate something illuminating about the content and the degrees of consciousness, and about the associative processes of the waking as well as the sleeping state?   And what of trances, oracles, mesmerism? Need these, from Pythagoras to the contemporary animal magnetists, be put down to

---

[3] *Collected Letters of Samuel Taylor Coleridge*, ed. E. L. Griggs, 4 vols. (London, 1956 [I and II] and 1959 [III and IV]), I, 71; hereafter cited as *CL*.

[4] *BL*, p. 80.

[5] *Ibid.*

[6] *Inquiring Spirit*, ed. Kathleen Coburn (London, 1951), p. 30; hereafter cited as *IS*.

trick and imposture? How does one mind work on another? What do we know about the imagination? In the tales of demonology and witchcraft, are there not many cases that suggest pathological states?... The more one reads Coleridge the more impressed one becomes with what can only be called a psychological approach to all human problems. Whether it be punctuation, or political sovereignty, a criticism of *Richard II*, the position of the mediaeval Church, or the baby talk of children, the state of Ireland or the work of the alchemists, he sees it as a piece of human experience, understandable in relation to the whole human organism, individual or social, so far as that organism can be comprehended as a whole.... In personality, clearly or obscurely, everything is connected with everything else. The necessity of seeing every problem in its relations and perspective, in a perspective increasingly multiple the more one knows, accounts for that sense of defeat by the complexity of his materials that sometimes paralysed him before he fairly set out.[7]

When Coleridge opened the first volume of Vico and started reading the *Autobiography*, he must at least have sympathized with him as a man—the neglect, the illness, the dependence and poverty. In the *Biographia literaria* he had pointed to the fact that for the past two or three centuries there seemed to have existed "a sort of secret and tacit compact among the learned not to pass beyond a certain limit in speculative science," and how "the few men of genius among the learned class" had had to overstep the boundary very circumspectly. "Therefore [he continues] the true depth of science, and the penetration of the inmost centre, from which all the lines of knowledge diverge to their ever distant circumference, was abandoned to the illiterate and the simple, whom unstilled yearning and an original ebulliency of spirit had urged to the investigation of the indwelling and living ground of all things.... All without distinction were branded as fanatics and phantasts; not only those whose wild and exorbitant imaginations had actually engendered only extravagant and grotesque phantasms . . .; but the truly inspired likewise, the originals themselves!"[8] And as he read on into the *Scienza nuova* he must have found himself on very familiar ground.

... we shall reduce these beginnings to scientific principles, by which the facts of certain history may be assigned their first origins, on which they rest and by which they are reconciled.

Uniform ideas originating among entire peoples unknown to each other must have a common ground of truth.

In the night of thick darkness which envelops the earliest antiquity, so remote from ourselves, there shines the eternal and never failing light of a truth beyond all question: that the world of human society has certainly been made by men, and its principles are therefore to be found within the modifications of our own human mind.

There must in the nature of human things be a mental language common to all nations,

---

[7] *Ibid.*, pp. 14–15.
[8] *BL*, p. 81.

which uniformly grasps the substance of things feasible in human social life, and expresses it with as many diverse modifications as these same things may have diverse aspects. . . . This common mental language is proper to our Science. . . .[9]

Coleridge took the book, probed, tested, argued with it, in order to enlarge and confirm the foundations of Vico's thought and with luck his own.

Even the circumstances of Coleridge's first encounter with Vico's "great Work" were unexpected but strangely apt. The story has been told in detail by Max H. Fisch and will be well known to Vichian scholars; but it deserves to be retold, at least in summary, in order to trace Coleridge's response to Vico.[10] Gioacchino de' Prati, born near Trent in 1790, came to England first in 1823 from Switzerland to take political asylum, accompanied by an unmarried female companion who went by the name of Giuseppe Maffei. De' Prati had been educated at Salzburg, Innsbruck, Vienna, Landshut, and Pavia; though he had had extensive training in medicine, he took a law degree at Pavia in 1810. In England he was befriended by a group of literary men of liberal political sentiment, one of whom was Coleridge's nephew Edward. Edward Coleridge brought de' Prati to Highgate to meet Coleridge in April, 1825. Coleridge took to him immediately and offered to help him in any way he could. As a tutor in German involved in small-scale educational enterprises and trying to establish himself as an occasional writer, de' Prati did not prosper. By 1829 he was in debtor's prison; but being already "deeply engaged in physiological and medical studies"—Coleridge in his earliest reference to him gives him the title of "Doctor"—he used his time well, receiving instruction from Joseph Henry Green, Coleridge's philosophical collaborator and later his literary executor. When de' Prati was released from prison he went to Brussels for a time; then, after a short stay in England, he left for France on revolutionary concerns of his own—for de' Prati is described by the historian of the Italian irredentist revolution as "the most dangerous Irredentist of southern Tirol" and "one of the most dangerous innate revolutionists of the time."[11]   He

[9] Throughout this essay I have used Max H. Fisch and Thomas G. Bergin's translation of the *Autobiography* and of the *Scienza nuova*, published in Ithaca in 1944 and 1948 respectively.

[10] Max H. Fisch, "The Coleridges, Dr. Prati, and Vico," *Modern Philology*, XLI (1943–44), 111–12. The central purpose of the article was to reprint from de' Prati's autobiography in the 1838 *Penny Satirist* (London) Coleridge's letter of May 14, 1825, to de' Prati. But the biographical information about de' Prati, and the account of his relations with Coleridge and of the part played by Coleridge in disseminating the Vichian philosophy make it a document of major importance. My debt to Professor Fisch's article will be clear to anyone who has read it. It should be pointed out, however, that Professor Fisch did not have access to Coleridge's Notebook 21. (The name "Prati" was used by his son Luigi: it would have been more convenient to use the name in this form—as Coleridge almost always did—throughout the essay. But the editors opted for the form "de' Prati".)

[11] It is not clear whether Coleridge knew of de' Prati's career as a revolutionist,

settled again in England in July, 1830, first as a lay preacher, then as a medical practitioner.   After repeated applications, he succeeded in getting himself repatriated to Austrian Italy in 1852 and died in Brescia in 1863.   Coleridge had died in July, 1834.

No descriptive account of de' Prati survives.   The clear impression given by the records and by Coleridge's response to him is that he was an intelligent, perceptive, and personable young man, well educated, widely read, and master of French and German, as well as of his native Italian.   His obscure autobiography, printed serially in the *Penny Satirist* between 1837 and 1840, shows that he came to write—one hopes as the eventual result of Coleridge's coaching—a nervous, direct, and even felicitous English prose, without many foreign mannerisms.

An unpublished fragment of a letter from Coleridge to his son Derwent, postmarked April 15, 1825, gives the date of their first meeting: Edward Coleridge brought him with two other friends, and Coleridge refers to him as "a Dr Prati, a literary German." [12]   They began to converse together in German—"Coleridge spoke this language," de' Prati tells us, "quite correctly, and with a soft Hanoverian accent"—and Coleridge was so taken with him that he invited him to walk with him in the garden the next morning. Thereafter, de' Prati says, he visited Coleridge at least once a week for two years.   No wonder: de' Prati's reading and literary enthusiasms were thoroughly Coleridgean—Boehme, Bruno, Spinoza, Schelling; he ascribed his intellectual awakening to Lessing's *Erziehung des Menschengeschlechts* (*On the Education of the Human Race*) (and promptly borrowed some volumes of Coleridge's set of Lessing); he had personal acquaintance with Jacobi, Schelling, Friedrich von Schlegel, Ritter, Oken—all men whose work Coleridge is known to have read and, all but Ritter's, to have annotated; and, as an additional treat to cap so detailed a series of coincidences, de' Prati had spent a few days in Mesmer's house, had witnessed experiments in zoomagnetism, and had discussed with the Mesmer the medical implications of what they

----

though there may be conniving emphasis when he underlines the word "revolutionists" in the letter of May 14, 1825.   Coleridge had known a few revolutionists in his earlier years.

[12] Victoria College Library, MS F 3.19.   Fisch gives the date of the first meeting as May, 1824, on the evidence of the autobiography; but de' Prati seems to have made a mistake.   The letter of April 15, 1825, names "Sir James Stuart & Mr Woodcock" as Edward's two companions—the same two men named in de' Prati's account of his first meeting with Coleridge.   The preparations for this visit seem to be recorded in the undated letter in *Unpublished Letters of Samuel Taylor Coleridge*, ed. E. L. Griggs, 2 vols. (London, 1932), II, 339; hereafter cited as *UL*.   I am grateful to Miss Kathleen Coburn for bringing the manuscript fragment to my attention and for the use of material in Notebook 20 before the publication of it in her edition.

had observed.[13]   Vico must have been discussed in one of their earliest con-versations.   In a letter of May 14, 1825, Coleridge acknowledges the receipt of books from de' Prati, and continues in a postscript: "I am more and more delighted with G. B. Vico, and if I had (which thank God's good grace I have not) the least drop of *Author's* blood in my veins, I should twenty times successively in the perusal of the first volume (I have not yet begun the second) have proclaimed: 'Pereant qui ante nos nostra dixere.' "[14]

The date of Coleridge's first reading is recorded in one of his notebooks: "2 May, 1825.   Began to read Giambattista Vico's Autobiography—born in Naples 1670.—The original Discoverer of the true Theory of the ʹΟμηροι vice ʹΟμηρος, & of the character of the Ancient History of Rome—.   The Work in 3 vol. which D^r De Prati has lent me, contains only his Principi di Scienza Nuova D'intorno alla commune Natura Delle Nazioni."[15]   The edition was correctly identified by Professor Fisch as the sixth edition (Milan, 1816); a further page reference in the Coleridge notebook confirms the identification.[16]   There is no way of saying what eventually became of the volumes.   In October, 1825, Coleridge told Gillman that he had left one volume behind in Highgate when he went to Ramsgate on holiday, and asked to have it sent to him.[17]   On October 29, 1833, he wrote to de' Prati after an interval in their association, having read in "The Times of today" of his return to England: "I have (or rather, ought to have) two volumes of your's—Vico's Nuova Scienza *but* unfortunately I had yielded to the request of a friend and relation [Henry Nelson Coleridge], to lend them to him— and he is now in Devonshire and will not return till the end of November— but I should be most happy to order another Copy for you, if one can be

[13] Cf. a marginal note on Southey's *Life of Wesley* (1820), I, 301, written in late 1825 or in 1826 (also printed in *Table Talk*, April 30, 1830, note): "Nine years has the subject of Zömagnetism been before me.   I have traced it historically—collected a Mass of documents in French, German, Italian, the Latinists of the 16 Century—have never neglected an opportunity of questioning Eye witnesses (ex. gr. Tieck, Treverinus, De Prati, Meyer, and others of literary or medical celebrity) and I remain where I was, where the first perusal of Klug[e]'s Work had left me, without having advanced an Inch backward or forward.   Treverinus the famous Botanist's reply to me, when he was in London, is worth recording. . . . I have seen what I am certain I would not have believed on *your* telling; and in all reason therefore I can neither expect nor wish that you should believe on mine."   For Coleridge collecting materials on animal magnetism in May, 1817, see *CL*, IV, 730–31.

[14] First printed by de' Prati in the *Penny Satirist*, reprinted by Fisch.

[15] Notebook 20, folio 16*v*.

[16] Coleridge notes: "Vico. I. p. 135.   Sacra i.e. secreta—a capital stroke of Jesuitry— in an *uom di religione*—It would not surprize me to see it shot off against the Irish Bible Society."   The reference is to vol. I, p. 135, sec. 91 in the Bergin-Fisch translation.   There is no copy of the Milan 1816 edition in the British Museum (see also note 33 below), but there is one in the London Library.

[17] *Letters of Samuel Taylor Coleridge*, ed. E. H. Coleridge, 2 vols. (London, 1895), II, 744; hereafter cited as *L*.

found in London—or any other work, as a quid pro quo—."[18]   Other
instances are known of Coleridge's keeping a borrowed book for rather a
long time—Sotheby's folio Petrarch, and a copy of Cocceius's biblical commentary belonging to a clerical acquaintance—and of his apologizing for the
delay and promising to return them.   On this occasion he was perhaps not
informed by simple contrition: at the end of the letter he asked de' Prati for
"the volumes of Lessing's Works which you once took home with you."
De' Prati returned the Lessing volumes: the set is intact in the British
Museum.   There was no copy of Vico in the sale of the books J. H. Green
received from Coleridge after his death; so presumably Coleridge played
his part.

On May 2, 1825, Coleridge set to work in his own way.   He seldom
ignored the forepages of any book he handled; and the notes in this case
begin with the *Autobiography* (pages iii–lxxiv).   Although Coleridge at their
first meeting conversed with de' Prati in German, and agreed in an early
letter at least that each would employ "the most suitable vehicle for its [the
heart's] utterance, our mother tongue," he had learned Italian when he was
in the Mediterranean in 1804–6, part of the time in the post of secretary to
the governor of Malta.   Since that time he had read extensively the major
classics of Italian literature and much else, including a certain amount of
curious, proscribed, and contemporary matter.[19]   When he took up Vico,
he read the original with ease—an advantage that the earliest English translators and exponents of Vico seem not to have enjoyed.[20]   His first comment
in Notebook 20 refers to page 54 of the *Autobiography*: "Plato, Tacitus,
Bacon, and—Grotius! li quattro Autori, che egli ammicava sopra tutt' altri."
Plato and Bacon were also very much Coleridge's men; he had no special
regard for Tacitus; but Grotius stood in Coleridge's mind for a strain of
dangerously infectious, because narrow, rationalism in the theology of his
own time, and any position that could be seen as "Grotio-Paleyan" he
treated with suspicion or scorn.   He next notes that Vico had made a commentary on part of Grotius' *De jure belli et pacis*, quotes a sentence in Italian,
and on Vico's phrase "Opera di Autore Eretico" notes: "Striking instance
of the Romish Superstition—even on the noblest Minds.—"   The next note
is more interesting: a sentence in Latin referred to as "P. 60.   Vita di G. B.
Vico"—"Omnis divinae atque humanae eruditionis elementa tria, Nosse,
Velle, Posse: quorum principium Unum Mens; cujus Oculus Ratio, cui
aeterni Veri lumen praebet Deus."[21]   This sentence appears on the verso of

---

[18] *UL*, II, 453.
[19] Coleridge's knowledge of Italian is considered in detail in an appendix to *The
Notebooks of Samuel Taylor Coleridge*, ed. Kathleen Coburn, 2 vols. (4 pts.) (New York
and London, 1957 and 1961), II (Notes).
[20] See nn. 33 and 36 below.
[21] The Latin sentence appears on pp. 50–51 of vol. I of the 1816 edition, in the *Vita*,

the contents leaf of *Aids to Reflection* as the leading epigraph. *Aids to Reflection*, a considerable series of aphorismic extracts mostly from the works of Archbishop Leighton, with Coleridge's interpolated comments, had the following objects as announced in his preface: "1. To direct the Reader's attention to the value of the Science of Words, their use and abuse. . . . 2. To establish the *distinct* characters of Prudence, Morality, and Religion. . . . 3. To substantiate and set forth at large the momentous distinction between REASON and Understanding. . . . 4. To exhibit a full and consistent Scheme of the Christian dispensation, and more largely of all the *peculiar* doctrines of the Christian Faith; . . ." Coleridge had always been a keen "mottophilist" and had a sharp eye for the sort of quotation that would focus the reader's mind allusively upon his central intention. He now takes up, as leading epigraph to a book long in preparation and completely printed in text, the thesis that Vico had proposed "at the solemn public opening of studies in 1719": "All divine and human learning has three elements: knowledge, will and power, whose single principle is the mind, with reason for its eye, to which God brings the light of eternal truth." On May 19, 1825, Coleridge wrote: "My book [*Aids to Reflection*] will be *out* on Monday next, and Mr Hessey hopes that he shall be able to have a copy ready for me by to-morrow, so that I may present it to the Bishop of London."[22] Five days earlier the book had not yet "left the printer's office in the shape of a volume." At most, eighteen days elapsed between his finding the Vichian thesis and the issuing of the completed copies of *Aids to Reflection*, where the thesis was printed on the verso of the contents leaf. Coleridge might playfully have claimed to feel annoyance with those who had anticipated him, but he was more inclined to rejoice in them.

The notes then move to Book I, sections 53–54, of the *Scienza nuova*, and Zoroaster, beginning with a trenchant summary of Vico's argument and overflowing into the comment: "O the notable Chain of such Dandelions as grow in the garden of Morpheus—the fallen-out teeth of the old Lion, Tempus edax!"; then come four lines of improvised and slightly indelicate verse, with more exuberant wordplay and the characteristic remark: "And these Chaldean Sages—what do we learn from the recorded FACTS of History, as opposed to the fancies, the putamenta, of Theorists—that they were Fortune-tellers, who practised divination by the trajectory of Shooting Stars, and after a time improved this trade into the noble Science of judicial

---

the epigraph to *Aids to Reflection* citing "p. 50." The notebook clearly reads "p. 60": I cannot account for the slip in the manuscript, since the *Vita* is paginated in arabic numerals. Volume I is paginated in one series, pp. iv, 211 [1], the *Vita* ending on p. 68.

[22] *UL*, II, 739; an undated letter to Hessey, *UL*, II, 342, must have been written two or three days at most before May 18, 1825, and seems to have gone with the final corrected proofs of the forepages.

Astrology!—"[23]   He makes a memorandum to "Compare and collate the romantic tales and exaggerations imported into Europe by the Chinese Jesuits— & again magnified by the Solar Microscope of the Infidel Kalterfeltos of France, with the stories of the Greek Sophists & (not improbably) the Priests from their enmity to Philosophy, the true *Religion* of Greece, respecting Ægypt and Scythia—"   The next comment is less respectful: "Mem.   The Science of Comparative History—Comparative Anthropotomy."   After some four pages of summary notes on the way human groups grow, he notes a resemblance between patricians and plebeians, on the one hand, and "the Planters and the Negros in our Colonies," on the other—a thought that Henry Crabb Robinson's diary shows Coleridge expounding in conversation on June 16, 1825.[24]   In these notes he has advanced at least to page 135 of Volume I—a reference given in the manuscript; but the book has been turned upside down and notes have been written from the back, so that there are notes on folios 39*v–r* referring (without citation) to Book I, sections 50–52.   At the end of these notes he sets down ten "Tests of Tradition," all arriving at the same conclusion: "Ergo, the Hebrew Chronology is the more probable."   Four of these tests are peculiarly Coleridgean, and all expand and support the argument in Vico's section 54.

3. That which best harmonizes with our own experience, ex. gr. of Americas, New Holland &c. . . .

7. That which is INDIVIDUALIZED and *ordinary* human. . . .

9. That which has fewest of the *common* to all other nations— . . . This ~~argument~~ fact has been hitherto historically interpreted instead of anthropologically & psychologically, as it should have been— & hence the arguments applied to the opposite conclusion.— . . .

10. That which tho' most unlike all the rest will yet, if admitted & layed down as the Ground, best explain all the others, when taken in conjunction with Anthropognosy & Psychology— . . .

I am not informed whether or not other notes and comments on the *Scienza nuova* are to be found in later notebooks.   There was no room for any more in Notebook 20 by the time he had reached the text of about Book I, section 91, and since that notebook seems to have been in use into September, 1825, it may include all that he had to write on Volume I—that is, on the *Autobiography*, the *Idea of the Work and Explanation of the Chronological Table*, and Book I, "The Establishment of Principle."   But a few more direct traces of the reading can be recorded.

On May 23, 1825, Coleridge wrote to Hessey, the publisher of *Aids to Reflection*:

[23] Notebook 20, fol. 17*v*.
[24] See pp. 235–36 below.

It is singular that on my return to Highgate much impressed with the Light, you had
flashed upon my mind with regard to the cure of Stammering, one of the very first
sentences I met with in Giambattista Vico was the following—
  "I *mutoli* mandan fuori i suoni informi *cantando*—e gli *scilinguati* par *cantando*
  spediscono la lingua a pronunziare!"—
i.e. Mutes or Dumb Persons send forth indistinct sounds in a sing-song: and Stam-
merers by chaunting gradually unloose and accustom or facilitate the tongue to
pronounce freely.   A curious coincidence—I have myself repeatedly observed that
children in being taught to read begin to stutter when you prevent them from *singing*
their words.[25]

Here Coleridge finds a coincidence between one of Vico's principles and his
own absorbed observation of the behavior of children: here, he felt sure, if
nowhere else—before the moment of evanishment, before the "shades of the
prisonhouse" close upon the adult psyche—he might come upon some
elemental clue to the continuously integrative workings of the human mind.
And did not Vico write: "every theory must start from the point where the
matter of which it treats first began to take shape"?

In the very first notebook entry, even before the notes on the *Autobiography*
begin, Coleridge characterized Vico as "The original Discoverer of the true
Theory of the ʽΟμηροι vice ʽΟμηρος, & of the character of the Ancient
History of Rome." Is this what de' Prati had told him to expect?
Coleridge was already versed in the details of the Homeric question, but his
interest, unlike that of a textual critic, was primarily anthropological and
psychological.   The way Coleridge's mind in conversation flickered over a
host of unexpected relations—if "flickered" is a possible word for so extended a process—is well illustrated in Henry Crabb Robinson's account of
a conversation during which de' Prati was present and in the course of which
Coleridge talked about Vico.   An informal account, and one that is less
epigrammatic and condensed than most of the records taken by Henry Nelson
Coleridge for the *Table Talk*, it is of further interest because Robinson was
not always a sympathetic or patient auditor.   Robinson, Edward Irving
(founder of the Catholic Apostolic Church and a spell-binding preacher),
Irving's brother-in-law Martin, and Basil Montague (an old disciple of
Coleridge's and, with Coleridge's encouragement, editor of Bacon), placed
themselves "in a chariot" on June 16, 1825, rode to Highgate, and took tea
at the Gillmans.

I think I never heard Coleridge so very eloquent, and yet it was painful to find myself
unable to recall anything of what had so delighted me, that is, anything that seemed
worthy to be noted, so that I could not but suspect some illusion arising out of the
impressive tone and the mystical language of the orator.   He talked on for several
hours without intermission, his subject the ever recurring one, religion, but so blended

---

[25] *UL*, II, 352.   The quotation (or rather misquotation) is from Vico, *Scienza nuova*,
par. 461.

with mythology, metaphysics and psychology that it required great attention to find really the religious element.   I observed that when Coleridge quoted Scripture or used well-known religious phrases Irving was constant in his exclamations of delight, but that he was silent at other times.   Dr. Prati came in, and Coleridge treated him with marked attention.   Indeed Prati talked better than I ever heard him.   One sentence (Coleridge having appealed to him) deserves repetition: "I think the Old Pantheism of Spinoza far better than modern Deism, which is but the hypocrisy of Materialism"—in which there is an actual sense and I believe truth.   Coleridge referred to an Italian Vico who is said to have anticipated Wolf's theory concerning Homer (which Coleridge says was his at college.)   Vico wrote *Sur une nouvelle science*, viz. Comparative History.   Goethe notices him in his *Life* as an original thinker and great man.   Vico wrote on the origin of Rome.   Coleridge drew a parallel between the West Indian planters and the negroes, the subjection between them, and the condition of the plebs of Rome towards the patricians; but when I inquired concerning the origin of the inequality Coleridge evaded giving me an answer. Coleridge very eloquently expatiated on history and the influence of Christianity on society.   His doctrines assume an orthodox air, but to me they are unintelligible.[26]

Robinson's mention of the talk that included "religion . . . blended with mythology, metaphysics and psychology" reminds us that on May 18, 1825, Coleridge, as a newly appointed associate, had delivered to the Royal Society of Literature his first and only annual paper, on the theme of the *Prometheus* of Aeschylus, in which he said: "I flatter myself I have thrown some light on the passages in Herodotus respecting the derivation of the Greek Mythology from Egypt. . . ."[27] Coleridge had not finished the paper by April 8, but he delivered the manuscript—possibly a draft—to the secretary of the Royal Society of Literature on April 26.[28]

Vico, then, cannot have influenced the *Prometheus* essay unless through de' Prati's conversations.   Indeed, nothing in the essay recalls Vico clearly,

[26] *Crabb Robinson on Books and Their Writers*, ed. E. J. Morley, 3 vols. (London, 1938), I, 320–21.   De' Prati should be allowed to give his version of Coleridge's monologue: "All around him were so taken up with his speech, that seldom a word or a whisper was heard during the whole time he was addressing the company.   I remember with delight the instruction and pleasure I derived from these discourses, which cannot be better compared than with the dialogues of Plato.   The finest loftiest ideas, pouring forth amidst the most blooming poetical phrases, allegories, and types, now spiced with Socratic irony, now strengthened by close and all-penetrating argumentation, afforded men an intellectual banquet, nowhere to be met either here or in any part of the continent."

[27] *L*, II, 738.

[28] *Ibid.*, pp. 737–38; *UL*, II, 339.   T. J. Wise was wrong in stating in the *Ashley Catalogue* that his copy of "On the *Prometheus* of Aeschylus" was the only one surviving from a small number of printed copies issued to Fellows at the lecture.   The pamphlet has a printed heading: "Extracted from Vol. II. Part II. of the *Transactions of the Royal Society of Literature*"—"Read May 18, 1825."   The working copy, which Coleridge may even have read from at his lecture, was torn from a notebook and was originally composed in 1823.

except perhaps a passage at the opening, where Coleridge writes: ". . . to a man of sound judgment and enlightened common sense—a man with whom the demonstrable laws of the human mind, and the rules generalised from the great mass of facts respecting human nature, weigh more than any two or three detached documents or narrations, of whatever authority the narrator may be, and however difficult it may be to bring positive proofs against the antiquity of the document. . . ." [29] Shortly afterward he claims that the Book of Genesis is "in perfect accordance with all analogous experience, with all the facts of history, and all that the principles of political economy would lead us to anticipate." These two passages have a Vichian color to them, but they are also typically Coleridgean. Coleridge is arguing for the greater antiquity of the Hebrew culture and for the greater reliability of Hebrew chronology against the claims of contemporary French Egyptologists for the primacy of the Egyptians. Vico at the very opening of the *Scienza nuova* argues also for the primacy of the Hebrews and in his chronological table dislodges the Egyptians from the first place, where John Marsham had placed them in his *Canon*, of 1672, to the fifth place below the Hebrews, Chaldeans, Scythians, and Phoenicians. But this controversy had been going on one way and another for a century or so; Coleridge was already versed in some of the literature of the debate and followed with interest the reports of Napoleon's Egyptologists, who, on fresh inscriptional evidence, sought to restore the claim for Egyptian antiquity. Vico himself, at the beginning of his chronological section, makes it clear that in this issue he stands at the end of a process, not at the beginning. Coleridge, though belatedly, had on March 16, 1824, proposed for the Royal Society of Literature "a series of Disquisitions" on the relations between philosophy, poetry, and religion in the gentile world, especially in early Greece. The details of the proposal were altered a little before the *Prometheus* lecture was given, but there was no important change; for this was an area in which Coleridge was at home and where he had speculated independently—the essay even makes strong use of a substantial key passage from *The Friend* of 1809.

The parallel between the opening of the *Prometheus* essay and certain parts of the manuscript "Tests of Tradition" is striking, but it is difficult to avoid the conclusion that the essay informed the "Tests," rather than the reverse, and that the notebook entries—including the quizzical and facetious touches —show Coleridge testing another man's theory by seeing what happens when he expands and develops it with his own store of knowledge and through his own sense of relations. The Vichian turn of Coleridge's mind, as shown in an essay written before he had read the *Scienza nuova*, perhaps accounts for the absence of a strong sense of fresh discovery. De' Prati may well have given Coleridge the gist of Vico's theory in conversation; if he

[29] *UL*, II, 322–23.

did, it seems to have encouraged rather than modified what Coleridge had been considering for some time.   Whatever Vico may have contributed indirectly, it was not lucidity or grace: the essay, even in a concentrated reading now, is a dense, and incomplete tortuous document.   Coleridge was aware of this too.   "Yesterday," he told his nephew, "I had to inflict an hour and twenty-five minutes' essay full of Greek and superannuated Metaphysics on the ears of the Royal Society of Literature, the subject being the Prometheus of Aeschylus deciphered in proof and as instance of the connection of the Greek Drama with the Mysteries.   'Douce take it' . . . if I did not feel remorseful pity for my audience all the time.   For, at the very best, it was a thing to be read, not to read." 30

A few more comments on Vico are preserved in Henry Nelson Coleridge's collection of Coleridge's *Table Talk*.   The earliest of these is almost five years after the first reading—May 12, 1830: "I have no doubt whatever that *Homer* is a mere concrete name for the rhapsodies of the 'Iliad.'   Of course there was a Homer, and twenty besides. . . ." This is not a specific reference to Vico, but Henry Nelson Coleridge adds a note: "Mr. Coleridge was a decided Wolfian in the Homeric question; but he had never read a word of the famous Prolegomena, and knew nothing of Wolf's reasoning but what I told him of it in conversation.   Mr. C. informed me, that he adopted the conclusion contained in the text [above], upon the first perusal of Vico's 'Scienza Nuova'; 'not,' he said, 'that Vico has reasoned it out with such learning and accuracy as you report of Wolf, but Vico struck out all the leading hints, and I soon filled up the rest out of my own head.' " 31   Henry Nelson Coleridge published in 1830 *Introductions to the Study of the Greek Classic Poets*, for which he had read Wolf's *Prolegomena* in preparing the section on the origin of the Homeric poems.   The second edition, of 1834, only slightly revised from the first, contains his translation of Book III of the *Scienza nuova*—"Discovery of the True Homer."   There is no reference to it in his introduction, and no prefatory comment to account for the abrupt interpolation of some forty pages of Vico in translation.32   But this was the first translation of Vico to appear in English; it was probably undertaken at

30 *L*, II, 739–40.
31 *Table Talk*, May 12, 1830, and note.
32 Kenrick's condensation of Michelet, however, had been published a year earlier; see note 36 below.   In his first edition, Henry Nelson Coleridge ascribed the view that Homer wrote the existing poems and rhapsodies and that they were first put into a body by Pisistratus and his son, to Wolf and Bentley, and in the second edition ascribed it to Wolf only.   The view that certain poetic nuclei composed by one or more principal bards were interpolated with episodes composed by other subordinate bards, he said in the first edition, "is Heyne's, and was, I believe, the opinion of the late Dr. Parr, and is, I know, the firm conviction of one or two of the most eminent English poets and philosophers of the present day"; in the second edition he simply said that this view "is Vico's, Wolf's, and Heyne's" (see p. 54 of the 1st ed., p. 70 of the 2d).

Coleridge's instigation, and it explains why de' Prati's volumes were in Devonshire in October and November, 1833.[33]

The *Table Talk* entry for July 9, 1832, is very similar to the earlier one, but it ends with several interesting observations: "The want of adverbs in the Iliad is very characteristic. With more adverbs there would have been some subjectivity, or subjectivity would have made them. The Greeks were then just on the verge of bursting forth of individuality." Two other entries are more circumstantial—one earlier, the other later.

23 April 1832. To estimate a man like Vico, or any great man who has made discoveries and committed errors, you ought to say to yourself—"He did so and so in the year 1720, a Papist, at Naples.[34] Now, what would he not have done if he had lived now, and could have availed himself of all our vast acquisitions in physical science?"

After the *Scienza nuova* read Spinoza, *De monarchia ex rationis praescripto*. They differed—Vico in thinking that society tended to monarchy; Spinoza in thinking it tended to democracy. Now, Spinoza's ideal democracy was realised by a contemporary—not in a nation, for that is impossible, but in a sect—I mean by George Fox and his Quakers.

9 April 1833. I have a deep, though paradoxical, conviction that most of the European nations are more or less on their way, unconsciously indeed, to pure monarchy; that is, to a government in which, under circumstances of complicated and subtle control, the reason of the people shall become efficient in the apparent will of the king.[35] As it seems to me, the wise and good in every country will, in all likelihood, become every day more and more disgusted with the representative form of government, brutalised as it is, and will be, by the predominance of democracy in England,

---

[33] Henry Nelson Coleridge evidently relied upon Michelet's *Principes de la philosophie de l'histoire, traduits de la scienza nuova de Jean Baptiste Vico, et précédés d'un discours sur le système et la vie de l'auteur* (Paris, 1827), which he commends in a footnote to *Table Talk* April 23, 1832, as "An admirable analysis of Vico." One of the few surviving entries from the early nineteenth-century borrowing ledgers of the British Museum Library is for Henry Nelson Coleridge and is dated only three months before Samuel Taylor Coleridge's death: "21. April 1834 Vico/ Giambattista/ Principi di Scienza Nuova &c. 1801 Principes de la Philosophie de Vi[c]o par *Jules Michelet. Michelet* 1827." There can be little doubt that the copy of Vico's *Principi* used in preparing this essay (Milan, 1801; 3 vols. in 1: British Museum, 800, f. 5) is the same copy that Henry Nelson Coleridge borrowed in 1834, or that the British Museum's copy of Michelet's *Principes* is also the copy Henry Nelson Coleridge used. Both were acquired by the end of 1833, the Vico probably much earlier; and they are the only copies of these editions in the museum. At the sale of the library of Derwent Coleridge, the poet's younger son, there was a copy of Michelet with Henry Nelson Coleridge's autograph in it.

[34] Coleridge seems not to be aware of the prolonged and dangerous process by which Vico freed himself of his "Catholic piety" in order to found what Fisch and Bergin have called "a thoroughly secular, even heretical philosophy."

[35] Henry Nelson Coleridge adds a note: "This is backing Vico against Spinoza. It must, however, be acknowledged that at present the prophet of democracy has a good right to be considered the favorite."

France, and Belgium. The statesmen of antiquity, we know, doubted the possibility of effective and permanent combination of the three elementary forms of government; and, perhaps, they had more reason than we have been accustomed to think.

Max H. Fisch, in his and Thomas G. Bergin's edition of *The Autobiography of Giambattista Vico*, has traced out the lines of the transmission of Coleridge's interest in Vico to his young Broad-Church admirers—Thomas Arnold, Julius Hare, Thirlwall, F. D. Maurice; how Henry Hart Milman's review of Henry Nelson Coleridge's *Introduction* in the 1831 *Quarterly Review* clarified the Homeric question and gave Vichian direction to further discussion; how John Kenrick, encouraged by Hare and Thirlwall, prepared for the *Philological Museum* in 1833 an able exposition of Vico's doctrine which was to be the most reliable English source for almost fifty years.[36] Some of the influence is clear, but in this case, as with others, it is very difficult to trace Coleridge's influence with any precision. There can be no doubt that, in Vico's case, he fulfilled his persistent desire to make current and vital the work of neglected genius. It is tantalizing to wonder whether James Joyce might somehow have discovered the Vico who was to be important in *Ulysses* through Coleridge, in whose poem he found the recurrent phrase "He listened and looked sideways up."

It is not, however, correct, I think, to see an almost exclusively Vichian strain in the theological inheritance the young Broad Churchmen received from Coleridge. Coleridge's scrupulous and detailed study of the Bible goes much farther back than 1825, nourished by a study of the Fathers, certain Caroline Divines, and the leading commentators of the Reformation, particularly Luther. After his life became regular and quiet in Highgate—after about 1819 when the *rifacciamento* of *The Friend* and the philosophical lectures were finished—the notebooks and marginalia show an insistent, almost daily, study of the Bible, book by book, in the light of his own sense of history, his prolonged reflection upon psychological phenomena, and his reflections upon the materials that were beginning to provide a focus for the emergent disciples of anthropology, comparative literature, and the higher criticism. The commentaries and analyses of Eichhorn and Cocceius, and later of Schleiermacher, were at his elbow as he sought to dispel the superstition and the panic-stricken irrationality of blind enthusiasm that he saw around him. He insisted upon reading the Bible as a human and historical

---

[36] "Vico," *Philological Museum*, 2 (1833): 626–44, signed "I. K." and "M. C. Y.," which Professor Fisch has identified as John Kenrick and Manchester College, York. Kenrick, like Henry Nelson Coleridge, cheerfully recommends Michelet: "Whoever is not in love with difficulty for its own sake, will do well to seek their knowledge of Vico's system in M. Michelet's work; for Vico himself is the Heraclitus of modern philosophers" (p. 630). Michelet's translation of Vico was based on his own selective recension of the 1725 and 1730 editions in order to give a single intelligible account; Kenrick follows Michelet.

document. His prime resolve was to drive the resources of intelligence and knowledge to the limit and, by so doing, to reinforce the reality of religious experience. He could foresee clearly the rationalistic assault that would be made upon the Bible, upon religion, upon the Church; he could even see what strategy would be used and tried to teach his young admirers how to meet that assault. To renounce any human resource was to capitulate. All the strength of ingenious and disciplined inquiry must be brought to bear to secure man's great birthright—the wholeness of imagination and that larger completeness of the individual which Coleridge called reason. In an early notebook, he had written down a question from Plato in Greek, and then had translated it: "Do you suppose the nature of the soul can be sufficiently understood without the knowledge of the whole of nature?"[37] He might well have added, even before reading Vico: "Do you suppose that the whole of nature can be sufficiently understood without the knowledge of the nature of the soul?"

Coleridge for years had been swimming against the dominant current of his times and had suffered for his temerity. In his letter of May, 1825, offering to help de' Prati as best he could, he admitted that although he had "some influence . . . a growing influence," it was "disproportionate to what it ought to be"—"at which you will not wonder when you know that during five and twenty, I might say thirty years, I have been resolutely opposing the whole system of modern illumination, in all its forms of Jacobinism, and Legitimatism, Epicurean (and in our country Pelagian) Christianity, Pelagian morals, Pelagian politics. . . ." In saying this, he was declaring himself as being of the party of Plato, Bacon, Boehme, Bruno: men whose work and spirit had encouraged and sustained him in his isolation. For in the postscript he suggests to de' Prati a project which he himself had had in mind since—at the latest—January, 1810. "By the bye, when I see you on Thursday I will mention a set of articles, on which I myself for a long time had set my thoughts, a critical and biographical account of the great *revolutionists* in the intellectual world, philosophical and religious. I am pretty certain that I could dispose of them, so as to make it worth your while. . . ." On May 8, 1826, he mentions this proposal again. De' Prati had sent for his comment an essay on Schiller, and Coleridge was troubled because Thomas Carlyle had recently published an impressive essay on Schiller in the *London Magazine* which rendered de' Prati's essay unsalable. Probably the writing was not very accomplished: Coleridge offers to help revise his work if he will send "Half a dozen pages fresh from your hand (if you did feel yourself equal or disposed to a biography of Bruno: yet a spirited Sketch of Vico's Life and great Work, your copy of which I have, would be more attractive to the Learned Public, and easier and *readier* to

[37] *Coleridge Notebooks*, vol. I, entry 1002.

yourself)—. . ."[38] "Great *revolutionists*"; now two are named—Bruno and Vico—and the circle closes.

On January 21, 1810, Coleridge wrote Lady Beaumont a long letter about his periodical *The Friend*, which had started in June, 1809, and was to continue until March, 1810. He goes on to speak about Jacob Boehme and to discuss what he was elsewhere to call "Vindiciae Heterodoxae" as part of a comprehensive philosophical work.

> Of Jacob Behmen I have myself been a commentator, from Plato, Plotinus, Proclus, & some Catholic Writers of the Vie Interieure.—But for myself I must confess, I never brought away from his Works any thing I did not bring to them—It is a maxim with me, always *to suppose myself ignorant of a Writer's Understanding, until I understand his Ignorance.* This I have not yet deciphered to myself in the Teutonic Theosopher [Boehme]: yet I conjecture that being ignorant of Logic & not versed in the Laws of the Imagination, he rendered many *Intuitions* in his own mind, perhaps of very profound Truths, and, as it were, *translated* them into such *Images* and *bodily* feelings as *by accident* were co-present with his Intuitions. . . . Yet Jacob Behmen was an extraordinary man. . . . If it please God, I shall shortly publish, as a Supplement to the first Volume of the Friend, a work of considerable size & very great Labor—the toil of many years—entitled, The Mysteries of Religion grounded in or relative to the Mysteries of Human Nature: or the foundations of morality laid in the primary Faculties of Man. . . . Either in this or in some after Number of the Friend I shall give the character of Jacob Behmen & compare him with George Fox—and both with Giordano Bruno.—The most beautiful and orderly development of this philosophy, which endeavors to explain all things by an analysis of Consciousness, and builds up a world in the mind out of materials furnished by the mind itself, is to be found in the Platonic Theology of Proclus. . . .[39]

In September, 1814, the proposal has changed somewhat: it is to be "a large volume on the LOGOS, or the communicative intelligence in nature and in man, together with, and as preliminary to, a Commentary on the Gospel of St. John; and in this work I have labored to give real and adequate definitions of all the component faculties of our moral and intellectual being, exhibiting constructively the origin, development, and destined functions of each."[40] In the *Biographia literaria* (written in 1815) he says that the work is in progress, refers to it as *Logosophia*, promises an announcement of it "at the end of this volume" (but did not carry it out), and implies that it will consist of at least five treatises, in the fifth of which there will be a discussion of Spinozism.[41] The design is refined further on September 27, 1815: "LOGOSOPHIA: or on the LOGOS, divine and human, in six Treatises." Here, for the first time, the context into which Coleridge was to place Vico appears clearly:

[38] *UL*, II, 374.
[39] *CL*, III, 278–79. Coleridge's annotated copy of Law's edition of Boehme is in the British Museum Library.
[40] *Biographia literaria*, ed. J. Shawcross, 2 vols. (Oxford, 1962), II, 230.
[41] *Ibid.*, I, 92, 179, 180, 182*n*.

"The vth. [Treatise] (Λόγος Ἀγωνιστής) on the Pantheists and Mystics; with the Lives and Systems of Giordano Bruno, Jacob Behmen, George Fox, and Benedict Spinoza.—"[42]   The *Logosophia* was not so easy to finish as the confident letters of 1815 suggested it might be; and the "Vindiciae Hetero-doxae" ran into difficulties at once—the Bruno essay never got started, because copies of Bruno were, and are, extremely rare, and Coleridge was refused the loan of the only complete collection he knew of.[43]   Another revised form of the work appears in September, 1816: there is to be a large new poem at the beginning and at the end; and the Λόγος Ἀγωνιστής persists as "Biography and Critique on the Systems of Giordano Bruno, Behmen, and Spinoza."[44]   Thereafter, except for the proposal that de' Prati should write something of the sort, there is no further mention of the "Lives" except in a wistful marginal note, perhaps written in 1830 or even later, in *The Works of the Late Reverend Mr. Samuel Johnson, sometime Chaplain to the Right Honourable William, Lord Russell* (London 1710): "Among my count-less intentional Works, one was—Biographical Memorials of Revolutionary Minds, in Philosophy, Religion, and Politics.   Mr. Sam Johnson was to have been one.   I meant to have begun with Wickcliff, and to have confined myself to Natives of Great Britain—but with one or two supplementary Volumes, for the Heroes of Germany (Luther and his Company) and of Italy (Vico)."[45]

When Coleridge first met Charles Augustus Tulk, the exponent of yet another heterodox genius, Emanuel Swedenborg,[46] he told him: "If I had met a friend & a Brother in the Desart of Arabia, I could scarcely have been more delighted than I was in finding a fellow-laborer and in the only Country in which a man dare exercise his *reason* without being thought to have lost his Wits, & be *out of his Senses*"; and added—"My main Object is to demonstrate that while my Opponents (I speak not of my Libellers; but of the warm Adherents of the Tabula rasa and Nil nisi ab extra Scheme) call out for Facts, Facts, Facts—*all* the Facts of Experience are on my side."[47] It is a pity that the "Lives" were never written.   It is a pity that Coleridge never made the projected translation of Bacon's *Organum* with parallels from Vico: it might have been a powerfully influential book.   It is disappointing that in the end there is no direct celebration of the imaginative sweep of Vico's thought, or any forecast of the effect that it would eventually have upon the development of historical imagination and the concept of historical science and the basis for a scientific history.

[42] *CL*, IV, 589–90; cf. *ibid.*, p. 592.
[43] *Ibid.*, pp. 656, 926.
[44] *Ibid.*, p. 687; cf. *ibid.*, p. 775.
[45] *IS*, p. 183.
[46] Coleridge annotated several of Swedenborg's books.
[47] *CL*, IV, 589.

As early as 1804 Coleridge had set down his view of the timelessness and privileged vitality of "true genius": "a Shakespere, a Milton, a Bruno, exist in the mind as *pure Action*, defecated of all that is material & passive.   And the great moments, that formed them—it is hard and an impiety against a Voice within us, not to regard [them] as predestined, & therefore things of Now & For Ever and which were Always"[48]   That Coleridge should instantly have included Vico in the company of his chosen mystics and neglected geniuses is the tribute of powerful and penetrating intelligence; the recognition of a fellow spirit across the gulf of time, a most hospitable greeting in that country where all things are one through the dynamic integrity of the human mind.   Some words Vico had written about the *Scienza nuova* must have struck Coleridge's ear almost like a reverberation of Giordano Bruno's voice: "The composition of this work, if I am not deceived, has filled me with an heroic spirit, which places me above the fear of death and the calumny of my rivals.   I feel myself on a rock of adamant, when I think on the judgment of God, who does justice to genius by the esteem of the wise."

[48] *Coleridge Notebooks*, vol. II, entry 2026: 19 Apr 1804.

A. Walton Litz   VICO AND JOYCE

To the student of modern European literature, Vico's name is inevitably linked with that of James Joyce. Although it was Croce who first defined Vico's crucial role in the history of "aesthetic science," it was Joyce who demonstrated that Vico's ideas hold a special vitality and relevance for the modern artist. The *New Science* did more than supply raw materials for Joyce's art: the form of Vico's thought made a deep impress upon Joyce's imagination, and in his complex last work, *Finnegans Wake*, Joyce took for his model Vico's "ideal eternal history traversed in time by the histories of all nations." [1] It would be a mistake to think of Vico and Joyce in terms of our conventional notions of literary "influence"; the relationship between their works was fundamentally creative, and in the long run Joyce's art may condition our reading of Vico as much as the *New Science* conditions our understanding of *Finnegans Wake*. Late in his life, when the Danish writer Tom Kristensen confessed that he needed help with *Finnegans Wake* (then known simply as *Work in Progress*), Joyce suggested a reading of Vico. " 'But do you believe in the *Scienza Nuova?*' asked Kristensen. 'I don't believe in any science,' Joyce answered, 'but my imagination grows when I read Vico as it doesn't when I read Freud or Jung.' " [2]

There is no simple explanation for Vico's extraordinary power over Joyce's imagination. In a letter to Harriet Shaw Weaver written during the first years of his work on *Finnegans Wake*, Joyce remarked on the "philosophical" theories underlying his book: "I would not pay overmuch attention to these theories, beyond using them for all they are worth, but they have gradually forced themselves on me through circumstances of my own life. I wonder where Vico got his fear of thunderstorms. It is almost unknown to the male Italians I have met." [3] Obviously the *New Science* appealed to all levels of Joyce's mind, and his initial interest may have been stirred as much by his pathological fear of thunderstorms as by his rational

1 *The New Science of Giambattista Vico*, trans. Thomas G. Bergin and Max H. Fisch (Ithaca, N.Y., 1948), pars. 393 and 349.
2 Richard Ellmann, *James Joyce* (New York, 1959), p. 706.
3 *Letters of James Joyce*, I, ed. Stuart Gilbert (New York, 1966), 241.

admiration for Vico's theories. As we shall see later, Vico's awe-inspiring thunder echoes throughout *Finnegans Wake.*

The "circumstances" of Joyce's life which promoted Vico's influence deserve some comment, since they help us to understand Vico's ultimate appearance as "Mr John Baptister Vickar," the producer and ubiquitous stage-manager of *Finnegans Wake.*[4] We cannot date Joyce's first reading of Vico with any precision, but it certainly occurred soon after 1905, when he took up residence in Trieste, and it may have been connected with his interest in Homer. Although Joyce did not begin work on *Ulysses* in earnest until 1914, he had conceived as early as 1906 the idea of a Dublin story based on the *Odyssey*, and in the period 1906–14 he read extensively in Homeric scholarship. He may well have been attracted to the *New Science* by Vico's chapters on the "Discovery of the True Homer," where he would have found strong support for his plan to reincarnate Homer's hero in modern Dublin; but soon every aspect of the *New Science* was working on his imagination. Paolo Cuzzi, a Triestine lawyer who took English lessons from Joyce in 1911–13, discovered that Joyce was "passionately interested" in Vico. "Cuzzi was reading Freud's *Five Lectures on Psychoanalysis*, and he talked with Joyce about slips of the tongue and their significance. Joyce listened attentively, but remarked that Freud had been anticipated by Vico."[5]

Joyce came to know the Italian language quite well during the years in Trieste (1905–15, 1919–20), and several of his references to Vico reveal a familiarity with the original text; but, like most other students of Vico, Joyce sought help from the commentators and translators. Sometime before the first World War he borrowed a copy of Croce's *Estetica*,[6] and in the chapter on Vico must have found confirmation of his own enthusiastic responses. Those aspects of the *New Science* emphasized by Croce could stand as headings for any discussion of Vico's influence on Joyce, and one passage in Croce's study—a quotation from Vico's letter to Solla of January 12, 1729—must have reminded Joyce of his own aim in constructing a modern Odyssey.

. . . such a Captain as, for instance, Tasso's Godfrey is the type of a captain of all times, of all nations, and so are all personages of poetry, whatever difference there may be in sex, age, temperament, custom, nation, republic, grade, condition or fortune; they are nothing save the eternal properties of the human soul, rationally discussed by politicians, economists and moral philosophers, and painted as portraits by the poet.[7]

But it was probably from Michelet's famous *Oeuvres choisies de Vico* that

---

[4] *Finnegans Wake* (New York, 1939), p. 255, l. 27; all subsequent references to *Finnegans Wake* will be inserted directly into the text.

[5] Ellmann, *James Joyce*, p. 351.

[6] *Ibid.*

[7] Benedetto Croce, *Aesthetic*, trans. Douglas Ainslie (London, 1922), p. 224.

Joyce received most help. This was the text he recommended to his friends who had no knowledge of Italian,[8] and—as James S. Atherton has noted—Michelet's prefatory "Discours sur le système et la vie de Vico" is a summary of the *New Science* which "contains nearly everything that Joyce used from Vico."[9] Joyce also knew Edgar Quinet's discussion of Vico and Herder,[10] and, in a sentence from *Finnegans Wake* which I shall analyze later, he playfully acknowledged his debt to Quinet and Michelet. It seems only fitting that Michelet, whose 1824 discovery of the *New Science* inaugurated a new era in Vico's reputation, should have served as a guide to Joyce's explorations.

Turning now to the impact of Vico's theories upon Joyce's art, we are faced with the problem of determining just when these theories entered the "public" structure of his work. The explicit role Vico plays in *Finnegans Wake*—a role Joyce discussed and publicized—has tempted many critics to discover Vichian patterns in the earlier works, *A Portrait of the Artist as a Young Man* (written 1904-14) and *Ulysses* (written 1914-22). Certainly Joyce was well acquainted with Vico during the years when he was finishing *Portrait*, and one may see in the novel's use of myth some suggestions of Vichian influence.[11] But the resemblances are too general to be persuasive, and without the evidence of the later works no reader would suspect *Portrait* of containing Vichian patterns. The most we can say is that *A Portrait of the Artist* displays that interest in heroic types and cyclic form which made Joyce so receptive to the *New Science*.

In *Ulysses*, however, we witness the transition from subconscious influence to conscious intention. By the time he had finished writing *Ulysses* Joyce was prepared to use Vico's cyclic view of history as the framework for his next book, but Vichian ideas played a much more ambiguous part in the making of *Ulysses* itself.[12] As W. Y. Tindall has observed, "the general

[8] Joyce recommended Michelet's translation to his friend Padraic Colum (Mary and Padraic Colum, *Our Friend James Joyce* [New York, 1958], p. 122), and Stuart Gilbert quotes from Michelet's preface in his "Prolegomena to *Work in Progress*," an essay written under Joyce's supervision (*Our Exagmination Round His Factification for Incamination of Work in Progress*, ed. Samuel Beckett *et al.* [Paris, 1929], p. 51). Sylvia Beach's famous bookshop, Shakespeare and Company, which served as headquarters for Joyce and his friends during the 1920's and 1930's, owned an 1894 reprint of the *Oeuvres choisies de Vico* (first published in 1835). This unmarked copy is now in the Sylvia Beach Collection of the Princeton University Library.

[9] James S. Atherton, *The Books at the Wake* (New York, 1960), p. 267.

[10] One of the most important motifs in *Finnegans Wake* revolves about a long quotation from Quinet's *Introduction à la philosophie de l'histoire de l'humanité* (1825). See Atherton, *Books at the Wake*, p. 276.

[11] See Adaline Glasheen, "Joyce and the Three Ages of Charles Stewart Parnell," in *A James Joyce Miscellany: Second Series*, ed. Marvin Magalaner (Carbondale, 1959), pp. 167-68.

[12] Two unpublished dissertations have been devoted to the Vichian aspects of *Ulysses*: Ellsworth Mason's "James Joyce's *Ulysses* and Vico's Cycles" (Yale University, 1948),

structure of *Ulysses* is cyclical," and these "cyclical patterns suggest the philosophy of Giambattista Vico"[13]—but only to a reader familiar with Joyce's use of Vico in *Finnegans Wake*. The larger cycles of *Ulysses* are too general to be assigned to any one source, and although Joyce clearly had Vico in mind, he did not demand that the reader share this association. On one of the note-sheets for the novel Joyce jotted down the entry "Vico prince Consort," indicating that he associated Vico's cycles with the viceregal circuit described in the "Wandering Rocks" chapter, but this connection is not mentioned in the text: the Vichian reference existed for Joyce, not for the reader. Most of the Vichian cycles that have been discovered in *Ulysses* since the publication of *Finnegans Wake* would seem to lie on the borderline between the private imagination of the author and the public structure of the novel.

The same status would apply to Joyce's "Vichian" uses of Homer. In his attempt "to transpose the myth *sub specie temporis nostri*,"[14] to adapt the Homeric types to the conditions of modern bourgeois life, Joyce clearly found support in Vico's theory that the Homeric poems are a collective record of racial and historical forces. In his *James Joyce's 'Ulysses*,' a study written under Joyce's guidance, Stuart Gilbert points out the obvious connections:

Vico contemplated the writing of an "ideal and timeless history, in which all the actual histories of all nations should be embodied." . . . National heroes were, for him, not so much pre-eminent individuals, accidentally born out of their due time, as the embodiment of actual tendencies of their nations as a whole. They were led rather than leaders. Thus, as the past renews itself and civilizations rise and wane, the figures of antiquity will, *mutatis mutandis*, be reproduced. It does not, of course, follow that each avatar of a hero of legendary times will attain equal eminence. A Nestor may reappear as an elderly pedagogue, a Circe as the "Madam" of a one-horse brothel. As the cycle of history turns the light of fame may touch now one, now another, facet of the whole. But there will always be a substantially exact reproduction, a recall, of a set of circumstances which have already existed and of those personalities who, in a remote past, expressed better than their fellows the spirit of their age.[15]

But, as with the cyclic structure of the novel, Joyce's adaptations of the myth do not derive directly from Vico—many other sources suggest themselves— and it seems evident that Joyce did not wish to limit the novel's major motifs by linking them to a specific theory.

---

and Patrick T. White's "James Joyce's *Ulysses* and Vico's 'Principles of Humanity'" (University of Michigan, 1963).

[13] W. Y. Tindall, *James Joyce: His Way of Interpreting the Modern World* (New York, 1950), p. 70.

[14] *Letters*, I, 146–47.

[15] Stuart Gilbert, *James Joyce's "Ulysses*," rev. ed. (London, 1952), pp. 50–51.

The explicitly Vichian references in *Ulysses* are to be found on the level of verbal detail, and are easily glossed by the experienced reader of *Finnegans Wake*. The "Vico Road, Dalkey" appears as early as the "Nestor" episode; the thunder heard in "Oxen of the Sun" ("a black crack of noise in the street") suggests Vico's divine thunderclap; and it is significant that at the end of the day the weary Leopold Bloom thinks of "the vogue of Dr Tibble's Vi-Cocoa." [16]   Appropriately enough, most of the Vichian allusions cluster in the "Nestor" episode, where the subject is history, and in the "Cyclops" episode, where the "cave man" mentality of blind patriotism is linked with the behavior of men in Vico's "cyclopean" period (the first and most primitive stage of social development).   A. M. Klein, a critic whose ingenuity can equal that of Joyce himself, finds the four-part Vichian cycle (age of gods—age of heroes—age of men—*Ricorso*) re-enacted throughout the "Nestor" episode.   He makes the following claims at the beginning of his essay, claims which he then makes good through detailed and subtle analysis.

[This essay] is an attempt to show that the entire chapter, from beginning to end, has been shaped and influenced by Vico's paradigms of providence; that there is hardly a phrase which has not been, at least in its sequence in the text, predetermined by this pattern; that even the proper names occurring in this chapter find their place therein, not only in an order dictated by the course of the narrative, but also in an order dictated, in true Viconian style, by the nature of their etymologies; that every numeral appearing in the text has a significance which goes beyond its immediate one in relation to the narrative. . . . It will be shown, in fact, that throughout the chapter, in its very style and in the sequence of its paragraphs, the unrelenting winding workings of Providence are being continually simulated.[17]

Although Klein's argument often seems forced, he has clearly demonstrated a hidden, Vichian level in the narrative of one chapter.   Matthew Hodgart has applied the same method of analysis to a sentence in the "Cyclops" episode, demonstrating that a single proper name suggests "the three stages of human history according to Vico";[18] and one suspects that this method, if applied to the entire "Cyclops" episode, would yield a pattern as intricate as that discovered by Klein in "Nestor."

Once again we return to the question: "To what extent are these hidden Vichian allusions an essential part of the novel, and to what extent were they an elaborate game Joyce played with himself as he rehearsed the themes and techniques that were later to dominate *Finnegans Wake*?"   There is no simple answer to this question, but Hodgart is surely mistaken when he says

16 *Ulysses*, rev. ed. (New York, 1961), pp. 24, 394, 635.
17 A. M. Klein, "A Shout in the Street," *New Directions in Prose and Poetry*, no. 13 (1951): 331.
18 Matthew Hodgart, "A Viconian Sentence in *Ulysses*," *Orbis Litterarum*, no. 19 (1964): 203.

that, if the artistic effects of these Vichian references in *Ulysses* "cannot be defended, then neither can any part of *Finnegans Wake*." [19] In *Finnegans Wake* the Vichian patterns are part of the work's "public" meaning, they pervade every aspect of its structure and language, and we would expect— even demand—that they should be present in the smallest details. But Joyce chose not to declare his debt to Vico when he constructed the general design of *Ulysses*; the novel stands on its own without any support from the *New Science*; and therefore the Vichian elements in "Nestor" and "Cyclops" must be defended on quite different grounds, as part of the novel's incredible range of reference. Perhaps the most sensible solution is to regard Joyce's artistic career as a continuous performance, the making of a single multi-chaptered book, and to view the Vichian references in *Ulysses* as fore-shadowings of *Finnegans Wake*.

Although he had been collecting materials for many years, Joyce did not begin work on *Finnegans Wake* until March, 1923, over a year after the publication of *Ulysses*. From the beginning the *New Science* provided him with a stable framework, just as the narrative pattern of the *Odyssey* had given him certain "ports of call" in his work on *Ulysses*. Vico acted as a constant stimulus to his imagination, and in March, 1925, during a period of ill-health and near-blindness, Joyce dictated a letter which contained this sentence: "I should like to hear Vico read to me again in the hope that some day I may be able to write again." [20] To his friends who were baffled by the new work-in-progress, Joyce recommended Vico as a guide, and he made certain that *Our Exagmination Round His Factification for Incamination of Work in Progress*, a collection of "explanatory" essays published in 1929, contained two essays summarizing his debt to Vico: Samuel Beckett's "Dante . . . Bruno. Vico . . Joyce" and Stuart Gilbert's "Prolegomena to *Work in Progress*." *Our Exagmination* was a mock-serious production, but Joyce saw to it that the Vichian background was included in the two most informative essays.

Finnegans Wake is founded on an elaborate theory of cyclic recurrence which Joyce drew from many sources, but primarily from the *New Science*.[21] In his brilliant study of literary sources, *The Books at the Wake*, James S. Atherton has summarized the Vichian "axioms" that apply to *Finnegans Wake*:

1. History is a cyclic process repeating eternally certain typical situations.

---

[19] *Ibid.*, p. 204.

[20] *Letters of James Joyce*, III, ed. Richard Ellmann (New York, 1966), 117–18. Joyce had advertised for someone who could read Vico to him in Italian.

[21] The following studies contain useful summaries of those aspects of the *New Science* which were most important to Joyce: Clive Hart, *Structure and Motif in "Finnegans Wake"* (London, 1962), pp. 47–52; Klein, "A Shout in the Street," pp. 327–30; Tindall, *James Joyce*, pp. 70–71.

2. The incidents of each cycle have their parallels in all other cycles.
3. The characters of each cycle recur under new names in every other cycle.
4. Every civilization has its own Jove.
5. Every Jove commits again, to commence his cycle, the same original sin upon which creation depends.[22]

For Joyce, history "moves in vicous cicles yet remews the same" (134.16–17), and his archetypal hero, Humphrey Chimpden Earwicker, constantly re-enacts the basic patterns of behavior which apply to all men in all ages. The title of the book is that of an anonymous Irish ballad whose hero, Tim Finnegan, is thought to be dead but suddenly undergoes a comic resurrection, just as the great hero of Irish legend, Finn MacCool, is born again in every cycle: Finn-again-wakes.

In recounting the history of civilizations, Joyce adopts Vico's three ages—the age of gods, the age of heroes, the age of men—and retains many of Vico's imaginative details: a divine thunderclap, always represented in *Finnegans Wake* by a hundred-letter thunder-word (see 3.15–17), drives primitive man into caves, where religion, language, and social customs develop. But, as Clive Hart has pointed out, Joyce alters Vico's tripartite cycle into a four-part cycle and exalts the brief Vichian *ricorso* until it becomes the crucial moment in history.[23] Influenced by Indian philosophy, by theosophy, and perhaps by the apocalyptic theories of William Butler Yeats's *A Vision*, Joyce made the moment of "reflux" central to his vision. And by emphasizing the fourth period of destruction and reconstitution he strengthened the personal application of his cyclic theory: Vico's institutions of religion (baptism), marriage, and burial combine with the mystic notion of resurrection to provide a personal analogue to the four-part progress of universal history. Just as each civilization passes through the four-part cycle, so each individual re-enacts in miniature the life of his race. As Thornton Wilder once remarked in a lecture on "Joyce and the Modern Novel," *Finnegans Wake* culminated Joyce's lifelong search for an art form in which the individual would be both unique and archetypal.[24]

This four-part cycle, with its historical and personal implications, pervades every aspect of *Finnegans Wake*, governing the construction of words and sentences as well as the largest structural patterns. W. Y. Tindall has given the best description of the book's general design:

[22] Atherton, *Books at the Wake*, p. 32.

[23] Hart, *Structure and Motif in "Finnegans Wake,"* pp. 50–53.

[24] Thornton Wilder, "Joyce and the Modern Novel," in *A James Joyce Miscellany*, ed. Marvin Magalaner (New York, 1957), pp. 11–19. Wilder's comments on *Finnegans Wake* are especially interesting because his own play, *The Skin of Our Teeth*, closely follows the cyclic form of Joyce's work (see Joseph Campbell and Henry Morton Robinson, "The Skin of Whose Teeth?" *Saturday Review of Literature*, 25 [December 19, 1942]: 3–4). Similarly, Samuel Beckett may have been influenced by Joyce's adaptations of Vico.

Finnegans Wake is divided into four books, the first three long and the last one short. The first book has eight chapters, the second and third books have four chapters apiece, and the fourth has one chapter.   The first book is Vico's divine age, the second his heroic age, and the third his human age.   The fourth book is the reflux that leads to the divine again.   In the first book we occupy a gigantic and fabulous world, but since subsequent history grows out of this world, the elements of the later ages are present in it.   Each book contains the elements of the others, and each book contains the whole pattern.   Each chapter of each book is one of Vico's ages.   In Book I the first four chapters represent a complete cycle with its reflux.   The second four chapters repeat the cycle on another level.   The four chapters of Book II and the four chapters of Book III constitute two more cycles.   Joyce indicated the end of a cycle by the word Silence.   This word occurs in the third chapters of Book II and Book III before the reflux.   The main structure, therefore, is one large cycle, containing four smaller cycles.[25]

Book IV of *Finnegans Wake* ends in the middle of a sentence, the last half of which opens Book I; thus the work literally acts out the Vichian *ricorso.*

>   . . . A way a lone a last a loved a
> long the
>   riverrun, past Eve and Adam's, from swerve
> of shore to bend of bay, brings us by a commodius vicus of recirculation back to Howth Castle and Environs.
>   Sir Tristram, violer d'amores, fr'over the short sea, had passencore rearrived from North Armorica. . . .

"Howth Castle and Environs," the geographical center of the book, conceals the initials of Joyce's hero, H. C. E.—both the landscape and the hero are reconstituted as we move along Vico's road, "a commodius vicus of recirculation."   In a letter explaining the opening lines of *Finnegans Wake* Joyce glossed the phrase "passencore rearrived" as the "*ricorsi storici* of Vico."[26]

The Vichian patterns that determine the architecture of *Finnegans Wake* are also present in the smallest units of construction, since it was Joyce's aim to demonstrate the universality of his cycles.   Just as an archetypal pattern may apply to an individual as well as a nation, so Joyce can compress his major affinities with Vico into a single passage.   "Teems of times and happy returns.   The seim anew.   Ordovico or viricordo.   Anna was, Livia is, Plurabelle's to be." (215.22–24.)   This passage occurs near the end of the famous chapter devoted to Joyce's archetypal heroine, Anna Livia Plurabelle, and its theme is entirely Vichian.   "Seim" is a combination of "same" and "Seine," emphasizing the river-like nature of Joyce's heroine.   "Ordovico" is Vico's order, compounded with the Ordovices (an ancient British tribe) and the Ordovicean period in geology.   "Viricordo" contains both *viri*

---

[25] Tindall, *James Joyce*, p. 72.
[26] *Letters*, I, 248.

cordo (the heart of man) and *vi ricordo* (I remember you). "Anna" is the heroine's title as a goddess of old; "Livia," her name as a heroic mother figure; while "Plurabelle" represents her future as many women in the civil age. "Plurabelle" also suggests Vico's *pura et pia bella*, the wars of the heroic peoples.[27] The gist of the entire passage is this: whether we look at the larger patterns of history or within the heart of man, whether we examine past or present or future, we find Vico's "order" in the cyclic recurrence of certain types and situations.

One of Joyce's favorite devices in *Finnegans Wake* is to compress the Vichian cycle into a rhythmic four-part sentence. Thus a late addition to Book II—"in deesperation of deispiration at the diasporation of his diesparation" (257.25–26)—is a pedantic (and strictly alphabetical) recapitulation of the Vichian ages. "Deesperation" (French *déesse*) suggests the gods and goddesses of the divine age; "deispiration" (*deis* is an old form of *dais*) hints at the grand stage of heroic action; "diasporation" is the fragmentation of the civil age; while "diesparation" alludes to the *Dies irae* and the Last Judgment.

Perhaps the most interesting of these four-part sentences is to be found in Book I, in a section rich with Vichian allusions. "From quiqui quinet to michemiche chelet and a jambebatiste to a brulobrulo!" (117.11–12). "Quiqui" suggests the first of Vico's ages, the obscure origin of language in primitive man's first questions ("Who?" "What?") when faced with natural mysteries. It is analogous to the stuttering "pa! pape!" which Vico posited as man's first verbal reaction to the awe-inspiring thunderbolt, and from which "was subsequently derived Jove's title of 'father of men and gods.'"[28] But it also suggests childhood, the questioning child; the individual reflects in his development the cyclic pattern of the race.

"Miche" means "to pilfer" or "to skulk"; it is also French for a round loaf of bread, and in French slang means "buttocks." All these meanings suggest the Fall and Adam and Eve hiding from the Lord, as well as the guilty retreat of Vico's primitive men into caves. "Michemiche" is reminiscent of "mishe mishe" (Irish "I am, I am," i.e., Christian) on the first page of *Finnegans Wake*, where the phrase is associated with baptism; hence Vico's institution of religion is suggested, just as "miche" (a loaf of bread) and "chelet" (*châlet*) remind one of the homemaking aspects of life and Vico's institution of marriage.

Compared with the complexity of "michemiche," "jambebatiste" is quite simple. "Jambe" and "batiste" present an image of legs covered by cloth— the shrouded body at the wake, Vico's institution of burial. "Brulobrulo" (French *brûler*) logically follows as the hell which must precede resurrection.

[27] Bergin and Fisch, *New Science*, par. 1049. Adaline Glasheen has noted this Vichian wordplay in her *Second Census of "Finnegans Wake"* (Evanston, 1963), p. 9.
[28] Bergin and Fisch, *New Science*, par. 448.

Taken together, these two portmanteau words represent the death and re-birth of every individual and every civilization.

But, in addition to outlining the historical and personal applications of the Vichian cycle, this sentence traces the philosophical heritage of *Finnegans Wake*: from Edgar Quinet to Jules Michelet to Giambattista Vico to Giordano Bruno, "burnt Bruno" (whose speculations on the identity of opposites had early attracted Joyce). Thus the sentence comments upon the history of the world-view it embodies.[29]

The linguistic complexity of these passages from *Finnegans Wake* should remind us that Joyce was deeply influenced by Vico's treatment of language as well as by his cyclic view of history. Vico's "three languages" (cere-monial—heraldic—articulate) are put to artistic use in *Finnegans Wake*, but much more important to Joyce was the general example of Vico's use of etymological evidence. Vico looked upon language as fossilized history and sought to recover the past from the radical meanings of words; Joyce reversed this process and sought to create new verbal units which would embody the entire history of a theme or motif. As James S. Atherton has observed, the word units of *Finnegans Wake* "are constructed so as to contain within them-selves sufficient data to allow the structure of the entire work to be deduced from any typical word."[30] Ideally, each word in *Finnegans Wake* should be a tiny mirror reflecting "all marryvoising moodmoulded cyclewheeling history" (186.1–2). Joyce lived in an age which had witnessed the "ab-nihilisation of the etym" (353.22), and he believed it was the job of the artist to build a new world of language out of the ruins of the old.

Surveying Joyce's many uses of Vico in *Finnegans Wake*, it is tempting to seize upon the historical patterns as the point of most profound influence. This is probably a mistake. The historical speculations of the *New Science* provided a neat structural scheme and a wealth of supporting detail, but we must remember that Joyce was an artist who needed rather mechanical schemes to support the verbal elaborations of his late style. "Of course," he once told a friend, "I don't take Vico's speculations literally; I use his cycles as a trellis."[31] Like the mosaic-worker or the illuminator of a medieval manuscript (two of his favorite comparisons), Joyce needed a simple and all-encompassing design to control his passion for intricate detail. As we come to know *Finnegans Wake* better, we shall probably place less importance on those obvious debts to Vico revealed by the early com-mentators, and more upon the deep affinities between Joyce's mind and Vico's. After the publication of *Finnegans Wake* Joyce was still interested

[29] For further discussion of these two sentences see my *The Art of James Joyce* (London, 1961), pp. 59–62 and 94–97.

[30] Atherton, *Books at the Wake*, p. 34. Atherton's entire discussion of Joyce's debt to Vico's linguistic speculations (pp. 32–34) is relevant here.

[31] Colum, *Our Friend James Joyce*, p. 123.

in obtaining the latest study of the *New Science*;[32] clearly, Vico's power to stir his imagination had not lessened.   At bottom it was Vico's creative interpretations of poetry and language that appealed to Joyce, and the motto of *Finnegans Wake* might well be that which Michelet gave to the *New Science*: "Humanity is its own creation."[33]

[32] *Letters*, III, 480.
[33] *Oeuvres choisies de Vico*, ed. Jules Michelet (Paris, 1835), I, iii.   " 'Le mot de la *Scienza nuova* est celui-ci: *l'humanité est son oeuvre à elle-même.*' "

Part III

VICO AND
CONTEMPORARY
SOCIAL AND
HUMANISTIC THINKING

David Bidney

VICO'S NEW
SCIENCE OF MYTH

Scholars have been concerned with the problem of the interrelation of
language, thought, and myth from the time of Plato onward, but it was not
until the eighteenth century that Giambattista Vico made a serious attempt
to introduce a new science of historic myth as part of his *New Science* of
cultural history. Vico interpreted the Greek maxim "Know Thyself" as
signifying the possibility of a science of mankind as revealed in the ethnohistory of man. Man, he maintained, acquires an objective knowledge of
himself, not through critical reflection and analysis of his individual ideas as
Socrates and Plato attempted to do, but rather through reflection on the
historical evidence of the mental and cultural development of man in society.
Vico thought that a critical, etymological study of the classic myths of the
Greeks and Romans would prove invaluable for reconstructing the prehistory of classical civilization. He devoted himself especially to the study
of Homer, with the aim of demonstrating that the Homeric myths can be
understood best from the perspective of ethnohistory and that, if properly
interpreted, they would provide the key to the door to the mysteries of
prehistoric times. Thus the study of myth became for Vico an integral part
of his science and philosophy of history—a thesis which has since been
developed by the ethnologists E. B. Tylor, in *Primitive Culture*, and Max
Müller, in *Science of Thought*, and by Ernst Cassirer, in his classic *Philosophy
of Symbolic Forms*.

Vico's studies of Francis Bacon, Descartes, and Spinoza led him to reflect
on the possibility of a science of universal human history or ethnohistory.
From the seventeenth-century philosophers he learned that all natural
phenomena are subject to natural law because they are subject to an immanent, immutable, divine providence. Science and metaphysics were
considered to be ultimately inseparable, and God, as the divine principle
immanent in nature, was conceived of not only as the First Cause or Creator
but as the *natura naturans*, the nature-engendering principle or power which
sustains and maintains the system of nature in operation. Natural law, then,
was considered to be an empirical manifestation of divine providence in
nature because natural law was conceived of as a manifestation of divine
nature and will.

The idea then occurred to Vico that, if Providence is immanent in the whole of nature, it may be present in the processes of human history also, since man, as Spinoza had demonstrated in his *Ethics*, was an integral part of the order of nature and was subject to natural law. Indeed, philosophers and theologians in the past had fully admitted and recognized the idea of providence in human affairs and, in the Middle Ages, had debated the question of whether divine providence was concerned only with the order of nature as a whole or extended itself to individual human affairs as well. Theologians who based their thinking on the Hebrew Bible and the New Testament were especially concerned with the idea of special providence (as was St. Augustine in his *City of God*), and they sought to interpret special events of history, such as the birth of Jesus of Nazareth and the founding of the Christian Church, as manifestations of divine providence in human history. Even Spinoza, who tended to interpret divine providence in naturalistic terms in his *Tractatus theologico-politicus* and who denied supernatural miracles, did not conceive of the possibility of a science of history comparable to that of physics. Human affairs appeared to him, as they did to Descartes, as being full of contingencies, and human history was a record of human folly and superstition which at most provided material for the moralist and statesman to reflect upon. Human history did not contravene natural law, but neither did it (when taken as a whole) manifest any specific natural laws of its own; at most it served to illustrate the laws of human nature or psychology. Vico, however, extended the idea of natural law and Providence to universal human history while maintaining the reality of individual freedom of will. There was, he maintained, an immanent, *civil* providence manifested in the history of civilization which corresponded to the *natural* providence immanent in nature as a whole. This universal civil providence became manifest in the history of the gentile peoples, that is, of all peoples other than the biblical Hebrews; the latter, as the Chosen People, were subject to a special providence.

In his way Vico repeated the anthropological thought of Socrates, who had admonished Greek thinkers of the fifth century B.C. to study and examine man and the problem of education for living in civilized society, rather than to speculate about cosmic nature and the heavens, as their predecessors had done. For Socrates and Plato the state was the individual magnified, and human society was to be understood on the analogy of the individual, his nature and his character.[1] Vico, however, introduced a new heuristic argument to the effect that the human mind can know best those things of which it is the efficient cause or which are man-made.[2] This, he maintained, was

[1] David Bidney, "The Philosophical Anthropology of Ernst Cassirer and its Significance in Relation to the History of Anthropological Thought," in *The Philosophy of Ernst Cassirer*, ed. P. A. Schilpp, The Library of Living Philosophers, VI (Evanston, Ill., 1949), 465–544.

[2] Vico, *New Science*, par. 331.

the reason for man's success in mathematical studies, since numbers and figures are products of human imagination and intellectual construction. Similarly, he reasoned, human thought and ethnic or cultural history could be the subjects of a scientific study, since human thought and its products or mentifacts are also man-made and subject to the control of the human intellect and will. In principle, therefore, it should be possible to achieve greater success in the science of cultural history or civilization, of which man himself is the author, than in the physical sciences of cosmic nature, of which God is the direct author. History, far from being least subject to scientific analysis, is, and should be, most amenable to scientific study. Man can know himself directly through historical and comparative analysis of his social and cultural achievements, whereas he can understand and explain nature only by inference from effect to cause.

The Greek philosophers recognized cycles in human history and in the gradual development of the arts and sciences from crude, primitive beginnings to a state of refinement and maturity—as may be seen also in the *History* of Herodotus. But they were primarily interested in the present, functional interrelation of institutions and did not concern themselves with reconstructing their past, of which there were no written records. In his *Republic* Plato had reflected on the sequence of political institutions—from monarchy, through aristocracy, to democracy—and had sought to construct an ideal, rational republic which should not be subject to the vicissitudes of political and cultural change that had plagued all known historical Greek states. The ideal republic, once established under the guidance of the philosopher-king, would remain fixed by law and would no longer be subject to radical change in laws or institutions. As conceived by Plato, the ideal republic was to be modeled after the type that was an intellectual idea perfect in its kind. Any change, therefore, could only be a change for the worse, not for the better. The ideal republic was to exist in an eternal present, imaging on earth the absolute, eternal idea.

Change and flux were evils inherent in the natural order, and Plato sought a fixed, absolute human social order governed by rational law. His thought followed the Parmenidean metaphysical tradition that being and permanence were the antitheses of becoming and change, and that objective certainty in knowledge involved knowledge of being, of fixed principles of reality which could be intuited or deduced by the human intellect. Science, in the sense of demonstrable true ideas, could be attained in mathematics, astronomy, and metaphysics, but not in the study of natural phenomena subject to change and contingency; in the latter, probability based on experience was the most that could be expected. Hence, a science of history appeared to be impossible. Cycles of history lasting some 25,000 years were mythic traditions mentioned by Plato,[3] and they emphasized the flux of human civilizations and the need

[3] Plato, *The Statesman.*

for divine providence in human affairs; but they were not to be taken seriously as expressions of fixed principles.

In the Middle Ages the Arab historian Ibn Khaldûn suggested the possibility of a new science of history in his *The Muqaddimah*,[4] or *Introduction to History*, which was modeled after the Greek idea of cycles, but he limited himself to the study of the Arabic people of the Near East and was concerned primarily with political organization, just as Plato and Aristotle had been. He realized that the nomadic, tribal phase of society preceded the urban, civilized stage, and he demonstrated the need for a clear understanding of these stages of social and political development before an attempt to describe the history of ancient societies could be made. It was, he argued, a mistake to assume that ancient societies were identical in structure to those of contemporary times. But Ibn Khaldûn's *Muqaddimah* lacked the concept of natural law, as did the work of Plato and Aristotle, and he did not attempt to apply his idea of stages of social development to all aspects of civilization. He simply had applied the Aristotelian idea of historico-political development to Arabic society and had shown in the Greek manner how cycles of social history tend to repeat themselves.

The revolution in scientific knowledge and methodology achieved by Bacon, Galileo, Descartes, Spinoza, and Leibniz in the sixteenth and seventeenth centuries consisted precisely in the new vision of natural phenomena and processes as being subject to mathematical law, to mathematical measurement and expression. One did not have to choose between Heraclitus' principle of becoming and Parmenides' principle of being. There were *laws of becoming* in nature, and thus the old antithesis of being and becoming was resolved. Scientific knowledge of the laws of nature was possible because the principles of being, in the form of natural laws, were immanent in the very processes of nature's becoming. Scientific knowledge was not the prerogative of the intellect alone; it required careful observation of empirical data, together with intellectual and imaginative intuition and deduction.

When applied to the study of history by Vico, this new concept of a science of nature led to the principle that human historical processes are subject to dynamic laws which enable the historian to understand and integrate the sequence of historical epochs or stages of development in human civilization. Change in human civilization is inevitable and necessary; man cannot arrest the development of society by constructing philosophical, utopian republics. At most the historian and philosopher can describe and evaluate the order of historical changes and the laws that governed civilization at each stage of its development. The metaphysical philosopher and theologian can explain the order of civilization as the

[4] Ibn Khaldûn, *The Muqaddimah: An Introduction to History*, trans. Franz Rosenthal, 3 vols. (New York, 1958).

manifestation of a divine, civil providence which orders the affairs of men in spite of themselves.

It was Vico's unique achievement to have expressed clearly the idea of a comparative science of ethnology or socio-cultural history, even though that idea was based on the Greek model of cycles of history and civilization. Vico relied primarily on Greek and Roman history and projected his law of historical development to other gentile peoples. It remained for Auguste Comte to apply a similar principle of development to European civilization from the Middle Ages to the beginning of the nineteenth century, and for E. B. Tylor to trace the development of primitive culture from savagery, through barbarism, to civilization. The main difference between Vico and his nineteenth-century successors concerns the idea of unilinear progress, which is lacking in Vico. As stated, Vico retains the Greek idea of cycles and of the eventual decline of a society and its civilization—a thesis which Nietzsche and Spengler rediscovered in their own ways—but nineteenth-century sociologists and ethnologists adhered to the idea of progress introduced by the French philosophers of the eighteenth-century Enlightenment. However, the basic principle of a law of historical development is present first in Vico, then in Kant, and finally in Comte and Tylor and their followers.[5]

Vico designated three ages or stages in the development of mankind, the age of the gods, the age of heroes, and the age of man. The age of the gods is the prehistoric, primitive age of culture or civilization and corresponds to the infancy of mankind. The age of heroes marks the beginning of the civil or political state and corresponds to the youth of the human race. The age of man represents the stage of development to mature, rational humanity. In the third stage of civilization, men realize their rational powers and achieve the ability to organize their social life according to the principles of reason and justice for all. Finally, in the fourth or final stage, decline sets in, as in the old age of the individual, and the civilization disintegrates. The cycle from the birth to the death of a civilization is a course preordained by divine, civil providence and tends to be fulfilled regardless of the plans and motivations of the individual actors at a given time and place.

The essential point in Vico's thesis, and the one in which he most nearly anticipates modern ethnological science, is his conception of the evolutionary, social mentality of human societies and the corresponding stages of socio-cultural evolution. Utilizing the concept of the state of nature which he derived from Hobbes and Spinoza, Vico imagined that mankind was actually in such a state of nature following the Noachian flood mentioned in the Bible.[6] Primitive man was postdiluvial man. Vico lacked entirely the

[5] David Bidney, *Theoretical Anthropology* (New York: Columbia University Press, 1953).

[6] Vico, *New Science*, pars. 369, 370.

concept of prehistory introduced in the nineteenth century by the geology of
Charles Lyell and the evolutionary biology of Charles Darwin, which pushed
back the horizons of time millions of years. Working within the biblical
framework of time, he imagined mankind as having evolved from a precultural state of nature to a primitive state of culture, the age of the gods,
through a semibarbaric age of heroes, to a final state of rationality and
civilization. Rousseau's criticism[7] that the concept of the state of nature as
put forward by Hobbes and Locke tended to presuppose human culture in a
prepolitical stage of development was clearly anticipated by Vico, whose
state of nature is precultural.

Unlike his seventeenth-century predecessors, Vico did not regard the state
of civilization as one artificially introduced through the convention of a
"social contract" with a sovereign. For Vico the state of civilized society
was the result of a gradual, natural process of development. Beginning
with the establishment of the first families in caves, he attempts to reconstruct
in Aristotelian fashion the gradual extension of social organization to include
non-consanguineous dependents who sought the protection of the original
families. In time the families became clans or *gentes*, with their patriarchal
leaders, and these in turn merged into tribes and finally into sovereign states.
Vico seems to have had no idea of matrilineal clans, since he derived his
information from Graeco-Roman sources, which followed patrilineal descent. The three primary socio-cultural institutions were, according to
Vico, religion, the family (with its associated incest taboos), and burial of the
dead—the three institutions that serve to differentiate man and humanity
from the beasts.[8] Vico's thesis of the primacy of religion in the civilizing
process reappears in the classic work *The Ancient City*, by Fustel de Coulanges,
although the latter fails to mention Vico's work.

In the first cultural age, the age of the gods, man has not yet discovered
himself. He attributes all causal action to divine, supernatural beings who
regulate all the powers of nature. As Thales put it, originally "all things are
full of gods," and man is thought to be impotent in relation to them.
Aboriginal, cultural man speaks a poetic, metaphorical language and tends
to regard all nature as animated by spiritual beings or powers. When he
describes the phenomena of nature or narrates the events of his life, he tends
to do so in poetic language that expresses his feelings of awe and reverence
before the supernatural powers, which he believes to be immanent in all
things. This is *the age of myth*, properly so called because it marks the beginning of those oral narratives and traditions concerning the nature of the gods
and their relations with men.

In the second age of civilization or culture, the age of heroes, there emerge

[7] J. J. Rousseau, "Discourse on the Origin of Inequality," in *The Social Contract and
Discourses* (New York: E. P. Dutton & Co., 1913).

[8] Vico, *New Science*, par. 333.

the traditional, semidivine culture heroes, the superhuman benefactors of mankind who allegedly introduce the basic social institutions and laws of human society. This is the age of semidivine kings and lawgivers who are simultaneously the founders of the first cities. This is also *the age of the professional bards or poets* who sing of the deeds of the culture heroes. The poets, as Plato informs us in the *Republic*, are the true authors and makers of the recorded myths that later generations of scholars have found so incredible. The poets selected and created the body of narratives concerning the culture heroes which has been recorded; it is they, too, who formulated the first genealogies of the gods, as may be seen from the works of Hesiod and Homer. The poets, however, were not the authors of the mythical traditions concerning the gods; the latter originated with primitive, cultural man in the age of the gods.

In the third age of man, men became conscious of their own intellectual powers and of their ability to regulate social institutions. It is *the age of the discovery of man* as a free, creative agent capable of directing his own destiny and of expressing himself and his ideas in rational, logical concepts. It is the age of prose and philosophico-scientific literature. It also marks the beginning of republican forms of government in which the people are recognized as the source of political power and authority. The mythical narrative concerning the culture heroes tends to be questioned and criticized as incredible. Even when accepted in part, myths are often reinterpreted as philosophical allegories in order to render them more rational and in accord with the axioms of reason and logic. In the rational age of mature humanity, scholars tend to forget the poetic, metaphorical thought of previous ages and to accuse the ancients of irrationality and immorality, or else they attribute to them philosophical wisdom of which they are quite incapable. The wisdom of the ancients, Vico insists, was a poetic, mythical wisdom—not the wisdom of the philosophers and theologians.

Viewed from a historical and evolutionary perspective, the significance of the ancient myths for the scholar lies in the ethnological information they may convey. Myths constitute a record of the mentality and culture of primitive and ancient man. They have both a subjective and objective ethnological value. Subjectively, and psychologically, they tell us how primitive man thought and expressed himself in his narratives and traditions, regardless of the truth of his beliefs. Objectively, when properly analyzed the myths may reveal to the scholar historical truths concerning the socio-cultural life of primitive man. Vico further insists that through semantic, etymological analysis the scholar may reconstruct the prehistory of primitive man, since the myths contain references, in allegorical form, to significant historical events in the life of primitive man. The latter assumption concerning the allegorical significance of the myths is one that Vico stresses as a major thesis, even though it is highly problematical. The former of Vico's assumptions, concerning the subjective, psycho-cultural value of myths in revealing the mentality of primitive man, the subject of the myths, is one that was later developed at length in the ethno-linguistic theories of Max Müller and in the evolutionary ethnology of E. B. Tylor.

Furthermore, according to Vico, the myths themselves are subject to a process of evolution and degeneration. Primitive, aboriginal myth in the age of the gods is the true narrative of man's historical, social experience expressed in poetic, metaphorical language that can scarcely be understood by the modern scholar without minute, etymological and comparative, linguistic analysis. The myths of the second period, the age of heroes and professional poets, are artistically consciously formulated myths that reflect the ideas, prejudices, and morals of the poets themselves and of the society in which they lived. In the second period the myths first become partially falsified because the poets themselves have misunderstood the metaphorical language of the ancients; they are later corrupted, as new generations of poets reconstruct them to suit their own fancies and dissolute customs. Vico states this thesis very clearly in different parts of his work. Thus he writes: "Such fables in their beginnings were all true and severe and worthy of the founders of the nations, and only later (when the long passage of years had obscured their meanings, and customs had changed from austere to dissolute, and because men to console their consciences wanted to sin with the authority of the gods) came to have the obscene meanings with which they have come down to us" (*New Science*, paragraph 81). And again: "The fables originating among the first savages and crude men were very severe, as befitted the founding of nations emerging from a state of fierce, bestial freedom. Then, with the long passage of years and change of customs, they were impropriated, altered, and obscured in the dissolute and corrupt times, even before Homer. Because religion was important to the men of Greece, and they feared to have the gods opposed to their desires as they were to their customs, they attributed their customs to the gods and gave improper, ugly, and obscene meanings to the fables" (*New Science*, paragraph 221). Finally: "The fables in their origin were true and severe narrations (whence *mythos*, fable, was defined as *vera narratio*, as we have frequently noted). But because for the most part they were originally monstrous, they were later misappropriated, then altered, subsequently became improbable, after that obscure, then scandalous, and finally incredible. These are the seven sources of the difficulties of the fables, which can all easily be found throughout the second book" (*New Science*, paragraph 814).

Here we see that Vico repeats in various contexts his firm belief that the original myths in the age of the gods were true narrations which were later misunderstood and still later deliberately altered and corrupted to suit the poet's fancies and the customs of the times. Vico does not, however, tell us how to differentiate a true or genuine myth from a false or corrupt one. He admits that even the aboriginal, genuine myths were monstrous, and he fails to inform us how a monstrous myth differs from a corrupt one.

Thus, while the poets as a class may be regarded as the originators of myths, Vico distinguishes two ages of poets before Homer: "The first was the age of the theological poets, who were themselves heroes and sang true and austere fables; the second, that of heroic poets, who altered and corrupted the fables; and the third, that of Homer, who received them in their altered and corrupted form" (*New Science*, paragraph 905).

Vico himself regarded his theory of myth and especially his study of Homer as his greatest single achievement and as the vindication of his new science of history. Aboriginal myth is thought to be a direct expression of the mind and spirit of a people. True and genuine myth must be distinguished from the falsified and corrupt myth of later poets. All myths must not be put into one category based on an indiscriminate study of genuine and corrupt examples. Myths must be understood in their historical contexts, and they require meticulous philological analysis of the language in which they are expressed. Through the study of the folklore of a people, the ethnologist and folklorist may reconstruct its ethnic history and provide new generations of poets and artists with a genuine source of inspiration for further ethnic creativity. This is the vision and inspiration of Vico's theory of myth, and it is this positive evaluation of primitive and classic mythology which influenced the originators of the Romantic movement, such as Herder and Schlegel, in Germany.[9]

Vico's great literary "discovery" was that Homer never existed as an individual, historic poet. Instead, "Homer was an idea or a heroic character of Grecian men insofar as they told their histories in song" (*New Science*, paragraph 873). "The Greek peoples were themselves Homer" (*New Science*, paragraph 875). "The Homer who wrote or put together the *Iliad* preceded by many centuries the Homer who was the author of the *Odyssey*" (*New Science*, paragraph 880). Vico arrived at this momentous conclusion by comparing the two texts and noting that the *Iliad* refers to a primitive period when the peoples of Greece practiced villainy, savagery, and cruelty, whereas the *Odyssey* belongs to a period of luxury and moral decadence. Etymologically, the name *Homer* may be said to derive from *homou* (together) and *eirein* (to link), thus signifying "stickers together of songs," which is precisely what the rhapsodes were (*New Science*, paragraph 852). Homer is the class name for the rhapsodes who put together in song the many tales of the history of prehistoric Greece. Homer is not the author of the book attributed to him; he is himself part of the Greek *mythos*.

From the perspective of ethnohistory, it appears that there are two distinct

9 Max H. Fisch, Introduction to Vico's *Autobiography*, trans. Max H. Fisch and Thomas G. Bergin, p. xx; Stephen Toulmin and June Goodfield, *The Discovery of Time* (New York, 1965), pp. 125–40.

sources of poetry and myth: the theological poets and the heroic poets.   The primitive theological poets were the earliest wise men in all the gentile nations (*New Science*, paragraph 916), and it is they who produced the first myth of the gods whom they themselves had created out of their own imaginations, motivated by fear of thunder and lightning.   In Vico's words: "In this fashion the first theological poets created the first divine fable, the greatest they ever created; that of Jove, king and father of men and gods, in the act of hurling the lightning bolt; an image so popular, disturbing, and instructive that its creators themselves believed in it, and feared, revered, and worshiped it in frightful religions" (*New Science*, paragraph 379).   This great religious myth marked the origin of a poetry whose proper material has always been "the credible impossibility."   "It is impossible that bodies should be minds, yet it was believed that the thundering sky was Jove" (*New Science*, paragraph 383).   The theological poets were also the first historians of the gentile nations and recorded significant events in the development of civilization among their peoples.   Vico states it as a principle "that the first fables must have contained civil truths, and must therefore have been the histories of the first peoples" (*New Science*, paragraph 198).   "The poets must therefore have been the first historians of the nations" (*New Science*, paragraph 820).

Thus, both theological and heroic poets may be said to have produced historical myths which referred to facts and events that actually happened. "Since barbarians lack reflection, which, when ill used, is the mother of falsehood, the first heroic Latin poets sang true histories; that is, the Roman wars. . . . And here we have a luminous proof of the fact that the first fables were histories.   For satire spoke ill of persons not only real but well known; tragedy took for its arguments characters of poetic history; the Old Comedy put into its plots illustrious living persons; the New Comedy, born in times of the most lively reflection, finally invented characters entirely fictitious . . . and neither among the Greeks nor among the Latins was an entirely fictitious character ever the protagonist of a tragedy" (*New Science*, paragraph 817). According to Vico, primitive, savage, and barbaric man expressed his feelings and the impressions of his senses in true, mythical narratives; the myths were true narratives, in poetic language, of actual, ethno-historical events.   Lacking developed rational powers of reflection, primitive, poetic man was still incapable of creations, fictions, and falsehoods.

According to Vico, then, there are two basic types of myth: theological myths, concerning the nature of the gods, and historical myths, concerning culture heroes and social institutions.   The question may well be raised: "Are the two types of myth coeval, or does one precede the other in time?" Vico's answer appears to be that the myth of Jove, the god of thunder and lightning, certainly came first; it was the first divine fable and the greatest ever created (*New Science*, paragraph 379).   Although this theological myth contained elements of falsehood and fiction in portraying the father of the gods in material form, it contained the great truth "that divine providence watches over the welfare of mankind" (*New Science*, paragraph 385). Subsequent theological myths, like the myths of the heroic age, were essentially historical myths in symbolic, allegorical form. There was, in principle, only one genuine theological myth, that of the myth of Jove, the god of thunder and lightning. This would imply a primitive, mythical monotheism—a thesis later developed by Schelling[10] and by Max Müller.[11]

All genuine myth is, in principle, *vera narratio*. Theological myths concerning the father of gods and men, whether he be called Zeus or Jove or by any other name, are true in principle inasmuch as they contain implicitly the great truth of the reality of divine, civil providence. As myths they also contain elements of imagination which are false and fictitious, since the deity is imagined in material form and body. That is why Vico calls them "credible impossibilities"; they were believed by the poets and the people, but they are incredible to us from the perspective of reason and revelation. Historical myths employ two types of symbols, namely, symbols of lesser gods and symbols of cultural heroes. In either type of historical myth the poets narrated symbolic facts and referred to real people and events. In the age of the gods the poets employed symbols of deities; in the age of heroes they utilized type images of culture heroes. In both instances they were narrating and recording *vera narratio*, historical facts that are credible and possible by our rational standards. In a prereflective age, such as the age of the gods and the age of heroes, poets had not yet learned to fabricate deliberate, systematic fictions and falsehoods, and it may therefore be assumed that they spoke theological and historical truths.

Vico's method of interpreting myths may be termed "ethnic Euhemerism,"[12] for he reduces the classic Greek and Roman gods and heroes to class symbols of the societies they represented at given periods of history. With the exception of Jove, the gods and heroes were symbolic, imaginative universals who represented in allegorical and metaphorical form individuals and classes in relation to one another (*New Science*, paragraph 209). While Vico is critical of Francis Bacon for attributing philosophical wisdom to the ancients, on the ground that savage, aboriginal man was incapable of rational, metaphysical wisdom, he is himself prepared to attribute to the theological and heroic poets *historical wisdom* and allegorical symbolism in describing the institutions and customs of civilized life with amazing insight. "The wisdom of the ancients," he explains, "was the vulgar wisdom of the lawgivers who founded the human race, not the esoteric wisdom of great and

[10] F. W. J. Schelling, *Einleitung in die Philosophie der Mythologie*, in *Sämmtliche Werke*, I (1856); Ernst Cassirer, *The Problem of Knowledge* (New Haven, 1950).

[11] Max Müller, *Natural Religion* (New York, 1889).

[12] Bidney, *Theoretical Anthropology*, pp. 306–7.

rare philosophers" (*New Science*, paragraph 384). Vico ends by *explaining away* the reality of the gods and cultural heroes—just as he had explained away the reality and existence of Homer—as being nothing more than allegorical symbols of the Greek and Roman people themselves. Anticipating Émile Durkheim's sociological method in *The Elementary Forms of the Religious Life*, Vico does not treat the myths of the gods and heroes as mere fictions or irrational tales, as the rationalistic philosophers of the seventeenth and eighteenth centuries tended to do, but endeavors to explain and indicate the social and ethnic reality behind the mythical symbols and forms. Just as Durkheim attempted to indicate that society was the objective reality behind the variety of religious symbols of the gods, so Vico maintained that *historical societies and their forms of civilization* were in fact symbolized by gods and heroes.

Thus Vico attempts to provide a natural theogony, or generation of the Greek and Roman gods, indicating the allegorical significance of the historical, theological symbols of the twelve major gods (*New Science*, paragraph 317). Regardless of the problematic validity of his interpretation, it is a coherent, ingenious attempt to rationalize Greek and Roman mythology and theology which would have done credit to any pre-Christian philosopher. Were it not for the fact that Vico was a good Roman Catholic in eighteenth-century Italy, he could easily be mistaken for a philosopher of the time of Julian the Apostate, such as Sallustius, pleading for an allegorical interpretation of the ancient myths.[13]

Following Vico's interpretation, we learn that Hercules is said to have been born of Alcmena by a thunderbolt from Jove; another great hero of Greece, Bacchus, was born of thunderstruck Semele. The notion of the gods as sons of Jove was "a truth of the senses" for the Greeks in the age of the gods. So the "Muses were held to be the daughters of Jove (for religion gave birth to all the arts of humanity)" (*New Science*, paragraph 508). Similarly, out of solemnized marriages, the theological poets fashioned another divine character called Juno, who is both wife and sister of Jove. She is queen of gods and men because the kingdoms were afterward born of these legitimate marriages. So, too, Venus is originally the patron goddess of solemn marriage, but later, as the times became corrupt, Venus was believed to have lain with men, as had Jove with women, and to have conceived Aeneas by Anchises. Juno is said to have been jealous because the Roman nobles excluded the plebs from lawful marriage down to the 309th year of Rome. "By the Greeks, however, she was called Hera, whence the name the *heroes* gave themselves, for they were born of solemn nuptials" (*New Science*, paragraph 513). The tale that the goddess Juno imposes great labors on Hercules symbolizes the truth "that piety and marriage form the school wherein are learned the first rudiments of all the great virtues" (*New Science*,

[13] Gilbert Murray, *Five Stages of Greek Religion* (New York, 1951), appendix.

paragraph 514). In later times the austere myths of Juno and Hercules became corrupted, and "Hercules was made a bastard son of Jove who by Jove's favor, and despite Juno, had carried out all his labors (*New Science*, paragraph 514). Vico explains that the later Greek and Roman fables were invariably corruptions of the original virtuous myths of men in the golden age of the gods. "For in the golden age of the theological poets, men insensible to every refinement of wearisome reflection took pleasure only in what was lawful and useful, as is still the case, we observe, with peasants" (*New Science*, paragraph 516).

Vico postulates a golden age of the gods among the Greeks of some nine hundred years' duration (*New Science*, paragraph 69). The golden age began when men first acquired a degree of humanity through religion, that is, through the belief in a supreme being which they acquired through their experience of thunder and lightning and their animistic mode of thinking. Then followed the institution of marriage and the burial of the dead. These three primary institutions were the sources of all subsequent developments of civilization in society. In the golden age man was god-fearing and virtuous, but also superstitious and fanatical. Primitive man was prudent, just in his dealings with his fellow men, temperate in being content with monogamy, strong, industrious, and magnanimous (*New Science*, paragraph 516). In this golden age men had the virtue of the senses with an admixture of religion and savage cruelty which led them to practice the "inhuman humanity" of human sacrifice to the gods (*New Science*, paragraph 517).

The concept of the golden age of the gods is relevant to our discussion of myth because Vico assumes that this age of piety and virtue was one in which theological poets created unconscious, allegorical myths that were true narrations of divine providence and of the development of human civilization. It was an age of prereflection, and men were still incapable of deliberate falsehoods. Only with the development of reflective thought and of the refinements of civilization did human nature become subject to corruption— a thesis which obviously anticipated that which Rousseau set forth in *On the Origin of Inequality* and *Discourse on the Moral Effects of the Arts and Sciences*. This state of corruption in human nature led to corruption of the theological myths in that the poets began to imagine the gods in their own image. The myths reflect the state of civilization of the times, and the poets may be said to tell us more about themselves and their times than about the gods of whom they profess to sing. The corrupt myths reveal a subjective rather than an objective ethnological and historical truth.

Thus Vico's distinction between genuine or true myths of the golden age of the gods and corrupt myths of the age of heroes and of the age of man presupposes the historical principle of an age of virtue and innocence which is necessarily followed by an age of corruption. The fall of man is, for him, a recurring event which happens inevitably as civilization develops. Vico lacks the idea of unilinear progress and tends to think rather in terms of the Greek and biblical theories of human degeneration. Only a special providence and revelation can save a chosen people from the fate of the rest of gentile mankind. Vico's philosophical anthropology combines a theory of evolution and maturation in the development of thought from the age of the gods to the age of man with a theory of concomitant degeneration of the moral character of mankind. Nineteenth-century sociologists and ethnologists retained his theory of mental evolution and cultural evolution but disregarded his theory of moral degeneration.

The corruption of the myths is said to be attributable to two distinct factors. First, there is a kind of collective amnesia in the long passage of time which makes men of the heroic age forget the allegorical meanings implicit in the poetic language of the ancients—a thesis later put forward by Max Müller as "the disease of language" to explain the origin of myth in metaphor.[14] Second, moral corruption is caused by the abuse of reflective thought whereby men rationalize their vices by attributing them to the gods in their mythical narratives. Corrupt man and corrupt society become the measure of the gods.

Vico's theory of the origin of myth involves certain psychological and epistemological assumptions which he states explicitly and which have been developed by later writers. First, Vico postulates that aboriginal man was subject to strong feelings and a powerful imagination but lacked the power of reflective thought and conceptual analysis. Primitive man thought in terms of images and "imaginative universals" but not in terms of abstract intellectual concepts. Thus, when man in the age of the gods or in the age of heroes wishes to designate a universal property or characteristic of something, he selects some particular example, actual or imaginary, to which he attributes all the qualities of the type. As Vico puts it: "The first men, the children, as it were, of the human race, not being able to form intelligible class concepts of things, had a natural need to create poetic characters, that is, imaginative class concepts or universals, by reducing to them, as to models or ideal portraits, all the particular species which resembled them" (*New Science*, paragraph 209). Thus the type or genus of the "civil sage" or culture hero was imaged forth by the ancient Egyptians as "Hermes Trismegistus," to whom they attributed all the "inventions useful or necessary to the human race." Such type images are the basis of the true poetic allegories to be found in the myths or fables. "These fables are ideal truths conforming to the merits of those of whom the vulgar tell them; and such falseness in fact as they now and then contain consists simply in failure to give their subjects their due. So that, if we consider

---

[14] Ernst Cassirer, *The Myth of the State* (New Haven, 1946); Max Müller, *Chips from a German Workshop* (New York, 1881).

the matter well, poetic truth is metaphysical truth, and physical truth that is not in conformity with it should be considered false" (*New Science*, paragraph 205).

Imaginative universals, like Platonic universals, are ideal types to which existential reality is made to conform. Imaginative universal types are mythical because there no clear distinction is made between the universal ideal type and the particular individual who exemplifies it; the two are merged to create a concrete universal, a historical figure who is also an allegorical symbol of all particular individuals of the type and ultimately of the people as a whole. Thus the imaginative ideal type is a concrete universal rather than an abstract logical construct. This is the chief difference between the imaginative idealism of primitive, poetic man and the intellectual idealism of rational, philosophical man. Thus Jove is an imaginative universal of the character of God contemplated under the attribute of his providence (*New Science*, paragraph 381). Primitive, mythical monotheism is to be differentiated from intellectual, philosophical monotheism, which involves abstract conceptualization. Similarly, "Every gentile nation had its Hercules, who was the son of Jove; and Varro, the most learned of antiquarians, numbered as many as forty of them" (*New Science*, paragraph 196).

Vico's second assumption is that primitive man tends to think in animistic terms because he imagines, in his ignorance, that he is the measure of all things and attributes to all things in nature life and feelings analogous to his own (*New Science*, paragraph 120). "The human mind, because of its indefinite nature, wherever it is lost in ignorance makes itself the rule of the universe in respect of everything it does not know" (*New Science*, paragraph 181). "When men are ignorant of the natural causes of things, and cannot even explain them by analogy with similar things, they attribute their own nature to them. The vulgar, for example, say the magnet loves the iron" (*New Science*, paragraph 180). This human tendency to think anthropomorphically and animistically is the basis of metaphor, which in turn is an essential ingredient in the formation of myths. Vico is prepared to say that "every metaphor so formed is a fable in brief" (*New Science*, paragraph 404). In the myth of metaphor "man becomes all things by *not* understanding them" (*New Science*, paragraph 405). Vico's thesis ridicules the Greek Sophists' thesis that man is the measure of all things as being unworthy of a philosopher, although characteristic of primitive, mythical thought. This epistemic assumption was later developed in E. B. Tylor's famous theory that animism underlies primitive religion and myth. Tylor, however, continued to speak of primitive man as a philosopher who infers the idea of a soul in order to differentiate the living from the dead,[15] whereas Vico clearly

---

[15] E. B. Tylor, *Primitive Culture*, vol. I: *Origins of Culture* (New York, 1958), chap. xi.

regarded animistic thought as a product of prephilosophical, poetic thought. In this respect Vico was followed by Max Müller, who also attributed poetic, metaphorical thought to primitive man.

Thirdly, Vico tends to assume the psychic unity of aboriginal man. Uniform ideas are said to have originated independently "among entire peoples unknown to each other" (*New Science*, paragraph 144). He speaks of the common sense of the human race in recognizing principles of the natural law of nations (*jus gentium*). "Common sense is judgment without reflection, shared by an entire class, an entire people, an entire nation, or the whole human race" (*New Science*, paragraph 142). Vico is opposed to the notion that the natural law of nations originated in one nation and then passed by diffusion to others, as the Egyptians and Greeks claimed to have spread civilization throughout the ancient world (*New Science*, paragraph 146). In this respect he anticipated the arguments of modern evolutionary ethnologists, who cite examples of the independent evolution of Old World and New World civilizations against the claims of either racists, who would derive modern civilizations by diffusion from the "Aryan race," as in the case of Houston Chamberlain, or extreme diffusionists, such as G. Elliot Smith, who, on the assumption that civilization originated only once, attempted to derive ancient civilization by diffusion from Egypt.[16] Vico accepted mental universals, or common, folk wisdom, "a mental language common to all nations, which uniformly grasps the substance of things feasible in human social life" (*New Science*, paragraph 161). An example of this is "afforded by proverbs or maxims of vulgar wisdom in which substantially the same meanings find diverse expressions" (*New Science*, paragraph 161). He also finds a universal principle of etymology in all languages: "words are carried over from bodies and from the properties of bodies to express the things of the mind and spirit" (*New Science*, paragraph 237).

Fourthly, Vico assumes that the aboriginal myths have a unity of object or subject matter; the original myths are supposed to deal with the ethnohistory of the peoples who produced them. The theological poets produced historical allegories of their own peoples, even while they appeared to narrate the genealogy of the gods and their supernatural deeds. Vico's science of mythology consists of ethnic Euhemerism, which explains away the reality of gods and heroes, and even the authors of the myths themselves (such as Homer), by reducing them to imaginative, concrete universals or class symbols. The poets do not make the ethnic myths; they simply record in allegorical, poetic form the history of their peoples. *Vico did not demonstrate this unity of subject matter of the myths; he simply assumed it and interpreted the myths to fit his theory. The argument is really circular, since he selects only those*

---

[16] G. Elliot Smith, *The Ancient Egyptians and Their Influence Upon the Civilization of Europe* (London, 1911).

myths which lend themselves to his ethnic interpretation and uses his interpretation as proof of the unity of object or subject matter. Myths that do not lend themselves to his ethno-historical interpretation are labeled "corrupt" and are dismissed as products of later generations of dissolute poets. No one but Vico could possibly interpret the myth that Vulcan split the forehead of Jove, from which sprang Minerva, to mean that "the multitude of *famuli* practicing servile arts broke . . . the rule of Jove" (*New Science*, paragraph 589). Socrates and Plato would have censored this myth as being unbecoming and indecent for the education of children. There is no more evidence to prove that the genealogy of the gods is a series of historical allegories than there is for Francis Bacon's thesis that the myths were meant to symbolize cosmic processes of nature. As Ernst Cassirer was to argue in his *Essay on Man* and *Myth of the State*, there simply is no evidence for the unity of subject matter in the classic myths and there is no clear proof that the classic myths have a specific allegorical meaning. The allegorical interpretations tell us more about the interpreters than they do about the aboriginal myths.

It is necessary to distinguish, as Vico failed to do, between imaginative universals and allegories. An imaginative universal is an epistemic fact; it is an ideal class image based on the experience of particulars. Each people has its own prehistoric culture heroes, whom it idealizes and to whom it attributes comparable wisdom and virtue. The ideal imaginative universal of the culture hero is not incompatible with the actual historical existence of outstanding individuals who were cultural innovators and poets. Myths of the culture hero may presuppose the existence of the hero about whom the myths are told. Many historical figures have accumulated mythical tales that serve to glorify them in the eyes of their people. The Euhemeristic method of interpretation of theological myths was simply an attempt to explain the cult and myth of divine culture heroes by reference to historical individuals who were later deified. Euhemerus, in other words, tried to explain myths of the supernatural by means of naturalistic, historical facts and people. By contrast, Vico's ethnic Euhemerism *explains away* the historical culture hero and tends to reduce the hero to the people who produced him. Homer ceases to be a real historical individual and becomes instead the Greek people in various stages of development. In the same manner, modern imitators of Vico tend to explain away the historical Moses and the historical Jesus as symbolic creations of the people themselves. In sum, an imaginative, concrete universal is not, *ipso facto*, an allegorical universal symbolizing some social reality other than itself. It is possible to have imaginative universals of cultural heroes without reducing the heroes to allegories. An allegory presupposes a degree of conscious reflection and intellectual development which is incompatible with the mind of pre-reflective, mythopoeic man. Contrary to Vico, an imaginative universal is not, in principle, an allegorical symbol; it is rather an existential merging of the actual and ideal in the image of a single historical individual.

Vico's argument that primitive, savage man necessarily spoke the truth and created true ethno-historical myths and allegories because he was incapable of reflective thought may be good satire on the concept of rational man, but it is neither good ethnology nor good psychology. One might as well argue that young children are incapable of telling lies and falsehoods because their intellects are not fully developed. In fact, however, a lively imagination combined with animistic thought is a very fertile source of fictions and false-hoods, regardless of the moral intentions of the subjects. As later ethno-logists—notably Tylor—have pointed out, the mythopoeic mind is a source of mythical fancies and fictions precisely because it has not achieved a clear distinction between subjective and objective truth, between idea and object. The intellect, when abused, may indeed become an added source of deliberate falsehoods, but it is also our basic safeguard against the irrational myths of the imagination, and a potent source of moral allegories. A myth may indeed be a *vera narratio* for the primitive poet and those who believe his tales, but this is no ground for maintaining that primitive myths are objectively true and poetic allegories of ethno-historical facts. The claim for the truth of the myths may be no more than a mark of overcredulity on the part of the poet as well as of his interpreters.

Vico did appreciate the historical value of mythical narratives as containing evidence of the evolution of thought and civilization in prehistoric times. In this he was a pioneer and exercised considerable influence on the Romantic movement in the late eighteenth century and on evolutionary sociological and ethnological thought in the nineteenth century. But, instead of treating myths historically as expressions of prehistoric culture and thought which inform us primarily about the authors and subjects of the myths, as Tylor insisted, he proceeded to interpret them, in addition, as allegories, after the fashion of Francis Bacon, whose work *On the Wisdom of the Ancients* he read. Thus he tended to assume that the myths were primarily vehicles for the symbolic expression of historical truths that the poets in their wisdom wished to record for posterity. He confused the subjective, historical truth of the myths with their objective, historical truth by assuming a unity of object for myths, for which he had no evidence but that of his own fertile imagination. He was further misled by his philosophy and theology of history, which led him to postulate a golden age of primitive man dedicated to mythical truth and moral virtue, followed by an age of mythical and moral corruption. This strengthened his conviction that the theological myths contained allegorical, ethno-historical truths which, in order to be rediscovered and interpreted, required the historical imagination and learning of the etymol-ogist and philologist.

Following Vico's example, we might well say, it is a mark of civil, divine providence in human civilization that his work the *New Science*, although mistaken in its allegorical interpretation of myth as ethnohistory, was nevertheless destined to promote ethnological and sociological thought and to open up new horizons in the history of civilization for the scholarly research of future generations.

Tullio de Mauro   GIAMBATTISTA VICO:
                         From Rhetoric to
                         Linguistic Historicism

I

Vico came comparatively late to the consideration of language and he came by indirect ways. Among the duties of the Professor of Eloquence of the University of Naples was that of delivering the inaugural address at the opening of the school year; so Vico, who was the incumbent of that chair, delivered seven inaugurals, from 1699 to 1708, which, in his opinion "at least at a certain moment, formed a single unit, and were covered by a single title: *On the Aims of the Studies That Are Suited to the Nature of Man.*" The humanistic problem of the *ratio studiorum* is taken up again and is treated polemically, in opposition to solutions of the rationalistic type, which emphasize the role of logic and mathematics in education. The problem is solved by Vico through references to the Ciceronian and humanistic *scientia civilis* and through an underscoring of the primacy of literary and rhetorical education. While the *ratio studiorum* of scientific cast, repudiating rhetoric, "presents these disadvantages insofar as youthful students are concerned, that they are [when they enter life after the end of their school years] at once incapable of acting with prudence and are unable to speak in public with a knowledge of psychology and in terms apt to gain persuasion by skillful use of intensely emotional power," the type of education fostered by humanistic study is conformable "to human prudence, in both of its aspects: the moral one, which molds man in general, and civil prudence, which molds the citizen." Thus Vico, at forty years of age, posits the problem of the role fulfilled by language in the educational process, and deals with it, in the last and best known of his orations, *On the Study Methods of Our Time (De nostri temporis studiorum ratione),* from the perspective of rhetorical training.[1]

[1] See, in particular, chap. VII of the *De nostri temporis studiorum ratione* (English translation by Elio Gianturco, *On the Study Methods of Our Time* [Indianapolis, Ind.: Bobbs-Merrill, 1965]). On the meaning of the seven inaugurals in Vico's work see E. Garin, *Storia della filosofia italiana* (Turin, 1967), II, 928–34. Relationships with the rhetorical-linguistic conceptions of humanism are analyzed by K. O. Apel in *Die Idee der Sprache in der Tradition des Humanismus von Dante bis Vico,* vol. VIII of *Archiv für Begriffsgeschichte* (Bonn, 1963). Attention was first drawn to Vico's inaugurals within the framework of his linguistic conception by A. Sorrentino, *La retorica e la poetica di Vico: Ossia la prima concezione estetica del linguaggio* (Turin, 1927). See, however, the beneficially restrictive

In chapter VI of the *De nostri*, Vico epitomizes and sets forth again those ideas on the different "character" of languages which circulated in Europe at least as far back as the late Middle Ages and contraposes, in accordance with usual formulas, the geometrical French to the imaginative Italian tongue. Professor Fubini has found punctual parallelisms between the sentences contained in that chapter and those found in analogous writings of the epoch.[2] However, whereas the literati of the time are debating the primacy of language from viewpoints that are merely poetico-literary and, following the path blazed by Dante's *De vulgari eloquentia*, are striving to determine which language is best suited to artistic composition, Vico focuses his interest on the services that a certain language can render in view of the attainment of rhetorical proficiency, a proficiency which he, as the heir to Italian humanism, conceives of as a mastery of the *scientia civilis*. An as yet tenuous link is thus established between civil life and linguistic patrimony. The first glimmer illuminates, in an original manner, a material destined to become more and more the center of Vico's "continuous meditation" in his mature years.

II

As Professor Antonino Pagliaro remarks, considerations of language and linguistic expression occupy a central place in Vico's thought. This, however, has not always been properly emphasized.[3] According to common opinion, Vico is a thinker who evolved a certain conception of history, and from that conception drew, as a corollary, a certain view of language and of linguistic expression.[4] In reality, truth lies in the opposite viewpoint. What is deemed to be a corollary is, instead, the *major theorem* of that mental "geometry" at which Vico aimed. In other words, considerations of language and linguistic expressions are a primary *datum* in the formation of Vico's conception as a whole.

---

judgment made by A. Pagliaro, "Lingua e poesia secondo Vico," in his *Altri saggi di critica semantica* (Messina-Florence, 1961), pp. 299–444, esp. p. 302.

[2] See the whole essay entitled "Vico e Bouhours," in M. Fubini's volume *Stile e umanità di G. B. Vico* (Bari, 1946), pp. 158–72, esp. pp. 165–69. For the idiomatology *in nuce*, which evolved in Europe during the late Middle Ages, and its importance in the history of linguistic thought, I take the liberty of referring to what I have written in *Storia linguistica dell'Italia unita* (Bari, 1963), pp. 285–87, 320–24, and in *Introduzione alla semantica*, 2d ed. (Bari, 1966), pp. 47ff.

[3] A. Pagliaro, "Lingua e Poesia," pp. 308–10.

[4] Typical in this regard is the exposition of Vico's thought given by M. Leroy, *Les grands courants de la linguistique moderne* (Brussels-Paris, 1963), pp. 12–13 (Italian translation [Bari, 1965], pp. 19–20). Garin, too, in his considerations on Vico, refers only briefly to Vichian linguistics; see Garin, *Storia della filosofia italiana*, pp. 948–49.

Such is clearly the case as far back as the earliest "form" of Vico's "metaphysics." In the Preamble to the *De antiquissima Italorum sapientia* (*On the Most Ancient Italic Wisdom*) a task is outlined which, shortly afterward, appeared debatable to Vico himself: the task of reconstructing ancient Italic wisdom through the etymological and semantic analysis of the Latin vocabulary, in order to detect therein the elements of a true epistemology and ontology. The myth of the primeval, the primordial (what the German language expresses in the particle *ur*), which exerted such powerful influence upon the German and Anglo-Saxon world, from Leibniz to about the middle of the nineteenth century, has, in Vico, an authoritative advocate. Beneath the mythical vesture, however, and from among the slags of unacceptable etymologies, there shines a conviction which, after the lapse of centuries, holds the future as its own. Corsano felicitously spotted that point, assigning to Vico credit for having intuited that philosophical research cannot be separated from linguistic research.[5] It is therefore easy to see why, as early as 1710, linguistic research stands in the center of Vico's concerns.

In the later works, after having rectified the hypothesis of a most ancient Italic wisdom, Vico does not forsake the path of linguistic analysis. He himself gives us information on the role that the latter plays in his thought; and this very fact should give pause to those interpreters who relegate his remarks on language to a marginal place. In the *Scienza nuova prima*, paragraph 261,[6] he writes:

After twenty-five years of continuous meditation, I have found out that the principle stated by me at the outset is the major principle of this Science. It is of such a basic importance to it, as the ABC is to grammar, or the geometrical forms are to geometry. That principle asserts: It is hardly feasible to understand, it is even impossible to grasp with our imagination, what were the modes of thinking, and of expressing his ideas in words, of primitive man as portrayed by Grotius, Hobbes, and Pufendorf (translation by Elio Gianturco).

The same passage in the version of the *Scienza nuova seconda*, paragraph 34, gains in perspicuity:

We find that the principle of these origins both of languages and of letters lies in the fact that the first gentile peoples, by a demonstrated necessity of nature, were poets who spoke in poetic characters. This discovery, which is the master key of this Science, has cost us the persistent research of almost all our literary life, because with our civilized natures we [moderns] cannot at all imagine and can understand only by great toil the poetic nature of these first men. The [poetic] characters of which we speak were certain imaginative genera . . . to which they reduced all the species or

---

[5] A. Corsano, *G. B. Vico* (Bari, 1956), p. 90.
[6] Both the *Scienza nuova prima*, ed. F. Nicolini (Bari, 1931), and the *Scienza nuova seconda*, 4th ed. (Bari, 1953), reprinted also in G. B. Vico, *Opere*, ed. F. Nicolini (Milan-Naples, 1953), pp. 365–905, are quoted according to the paragraph numbering adopted by Nicolini.

all the particulars appertaining to each genus (translation by Max H. Fisch and Thomas G. Bergin).

Finally, in the *Autobiography*, Vico reconfirms this exact valuation of the role played in his thought by the discovery of the prelogical nature of meanings. A "philology" conscious of this, coupled with what he calls (and we all know how arbitrarily) "Platonic philosophy," is the basis of his system.[7] In conformity with this statement the principles of the *Scienza nuova* appear to him to be divided into two sections, one dealing with ideas, the other with languages.[8] In Book II and Book III of the *Scienza nuova prima* the principles are set forth according to this distinction.

In the eyes of Vico himself, then, discussions dealing with language and linguistic expressions are not on the same level with other components of his thought. They are of foremost importance and give rise to one of the *roots* of the *ingens sylva*. Only the "Kantian" insensitivity to philosophical historiography, which prevailed until the twentieth century, can explain how this fact was obscured for so long.[9]

III

Apropos of Vico's linguistic conception, G. Mounin has recently written a sentence which we take pleasure in quoting here. "It [that is, Vico's linguistic conception] represents, probably in a typical way, one of the problems of linguistics most frequently encountered: that of the correct scientific assessment of an intellectual heritage."[10] In fact, in the assessment of this heritage, diametrically opposite opinions are predominant. Let us examine the two most recent treatments of this topic.

G. Mounin, after asserting that the *Scienza nuova* is a theory of the origin of language and that this "greatly limits the credit one may assign to Vico as a linguist," mentions (endorsing an opinion of F. Nicolini's) that Vico's philological scholarship was poor, disordered, and obsolete, and draws the conclusion that Vico's theories, from a general theoretical viewpoint, have little validity. "Nothing forces us to revise the generally current, unformulated judgment that Vico, rather than being a precursor, trails behind, is a belated thinker."[11] However, another linguist of the structuralist

---

[7] Max H. Fisch and Thomas G. Bergin, trans., *The Autobiography of Giambattista Vico* (Ithaca, N.Y., 1944), p. 155.

[8] *Ibid.*, p. 167.

[9] For the development of this suggestion see my *Introduzione alla semantica*, pp. 63–73.

[10] G. Mounin, *Histoire de la linguistique: Dès origines au XX siècle* (Paris, 1967), p. 133.

[11] *Ibid.*, pp. 135ff., 140–41. Nicolini's opinion, mentioned by Mounin, stems from G. B. Vico, *La science nouvelle*, with an introduction by F. Nicolini (Paris, 1953), p. xxxvii;

school, Rosiello, judges Vico in the opposite way: "Vico's historicism anticipates modern linguistic theories."[12]   Even if we turn to less recent studies, the disagreement remains.   On one side are ranged scholars, such as Arens, Hall, Jr., and Raggiunti, who ignore or assess Vico negatively; on the other side are scholars who are bent on reconstructing his thought and who find therein aspects which are still productive: Verburg, Apel, Pagliaro, Leroy.[13]

Vico's case is not isolated.   Think of Leibniz.   To nineteenth-century thinkers it still seemed clear that Leibniz was the fountainhead of the modern tradition of scientific studies.[14]   In our century, both historians of philosophy and historians of linguistics have failed to see Leibniz's historically decisive

---

here Nicolini epitomizes the remarks expounded in his volume *La giovinezza di Giambattista Vico (1668–1700)* (Bari, 1932), pp. 64ff., 132ff.   Discussing the scholarly aspects, Nicolini thinks that, "concerning the basic historical problems of the last *Scienza nuova* (1730–1744), he [Vico] fails to take into account the ever larger contributions made to the single questions by French writers."   Mounin's opinion that "everyone," even though not voicing this idea loudly, judges Vico to "lag behind his times" derives from Nicolini's judgment, coupled perhaps with the stress placed by R. A. Hall, Jr., on the connection between Vico and humanistic thought; see R. A. Hall, Jr., *Idealism in Romance Linguistics* (Ithaca, N.Y., 1963), pp. 21ff.   It is regrettable that Mounin does not know (or at least fails to discuss) the quite different opinions formulated by a philologist such as U. von Wilamowitz-Moellendorf, "Geschichte der Philologie," in *Einleitung in die Altertumswissenschaft*, A. Gercke and E. Norden, eds., 1st ed. (Leipzig, 1921), p. 41, and by linguists such as Pagliaro, "Lingua e poesia."   Naturally, I do not intend to deny the nexus (from the viewpoint of linguistic conception) between Vico and Italian humanism.   A penetrating analysis of that nexus is given by Apel, *Idee der Sprache*, pp. 83, 102–3, 156, 242, 285, 318ff.

[12] L. Rosiello, *Linguistica illuminista* (Bologna, 1967), p. 61.

[13] H. Arens, *Sprachwissenschaft: Der Gang ihrer Entwicklung von der Antike bis zur Gegenwart* (Munich, 1955), totally ignores Vico's name.   This gap, already pointed out by Pagliaro, "Lingua e poesia," p. 301, no. 2, and subsequently by the present author in *Introduzione alla semantica*, p. 53, certainly is not such as to impair the value of a book otherwise quite notable; but for a contrary opinion see T. Bolelli's *Per una storia della ricerca linguistica* (Naples, 1965), p. 19.   It should be noted that in Bolelli's "historical" volume, although Vico is duly mentioned, there is no account whatever of the linguistic theories of Condillac, Turgot, Leibniz, Boas, or Noreen, and no reference is ever made to Locke, Berkeley, Hume, Hamann, Wittgenstein, Madvig, or Kruszewski.   Violent critical barbs are shot at Vico by Hall, Jr., in *Idealism in Romance Linguistics*; more moderate, but essentially hostile, is the criticism of R. Raggiunti, *La conoscenza e il problema della lingua* (1956), pp. 45–54.   Different is the attitude expressed by P. Verburg in *Taal en Functionaliteit: Een historisch-critische Studie over de opvattingen Aangande de Functies de Taal* (Wageningen, 1952), pp. 335–36 and *passim*; see also Pagliaro; *idem*, *Il segno vivente: Saggi sulla lingua e altri simboli* (Naples, 1952), pp. 47–52; Apel, *Idee der Sprache*, *passim*, esp. pp. 318–80; Leroy, *Linguistique moderne*.

[14] To what was said in my *Introduzione alla semantica*, pp. 62–63, should be added W. Thomsen's discussion in *Sprogvidenskapens historie* (Copenhagen, 1902), chap. VI (Spanish translation [Barcelona, 1945], pp. 55ff.).

commitment to general theory and to the investigation and historical collection of linguistic data.[15] Scholars other than the historians of philosophy
and those of glottology mention Leibniz as a linguist, but only in order to
evaluate or criticize single aspects of his contributions, as if the German
philosopher had had merely the distinction of understanding that Hebrew
could not have been the mother tongue of mankind and could have been
guilty only of a failure to guess correctly this or that particular etymology.[16]
In the final analysis, very few scholars render full justice to Leibniz's linguistics by devoting their efforts to thinking it through with the care it
deserves because of the superior excellence of its concepts, the importance
it has within the framework of Leibnizian thought, or the decisive impact it
exerted, in the eighteenth century, on the rise of historical and comparative
linguistics.[17] Just as the scanty attention paid by cultural and intellectual
historians to linguistic conceptions was based (as I have tried to show) on the
acceptance of a philosophical problematics of the Kantian type, so the disparity of judgments, which is still predominant among the historians of
linguistics, derives from a substantial dissimilitude of basic criteria—that is,
from different conceptions of linguistics. If it is held that the proper
function of linguistics consists exclusively in producing scientifically correct
etymologies, that is, etymologies conformable to the "laws" which summarize the diachrony of phonematic systems, Vico and Leibniz will not
arouse any deep interest in the historian of linguistics. When they engaged
in etymological research the results were absurd;[18] thus, in that respect, they
deserve a negative verdict or a compassionate silence.

[15] Here too, for brevity's sake, I shall refer to my *Introduzione alla semantica*, pp. 62–63;
for a history of linguistic research which ignores Leibniz, see *ibid.*, n. 9.

[16] See Leroy, *Linguistique moderne*, pp. 11–12, and, also by Leroy, "Les curiosités
linguistiques de Leibniz," *Revue internationale de philosophie*, no. 76–77 (1966): 193–203.

[17] Verburg, *Taal en Functionaliteit*, pp. 265–97 and *passim*; Arens, *Sprachwissenschaft*,
passim; J. T. Waterman, *Perspectives in Linguistics* (Chicago-London, 1953), pp. 13–15;
Rosiello, *Linguistica illuminista*, pp. 44–50. In my *Introduzione alla semantica* I have tried
to show the centrality of the position of Leibniz in the history of ideas and of linguistic
research.

[18] In Leibniz, for instance, we can still read that "the ancient Germans, the Celts, and
other nations akin to them, made use of the letter *R* in order to designate an impetuous
movement and a sound similar to that produced by that letter." On the basis of this
idea, whose archetype is doubtless to be found in Plato's *Kratilos* (426d), a work to which
Vico himself reverts (Preamble, *De antiquissima*, ed. G. Gentile and F. Nicolini, I [Bari,
1914], 126), Leibniz thinks that ῥέω, *rinnen*, *rühren*, *rauben*, *rauchen*, and *regula*, are
related; see *Nouveaux essais*, III, II, Gerhardt's ed., 5 : 261ff. (Students of "impressive"
phonetics may be interested to know that the same queer idea about "vibrant articulation" cropped up in the mind of Saussure, too; it is set forth in a youthful work of his,
Corso di linguistica generale, Introduction and Commentary by T. de Mauro [Bari, 1967],
p. 289.) Strained interpretations and untenable etymologies are scattered throughout
Vico's work. In the *De antiquissima* he maintains, for instance, the synonymy of *verum*
and *factum*, of *aequum* and *verum*, etc., a synonymy which he vainly champions in a

It is debatable, however, whether the only or most important task of linguistics is to formulate etymological assumptions. If we are to judge from the current output, we must say that the task of linguistics does not consist in that. The strong emphasis placed on synchronic research by Leonard Bloomfield in American linguistic scholarship, or, more generally, in modern scholarship, is one of the deep-lying reasons for that fact. The other reason may be seen in Ferdinand de Saussure's attitude as manifested in the most widely circulated book of linguistics in modern times. Although he is the discoverer of many fine and well-worked-out etymologies, Saussure under-scores in his *Course of General Linguistics* the scanty importance of etymo-logical research within the total framework of linguistics. As for this framework itself, Saussure determines it by pointing out three basic tasks that transcend the narrow realm of etymology. Such tasks, for him, are: "(1) endeavoring to give the description and history of all the languages that can be got hold of; (2) discovering the forces that, permanently and uni-versally, play a role in all languages; (3) delimiting and defining its own fundamental being [that is, answering the question: 'What is linguistics?'].""19

As may be seen, etymology, according to Saussure, is only a partial aspect of a section of task (1) (the history of words). It is a partial aspect, not the principal task, and much less is it the *whole* of linguistics. Vico, who by consensus is an extremely poor etymologist, made his contributions in other fields. (Professor Pagliaro, however, advances some reservations, and observes that in the chaos of Vichian etymologies some "priceless gems" can be detected.) These contributions are, as we shall see, in the second of the research directives indicated by Ferdinand de Saussure.

IV

Like Aristotle,[20] but unlike a considerable number of thinkers belonging

---

Risposta to a reviewer (see this reply in Nicolini's *Opere*, pp. 310–11). In the *De uno uni-versi iuris principio et fine uno, auctoritas* is made to derive from αὐτός (bk. I, chap. LXXXIX conditio from *cum* and *ire* (bk. I, chap. C), ἥρως from *haereo* (bk. I, chap. CIV); *fides* (faith) is confused with *fides* (string of a musical instrument) (bk. I, chaps. C, CLXXXIII). Frequently, specimens of etymologies of this type are to be found throughout the *Scienza nuova seconda*, where Vico assumes the existence of etymological affinities between *jus* and Jupiter (par. 15), ὄψις and ὠφέλεια (par. 541), μέλι and μῆλον (par. 545), etc.

19 On Saussure's attitude toward etymology see: *Cours de linguistique générale*, 2d ed. (Paris, 1922), pp. 259–60 (Italian trans., pp. 229–30 and n. 290); as for the tasks of linguistics see p. 20 of the French text, p. 15 of the Italian translation, and nn. 40–43 of the commentary.

20 See: L. Scaravelli, *Critica del capire* (Florence, 1942), pp. 5ff.; Pagliaro, "Lingua e poesia," pp. 313ff.; De Mauro, *Introduzione alla semantica*, pp. 41ff.

to the Aristotelian tradition, Vico is aware of the basic importance that must be attached to the study of linguistic phenomena in the construction of the science of linguistics. Having committed himself from the outset to the investigation of linguistic phenomena, he encounters a conception which had been dominant for centuries—rationalistic and logicalizing conventionalism (of remote Aristotelian ancestry).

The conventionalistic conception of language has a long and complex history, out of which there emerge certain essential and constant features. Such features are present in Aristotle's *De interpretatione*, in Descartes, in the *Grammaire raisonnée de Port Royal*, as well as in more recent works, such as the theoretical writings of Whitney or the *Tractatus* of Wittgenstein.[21]   We can sum up those features in the following statements:

1. The world is organized into distinct situations made up of distinct objects, and such distinctions are prior to any human intervention.

2. Distinct objects are reflected in the mind of man and there make up ideas, concepts, representations, and categories which are identical for all.

3. The vocabulary of languages is an ensemble of phonic labels denoting mental entities to which they bear a relationship of biunivocal correspondence.

4. The vocabulary of one language differs from that of another only insofar as the phonic "rind" of the language is concerned; the semantic core, the series of meanings, is a universal, interlinguistic datum.

5. The phonic form of words varies from language to language in words of identical meaning; it is therefore a datum dependent upon the arbitrariness of collective convention. The phonic form is a *placitum*; it exists *ex instituto*.

6. First we have an idea, then we create a name for it (Whitney).

A complete criticism of this viewpoint, which still circulates widely in common circles and even among linguists, has been made only in our century, particularly by Saussure and by Wittgenstein (in his last writings).[22] But such criticism had already begun in the seventeenth and eighteenth centuries, with Locke, Leibniz, Hume, and G. B. Vico.[23]

[21] For the texts quoted here, and for their place in the history of linguistic thought, see, besides Verburg's *Taal en Functionaliteit* and my *Introduzione alla semantica*, E. Coseriu, "L'arbitraire du signe: Zur Spätgeschichte eines aristotelischen Begriffes," *Archiv für das Studium der neueren Sprachen und Literaturen*, 119 (1967): 81–112; as for Wittgenstein in particular, reference is made to my essay *Ludwig Wittgenstein: His Place in the Development of Semantics* (Dordrecht, 1967). In regard to Whitney's conventionalism and to the objections brought up against it by Saussure in his unpublished notes, see my commentary to his *Cours de linguistique générale*, Italian translation, pp. 352–53 and n. 137.

[22] De Mauro, *Introduzione alla semantica*, pp. 122ff., 175ff.

[23] On the relationships of partial analogy and divergence between the linguistic conceptions of Vico, Locke, Leibniz, and Hume see Apel, *Idee der Sprache*, pp. 102–3, 239, 297, 318ff.; De Mauro, *Introduzione alla semantica*, pp. 51–58; Rosiello, *Linguistica illuminista*, pp. 33ff.

According to Vico, conventionalism must be objected to because, as he puts it sarcastically, it compels us to assume that "the nations which invented their own languages must previously have gone to school to Aristotle" (*Scienza nuova seconda*, paragraph 455). This is not a flash of humor which would acquire a modern flavor only if it were arbitrarily wrenched out of context; [24] it is a remark which reappears, more amply developed, in another passage. If we compare the two passages, we become cognizant, beyond all doubt, of the fact that Vico has meant to epitomize in them, in a pungent form, the substance of his opposition to rationalism. The "philologians" are too easily convinced that the meanings of the words (of all languages) have been determined by stipulation (*ad placitum*) (*Scienza nuova seconda*, paragraph 444). Philological scholars are wrong in attributing to the "nations, which invented language," and to the "popular masses, which hold the lordship over common speech" (*Scienza nuova seconda*, paragraph

[24] This seems to be the opinion of Mounin (see *Histoire*, p. 138), who, although he contextualizes the quotation from Vico, thinks that it is anchored to the immediately preceding paragraphs (448–54) devoted to delineating, in a manner that today seems unacceptable (just as the Port Royalist definitions seem unacceptable to us), the genesis of the parts of discourse (*partes orationum*). The Vichian passage reads: "All these things seem more reasonable than those made by Julius Caesar Scaliger and Francisco Sanchez concerning the Latin language. Scaliger's and Sanchez's opinions are predicated upon the absurd assumption that the primeval nations went to school to Aristotle, whose principles stand at the basis of the reasoning of those two scholars" (translated by Elio Gianturco). Nevertheless, the collocation of the sentence, which constitutes the conclusion of all the "Corollaries concerning the Origins of Languages and Letters" (pars. 428–55), the addition of the word "all" to "these things," and, finally, the reference to Aristotle's principles, lead us to think that the passage we have quoted intends to take up anew and to conclude sarcastically the total ensemble of paragraphs devoted to outlining, in opposition to Aristotelian conventionalism, the "historicistic" conception of language. That this was Vico's intention is proved by the fact that the concept expounded here recurs, with explicit statements that clear away all doubt, in another Vichian writing as well. In 1740, in reference to a *Grammatica* by Antonio d'Aronne, Vico declared:

Since, in conformity with natural order, veracious speaking should precede "properly arranged" speaking, Giulio Cesare della Scala (followed by all the best grammarians of later times) endeavored, with a generous effort, to discourse on the causes of the Latin language by basing his arguments on the rules of logic. The result, however, was a failure because, instead of availing himself of the principles of logic, he chose to follow all too slavishly those of a particular philosopher, that is, Aristotle. Now, the principles of the Aristotelian logic being too general, it is impossible to explain through them the almost countless details that harass the scholar's research. Hence, Francisco Sanchez, one of Scaliger's courageous disciples, who in his *Minerva* follows in the master's footsteps, vainly endeavors by means of his famous ellipsis to account for the innumerable particularities of the Latin language. Striving to "save" the universal principles of Aristotelian logic, poor Sanchez becomes strained and tedious by presenting us with an immense abundance of Latin idioms, with which he claims to remedy the elegant, expressive shortcomings that the Latin language manifests in the process of expression (Nicolini's *Opere*, pp. 944–45).

There is therefore no doubt that Vico intended to summarize his point of view as a conclusion to the entire set of his corollaries.

32), a rational knowledge and a capacity to stipulate, with which it is impossible to endow them.   At the time when languages originated, there was no scientific knowledge available, and no human being was in a position to discriminate rationally between the various classes of objects and the categories of reality.   The earliest men, "like children of mankind," were incapable of framing abstract, general concepts of things (*Scienza nuova seconda*, paragraph 209).[25]

Hence, Vico asks himself, of what were the men of that primitive age capable?   And, in a more general way, what was the mental range of the men of that time whom we consider to have been "lords," or "creators," of

[25] Mounin (*Histoire*, p. 135) criticizes Vico for setting forth his ideas (to be more precise: setting forth only a part of his ideas) under the guise of "*une théorie de l'origine du langage.*"   According to the keen-minded French scholar, "ceci limite déjà beaucoup le mérite que l'on pourra trouver à Vico linguiste."   In reality, the glottogonic way in which a large part of the Vichian conception is posited simply indicates that Vico writes, not in 1968, but in the first part of the eighteenth century.   In a different phrasing, the *glottogonic* presentation was suggested to Vico by the whole cultural setting within which he moved and, in particular, by the opponents against whom he was battling.   As Professor Pagliaro has shown ("Lingua e poesia," p. 317), while Aristotle's conventionalism was of the "synchronic" type—since it originated from a phenomenological assertion of the fact that the name is not by nature intrinsic to the object—in the transition from Aristotle to his Aristotelian interpreters there took place a "slipping," a sliding, from the phenomenological to the glottogonic plane.   This is especially noticeable in Boethius, "in whom we can observe a shift from the functional and logical consideration to the genetic one.   The shift takes place by imperceptible degrees.   If the 'significant' *in actu* is naturally arbitrary—and it is but a phonic symbol—this leads us to think that the person who has 'set' the name has merely followed the prompting of a personal criterion. Thus the question is shifted to the genetic plane."   Hence, the mere fact of having to defend a polemical position drives Vico toward a genetic viewpoint.   But there is something else.   In fighting against the conventionalistic-rationalistic idea of the logical, intellectualistic nature of lexical meanings, Vico was aware that his arguments would have a more cogently persuasive force if he emphasized that even the development of prose languages originated in remote historical stages when no Aristotle was present, that therefore there could not have existed any possibility of apprehending reality and its categories in a lucid rational way, and that consequently there was no likelihood of transposing such a rational mode of apprehension into a system of symbols.   The reader should finally take into account the fact that the attraction Vico felt toward the period of origins (which Mounin so roundly condemns) has lasted much longer than Vico's times.   Strangely enough this is egregiously shown by Mounin himself.   In the very book where Vico is "flunked" for his glottogonic propensities, Mounin relates that even "un savant aussi positif, aussi moderne que Whitney, en 1876, résiste encore très mal à cette tentation" to go back to "l'étape initiale du langage" (*Histoire*, p. 22).   Furthermore, "même Tovar, en 1954, ne semble pas entièrement dépris de ces mirages lorsqu'il conclut ainsi, de manière au moins ambigue, son article: "En résumé, dans la mesure où la linguistique nous permet de sonder les profondeurs de l'esprit humain, elle nous permet aussi de remonter le cours de la préhistoire jusqu'à ce que nous atteignons les origines de l'homme lui-même. ...' "   If the glottogonic mirage still persists in our day, it is quite understandable that it may have held a dominant fascination even for an original mind like Vico's.

language? He answers: "The nature of children is such that by the ideas and names of the men, women, and things they have known first, they afterward apprehend and name all the men, women, and things that bear any resemblance or relation to the first" (*Scienza nuova seconda*, paragraph 206, Bergin and Fisch's translation).

As we shall see, the same tendency is to be found among the primitives; but, in children as well as in primitives, it is a question not so much of a particular and exclusive character as of a more or less emphasized general propensity of human nature: "Whatever appertains to men but is doubtful or obscure, they naturally interpret according to their own natures and the passions and customs springing from them" (*Scienza nuova seconda*, paragraph 220, Bergin and Fisch's translation).

Metaphorical expressions, traditionally viewed as an extrinsic ornament, as rhetorical luxury, actually did originate, and do now originate, from the exigency of adhering, with limited lexical resources, to the complexity of reality. They spring from "poverty of language and necessity of self-expression" (*Scienza nuova seconda*, paragraph 456), in accordance with a process which Vico reconstructed in its conceptually essential aspects as far back as the *Scienza nuova prima*, where we read (paragraphs 261-62):

We have thus discovered that the "poetic characters" constitute the primary elements of the languages that were spoken by the pagan nations in primitive times. We must start with the assumption of a nation extremely limited from the intellectual viewpoint and incapable of inventing words designating an abstract or generalized notion. Such a nation would be apt, for instance, to call a man by a name indicating the quality, in that man, which was perceived first. Let us take, for instance, the type of (character of) a man who has performed an important labor imposed on him by the needs of his family or clan: let us assume that he gains renown on account of that labor, for having, through such a deed, preserved his family or his clan (and consequently, a part of mankind). Let us suppose that a certain nation, let us say the Greek nation, calls him Hercules (that is, "Ηρας κλέος, meaning Juno's glory, Juno being the goddess presiding over nuptial rites, therefore over the welfare of families). Without doubt, such a nation, in subsequent times, will call by the name Hercules all the various men who, in different epochs, perform labors similar in kind to those performed by the hero on whom the name Hercules was originally bestowed. And, since we assume that such a nation was primitive and coarse, we should also assume the mind of such a nation to be so blunt-edged, so dull, as to be unable to perceive any but the most sensational events. As a consequence, all the most famous deeds achieved by different men at various times, that is, deeds belonging to the same category, namely, such as grand labors performed in order to fulfill the pressing needs of a family or a clan, will be connected with the name of the man who first received that name deriving from the deed he performed. All those who fulfill grand labors on behalf of their family or clan will therefore receive the appellative of Hercules. We must therefore say that, in this respect, all the pagan nations of primitive times were made up of poets, were endowed with poetical imagination. The vernacular languages still preserve evident vestiges of this imaginativeness of the primeval nations. . . . (translated by Elio Gianturco).

Vico continues, quoting examples of antonomasia common in Latin, and concludes that this rhetorical figure (and, for that matter, all others of a similar kind): "were thought . . . to have been created by the caprice of particular poets; [but] . . . arose from the natural necessity of thinking and explaining things thus, an expedient common to all of the pagan nations" (paragraph 263).

In a nutshell, this long excerpt from The *Scienza nuova prima* contains all the essential elements of anticonventionalist criticism and of Vico's original semantic-linguistic conception. Let us now rapidly point out the most conspicuous elements:

1. During the remote stages when languages orginated, men were not in a position to evolve abstract ideas, generalized concepts; they were capable of only some general "constructs" of the imagination (*Scienza nuova seconda*, paragraph 34).

2. During the remote stages when the corpus of vernacular languages was formed, and during the mythico-heroic phase into which Vico projected his considerations (see note 26 below), men were incapable of arriving at general ideas, at class concepts, concerning things (*Scienza nuova seconda*, paragraph 209).

3. They could strive to express themselves only through "imaginative universals" (*generi fantastici*) that were bound up with their "extremely weak ratiocinative powers" and with the "poverty of linguistic resources and the necessity of self-expression" (*Scienza nuova seconda*, paragraphs 34, 209, 456ff.).

4. Universal realities, which appear identical to the rational mind, take on different aspects on the linguistic level. The "mental dictionary," that is, a roster of universal categories, which Vico envisaged, finds realization, in the realm of languages, through "heroic characters" (*De constantia jurisprudentis, pars posterior*, chapter XIII, section III, Nicolini's edition), that is, through words whose meaning is "an imaginative universal" springing from a "contraction of imaginative universals." [26]

[26] The "contraction" to which Vico refers is—unlike that postulated in imaginative fashion by Plato in his *Kratilos*—a procedure which concerns, not the "significants," but the signified. This is quite clear, for instance, in a passage (*De constantia jurisprudentis, pars posterior*, chap. I, n.) where Vico, illustrating the relationship between poetical locution (which, in his opinion, is "uniquely appropriate") and prose locution (less appropriate, because more abstract), makes the following statement:

Intrinsically appropriate is that locution which cannot be used to designate with equal appropriateness a thing different from that of the specific feature of which it indicates. For example, the Latin expression "the boiling of the blood around the heart" cannot denote any other passion but angriness . . . and the reason is that the poetical locution is made up of features uniquely and intrinsically peculiar to the thing designated, so that it describes the most characteristic and

5. If it is true that natural or mental needs common to all men preside over the production of "imaginative universals" (*generi fantastici*), it is also true that these universals realize themselves in manners and ways that are different according to the various human communities. Events occasionally rational, bound up with the accidentality of customs and of particular historical vicissitudes, are the kernel around which the "extremely weak ratiocinative powers" condense the first general experiences, the first "elements of knowledge." These elements assume a different configuration in the various languages (*Scienza nuova seconda*, paragraph 445). After Locke and Leibniz, with an equally penetrating genius, Vico clearly perceives that the vocabularies of the various languages are not nomenclatures of concepts universally identical. Vocabularies, as well as the entire grammatico-syntactical corpus of languages, are made up of "almost infinite particulars" that are not capable of being reduced to the universal logic of a "specific philosopher," that is, to the logic of Aristotle. (See Vico's *Opere*, Nicolini edition, pages 944–45.)

6. In the origins of languages, therefore, we find not a convention, a collectively agreed upon stipulation, but a natural need to grasp, an exigency of explaining, the phenomena of experience within a prerational mental framework which is defective, coarse, and weak-minded (*De constantia jurisprudentis*, pars posterior, chapter XIII, section XXVI).

From this criticism there springs forth an original conception of language. For Vico, "language is not an artificial medium which men have deliberately constructed to give expression to pre-existent ideas, but has evolved naturally, the course of its development being inseparable from that of the human mind itself."[27]

This profoundly new conception of language is, as everyone knows full well, awkwardly wrapped up in Vico's mythical conception of the perpetual succession of the three stages (divine, heroic, human). According to Vico, the historical developments of languages are inescapably governed by this diachronic tripartition (*Scienza nuova*, paragraph 32). Mounin is right when he protests against those who consider this baroque tripartition alone (or almost alone) to be the most glorious achievement of Vico's linguistics. But a similar error is committed by those scholars who, having emphasized the mythical character of Vico's periodology, strive to throw away the whole of the *Scienza nuova*.[28]

---

ultimately constituent qualities of that object. Prose locution, instead, subjects the specific features of any object to a process of abstraction, the result of which is a single term: for example, from the words "boiling," "blood," and "heart," prose locution makes the single verb "to get angry."

[27] P. Gardiner, "G. B. Vico," in *The Encyclopaedia of Philosophy* (New York–London, 1967).

[28] Mounin, *Histoire*, pp. 135–36: "Il (Vico) est célèbre pour la théorie des trois étapes linguistiques." As we hinted, if Mounin had taken a look at the recent contributions by

The twofold error by now is obvious; but, unfortunately, the persistent dearth of scholarly inquirers into the history of linguistics makes it necessary to re-emphasize what, in other cultural sectors, is an obvious recommendation. The interpreter's duty is that of discriminating between mythological or non-documented elements and elements better substantiated and proved. The interpreter, furthermore, should understand the connection (if there is one) between the elements of one nature and those of a different nature; that is, he should delineate the structure of an intellectual system. The interpreter's task should by no means be that of "liquidating" a conception rich in stimulative suggestions (not yet fully grasped by most members of the venerable confraternity of specialists) merely on the ground that such a conception is impaired by still-persistent elements of a fantastic, mythological nature.

If we read Vico, not with the purpose of finding reasons for condemnation, but with the aim of grasping his thought, we notice that he was perfectly aware of the weakness of the temporal tripartition (*Scienza nuova seconda*, paragraph 629), and with particular clarity insofar as the domain of language is concerned. Vico decidedly and explicitly warns that the three languages corresponding to the three ages, that is, "silent" language, "poetical" language, and language by words conventionally agreed upon by a collectivity, "began at the same time"; thus it can be stated, on the one hand, that, even in the remotest stages, the "*placitum*," that is, the rational and conventional reorganization of the materials of expression, must have been in operation (*Scienza nuova seconda*, paragraph 446); on the other hand, even in culturally more advanced stages, "poetical logic" has been and is at work (*Scienza nuova seconda*, paragraph 412): "The poetic speech which our poetic logic has helped us to understand continued for a long time into the historical period, much as great and rapid rivers continue far into the sea, keeping sweet the waters borne on by the force of their flow" (translated by Bergin and Fisch).

In concluding this section it is profitable to dwell for a moment on two aspects of the Vichian conception of language. When Vico underscores the presence of a poetical component in language, he intends to refer, beyond any doubt, to the total aggregate of rhetorical figures, such as "tropes," "metaphors," and "poetical expressions," with which every language is saturated, and of which, in his opinion, poetry is made up (*Scienza nuova seconda*, paragraphs 404ff. and 456ff.). His position is far different from Croce's, and Croce himself was aware of this.

Verburg, Pagliaro, Apel, and others, he would have discovered that Vico is by now "famous" also for other less transient and less easily criticizable reasons. Coming from a scholar like Mounin, who is the author of a book so *naturaliter vichianus* as *Les problèmes théoriques de la traduction* (Paris, 1963), that criticism is somewhat puzzling.

Croce, through his criticism and his attempted rejection of the cognitive and actual validity of any general entity, mediating between unrepeatable individuality and the ubiquitous universal, was led to deny (among other things) the cognitive and actual validity of the division (which we have adopted) of linguistic signs into phonemes and syllables, vocables and parts of speech.   In the final analysis, speaking appeared to him as a kind of free song, and language was dissolved into the indistinct splendor of poetry.[29]   Vico, however, is firmly persuaded of the complex nature of linguistic signs, and he merely points out, in signs and in their elements, the character which they frequently possess, that of being "poetical locutions."   The latter are, in his view, the essence of poetry.   To condense this into a quick formula, we may phrase our thought as follows: whereas Croce tries to dissolve language into poetry, Vico, on the contrary, dissolves poetry into language, that is, into a particular way of utilizing language.[30]   It should also be emphasized that "poetical locution," which in Vico's opinion is generally present in "prose languages," is not a luxury of the sophisticated literatus, but corresponds to the natural needs of understanding, of expressing one's ideas, of communicating.

More generally, in Vico's philosophical and historical view, the whole of speech (and of languages, which are the instruments of it) interweaves with other activities and institutions of human communities.   In particular, Vico underscores the relationship of reciprocal exchange which exists between the religious, juridical, and linguistic traditions of a nation (*De constantia jurisprudentis, pars posterior*, chapters XII, XIII, XXIV; *Scienza nuova seconda*, paragraphs 32, 443, 936).   The whole nature of man in its temporal unfolding along the course of history is connected with speech and languages, as with its tools and, simultaneously, its conditions.   "*Humanitas potissimum linguis conciliata*" (Mankind is, most of all, linked together by linguistic bonds) (*De constantia jurisprudentis, pars posterior*, chapter II, section 1).

V

From this conception of languages as historical formations in which the whole experience of human communities and of single individuals (insofar as they share in history) is reflected and molded, Vico draws two noteworthy conclusions.   We have already pointed out the first, that is, the recognition

---

[29] For this interpretation of Croce's linguistics I refer to the discussion of the various exegetical theses developed in my *Introduzione alla semantica*, pp. 90–111.

[30] In regard to all this, and specifically in regard to Vico's alleged "Croceanism," see once again Pagliaro's basic essay: "Lingua e poesia," esp. pp. 300–1. Pagliaro previously dealt with the same topic in *Il segno vivente* (Naples, 1952), pp. 47ff.

of the central importance of both the philosophical and the historico-philological considerations of linguistic phenomena (the significance of the latter consideration being even greater than that of the former). Recognition of such centrality (see section II of this essay) is not a whim, a gratuitous mental quirk. It is, instead, the rigorous consequence of a discovery which places self-expression at the roots of the complex historicity of man. Through such discovery, philology is placed on a par with philosophy, as the other foundation-layer of the *Scienza nuova*; and a linguistic reflection of this may be seen in the fact that the very words "philologian" and "philology," in the Vichian *usus scribendi*, are stabilized in that meaning which, in Europe, becomes common only with, and after, Fr. A. Wolf.

The second conclusion belongs to the set of problems which had most interested the young Vico: the problems of the *ratio studiorum*. Linguistic pedagogy had been viewed by Vico, when he was not yet forty, as the mere acquisition of a skill through which the individual could best enter civil life and effectively engage in debate or, rather, cogently induce persuasion in regard to ethical matters (see above, section I). The expression of one's thought was still considered exclusively as an extrinsic effort to clothe, more or less effectively, a certain conceptual and human substance which would be unaffected by that garb.

The linguistic conception that Vico elaborates in the years of his maturity radically changes the terms of the problem. Languages by now appear to him as vehicles of a complex and differentiated historicity which is not reflected but *actualized* therein. "Languages," writes Vico to Solla, "are, so to speak, the vehicle by which the spirit of a nation is transfused into the soul of the person who learns them." Because languages are such complex and rich organisms, learning and mastering them are decisive events in the life of the individual. Language does not transmit experience; it conditions it. Vico is fully aware that such conditioning may not, at times, have a *positive* result. He quotes, for instance, prose languages, whose vocabularies are generally characterized by the presence of words having abstract meanings: since "those who speak in generalized statements never speak of any subject with cogent, expressive appropriateness," such languages may exert a *negative* influence. "Hence it happens at times that vernacular languages constitute great obstacles standing in the way of philosophers who wish to distinguish the true essences of things" (*De constantia jurisprudentis, pars posterior*, chapter I).

However, Vico views the conditioning exerted by languages upon the mind of man, which is molded by them, as an undeniable fact, and, all told, a positive one, "since languages render the human mind ingenious, whenever, in order to express any object pertaining to physical nature, to morality, to household matters, to civil matters (which are almost without number), the mind is compelled, by its power of memory, to run over the notably extensive vocabulary of life, and to discover the most appropriate word which designates that object" (*De constantia jurisprudentis, pars posterior,* chapter XII, section 11).

Language learning, then, is conceived by Vico no longer in rhetorical terms, but instead, and exclusively, as a basic aspect of the education of the mind, by which the individual becomes a partaker of a historically definite patrimony of culture. Thus, in the *Scienza nuova prima*, he writes (paragraph 42): "Seven-year-old children are found to have already learned an extensive vocabulary. When an idea is awakened in their minds, they quickly run over the totality of that lexical storehouse in order to find the agreed upon word and to convey it to others. Every word they hear awakens the idea connected with it. . . . As a consequence, every language is like a great school where human intellects are trained to become more dexterous and quicker in expressing themselves" (translation by Elio Gianturco).

Vico does not insist on developing in detail the (decidedly antirhetorical) pedagogical consequences of his linguistic historism.[31] On this, more than on any other aspect of his thought in the *Scienza nuova*, "few things are said, but much is left for the reader to think."

Translated by Elio Gianturco

---

[31] The evident pedagogical scope of Vico's thought is keenly perceived by M. T. Gentile, *Educazione linguistica e crisi della libertà* (Rome, 1966), pp. 57, 348, 365, 366; in connection with the problem of the humanistic *ratio studiorum* and of the Ciceronian *scientia civilis*, see Apel, *Idee der Sprache*.

Werner Stark   GIAMBATTISTA VICO'S
                      SOCIOLOGY
                      OF KNOWLEDGE

The historical development of social theory has followed a curious zigzag pattern. It has taken place within two clearly defined extreme positions and sometimes has approached one of these outer limits, sometimes the other. There were periods when the unity of society was stressed at the expense of the multiplicity and diversity of its members, and it was then that the great simile of the "body social" made its appearance and passed for an ontological truth; there were other periods when the multiplicity and diversity of individuals were stressed at the expense of the unity of society, and then there was talk of human atoms or human monads, and of a tension and balance between them as constituting the social bond. In Vico's childhood, the latter opinion was in vogue. Cartesian rationalism tended toward atomism, mechanism, and contractualism; society was a nominal, rather than a real, entity. Both Spinoza and Berkeley formulated sociologies in this style. The reaction was to come after the French Revolution, in the Romantic age, which opposed the rationalistic conception of social life with consistency and passion. To Comte it was the individual, not society, who was an abstraction. Only society was real; the individual was merely a cell in an organism and would lose his meaning, and even his life, if he were taken out of the vital frame that had given him existence and sustained him to his dying day.[1]

As soon as Vico had freed himself from his early Cartesianism, he began to share the incipient "pre-Romantic" tendency toward more collectivist, organicist forms of sociological thinking. One fruit of this new tendency was "the discovery of the true Homer." The Rationalists, in their anxiety to exclude all mystery, even relative mystery, from their world, had tried to find for every social phenomenon one assignable cause, and, if possible, one assignable will, that would explain it. Thus the University of Cambridge, which was, in fact, the product of slow evolutions and accretions, was fathered by a certain "Prince Cantaber." In this case, the fictitiousness of the character was obvious. But it was not so obvious in the case of the supposed author of the *Iliad* and the *Odyssey*. Did a poem not presuppose a poet? Vico saw the shallowness of this individualism. He recognized that even the so-called Homeric epics were the results of collective, rather than

[1] W. Stark, *The Fundamental Forms of Social Thought* (London, 1962).

of highly personalized, forces, of many bards rather than of one bard; they were precipitations of a whole nation's romancing. Research since his time has borne him out. The discovery of the true Homer was in this way a discovery of the *real* existence of social wholes; they were real, as real as any concrete man, because, like him, they could *create*. With this insight Vico took a tremendous step in the direction of sociological "realism," in the philosophical meaning of the term.[2] But—and this shows his incomparable originality, indeed, the uniqueness of his mind—he did not end up by presenting a new version of the old and about-to-be-revived doctrine of the "body social." He could have taken such a doctrine almost intact from his master Plato, but he preferred to fashion his own social theory from other, and deeper, elements in the Platonic system. This was a feat of the first magnitude. It was, in fact, the beginning of a third sociology which since his time has taken its place alongside organicism and mechanicism and now bids fair to overcome them both.

The radically new conception which Vico thrust into the discussion was the idea that the social order—the whole sociality of man—was not an artifact as Descartes and his disciples believed, nor yet a natural datum as Comte and his followers were to assume, but rather a potentiality which can be developed, and which has to be developed if it is to become a reality. When God created man, he envisioned him as a social creature, that is to say, as reasonable and benign; yet he also envisioned him as a creature endowed with freedom. Because of this freedom, he could not be given sociality straight away, like the ant or the bee. Sociality had to be held out to him as a developmental goal, an ideal which the real could and would approximate if man in his freedom would only try to become himself, that is, if he would try truly to humanize himself. In Platonic language, the end was before the beginning; expressed differently, man was meant to become Man; the crude savage was destined to become the cultured personality. To Vico, human development was essentially a realization of this scheme. The ideal eternal history of which he so often spoke, the *corsi* and the *ricorsi* that it entails, is the implementation of the Demiurge's idea of man through man himself.

But Vico drew from Plato more than the rudiments of a general sociology. He also derived from him the bases of a more restricted subscience, the discipline that in the present century has come to be called the "sociology of knowledge." In the context of his struggle against the Sophists, Plato developed the conviction that it was vain to expect all men to be receptive to all truths: for instance, only those can know the gods who are, to some extent, godlike themselves. Every class has, in principle, a mentality appropriate to itself. The Neo-Platonism of Husserl summed this up as the correspondence of *noesis* and *noema*. Many were the thinkers between Plato and Husserl

[2] See esp. *Scienza nuova*, pars. 873, 875, 877, 878.

who upheld the same conception.   Perhaps it was most clearly formulated
by Goethe in one of his *Zahme Xenien*:

> Were not the eye a-kindred to the sun,
> It never could perceive the sky-sun's image.

One of the classical writings in which this basic intuition is most fully and
most lucidly explored and expounded is Vico's *Scienza nuova*.   Indeed, it is
doubtful whether there was a more conscious and accomplished sociologist
of knowledge in the field before the middle twenties of our century, when
Max Scheler, Husserl's comrade-in-thought, gave the subject its first
systematic presentation.[3]
    Before turning to the substance of Vico's analysis, a preliminary remark is
necessary because it will help us to appreciate the greatness and the modernity
of the Neapolitan's contribution.   It is presently recognized that the sociology of knowledge (the term taken in its widest connotation) has two
subjects rather than one: the social roots of knowledge in the proper sense
of the word, of truthful, valid knowledge; and the social roots of pseudo-
knowledge, that is, of error, of "ideology."[4]   For a long time this crucial,
all-important distinction was not made, and a panideological doctrine held
sway; to Marx, for instance, or, at the other end of the political spectrum, to
Pareto, all thought was ideological and had to be "unmasked" as such.
Vico, however, makes the distinction, even though he does not spell it out.
What later writers called an ideology or a *derivazione*, he called a "conceit."
In its vanity and pride, every nation makes itself believe that *it* has "invented
the comforts of human life," just as every scholar flatters himself that the
wisdom which *he* retails is "as old as the world."   Such wish-determined
conceptions cannot but inhibit the recognition of the facts as they really are.
But, though there are these un- and antiscientific tendencies operative in our
minds, it does not follow—of this Vico is convinced—that the whole cargo of
our culture, or any culture, is hopelessly contaminated.[5]
    Coming, then, to the core of the problem—the relation of the social sub-
structure to the mental superstructure—we can best characterize the Vichian
doctrine by holding it against the two main alternatives that, between them,

---

[3] P. Landsberg, in *Schmollers Jahrbuch für Gesetzgebung, Verwaltung und Volkswirtschaft*,
1931, esp. pp. 790, 791, 804, 805, and E. Tuchtfeld, in *Zeitschrift für die Gesamte Staats-
wissenschaft*, 1951, pp. 723, 724.

[4] W. Stark, *The Sociology of Knowledge* (London, 1958), chap. 2; see also *idem*,
Montesquieu: Pioneer of the Sociology of Knowledge (London, 1960).

[5] On the "conceits" see *Scienza nuova*, esp. pars. 26, 120–28, 330, 361, 380, 430, 761,
772, 779.   Of special interest in this context is Vico's handling of the two opposite conceptions of culture migration which since his day have come to be known as diffusionism
and convergionism.   While adducing a case of diffusion (par. 440; see also pars. 441 and
737), he regards diffusionism as being largely ideological (pars. 144, 145, 146, 198, 284,
285) and opts for convergionism.

have always dominated the discussion.   Some writers, such as Alfred Weber in the last generation and Pitirim Sorokin in our own, have tended to think in terms of a culture-entelechy or culture-soul which is ontologically basic and pre-existent and which generates, by a process of emanation, a whole social cosmos comprising both a material and a mental order.   Other writers, such as Karl Marx or Émile Durkheim, have rejected this approach as too idealistic and have presented instead a more "materialistic" conception of the history of ideas.   To them, the extramental, objective reality of the socio-economic world is first, and it is from that tangible reality—for example, from the reality of production and property relations or of the given division of labor—that ideas arise as its necessary and sufficient complement, as an image of the hard facts, as it were, reflected in the mirror of the mind.   It is not difficult to see that this divergence of opinion is fated to continue until the last battle between idealism and materialism is over and done with.   Yet to Vico the whole discussion appeared, or would appear, almost without substance.   In his system the intramental and the extramental, subjective metaphysics and objective ordering, are flawlessly combined.[6]

We can best enter into Vico's root conception by looking at one of those semantic analyses—or should we say playful speculations?—of which he was so fond, and which are always revealing, even if they sometimes err on the side of imagination.   The Greeks called their high god *Dios* (or Zeus) and their law *dikaion* (originally *diaion*); the Romans paralleled this by deriving both *Jovis* and *ius* from an original *Ious*, an expression in a manner halfway between the two.   The reason for this philological phenomenon is the initial connection between, nay, the unity of, the intramental religious philosophy of primitive man and his extramental social ordering.   That which reduced the semibestial giants who roamed the earth after the Flood to discipline and thereby started the humanization of man, that which constituted the source from which everything else was to flow in the fullness of time, was an idea in the mind which was at the same time also an agency outside the mind, a rudimentary system of metaphysics as well as a rudimentary system of social control, namely, the conviction that man was in the grip of a supervising and, if necessary, avenging deity.   Nor was the situation different in later ages.   The customs of "heroic" societies and the laws of "human" ones have both intramental and extramental aspects, and these aspects together—elements which in reality are but one—are to Vico the substructure on which the whole cultural superstructure of a given epoch rests.[7]

When we look upon the cultural content of any historical constellation from this theoretical vantage point, even the strangest, and at first sight most incomprehensible, conceptions become comprehensible.   At the threshold of all social developments there stands an act of the human imagination, and

---

[6] See Stark, *Sociology of Knowledge*, chap. 5, esp. pp. 224, 225, 226, 229.
[7] *Scienza nuova*, pars. 398, 433, 1015, 1098.

so the mentality of primitive man necessarily was permeated by the imagination. That is, as it were, its style. But the intuition that thought to discern
behind the rolling thunder and the flash of lightning a divinity called Zeus
or *Jovis* was not purely phantasmagoric. There *is* a god whose existence
was (poetically) apprehended by the childlike mind of early man, as it was by
the more rational conceptions of later ages. In other words, even early man
was in contact with the facts, and it makes little difference that he apprehended
them in his way and not in ours. How could he have done otherwise? If
we, however, would like to understand the primitive mentality properly, if
we would (as the scholar should) try to see the realistic kernels through the
imaginative shell in which the "age of the gods" (the age of social control
through fear) encased them, we must practice a certain method of analysis;
we must "demythologize" the mythologies, to use a modern phrase which
suits Vico to perfection. This is what our philosopher tried to do throughout his great work. Vico was a prime practitioner of the hermeneutic
method, the method of "understanding," which is the very heart of any
sociology of knowledge.[8]

Anything even remotely resembling adequate documentation is out of the
question here, but one example can and must be given. We take it from
paragraph 989 of the *Scienza nuova*. The Romans had a "Salic Law," just
as the French did in the Middle Ages: women could not succeed to the royal
throne. Yet there is a tradition according to which a woman, Tanaquil, at
one time governed the Roman kingdom. How can the origin of this
curious piece of mock-historical lore be explained? What was its deeper
meaning, and what its factual core? Behind the name of Tanaquil, Vico
surmises, there hides a weak-kneed king, a king who was a woman in his
will, even though he was a male in his body. We have before us a "heroic
phrase," a reflection of the maleness of heroic society, in which any deficiency
in imperiousness was immediately decried as womanly. The famous fable
of the She-Pope Joan can be explained in the same way. There never was a
Pope Joan, but there was a Pope John who did not show the firmness
expected of any and every public figure in "barbarian times": when it came
to dealing with the Patriarch of Constantinople, Photius, he exhibited great
weakness. His was the softness of a lady rather than the hardness of a lord.[9]

Behind the fictions of Tanaquil and Joan there hide simple historical facts,
or, rather, concrete historical figures, but sometimes the mythologies that
fill ancient thinking are symbolic in a wider and vaguer sense. Yet they can
and must be handled in the same fashion: they, too, are reducible to real

[8] A fuller consideration of this method and its application would have to be based
mainly on the following paragraphs of *ibid.*: 59, 68, 78, 79, 82, 91, 414, 425, 432, 508,
514, 734, 802; see also par. 1036: ". . . all the fictions of ancient jurisprudence were truths
under masks."

[9] See *ibid.*, par. 1035.

events. What, for instance, was the meaning of the story of the rape of Proserpine, whom Pluto was said to have carried off to the underworld? Proserpine is the seed corn and Pluto the earth, just as, in the fable that makes Zeus, in the form of a shower of gold, do violence to Danae in a tower, Zeus is the fertility-giving rain and Danae the fertility-receiving soil, while gold is the ripened grain and the tower the granary in which it is preserved. Even bolder is the use of the serpent as a symbol of the cultivated land: the imagination of early men flew high, but not so high that the scholar would be unable to follow it and to catch it, as it were.[10]

Vico notes that the meanings thus elicited are not stable throughout history. With a change in outer life comes a change in inner meaning—a conception supremely characteristic of any "sociology of knowledge." Pluto and Zeus were not, originally, lustful types who pursued the objects of their lust. But, when the moral tone of Greek society degenerated, when dissoluteness began to take the place of discipline, the traditional fables were pressed into the service of a lascivious generation. If even the gods went gallivanting, it was asked, why should humans not indulge in the same sport? Such ideas, Vico asserts, were far from the minds of the family fathers of the first rude ages; different societies have different mentalities, each its own.[11]

The mode of analysis which we have so far investigated would have been quite sufficient by itself to make Vico one of the greatest protagonists of the sociology of knowledge the world has ever known. But he has yet another profound and epoch-making intuition to add. Societies are not unities: they are, as a rule, riven by strife. Vico was one of the first theorists of the class war. Maintaining, as he did, that the commonwealths of early history were ordained to preserve the power of the nobles, and that the privileged heroes "swore eternal enmity" to the power-seeking plebeians who were "guests" in their cities, he anticipated much of the Marxist theory of history and the state. Such writers of the intellectual left as Georges Sorel and Max Adler freely acknowledged his genius: they saw him as one of themselves, and not without good reason.[12] Like Marx later on, he was convinced that thought-forms and thought-content reflect, not only the inclusive societies within which they arise, but also, and more specifically, the social struggles that rend these societies. Perhaps most in line with Marxism is Vico's assertion that, because of the class war, the gods of the Graeco-Roman Pantheon tended to split in two, each of the classes having their own. The same goddess was called Minerva in the nobleman's *curia*, he records, but Pallas in the plebeian assemblies. Hercules was the symbol of the upper

[10] *Ibid.*, pars. 546, 548; see also pars. 605, 629, 634, 635, 679, 721, 747.

[11] *Ibid.*, pars. 814, 817, 818; see also pars. 81, 221, 569; finally, see pars. 512, 514, 533.

[12] G. Sorel, in *Le Devenir Social*, 1896, and M. Adler, in Grünberg's *Archiv für Geschichte des Sozialismus und der Arbeiterbewegung*, 1929.

classes, Antaeus of the lower; their wrestlings were the historical contentions in which the latter endeavored to snatch rights from the former. Following this model, a whole chain of paragraphs in the *Scienza nuova* (647–59) interprets fables as imaginative conceptualizations of the class war.[13]

Most sociologies of knowledge which have been presented have a weak spot. The general assertion that intellectual superstructures were dependent on "real" social substructures has hardly ever been supplemented by a specific investigation of the mode of that dependence.[14] Vico, too, is not too clear on this point. Yet the elements of an opinion can be discerned. The sciences, he says in one context, had their beginnings in the public needs or utilities of the peoples; later he gives it as his conviction that the thirty thousand gods whose names Varro has assembled were related to as many needs of the physical, moral, economic, and civil life of the earliest times. Admittedly, it is not easy to make much of such *obiter dicta*. Yet, if it is allowable to bring the wisdom of hindsight to bear upon them, a definite theoretical tendency can—to say the least—be read into them. There is a fairly large school of authors who maintain that forms of thought arise because they have a *function* to fulfill in the societies in which they are born and find formulation. Expressed differently, and pushed more closely to Vico's mode of expression, forms of thought are answers to human needs and, in this sense, of utility to the people who entertain them. The mode of dependence between the conditioning outer life and the conditioned inner life appears as one of interfunctioning or interrelation (mutuality). Such a functionalist approach is entirely reconcilable with Vico's general philosophy; indeed, it is not overbold to assert that it is germane to it.[15]

We hear a good deal more on yet another of the basic problems of the sociology of knowledge. The questions were not raised until the twentieth century, but Vico answered them by anticipation in the eighteenth. Granting that the mental superstructure depends (in the manner just characterized) on the social substructure, how complete is that dependence? Are only the contents of some minds conditioned, or are all? All of Book IV of the *Scienza nuova*, and more particularly section I, opts for the latter alternative. Vico clearly thinks in terms of all-pervasive culture-mentalities. Each system of social control—control by the gods, control by the nobles, and the mutual control which is the essence and the secret of democracy— has its own appropriate style of thought. It shapes all the ideas that prevail under it, from law and philosophy to the technique of writing. The only modifying fact which Vico acknowledges (again in surprising agreement with much later theorizing on the subject) is the possibility of anticipations

13 Cf. pars. 586, 611, 590, 618, 104–15, 271–76, 286, 290, 293, 414, 439, 443, 579, 580, 583, 584, 609, 668, 985, 1076.
14 Stark, *Sociology of Knowledge*, chap. 6.
15 Above all see *Scienza nuova*, pars. 51, 69, 175; see also pars. 147–52.

and survivals, especially the latter.   The germs of the aristocratic regime can be discerned in the theocratic one, yet many phenomena which were the products of the theocratic regime, and which were in line with its constitution, spilled over, so to speak, into later periods and continued, perhaps with appropriate adjustments, to "function" in them.[16]

But, by saying that the totality of a culture-mentality is conditioned or determined by the type of social ordering which prevailed at the hour of its birth, nothing is yet decided about the degree of that determination.   All contents of the mind may be dependent on their bases in life, but not all need be equally dependent.   Some later sociologists of knowledge have asserted that certain kinds of ideas are relatively bound and others relatively free; notably Georges Gurvitch but even Friedrich Engels has left statements to this effect.[17]   This is a point on which Vico is very clear, and he thinks like Gurvitch and Engels.   His thesis, more particularly, is that law is comparatively close to the base, philosophy relatively remote from it; indeed, he is even more specific.   Law arises first from the matrix of life; philosophy is added later, as a more distant link in a chain of connections.   In paragraph 1040 of the *Scienza nuova* this conception is stated with all desirable precision: "It must have been from observing that the enactment of laws by the Athenian citizens involved their coming to agreement in an idea of an equal utility common to all of them severally, that Socrates began to adumbrate intelligible genera or abstract universals by induction; that is, by collecting uniform particulars which go to make up a genus of that in respect of which the particulars are uniform among themselves."[18]

What we have considered thus far is the positive side of the sociology of knowledge—sociology of knowledge as a tool of scholarship which contributes to the proper understanding of the facts.   The subject has, however, another and distinct aspect, namely, a philosophical side; it is concerned not only with the origin of ideas but also with their validity, or at least with the problematic judgment of their validity.   It asks not only where ideas come from and what the analysis of their genesis can contribute to their comprehension, but also in what relation they stand to the truth. On this point, several sharply defined schools of thought have sprung up, and two of them are of the greatest importance.[19]   The first, best represented in our time by Karl Mannheim, was relativistic.   Every age has its own truth, so Mannheim taught; absolute truth is beyond human reach.   The other school, whose chief protagonist was Max Scheler (in America, Florian Znaniecki), embraced the opposite opinion.   It conceded that absolute truth *in its fullness* is beyond

---

[16] See *ibid.*, esp. pars. 835, 936, 991, 994, 996; see also pars. 371, 372.

[17] *Re* Gurvitch see G. Eisermann, *Die Lehre von der Gesellschaft* (Stuttgart, 1958), pp. 408 *et seqq.*, esp. pp. 432 *et seqq.*; *re* Engels see Stark, *Sociology of Knowledge*, pp. 284, 285.

[18] See also pars. 1041–43.

[19] Stark, *Sociology of Knowledge*, chap. 8.

human reach, but asserted at the same time that every age apprehends and comprehends a part of it—an *aspect* of it, to use Max Scheler's technical term. While the Mannheimian alternative has its roots in pragmatism, the Scheler-Znaniecki theory is in the last resort Platonistic in inspiration.[20]

It is obvious that the two conflicting attitudes are almost impossible to reconcile: according to the one, we never have the truth; according to the other, we always have it. Because he was with every fiber of his being a Platonist, Vico could not but join the tradition that in the fullness of time was to lead to Scheler and Znaniecki. But even in this area, his genius, which was essentially one of synthesis, asserted itself and showed its strong side. Without making any damaging concessions to relativism, and without taking even a single step in the direction of that philosophical and ethical anarchy which is the inherent danger of all relativism, he yet knew how to avoid giving the impression that all ideas are equally true, or that there is little from which to pick and choose among societies insofar as contact with the truth is concerned. This position can be formulated succinctly by saying that, according to him, the objective truth in itself is indeed always the same, but it is not always equally well received and reflected by men's subjective consciousness.[21]

We can almost grasp Vico's specific reconciliation of relativism and absolutism with our hands in the important paragraph (1096) that closes the fifth book of the *Scienza nuova*.* Summing up all that has gone before, this is what he writes:

> Now, in the light of the recourse of human civil institutions to which we have given particular attention . . . let us reflect on the comparisons we have made throughout this work in a great many respects between the first and last times . . . of the ancient and modern nations. There will then be fully unfolded before us, not the particular history in time of the laws and deeds of the Romans or the Greeks, but (by virtue of the identity of the intelligible *substance* in the diversity of their *modes* of development) the ideal history . . . of the eternal laws which are instances by the deeds of all nations . . . in their rise, progress, maturity, and dissolution.[22]

---

[20] M. Scheler, *Die Wissensformen und die Gesellschaft* (Leipzig, 1926); Fl. Znaniecki, *The Social Role of the Man of Knowledge* (New York, 1940); K. Mannheim, *Ideologie und Utopie*, 3d ed. (Frankfurt, 1952).

[21] Certain passages of the *Scienza nuova* show a tendency to emphasize the specific weaknesses of earlier man insofar as the recognition of the truth is concerned (pars. 180–87, 218, 236, 367, 374, 383, 384, 385, 833; see also pars. 670, 783, 786, 787); others point out the parallel, yet opposite, weaknesses of modern man (pars. 204, 704, 707, 1102, 1106). The conviction that each society has its inherent handicaps is a form of relativism, but the limitations that Vico brings to our attention concern always the pursuit of truth, never *truth itself*.

[22] Italics added. The substance of Vico's sociology of knowledge (insofar as it is an epistemology) is contained in the following paragraphs of the *Scienza nuova*: 29, 34, 161–64, 205, 209, 218, 219, 311, 312, 332, 333, 348, 350, 363, 375, 381, 424, 445, 495–98, 499, 501, 502, 520, 699, 768, 769, 779, 816, 818, 932–34, 941. On the parallel problem

To anyone who knows his Vico this is a splendid formulation of the basic insight on which all his thinking rests, and the words that fill the parenthesis present us with a characterization of his attitude toward the problem of truth which is as clear and as sufficient as it is terse. Truth is always absolute because there is substantial identity of meaning (—of reference, as some might prefer to say); but there is also relativity, for that absolute truth is, and must be, presented in a diversity of modes of expression.

It is the most problematical philosophical concept that shows Vico's thinking on this all-important point in the most unproblematical manner. All societies need such ideas as "strength" and "beauty"; without them they could not carry on any conversations, either simple or refined; and there is little difference between one culture and another as to what really constitutes strength or beauty. The essential attributes are always the same. But only in some societies—only in mature societies—can strength and beauty be described in abstract terms. Our own is among them. In other societies— in societies not yet mature—they can be envisaged only in concrete terms, by visual images, by pictorial representations. Where we say strength, the early Romans said Hercules; where we say beauty, they said Venus. The reference is to the same thing-in-itself (if we may borrow for a moment from Kant), but the mode of apprehension is different: the one *noumenon* fractures itself into many *phenomena*, of which every society has its own variety. Reality is one, appearances are diverse. Can there be a more convincing solution to the conflict between absolutism and relativity?

Vico supports and perfects this theoretical analysis by introducing two further considerations. The first concerns the concept of truth itself. There are really two such concepts, although they are, in principle, equivalents: there is the concept of the abstractly true, and there is the concept of the concretely certain. Primitive man apprehended the concretely certain; modern man formulates the abstractly true. The image of strength in the shape of Hercules is as certain in its outlines as is the image of a wall or a tree which I see before me: both rest on the sense of vision, and our eyes do not deceive us. What I see, I see, and there can be no discussion about its truth. But the idea of strength can also be expressed in a series of general propositions, and we can make these propositions as true as the purely mental operation which states that thrice three is nine. Thus we have embodied, and, as it were, disembodied, truth. With this distinction in the definition of truth goes a difference in method. Pictorial truth is caught and conveyed

---

of the "absolute" and "relative" aspects of law see *De uno universi iuris principio et fine uno*, chaps. XXI *et seqq.*, XLVIII *et seqq.*, LXXXII *et seqq.*, and CXIV *et seqq.* The title of chap. LXX is "Iustitia particularis et universa, doctrina aliae, reipsa idem" (Particular and Universal Justice Are Different in Doctrinal Formulation but Are Identical in Substance). (The references in this note refer to both the contents of the foregoing lines and the rest of the essay.)

by means of example, of the revealing instance; conceptual truth is formulated by means of induction, of the step-by-step reduction of that which is incidental and accidental outside to the essential within.   Speaking of poets and philosophers, Vico asserts that the former may be said to have been the sense, the latter the intellect, of the human race (*Scienza nuova*, paragraph 363).   Earlier societies were poetic: they saw the truth through their senses. Later societies are philosophical: they grasp it with their intelligence.   But the truth is always the truth.   Yet, to Vico, the conquest of truth by the earlier societies is only a second best, as can be seen from what he says in paragraph 1027 of the *Scienza nuova*: ". . . as men are naturally drawn to the pursuit of the true, their desire of it, when they cannot attain it, causes them to cling to the certain. . . ." It is better to see things in the abstract than to see them in the concrete.   And why?   Because man, as God envisioned him in the beginning, was meant to be a creature of intelligence rather than a creature of sense.   Our perfected self is centered on our reason; so long as we are bound to our bodies, we are not entirely what we could be and should be.   Our study of Vico's sociology of knowledge thus leads us back to his basic doctrine of man.   Everything in his system is magnificently consistent: his philosophy is all of one piece, as Michelangelo's "Pietà" is all of one block of marble.

As we mature, then, we progress from more concrete to more abstract modes of thought, just as we progress from a more fear- and force-controlled existence to one more informed by the spirit of neighborliness and benignity. The development is loss as well as gain.   Earlier man had the glory, as well as the limitations, of the senses; he was a great artist.   Later man has the limitations, as well as the glory, of the intellect; he is apt to evolve that remoteness from reality, that color blindness, that general anemia, which is the bane of full-fledged intellectualism.   Vico's philosophy contains, in addition to its over-all optimism, a definitely tragic element which is some-times overlooked.   The truly perfect man would be both artist and intel-lectual, just as he would have both the chivalric virtues of the heroic ages and the civic virtues of the newer democracies.   That perfection is forever denied us: we are imprisoned in an inescapable "either/or."   But, in whatever we think and in whatever we do, the mode of our thinking and the mode of our action are closely—vitally—associated.   They are so in fact, in historical reality; they would be so even in the ideal, in that total fulfillment which we can envisage but never attain.[23]   In the last analysis, all of Vico's thinking and feeling is permeated by the conviction that man and society, the inner processes of mind and the outer processes of conduct, are in the deepest and fullest sense of the word linked and locked; this is the conviction which is the life principle, as it were, of the discipline known as the sociology of knowledge.

[23] See esp. the *Scienza nuova*, par. 821.

Edmund Leach   VICO AND LÉVI–STRAUSS
ON THE ORIGINS
OF HUMANITY

I am not aware that Claude Lévi-Strauss has ever invited his readers to examine the writing of Giambattista Vico, and, if Lévi-Straussian arguments seem occasionally to echo a Vichian theme, this is probably no more than an accident. If Vico influenced Lévi-Strauss across the centuries, the route was devious and indirect. Lévi-Strauss' eighteenth-century patron was J. J. Rousseau, and certain of Rousseau's problems, particularly those which are raised in the *Discours sur l'origine et les fondamens de l'inégalité parmi les hommes* (1755), have repeatedly served as main points of departure for Lévi-Straussian analysis (for example, Lévi-Strauss [1961], pp. 389–90; [1962a], pp. 142–43; [1962b], p. 326). Now, at certain points Rousseau and Vico seem to talk much the same language, not because they influenced each other,[1] but because both were reacting to Hobbes. Hobbes seems to have imagined a primeval state of affairs in which natural men were animals living outside society but were endowed with a special faculty—*reason*—and a special appetite—*lust for power*. The special appetite would have driven these brute men toward mutual annihilation, but reason would then have shown the advantages of civilization, that is, of attaining peace through submission to the disciplined institutions of an organized commonwealth.

Vico and Rousseau both reject Hobbes's assumption that the human animal is naturally endowed with reason, but they are inclined to agree that the first forms of civilization were established when men came together to form

All quotations from Vico's New Science *are taken from Thomas G. Bergin and Max H. Fisch's Anchor Books edition (Garden City, N.Y., 1961).*

[1] I have no evidence that Rousseau ever read Vico, but at the beginning of chapter 15 of *Structural Anthropology* [1963a] Lévi-Strauss quotes the following passage from Rousseau: "The investigations we may enter into in treating this subject, must not be considered as historical truths, but only as conditional and hypothetical reasonings, rather calculated to explain the nature of things, than to ascertain their actual origin; just like the hypotheses which our physicists daily form respecting the formation of the world" (Rousseau [1755], p. 6). A pedant might argue that this position is distinguishable from that of Vico because the latter argued specifically that the nature of things is in their true origins. But the truth in question is "poetic truth," and we must surely suppose that Vico means for us to understand his history of mankind "only as conditional and hypothetical reasonings" precisely in Rousseau's sense.

societies for their mutual advantage. Thus they share a common interest in the following questions: If, at some point in the historical past, savage brutes outside society turned themselves into civilized men inside society, how did this come about? What mechanism of evolution could turn a man-animal into a man-human?

In some respects Vico and Rousseau give the same kind of answer. Both assume that reason is a by-product of civilization intimately bound up with the use of language. Both recognize that, in an evolutionary scheme, one must postulate a primeval stage of brutality in which "men" could not talk and therefore could not reason. Both persuade themselves that the invention of speech must have preceded the development of *reason*; they are thus led to a romantic conception that speech was first invented as a means of communicating *emotion*—the first men expressed their ideas as poetry.[2]

As is well known, Rousseau carries his romanticism a good deal further than this and seems at times to idealize completely the prehuman animal state of man: where Hobbes's proto-men are aggressive criminals conducting a war of all against all, Rousseau's original savage lives in a placid and happy state of cowlike ignorance. But because he is devoid of language he is not yet human.[3]

Rousseau understands very clearly the extreme difficulty of imagining just how a spoken language might come into being. The relationship between the creation of a spoken language and the creation of society is a "chicken and egg" problem. Neither, it seems, can begin to develop without the prior existence of the other (Rousseau [1755], p. 60). Rousseau offers no solution to this puzzle, but he continues to insist that it is the possession of language which distinguishes civilized man in society from animal man in nature. Lévi-Strauss shares this view,[4] although he has added to it in various

[2] "Poetic wisdom, the first wisdom of the gentile world, must have begun with a metaphysics not rational and abstract like that of learned men now, but felt and imagined as that of these first men must have been, who, without power of ratiocination, were all robust sense and vigorous imagination. This metaphysics was their poetry, a faculty born with them" (*New Science*, par. 375). "D'abord on ne parla qu'en poésie; on ne s'avisa de raisonner que long-temps après" (Rousseau [1782], p. 365, quoted in Lévi-Strauss [1962a], p. 146).

[3] References to Rousseau's noble savage usually misrepresent what he actually wrote—although he was not a consistent writer. Rousseau imagined a prehuman state of man, in which man was isolated and peaceful because he could not speak. The noble savage appears at a later stage of development but is an ideal type, an imaginary first human being who possesses speech and lives in society but who has not been corrupted by the evils that civilization brings with it. The identification of this ideal type with actual South Sea Islanders of the eighteenth century and the idea that they represent natural man, who is permanently contrasted with civilized man—an idea which sentimentalizes the whole conception—is attributable to Diderot, not Rousseau. On this point see Lévi-Strauss [1961], pp. 388–89.

[4] "Whoever says 'Man' says 'Language', and whoever says 'Language' says 'Society'" (Lévi-Strauss [1961], p. 389).

ways, in particular by suggesting that the philosophical puzzle embodied in the question "In what way does a human being differ from a non-human animal?" is one which worries all mankind. The distinction between the time-now of experience, when men talk and animals do not, and the time-then of myth, when men and animals both talked, is for Lévi-Strauss an expression of this universally persistent interest in the problem of what constitutes the humanity of man, the contrast between culture and nature.

Vico not only shares Rousseau's views about the imaginative capacities of natural man; he likewise agrees that we must presuppose an initial stage in which natural men existed in a state of blissful peace:

Freshly emerged from bestial liberty, in the extreme simplicity and crudeness of a life content with the spontaneous fruits of nature, satisfied to drink the water of the springs and to sleep in the caves, in the natural equality of a state in which each of the fathers was sovereign in his own family [in those times], one cannot conceive of either fraud or violence by which one man could subject all the others to a civil monarchy (*New Science*, paragraph 522).

Even so, Vico, unlike Rousseau, reaches essentially Hobbesian conclusions. In the Vichian scheme the first cultural development is not language but a sense of property—manifested in the rights that men assert over women in a state of matrimony (*connubium*)—and it is from this sense of property that the natural aggressiveness of Hobbes's savage derives: "natural liberty is fiercer in proportion as property attaches more closely to the persons of its owners" (*New Science*, paragraph 290). From this Vico deduces (like Hobbes) that one major function of the institutions of organized society is to curb the aggressive acquisitiveness of human individuals. Finally, again like Hobbes, he reaches the very un-Rousseau-like conclusion that, in a state of civilization, a monarchy is always the ideal form of political order (*New Science*, paragraph 1008).

Some of these Vichian opinions, it may be remarked, have received a good deal of support from contemporary studies of animal behavior. Ethologists now tell us that "territoriality"—that is, a sense of property in relation to territorial space—is innate throughout large parts of the animal kingdom, and is closely linked with mating behavior. It has been shown that aggressive defense of such property serves important evolutionary functions, but that, in addition, in all species where this applies, aggressiveness is inhibited by social mechanisms ("ritualization") which prevent mutual annihilation of members of the same species (see, for example, Lorenz).

However, in the context of Lévi-Strauss' work, our interest in Vico focuses primarily on his views about mythology and the poetic imagination.

Some of Lévi-Strauss' more down-to-earth commentators have complained that, at critical points in his exposition, he tends to become "ambiguous," "obscure," etc. Others, more kindly disposed, have remarked that, because he is trying to display, in formal verbal argument, facts that are more easily expressed in music or in poetry, the tendency toward opacity is only to be expected. In his most illuminating moments Lévi-Strauss himself resorts to poetic devices. The same, I think, might be said of Vico. In order to explain how his proto-men, the hero-giants, might have exercized their imaginations creatively even before they had devised a spoken language, he resorts to poetic imagery. For example, in the following quotations, consider how the intricacy of the argument eventually leads Vico to argue like one of his own "theological poets":

And because in such a case [a clap of thunder] the nature of the human mind leads it to attribute its own nature to the effects, and because in that state their nature was that of men all robust bodily strength, who expressed their very violent passions by shouting and grumbling, they pictured the sky to themselves as a great animated body, which in that aspect they called Jove, . . . who meant to tell them something by the hiss of his bolts and the clap of his thunder (*New Science*, paragraph 377).

The first men, who spoke by signs, naturally believed that lightning bolts and thunderclaps were signs made to them by Jove. . . . that such signs were real words, and that nature was the language of Jove (*New Science*, paragraph 379).

Their poetic wisdom began with this poetic metaphysics, which contemplated God by the attribute of his providence (*New Science*, paragraph 381).

Thus it was fear which created gods in the world; not fear awakened by men in other men, but fear awakened in men by themselves (*New Science*, paragraph 382).

That such was the origin of poetry is finally confirmed by this eternal property of it: that its proper material is the credible impossibility. It is impossible that bodies should be minds, yet it was believed that the thundering sky was Jove (*New Science*, paragraph 383).

"Logic" comes from *logos*, whose first and proper meaning was *fabula*, fable. . . . In Greek the fable was also called *mythos*, myth, whence comes the Latin *mutus*, mute. For speech was born in mute times as mental [or sign] language (*New Science*, paragraph 401).

For that first language, spoken by the theological poets, was not a language in accord with the nature of the things it dealt with . . . but was a fantastic speech making use of physical substances endowed with life and most of them imagined to be divine.
This is the way in which the theological poets apprehended Jove, Cybele . . . and Neptune, for example, and, at first mutely pointing, explained them as substances of the sky, the earth, and the sea, which they imagined to be animate divinities. . . . And similarly by means of the other divinities they signified the other kinds of things appertaining to each, denoting all flowers, for instance, by Flora, and all fruits by Pomona. We nowadays reverse this practice. . . . For when we wish to give utterance to our understanding of spiritual things, we must seek aid from our imagination to explain them and, like painters, form human images of them. But these theological poets, unable to make use of the understanding, did the opposite and more

sublime thing: they attributed senses and passions . . . to bodies, and to bodies as vast as sky, sea, and earth.   Later, as these vast imaginations shrank and the power of abstraction grew, the personifications were reduced to diminutive signs. . . . Jove becomes so small and light that he is flown about by an eagle. . . . Cybele rides seated on a lion.

Thus the mythologies . . . must have been the proper languages of the fables; the fables being imaginative class concepts, . . . the mythologies must have been the allegories corresponding to them (*New Science*, paragraphs 401–3).

It is noteworthy that in all languages the greater part of the expressions relating to inanimate things are formed by metaphor from the human body and its parts and from the human senses and passions.   Thus, head for top or beginning; the brow and shoulders of a hill; the eyes of needles and of potatoes. . . . the wind whistles; the waves murmur. . . . All of which is a consequence of our axiom that wherever man is lost in ignorance he makes himself the measure of all things.   Where rational metaphysics teaches that man becomes all things by understanding them . . . , this imaginative metaphysics shows that man becomes all things by *not* understanding them (*New Science*, paragraph 405).

It is far from my intention to imply that all (or indeed any) of this is a direct forestalling of Lévi-Strauss, although certainly the final sentence in this group of quotations is completely in line with the modern master's style; it is strictly comparable to the now notorious remark that "nous ne prétendons donc pas montrer comment les hommes pensent dans les mythes, mais comment les mythes se pensent dans les hommes et à leur insu" (Lévi-Strauss [1964], p. 20).

But I would suggest that Lévi-Strauss stands a great deal closer to Vico on these issues than do many later authorities.

Late nineteenth-century writers, taking their lead from Max Müller, were all too willing to find the explanation of myth in a crude theory of metaphorical confusion.   It was presumed that the personification of nature, so characteristic of mythology, has its ultimate root in linguistic ambivalence; it is "a disease of language."   The fact that sane men were apparently unable to distinguish between the ambiguities of poetry was taken as evidence of the childish mentality of primitive man.   Vico also seems to regard the personification of nature as the prototypical characteristic of mythical thought, but his approach is quite different.   Vico's hero-giants are in no sense childish and trivial; on the contrary, it is the gigantic creative power of their imaginations which makes them what they are.

In this discussion Vico is really concerned with the same basic problem that repeatedly confronts the anthropologist when he meets with totemic phenomena.   What is really meant when the Bororo Indians say that they are red parrots, the Dinka say that they are lions, or the Nuer say that human twins are birds?[5]   Ethnography shows us that, for the purposes of myth,

[5] For a discussion of various styles of argument in such matters see Cassirer, p. 65, and Firth.

categories derived from an observation of nature are again and again endowed with human characteristics and vice versa. Why should this be so? What does it signify? Is this just nonsense, or is there a subtle sense behind the nonsense?[6]

One answer that has been fashionable among functionalist social anthropologists for the past forty years is that when things (including categories of materials and species of plants and animals) are endowed with attributes of human personality this marks their social importance—personification is an index of social and/or economic value (cf. Radcliffe-Brown). It was in a critique of this position that Lévi-Strauss came up with his now celebrated aphorism to the effect that totems are valued "not because they are good to eat but because they are good to think" (Lévi-Strauss [1962a], p. 128); that is, totems are categories of a kind which make thinking possible.

Now Vico knew nothing of the ethnography of totemism, but his attitude toward the deities of classical mythology seems to imply an intellectual position which is close to that of Lévi-Strauss. Vico affirms that primeval man personified as deities the "imaginative class concepts" in order to be able to think about them.

Proto-man's direct experience was limited to the feelings and emotions of his bodily senses; therefore, the only way in which he *could* impose an orderly frame of logic upon the world of observation was by using categories derived from experience of his own body to sort out the attributes of the external world (cf. Cassirer, p. 90). This thesis is not identical to that formulated by Lévi-Strauss but it is of the same kind. Instead of dismissing mythical thought as non-logical or prelogical (and therefore naïve), it presumes that it rests on logical principles. The purpose of Vico's inquiry, like that of Lévi-Strauss, is to discover what these principles are.

As Vico's investigation into the meaning of mythology proceeds, he encounters what Lévi-Strauss would now refer to as "structural" data. Vico realizes that mythical stories do not exist as isolate units but as sets, and that the elements in the units of a set must somehow fit together. Because of this over-all (structural) unity, deductive inferences may be made from one particular story to another. For example, Vico (*New Science*, paragraph 712) observes that, since the "lower world" of Ulysses is no deeper than a *ditch*, it follows that Homer's idea of "heaven" must have been equally simple—no higher than the summits of the mountains. Later Vico points out that it is precisely this kind of logical consistency which makes it sensible to equate the so shallow "lower world" not only with a *grave* but also with a *plough furrow* into which seed corn is sown (*New Science*, paragraphs 715–17).

---

[6] Cf. "dans ma perspective, le sens n'est jamais un phénomène premier: le sens est toujours reductible. Autrement dit, derrière tout sens il y a un non-sens" (Lévi-Strauss [1963b], p. 637).

The whole argument in this series of paragraphs is virtually a sequence of mathematical relations which Lévi-Strauss might have presented thus:

underworld : earth :: earth : heaven

water
rising from below ground : earth :: earth : streams falling from above ground

springs :: mountains
depressions in ground :: things above ground
ditch :: ridge
grave :: (house, temple)
seed in furrow :: standing grain in ear
plebeians (savages) living in valley :: nobles (heroes) living in mountains
promiscuity :: marriage
chaos :: order
[nature] :: [culture]

Nor is this just a formal exercise of arranging categories in binary opposi-tions. Vico uses his structural insights to throw light on the *meaning* of classical mythology in a way which I myself find quite convincing. For example, he argues that it is a mistake to suppose that Prometheus was condemned to punishment in the *underworld*. He was "chained to a crag" and his entrails were "devoured by a mountain eagle." Therefore, his punishment occurred in *heaven*. Once we have understood this, many aspects of Prometheus' mythological role take on new meaning. Logic of this kind did not reappear in myth analysis until Lévi-Strauss published "La Geste d'Asdiwal" in 1960!

The reader will need a fairly close familiarity with Lévi-Strauss' writings to fully understand what is here under discussion, but a passage in which Lévi-Strauss comments on the Nuer equation "twins are birds" illustrates my point and is equally applicable to the classical proposition "Prometheus is chained to a mountain crag."

What we are presented with is a series of logical connections uniting mental relations. Twins "are birds" not because they are confused with them or because they look like them, but because twins, in relation to other men, are as "persons of the above" to "persons of the below" and, in relation to birds, as "birds of the below" are to "birds of the above." Thus they occupy, as do birds, an intermediary position between the supreme spirit and human beings (Lévi-Strauss [1962a], p. 116).

I am claiming that in a very tentative way Vico was already groping after this kind of analysis in 1725.

Lévi-Strauss' "structural" interpretation of mythology and of other varieties of ethnographic data—for example, his analysis of kinship systems—takes its starting point from his interest in structural linguistics. There is a sense in which the structure of spoken languages provides Lévi-Strauss with a "basic model" through which he can begin to talk about structure in other kinds of cultural data.[7] The equivalent "basic model" for Vico was his interest in etymology, which often owed more to a vivid imagination than to sound knowledge of the facts, but which, even so, provided him with the wherewithal for many very shrewd observations. Some of these are decidedly Lévi-Straussian in tone. For example, in Vico (*New Science*, paragraphs 567–69) we find it argued that (1) the crucial distinction between the social order of the nobles and the social disorder of the plebeians depends on (2) the distinction between formal marriage (*connubium*) and sexual promiscuity (*more ferarum*: the morality of beasts) which is expressed by (3) the difference between "Venus *pronuba*," who wears a girdle and is worshiped by the nobles, and "Venus naked," who was worshiped by the plebeians; and then, by a sequence of etymological shifts, this becomes equivalent to (4) the distinction between stipulated contracts (*pacta stipulata*), where the *stipulata* means "clothed" and derives from the blade that clothes the grain (hence "vested" interests), and "simple agreements, which involve only natural obligation" (*pacta nuda*: naked contracts). This kind of procedure in which a single "opposition" is chased from pillar to post through a whole series of transformations is a typical Lévi-Straussian device. It will be observed that the details of the argument link up directly with the sequence of binary oppositions mentioned previously.

My final Vichian–Lévi-Straussian link is provided by Hegel. Vico is Hegel's forerunner by a hundred years but he too is at pains to emphasize the recurrent contradiction between political intention and political performance:

> It is true that men have themselves made this world of nations . . . but this world without doubt has issued from a mind often diverse, at times quite contrary, and always superior to the particular ends that men had proposed to themselves. . . . Men mean to gratify their bestial lust and abandon their offspring, yet they inaugurate the chastity of marriage from which the families arise. The fathers mean to exercise without restraint their paternal power over their clients, yet they subject them to the civil powers from which the cities arise. The reigning orders of nobles mean to abuse their lordly freedom over the plebeians, yet they are obliged to submit to the laws which establish popular liberty. The free peoples mean to shake off their laws, yet they become subject to monarchs (*New Science*, paragraph 1108).

Lévi-Strauss admits no debt to Hegel, although on occasion he has claimed to be a Marxist (Lévi-Strauss [1961], p. 61). The following passage comes from the end of *Tristes Tropiques*. Lévi-Strauss is outlining the plot of an imaginary revision of Corneille's *Cinna* which he entitles *The Apotheosis of Augustus*:

---

[7] See Lévi-Strauss [1963a], especially chaps. 1–5, 11.

I put on the stage two men who had been friends in childhood and re-met at a moment of crisis in both their very different careers. The one had opted, as he thought, against civilisation, only to find that he was heading back towards it by a very complicated route and had destroyed in so doing the sense and value of the alternative, which he had supposed to be his concern. The other had been marked out from birth for the world and its honours only to find that all his efforts had tended towards the abolition of that world and those honours. Each sought, therefore, to destroy the other, and in so doing to save, even at the price of his own death, the significance of what had gone before (Lévi-Strauss [1961], pp. 376–77).

If we remember that in Vico's dream of the beginning of civilization the proto-men (the giants) are initially one, but that they later divide themselves into two groups, (1) the heroes, who withdraw to the mountains and develop as nobles, the poetic creators of civilization, and (2) the plebeians, who remain in the valleys as savages and become "clients" of the nobles, we can see that Vico and Lévi-Strauss, in the passages quoted, were both letting their imaginations run in very similar directions. When I first encountered the Lévi-Straussian item it struck me that this was a very peculiar variety of Marxism, although plainly infused with elements from Hegelian logic; now I might say: "It is almost Vichian." Or, to turn the analogy the other way round, nothing could be more Lévi-Straussian than the following:

But in the night of thick darkness enveloping the earliest antiquity, so remote from ourselves, there shines the eternal and never failing light of a truth beyond all question: that the world of civil society has certainly been made by men, and that its principles are therefore to be found within the modifications of our own human mind (*New Science*, paragraph 331).

Lévi-Strauss' version of this argument is much more complex and cannot be fairly condensed into a few sentences. He emphasizes that man's brain, which is the apparatus through which he thinks, is a part of nature just as are the things in the world external to man, and because these objects—human and non-human—are a part of nature they obey laws of nature which are discoverable by man. This process of discovery depends on the fact that a common "structure" permeates not only nature external to man and nature internal to man but also non-natural (cultural) phenomena, which are the products of human minds. The cultural data constitute a "language" through which man is able to apprehend and therefore to control not only the natural world of things external to himself but also the artificial world of human society itself. Thus, in effect, Lévi-Strauss, like Vico, affirms that "the principles of the world of civil society are to be found within modifications of our own human mind." This is an elusive kind of doctrine, though my formulation is no more opaque than are some of Lévi-Strauss' own. The following have been quoted frequently:

Sans mettre en cause l'incontestable primat des infrastructures, nous croyons qu'entre *praxis* et pratiques s'intercale toujours un médiateur qui est le schème conceptuel par l'opération duquel une matière et une forme, dépourvues l'une et l'autre d'existence indépendante, s'accomplissent comme structures, c'est-à-dire comme êtres à la fois empiriques et intelligibles (Lévi-Strauss [1962b], p. 173).

Ainsi peuvent être simultanément engendrés, les mythes eux-mêmes par l'esprit qui les cause, et par les mythes, une image du monde déjà inscrite dans l'architecture de l'esprit (Lévi-Strauss [1964], p. 346).

The second of these, in particular, in its final phrase comes close to Vico's expression.

The editors of the English translation of the *New Science* declare that "it is the most impressive and most interesting attempt prior to Comte at a comprehensive Science of human society. It contains the most thorough-going class-struggle analysis prior to Marx." [8] Few English writers on the history of sociology would, until recently, have made this kind of assessment, but the fact that I have been able to show that Vico had so many premonitions of the work of Europe's foremost living anthropologist could surely imply that this is a judgment which we should take seriously.

References

Cassirer, E. 1955. *The Philosophy of Symbolic Forms.* Vol. II: *Mythical Thought.* New Haven: Yale University Press.

Firth, R. 1966. "Twins, Birds and Vegetables: Problems of Identification in Primitive Religious Thought." *Man,* n.s., 1, no. 1: 1–17.

Hobbes, T. 1651. *Leviathan, or the Matter, Form, and Power of a Commonwealth Ecclesiastical and Civil.* London.

Lévi-Strauss, C. 1960. "La Geste d'Asdiwal," in *Annuaire de l'École Pratique des Hautes Études* (5th sec.: Religious Sciences). Paris, 1958–59.

———. 1961. *World on the Wane.* London: Hutchinson. An incomplete translation of *Tristes Tropiques.* Paris: Plon, 1955.

———. 1962a. *Le Totémisme aujourd'hui.* Paris: Presses Universitaires Françaises.

———. 1962b. *La Pensée Sauvage.* Paris: Plon.

———. 1963a. *Structural Anthropology.* New York: Basic Books.

———. 1963b. "Réponses à quelques questions," in *Esprit* (Paris), November: 628–53.

———. 1964. *Mythologiques: Le Cru et le Cuit.* Paris: Plon.

Lorenz, K. 1966. *On Aggression.* New York: Harcourt, Brace & World.

Radcliffe-Brown, A. R. 1922. *The Andaman Islanders.* Cambridge: At the University Press.

Rousseau, J. J. 1755. *Discours sur l'origine et les fondamens de l'inégalité parmi les hommes.* Amsterdam.

———. 1782. "Essai sur l'origine des langues," in *Collection complète des Oeuvres de J. J. Rousseau, Citoyen de Genève.* VIII, 355–434. Geneva. (This essay is posthumous. Rousseau died in 1778.)

[8] Thomas G. Bergin and Max H. Fisch, trans., *The New Science of Giambattista Vico* (Garden City, N.Y.: Anchor Books, 1961), p. xiii.

H. Stuart Hughes

VICO AND CONTEMPORARY SOCIAL THEORY AND SOCIAL HISTORY

It would be presumptuous to attempt in a single brief essay an assessment of Vico's influence on the past three generations of social theorists and social historians. A full account of such influence would require an entire volume —or perhaps several volumes—and, even then, many important derivations or connections might remain undiscussed. My purpose is far more modest. I should like to locate a few of the areas in which Vico's thoughts have been echoed and his suggestions followed, but in which little or no credit has been given to Vico himself. At the same time, I shall speculate on the reasons why his example has manifested itself in so remote and indirect a fashion. For the very fact that Vico has so seldom been explicitly cited may well be a sign of the pervasiveness of his contemporary influence.

At the start we should distinguish between two aspects of the Vichian inheritance. The first is what Vico called "ideal eternal history"—his schematic account of the successive ages through which "nations" have run their course, and of the *ricorsi* in which subsequent ages have repeated the patterns of those that came before. The second is the *verum-factum* principle —the basic insight that enabled Vico to understand the "civil world." The influence of these two lines of thought has been far from equal: the first has been restricted to a special and rather eccentric type of investigation; the second has been at the very center of contemporary social theory and social history. It may be well, then, to begin with the simpler and more narrowly delimited of the Vichian legacies—the question of "ideal eternal history."[1]

A number of years ago when I undertook a critical analysis of the work of Oswald Spengler[2]—which attempted to relate *The Decline of the West* to certain of its predecessors, such as Danilevsky's *Russia and Europe*, and to successors like Toynbee's *A Study of History*—I quite naturally assumed that Vico would figure prominently among Spengler's intellectual antecedents. A closer study revealed nothing of the sort. Far from acknowledging a debt

[1] See Vico's own statement in the *New Science*, trans. Thomas G. Bergin and Max H. Fisch, Anchor Books ed. (Garden City, N.Y., 1961), pp. 375–81.

[2] H. Stuart Hughes, *Oswald Spengler: A Critical Estimate*, rev. ed. (New York, 1962).

to Vico, Spengler (and Toynbee also) seemed almost systematically to avoid making reference to him. In Spengler's case the explanation I arrived at was that he had never read Vico's work; in the case of Toynbee, an encounter with Vico came too late to alter appreciably an understanding of comparative history which had already established itself in the historian's mind.[3]

Further reflection has suggested that, besides mere ignorance, there were more general reasons that prompted the "metahistorians" of the twentieth century to neglect their great intellectual ancestor. By the time that Spengler and Toynbee arrived at their own individual conceptions of a cyclical pattern of history—in both cases on the eve of the First World War—Vico had already been absorbed into the stream of current speculation on history and society: one no longer had to go directly to Vico himself to learn the outlines of what he had taught. But this absorption had come about in a partial and fragmentary fashion which made it difficult to appreciate his full worth. By the late nineteenth century, in both Germany and England, historians were seeking confirmation for their conviction that events followed a course which could be rationally determined and that this course was in the direction of human progress. Such a principle of explanation—positivist in a broad meaning of the term—could and did find in Vico an anticipation of the truth; but the tributes paid to his work tended to be grudging and patronizing—Vico's "metaphysical" cast of mind had permitted him to catch no more than glimpses of the underlying movement of history.[4] Hence it was only natural that younger men like Spengler and Toynbee, who in their different ways were combating the reigning cult of progress, should have failed to see in Vico's teaching of the *ricorso* an anticipation of the comparisons they too would draw among the life cycles of civilizations.

Moreover, by the time Croce's magisterial study had finally revealed the full scope of Vico's thought (the date of its publication, 1911, was also that of Spengler's sudden awareness of his own historical principle), the emphasis had shifted: what Croce was after was not a cyclical view of the past but a source of inspiration for his personal effort to revivify philosophy by "suffusing" it with history.[5] As an unremitting foe of positivism, Croce saluted in Vico the progenitor of the idealist canon of historical study which he himself had formulated. In such a perspective the theory of the *ricorso* necessarily took second place. In Croce's mind, as in that of the other imaginative social thinkers of his generation, Vico's most precious legacy

[3] Arnold J. Toynbee, *A Study of History*, vol. XII: *Reconsiderations* (London, 1961), 584–87.

[4] Max H. Fisch's Introduction to *The Autobiography of Giambattista Vico*, trans. Max H. Fisch and Thomas G. Bergin, Great Seal ed. (Ithaca, N.Y., 1963), pp. 90–94.

[5] Benedetto Croce, *La filosofia di Giambattista Vico* (Bari, 1911), trans. R. G. Collingwood as *The Philosophy of Giambattista Vico* (New York, 1913), pp. 33–34.

was his tremendous insight that man could understand the "civil world" because he had made it.

In undertaking to assess this second (and predominant) aspect of Vichian influence, it is perhaps worthwhile to cite once more the key passage from the *New Science*:

> But in the night of thick darkness enveloping the earliest antiquity, so remote from ourselves, there shines the eternal and never failing light of a truth beyond all question: that the world of civil society has certainly been made by men, and that its principles are therefore to be found within the modifications of our own human mind. Whoever reflects on this cannot but marvel that the philosophers should have bent all their energies to the study of the world of nature, which, since God made it, He alone knows; and that they should have neglected the study of the world of nations, or civil world, which, since men had made it, men could come to know.[6]

For Croce the governing terms in Vico's injunction were "the modifications of our own human mind." He was less interested in the concept of "making." Or, more precisely, to use a distinction of verb that exists in English but not in Latin or Italian, he was concerned with *facere* or *fare* in its sense of "doing" rather than in its sense of physical creation. According to Croce, the historian's overriding problem was how to get inside the minds of historical actors—to understand why the protagonists of past events had behaved as they did; the matter of motive was primary. And here Vico offered a ready answer: since the historian could reproduce in his own mind the "modifications" that the thoughts of men in earlier ages had undergone, he could reconstruct through a process of intellectual sympathy the chain of reasoning that lay behind a sequence of historical actions.

To most of Croce's intellectual generation this answer seemed satisfactory. What was true of Croce himself applied also to such diverse contemporaries as Georges Sorel, Friedrich Meinecke, or Max Weber.[7] In Sorel's case, the debt to Vico was clear and was explicitly recognized. In Weber's case, one searches his *Wirtschaft und Gesellschaft* in vain for a reference to the author of the *New Science*; as in most German thought of the early twentieth century, Vico's influence comes mediated through a writer of the intervening century, such as Marx or Dilthey. Yet, for Sorel and Weber alike, a similar Vichian principle of historical understanding applied. The devices that Sorel referred to as *diremptions* and that Weber described as ideal types were artificial mental constructions—self-induced modifications of the mind—that enabled the historian or the social theorist to penetrate the raw data of his craft which had previously remained opaque.

[6] Bergin and Fisch, *New Science*, pp. 52–53.

[7] For these relationships, see H. Stuart Hughes, *Consciousness and Society* (New York, 1958).

Down to about 1930, this neo-idealistic procedure held firm.   And as of today no other social-science epistemology has replaced it.   But, from the start, the practice of understanding the past—or a present social reality— through an act of mental sympathy had distinct limitations.   It worked better for specific actions and events than it did for the general process of slow change; it was far easier to apply to individuals or small groups than to masses of mankind; and by the same token, while it offered an avenue to the minds of the articulate and the educated, it gave few clues to the thoughts and feelings of those unschooled in writing or formal speech.   In short, the neo-idealistic procedure almost of necessity gave the preference to elites and to logical reasoning.   Still more, its findings remained unproved; it offered no objective criterion against which the sympathetic insight of the historian could be tested.

Yet, all along, Vico's own work had suggested a supplementary procedure that could provide precisely the kind of irrefutable evidence required. There were, Vico saw, manifestations of the past lying all about us:

> Truth is sifted from falsehood in everything that has been preserved for us through long centuries by those vulgar traditions which, since they have been preserved for so long a time and by entire peoples, must have had a public ground of truth.
>
> The great fragments of antiquity, hitherto useless to science because they lay begrimed, broken, and scattered, shed great light when cleaned, pieced together, and restored.
>
> . . . .
>
> Here emerges a great principle of human institutions . . . : that since the first men of the gentile world had the simplicity of children, who are truthful by nature, the first fables could not feign anything false; they must therefore have been . . . true narrations.[8]

Such direct evidences of a vanished reality—architectural monuments, artifacts, folklore, myths, language, and the like—very early furnished the raw material for archaeologists and philologists.   Historians and social scientists, however, were slower to exploit evidence of this kind and slower still to realize how it might alter the critical definition of human study and aid in the solution of the philosophical problems with which Croce's generation had wrestled.   It was not until the 1930's in France that men like Lucien Febvre and Marc Bloch began to experiment systematically with what they called a "regressive" method of historical study.

The *locus classicus* of the new method was Bloch's *Les caractères originaux de l'histoire rurale française*.[9]   As a student of the West European—and more

[8] Bergin and Fisch, *New Science*, pp. 64, 90.

[9] Originally published in Oslo in 1931, *Les caractères originaux* was reissued in Paris in 1952, with a supplementary volume of Bloch's subsequent notes and expansions on the same theme.   An English translation by Janet Sondheimer, entitled *French Rural History: An Essay on Its Basic Characteristics*, was published in Berkeley, Calif., in 1966.

particularly of the French—countryside, Bloch had recognized that in this area it was out of the question for the investigator to proceed in the conventional chronological order.   Prior to the eighteenth century, no even remotely adequate documentation existed: rural society had made its appearance in written records only a few generations ago.   Hence the most promising course for the historian was to work backward—to start with the present day, or with "a past very close to the present," and to feel his way by cautious stages through centuries that grew steadily more obscure.   The countryside, Bloch realized, altered its character only very gradually; even in his own time there was much about it that had retained its medieval aspect. A highly trained scholar who knew how to use his eyes and was not afraid of long tramps through the mud could reconstruct its history through extrapolating from direct, on-the-spot observation.

Bloch similarly applied this regressive method to his synthesizing work on feudal society and to a number of shorter studies dealing primarily with technological themes.[10]   And after him a talented group of his own and Febvre's students expanded its range and refined its procedures; by the 1950's the kind of social history associated with the *Annales* that Bloch and Febvre had founded had become the dominant current in French historiography.[11]   There was no question that its ultimate inspiration was Vichian. Yet the masters who established the new canon of historical study referred to Vico himself scarcely at all.

The explanation for such apparent ingratitude is very simple: the lessons of Vico reached the more imaginative French historians of the twentieth century through the mediation of Michelet.   In Febvre's work, in particular, expressions of respect and indebtedness to Michelet are not difficult to find; for the cofounder of the *Annales*, the nineteenth-century rediscoverer of Vico was the artist who had attempted to "resurrect" the full complexity and variety of the past, who had thought in terms of a history that extended beyond governing elites to embrace the doings and aspirations of entire populations, a history in which all aspects of life were seen as a continuous whole and which was not ashamed to draw on the lowly or the long-neglected in its search for evidence.[12]   The example of Michelet, who was restored to favor after a generation or more of positivist-minded denigration, acted as a tonic to the minds of twentieth-century historians; in recognizing

---

[10] *La société féodale*, 2 vols. (Paris, 1939–40), trans. L. A. Manyon as *Feudal Society* (London, 1961); *Mélanges historiques*, ed. Charles-Edmond Perrin, 2 vols. (Paris, 1963).

[11] Jean Glénisson, "L'historiographie française contemporaine: tendances et réalisations," Comité français des sciences historiques, *Vingt-cinq ans de recherche historique en France (1940–1965)* (Paris, 1965), I, xi, xxiv–xxv, lxiii.

[12] See, for example, the Introduction to a volume of selections entitled *Michelet*, in the series *Les classiques de la liberté* (Geneva-Paris, 1946), p. 11; "Vivre l'histoire: Propos d'initiation" (1941), *Combats pour l'histoire* (Paris, 1953), pp. 25–26.

their debt to him they forgot Michelet's own master, whose precepts had similarly revivified French historical study a century before.

The exploitation by Febvre and Bloch of Vico's *verum-factum* principle had epistemological advantages that its proponents never fully appreciated. As men little inclined toward philosophical analysis of their own work, the founders of the *Annales* failed to realize the extent to which it might lead them over some of the stumbling blocks that the generation of their immediate predecessors had bequeathed them.   The new technique of extrapolation from direct and tangible evidence offered greater certainty than did the subjective methods of a Croce or a Meinecke.   In providing a number of fixed points of reference from which the historian could take his bearings, such evidence suggested the possibility of a more solid grounding for what historians and social scientists conventionally referred to as the "truth"; the realities that artifacts or tradition revealed—techniques, attitudes, economic or social structure—were the things least likely to have been concealed or to have suffered distortion at the hands of subsequent commentators.   Alternatively, if these evidences had in fact been deformed through time, they could, in Vico's own words, be "cleaned, pieced together, and restored." In short, as Bloch himself surmised, what was "most profound in history" might "also be the most certain." [13]   And this "bedrock" evidence offered precisely the clues to those questions of imperceptible change and of the mentality of the inarticulate which had proved most troubling to the historians and social theorists of the early twentieth century.

So much at least was true of monuments hewn in stone.   The matter of myth or unwritten memory was more tricky.   Vico had spoken of "fragments of antiquity" and of "vulgar traditions" almost in the same breath: for him they were but two aspects of the same man-made evidence that later generations of humanity were free to decipher.   And in his own efforts at decoding he had gone on to offer some hypotheses about the origins of myth and the workings of the mind of primitive man:

It is . . . beyond our power to enter into the vast imagination of those first men, whose minds were not in the least abstract, refined, or spiritualized, because they were entirely immersed in the senses, buffeted by the passions, buried in the body.

or again:

The first men, the children, as it were, of the human race, not being able to form intelligible class concepts of things, had a natural need to create poetic characters; that

---

[13] *Apologie pour l'histoire ou métier d'historien* (Paris, 1952), trans. Peter Putnam as *The Historian's Craft* (New York, 1953), p. 104; see also H. Stuart Hughes, *History as Art and as Science* (New York, 1964), pp. 15–19.

is, imaginative class concepts or universals, to which, as to certain models or ideal portraits, to reduce all the particular species which resembled them.

or once again:

In that human indigence, the peoples, who were almost all body and almost no reflection, must have been all vivid sensation in perceiving particulars, strong imagination in apprehending and enlarging them, sharp wit in referring them to their imaginative genera, and robust memory in retaining them.   It is true that these faculties appertain to the mind, but they have their roots in the body and draw their strength from it.[14]

A generation ago such a view of the "bodily" and "poetic" character of preliterate thought was almost universally accepted.   Indeed, one of Vico's most fruitful suggestions for subsequent social theory was his notion that the mind of primitive man, however odd it might appear at first glance, deserved more sympathetic and discerning treatment than the polite denigration that was usual among his contemporaries.   In this guise, Vico stands at the origin of modern cultural anthropology.   Yet even he denied his heroes and savages the power of abstract reasoning; while he admired the sharpness of their sensations, the retentiveness of their memories, and the power of their imaginations, he was sufficiently in accord with the mental patterns of his own time to contrast eighteenth-century refinement with what he presumed to be the uncontrolled passion of the primitive way of thought.

Now just within the last twenty years Claude Lévi-Strauss has advanced the hypothesis that the savage and the civilized minds may not be as different as, until recently, the anthropologists themselves assumed.   For Lévi-Strauss the reasoning of primitives is neither simple nor erratic.   It is frequently complicated in the extreme, and it excels in establishing detailed and even sophisticated systems of classification.   Moreover, its deepest patterns follow a logic similar to that of mankind in the civilized West: at bottom, savage and city-dweller are both neolithic in temper.[15]   The task for the anthropologist, then, is to locate and to delineate the eternal structures of the mind which lie below the vast heterogeneity of primitive imaginings and scientific chains of reasoning.   And the way to arrive at such a universal mental "architecture" is through a systematic study and coding of mythical material[16]—a Vichian enterprise if ever there was one!

A third generation of twentieth-century social theorists, then, has used this tradition—and once more without attribution to the author of the *New*

[14] Bergin and Fisch, *New Science*, pp. 32, 76, 260.

[15] Such is the central contention of Lévi-Strauss' *La pensée sauvage* (Paris, 1962), translated as *The Savage Mind* (Chicago, 1966).

[16] This is the task Lévi-Strauss has set himself in his four-volume series entitled *Mythologiques*, the first three volumes of which have appeared to date: *Le cru et le cuit* (Paris, 1964), *Du miel aux cendres* (Paris, 1966), and *L'Origine des manières de table* (Paris, 1968).

Science—as a point of departure for still another approach to the "civil world." Just as Croce found inspiration in Vico's pronouncement that man's intelligence could penetrate to an understanding of what he himself had made, just as Bloch discovered in the "great fragments of antiquity" the clues to what was most continuous and certain in the human experience, so Lévi-Strauss and the present generation of "structuralists" have exploited a third possibility which, to use Vico's own expression, had been "hitherto useless to science." That the effort to discover in mythology a universal code entails a change in Vico's definition of the primitive is a matter more of emphasis than of basic approach. Indeed, one might go so far as to say that Lévi-Strauss' search for a common denominator in the mind of the savage and in the mind of civilized man is only a logical extension of the principle of imaginative understanding which Vico himself propounded.

Still more: in at least one flash of insight Vico anticipated the structuralist program: "In the nature of human institutions," he maintained, "there must ... be a mental language common to all nations, which uniformly grasps the substance of things feasible in human social life and expresses it with as many diverse modifications as these same things may have diverse aspects."[17] Or to put the same thought in the language of the 1960's, these "diverse modifications" may be thought of as corresponding to as many different structural codes.

So perhaps we are back once more to the hope of establishing an "ideal universal history." But this time it will be history in a more abstract and conceptually rigorous sense than was true of the cyclical constructions of a Spengler or a Toynbee. From our present vantage point, the search for a method of coding which is universally applicable to human experience appears to mark the current frontier of Vico's protean legacy.

---

[17] Bergin and Fisch, *New Science*, p. 25.

Elio Gianturco   VICO'S SIGNIFICANCE
                          IN THE HISTORY OF
                          LEGAL THOUGHT

Introduction

It is a matter of general knowledge that the so-called revival of Vico's
reputation in our century was given decisive impetus by B. Croce's monograph published in 1911.[1]   In retrospect, with this monograph Croce appears
to have performed for Vico in the twentieth century the same service that
Michelet did in the nineteenth.   Croce bestowed on Vico's renown a new
lease on European and trans-European life.   His book, though fully deserv-
ing the applause that greeted it on its appearance and that it continued to
enjoy in subsequent years, and though admirable in the masterliness of its
"cut," in the harmonious proportionality of its structure, in its close
empathetic adherence, and in the consummate skill with which large masses
of the original texts are melted into the substance of the critical exposition, is
nevertheless marked by certain blemishes.   At the time of writing, Croce's
antagonism toward all forms of positivism had reached its acme.   We must
hold fast to the fact that Italian positivism between 1890 and 1910 was
especially dominant in the field of sociological and legal studies.   Vico
had been set up as an idol by the positivistic jurists, especially those of
southern Italy.   It had become the vogue among them to portray him
as a jusphilosophical precursor of Hegel and to interpret his thought
through Hegelian spectacles.   Croce views Vico through these spectacles,
but he is firmly determined to wrest the "Vico monopoly" from juristic
circles.

    Accordingly, he portrays Vico as his lineal forebear in idealistic im-
manentism, as preponderantly a metaphysician, and as the discoverer, before
Baumgarten, of the modern discipline of aesthetics.   (Croce had published
his own *Aesthetics* in 1901; in it, Vico's role in the revaluation of the imagination is duly brought out.[2])   In the 1911 monograph the epistemological

    [1] B. Croce, *La filosofia di G. B. Vico* (Bari: Laterza, 1911).   This work was reprinted
in paperback form in 1965.   The English translation by R. G. Collingwood, first
published in 1913, was reprinted by Russell and Russell (New York) in 1964.   The most
recent Croce bibliography, which supplements the previous one by E. Cione (Rome,
1956), is that edited by Silvano Borsari for the Istituto Italiano di Studi Storici (Naples,
1964), entitled *L'opera di Benedetto Croce*.
    [2] *Estetica*, 6th ed. (Bari: Laterza, 1928), pp. 242–58.

aspects of Vico's thought are thrown into prominent relief.[3]   Now these
are not as important as the sociological aspects (it has been said that Vico is
the greatest sociologist of the pre-Comtean period)[4] or, as I will try to show,
his juristic contributions.   Nevertheless, the net result of Croce's monograph
was that of focusing a dazzling light on the *Scienza nuova*: of fixing the
Scienza nuova, so to speak, at the central spot of the firmament of research,
and hence of obscuring and eclipsing Vico's immeasurably significant
achievements in the fields of law.   These achievements are embodied principally in the *Il diritto universale*.[5]

As a consequence of the foregoing, in order adequately to approach the
topic that I have undertaken to treat, it is necessary for us to perform a kind
of "Copernican" turning, a reorientation of our categories.   It is necessary
to assume that the North Star of our research, the cynosure of our attention,
is no longer the *Scienza nuova*, but *Il diritto universale*.   If we perform this
reorientation, not only will the usual ranking of the two works be inverted
(the *Diritto universale* will appear more important than the *Scienza nuova*),
but the character, the content, and the significance of the latter opus will
appear in a new dimension.   Moreover, the meaning of the transition from
Diritto universale to *Scienza nuova* will become crucial to an understanding of
the whole intellectual evolution of our author.

The momentousness of the *Diritto universale* in the history of legal thought
is so pivotal, so irrefutably patent, that one experiences a certain shock in
realizing the almost total absence of Vico's juridical ideas from modern
histories of legal philosophy and from source books on jurisprudence.   The
Diritto universale logically fills the hitherto empty interval (not to call it the
yawning gap) between the appearance of the *Jus belli ac pacis* (1625) and that
of the *Esprit des lois* (1748), and it rightfully claims its place between them.
In Vico, we are confronted with the greatest legal intellect between Grotius
and Montesquieu.   The remark has been made that Vico is one of the few
philosophers who have been thoroughly acquainted with law and its history
and have therefore been able to make contributions of the highest value to

---

[3] Croce, *La filosofia di G. B. Vico*, paperback ed., chaps. I and II.   The chief viewpoints
guiding Croce's presentation of Vico are detailed in A. Scrocca's *G. B. Vico nella critica
di B. Croce* (Naples: Giannini, 1919); among more recent treatments see A. M. Jacobelli
Isoldi, "Il pensiero di Vico nell'interpretazione di Croce," *Giornale critico della filosofia
italiana*, 1950.

[4] See Jean Lamure, "G. B. Vico, un précurseur de la sociologie en Italie," *Revue de
l'Institut de Sociologie*, 3 (July–September, 1949): 321–36; see also Lucio Mendieta y
Nuñez, "J. B. Vico, precursor de la sociologia," *Revista Mexicana de Sociologia*, 15,
no. 1 (1953).

[5] Ed. Fausto Nicolini, 2 vols. (I: *Sinopsi, e De uno universi iuris principio et fine uno*.
II: *De constantia jurisprudentis*) (Bari: Laterza, 1936).

juridical philosophy. The growth of legal thought during the period separating the creator of the doctrine of international law from the most luminous of all theorists of modern liberal constitutionalism becomes unintelligible if we choose to disregard the towering jusphilosophical framework of the *Diritto universale* (1720). Vico is the direct successor and continuer of Grotius; and he leads us from Grotius to Montesquieu, from jusnaturalism to sociological historicism. His vehement attacks against the three major representatives of "baroque" jusnaturalism—Grotius, Selden, and Pufendorf—may induce uncautious readers to think that he completely disavowed the jusnaturalistic position. But Vico is no Bergbohm.[6] He disavowed that position, yes, but by *devouring* it, by transfusing it into a system animated by a contrary spirit. The identical thing took place in the case of Montesquieu, and it has continued to puzzle the interpreters of both men. One of Hegel's concepts will help us to realize what happened. If there ever was a typical, a "classical," case of *Aufhebung*, it is this. In Vico the two *frères ennemis*, jusnaturalism and historicism, are coupled; the two reluctances are made to coexist, to act together. The Neapolitan jurist creates a synthesis superior to both jusnaturalism and historicism, a synthesis in which neither is impaired or sacrificed to the other. There is a subsumption of the two under a viewpoint which transcends them both. The reciprocal revulsion, the dialectical relationship, between jusnaturalism and historicism is preserved; Vico feels no impulse to destroy the duality by wrecking, mutilating, or, worse still, by altogether suppressing one of the factors. The ideal of law, the archetype of justice, looses none of its radiance, but, *corre in tempo*, incarnates itself in multiple historical *avatars*, in a ceaselessly asymptotic effort to realize the idea. In Vico the synthesis of jusnaturalism and historicism (or, shall we say, of idealism and positivism) does not result in cacophonous discord, does not bring into existence a hybrid monster. Rather, what we have is the portrayal of a process of antagonistic collaboration, a contrasting synergy of opponents. It is a co-participation of mutually repellent adversaries, winding up in a propitiation of their dissidences, in a seemingly conclusive (but not final: *corsi e ricorsi*) unfolding of all the intellectual powers of mankind. The outcome is the advent, or rather epiphany, of the totality of reason. *Verum*, the timeless paradigm of justice, and *certum* (whose other name is *auctoritas*, in the meaning that Vico attaches to it), that is, man's inevitably unsuccessful, ever-renewed attempts at carrying that paradigm into phenomenic existence, at making societal reality coincide with that paradigm, appear, in the end (and here is the deep affinity of Vico with Dante, with Goethe), as the twin *Dioscuri* of the world pageant, as the ever-battling kindred foes of the time drama of history. Vico's glance

---

[6] Carl Bergbohm (1849–1929), was the most resolute and radical denier of natural law. His position is set forth in his major work, *Jurisprudenz und Rechtsphilosophie*, vol. I: *Das Naturrecht der Gegenwart* (Leipzig, 1892).

soars above them and sees them as fulfilling a grandiose commitment: as subserving, unbeknown to themselves, a superior providential mission, an astute superindividual purpose, of which the two battlers are unaware. Writhing in the inextricable folds of freedom and necessity, they do not know that their combat is foreordained to a higher end.   In the light of that end, the meaning of their struggle becomes manifest.

Vico and Universal Law

Together with Montesquieu, Vico is the intellectual progenitor of all the attempts that have been made—in the nineteenth century and in our own—at constructing a history of law on a universal scale and at deriving from it a general philosophy of civilization.[7]   It is the history of comparative law as a discipline (*vergleichende Rechtslehre*) which opens up for us this vast panorama of jural studies.   There were institutional comparisons prior to Vico (Aristotle, Theophrastus, Bodin, and, more immediately, Grotius); but the distinctive feature in the *Diritto universale* is that the comparative method is consciously and deliberately applied to the whole aggregate of ethnographical data known prior to 1720 and is made to subserve a new investigation: the universal history of law.   After the *Diritto universale*, after the *Esprit des Lois*, we begin to hear voices calling no longer for national histories of law but for histories based on a multinational, panchronic viewpoint; the desideratum, in other words, is a jural history which would take in, as Vico says, the extent of all epochs and the expanse of all peoples.   It is a peculiar feature of Vico that, while he constructs a "general" history of law, and therefore abandons the time-space limitations of Romanistics, he still patterns the history of all laws on the normal, prototypical "model," which for him is Roman law.   As the Greek sculptor constantly kept before his eyes Polikleitos' canon of the proportions of the human body, so Vico hypostatizes the image, the "eidolon" of Roman law, into a sort of Platonic *eidos* or perfect *paradeigma*, a perpetual "*étalon de valeurs.*"   There is, for him, an equation between the *optimum* of law, the ideal of law, and post-Constantinian *jus*, profoundly permeated by *aequitas*, which is equivalent to justice itself.   It is a conception not unlike that held by one of the eighteenth-century commentators on Grotius, Samuel Coccei.   Vico's conception of Roman law is the feature that distinguishes him from Montesquieu.   In this

[7] The latest attempt along this line is René Dekkers' book *Le droit des peuples* (Brussels, 1963).   Those which Professor Dekkers in this book calls "*analogies sans contact*" are exactly what Vico terms *jus naturale gentium*.   The review of Dekkers' work by Franz Wieacker, in *Zeitschrift der Savigny Stiftung für Rechtsgeschichte*, 71 (1953): 539–46, is important; see esp. pp. 539–40 and 544.   Among the works preceding that of Dekkers, I would select for special notice H. Decugis, *Les étapes du droit, des origines à nos jours*, 2 vols. (Paris: Sirey, 1946).

respect it is symptomatic that, whereas in the *Diritto universale* and in the *Scienza nuova* Roman law is considered to be the prime factor of Rome's greatness as a political state, Montesquieu,[8] in his *Considérations sur les causes de la grandeur et décadence des Romains* (1734), hardly places any emphasis at all on the jural factor as a possible component of that *grandeur*.

The earliest voice calling for the new universalistic approach to law is that of Thibaut;[9] and, as it is natural, considering Thibaut's antagonism toward Savigny, that voice has a pronouncedly anti-Romanistic ring. In the Thibaut-Savigny controversy the idea of universal law stands out in the challenging posture conferred on it by Thibaut: "In order that legal history may become truly pragmatic," he writes, "it will be necessary for it to set about studying the legislations of *all* ancient and modern peoples."

Special interest attaches to the fact that, while Vico crosses the boundaries of Romanistics over into the immense territory of universal law, Savigny categorically refuses to do so. The difference between Vico's and Savigny's attitude toward Roman law helps us to fix their respective positions in the history of jural thought.[10] Savigny deals with Vico in his *Vermischte Schriften*, IV (1850). While Thibaut's acrid, irony-spiked remarks against Savigny's "romano-centrism" are the reflections of a polemically exacerbated animus, the drift of Thibaut's argument is fully convincing and is particularly important for the Vico-originated idea of a universalistic approach to law. Thibaut's much-quoted pronouncement reads:

The really vivifying legal history is not the one which looks with spell-bound eyes at the history of a single nation, plucks out its most minute details with a puny pettiness, and, in its *micrology*, resembles nothing more than the dissertation of that great hack-writer on the topic of *"Et caetera."* Just as one should give to a European traveler, desirous of having his mind powerfully stimulated and his inner feelings stirred, the advice to seek his salvation outside of Europe, so should our histories of law, in order to become truly pragmatic, embrace the legislations of all nations, ancient and modern. Ten valuable lectures on the structure of Persian or Chinese law would awaken in our

---

[8] On the history of juridical comparison after Montesquieu, see M. Gutzwiller, "Rechtsvergleichung in kontinentaler Sicht," *Schweizerische Beiträge zum vierten Kongress für Rechtsvergleichung*, 1954, pp. 14ff. Important is J. Kohler's chapter, "Rechtsphilosophie und Universalrechtsgeschichte," in Holtzendorff's *Rechtsphilosophie und Universal Enzyklopädie der Rechtswissenschaft* (Munich, 1915), pp. 1–62; see also Leonhard Adam, "Die vergleichende Rechtswissenschaft, unter besonderer Berücksichtigung der ethnologischen Rechtsforschung," *Juristische Blätter* (Vienna), 1930, pp. 472–76.

[9] On Thibaut see Hans Kiefner, "A. F. J. Thibaut," *Zeitschrift der Savigny Stiftung*, 77 (1960): 304–44. Kiefner emphasizes Thibaut's opposition to the *Historische Schule*, to the so-called *jurisprudentia elegans*, and to the unhistorical axiomatics of jusnaturalism.

[10] On this question of Savigny's attitude toward Roman law see Sachers, *Die historische Schule Savignys und das roemische Recht*, Atti del Congresso Internazionale di Roma, 1933 (Bologna, 1933), II, 215; and Savigny, in *Vermischte Schriften*, IV (1850).

students more juridical sense than a hundred lessons on the miserable patching-up treatments undergone by intestate succession from Augustus to Justinian.

This is enough to endear Thibaut's memory to all present and future Romanists; and so it happens that intestate succession in Roman law is one of Vico's favorite *chevaux de bataille*.

The Thibaut-Savigny codification debate took place during the first half of the second decade of the nineteenth century (1814). And a few years later, in 1820, two jurists simultaneously rose to advocate the universalistic approach to legal history: Pellegrino Rossi and Wening. Rossi, writing on the "Study of Law in its Relation to the History of Civilization,"[11] made a fervent plea for that approach, while Wening, in a little-known passage of his *Lehrbuch der Enzyklopaedie und Methode der Rechtswissenschaft*,[12] insisted on the necessity of investigating "the whole development of the law of mankind," and of "studying it in its causes, or sources." But the most outstanding figure in the history of the idea of a *Universaljurisprudenz* in the 1830's[13] was Anselm von Feuerbach. His renown in the history of criminal law is outstanding, whereas his achievement in the province of *Universaljurisprudenz* has remained hidden until our own epoch, when Professor Radbruch, in his masterful biography of this jurist, highlighted it.[14]

I should like at this point to refer to a fact which is characteristic of the posthumous reputation of Vico in the nineteenth century, that is, to the fact that his influence becomes inextricably intertwined with that of Montesquieu and Hegel. It is, for instance, difficult to say which force, Vico or Hegel, stands behind Gans's *Universal History of Inheritance Law*[15] or behind Unger's *Die Ehe in ihrer Weltgeschichtlichen Entwicklung*.[16] (Gans was familiar with both; Unger, I surmise, did not know Vico.) If Feuerbach did not know Vico's *Diritto universale*, his reaffirmation of Vico's conception of jural science is, it seems to me, all the more significant. Feuerbach writes: "A complete, all-sided cultivation of jurisprudence will prosper only when

---

[11] *Annales de Legislation de Genève*, I (1820), 1.

[12] (Landshut, 1820), bk. I, sec. V, par. 83.

[13] But the idea goes back to the early 1890's insofar as Feuerbach is concerned; in his *Kritik des naturalischen Rechts* (Altona, 1796), he traces the program of a universal science of positive law on a comparative basis.

[14] See G. Radbruch, *Paul Johann Anselm Feuerbach*, 2d ed. (Göttingen, 1957), Bibliography, p. 210; *idem*, *Elegantiae Juris Criminalis*, 2d ed. (Basel, 1950), pp. 193ff.

[15] Eduard Gans (1798–1839) is sometimes referred to as "the founder of comparative legal science in Germany." The German title of his major work is *Das Erbrecht in Weltgeschichtlicher Entwicklung*, 4 vols. (Berlin: Maurer, 1824–35).

[16] Joseph Unger (1828–1913), President of the Austrian Reichsgericht, was the first legal scholar who undertook to systematize Austrian private law; see his *System des österreichischen allgemeinen Privatrechts* (Leipzig, 1856–59); his *Die Ehe* came out in Vienna in 1850. On Unger see M. Wlassak, "Josef Unger," an obituary note (Vienna, 1913); and G. Walker, *Josef Unger* (Vienna, 1928).

philosophy, classical philology, and history [conspiring in unison] . . . collaborate toward the common goal." [17]   The indispensable tool for the study of legal history on a universal scale is, of course, the comparative approach; and on this point Feuerbach convincingly argues: "Why does the anatomist possess a comparative anatomy? Why do we *not* yet possess any comparative jurisprudence? The richest source of all discoveries, in every science based on empirical materials, is comparison and combination." [18] The affinity between language and law, on which Vico insisted, is for Feuerbach an equally valid criterion in regard to the method to be employed in the study of the respective sciences.   "Just as the philosophy of language, which constitutes the real science of linguistics, stems from a comparison of languages, so will *Universaljurisprudenz*, which is *the* juridical science *tout court*, result from the comparison of the laws and customs of the . . . nations of all epochs and regions of the earth." [19]   Feuerbach is unaware that this is the *leitmotif* of Vico's *Diritto universale*; hence he attributes the idea of *Universaljurisprudenz* to Montesquieu.   "Montesquieu conducted us as far as the steps of the temple, and allowed us, with singular ingeniousness, to cast many a glance into its inner rooms; but no one has led us yet into its very center." [20] Radbruch relates that Feuerbach accumulated a considerable mass of materials toward the realization of his project, but that various circumstances prevented him from forging them into the *magnum opus* that he had envisaged. Twenty-four years later, in 1857, the Palermitan Emerico Amari (1810–70) published a critique of the "Science of Comparative Legislation," thereby creating both the name and the bases of this discipline which has undergone such prodigious expansion in our day.   Amari formally acknowledged that he had derived his inspiration from Vico, and that he looked upon himself as Vico's direct continuer. [21]

But the *annus mirabilis* in the history of *Universaljurisprudenz* was 1861. In that year both Bachofen's (1815–87) *Mutterrecht* [22] and Sumner Maine's (1822–88) *Ancient Law* were published. [23]   Apropos of Bachofen's *Mutter-*

[17] Paul Johann Anselm Feuerbach, *Kleine Schriften* (Nürnberg, 1833), p. 161.

[18] *Ibid.*

[19] *Ibid.*, p. 163.

[20] *Ibid.*, p. 164.

[21] On Emerico Amari see the thorough biographical account given in the *Dizionario Biografico degli Italiani*, with complete bibliography.

[22] Bachofen's *Mutterrecht* is now available in English for the first time: see *Myth, Religion, and Mother Right*, trans. Ralph Manheim, with a preface by George Boas and an introduction by J. Campbell, Bollingen series, no. 84 (Princeton: Princeton University Press, 1967).   See also J. Kohler's necrological notice on Bachofen in *Zeitschrift für vergleichende Rechtswissenschaft*, 8 (1888): 148.

[23] Sir Henry James Sumner Maine was Professor of Comparative Jurisprudence at Oxford in 1869.   According to Chambers' *Encyclopaedia* (Oxford, 1966), 8: 846, *Ancient Law* was one of the most influential works of its time.   On Maine, well worth reading are: E. Grant Duff, *Sir H. Maine* (London, 1892), and F. Pollock, *Oxford Lectures*

recht, it would be interesting to find out whether he was familiar with a passage from the *Scienza nuova prima*, chapter V, entitled "Ordine naturale dell'idee umane intorno ad un giusto universale," in which we find the following: "Primitive men acquired a 'cyclopean' power over their wives and consequently over their children . . . , preserving, however, the primal custom of beastlike [sexual] communion, in *which the offspring follows the condition of the mother.* . . ." If Bachofen knew this passage, in which the "matriarchal" theory is contained in a nutshell, then we would have to credit Vico with this impressive contribution to ethnological jurisprudence. Bachofen, who was professor of Roman law in Basel from 1841 to 1844, had as his objective (as Schnitzler points out) the establishment of a philosophical legal science, a general jurisprudence based on a comparative study of ethnological materials.   Later, Albert Hermann Post (1839–95) [24] actually created this discipline with his *Einleitung in die Naturwissenschaft des Rechts* (1873). [25] The next important names are those of A. Bastian, Bernhoeft, Dahn, and Josef Kohler. Bastian's name remains bound up with the theory of the *Elementargedanken*. This *Elementargedanken* is nothing more than Vico's conception of the *jus naturale gentium* as it is clearly set forth in *Scienza nuova seconda* (1744), Book I, section II, axiom XIII: "Uniform ideas that we find in entire nations, having had no contacts with one another, must have a fundamental motive of truth."

In 1878 (this being a date that marks a milestone in the history of the posthumous diffusion of Vico's thought) the first journal of comparative jurisprudence began to be issued: it is the *Zeitschrift für vergleichende Rechtswissenschaft*, which has survived two world wars and is still being published. Its first editor was Bernhoeft, who gave a formulation of its goals in the first issue; but these goals were still more lucidly, persuasively, and thoroughly set forth in the second issue, by Felix Dahn, Bernhoeft's coeditor. Dahn's felicitously phrased statements could have been signed by Vico himself, so faithfully do they express the criteria that had guided him in composing the *Diritto universale*. [26] After a few issues, Joseph Kohler (1849–1919) joined the

---

and Other Discourses, vol. VI: *Sir H. Maine and His Work* (London, 1890); see also I. Vanni, *Gli studi di H. S. Maine e la filosofia del diritto* (Verona, 1892); K. B. Smellie, "H. S. Maine," *Economica*, 1928, W. A. Robson, "Henry Maine Today," in *Modern Theories of Law* (London, 1933); and the article by E. Adamson Hoebel in the *International Encyclopedia of the Social Sciences*, 9 (1968): 530–33; and last, but not least, Paul Vinogradoff, "H. S. Maine," *Law Quarterly Review*, April, 1904, an article which J. H. Morgan terms "the best short study of Maine."

[24] On Post see A. Achelis, *A. H. Post und die vergleichende Rechtswissenschaft* (Hamburg, 1896), and J. Kohler's article "A. H. Post," *Zeitschrift für vergleichende Rechtswissenschaft*, 12 (1896): 454ff.

[25] Post's major work, however, was *Bausteine für eine allgemeine Rechtswissenschaft auf vergleichend-ethnischer Basis*, 2 vols. (1880–81).

[26] Felix Dahn, "Vom Wesen und Werden des Rechts. Einleitung: Die Rechts-

editorial staff of the *Zeitschrift*. In Kohler we have an intellectual figure of truly impressive stature.[27] The scope of the jurist's intellectual interests becomes coextensive with that of legal phenomenology itself. Kohler's universalistic aspirations make him a sort of *Vicus modernus*, a kind of Faustian *Allwisser*, a miracle of encyclopedic legal scholarship. Vico's idea of the *diritto universale* is resurrected in a post-Hegelian garb; Kohler's Weltanschauung is Hegel's absolute, immanental idealism. Jural science becomes the "philosophy of the universal history of law"; it is the attempt to ascertain the permanent aspects of the juridical development of mankind, a real *sistema di diritto natural delle genti*.[28] The persuasion of the essential unity of the human mind, of the *natura comune delle nazioni*, a final inference to be drawn from the comparison of *all* legal materials of the human race, a conclusion predicated upon Vico's assumption of the independent, separate development of human groups, an assumption which the modern *Kreislehre*, so resolutely diffusionist and therefore anti-Vichian, has done its best to shatter—this conclusion, which is a peculiar feature of Vico's system, and the demonstration of which was the objective that he pursued throughout his life with undeflecting ardor, comes to life again and bears fruit in Joseph Kohler. "Continuing the work of Post," writes A. Schnizler, "he [Kohler] gives to legal research guidelines for the procurement of materials concerning the conditions of the primitive tribes of Africa and Australia, as well as of those of the American Indians. He draws within the circle of his investigations the legal institutions of the ancient culture-nations. The laws of the Orient, Talmudic law, Islamic, Far Eastern, and Slavic peoples, are collected and worked on; in a great number of studies and essays, in publications of monographs issuing from his academic seminar, in countless book reviews, Kohler promotes ethnological research and drives toward a *Universalrechtsgeschichte*. In contrast to the idea of a motionless, metaphysical jusnaturalism, Kohler constantly keeps in view the developmental aspect of law and portrays it in

---

vergleichung als Grundlage der Rechtsphilosophie," *Zeitschrift für vergleichende Rechtswissenschaft*, 2 (1880) : 1–10; see esp. p. 8, the characteristic statement: "The indispensable presupposition of all legal philosophy is a discipline of comparative legal history."

[27] See the extremely competent analysis of Kohler's achievements given by Leonhard Adam, "Joseph Kohler und die vergleichende Rechtswissenschaft," *Zeitschrift für vergleichende Rechtswissenschaft*, 37 (1919): 1–31; in the same issue of the *Zeitschrift* see Max Schmidt's important article "Die Bedeutung der vergleichenden Rechtswissenschaft für die Ethnologie," pp. 348–75, esp. pp. 368–75. A moving tribute is "In Memoriam J. Kohler," by Leonhard Adam, in the *Zeitschrift*, 38 (1920): 1–30, esp. pp. 26ff.: "in attempting to survey the monumental work of Kohler, we are constantly compelled to revert to his universal history of law, to his comparative jurisprudence, to his ethnological legal research." A complete history of all of Kohler's writings is given in V. Eschke and A. Kohler's *Joseph Kohlers Bibliographie* (Berlin, 1931).

[28] See *Scienza nuova seconda*, bk. II, sec. I, chap. II.

its connection with the general conditions of the culture of each people."[29]

In 1911, reviewing Croce's monograph for the *Archiv für Rechtsphilo-sophie*,[30] Kohler pays homage to his great intellectual ancestor in these words: "All of these grandiose thoughts are to be found in Vico. Through them he has anticipated the whole of ethnology, as well as the universal history of law, and has done pioneer work in the philosophy of history. He is the grand anticipator of Herder and Hegel. In the future the philosophy of law and the comparative history of law cannot afford to pass Vico by."[31]

Labels are notoriously either bereft of meaning or inadequate, and that of "Neo-kantian," it seems to me, fails to give an idea of the rich substance of the jusphilosophical theory of Giorgio del Vecchio, the grand old *doyen* of Italian jurisprudence, the founder of the *Rivista internazionale di filosofia del diritto*, and professor for many years at the University of Rome. In his classroom, succeeding generations of Italian law students have learned the philosophical principles of their life trade. His textbook *Lezioni di filosofia del diritto* (whose thirteenth edition came out in Milan in 1965) has been for almost thirty years the daily bread of legal tyros.[32] If a label has to be chosen, the label "Neo-Vichian" would suit Del Vecchio better than "Neo-Kantian." In the *Lezioni* his indebtedness to Vico, which Del Vecchio takes no pains to conceal, is quite evident. Del Vecchio's conception of the "three tasks of legal philosophy" (these three *richerche* have become almost a byword among Italian law students) stems from the *Diritto universale*: the relationship between jusnaturalism and positive law, between law as an ideal and law as experience, is envisaged in the purest Vichian fashion. The polemical juggernauts that are fought against are the same (utilitarianism, formalism, skepticism, Hobbesianism); and last, but not least (Del Vecchio was, in his youth, a student of Kohler), "In order to obtain the knowledge of the entire phenomenon of law, both from the static and the dynamic view-point, we should study the juridical history of mankind in an all-embracing fashion. We should study the 'ideal eternal history' to which Vico refers, and through the stages of which the histories of all nations pass. We should draw up a possible integral picture of the life of law, in its origin and growth." "That this is possible," Del Vecchio emphasizes, "is shown . . . by the fact that there is no human existence without a legal order [governing

[29] A. F. Schnitzler, *Vergleichende Rechtslehre*, 2d ed., I (Basel, 1961), 18–19.

[30] "Vico als Rechtsphilosoph," pp. 261–65.

[31] *Ibid.*, p. 265.

[32] Del Vecchio's *Lezioni* has been translated into ten languages (English, French, Spanish, Portuguese, German, Japanese, Turkish, Rumanian, Greek, and Persian). The valuable bibliography prefixed to the 1965 edition has been brought abreast of the specialized literature up to 1962. See also Enrico Vidal's valuable monograph *La filosofia giuridica di G. del Vecchio* (Milan, 1951).

it], by the great number of similarities and analogies which are to be found in the legal systems of all peoples."[33] The "substantial units" of the *diritto natural delle genti*, "in which, with various modifications, all nations agree"[34] (as we saw, Bastian calls them *Elementargedanken*), attest and "confirm the fundamental identity of the nature of man in which law is rooted."[35] In the next sentence we feel the pulse of the Vichian tradition: "So that we have here a new field of philosophical investigation which presents, it is true, a phenomenic and historic character, but which it would be more appropriate to call *metahistorical*, since it goes beyond the sphere of jurisdiction of the sciences that deal with the law of a particular nation."[36] The spirit of the *Diritto universale* appears in this pronouncement in concentrated essence. No less genuinely Vichian is Del Vecchio's definition of legal philosophy: "It is the discipline that defines law in its logical universality, seeks the origins and the general characteristics of its historical development, and evaluates law according to an ideal of justice derived from pure reason."[37] Kant, as the reader sees, appears at the end, asserting the a priori value of the *Rechtsbegriff* (which Vico had preserved under the name of *jus naturale philosophorum*). But is this last-minute appearance of Kant sufficient to label Del Vecchio as a Neo-Kantian *tout court*? Undoubtedly Del Vecchio has fought all his life (all honor to him) to maintain the pre-eminent value, the primacy, of the a priori in legal philosophy; but Vico's historicism and universalism have also influenced him profoundly.

[33] *Lezioni di filosofia del diritto*, 6th ed. (Milan, 1943), p. 3.

[34] *Scienza nuova*, 3d ed., bk. I, sec. XIII, chap. II.

[35] Del Vecchio, *Lezioni*, 1943 ed., p. 3; see also *idem*, "L'unità dello spirito umano come base della comparazione giuridica," *Rivista internazionale di filosofia del diritto*, 3–4 (1950): 436.

The first scholar who drew the attention of his fellow scholars to the "substantial units on which, with various modifications, all nations agree" (*Scienza nuova*, 2d ed., bk. I, axiom XIII, On Method) was Vico, who infers from this agreement the existence of an "eternal and universal law, uniform among all nations although such nations may have arisen in very different epochs. Wherever the same needs are present, the institutions of that law spring into existence, and their origins and progress are constantly grounded on that basis" (*Scienza nuova*, 1st ed., bk. I, p. 34). The unity of the human mind accounts not only for the logical unity of the juridical category but for the phenomenic unity as well, which transpires in that constancy of manifestations. Hence Vico posits a law which is at the same time both natural and historical; it is natural inasmuch as it is based on an absolute criterion, namely, the common sense of mankind, which God's providence has bestowed on all nations (*Scienza nuova*, 2d ed., axioms XI, XII); it is historical inasmuch as it is put into practice by folkways. Vico is fully conscious of this twofold character of "his" law. It is a law whose institutions "have sprung from the customs themselves of the nations, and are based on the ideas that the nations have had concerning their own nature" (*Scienza nuova*, 1st ed., bk. II, sec. IV, p. 69).

For this quotation see Felice Battaglia, *Corso di filosofia del diritto* (Rome, 1942), III, 233–35.

[36] Del Vecchio, *Lezioni*, 1943 ed., p. 3.

[37] *Ibid.*, p. 4.

The Presence of Vico's Juridical Thought in Italian Culture

Professor De Mas, with brilliant expertise, has sketched in the present symposium the history of Vico's presence in the general Italian intellectual tradition. I feel that it is necessary to insert here some supplementary information in regard to the jural aspect of that tradition.[38]

From 1850 to about 1900, positivism in Italy was in the ascendant. There were, of course, countercurrents, of which Neo-Kantianism was the most notable. Italian positivism, it has been observed repeatedly (*cela saute aux yeux*), is of Anglo-French derivation (Comte, Darwin, John Stuart Mill, Herbert Spencer), but it also has indigenous roots in the inductivism of Machiavelli, Galileo, and Carlo Cattaneo.

A startlingly original thinker, Cattaneo (1801–69) "invented" sociology almost simultaneously with, but independently of, Comte. He planned, but left incomplete, a vast work entitled *Psicologia delle menti associate*, which is the earliest configuration of the science today called social, or collective, psychology. In pre-Diltheyan accents, Cattaneo writes:

> We cannot get hold of the human spirit, we cannot scrutinize its essence, we cannot know it, unless we study it in its actual operations and manifestations. . . . We should study it in as many and as different situations as we can. It is only when we have contemplated the polyhedron of human ideas in the greatest number of its countless facets that the traits common to all of them will disclose to us its fundamental and constant nature. These traits are scattered in the histories [of the various peoples], in their laws, in their religious rites, their languages; and the knowledge of man, which we seek in vain in the hidden regions of the solitary conscience, will arise from this wholly historical and experimental ground.[39]

Cattaneo makes clear to us how closely the genesis of social psychology is connected with the reaction against "individualistic" psychology when he stresses that "the study of the individual in the bosom of humanity, *l'idéologie sociale*, is the prism that enables us to break down into distinct and brilliant colors the blurred whiteness of inward psychology."[40]   The idea that man's intelligence is, and cannot but be, a social product is a typically Vichian one: for Vico, mentality and sociality are interconvertible terms. Cattaneo scrutinized and assimilated Vico's doctrines and left us a fine essay on the *Scienza nuova*.

Cattaneo had a precursor, Gian Domenico Romagnosi (1761–1835).

[38] For Vico's influence on political thought in the South during the *Risorgimento*, see A. Romano, *Vico e il pensiero politico meridionale del Risorgimento*, Atti del XX Congresso della Società Nazionale per la Storia del Risorgimento (Rome, 1933).

[39] I am borrowing this quotation from Carlo Cattaneo, *La società umana*, ed. Paolo Rossi, 2d ed. (Milan: Mondadori, 1961), pp. 77–78. A fine anthology of Cattaneo's writings is that edited by G. Salvemini (in the collection *Le più belle pagine degli scrittori italiani*, 2d ed. [Milan: Garzanti, 1947]).

[40] Cattaneo, *La società umana*, p. 78.

Romagnosi's juristic genius is eminent: he made essential contributions to constitutional and criminal law and practically created the Italian "brand" of administrative law. Like Cattaneo, Romagnosi had a wide-ranging mind, which enabled him to master a variety of cultural fields. This mastery resulted in a rather eclectic system in which elements of empirical naturalism, verging on materialism, were amalgamated (in a rather incongrous *mélange*) with some Vichian elements. As is to be expected, the latter elements are by no means predominant in Romagnosi. It is noteworthy, however, that he makes his own the Vichian conception of justice as the eternal measure of utility, as *utile aeterno commensu aequale*. In Romagnosi's words: "Utility and justice are not contrary things, just as force and law are not opposites. Just as law, in its essence, cannot be anything but a force subject to regulation, so justice cannot be anything but a regulated utility, a utility conformable to the social order instituted by reason."

Vico and the Positivistic Period in Italy[41]

"The combination of jural studies, psychology, and sociology," as B. Brugi remarks, "is traditional in Italian legal philosophy and goes at least as far back as Vico."[42]   In 1890 an Italian jurist observed: "Positivism, in our day, attaches great importance to psychology and, through the characteristics of human psychology, explains the most salient facts that come under juristic observation." During the 1880's and 1890's, many Italian jurists cultivated the study of the relationship between law and psychology. Vadalà Papale examined the *Psychological Data in the Juridical and Social Doctrines of Vico* (Rome, 1889). Psychology became one of the major *fulcra* of Italian positivism, a positivism which, in its most eminent leader, Roberto Ardigò (1828–1920), became strongly tinged with immanentism and materialism; Ardigò composed a *Psychology as Positive Science*. Psychology penetrated even the inner sanctum of constitutional law. Vacchelli published a work entitled *The Psychological Bases of Public Law*; it was, to my knowledge, the first attempt to apply psychology to public law. In our day such studies have taken a great *essor*, especially in American political science, thanks to Professor Laswell, Professor Merriam, and a pleiad of distinguished American scholars. The psycho-jural trend, so obviously a phase of Vichian influence, was strengthened by the hegemony of positivistic sociology. At

---

[41] N. Bobbio, *La filosofia del diritto in Italia nella seconda metà del secolo XIX* (Rome, 1942).

[42] This trend has been studied by V. Miceli, "L'indirizzo psicologico nella filosofia del diritto," *Rivista di sociologia*, 1903, pp. 7–28, and by Vacchelli, *Le basi psicologiche del diritto pubblico* (Milan, 1895). On V. Miceli, see W. Cesarini Sforza's commemoration entitled "Per la storia della filosofia del diritto: V. Miceli," in his *Vecchie e nuove pagine di filosofia, storia e diritto* (Milan, 1967), pp. 237–49.

the beginning of the twentieth century, the history of this trend was traced by Gioele Solari, Vincenzo Miceli, Icilio Vanni, and Professor Bonucci.

Vico and the Neapolitan Jurists

The nineteenth century in Italy, especially its second half, was marked by a triumphal entrance of Vico's ideas into all spheres of jural thought. Hints that he had dropped were picked up and elaborated. Directions in which he had pointed were followed. Investigations that he had started came to full fruition. His achievements were remembered, treasured, and constantly held out as examples. This was the case particularly in Naples, where we observe a continuous line of *vichismo*, a Vichian school of jural studies, from Genovesi, Filangieri, Pagano, Cuoco,[43] through Nicola Nicolini, Savarese, Capitelli, Cenni, Pessina, etc. In the *Proceedings* of the Naples Academy of Moral and Political Sciences (founded in 1869), Vico's name recurs continually. In the field of jural didactics his authority was canonical. Specifically operative was his influence on the *Report on Legal Education* drawn up by Professors Luigi Capuano and Francesco Pépere (printed in the Academy's *Atti* in 1874). The two scholars were asked to discuss this problem: "Which are the subject matters whose study is imperative for the attainment of a complete juridical culture; and according to what methods are they to be organized?" Capuano and Pépere give this answer: "Concerning this question, we meet with two similar views: one by Leibniz, the other by Vico. The former, in his *Nova methodus*, lays it down that three disciplines are mainly necessary: that is, natural law, history, and *nomethesia* (in addition to geometry, mathematics, physics, etc.). In the *Diritto universale* Vico states: "The whole of jural science coalesces out of three parts: philosophy, philology, and a certain 'art' enabling us to fit law to facts." Specifically speaking [we read in the *Report*], the first part is the philosophy of law, the second ('philology') is legal history; the third is the art (or science) of legislation." [44] The *rapporteurs* conclude by saying that, for both Vico and Leibniz, the most important of these subject matters is the philosophy of law, which constitutes the primary base on which a jural science should be constructed.

Vico and Hegel

In the writings on law by authors of the positivistic school of nineteenth-century Italy, we often come across a characteristic phenomenon: the

[43] See the excellent study by Fulvio Tessitore, *Lo storicismo di V. Cuoco* (Naples, 1965).

[44] Vichian influence is also detectable in F. Pépere's *Enciclopedia e metodologia del diritto* (1864) and in his *Storia del diritto*, 1st ed. (Naples, 1871–73); it is strongest in Luigi Capuano, whose *Dottrina e storia del diritto romano* (Naples: Marchese, 1878) is entirely patterned after, nay, constructed from, Vichian materials.

doctrines of Vico are closely interlaced with those of Hegel's *Rechtsphilosophie* (this trend is particularly observable in the jurists of the Neapolitan school—Miraglia, Lioy, Bovio, etc.). In his paper of the present symposium, Professor Piovani has dealt masterfully with this theme. The "interlacement" often results in such a shocking hybridism that we are tempted to exclaim, like the two witnesses at the metamorphoses of Agnolo Brunelleschi in Dante's *bolgia* of the thieves: "Vedi che già non sei nè due nè uno!"[45] It is, however, both astonishing and comforting to find a dissenter's voice in that chorus of "confusionists." Because that voice is rare, it deserves to be heard. "Vico," points out Soro Delitala, "draws from every system the elements of truth which it contains: he is not entirely authoritarian or dogmatic, nor wholly an experimentalist." For Delitala the formula coined by Vico in order to indicate the reciprocity of truth and fact (*verum et factum convertuntur*) is by no means identical in meaning to Hegel's lemma that *alles wirklich ist vernünftig, alles vernünftige ist wirklich*; on the contrary, it is utterly different. Whereas, by his lemma Hegel means that thought is the same as being, so that everything real is rational (and conversely), for Vico the convertibility of truth and fact means that fact is the necessary precondition for achieving truth. Consequently, as soon as truth is generally acknowledged, it cannot fail to permeate, pervade, and transform fact—that is, factual conditions, positive situations. The fact that Delitala is correct in this interpretation of Vico may be evinced by Vico's portrayal of the patrician-plebeian struggles in Rome. The moment in which the plebeian masses become convinced of the truth that all men are by nature equal marks the inception of their attempts to vindicate for themselves full juridical equality, that is, to transform the *vernünftig* into the *wirklich*. This obviously has nothing to do with the meaning of Hegel's lemma, which, on the one hand, is the slogan of the epistemology of absolute metaphysical idealism and, on the other hand, constitutes an argument for justifying political quietism.

Vico and Criminal Law[46]

Vico's influence is clearly discernible in the history of the Italian doctrines concerning criminal law and criminal-law procedure. In the latter province the major figures are Mario Pagano (1748–99), Gaetano Filangieri (1752–88), and Nicola Nicolini (1772–1857). Vichian ideas are threaded into Pagano's *Considerazioni sul processo criminale* (Naples, 1787),[47] while, in the *Logica dei*

[45] *Inferno*, canto XXV, l. 69.

[46] D. A. Cardone, "Delitto e pena nel pensiero di Vico," *Scuola positiva*, no. 11–12 (1928); G. Contursi Lisi, "Idee penali di Vico," *ibid.*, no. 5–6 (1928).

[47] See Marcello Finzi, *M. Pagano criminalista* (Turin, 1915). No scholar can afford to overlook Professor Gioele Solari's studies on M. Pagano; see, in particular, *Le opere di M. Pagano: Ricerche bibliografiche* (Turin, 1936), as well as his essay "Vico e Pagano," in

probabili applicata ai giudizi criminali (published in a posthumous edition in Naples in 1803), he presents us with a most original application of Vico's theory of *conoscenza probabile* to the theory of judicial evidence in criminal cases.   As for Nicola Nicolini, professor of criminal law at the University of Naples, magistrate of the Supreme Court, and Minister of State, he, as Del Giudice informs us, played an important role in the compilation of the penal codes of the Kingdom of the Two Sicilies.   "His knowledge of Vico's theories was so thorough that it enabled him to give a highly scientific and systematic turn to the treatment of legal procedure.   His *Procedura penale del Regno delle Due Sicilie* (9 volumes, Naples, 1828–31), by its constructive power and scholarship, is superior to all similar works of Nicolini's time."[48] No less notable, and thoroughly impregnated with Vichianism, is Nicolini's *Questioni di diritto* (Naples, 1834–41).   To Filangieri I have already referred. Vico's inspiration is present also in Francesco Carrara (1805–88), author of the famous *Programma del corso di diritto criminale* (Lucca, 1867–70).[49]   Carrara was the major leader of the so-called classical Italian school of criminal law. The central canon of this school was that of the *tutela giuridica*.   The idea is set forth and elaborated in one of Carrara's essays printed in his *Opuscoli di diritto criminale* (Lucca, 1870) entitled, precisely, "Dottrina fondamentale della tutela giuridica."   The link between Carrara's *tutela* and Vico's concept that bears the same name in the *Diritto universale* is too obvious to escape the attentive reader.   The ideas on criminal law which are expressed in the *Diritto universale* apparently had no effect on Lombroso and the members of his school; but they are found to be fully operative in Lucchini's *Teorica della pena*[50] and especially in Zuppetta's (1810–89) *Corso completo di legislazione penale comparata* (Bologna, 1856).   Zuppetta was an appellate judge in the Republic of San Marino and compiled its *Code of Criminal Law* (1865).   His *Corso completo* stands out because of its technical excellence and the unusual breadth of its intellectual vision.   The comparative approach, so splendidly used by Vico, enables Zuppetta to survey and dominate his extensive subject matter in the entire range of its complex relationships.

---

his *Studi su F. M. Pagano*, ed. L. Firpo (Turin, 1963), where (p. 48) we read: "*La Logica dei probabili* costituisce il superamento del dualismo fra verità oggettiva e certezza, consacrato nel processo penale del diritto comune, contro cui il Pagano proclama il principio che nelle scienze morali ciò che vale è la certezza, la verità oggettiva, cioè *probabile*."

[48] *Storia del diritto italiano*, ed. Pasquale del Giudice (Milan, 1923), II, 337.

[49] See U. Spirito, *Storia del diritto penale italiano* (Rome, 1925); E. Ferri, "F. Carrara e l'evoluzione del diritto penale," *Nuova Antologia*, 1899; E. Brusa, "F. Carrara," *Revue de droit international*, 20 (1889); E. Ferri, "Da C. Beccaria a F. Carrara," *ibid.* and *Archivio giuridico*, 44 (1890); and the memorial volume *Per le onoranze a F. Carrara* (Lucca, 1899).

[50] See also L. Lucchini, *Critica della pena, e svolgimento di alcuni principii intorno al diritto di punire, esposti dal Vico* (1868).

Vico and Contemporary Italian Juridical Literature [51]

The situation of Italian jusphilosophical researches at the beginning of the twentieth century has been delineated with photographic precision by Giorgio del Vecchio. "Legal philosophy," he writes, "had reached a critical point. While traditional trends of a prevalently dogmatic nature still persisted, positivistic tendencies appeared to be preponderant. Strong was the Hegelian current, dogmatic in its form, but empirical (hence akin to positivism) in its substance, while similarly ambiguous was the historicist trend [this was the trend followed by Cavagnari, Carle, Solari], which made frequent references to some solemn formulas of Vico, but which did not really accept its metaphysics and instead was rather close to positivistic relativism." [52] This situation was pre-eminently favorable for an integral re-emphasis upon Vico's conception of the philosophy of law as it was formulated in the *Diritto universale*. Del Vecchio, although recognizing his own debt to Kant's epistemological critique ("although not becoming a slave to it and, instead, striving to complete and surpass it" [53]), interprets his own position and role in Italian jusphilosophy as centering on that integral re-emphasis upon Vico's conception of the essence and task of jurisprudence. "From the contrast between these opposite currents there arose a stimulus for the critical solution of jusphilosophical problems: a solution which would be capable of reconciling the legitimate requirements of historical and positive research with the equally legitimate exigencies of pure speculation, that is, with the awareness of the absolute validity of justice." [54] It is noteworthy that Igino Petrone, whose keen mind was goaded by that same exigency into subtle epistemological speculations (he styles himself "a critical idealist") should take over entirely not only Vico's conception of jusphilosophy but his idea of the *circulus et constantia* (*De uno universi iuris principio et fine uno*, paragraph 6), naturally divesting the latter of its theological terms and changing Vico's God into a Kantian "ontological principle." In his *Problems of the Moral World Meditated by an Idealist*, Petrone writes:

Philosophy follows a circular process: it starts from phenomenology in order to discover the primal ontological principles; and from these it returns to the world of experience in order to understand it better. Philosophy is not only an analysis of first principles but also an intuition of the world in the experimental sense of the term, namely, a scientific understanding both of the phenomenology of the juridical conscience and of the history of legal evolution. However, it remains true that philosophy is a positive intuition of the juridical world only because of its having been an analysis of first principles.

---

[51] R. Orecchia, *Filosofia del diritto in Italia* (Milan, 1967).
[52] Del Vecchio, *Lezioni*, 1948 ed., p. 126.
[53] *Ibid.*
[54] *Ibid.*

It is by now a trite observation that the vivacious reaction against positivism, represented on the one hand by the absolute idealism of Croce and,
on the other, by Gentile's *attualismo*, failed to energize significant activities in
the field of jural philosophy.[55]   And the current explanation for this in-
fertility is, I think, correct.   Croce, for one, utterly expunges the "ideal"
element from jusphilosophy and reduces the whole of the speculative and
material world of law to a mere function of utilitarianism (he out-Benthams
Bentham, so to speak); the formula in which he concentrates his view is
"*riduzione del diritto all'economia*."   Thus, all jural phenomena are categorized
under the caption "economic activities"; there is no room left for meta-
empirical aspects, and from the Vichian dyad (*verum-certum*) the *verum* is
excised.

The situation of Italian jusphilosophy in 1950—it is not much changed
today—was cogently described by Enrico Paresce in his *Report* to the London
Conference on Comparative Law.[56]   The situation was (as the diplomatic
jargon has it) "fluid."   As Paresce summarizes: "The latest developments of
jusphilosophical speculation have, most of them, lost a decided, clear-cut
philosophical orientation.   Many scholars, it may be said, appear weighed
down, as it were, by the multiplicity and breadth of speculative themes, and
engage in informational studies and ample historical reconstructions;
Husserlian phenomenology, ontologism, Marxism, intertwine and at times
contradict each other; but philosophical speculation resorts, in a constructive
sense, to methodological inquiries, which the jurists are compelled to grapple
with."[57]   On the whole, Paresce considers the bewildering luxuriance with
optimism: "The value of dogmatics, the complex problems of interpretation,
are posited by the most thoughtful of these jurists in ways which attest to
genuine philosophical viewpoints.   Philosophy certainly does not consist in
the fruitless cataloguing of problems historically propounded, but in the
birth of ever-new questions.   Thus, Carnelutti and Santi Romano have
given the start to speculations concerning the problems of jural science;
Salvatore Pugliatti, Arturo Carlo Jemolo, Emilio Betti, Esposito, Mortati,
and, more or less, all "practical" jurists, have a doubt to advance, a problem
to tackle and solve."   Paresce concludes by saying that "Italian jural science
is seeking its *ubi consistam*, the solid ground of a philosophical *organon* on
which to rest."[58]

[55] See A. Tozzi, *L'eredità del neo-idealismo italiano* (Florence, 1953).   On Croce's conception of law see G. Fassò, "Croce, Benedetto," *Nuovissimo Digesto italiano* (Turin,
1960), V, 16–18 (full bibliography on pp. 17–18).
[56] Enrico Paresce, "La filosofia del diritto in Italia nel secolo XX," *Rivista internazionale
di filosofia del diritto* (1951), pp. 21–39.   Pietro Piovani, "Die jüngste Rechtsphilosophie
in Italien," *Archiv für Rechts und Wirtschaftsphilosophie*, 29, no. 3 (1951): 361–85; Luigi
Caiani, *La filosofia dei giuristi italiani* (Padua, 1955).
[57] Paresce, "La filosofia del diritto," pp. 38–39.
[58] *Ibid.*, p. 39.

It is in this situation, so variegated, so restlessly mobile, so dynamic, full of vital freedom, tossed by the currents of many doctrines, that the presence of Vico is particularly noticeable. His influence on modern Italian jus-philosophers and jurists is pervasive and ubiquitous. It prompts, supports, cautions, confirms, dissuades, warrants, deflects from illusive paths, dispels falsity, orients, mirrors, and multiplies itself in a variety of kaleidoscopic transformations. Pietro Piovani continues Vico's tradition at the University of Naples,[59] contributing to it a consummate conceptual virtuosity joined with a superb literary elegance. Vichian substance feeds the grave density of Capograssi's thought.[60] It inspires Guido Fassò's researches on the historical and logical genesis of the *Scienza nuova*,[61] Ambrosetti's reflections on rationality and historicity in law,[62] Frosini's meditations on philosophy and jurisprudence;[63] it presides over debates concerning the relationships which dogmatics entertains (or should entertain) with other aspects of the legal prism. Vico is present at the dogged battle that practical jurists and jusphilosophers are fighting over the concept of jural science, over formalism, over the content, articulations, and purposes of legal methodology. The renaissance of jusnaturalism (so characteristic a facet of postwar European jusphilosophy, especially in Italy and Germany) gives new topicality and freshness to the Vichian dialectic between *verum* and *certum*. The impulse Vico had given, in its formative phase, to ethnological jurisprudence, and which, during the late positivistic period (and subsequently), had manifested itself in the complex studies of Giuseppe Mazzarella,[64] propagates its waves into the rich researches of Fulvio Maroi,[65] into the writings of Evaristo

[59] P. Piovani: *Normatività e società* (Naples, 1949); *Momenti di filosofia giuridico-politica italiana* (Milan, 1951); *Il significato del principio di effettività* (Milan, 1953); *La filosofia del diritto come scienza filosofica* (Milan, 1963); *Linee di una filosofia del diritto* (Padua, 1964).

[60] Capograssi's major work is *Il problema della scienza del diritto* (Milano, 1937). After his death (1956) an edition of his *Opere complete* was published by Giuffrè (Milan, 1959). See R. Orecchia, "G. Capograssi: cristiano, filosofo e giurista," *Rivista internazionale di filosofia del diritto*, 34 (1957): 40–55; see also the moving re-evocation by P. Piovani, "Itinerario di G. Capograssi," *Rivista internazionale di filosofia del diritto*, 1956, p. 418.

[61] G. Fassò: "Genesi storica e genesi logica della filosofia della Scienza nuova," *Rivista internazionale di filosofia del diritto*, 1948, pp. 319–36; *I "quattro autori" del Vico* (Milan: Giuffrè, 1949); *La storia come esperienza giuridica* (Milan: Giuffrè, 1953) (in the publications of the *Seminario giuridico* of the University of Bologna, vol. 16).

[62] Giovanni Ambrosetti, *Razionalità e storicità del diritto* (Milan, 1953).

[63] V. Frosini: *La struttura del diritto* (Milan, 1962); "Genesi ideale e storica della filosofia del diritto nel pensiero vichiano," *Annali del Seminario Giuridico, Università di Catania*, 1942.

[64] G. Mazzarella: *Gli elementi irriduttibili dei sistemi giuridici* (Catania, 1918–20); *Studi di etnologia giuridica*, 16 vols. (Catania, 1903–30); *Les types sociaux et le droit* (Paris, 1908); *Le unità elementari dei sistemi giuridici* (Messina, 1922).

[65] F. Maroi, *Scritti giuridici*, 2 vols. (Milan: Giuffrè, 1956).

Carusi,[66] Mario Sarfatti,[67] T. Ascarelli,[68] and F. Messineo. Special mono-graphs and studies, like those of Cantone[69] and Bellofiore,[70] bring out Vico's message as a jural philosopher. Bobbio,[71] Ascoli,[72] and Semerari,[73] deter-mine Vico's place in the trajectory of eighteenth-century thought. A. Passerin d'Entrèves' substantial pages contribute to the better evaluation of Vico's position in the "cadre" of jusnaturalism.[74] In his books on legal philosophy, Perticone follows Vico's footprints in his analysis of justice, as does Olgiati, the latter to a more marked extent.[75] Frosini, one of the most agile and original of Italian jusphilosophers, in subtle analyses underscores Vico's topicality and illustrates the pertinence and profundity of some of his intuitions.[76] C. Ghisalberti, B. di Giovanni, N. Badaloni, and Giuliana d'Amelio, throw floodlights on the immediate background of Vico's legal historicism. Paolo Rossi draws the major outlines of the new Vichian research. While Piazzese and Graneris sift the problems of the *certum*, Vassalli, in the wake of a lively polemic between Betti and his opponents, grapples with the complex question of the relationship between dogmatics and legal history. Enrico Paresce (at the present time perhaps the finest connoisseur of legal dogmatics) pursues, along lines analogous to those followed by Perticone, the meta-empirical genesis of law. In the very title of Cajani's book *Value Judgments in Legal Interpretation* (Padua, 1954) we recognize Vico's suggestions. As an inspirational motto, Cajani's book could wear Vico's "*autoritas pars rationis,*" with the proviso that the title of his volume would be understood in inverted order: that is, as *ratio pars auctoritatis.*

The problems so brilliantly debated by Bagolini, Cesarini Sforza, Leone, and Piovani, concerning the relations among dogmatics (or what may be

---

[66] E. Carusi, "Folkloristica giuridica e storia del diritto," *Rivista di storia del diritto italiano*, 2 (1929): 129ff.

[67] M. Sarfatti, *Introduzione allo studio del diritto comparato* (Milan, 1952).

[68] T. Ascarelli, *Studi di diritto comparato* (Milan, 1952).

[69] C. Cantone, *Il concetto filosofico del diritto in G. B. Vico* (Mazara del Vallo, 1952).

[70] L. Bellofiore, *La dottrina del diritto naturale in Vico* (Milan, 1954); see the review of this monograph by B. de Giovanni in *Rivista internazionale di filosofia del diritto*, 1954, pp. 456–58. Bellofiore gives a clever analysis of the relationship between *verum* and *certum* on pp. 15, 44, 54ff., of his work.

[71] N. Bobbio, *Il diritto naturale nel secolo XVIII* (Turin: Giappichelli, n.d.).

[72] Max Ascoli, *Saggi vichiani* (Rome, 1928). Ascoli grasps and expounds with incisive exactness Vico's position within the currents of eighteenth-century jusnaturalism.

[73] G. Semerari, *Storicismo critico* (Bari, 1960).

[74] A. Passerin d'Entrèves, *Natural Law: An Introduction to Legal Philosophy* (London, 1951); *idem*, *Natural Law: An Historical Survey* (New York, 1965).

[75] See F. Olgiati, *Il concetto di giuridicità nella scienza moderna del diritto*, 2d ed. (Milan, 1950).

[76] V. Frosini, "Vico e la giurisprudenza," in his *Filosofia e giurisprudenza* (Catania, 1955).

called Vico's "systematicity"), the general theory of law, and jural science, are "à l'enseigne de Vico." And so, in a way, are the discerning explorations of Bobbio in the domain of juridical positivism (Vico's *certum*). Even the recently manifested turn toward modern American realism, documented by a couple of excellently crafted Italian monographs, is a sign of the continuing vitality, in Italy's jusphilosophical thought, of Vico's interest in the "art of applying law to facts." The problems of juridical experience (again, the *certum*, conceived in the complete expansion of its range) are skillfully analyzed by Capograssi, Renato Treves, and Pietro Piovani. In legal history, Vico's influence seems to be less vigorous,[77] but one perceives Vichianism at work in the attempts of Giuliana d'Amelio, Opocher, Mosco, and Cassandro to unravel the coils and straighten the tangles of the difficult problems connected with legal historiography, while the resumption of interest in juridical sociology, attested to by the researches of Franco Leonardi and Giuseppina Nirchio, are clearly oriented along Vichian directives.[78]

---

[77] G. Graneris, "Il diritto vero e il diritto certo," *Rivista di filosofia neoscolastica*, 1945, pp. 244ff.

[78] For this trend see R. Treves, "La sociologia giuridica in Italia e i suoi possibili sviluppi," *Quaderni di sociologia*, no. 3 (1962): 10; and Franco Leonardi, "Sociologia giuridica e teoria generale del diritto," *Rivista internazionale di filosofia del diritto*, 1951, pp. 724–52; Giuseppina Nirchio, *Introduzione alla sociologia giuridica* (Palermo, 1957); see also the substantial treatment of this topic by B. Bruni Roccia, entitled "Sociologia e scienza comparata del diritto," *Rivista trimestrale di diritto e procedura civile*, 16 (1962): 260–79.

Giorgio Tagliacozzo

ECONOMIC
VICHIANISM:
Vico, Galiani, Croce—
Economics,
Economic Liberalism

1. As every reader of the *New Science* knows, Vico's book contains a section on "poetic economy"—the economy of the "age of heroes." This was the first study of such a topic ever conceived. Vico also dealt with some socio-economic problems of later stages of social evolution. In none of his works, however, did he pay specific attention to problems of economics *stricto sensu*. In spite of this, studies of (*a*) the set of direct and indirect inferences that can be drawn from the principles of the *New Science* in the economic field—what we might call economic Vichianism—and (*b*) the relationship or analogy, if any, of economic Vichianism to later economic theories or viewpoints, and its place in the history of economics, are justifiable and very interesting. Let us remember with Professor Fisch[1] that "just as Euclid's Elements as a system is susceptible of indefinite further development without addition or change in the definitions, axioms, or postulates, so Vico's new science is susceptible of indefinite further development without change in its principles."

2. In order to draw inferences in any field from the principles of the *New Science*, a person must previously have singled out such principles and have selected those most relevant to his field, be it philosophy, anthropology, psychology, economics, or any other. However, anyone interested in economic Vichianism need not single out the principles of the *New Science* by himself, or select those most relevant to economics, or even draw basic inferences from them concerning such problems as value, interest, or monetary and economic policy; for, as we hope this essay will demonstrate, these tasks have been performed already, perhaps unsurpassably. The scholar who accomplished this feat a few years after Vico's death—developing a full-blown economic viewpoint which is still worthy of attention—was Ferdinando Galiani.[2] Such being the case, our basic tasks in this essay will

[1] Max H. Fisch, Introduction to *The New Science of Giambattista Vico*, trans. Thomas G. Bergin and Max H. Fisch (New York: Doubleday, 1961), p. xlii; all quotations from the *New Science* in this essay, as well as page numbers, refer to excerpts from this edition.

[2] On Galiani's life, personality, and work see Giorgio Tagliacozzo, ed., *Economisti napoletani dei sec. XVII e XVIII* (Bologna: Cappelli, 1937), Introduction, pp. xvi–xx, and

be: (a) to single out those principles of the New Science which are the foundations of Galiani's economic thought; (b) to point out the inferences Galiani drew from those principles and, of course, to recall his rich and original elaborations upon them; (c) to relate the influence of Galiani's thought on, or analogy to, later theories; (d) more generally, to define the place of the economic viewpoint stemming from Vico and creatively developed by Galiani—Economic Vichianism—within the history of economic thought. A prerequisite for the performance of task (d), however, is a comparison between Galiani's and Benedetto Croce's economic ideas, and between economic Vichianism and economic liberalism. The foregoing explains the title of this essay and its subtitle. For the sake of brevity there will be some overlapping in the treatment of these topics.

3. There are singular analogies to be drawn between Vico's discussion of the principles of the New Science and Galiani's discussion of the principles of economic value. These may be condensed as follows:

a. Vico devoted Book I of the New Science to the "Establishment of Principles." Galiani opened his Della moneta with a "Declaration of the Principles from Which the Value of All Things Originates." [3]

b. In Vico's New Science, principle, in addition to its relatively abstract scientific definition, has the etymological meaning of "beginning," a relatively concrete genetic connotation. [4] Something similar can be said about principles in Galiani.

c. Before putting forth his principle that "the world of civil society has certainly been made by men" and that "its principles are therefore to be found within the modifications of our own human mind," [5] Vico blamed the "conceit of the nations, each believing itself to have been the first in the world," for leaving us "no hope of getting the principles of our science from the philologians," and the "conceit of the scholars, who will have it that what they know must have been eminently understood from the beginning of the world," for making us "despair of getting them from the philosophers," so that "for purposes of this inquiry, we must reckon as if there

---

Note, pp. xl–lxviii. This book also contains a bibliography on Galiani (pp. lxv–lxvi) and large excerpts from his Della moneta (pp. 93–214) and Dialogues sur le commerce des blés (pp. 217–63). All quotations from Galiani's works in this essay, as well as the page numbers, refer to excerpts included in the above volume. An extensive bibliography on Galiani has recently been compiled by Walter Braeuer ("Galiani, Ferdinando," in Handwörterbuch der Staatswissenschaften [Stuttgart: G. Fischer, 1965], IV, 200–201); see also Herbert Dieckman and Philip Koch, "The Autograph Manuscript of Galiani's Dialogues sur le commerce des blés," Harvard Library Bulletin, 9, no. 1 (Winter, 1955): 110–18.

[3] Della moneta, pp. 94ff. The words quoted in the text appear in the title of bk. I, chap. II.

[4] See Bergin and Fisch, New Science, p. xxii.

[5] Ibid., par. 331, pp. 52–53.

were no books in the world."[6]   Elsewhere Vico lashed out at the philologians for accepting "with an excess of good faith the view that in the vulgar
languages meanings were fixed by convention."[7]   He also stated that the
natural-law theorists failed in what they attempted, and they failed "by
beginning in the middle; that is, with the latest times of the civilized nations,
... from which the philosophers emerged and rose to meditation of a
perfect idea of justice," instead of "beginning the treatment of law [as he
does] ... at this most ancient point of all times. ..."[8] Finally, Vico censured
the viewpoint of the Enlightenment, according to which laws, names, family
coats of arms, medals, money, language, and writing, are created by convention, substituting for it his concept that, on the contrary, these are natural
creations of the human mind.[9]   Analogous to all this, Galiani on two
occasions[10]—that is, before presenting his basic principles on value in general
and on the value of precious metals in particular—denounced the "scholars"
(*saggi*), according to whom the value of precious metals is determined by
convention.   "How ridiculous," he said on the second of these occasions,
"are those who claim that men all gathered at one time and agreed to use
those metals, by themselves useless, as money, thereby endowing them with
value.   Where are these congresses, these agreements [*convenzioni*] of all
mankind? ..." His answer, which followed immediately, was: "One must
indeed say that, when all men share in a given sentiment and keep that
sentiment for many centuries, this is not the result of a decision made at
meetings held beside the Tower of Babel or the Ark; rather, it is attributable
to the dispositions of our souls and to the intrinsic qualities of things, because
these, indeed, are always the same and always will be."[11]   This passage—the
starting point of Galiani's explanation of the value of precious metals—is
closely related to a combination of the Vichian statements mentioned above.
Furthermore—as Nicolini was the first to point out in 1918[12]—it is a paraphrase of two Vichian axioms: "Uniform ideas originating among entire
peoples unknown to each other must have a common ground of truth";[13]
and "The nature of institutions is nothing but their coming into being

[6] *Ibid.*, par. 330, p. 52.
[7] *Ibid.*, par. 444, p. 104.
[8] *Ibid.*, pars. 394 and 398, p. 83.
[9] *Ibid.*, par. 434, p. 100 and *passim*.
[10] *Della moneta*, pp. 94–95 and 125–26.
[11] *Ibid.*, pp. 125–26. Galiani (*ibid.*, p. 124) also explains in an obviously Vichian vein
that, "since things have very small and invisible beginnings, a slow growth, an irresistible
power of forging ahead (because they are sustained by nature itself, which is ordained to
give them motion), man cannot either perceive their beginnings or stop their growth, or
undo them, once they are established."
[12] Fausto Nicolini, "G. B. Vico e F. Galiani," *Giornale storico della letteratura italiana*,
71 (1918): 159; see also Ferdinando Galiani, *Della moneta*, ed. F. Nicolini (Bari: Laterza,
1915), Note, p. 368.
[13] *New Science*, par. 144, p. 22.

(*nascimento*) at certain times and in certain guises. Whenever the time and guise are thus and so, such and not otherwise are the institutions that come into being."[14]

d. Galiani's view that the value of money stems from a natural relationship between "the dispositions of our souls" (that is, the natural inclinations of the human mind) and the "intrinsic qualities" of precious metals is, as he points out, only one instance of a natural relationship between the human mind and a particular type of thing. Another of the several instances mentioned by Galiani is the natural feeling of men for the "things capable of bestowing honor upon their owner."[15] These Galianean views are reminiscent of Vico's statement that ". . . all nations, barbarous as well as civilized, though separately founded because remote from each other in time and space, keep these three human customs: all have some religion, all contract solemn marriages, all bury their dead."[16]

e. Before dealing with any particular instance of a natural relationship of the type indicated, however, Galiani analyzed the natural relationship existing between the human mind and "things" in general. This is his value theory proper. "Any edifice erected on these bases" [that is, on the natural inclinations of the human mind in their relationship with 'things']," Galiani says, "will be durable and eternal."[17] This statement, *mutatis mutandis,* is reminiscent of the following words from Vico: "Now since this world has been made by men, let us see in what institutions all men agree and always have agreed. For these institutions will be able to give us the universal and eternal principles . . . on which all nations were founded and still preserve themselves";[18] "Doctrines must take their beginning from that of the matters of which they treat"; "This axiom . . . is universally used in all the matters which are herein discussed."[19]

4. Galiani's value theory proper, based on *utility* and *scarcity,* is well known to, and has been highly praised by, historians of economics. Therefore, we shall dispense with summarizing it here. The following statements, which appeared after the present writer's publication of a note on Galiani's economic theory,[20] will be sufficient to recall the main reasons for such praise:

a. Galiani developed an economic theory based entirely on subjective estimation. The outlines of his system are still valid today.[21]

---

[14] *Ibid.,* par. 147, p. 22. On the genetic meaning of "nature" in the *New Science* see *ibid.,* p. xxii. Similar remarks would apply to Galiani (see n. 11 above).

[15] *Della moneta,* p. 99.

[16] *New Science,* par. 333, p. 53.

[17] *Della moneta,* p. 96.

[18] *New Science,* par. 332, p. 53.

[19] *Ibid.,* pars. 314 and 315, p. 49.

[20] Tagliacozzo, *Economisti napoletani,* pp. xl–lxviii.

[21] Emil Kauder, "Genesis of Marginal Utility Theory," *Economic Journal,* 63 (September, 1953): 645.

b. Value in use, according to Smith, is a precondition of exchange value. But value in use does not directly constitute value in exchange or price. This is a crucial point in the history of economic theory. Smith observed what was later called the "economic paradox," i.e. that the most useful things, such as bread, are cheap, while things comparatively less useful, such as diamonds, are expensive. . . . The degree of usefulness, however, will not determine price; to do so will be left to the cost of production under the pressure of competition. It remained for the so-called modern or subjective theory of value, developed one hundred years later, to resolve the economic paradox by relating exchange value and price to the degree of value in use. The procedure for doing this had already been suggested by Galiani but was overlooked by Smith.[22]

c. Galiani, the critic of the physiocrats, had impressed Turgot; but his real successor, much older than himself, was the abbé and philosopher Étienne Bonnot de Condillac. . . . Condillac restated the doctrine of Galiani. . . .[23]

d. Galiani anticipated by one hundred years two important schools of thought—the neo-classical and the historical.[24]

e. Anyone who today reads Gossen, Jevons, Menger or Marshall is bound to recall Galiani's penetrating views. . . .[25]

f. [Galiani was] one of the ablest minds that ever became active in our field.[26]

g. He [Galiani] displayed sure-footed mastery of analytic procedure and, in particular, neatness in his carefully defined conceptual constructions to a degree that would have rendered superfluous all the nineteenth century squabbles—and misunderstandings—on the subject of value had the parties to these squabbles first studied his text, *Della Moneta,* 1751.[27]

h. . . . It was the "subjective" or "utility" theory of price that had the wind until the influence of the *Wealth of Nations*—and especially Ricardo's *Principles*—asserted itself. Even after 1776, that theory prevailed on the Continent, and there is an unbroken line of development between Galiani and J. B. Say. . . . Beccaria, Turgot, Verri, Condillac, and many minor lights contributed to establishing it more and more firmly.[28]

i. Galiani's contemporaries appreciated the new vistas which he opened. The French economist and statesman, Anne Robert Turgot, in an unfinished paper, "Valeurs and Monnaies," developed a price theory along Galiani's lines.[29]

---

[22] Eduard Heimann, *History of Economic Doctrines* (New York: Oxford University Press, 1945), pp. 67–68.

[23] *Ibid.,* pp. 108–9.

[24] *Ibid.,* p. 62.

[25] Luigi Einaudi, "Galiani economista," in *Rendiconti: Classe di scienze morali, storiche e filologiche,* Accademia Nazionale dei Lincei, ser. VIII, vol. IV, fasc. 3–4 (Rome, 1949), p. 123; see also *idem,* "Einaudi on Galiani" (partial English translation of the above), in Henry W. Spiegel, ed., *The Development of Economic Thought* (New York: John Wiley, 1952), p. 64.

[26] Joseph A. Schumpeter, *History of Economic Analysis* (New York: Oxford University Press, 1954), p. 292.

[27] *Ibid.,* pp. 300–1.

[28] *Ibid.,* p. 302.

[29] Emil Kauder, *A History of Marginal Utility Theory* (Princeton: Princeton University

j. With Galiani and Turgot subjective valuation becomes the keystone for a system of thinking. This theory had to be defended against the classical system which was based on labor costs. The defense of Galiani, his followers, and his friends was taken over by Condillac.[30]

k. Due to Adam Smith the Galiani school never went beyond the very promising start indicated in Turgot's unfinished work. Adam Smith had an unfortunate influence on the further development of the value explanation. . . .[31]

l. Most works which [Menger] perused for the publication of his *Principles* are quoted in two lengthy footnotes which read like a history of the value-in-use theories from Aristotle to Albert Schäffle. He examined, but not too carefully, Montanari, Galiani, Turgot, and Condillac. He dismissed the achievement of the earlier French and Italian writers with the remark that the German economists offer a more profound treatment of the subject.[32]

5. Neither the analogies that exist between Vico's and Galiani's principles nor the lavish praise bestowed upon Galiani's value theory by so many economists, however, specifically answers the fundamental questions concerning the extent of Vico's influence on: (*a*) Galiani's value theory proper, beyond its "principles"; (*b*) his other achievements in technical economic theory (that is, in the theory of *alzamento*, the theory of interest, etc.); (*c*) Galiani's views on applied economics and methodology of economics. What is to be said about that influence?

Schumpeter attempted an answer to question (*a*) when he said: "It must not be forgotten that the theory [of value] he developed was really that of the scholastics." And, he added: "Nicolini . . . in his *Note* to his edition of Galiani's *Della Moneta* (1915), . . . being a philosopher, . . . is inclined to exaggerate the dependence [of Galiani upon Vico], which amounted to little, so far as technical economic theory is concerned."[33]

These remarks deserve close consideration. Our viewpoint on the issues they involve will emerge in the following pages and in the conclusions of this essay. For the time being we shall simply add that, if the first of the

---

Press, 1965), p. 25. Turgot's paper "Valeurs et Monnaies" was written in 1769 (Kauder's "1796" is a misprint; Turgot died in 1781). On this and on the Galiani-Turgot-Condillac subjective value theory see Tagliacozzo, *Economisti napoletani*, pp. xlvi–xlvii.

[30] Kauder, *Marginal Utility Theory*, p. 27.

[31] *Ibid.*, p. 28.

[32] *Ibid.*, p. 83. Kauder refers to Carl Menger's *Principles of Economics*, first published in 1871 (English ed. [Glencoe, Ill: The Free Press, 1950], app. D, pp. 295ff.). Tagliacozzo (*Economisti napoletani*, p. xlviii) has demonstrated that Menger's statement is unjustified and misleading. Actually, according to F. H. von Hayek ("Carl Menger," *Economica*, November, 1934, p. 955) and to Tagliacozzo (*Economisti napoletani*, p. xlviii), Carl Menger owed to the Galiani-Turgot-Condillac subjective value theory much more than is generally realized.

[33] Schumpeter, *Economic Analysis*, p. 300, n.

above remarks was meant to imply, as it probably was, that the theory of the Scholastics was the *only* foundation of Galiani's modern construction, and that Galiani's construction on that weak basis was made possible *only* by his genius as an economist—that is, independently of Vico's influence—then in our opinion it does not go nearly far enough. As for the second remark, perhaps we should point out that, in his book, Schumpeter discussed only Galiani's value theory, although he added a few remarks on Galiani's economic methodology and applied economics. He did not mention, or elaborate upon, Galiani's other achievements in technical economic theory, such as his theory of the rate of interest. This means that Schumpeter's judgment, according to which Galiani's dependence on Vico "amounted to little," is based singularly on value theory *stricto sensu*.

6. We shall now make some remarks related to questions (*a*) and (*b*) in section 5 above. Question (*c*) will be dealt with in sections 7 and 8.

a. Nothing comparable to Galiani's typically Vichian "principles from which the value of all things originates" (see section 3[*a*]) can be found in any of his scholastic predecessors. Yet these "principles" are not just a fascinating reminder of Galiani's familiarity with the *New Science* or a tantalizing but unnecessary springboard for Galiani's value theory. As we hope to demonstrate, they are—in combination with another general statement related to them, which will be discussed below in (*d*) and (*e*)—the heart and blood of his value theory and the core and point of departure of his other achievements in technical economic theory, as well as of his applied economics and methodology of economics.

b. It might be observed, however, that the above-mentioned principles of value, with all their depth and beauty, were not sufficiently specific to lead necessarily to the sophisticated value theory elaborated by Galiani and that, therefore, this theory is basically a product of the latter's genius. At first glance, these two points appear to be fairly well justified; and, if Galiani's value theory were his only great theoretical achievement, and if that achievement were independent of the rest of his thought, they might even be conceded.

c. However, this is not the case. Galiani's "other" great achievements in technical economic theory (see [*f*], [*g*], and [*h*] below) are by no means few. Furthermore, these achievements, together with his value theory, form a unitary system which includes a theory of applied economics and one of economic methodology. The factor that, taken with the principles of value, unifies this system is the fundamental idea, derived from Vico, quoted in (*d*) below. Hence, even though we must acknowledge Galiani's genius in formulating his value theory, we must add that such a theory—a "quantum jump" compared to the theories of his predecessors—was made up of the same basic substance as his other achievements in technical economic theory, that is, of the same Vichian frame of mind, the same set of recollections, the same enthusiasm, generated by the *New Science*. In other words, Galiani's value theory was born and thrived within the framework of his way of thinking, which had been shaped at a very early age by the *New Science* and which cannot be fully explained independently of it.

d. The fundamental idea derived from Vico is the following: "Of the many errors by which our mind is beset and among which it perpetually wanders, very few would be left if it were possible to make people avoid those which stem from relative words taken in an absolute sense." [34] This statement—endowed with an almost Pirandellian flavor—is actually a re-affirmation, in a more general and more profound Vichian key, of the Galianean "principles from which the value of all things originates." It is more profound, we might explain, because, as Pagliaro points out, "Within the picture of the *New Science* the theory of language occupies a central place, or rather it is the nucleus around which the solid, or perhaps grandiosely baroque, edifice of Vico's thought has coherently, even though not always organically, developed." [35] Many affinities between Galiani's statement and Vico's specific formulation of certain basic tenets of the *New Science* (for example, its semantic emphasis, its diachronic conception and structure, etc.) could, of course, be mentioned as well.

e. Galiani's statement quoted in (*d*) is immediately followed by these words:

> If this [making people avoid the errors which stem from relative words taken in an absolute sense] were possible, all this third book would have been omitted because all that has been written by the scholars and decreed by the rulers concerning the value of money in most cases has been done without account being taken of the fact that value is a word expressing a relationship. What will shortly be said about the *alzamento*—that is, whether it is profitable or not—would not have been so inconsistently dealt with if it had only been kept in mind that utility is relative. [36]

This not only underlines the importance attached by Galiani to the statement cited in (*d*); it also confirms the strict relationship that existed in his mind between that statement and his relativistic conception and treatment of the problems of value in general and of the value of money in particular. (Galiani's discussion of the *alzamento* is part of the latter; see [*f*] below.) However, Galiani could have gone even further in his remarks than he did. His awareness of the tendency of the human mind to take "relative words . . . in an absolute sense," coupled with his views that "value is a word expressing a relationship" and that "utility is relative," is the basis not only

[34] *Della moneta*, p. 155.
[35] Antonino Pagliaro, "La dottrina linguistica di G. B. Vico," in *Memorie: Classe di scienze morali, storiche e filologiche*, Accademia Nazionale dei Lincei, ser. VIII, vol. VIII, fasc. 6 (Rome, 1959), p. 380.
[36] *Della moneta*, p. 155.

of his theory of the *alzamento* but also of his theory of the rate of interest and that of the rate of exchange[37] (see [g]), as well as of his views on applied economics and economic methodology (see sections [7], [8], and [9]).

f. Alzamento was the word, in Galiani's time, for what we now call devaluation. It was caused by the artificial reduction of the precious-metal content of a given currency by different means, such as by shearing or new minting. Following that reduction, prices tended to rise, and the purchasing power of the currency was apt to shrink. We shall not elaborate on Galiani's sophisticated discussion of the consequences of the *alzamento*.[38] For our purposes it will be sufficient to recall Galiani's definition of it: "a gain which the prince and the state derive from the slowness with which people change their connection of ideas concerning the prices of goods and money."[39]   In other words, as Galiani puts it, the *alzamento* "does not produce any change of things, but only of words";[40] "the prices of things, in order to remain the same in fact, must change as to the words."[41]   Or, if the change of the nominal prices "occurred the same day on which the *alzamento* took place, and occurred proportionally and uniformly throughout the market, the *alzamento* would have no consequence whatever."[42]   To sum up: The *alzamento* brings about its consequences because of the tendency of the human mind to take relative words in an absolute sense (or, we might say, because of the tendency of the human mind to alter its understanding of things more slowly than circumstances require).   Galiani's theory of devaluation, based on Vichian principles, is, of course, as sound today as it was yesterday.

g. According to Galiani, the rate of interest and the rate of exchange are not in the nature of unearned surpluses, but serve as means to accomplish equality in exchange—means used by the contracting parties with a view to equalizing values that are numerically equal but that are separated by time or space.[43]   A creditor who is afraid that the principal might not be repaid will suffer from palpitations of the heart.   But, "if someone suffers from palpitations of the heart, this is painful; hence it is only proper to pay for it. What is known as reward for pain is—if it is legitimate—nothing but the price for palpitations of the heart."[44]   Galiani further explains that a "loan," in substance, is "the surrender of a thing, with the proviso that an equivalent thing is to be returned, not more."[45]   However, what is *equivalent*?   The usual definitions [based on "relative words . . . taken in an absolute sense"]

---

[37] Our statement is confirmed *ad abundantiam* by Galiani's own words.   On p. 95 of *Della moneta* he emphasizes the relationship that exists between the "dispositions of the human mind" and the value of money, *alzamento*, interest rate, etc.

[38] Einaudi has devoted several fascinating pages to Galiani's discussion of *alzamento*; see *Galiani economista*, pp. 139–48.   In Spiegel, *Development of Economic Thought*, those pages have not been translated.

[39] *Della moneta*, p. 165.   [40] *Ibid.*, p. 166.   [41] *Ibid.*

[42] *Ibid.*   [43] *Ibid.*, p. 209.   [44] *Ibid.*, p. 211.

[45] *Ibid.*

relate equivalence to material, objective circumstances—for example, to "weight or similarity of form"[46]—and thus to the identity of the thing which is to be surrendered and returned (number of units of money, etc.). But those who adopt such definitions "understand little of human activities,"[47] for value is not an objective characteristic of goods; it is "the relationship of goods to our needs. Goods are equivalent when they provide equal convenience to the person with reference to whom they are said to be equivalent."[48] To sum up, Galiani's theory of interest is also an application of his general principle that value is a relationship and that relative words should not be taken as absolutes.

The theory of interest is, of course, one of the most important theories in the science of economics. It has been one of the latest, however, to receive adequate treatment by economists. According to Böhm-Bawerk—the founder of the modern viewpoint—the "germ" of his own theory can be found in Galiani (1750), Turgot (1769), then in Rae (1834), and later in Jevons (1871).[49] In an analysis of Böhm-Bawerk's elaboration of the above view,[50] however, the present writer pointed out that (1) Böhm-Bawerk acknowledged substantially Galiani's superiority over the other forerunners; (2) Menger, the founder of the Austrian school of economics, never achieved a theory of interest comparable to Galiani's; (3) Irving Fisher's viewpoint on interest was similar to that of Galiani and of Böhm-Bawerk. This analysis has been confirmed by Einaudi[51] and by Kauder.[52] However, while the chorus in praise of Galiani is certainly justified, one should not forget that such an achievement would have been impossible without those Vichian principles mentioned in (d) and (e).

7. Like his achievements in technical economic theory, Galiani's views on applied economics and the methodology of economics, expressed in the *Dialogues sur le commerce des blés*, are a series of variations on, or applications of, the Vichian principles that we mentioned in sections 6(d) and (e). At the same time, Galiani's views on methodology and applied economics bear a strong resemblance to much later, and even to contemporary, viewpoints on the same subjects. We shall explain both of these statements and point out their combined significance in sections 8 and 9. As background for that

---

[46] *Ibid.*
[47] *Ibid.*
[48] *Ibid.*
[49] See Tagliacozzo, *Economisti napoletani*, pp. xlix–l, which also contains bibliographical references.
[50] *Ibid.*
[51] Einaudi, "Galiani economista," p. 138; see also Spiegel, *Development of Economic Thought*, p. 80.
[52] *Marginal Utility Theory*, p. 24.

discussion, however, it is necessary to present here several quotations or statements referring to Galiani's views.

a. Galiani's remarks in *Della moneta* on the tendency of the human mind to take "relative words . . . in an absolute sense" and on the fact that "utility is relative," become, in his *Dialogues*, a criticism of the tendency of the "laissez-faire" economists of the physiocratic group to draw practical conclusions from abstract principles.[53]

b. The *Dialogues* are thus a plea for a relativistic judgment of economic matters, based on a realistic consideration of the "circumstances" and the "ends."[54]

c. As far as "circumstances" are concerned, Galiani points out that men in general, and statesmen in particular, have a tendency always to follow the same principles without realizing that circumstances are constantly changing.[55] For example, the physiocrats proclaim: "Laissez-faire; no hindrances, no prohibitions."[56] To which Galiani replies: "I am neither for nor against the export of wheat. . . . I am for nothing. . . . I am for people not to reason falsely. . . . The export of common sense is the only one which exasperates me."[57] In other words, Galiani is against abstract principles and metaphysical preconceptions. He is for the correct use of "reason."

d. Reason, however, cannot draw correct inferences directly from metaphysical generalizations. Yet this is what the physiocrats were doing. "They posit big principles that no one is supposed to oppugn; they draw their inferences boldly, sharply, right and left, without confronting obstacles. . . ."[58] Reason brings good results only when it elaborates upon sound theoretical assumptions and corrects and reformulates them in order to take into account the changing circumstances of time and place. Sound theoretical assumptions, according to Galiani, can and should be made. They are those arising from man's proper nature: "Let us establish principles that are derived from the nature of things themselves. What is man? What is the relationship between man and his food? Let us then apply these principles to time, place, circumstances. Which is the kingdom with which we are concerned? What is the situation? What are the mores, the opinions, the opportunities that are open, the risks to be avoided? Knowing all this, we may arrive at a decision."[59]

e. Human nature in Galiani's *Dialogues*, as well as in *Della moneta*, is not an abstract concept similar to the utilitarian and materialistic *homo oeconomicus* of so many generations of economists. Human nature for Galiani corresponds to man in his reality and can include any and all the "dispositions of

---

[53] See Tagliacozzo, *Economisti napoletani*, p. lii.
[54] *Ibid.*
[55] *Dialogues*, p. 219.
[56] *Ibid.*, p. 222.   [57] *Ibid.*, p. 224.   [58] *Ibid.*, pp. 236–37.
[59] *Ibid.*, pp. 231–32.

the human soul." This is explicitly stated in the *Dialogues* as follows: "Do you know what the mistake of your writers [the physiocrats] consists of—a mistake of which they have never become aware, but which is the cause of all others? It consists in the belief that men always consume the same quantity of food."[60] A few lines before, Galiani had explained that different groups of people live a different life, have different economic needs, behave differently toward spending or saving their money, etc.[61] What he had meant to say was substantially that men have different "ends" and that, therefore, "wealth" is not an absolute but a relative word and should not be implicitly or explicitly identified with given—material—things, as if the latter were the only possible aim of men.

f. What has been said about "wealth" relative to individuals could be repeated in regard to societies and states. For instance, the economic policy concerning grain may be directed toward different aims: commercial, political, military, etc.[62] As Einaudi has pointed out, wheat, according to Galiani, in certain circumstances could represent "veritable war ammunition."[63]

g. If economists consider man in his full nature and wealth, consequently, as a relative concept to be judged according to individual aims, with no moral or utilitarian implications involved,[64] then economics becomes a "science of man's behavior," a study of relationships between means and ends, a "science of administration."[65] According to Galiani, "it is absolutely the same science as that of pilotage and of the steering of a ship: the end is the route; the means are the maneuvers that it is necessary to make."[66]

8. The relationship between Galiani's views on applied economics and on the methodology of economics, as presented in the *Dialogues*, and the main themes, derived from Vico, that form the basis of *Della moneta*, is so evident as to require only a few words of comment.

a. A general remark applying to most of the above highlights is one concerning the striking parallelism that exists between Vico's frontal attack against Cartesianism and the criticism of the natural-law theorists, and Galiani's polemic against the physiocrats—the representatives, in the field of

[60] *Ibid.*, p. 235.
[61] *Ibid.*
[62] *Ibid.*, p. 237.
[63] Einaudi, "Galiani economista," p. 138; see also Spiegel, *Development of Economic Thought*, p. 81.
[64] Long before writing the *Dialogues*, Galiani had, in *Della moneta* (p. 99), rebuked those who "blame our nature for giving us this or that disposition of the soul." And he had added: "we have received that disposition [from nature], we cannot do away with it . . . and we cannot and should not submit it to anybody's judgment."
[65] *Dialogues*, p. 259.
[66] *Ibid.*

economics, of the basic viewpoint of rationalism and of the Enlightenment. As a matter of fact, just as Vico was one of the first and most authoritative critics of Cartesianism, so Galiani was the first and—until 1926, when John Maynard Keynes's *The End of Laissez-Faire* [67] appeared—the most forceful critic of "laissez-faire."

b. What has been said in sections 7(*e*), (*f*), and (*g*) seems somehow to be related to Vico's defense of passions, in which he dismisses "from the school of our Science the Stoics, who seek to mortify the senses, and Epicureans, who make them the criterion. . . . For both deny providence." [68]

9. A few remarks now are in order on the relationship between the Galianean viewpoint on applied economics and the methodology of economics, and much later and even contemporary theories on the same subjects.

a. From the end of the seventeenth century—or, more precisely, from about 1750—until a few decades ago economic thought was dominated by the "laissez-faire" maxim. In 1926 Keynes wrote in his *The End of Laissez-Faire*: "We do not dance even yet to a new tune. But a change is in the air." [69] Galiani had danced to that tune over one hundred and fifty years before.

b. The only important exception to the dominance of "laissez-faire" in economics during the period between Galiani and Keynes is the one represented by the German historical school and related German trends, which had their early roots in the philosophy of Fichte, Müller and Hegel.[70] Einaudi drew a parallel between Galiani and the historical school when he wrote: "Anyone who turns the pages of Roscher, Hildebrand and Knies is bound to recall Galiani's *Dialogues sur le commerce des blés*, where he insists that those who develop theories should keep in mind the specific circumstances of time and place." [71] Similarly, Schumpeter wrote: "[Galiani] was the one eighteenth-century economist who ever insisted on the variability of man and on the relativity, to time and to place, of all policies; the one who was free from the paralysing belief—that then crept over the intellectual life of Europe—in practical principles that claim universal validity." [72] In our opinion, however, neither Einaudi nor Schumpeter went far enough in his praise of Galiani from this standpoint. The present writer has pointed out that the economists of the historical school did criticize the extravagances of

[67] (London: The Hogarth Press, 1926).

[68] *New Science*, par. 130, pp. 19–20; see, in this connection, nn. 64 and 11 above.

[69] P. 5.

[70] For a broad panorama of these German trends see Ralph H. Bowen, *German Theories of the Corporative State* (New York: McGraw-Hill, 1947). On the German historical school see Giorgio Tagliacozzo, *Economia e massimo edonistico collettivo* (Padua: Cedam, 1933), pp. 53ff.

[71] Einaudi, *Galiani economista*, p. 123; see also Spiegel, *Development of Economic Thought*, p. 64.

[72] *Economic Analysis*, p. 292.

laissez-faire economics, as Galiani had done before them; unlike Galiani, however, they went too far in that criticism by denying the possibility of establishing general principles of economics.[73] Heimann has enlarged upon this opinion by praising Galiani's "historical-institutionalist criticism of abstract theorizing" and adding: "Galiani was not opposed in principle to economic theory. . . . He thus achieved a balance between abstract theorizing and historical analysis which neither orthodox theory nor orthodox historical school proved capable of maintaining."[74]

c. Many aspects of Galiani's methodological thought bear a strong resemblance to the most advanced contemporary viewpoints. Among them are his emphasis on the necessity of basing economic reasoning on a realistic consideration of the "circumstances" and the "ends"; his relativistic conception of "wealth"; his view of economics as being neutral between ends and as a "science of human behavior," a study of relationships between means and ends, a "science of administration." These resemblances will be made clear in (*d*), (*e*), and (*f*).

d. Lionel Robbins' *An Essay on the Nature and Significance of Economic Science*[75]—an authoritative book inspired basically by Max Weber's work on the methodology of the social sciences[76]—centers on the same methodological problems as those discussed by Galiani and reaches analogous conclusions. Robbins strongly criticizes the "definition of Economics" which, at the time when he wrote, still held sway over "most adherents, at any rate in Anglo-Saxon countries": "that which relates it [economics] to the study of the causes of material welfare."[77] He also points out that "attempts have certainly been made to deny the applicability of economic analysis to the examination of ends other than material welfare," adding that "no less an economist than Professor Cannan has urged that the political economy of war is 'a contradiction in terms,' apparently on the ground that, since Economics is concerned with the causes of material welfare, war cannot be part of the subject of Economics."[78] According to Robbins, then, "it is not legitimate to say that going to war is uneconomical if, having regard to all the issues and all the sacrifices necessarily involved, it is decided that the anticipated result is worth the sacrifice."[79] Obviously Galiani would

[73] Tagliacozzo, *Economisti napoletani*, p. liii.

[74] *Economic Doctrines*, p. 62.

[75] Lionel Robbins, *An Essay on the Nature and Significance of Economic Science* (London: Macmillan, 1st ed. 1932; 2d ed. rev., 1935).

[76] Max Weber, *The Methodology of the Social Sciences* (Glencoe, Ill.: The Free Press, 1964), esp. "The Meaning of 'Ethical Neutrality' in Sociology and Economics" (pp. 1–47) and " 'Objectivity' in Social Science and Social Policy" (pp. 50–112).

[77] Robbins, *Economic Science*, p. 4.

[78] *Ibid.*, p. 7.

[79] *Ibid.*, p. 145.

have agreed with Robbins (see section 7[*f*]). Macfie[80] and Morgenstern[81] have presented viewpoints quite similar to those of Robbins and of Galiani.

e. To Robbins and to most modern theorists—as to Galiani—"wealth," then, is relative. Robbins uses almost the same words as Galiani to express this concept: ". . . man wants both real income and leisure . . . [and] his want for the different constituents of real income and leisure will be different. . . . The ends are various. . . . Here we are, sentient creatures with bundles of desires and aspirations, with masses of instinctive tendencies all urging us in different ways to action."[82]   Elsewhere Robbins notes: "Any kind of human behavior falls within the scope of economic generalization."[83]   And: "The hedonistic trimmings of the works of Jevons and his followers were incidental to the main structure of a theory which—as the parallel development in Vienna showed—is capable of being set out and defended in absolutely non-hedonistic terms."[84]   Of course, Galiani was as far from hedonism and utilitarianism as any modern economist.

f. Robbins' delineation of the fundamental implications of a relativistic (that is, non-hedonistic) conception of "wealth" is analogous to Galiani's. The first implication of this viewpoint is that economics is "neutral between ends"[85]—that is to say, "economic analysis is *wertfrei* in the Weber sense. The values of which it takes account are valuations of individuals";[86] "it [economic analysis] assumes that human beings have ends in the sense that they have tendencies to conduct which can be defined and understood";[87] "what is of relevance to the social sciences is, not whether individual judgments of value are *correct* in the ultimate sense of the philosophy of value, but whether they are *made* and whether they are essential links in the chain of causal explanation."[88]

g. The following are examples of other interrelated implications of a relativistic concept of wealth as pointed out by Robbins:

"The generalizations of economics, in addition to being based on the psychological premise of individual valuation," also depend on the assumption of "rational conduct."[89]   (Galiani, it will be remembered, has much to say on "reason" in economics, and speaks of a "science of human behavior.")

Economics is "the science that studies human behavior as a relationship between ends and scarce means which have alternative uses."[90] (Galiani spoke of economics as a study of relationships between means and ends and as a "science of administration.")

[80] Alec L. Macfie, *An Essay on Economy and Value* (London: Macmillan, 1936).
[81] Oskar Morgenstern, *The Limits of Economics* (London: William Hodge, 1937).
[82] Robbins, *Economic Science*, pp. 12–13.
[83] *Ibid.*, p. 17.   [84] *Ibid.*, p. 85.   [85] *Ibid.*, p. 24.   [86] *Ibid.*, p. 91.
[87] *Ibid.*, p. 24.   [88] *Ibid.*, p. 90.   [89] *Ibid.*   [90] *Ibid.*, p. 16.

"Applied economics consist of propositions of the form 'If you want to do this, then you must do that.' "[91]   (For Galiani's analogous viewpoint see section 7[*f*].)

10. Before concluding this essay, we shall offer a few remarks on two topics that have an important bearing on it: Benedetto Croce's economic thought and economic liberalism.   The latter will be dealt with in section 11. In an earlier study[92] the present writer recalled the following facts:

a. Between 1881 and 1884 Croce became acquainted with the books that were to become the starting point of his intellectual pursuit: De Sanctis' works on literary history.   This means that Croce's first—at least indirect—acquaintance with Vico dates as far back as those years.   He read the *New Science* for the first time shortly before 1893.[93]   As is well known, De Sanctis' views on aesthetics—influenced by Vico's thought—were the point of departure of Croce's philosophical career, which began in the field of aesthetics and eventually led to a parallel view of aesthetics and (philosophical) economics.   Croce's first acquaintance with Galiani cannot be traced with exactness.   It can be pointed out, however, that it must have occurred well before the end of the nineteenth century[94] and that in 1908 Croce, in his *Philosophy of the Practical*, mentioned Galiani, as well as other important economists, and quoted one of his least known works.

b. Between 1895 and 1900 Croce plunged into economic studies, beginning with Marx and continuing with the classics of economic science.   By 1900 he had gone all the way, in his sympathies, from Marxism to what he called "purist" economic science.   This change is demonstrated by the following statements, the first made in November, 1897, the last two in October, 1899:

It is about time to confess that neither socialism nor "laissez-faire" (*liberismo*) are or ever could be scientific deductions.[95]

The scientific theory of value can only be found in the "purist" or Austrian trend.[96] I adhere to the "purist school."   However, while doing so, I would like to put forward a few warnings. . . . I think that pure economics must get rid of its illegitimate marriage with "laissez-faire" (*liberismo*) because "laissez-faire" is a very good moral-

---

[91] *Ibid.*, p. 149.

[92] Giorgio Tagliacozzo, "Croce and the Nature of Economic Science," *Quarterly Journal of Economics*, 59 (May, 1945): 307–29.   Cf. B. Croce, *Saggi filosofici* (Bari, 1952), p. 163, n. 2.

[93] Benedetto Croce, *Contributo alla critica di me stesso* (1918), also published as an appendix in Croce's *Etica e politica* (Bari: Laterza, 1931), p. 380.

[94] Croce (*Etica e politica*, pp. 377ff.) informs us that after 1886 he devoted a great deal of time to research on Neapolitan culture of the seventeenth and eighteenth centuries.

[95] Benedetto Croce, "Di alcuni concetti del marxismo," in his *Materialismo storico ed economia marxistica: Saggi critici* (Bari: Laterza, 1918), p. 98.

[96] Benedetto Croce, "Marxismo ed economia pura," *ibid.*, p. 177.

social-political creed, but it is not a scientific one. Therefore, one must let the "purists" in economics be whatever they want to be in any other field, without accusing them of being in contradiction with pure economics; in fact, the common acceptance of very general laws lends itself to different and even opposite concrete political programs.[97]

    c. In 1900 Croce exchanged letters with Vilfredo Pareto dealing with the "economic principle."[98]   After 1900 he abandoned his economic studies and began building up his philosophical system. Between 1902 and 1908 Croce published his *Aesthetics, Logic,* and *Philosophy of the Practical* (the last subtitled *Economics and Ethics*). Both in his second letter to Pareto and in the *Philosophy of the Practical* (in the chapter dealing with economics as a science[99]) Croce interestingly linked his concept of economics with that of rationality, and hence with the relationship between means and ends. The importance of the above facts will become apparent in the conclusions of this study.

    11. In another essay[100] the present writer quoted the following statement made by Croce in 1945:

Opening the socialist paper *Avanti* [September 19, 1944], I read that in England political liberalism has "died irremediably" and that "it has been supplanted . . . by Fabian socialism, which is diametrically opposed to it"; this in spite of the fact that (the paper adds) "the British are liberal by temperament." The foregoing appears to me, on the contrary, to be an acknowledgment of the real supremacy that liberalism still holds in England; and "Fabianism," namely, the concrete and progressive acceptance of economic reforms formerly found only in the programs of the socialists, is the proof that in England liberalism has freed itself from its old union with "laissez-faire." I have picked up a very instructive book on the "deflation of American ideals" [Edward Kemler, *The Deflation of American Ideals: An Ethical Guide for New Dealers* (Washington, D.C., 1941)]. What, in fact, is this "deflation"? It is the abandonment of the easy optimism characteristic of the nineteenth century, especially of the . . . decades between 1830 and 1870; it is the vindication of the ethico-religious nature of liberalism against the economic ties that liberalism had developed and the objections deriving therefrom; it is the arrival at the conviction that, on the one hand, the destruction of capitalism would not make us free, and, on the other, that the big corporations and the big concentrations of power must be directed and turned to social purposes.[101]

This statement is fully consistent with the position that Croce took on

   [97] *Ibid.,* p. 187.

   [98] Benedetto Croce, "Sul principio economico: Due lettere al Prof. V. Pareto," *ibid.,* pp. 243–65.

   [99] Benedetto Croce, *Filosofia della pratica* (Bari: Laterza, 1909), pp. 257–68, esp. p. 261.

   [100] Giorgio Tagliacozzo, "Croce e il liberalismo economico," *Studi Economici,* 8, no. 3–4 (May–June, 1953).

   [101] Benedetto Croce, *Considerazioni sul problema morale del tempo nostro* (Bari: Laterza, 1945), pp. 16–17.

applied economics after 1899.[102]   It is also in full harmony, *mutatis mutandis*, with Galiani's position, on the one hand, and with contemporary economic liberalism, on the other.

There is no need, here, to expand on economic liberalism or on its literature. This writer's essay on "Croce and Economic Liberalism"[103] discusses them extensively.[104]   We might just recall that the viewpoint on applied economics which began to be called economic liberalism in the early forties had its origins in 1926, with the appearance of Keynes's *The End of Laissez-Faire*, forged ahead in the United States after 1933 thanks to the New Deal, was immeasurably strengthened theoretically by the publication of Keynes's *General Theory of Employment, Interest and Money* in 1936, fought a winning battle in the years immediately following the Second World War, and has emerged triumphantly both in theoretical developments and in economic policy in the last decade or so.   It is also important to point out that economic liberalism, in addition to sharing with Galiani and Croce a common attitude toward "laissez-faire," also shares with them—implicitly or explicitly—the following tenets, which could, perhaps, be considered as premises for that attitude: (*a*) a relativistic conception of wealth; (*b*) a basic agreement with the "marginal utility" (or "subjective utility") value theory; (*c*) a methodological viewpoint based on such concepts as "rationality," "means-ends relationships," and "neutrality between ends."

12. These are our conclusions:

a. Galiani's singling out of some of the most significant principles of the *New Science* for use as foundations for his own economic thought was so

[102] On the same topic see also Benedetto Croce, *Liberismo e liberalismo* (Naples: Tipografia Sangiovanni, 1927), and *idem*, "Osservazioni sulla scienza economica in relazione alla filosofia e alla storia," *Quaderni della Critica*, November, 1946.

[103] See n. 100 above.

[104] From among the countless writings on topics related to economic liberalism we might quote the following books: William Beveridge, *Full Employment in a Free Society* (New York: Norton, 1945); Chester Bowles, *Tomorrow without Fear* (New York: Simon & Schuster, 1946); J. M. Clark, *Alternative to Serfdom* (New York: Knopf, 1948); *idem*, *Guideposts in Time of Change* (New York: Harper, 1949); Alvin Hansen, *American Role in World Economy* (New York: McGraw-Hill, 1945); Seymour Harris, ed., *Saving American Capitalism—A Liberal Economic Program* (New York: Knopf, 1948); Eduard Heimann, *Freedom and Order* (New York: Scribner, 1947); Horace Kallen, *The Liberal Spirit* (Ithaca: Cornell University Press, 1948); Frank H. Knight, *Freedom and Reform* (New York: Harper, 1947); Abba Lerner, *Economics of Control* (New York: Macmillan, 1944); Arthur M. Schlesinger, Jr., *The Vital Center: The Politics of Freedom* (Boston: Houghton, Mifflin Co., 1949); Morton G. White, *Social Thought in America: The Revolt Against Formalism* (New York: Viking Press, 1949).

We might also recall the following: Benedetto Croce and Luigi Einaudi, *Liberismo e Liberalismo* (Milan-Naples: Ricciardi, 1957); Amintore Fanfani, *Il neovolontarismo economico statunitense* (Milan: Principato, 1946); Norberto Bobbio, "Liberalism Old and New," *Confluence*, 5, no. 3 (Autumn, 1956).

skillful and faithful to its source that it made Galiani's economics a true corollary of Vico's ideas and established Galiani as the legitimate founder of economic Vichianism. It is very doubtful whether an analogous statement could be made about Vico's influence on any other thinker in any other field.

b. If Galiani had not been pervasively influenced by Vico, the founding principles of his economic thought could not possibly have been what they were. The philosophical background of his time, in that case, undoubtedly would have guided him on a different path. This conclusion is indirectly supported by the fact that, fourteen years after the appearance of Galiani's *Della moneta*, Antonio Genovesi—a philosopher-economist born sixteen years before Galiani, who frequented Vico's home[105] and lived in practically the same Neapolitan intellectual environment as did Galiani, but who was only sporadically and superficially influenced by Vico—published an unsystematic economic treatise, *Lezioni di economia civile* (1765), which did contain a poorly digested version of Galiani's ideas on value but which was loosely centered on the then fashionable problem of "public happiness."[106]

c. If Galiani had not been pervasively influenced by Vico, and if his *Della moneta* had not been based on principles derived from the *New Science*, his over-all achievement (including technical economic theory, applied economics, and economic methodology—what amounts to a full system derived from a few general principles) would have been impossible.

d. It is perhaps true, nevertheless, that, even if Galiani had not been influenced by Vico—that is, if his *Della moneta* had not been based on Vichian principles—his genius as an economist would have allowed him this or that sporadic "discovery" in technical economic theory, applied economics, or economic methodology. For instance, he could have improved upon the value theory of the Scholastics to some extent, even without Vico's influence. His treatment of that or of any other technical, applied, or methodological topic, however, would not have been equally compelling nor would his over-all economic thought have been systematic and unitary.

e. Galiani's founding of economic Vichianism probably would have occurred even if his faultless use of Vichian principles in the economic field had not been accompanied by his genius as an economist. In that case, however, his performance would have been weaker. This would have been the case more in the field of technical economic theory than in those of applied economics or methodology.

f. The remarks in (*e*) above are, in a sense, confirmed by Croce's position in the field of economics. Like Galiani, Croce was influenced by Vico.

---

[105] See Enrico De Mas, "Vico and Italian Thought," pp. 147–64 of this volume.

[106] On Genovesi's life, personality, and work see Tagliacozzo, *Economisti napoletani*, pp. xx–xxii and lviii–lxi; this book also contains a bibliography on Genovesi and excerpts from his *Lezioni di economia civile*. For a judgment on Genovesi see also Schumpeter, *Economic Analysis*, p. 177.

Unlike him, he was not a first-rate genius as an economist (in any case, in Croce's times the approach to technical economic theory pioneered by Galiani was no longer in need of a founding genius).   Croce's position was analogous to that of Galiani both in the field of technical economic theory and in those of applied economics and methodology; it was, however, less original, detailed, and forceful in the first of these fields than in the other two.

g. Galiani and Croce are both representatives of economic Vichianism—a way of economic thinking which stems from the use of Vichian principles as a frame of reference for the study of economic problems.

h. Because Vico was a genius as a philosopher, not as an economist, it is perhaps fortunate that economic Vichianism was founded by Galiani rather than by his inspirer.

i. If Croce's economic Vichianism was born independently of Galiani's— which is probably the case—then it can be said that Vico's principles gave birth to a Vichian approach to economic problems not just once but twice: first in 1750 (Galiani), then again around 1900 (Croce).

j. If—as F. A. von Hayek and the present writer have pointed out [107]—Carl Menger owed the Galiani-Turgot-Condillac subjective value theory much more than is generally realized, then: (1) Menger and the Austrian school, which he founded, are indirectly indebted to Vico; (2) the acknowledged analogy between Galiani's and Böhm-Bawerk's theory of interest becomes something more than mere chance; (3) Croce's adherence to the "purist" or Austrian trend becomes even more meaningful; (4) Menger's *Principles of Economics* becomes, in a way, an at least partly Vichian bridge between the first and second births of economic Vichianism.   It is an incomplete bridge, however, because Menger's range in technical economic theory is narrower than Galiani's, his methodology is far duller, and his applied economics is unsystematic and unrelated to technical economic theory.[108]

k. The striking analogies between economic Vichianism and contemporary economic liberalism are highly significant and deserve far more reflection than they have so far been granted.

[107] See n. 32 above.
[108] See Tagliacozzo, *Economisti napoletani*, p. xlviii and *passim*.   Menger's views on applied economics are briefly discussed by Kauder, *Marginal Utility Theory*, p. 64.

Part IV

VICO AND MODERN PHILOSOPHY, PEDAGOGY, AND AESTHETICS

Isaiah Berlin
A NOTE ON VICO'S
CONCEPT OF KNOWLEDGE

Vico's fundamental distinction, as everyone with the least acquaintance with his writings knows, is between *verum* and *certum*. *Verum* is a priori truth, and is attained in, for example, mathematical reasoning, where every step is rigorously demonstrated. Such a priori knowledge can extend only to what the knower himself has created. It is true of mathematical knowledge precisely because men themselves have made mathematics. It is not, as Descartes supposed, discovery of an objective structure, the eternal and most general characteristics of the real world but rather invention: invention of a symbolic system which men can logically guarantee only because men have made it themselves, irrefutable only because it is a figment of man's own creative intellect. "*Geometrica demonstramus quia facimus. Si physica demonstrare possemus, faceremus.*"[1] "The rule and criterion of truth is to have made it," Vico said a year later, in 1710.[2] *Faceremus*: but this is not possible: men cannot make the physical world. "*Physica a caussis probare non possumus, quia elementa rerum naturalium extra nos sint.*"[3] Only God can know these *elementa*, because he has made them all. This includes the "Zenonian" metaphysical "points," of which the attribute is *conatus*, the *conatus* which with *motus* makes the world go round, whereby *flamma ardet, planta adolescit, bestia per prata lascivit*, and so on. None of this is wholly transparent to us, for we did not make it; and, since this is not *factum* by us, it is not *verum* for us. So much is clear. There is no assumption of continuity between, on the one hand, natural forces of this kind and human activity, intellectual or imaginative, on the other. Other thinkers—Herder, Schelling, the *Naturphilosophen*, and the Romantics—believed in such continuity, and perhaps they counted earlier thinkers among their ancestors— Renaissance scientists and mystics and a tradition which stretches back to the Greeks and forward to modern theologians and metaphysicians. But this is not what Vico believed. He did not identify, but on the contrary sharply distinguished, natural processes, which are more or less impenetrable,

[1] *De nostri temporis studiorum ratione* (1709), ed. F. Nicolini (Bari: Laterza, 1914), sec. IV.
[2] *De antiquissima Italorum sapientia*, ed. F. Nicolini (Bari: Laterza, 1914), chap. I, p. 62.
[3] *Ibid.*, chap. III, p. 76.

from human volitions, thoughts, images, forms of expression, which we "create" ourselves. We do not know the natural processes *per caussas,* for we do not enter their workings. Hence, for us they are not a form of *verum* but of *certum;* of them we have not a (Platonic) *scienza* but only *conscienza.* This is Vico's dualism: it cuts across the metaphysical map in a different direction from that of Descartes, but it is no less sharply dualistic, with its obvious debt to Plato and to the Christian separation of spirit from matter.

What else, besides mathematics, falls on the *scienza-verum* side of the great division? That which earlier Renaissance thinkers—Manetti, Pico, Campanella—had spoken of, all that we had wrought ourselves: "houses, towns, cities, pictures, sculptures, arts and sciences, languages, literatures, all are ours," said Manetti in 1452; and Pico, Bouelles, and Ficino had spoken of man's autonomy. Vico echoes this. "*Tandem deus naturae artifex: animus artium, fas sit dicere, deus.*"[4] This is Vico's position in, say, 1709–10, the period of *De nostri* and *De antiquissima.* He has broken the spell of Cartesianism from which he had begun. Descartes is severely taken to task for recommending application of the geometric method to regions for which it is unsuitable, for example, poetry and rhetoric. The narrowing educational influence of the Cartesian insistence on the deductive method as the sole path to knowledge is condemned; it is denounced as a kind of pedagogic despotism which suppresses various other faculties and methods of mental development, especially the imagination. Nicolini is surely right in stressing that Vico was particularly opposed to Descartes' *Discours de la méthode,* with its fanatical monism and especially its contempt for scholarship and humane studies. But at this stage mathematics is still described by Vico as being "like a divine science, since in it the true and the made coincide." There are two types of knowledge: *scienza,* knowledge *per caussas,* which can give complete truth, truth one can have only of what one has made—for example, of logical, mathematical, poetical creations; and *conscienza,* the knowledge of the "outside" observer of the external world—nature, men, things, *motus, conatus,* and so on. Here Vico is undoubtedly influenced by Bacon and Hobbes, by experimentalism, the possibility of understanding processes and objects that we can to some degree reproduce artificially in the laboratory, and perhaps also by the Neapolitan empiricists of the seventeenth century. All this is novel enough. But his boldest contribution, the concept of "philology," anthropological historicism, the notion that there can be a science of mind which is the history of its development, the realization that ideas evolve, that knowledge is not a static network of eternal, universal, clear truths, either Platonic or Cartesian, but a social process, that this process is traceable through (indeed, is in a sense identical with) the evolution of symbols—words, gestures, pictures, and their altering

---

[4] *Opere,* vol. I: *Le orazioni inaugurali, Il de Italorum sapientia e le polemiche,* ed. G. Gentile and F. Nicolini (Bari, 1914), p. 7.

patterns, functions, structures, and uses—this transforming vision, one of the greatest discoveries in the history of thought, was still in the future. Descartes in a notorious passage in *La recherche de la vérité* observed that "a man needs Greek and Latin no more than Swiss or Bas-Breton; to know the history of the Roman Empire no more than of the smallest country there is,"[5] or in the *Discours* complained about the idle exaggerations of historians as a mere loading of the mind with superfluous information. On this Vico as yet has nothing to say. In 1709 he still accepts Descartes' gibe that all that classical scholars can at most hope to discover is what was known to "Cicero's servant girl." History is not rated higher than physics: the study of *certum—conscientia*—is entitled indeed to a province of its own, which *scientia* or geometric method must not invade, but it is an inferior discipline.

No doubt Vico had been deeply impressed by Lucretius and his account of the bestial beginnings of men; by Bacon's stress on the part played by myth and imagination in human progress (as expounded in *De augmentis*, that "golden book"); by Hobbes, not only on account of his doctrine of experiment as an imitation of—and thereby a means of insight into—nature, but also by his view that "civil philosophy," that is, political science, is demonstrative, and belongs to the realm of *verum*, because "we make the Commonwealth ourselves," not historically, but as a rational, deliberate pattern, an intellectual artefact. And Tacitus delighted him with his sharp insights into individual character in action, as he delighted Machiavelli. But none of this coalesced, none of it would have come to life in the new synthesis, the new conception of philosophy as the consciousness of the cumulative experience of entire societies, without the central principle which is Vico's ultimate claim to immortality: the principle according to which man can understand himself because, and in the process, of understanding his past—because he is able to reconstruct imaginatively (in Aristotle's phrase) what he did and what he suffered, his hopes, wishes, fears, efforts, his acts, and his works, both his own and those of his fellows. With their experience his own is interwoven, his own and his (and their) ancestors', whose monuments, customs, laws, but, above all, words, still speak to him; indeed, if they did not, and if he did not understand them, he would not understand his fellows' or his own symbols, he would not be able to communicate or think or conceive purposes, to form societies or become fully human.

Enough has been written on Vico's historicism, on his idea of a culture (a notion of which, if he was not the original begetter, he was the first to grasp the full importance for historians and philosophers alike), to make it unnecessary to stress its salient characteristics. Nor would this be an easy task: Vico had not (as Heine once observed of Berlioz) enough talent for his genius. Too many new ideas are struggling for simultaneous expression. Vico is

5 *Oeuvres de Descartes*, ed. C. Adam and P. Tannery, 12 vols. (Paris: Cerf, 1897–1913), 10: 503.

trying to say too much, and his notions are often mere sketches, inchoate, ill-formed; he cannot keep a cool head in the storm of inspiration; he is at times carried away by the flood of disorganized ideas, and differs greatly in this respect from such great intellectual organizers and architects as Descartes or Leibniz or Kant or even Hegel. Vico's exposition often attains to rhapsodic, at times volcanic, power; but this does not make for coherent exposition. There are, as his critics have not been slow to point out, many obscurities and contradictions in his tumultuous writing.

In what sense, we may well ask, do men "make" their history?[6] Conscious effort, deliberate attempts to explain the world to oneself, to discover oneself in it, to obtain from it what one needs and wants, to adapt means to ends, to express one's vision or describe what one sees or feels or thinks, individually or collectively—understanding, communication, creation—all these could be described as kinds of doing and making. But this omits too much: unconscious and irrational "drives," which even the most developed and trained psychological methods cannot guarantee to lay bare; the unintended and unforeseen consequences of our acts which we cannot be said to have "made" if making entails intention; the play of accident; the entire natural world by interaction with which we live and function, which remains opaque inasmuch as it is not, *ex hypothesi*, the work of our hands or mind; since we do not "make" this, how can anything it possesses be grasped as *verum*? how can there be a *scienza* of such an amalgam? Furthermore, what is the relationship of the altering categories and the forms of symbolism which embody them—the procession (the fact that it is cyclical is not relevant here) from the dark caves of the *grossi bestioni* to the divine, the mythopoeic, and the heroic, poetic, metaphor-creating cultures, and from them to the humane, prose-using democracies—the relation of these changing forms of vision to creation, to the eternal laws, the *storia ideale eterna*, and the principles of the "civil theology" to which all cultures are subject? Since not we but God made the everlasting laws of the *corsi e ricorsi*, how can *we* know them? What kind of a priori intuitions are being claimed? And is the Renaissance parallel between the microcosm and macrocosm self-evidently valid? Is it really so obvious that phylogenesis—the history of the tribe—can be deduced from ontogenesis, from our individual recollections of our own mental and emotional growth? What guarantees this a priori historical phenomenology? By what faculty do we divine it? And what is the role of Providence in the *storia ideale*? If men make their history, does Providence "make" them create it as they do? If Providence turns men's bestial lusts, terrors, vices, into means for social and moral order, security, happiness, rational organization, what part is played in all this by men's own

---

[6] Mr. Bruce Mazlish has formulated some of these difficulties in his interesting essay on Vico, in *The Riddle of History: The Great Speculators from Vico to Freud* (New York: Harper & Row, 1966).

motives, purposes, choices? In what sense are men free, as Vico maintained? And, whatever the answer to this ancient theological puzzle, how
do we know that it is indeed a providence that shapes our lives? What, if
any, is the relation of Vico's undoubted Christian faith, his Catholic orthodoxy, to his anthropological, linguistic, historical naturalism, or of his teleology to his belief that to each order of culture belongs its own peculiar modes
of consciousness, not necessarily superior or inferior to its predecessors or
successors? I do not know if answers can be found to such questions which
historians of ideas have not settled; perhaps Vico himself has not left us
sufficient means for solving them; they arose again with the German philosophers of history and, in new guises, remain to plague us to this day. Be
that as it may, the claim for Vico that I wish to make is more circumscribed.
It is this: that he uncovered a species of knowing not previously clearly
discriminated, the embryo that later grew into the ambitious and luxuriant
plant of German historicist *Verstehen*—empathetic insight, intuitive sympathy, historical *Einfühlung*, and the like. It was, nevertheless, even in its
original, simple form, a discovery of the first order.

To apply the old medieval maxim that one can fully know only what one
has made to such provinces as mathematics, mythology, symbolism, language, is evidence enough of philosophical insight, a revolutionary step on
which the cultural anthropology and the philosophical implications of the
new linguistic theories of our own time have cast a new and extraordinary
light. But Vico did more than this. He uncovered a sense of knowing
which is basic to all humane studies: the sense in which I know what it is to
be poor, to fight for a cause, to belong to a nation, to join or abandon a
church or a party, to feel nostalgia, terror, the omnipresence of a god, to
understand a gesture, a work of art, a joke, a man's character, that one is
transformed or lying to oneself. How does one know these things? In the
first place, no doubt, by personal experience; in the second place because
the experience of others is sufficiently woven into one's own to be seized
quasi-directly, as part of constant intimate communication; and in the third
place by the working (sometimes by a conscious effort) of the imagination.
If a man claims to know what it is like to lose one's religious faith—in what
way it transforms the shape of one's world—his claim may or may not be
valid; he may be lying or deluding himself, or misidentifying his experience.
But the sense in which he claims to know this is quite different from that in
which I know that this tree is taller than that, or that Caesar was assassinated
on the Ides of March, or that seventeen is a prime number, or that vermilion
cannot be defined, or that the king in chess can move only one square at
a time. In other words, it is not a form of "knowing that." Nor is it like
knowing how to ride a bicycle or to win a battle, or what to do in case of
fire, or knowing a man's name, or a poem by heart. That is to say, it is not
a form of "knowing how" (in Gilbert Ryle's sense). What then is it like?

It is a species of its own. It is a knowing founded on memory or imagination. It is not analyzable except in terms of itself, nor can it be identified save by examples, such as those adduced above. This is the sort of knowing which participants in an activity claim to possess as against mere observers: the knowledge of the actors, as against that of the audience, of the "inside" story as opposed to that obtained from some "outside" vantage point; knowledge by "direct acquaintance" with my "inner" states or by sympathetic insight into those of others, which may be obtained by a high degree of imaginative power; the knowledge that is involved when a work of the imagination or of social diagnosis or a work of criticism or scholarship or history is described not as correct or incorrect, skillful or inept, a success or a failure, but as profound or shallow, realistic or unrealistic, perceptive or stupid, alive or dead. What this capacity is, the part that it plays in the understanding of the simplest communication addressed by one sentient creature to another, and a fortiori in the creation of adequate vehicles of expression, of criticism, above all in the recovery of the past not as a collection of factual beads strung on a chronicler's string (or of "ideas," arguments, works of art, similarly treated by the taxonomists and antiquaries of the humanities), but as a possible world, a society which could have had such characteristics whether it had precisely these or not—the nature of this kind of knowing is Vico's central topic. The past can be seen through the eyes—the categories and ways of thinking, feeling, imagining —of at any rate possible inhabitants of possible worlds, of associations of men brought to life by what, for want of a better phrase, we call imaginative insight. There must exist a capacity for conceiving (or at least a claim to be able to conceive) what "it must have been like" to think, feel, act, in Homeric Greece, in the Rome of the Twelve Tables, in Phoenician colonies given to human sacrifice, or in cultures less remote or exotic but still requiring suspension of the most deep-lying assumptions of the inquirer's own civilization. It cannot be otherwise if one is to begin to achieve any understanding of the "inner" structure of something outside one's immediate range of vision whether or not it is real or a dream. This remains true, whatever view one takes of the great controversy about the methods of the natural sciences as against those of the humane studies.

The identification of this sense of "knowing," which is neither deductive nor inductive (nor hypothetico-deductive), neither founded on the direct perception of the external world nor a fantasy which lays no claim to truth or coherence, is Vico's achievement. His program for the "new" approach to the human sciences is founded upon it. His claim may be extravagant: to call something knowledge which is so obviously fallible and needs empirical research to justify its findings may be an error. But he did uncover a mode of perception, something entailed in the notion of understanding words, persons, outlooks, cultures, the past.

When did he conceive this? When did he move from criticism of the un-historical, indeed anti-historical, approach of Descartes, and of Grotius and Selden (whom he had admired so deeply), to his new conception of historical method? Perhaps not much before 1720, when in the *De uno*[7] (that is, the *Diritto universale*) the first bold application of the *verum-factum* principle to human history is made, an application which later will be fully formulated in the celebrated passage of the last edition of the *Scienza nuova*,[8] which is dedicated to the effort to show how the findings of "philology" can at last be united with "philosophy"—the eternal principles revealed through reason planted in us by God and developed with the help of his providence, the path from *certum* to *verum*, to the pure Platonic vision from which Vico all his life drew inspiration. Yet the rudiments of this thought already appear in 1710, in the second chapter of *De antiquissima*, where we are told that "*historici utiles non qui facta crassius et genericas caussas narrant, sed qui ultimas factorum circumstantias persequuntur et caussarum peculiares reserrunt.*" This un-doubtedly reflects the influence of Bacon, but the emphasis on the concrete and the unique in the writing of history is a presage of what is to come ten years later. Leibniz also tried to formulate a doctrine of a priori definitions of individual entities by purely rational-logical methods, a path which, unlike Vico's, proved to be philosophically sterile.

No one understood the full originality of Vico in his lifetime or for nearly a century after his death, not even those few who actually read him: neither his fervent Neapolitan and Venetian admirers in the eighteenth century nor the famous men who commented on him later so superficially—Goethe and Jacobi, Galiani and Chastellux, Hamann and Herder (who arrived at similar ideas themselves), Joseph de Maistre and Ballanche; no one before Michelet seems to have had an inkling that Vico had opened a window to a new realm of thought, still less that those who made the effort to unravel the terrible tangles of his immensely suggestive but often dark ideas would never again be able to return to their beginnings—to the blissful simplicity and sym-metry of Descartes or Spinoza, Hume or Russell (or even Kant), still less to that of the Positivist historians and historical theorists; not, at any rate, without an acute and constant sense of the defectiveness of their conceptions of the mind and its powers, and consequently of what men are and how they come to be what they are. Not until the days of Dilthey and Max Weber did the full novelty of the implications for the philosophy of mind and epistemology of Vico's theses about the imaginative resurrection of the past begin to dawn upon some of those who, in their turn, resurrected him.

---

[7] *De uno universi iuris principio et fine uno* (Naples: Mosca, 1720).
[8] (Naples, 1744), par. 331 in the Bergin and Fisch translation.

Hayden V. White   WHAT IS LIVING
                          AND WHAT IS DEAD IN
                          CROCE'S CRITICISM OF VICO

For better than half a century the late Benedetto Croce labored to establish Giambattista Vico's claim to originality and his right to a prominent, not to say unique, place in the history of European thought. Seconded and supported by his colleague Fausto Nicolini, Croce consistently reiterated his belief in the breadth and fecundity of Vico's achievement. And the extent of Vico's current fame, as well as the high prestige that Vico enjoys in so many different disciplines, is attributable in considerable part to their tireless advocacy of his cause. To deny as much would be both imprecise and niggardly.

Croce and Nicolini were formidable advocates, commanding an almost intimidating wealth of learning, wisdom, and polemical shrewdness. But they were impelled as much by national pride, regional possessiveness, and a presumptive personal ownership as by respect for Vico's philosophy. Moreover, the strategy of their defense was questionable. One of their aims was to show Vico as precursor of the Crocean "philosophy of the spirit," and, in order to do this, they had to deny the legitimacy of Vico's attempts to found a science of society and to construct a philosophy of history. For both of these activities were anathema to the Crocean world view. Thus, even though Croce and Nicolini worked mightily to establish Vico's reputation in the twentieth century, their conception of his achievement was both biased and restricted. And much of the current disagreement over the precise nature of Vico's contribution to modern thought arises from their narrow definition of "what is living and what is dead" in Vichian philosophy.

Now, the determination of "what is living and what is dead" in prior philosophical systems was a characteristic Crocean operation, pursued by him with a special urgency. As self-appointed arbiter of taste for European humanism in its modern phase, Croce felt compelled to display his assaying abilities with more than normal frequency. Ultimately, almost every major European thinker and writer came to rest in a precise place on a hierarchy of accomplishment where Croce's own philosophy provided the final test of orthodoxy. Thus, for example, Hegel nested next to the *summum bonum*; De Sanctis, Goethe, Kant, Dante, Aristotle, and Socrates were appropriately placed so as to catch sight of it; Marx was permitted only a reflected glimpse of it: while Freud was consigned to the lower depths, where the light penetrated hardly at all. Vico's position was more difficult to determine; for he was at once the discoverer of the hierarchy's informing principle and its possible subverter.

To Croce, Vico was (as Goethe had called him) *"der Altvater"*—the patriarch, paradigm of a peculiar way of "feeling" philosophy *italianamente* while simultaneously "thinking" it *cosmopoliticamente*.[1] Croce confessed to a feeling of filial attachment to Vico,[2] but, appropriately, the feeling was one of distinct ambivalence. He was grateful to the "patriarch" for providing him with a classical pedigree for his own rebellion against the prevailing orthodoxies of his generation, positivism and vitalism, thereby saving him from the charge of mere eccentricity. But he could not forgive Vico for seemingly providing similar warrants for the systems he wanted to reject. If Vico represented the first clear anticipation of Croce's own "philosophy of the spirit," he was also the first sophisticated practitioner of the intellectual aberrations Croce hated most, sociology and philosophy of history. Ultimately, therefore, much more so than the other thinkers whom Croce respected, Vico had to be both affirmed and denied, exalted and negated; for, if Vico was justified in his attempt to found sciences of society and of history, then Croce's whole system had been ill-conceived, his cultural role incorrectly defined, and much of his activity worthless.

The combination of reverence and reserve which consistently marked Croce's comments on Vico was present in his early references to him. Croce first read the *Scienza nuova* seriously during his period of antiquarian retreat in Naples between 1886 and 1892.[3] He turned to the systematic study of Vico's whole philosophy only after 1893, when his essay "History Subsumed under a General Concept of Art" involved him in the current debate over the nature of historical knowledge and turned him from an antiquarian into a philosopher. In this essay Croce maintained that, although history is an art rather than a science, it is nonetheless a form of cognition— and not mere illusion, narcotic, or entertainment, as the current schools of aesthetics taught. He did not, however, explain how a pure intuition (which he took to be the essence of art) could be immediate and also have a cognitive content (as he wanted to assert of historical intuitions); and apparently he had

---

[1] Benedetto Croce, *La filosofia di Giambattista Vico*, 5th ed. rev. (Bari, 1953), Preface to the 1st ed., p. viii. All quotations from this work will be given in the versions provided by R. G. Collingwood in his translation, *The Philosophy of Giambattista Vico* (New York, 1913). Since almost all of the quotations are drawn from chapters X, XI, XIII, and XX, I have not provided citations to specific page numbers of the English version. Moreover, I have altered Collingwood's renderings in those places where, in my opinion, his tendency to "English" Croce's thought has obscured its distinctive Italian tone.

[2] Fausto Nicolini, *Croce* (Turin, 1962), p. 252.

[3] Benedetto Croce, "Contributo alla critica di me stesso," in his *Etica e politica* (Bari, 1956), p. 392.

not settled the matter to his own satisfaction at that time. But he would settle it shortly, and his settlement of it as well as of his attitude toward Vico (which reduced to the same problem) is signaled in the passing references he makes to Vico's thought in this early essay. He cites Vico twice—once disparagingly (along with Herder), as a representative of "philosophy of history," and once approvingly, though vaguely, as an authority on the true nature of the poetic faculty.[4]

In his autobiographical sketch written some years later, Croce says that at the time of the essay Vico was merely one factor among many (along with De Sanctis, Labriola, and the German aestheticians) in the economy of his intellectual life.[5] During the following ten years, however, Vico progressively moved to the center of Croce's thought, suggesting the enabling postulates of the embryonic "philosophy of the spirit" and the means of finally distinguishing precisely between history, art, science, and philosophy. Thus, by 1902, when Croce published his *Aesthetics*, he had credited Vico not only with having discovered the science of aesthetics but also with having perceived, albeit dimly, the true relation between poetry and history.[6] More specifically, Vico had formulated "new principles of poetry" and had correctly analyzed the "poetic or imaginative moment" in the life of the spirit.[7] True, he had not comprehended the nature of the other moments of the spirit's life—the logical, ethical, and economic moments; and this want of understanding of the other dimensions of the spirit's activity had led him to merge "concrete history" with "philosophy of the spirit," thereby hurling himself into the abysses of "philosophy of history."[8] Fortunately, Croce argued, Vico's "new science," that is, his epistemology, had nothing to do with "concrete and particular history, which develops in time. . . ." It was rather a "science of the ideal, a philosophy of the spirit," which dealt with the "modifications of the human mind."[9] Therefore, it could be disengaged from its misapplication to concrete history; and Vico could be honored for having discovered it while criticized for having used it improperly.

According to Croce's early analysis, then, Vico had failed on two counts: his investigation of the life of the spirit had not been complete; and he had confused concrete history with philosophy of the spirit, thereby generating the fallacies of philosophy of history. Philosophy of history was impossible, Croce maintained, because it was founded upon the belief that "concrete history could be subjected to reason" and that "epochs and events could be conceptually deduced."[10] It was the philosopher's counterpart of the

---

[4] Benedetto Croce, "La Storia ridotta sotto il concetto generale dell'arte," in his *Primi saggi* (Bari, 1951), p. 21 and p. 23, n. 1.

[5] Croce, "Contributo," p. 392.

[6] Benedetto Croce, *Estetica come scienza dell'espressione e linguistica*, 9th ed. rev. (Bari, 1950), pp. 242, 246.

[7] *Ibid.*, pp. 255-56.   [8] *Ibid.*, p. 256.   [9] *Ibid.*, p. 255.   [10] *Ibid.*

fantasy entertained by the social scientist, that is, the belief that one could derive universal laws of social process from the study of individual events, which generated the fallacies of sociologism.   Actually, however, if correctly developed, Vico's insight into the "autonomy of the aesthetic world" and his discovery of the cognitive element in poetry provided an antidote to both philosophy of history and sociologism.[11]   Vico's genius was confirmed by the fact that he had, however unwittingly, provided the cure for the sicknesses to which he himself had succumbed.

It should be noted that, although Croce repudiated any attempt to construct a philosophy of history, he was not opposed to what he called "theory of history."   In an essay written for the *Revue de synthèse historique*, which appeared in the same year as the *Aesthetics*, Croce distinguished between "theory of history" and "philosophy of history."   The former, he argued, was concerned to establish the criteria by which historians gave to their narratives an appropriate form, unity, and content; the latter sought to discover the presumed laws by which human actions necessarily assumed the forms they did in different times and places.   A theory of history was permissible, but only if it proceeded by means of a logic of intuitions, not a logic of concepts, that is to say, only if it were understood that history operated within the confines of art.[12]   In fact, the only conceivable theory of history, Croce held, was aesthetics.   "Inasmuch as it is a science of pure intuition, science of the individual object of pure intuition, aesthetics constitutes a philosophy of art; however, inasmuch as it is a theory of a special group of intuitions (intuitions that have for their object the real individual), aesthetics constitutes a theory of historiography."[13]   It was possible, then, to "philosophize" about the ways in which historians, unlike "pure" artists, distinguished among intuitions "between the factually real (*réel de fait*) and the ideally possible."[14]   But—and here was the crux of the matter for Croce at that time—any attempt to "establish historical laws" had to be sternly suppressed.[15]   The search for laws was a scientific enterprise; science dealt with "the universal, the necessary, and the essential."   History, by contrast, dealt with the individual, the empirical, and the transitory ("that which appeared and disappeared in time and space").[16]   It followed, therefore, that historical knowledge was "by nature aesthetic and not logical, representational and not abstract," and "intuitive," not "conceptual."[17]   Obviously, for the Croce of this period, history was not yet the "method" of philosophy, as it would become later on; it was a second-order form of

[11] *Ibid.*, p. 258.

[12] Benedetto Croce, "Les études relatives à la theorie de l'histoire en Italie durant les quinze dernières années," originally published in *Revue de synthèse historique* (Paris, 1902), and reprinted in *Primi saggi*, p. 184.

[13] *Ibid.*   [14] *Ibid.*, p. 185.   [15] *Ibid.*, p. 186.   [16] *Ibid.*

[17] *Ibid.*, pp. 184–85.

art, nothing more and nothing less—art turned upon the representation of the individually real, rather than upon the imaginary. And it had to be kept free from the scientist's impulse to see its objects as occupying a field of causally determined relationships, on the one hand, and the metaphysician's inclination to regard those objects as functions of transcendental or immanent spiritual processes, on the other.[18] In the light of these rigid distinctions, Vico was bound to be found wanting, not only on specific issues, but also in the direction of his main enterprise, his attempt to make of history a science.

The decade following the publication of the *Aesthetics* was a period of prodigious creativity for Croce. During this time he completed the articulation of his "philosophy of the spirit," founded and edited his journal *La Critica*, and produced a number of important studies in the history of philosophy, of which his essays on Hegel and on Vico were the most important.[19] In the four volumes making up the "philosophy of the spirit," Vico figures prominently as guide and authority, though with the usual reservations about his incompleteness and the inadequacy of his total system. Actually, Croce's activity during this time could be characterized as a filling out, completion, and correction of Vico's system in the light of his original criticism of it. Certainly his reading of Vico, as offered in his magisterial *The Philosophy of Giambattista Vico* (1911), is little more than an evaluation of the "new science" in the light of its approximation to, or deviation from, the tenets of Croce's finished philosophy.

Chapter III of *The Philosophy of Giambattista Vico*, entitled "The Internal Structure of the *New Science*," sets forth the critical principles that guided Croce in his final reading of Vico. Vico's whole system, Croce explains, actually embraces three different "classes of inquiry: philosophical, historical, and empirical; and altogether it contains a philosophy of the spirit, a history (or congeries of histories), and a social science." The first class of inquiry is concerned with "ideas" on fantasy, myth, religion, moral judgment, force and law, the certain and the true, the passions, Providence, and so on—in other words, "all the . . . determinations affecting the necessary course or development of the human mind or spirit." To the second class belong Vico's outline of the universal history of man after the Flood and that of the origins of the different civilizations; the description of the heroic ages in Greece and Rome; and the discussion of custom, law, language, and political constitutions, as well as of primitive poetry, social-class struggles, and the

---

[18] *Ibid.*, p. 186.

[19] The four volumes that make up the "philosophy of the spirit" are: the *Estetica* (1902), the *Logica* (1908), the *Filosofia della pratica* (1908), and the *Teoria e storia della storiografia* (1917). The fourth volume did not appear in a complete edition until the date given, but the essays that were to make it up began to appear in periodicals in 1912. On the development of Croce's thought during this period, see Nicolini, *Croce*, chap. 23.

breakdown of civilizations and their return to a second barbarism, as in the early Middle Ages in Europe. Finally, the third class of inquiry has to do with Vico's attempt to "establish a uniform course (*corso*) of national history" and deals with the succession of political forms and correlative changes in both the theoretical and practical lives, as well as his generalizations about the patriciate, the plebs, the patriarchal family, symbolic law, metaphorical language, hieroglyphic writing, and so forth.[20]

Croce argues that Vico hopelessly confused these three types of inquiry, ran them together in his reports, and committed a host of category mistakes in the process of setting them out in the *New Science*. The obscurity of the *New Science* results, he maintains, not from the profundity of the basic insight, but from an intrinsic confusion, that is to say, from the "obscurity of his [Vico's] ideas, a deficient understanding of certain connections; from, that is to say, an element of arbitrariness which Vico introduces into his thought, or, to put it more simply, from outright errors."[21] Vico had failed to see correctly the "relation between philosophy, history, and empirical science." He tended to "convert" one into the other.[22] Thus he treated "philosophy of the spirit" first as empirical science, then as history; he treated empirical science sometimes as philosophy and sometimes as history; and he often attributed to simple historical statements either the universality of philosophical concepts or the generality of empirical schemata.[23] The confusion of concepts with facts, and vice versa, had been disastrous for Vico's historiography and for his social science. For example, Croce notes, when Vico lacked a document, he tended to fall back upon a general philosophical principle to imagine what the document would have said had he actually possessed it; or, when he came upon a dubious fact, he confirmed or disconfirmed it by appeal to some empirical law. And, even when he possessed both documents and facts, he often failed to let them tell their own story—as the true historian is bound to do—but instead interpreted them to suit his own purposes, that is, to accommodate them to his own willfully contrived sociological generalizations.[24]

Croce professed to prefer the most banal chronicle to this willful manipulation of the historical record. He could forgive Vico for the numerous factual errors that riddled his work; imprecise in small matters, Vico made up for it by his comprehensiveness of vision and his understanding of the way in which spirit operated to create a specifically human world.[25] But the cause of his confusion, his identification of philosophy with science and history, Croce could not forgive. This "tendency of confusion or . . . confusion of tendencies" was fatal to Vico's claim to the role of social scientist and the

---

[20] Croce, *Filosofia di Giambattista Vico*, pp. 37–38; cf. Nicolini, *Croce*, pp. 254–55.
[21] Croce, *Filosofia di Giambattista Vico*, p. 39.
[22] *Ibid.*, p. 40.   [23] *Ibid.*   [24] *Ibid.*, pp. 41–42, 157.   [25] *Ibid.*, p. 158.

cause of his fall into philosophy of history. An adequate reading of Vico, therefore, required a careful separation of the philosophical "gold" in his work from the pseudoscientific and pseudohistorical dross in which it was concealed.[26] And to this task of separation (or transmutation, for this is what it really was) Croce proceeded in the chapters that followed, with a single-mindedness exceeded only by his confidence that in his own philosophy he possessed the philosopher's stone which permitted the correct determination of "what is living and what is dead" in any system. Willing to judge, and even to forgive, Vico in the light of the *scholarly* standards prevailing in the eighteenth century, Croce was unwilling to extend this historicist charity to Vico's *philosophical* endeavors.

A perfect example—and a crucial test—of Croce's critical method appears in chapter XI of *The Philosophy of Giambattista Vico*, where Vico's law of civilizational change, the so-called law of the *ricorsi*, is examined. Briefly summarized, this law states that all pagan peoples must pass through a specific "course" of social relationships with corresponding political and cultural institutions and that, when the course is complete, they must, if they have not been annihilated, retrace this course on a similar, though significantly metamorphosed, plane of existence or level of self-consciousness. If they are destroyed at the end of the cycle, they will be replaced by another people, who will live through the course in the same sequence of stages and to the same end.

Now, Croce maintains that this law is nothing but a generalized form of the pattern that Vico thought he had discovered in Roman history.[27] Vico gratuitously extended this law to cover all pagan societies, which forced him to press the facts into the pattern that applied only, if at all, to the Roman example. This "rarefaction" of Roman history into a general theory of social dynamics showed Vico's misconception of how empirical laws are generated, Croce claimed. Instead of generalizing from concrete cases and thereby contriving a summary description of the attributes shared by all instances of the set, against which the differences *between* the instances could be delineated, Vico sought to extend the general characteristics of the Roman set to include all sets resembling the Roman in their pagan character. The inadequacy of Vico's law was revealed, however, by the large number of exceptions to it which even Vico had to admit existed.[28] If Vico had not been led astray by loyalty to his biased reading of Roman history, the "empirical theory of the *ricorsi*" would never have been forced to grant so many exceptions.[29] And freed from the necessity of forcing other societies into the model provided by the Roman example, Vico might have been able to apply the truth contained in the theory of the *ricorsi* to their several histories.

---

[26] *Ibid.*, pp. 43–44.   [27] *Ibid.*, p. 129.   [28] *Ibid.*, pp. 130–31.   [29] *Ibid.*, p. 133.

The truth contained in the theory was a philosophical one, namely, that "the spirit, having traversed its progressive stages, after having risen successively from sensation to the imaginative and rational universal, from violence to equity, must in conformity with its eternal nature retrace its course, to relapse into violence and sensation, and thence to renew its upward movement, to recommence its course."[30] As a general guide to the study of specific historical societies, this truth directs attention to "the connection between predominantly imaginative and predominantly intellectual, spontaneous and reflective periods, the latter periods issuing out of the former by an increase in energy, and returning to them by degeneration and decomposition."[31] In any case, the theory only describes what happens generally in all societies; it neither prescribes what must happen at particular times and places nor predicts the outcome of a particular trend. Such distinctions as those sanctioned by Croce, such as between "predominantly imaginative and predominantly intellectual . . . periods," are "to a great extent quantitative and are made for the sake of convenience."[32] They have no force as law. Vico stands convicted, therefore, of an error and a delusion: he erred in trying to extend an empirical generalization to all classes superficially resembling that to which the generalization could be legitimately applied, and he was deluded by the hope of treating a philosophical insight as a canon of historical interpretation valid for all societies at all times and places.

Croce considers two possible objections to his criticism of Vico: on the one hand, he says, it might be argued that Vico does account for the exceptions to his law, by referring to external influences or contingent circumstances that caused a particular people to halt short of its term or to merge with and become a part of the *corso* of another people. On the other hand, he notes, it might be held—on the basis of Croce's own interpretation of the true value of the "law"—that, since the law really deals with the *corso* of the spirit and not of society or culture, no amount of empirical evidence can serve to challenge it. Croce summarily dismisses the second objection. "The point at issue," he says,

is . . . precisely the empirical aspect of this law, not the philosophical; and the true reply seems to us to be, as we have already suggested, that Vico could not and ought not to have taken other circumstances into account, just as, to recall one instance, anyone who is studying the various phases of life describes the first manifestations of the sexual craving in the vague imaginings and similar phenomena of puberty, and does not take into account the ways in which the less experienced may be initiated into love by the more experienced, since he is setting out to deal not with the social laws of imitation but with the physiological laws of organic development.[33]

---

[30] *Ibid.*, p. 136.   [31] *Ibid.*, pp. 133–34.   [32] *Ibid.*, p. 134.   [33] *Ibid.*, p. 136.

In short, Vico's "law" either obtains universally—like the "physiological laws of organic development"—or it does not; one exception is enough to disconfirm it.

This was a curious line for Croce to take, however, for it required that he apply to Vico's "law" criteria of adequacy more similar to those demanded by positivists than to those required by Croce's own conception of physical scientific laws as expounded in his *Logic*. In fact, he had criticized positivists for failing to see that the function of laws in science was "subserving" and not "constitutive."[34] The laws of physical science, he said, were nothing but fictions or pseudoconcepts, contrived by men or groups of men in response to needs generated by practical projects in different times and places, the authority of which was therefore limited to the duration of the projects themselves.[35] Croce specifically denied that natural sciences predicted in any significant sense; the conviction that they did represented the resurgence of a primitive desire to prophesy or to foretell the future, which could never be done. Such beliefs rested on the baseless assumption that nature was regular in all its operations, when in reality the only "regular" phenomenon in nature was that of the mind in its effort to comprehend nature.[36] The so-called laws of nature were being constantly violated and excepted, from which it followed that, far from being able to claim predictability, the natural sciences were much more dependent upon a *historical* knowledge of nature than were even the human sciences, which at least had the constant phenomena of mind from which to generalize.[37]

But, if this is the true nature of law in the physical sciences, it must also be the true nature of whatever laws are possible in the social sciences; and, this being the case, what possible objection could there be to Vico's use of the law of the *ricorsi* to characterize the evolutionary process of all societies and to encourage research into them in order to discover the extent of their deviation from the Roman model? The objection would seem to lie solely in Croce's hostility to any attempt to treat society and culture, which he took to be products of spirit, *as if* they were determined effects of purely physical causes. Croce's distrust of any attempt to treat society as if it were a possible object of science is well known.[38] In trying to characterize the operations of spirit in their concrete manifestations, in the social forms they took, in terms of laws, Vico seemed to be unwittingly materializing or naturalizing them and thereby depriving them of their status as creations of spirit. At least, so Croce saw it. Vico treated society and culture as if they were products of an invariable material process (thereby, by the way, betraying his misunder-

---

[34] Benedetto Croce, *Logica come scienza del concetto puro*, 3d ed. rev. (Bari, 1917), p. 204.

[35] *Ibid.*, p. 227.

[36] *Ibid.*, p. 228.

[37] *Ibid.*, pp. 229–31.

[38] Cf. *Primi saggi*, pp. 190–91, for an early expression of Croce's distrust of the very concept of society.

standing of the true nature of nature); and Croce demanded of him that, once he had opted for this treatment, he be consistent and truly regard the process as invariable.   From this came the thrust of Croce's appeal to the analogy that anyone "studying the various phases of life" must limit himself to a consideration of "the physiological laws of organic development" and not deal with the "social laws of imitation."

But the analogy betrays the bias in the criticism.   For, to follow the analogy out correctly, what is at issue in Vico's case is not a mixture of laws operating in one process with laws operating in another; it is the convergence of two systems, each governed by similar laws, the one canceling out or aborting the operations of the other.   For example, even a person studying the various phases of human life is not—as a scientist—embarrassed by the fact that a given individual does not reach puberty but, let us say, dies.   The death of a person before puberty does not invalidate the "physiological laws of organic development" governing the pubertial phase; it merely requires, if we want to explain the particular failure to reach puberty, that we invoke other laws, specifically those which account for the death of the organism, to explain why the prediction that puberty would *normally* occur was not borne out.

So it is also with civilizations.   Our characterization of the "course" that we predict they will follow is not vitiated by any given civilization's failure to complete such a course, if the failure can be explained by the invocation of another law, that covering the disintegration of civilizations short of their normal terms.   Thus, no number of societies failing to complete the *corso* described by the Roman model, used by Vico as an archetype, can serve to disconfirm Vico's "law."   This is because the "law of the *ricorsi*" is less a "law" than a theory or an interpretation, that is to say, a set of laws the utility of which, for predictive purposes, requires specification of the limiting conditions within which those laws apply.   In principle there is nothing at all wrong with Vico's choosing to use the Roman example as a paradigm of civilizational growth against which the growth of all other civilizations known to him, the Jewish and Christian excepted, could be measured.   It is perfectly good socio-scientific procedure, however imperfectly the procedure was carried out in Vico's case.   What Croce objected to was *any kind* of socio-scientific procedure, for by his lights it represented an effort to treat a product of "free" spirit as something causally determined.   And so he applied an impossibly rigorous standard of adequacy —a standard which he himself had specifically repudiated in his rejection of the claims that Positivists had made for the physical sciences—to Vico's effort to construct a science of societies.   This inconsistency in Croce's use of the concept of "law" can only be explained by his desire to claim Vico's sanction for his own manner of philosophizing while denying any claim by modern social scientists to be following out Vico's program of social analysis.

A better case can be made for Croce's criticism of Vico's efforts to construct a universal history, or a philosophy of world history. Here a genuine mixture of categories appears to have occurred. On the one hand, Croce correctly points out, Vico wants to use the theory of the *ricorsi* as the model for *all* civilizational growth; on the other, he wants to except the Jewish and Christian examples by attributing to them respectively a special memory and a special capacity for renewal, which precluded their termination before the end of the world. This distinction *was* gratuitous, and Croce appears to be correct in finding its origin in the conflict between the Christian believer who lurked within Vico's breast and the social scientist who had triumphed in his head.[39] But, as most of Vico's commentators have pointed out, even this inconsistency does not negate the effort, consistently pursued on the socio-scientific side of his work, to construct a universal philosophy of history. Croce himself admitted as much when, commenting upon Vico's attempt to draw similarities between Homer and Dante, he granted that such classifications were the necessary bases of any true history; for, as he put it, "without the perception of similarity, how would one succeed in establishing the differences?"[40] But here again he deplored the search for similarities as an end in itself; the urge to classify, he said, had prohibited Vico from carrying out the historian's task, that of "representing and narrating."[41]

What, then, is "living" and what is "dead" in Croce's assessment of Vico's achievement? The clue to the solution of this problem is provided by two of Croce's judgments, one on Vico and one on himself. Sum-marizing his analysis of Vico in the last chapter of *La filosofia di Giambattista Vico*, Croce said that in the end Vico "was neither more nor less than the nineteenth century in embryo."[42] And a few months later, in response to Borgese's "D'Annunzian" criticism of this book, he wrote that ". . . the philosophy with which I interpret and criticize the thought of Vico, while in some respects my own, . . . is, in the main, nothing other than the idealistic philosophy of the nineteenth century."[43] To be sure, Croce claimed to have purified the idealistic philosophy of the nineteenth century, to have rendered it more "realistic" and more "critical" of itself; but in the end he remained within its horizons. Ample as they were, these horizons did not adequately encompass the operations of the physical sciences or of those social sciences founded upon similar aims and methods. Consequently, Croce's criticism of Vico did not really meet the main thrust of Vico's "new science," the effort for which many of the major socio-scientific theorists of the nineteenth century honored him.

[39] Croce, *La filosofia di Giambattista Vico*, pp. 149–50.
[40] *Ibid.*, p. 156.
[41] *Ibid.*, p. 157.
[42] *Ibid.*, p. 257.
[43] See Benedetto Croce, "Pretese di bella letteratura nella storia della filosofia," in his *Pagine sparse* (Naples, 1943), I, 333.

Nicola Badaloni   IDEALITY AND
                                 FACTUALITY IN
                                 VICO'S THOUGHT

When Vico opened his *De antiquissima Italorum sapientia* (1710) with the
problem of the *verum et factum* and entitled the first chapter accordingly,
neither had he discovered the problem nor was he simply expressing the
current state of it.   He was rather echoing a great debate, already underway
throughout European cultural life, over the relation between truth, or possibility, or ideality, and the real, or factual, world.   A number of solutions
had been offered to this problem, among which may be distinguished:
(1) the Gassendian solution; (2) the Malebranche-Cartesian solution; and
(3) an alternative to these, the philosophy of the *factum*.

    What were the basic characteristics of these solutions?   The first of them
was offered as a philosophy of the *factum* in the sense that it appealed to the
world of experience as the unique criterion of truth.   To be sure, in an effort
to broaden the sphere of experience, it also accepted a series of events which
we would prefer to classify as *ideal* or metaphysical.   An authoritative
Italian Gassendian, Tommaso Cornelio, trying to explain the connection
between the body and the soul in such a way as to remain faithful to the
philosophy of the *factum*, had, in a work on metempsychosis, united the soul
and corporeality.   Yet, in this respect, Gassendianism, uniformly favoring
the sphere of the physical, tended in the end to include even metaphysical
questions in this sphere.   To Vico, Gassendianism appeared to be a philosophy dominated by *sense*, and he tended, therefore, to relate it in its logic
to the philosophy of Locke.[1]

    When, however, Vico speaks of Descartes, he has in mind his metaphysics
and his theory of reason.   The Cartesian revival, which had flowered in
Naples at the end of the seventeenth century, had appeared under the aspect
of a kind of moral rigor (Stoicist and Jansenist), a kind of Augustinianism.
Vico saw in Cartesianism the desire to "prove the existence of an agent above
matter which would not be material, like Plato's God," and in the Cartesians
the practical aim of establishing, "some day, rule even over the cloisters."[2]

    In general, then, Cartesianism represented a revival of the notion of the

[1] Epicurus is likened to Locke in Vico's *L'Autobiografia, il carteggio, e le poesie varie*,
ed. B. Croce (Bari, 1911), p. 16.
[2] *Ibid.*, pp. 18–19.

ideal inasmuch as it elevated the ideal over the factual.   A similar kind of reconstructive purpose seemed to be behind the philosophies of Malebranche and Leibniz, although Vico does not mention the latter in the *De antiquissima*. As for Malebranche, Vico's judgment of him is strictly dependent upon his judgment of Descartes.   Malebranche, Vico says, had been unable to construct a Christian ethics according to Cartesian principles.[3]   Malebranche's system, then, signaled the inability of Cartesianism to deal with moral problems.

As thus represented, of course, Vico's judgment is rather vague.   It is developed better in that paragraph of the *De antiquissima* which deals with the problem of the *mind*.   Vico criticizes Malebranche's vision of God because of the way he reconciles it with the Cartesian consciousness of self. Vico sets up, so to speak, a choice between the origin of ideas in the mind and their origin in God; and he ends by asserting that self-cognition, and therefore the structure of human nature in general, is not a primitive datum, but a datum that is dependent upon God.   The mind's cognitive power (rooted in ideality) thus depends on God.[4]

In order to understand the meaning that Vico gives to the problem of the *factum*, we may invoke, finally, a last witness, the historian and philosopher Ludovico Antonio Muratori.   The latter, following closely the current philosophical discussion, had interpreted the recourse to the *factum* as being equivalent to the assumption of an antimetaphysical position.   As a reader of Bayle (and as a polemicist against Le Clerc), Muratori had interpreted the philosophy of the *factum* as an alternative to the philosophical choice of the possible (with all the metaphysical implications it entailed).   But the *factum* did not, according to Muratori, refer only to the world of experience; it signified defense of orthodoxy as well, because it included *authoritarian* elements and, above all, an appeal to scriptural texts.[5]   In this context, history was for Muratori the acceptance of facts and the exclusion of the necessary, even if, by means of the category of *taste*, he submitted to limited rational criticism the facts thus defined.

Therefore, in relation to the present discussion, we have differentiated at least three meanings of the term *"factum."*   First, it means *factual reality*, which is testified to by the senses and is inseparable from them; second, it can be regarded as the *actualization* of all the possibilities inherent in ideality in such a way that it takes on meaning only in relation to these; third, it can mean acceptance of the *fact* in a context that implies rejection of any reference to the possible and acceptance of *auctoritas*.

[3] *Ibid.*, p. 29.

[4] Vico, *Le orazioni inaugurali, Il de Italorum sapientia e le polemiche*, ed. G. Gentile and F. Nicolini (Bari, 1914), p. 174.

[5] But Vico was dissatisfied by Muratori's solution also, especially with respect to the problem of ethics. Cf. Vico, *L'Autobiografia*, p. 238.

At the height of this discussion Vico intervenes with his *De antiquissima*.[6] Our purpose is to clarify how he presents his theory of the *factum*, to determine, that is, whether he, like Muratori, used it primarily for antimetaphysical and authoritarian purposes or merged it with one of the metaphysical solutions mentioned above.   We are interested also in the way that Vico interprets the theory of the *verum* and in the sphere of possibility within which the meaning of *making* (*fare*) can be rendered precise.

We have noted above how Vico, with respect to Malebranche, raises the question of the origin of values or ideas whose validity we sense, and how he suggests a choice between the origin of ideas in the self and their origin in God.   If ideas originate in the self, then we are condemned to a radical scepticism, for who in fact can guarantee their objective perception?   On the other hand, the self-consciousness of the ego (Vico has already objected to Descartes) has limits; man is unable by means of it to attain self-knowledge; at most he gains awareness of his existence.[7]

It is a different matter if ideas or possibilities do not originate with man but derive from God, if they are found in man in some objective way as conditions placed there by an agent (*operatore*) that constitutes both the self and the world of nature.   It is true that at this point the superior *agent* would have to take upon itself responsibility for all human acts, including evil and vices.   Yet for Vico the ideas do not determine human actions as far as their contents are concerned; they serve only to indicate the necessity of relating diverse possible contents to their valuative significances.   In the different circumstances in which we act, we feel the need to justify the sense of our acts and to establish their validity.   It is only for this reason that

even while we err, we cannot lose sight of God; in fact, we comprehend the false under the aspect of the true, evil under the appearance of good; we see finitude, we feel ourselves to be finite, but this means that we think the infinite.   It seems to us that we are seeing movements excited and communicated by bodies, but these same excitations, these same communications, assert and confirm God, the mind-God who is author of movement; we see the bad as the good, the many as one, otherness as sameness, things in motion as being at rest; but, since there is in nature neither rectitude, nor unity, nor sameness, nor rest, self-deception in these matters means only that men, even if lacking in prudence and truth with respect to created things, perceive in these imitations themselves the best and greatest God.[8]

This passage is the key to Vichian metaphysics, for it testifies to Vico's interest in *idealities* and in the formal character that they sustain.   Human action is caused by motivations that have to do with the *real*, with the *actual* (*fatto*), which never possesses the purity and the absoluteness of value.   The

---

[6] Vico, *Le orazioni*, p. 85.

[7] *Ibid.*, p. 139.

[8] *Ibid.*, p. 174.

latter comes under consideration because of our awareness of our difference from it and because of man's pretense or need to compare the world of facts with that of value.

Yet the result would seem at this point to promote a disconcerting scepticism; on one side stands the formalism of values, on the other, an indefinable multiplicity of situations; their collation is a *desire*, a *necessity*, but in no case a *science*. That Vico's thought moved to the border of such scepticism is confirmed by the positions he assumed with respect to the possibility of arriving at a science of nature. But to move to the border of scepticism is not to adopt it completely. We have already stressed how, in order to establish the logical structure of the self, the formalism of values might be posited; we must now add that ideas are also rooted in *sensible reality*. Insofar as the idea is rooted in the latter, it is *forma plastae*,[9] a creative component which is not consumed in the vicissitudes of the birth and death of things. The derivation of this concept from Le Clerc's thought is obvious. Elsewhere Vico speaks of *essentiae* or *virtutes*: the vulgar among the ancients had identified them with the *dei immortales*[10] while the learned had recognized, beyond their multiplicity, the divine unity that constituted them.

It is clear, therefore, that the overcoming of scepticism is entrusted to the correspondence which is established between the ideal values contained in the self and the ideal values transferred into reality in the form of plastic forces. Yet how can such correspondence occur if (as we have noted above) the idealities intrinsic to consciousness remain merely formal entities? One answer lies in the fact that the same formal relation that we have seen making the self the medium of the higher, divine reality also governs the nexus between ideality and reality in the sphere of nature. Even here, in fact, plastic forms are indefinable. In nature motion and extension rule. All motions are composites. Metaphysical realities are on one side *rest*, on the other, *effort (conatus)*. But in nature there is no rest, only motion;[11] there are extended things and these are in motion, but there is no *effort* (that is, force-causing motion). Not even light can be called effort; it is motion, which implies its transmissibility in time and its materiality.[12] Plastic natures are therefore inaccessible to us; they assume the formalism of *metaphysical points* (a theory which Vico ascribes to Zeno, but which in reality derives from Galileo), but, as such, they escape all of our cognitive faculties.

The first answer to the question therefore leaves us with only a formal correspondence. We are aware of the presence within ourselves of a metaphysical dimension; we are conscious of the presence of metaphysical forces in nature. But both are for us indefinable. The specter of scepticism thus returns to the fore.

[9] *Ibid.*, p. 150.   [10] *Ibid.*, p. 151.   [11] *Ibid.*, pp. 164–65.   [12] *Ibid.*, p. 161.

The first answer, then, is inadequate and requires further development, either in the direction of the relationship between *virtus* and *factum* in nature or in that of the relationship between *ideality* and *experience* in the cognitive sphere. This development is facilitated on both sides by the notion of *operatio*. Let us consider the question in connection with nature; here, we know, all is motion, and neither rest nor effort exists. There is a *virtus metaphysica*, but when we try to define it, we cannot lay hold of it. We can comprehend only its formal absoluteness, but such absoluteness does not exist in nature; since rectilinear movement is not real,[13] rest is not real, *effort* is not real. If we desire a science, then our only recourse is to *feign* such absolutes in the mind. Mathematics is the use of such absolutes as logical organizers of the world of experience. And precisely because such mathematical fictions *aim* to grasp, not the sensible appearances of things, but their internal structures, the *mathematical organizers* function as limits of physical becoming. The relation that is established between mathematics and physics is a relation which, on the one hand, sanctions the idealization of nature and, on the other, confirms its reality. And it is because the arcane relation between idealizations and facts *in rerum natura* eludes us that man is forced to *contrive* by mental means a relation between factuality and ideality, in his own image and likeness.

Without taking account of the cultural components of his discourse, Vico has thus assumed a position in the great dispute between Le Clerc and Bayle. It had been the latter in fact who, against the tendencies of philosophy and science in the late seventeenth century, had energetically defended the pre-eminence of the factual over the possible. Beside Bayle, and against him, had risen the voice of Jean Le Clerc, who at the beginning of the eighteenth century had promoted Cudworth's *The True Intellectual System*. The basic thesis of this English philosopher and of his divulger was the inadequacy of mechanical arguments for explaining existence and the recourse to *plastic forces*. According to this thesis, the latter possess a limited creative capacity regulated by God. It seemed to Bayle that the recourse to *plastic forces* was little more than an importation of the "intelligences" of the ancients (that is, of the pagan gods) and of the theory of the world soul into the modern context. A certain halo of neopaganism was thus perceived by Bayle around the philosophy of Cudworth and Le Clerc. The latter had also declared himself a supporter of the philosophy of the *factum*; he even characterized himself as an anti-Spinozan. Yet, in the conception of the *plastic forces* as entities, there appeared to be a certain limit placed on the voluntative power of God; and so, to his charge against Le Clerc of encouraging a revival of the philosophy of the ancients, Bayle added another, that of wishing to rationalize Christianity, developing it in an anti-Augustinian, a philo-Erasmian and Arianizing direction.

[13] *Ibid.*, p. 162.

Vico enters the discussion by apparently taking the side of Le Clerc, and yet he does not pretend to define these plastic forces which, as entities, might operate *in rerum natura*. They are real and they operate effectively; but for us they are indefinable and ungraspable; science is rendered possible only by means of the *fiction of the idealities*. In this way the methodological moments proposed by Le Clerc are saved, but within a context in which the metaphysical aspects are played down and the Baylian theme of the *factum* dominates.

But, again, what does this *metaphysica ficta*, which is mathematics considered as the methodological principle of the idealities, have to do with the *factum*? How can *fiction* and *reality* converge in such a way as to satisfy the requirements of the formula *verum et factum convertuntur*? Vico answers this question with his second interpretation of the convergence of the ideal and the real, by fusing it with the theme of the *operatio* in connection with a theory of experience. In fact, the *fictio* apparently is only superimposed on the real structure of man and nature. Between the *fictio mentale* and the real structure of things there exists an element of correspondence: their common origin in the *facere*. The human structure and the formal structure impressed by God on nature have this in common, that both are sustained by the *facere* of God.

But is the *facere* really a central element in the constitution of our experience? And, preliminarily, what are sensations? Our soul is *virtus*; sensation (for example, seeing) is *act*; sense (for example, eyesight) is *facultas*. But for Vico *facultas* is nothing more than *faciendi solertia*, that is, activity. In other words, sensations are created by us; and, if in fact senses are faculties, then in seeing colors, savoring flavors, hearing sounds, touching things cold and hot, we are *making* these things.[14] The only level of being on which force manifests itself directly as *effort* is therefore the human soul. The soul is accorded a creative role with respect to sensations (a view which, on the whole, is not very different from Berkeley's). The objectivity of sensations is based on the fact that, since they are creations of the soul, they tend to transcend it (that is, go beyond the feeling subject), to move toward a deeper reality, of which the creative activity of the subject (the *facere*) is the medium.

The reality that sustains the *facultas* or *facilitas* (that is, the *faciendi solertia*) is defined by Vico as God. While in seventeenth-century epistemology the secondary qualities are interpreted as the modes of appearance of the primary qualities, for Vico the validity of the secondary qualities resides in the fact that they create our relations with things, on the basis of the possible utilization of those things. In general, the universal validity of this relationship lies in the fact that it is established by an active structure, of which human *facilitas* is the medium.

[14] *Ibid.*, p. 175.

Thus, by means of *facilitas* there is established a relation with things which, in the final instance, is centered on their possible utilization in the service of our existence and conservation. This relationship is not conscious, because, although the *facilitas* lives in us, it is not founded by us. The fundamental choices in terms of our existence are already contained in sensibility. We can only add to our natural capacities some artificial ones (*deus . . . naturae artifex, homo artificiorum deus*). The objective status of our knowledge lies, therefore, in living the suggestions of nature (in the *New Science* Vico will justify, on the basis of this presupposition, his belief in the *feral stage* of man) and in discovering new ways of acting by which to carry through projects in the same direction as nature, by imitating the creative capacities of God.

But, if all of the meaning of truth is exhausted in this pragmatic relationship, why have metaphysics at all? Would it not be simpler to found history directly on the search for the utilities, without resorting to the complex metaphysical justification of the idealities? And also, if the pragmatic relationship is the dominant one, why insist on the necessity of deepening and completing our knowledge of things by inductive methods? And why, finally, consider the mathematical fiction, which is another idealization, necessary to science, even if it is *ficta*?

It is obvious that the reduction of knowledge to its pragmatic elements does not exhaust it. For Vico, it is true, all experimental knowledge must be referred back to the principle of *facilitas*. Every sensation, he repeats, following Herbert of Cherbury, is like the manifestation within us of a new faculty, "which is the main argument of that metaphysics."[15] And yet Vico, again following Herbert, asks for a determination of our typical modes of inquiry into the facts of experiences. Such determination would have to be cast as a set of responses to the questions *an sit, quid sit, quanta sit, qualis sit, quando sit,* and so on,[16] that is, it would have to be cast in terms of an ordered induction.[17] From this point of view Herbert's rules serve as topics in the service of the experimental physicists. But not even this use exhausts the meaning of induction. Induction has the task of verifying the true and the false; and the falsity of judgments proceeds only from the fact that "ideas present to us more or less than what things are, of which we cannot be certain, unless we have tested things by all the proper questions that can be set to them."[18]

The relation to *ideality* as a model is not abandoned thereby, but the idealities are now profoundly transformed. Because the idealities are indefinable apart from the "distorted" world of facts, they tend now to place their indefinable absoluteness at the service of the ordering of the facts. Still following Herbert, Vico raises the problem of the *similitudines morum*, thereby approaching awareness of the question of the common sense of nations[19] which will assume so much importance in the *New Science*.

[15] *Ibid.*, p. 256.   [16] *Ibid.*, p. 182.   [17] *Ibid.*, pp. 183–84.   [18] *Ibid.*, p. 269.
[19] *Ibid.*, p. 183.

Metaphysical absoluteness thus tends to take on a methodological dimension. This transformation serves substantially to justify utilization, in the field of history, of certain mathematical and logical techniques that had been discovered in the physical sciences. In Vico's philosophy the *ideas* are no longer defined in their abstract substantiality, but rather serve to indicate the existence of constant structures in the flow of events. Of course, Vico, following his friend Doria, continued to attribute an absolute significance to ideality. As a result, in the field of natural science the methodological reduction of ideas is possible only if the ideas are presented in terms of the unverifiable *fictiones*. The situation is different in the field of history, for here the model of an ideal eternal history is derivable from the facts and can therefore be constructed in a completely scientific manner. It is true that also in the historical process there is a residue of absoluteness. In the *New Science* there is still the permanence of a relation with the absolute, in the vast arc of historical becoming, which permits the attribution of a direction to this becoming. In every discrete historical epoch a relationship with ideal values is established. To recognize such a relationship, however, means not only that one has grasped the unity of history but also that one is able to determine the different ways in which this relationship is constituted in different epochs and to measure the correspondence between the various forms of social cohabitation and their related mentalities. The science of history arises at the moment when it is possible to understand the means by which this relationship is constituted and its functional variations. It is rendered possible by (1) the formality of values in an original relationship of the ego with God; (2) the presence of the idealities in reality as *virtutes*, *formae rerum*, or *plastic forces*; (3) the *operatio* by which the idealities enter into sensible reality, on the one hand, and condition the human investigation of the *utilities*, on the other; and (4) the recognition of the *ideality of value* as the methodological instrument for understanding the possible variations of factual relations.

For Vico, history is thus the actual expression of an eternal ideal order, that is, of a determinable sequence of possibilities. The science of history is the human recognition of the possible relations between the *ideal* and the *fact*. Such relations imply an element of constancy from the standpoint of ideality, in the sense that each epoch is in itself fully realized and does not have to be related to other epochs in order to have its validity established. Facts, on the other hand, are always different; yet, because the attitude assumed by the subject before the facts, in a constant operative effort to utilize them, is itself constant, the eternal ideal history is constituted by fixing the possible modes of relationship of the facts to the uniqueness of value.

The absoluteness of value thus remains, but the methodological aspect explicitly comes to prevail. The limits of the theory of the historical cycle (*corso*) can also be set, by posing on the one hand the feral stage (that is, the return of man to the bestial state) and, on the other, the stage of reflective barbarism, that state of extreme civilization in which men, having acquired the most refined techniques of reason, use them (having lost all reference to value) to the exclusive advantage of the individual, menacing thereby the existence of the species itself.[20] The providential mechanism of conservation in this case acts spontaneously, forcing a return of man to the state of barbarism, in order to assure the conservation of the species. Between these two limits (ferality on one side, forgetfulness of the absoluteness of value on the other) are disposed the history of human civilization, that of social classes, of their struggle, of the diverse forms of cohabitation, and of the sequential order of their greater or lesser perfection in relation to pre-established models. Within these limits the Vichian problematical judgment of history implies the *factum*; but this, in turn, leads to the fixing of a determinate number of possibilities for the ordering of historical facts. Historical knowledge consists in relating the facts to the diverse modes of their possible systematization, including among the facts the historicity of the true, that is, the relationship which men historically establish with values.

However, precisely in this systematization the historicity of the true finds its limit. Truth is defined, on the one hand, in terms of the relation of the diverse, individual moments of history to the absolute, and, on the other, as the total and fluid structure of these moments. In the first instance the facts as such contain their truth. Thus, for example, the symbols used by the priests of the epoch of the gods have a validity of their own (not an arcane and philosophical validity, but a practical and political one). They serve to establish communication with the masses and to control them through fear of the divinities. In this sense the symbols maintain their utility; they are the only possible way of assuring the conservation of the species in those specific circumstances. The margin of truth is wider when, in the epoch of fantasy, poetic physics permits the disposition of concepts which, in their permanent, prevalent, political significance, have some real relationship to nature and suggest the formation of determinate techniques for utilizing nature. This margin is even wider in that phase of history dominated by reason, in which man apprehends logic and achieves inter-human communication by means of a common reference to concepts.

In all these moments of human history, truth, however, is strictly bound to fact through the mediation of the utilities. Truth is constituted in its dependency by practicability. It takes on a different sense in relation to the scientific knowledge of history. Here it is no longer a matter of determining the symbolic or logical communicability (in accordance with the epochs) of certain ideas, but of uncovering, by the study of the facts, their laws and therefore the moments of their cycle. The *New Science* gives us not only localizable instruments of understanding in determinate epochs of history and in connection with the utilities, but also an integrated science of history

[20] Vico, *La scienza nuova*, ed. F. Nicolini (Bari, 1928), II, 162–63.

which explains the character of all epochs of history.   From knowledge, we have thus passed to science.   The ideas no longer refer only to the unconscious *operator* that impels us and directs us along certain paths; they are now known in the form of an ordered arrangement of the historical cycle.

The logical systematization of facts is the work of the *limits* "within which the customs of nations run."[21]   Human nature is constituted according to an order, empirically revealed (even if connected with the permanence of the reference to value), and is expressed in the disposition of a series of events, precisely in relation to the afore-mentioned constitution.   The Vichian philosophy of the *factum* thus leads back, within the sphere of the science of history, to a philosophy of order, the significance of which is more than pragmatic.   Each moment of historical development is motivated by material necessities (beginning with the radical situation of *scarcity*, in which primitive man is immersed, up to the justification of tolerance and freedom, to the moment in which men have greater supplies of material goods),[22] but the series in which the events assume their order (that is, the series of human responses to the requirements of self-preservation) has a theoretical, and not merely a pragmatic, validity.

The relationship between possibility and reality is thus revealed in the indication of the series of events that are possible, given the constitutive conditions of nature and of the human mind.   In this indication the science of history has its role.   That its discovery might for the first time furnish to men an instrument for regulating events is a matter which Vico limits himself to anticipating.   To its full specification arises the obstacle (aside from the limits of the historical situation) of the tendency to transfer to the initiative of Providence that rhythm of the historical cycle which Vico extrapolated from the facts (with the consequence of postulating a metaphysical law of conservation which imposes itself as a mechanism of self-regulation).   This obstacle notwithstanding, between the two solutions of the *verum-factum* relationship which we juxtaposed at the beginning, a way to a third solution was being opened, in which the science of facts (in reference to the historical world) signifies an understanding of their possible results and regulation in conformity with our actions.   The idea of the conversion of the true and the factual has been carried through the moment of practicability (*pragmaticità*), but it was not completely absorbed by it; it has passed through the moment of ideality, but neither was it integrally absorbed by this. Conditioned by the two moments of practicality and ideality, Vico's thought begins to push them in the direction of a science of history, which is today one reason for its currency.

Translated by Hayden V. White

[21] *Ibid.*, I, 81.
[22] *Ibid.*, p. 76.

Max H. Fisch   VICO AND PRAGMATISM

There have been many revolts against Descartes. It is a mark of his great-ness that they still continue. Vico's was not the first, and the pragmatists' has not been the last, but they have been as radical as any. Vico's began two hundred and sixty years ago with his inaugural oration of 1708, *On the Study Methods of Our Time*, and was made explicit and decisive in 1710 by his *Ancient Wisdom of the Italians*. The pragmatic revolt began just a century ago with Charles Peirce's three papers on cognition in the *Journal of Speculative Philosophy* for 1868, and was made firm a decade later by his "Illustrations of the Logic of Science," which appeared in six issues of *Popular Science Monthly* during 1877 and 1878. Neither revolt attracted much notice at the time, and it is only in retrospect that their depth and scope have become apparent. Peirce nowhere mentions Vico, nor does any other American pragmatist. Direct influence is out of the question, and indirect influence would be hard to trace. But a kinship has been discerned,[1] and detailed comparative studies may be expected to shed fresh light both on Vico and on pragmatism. One such study has already appeared, carefully comparing Vico with Dewey, but in a particular respect, dialectically rather than historically, and in relation not to Descartes but to Hobbes.[2] What follows here is the outline of a tentative approach to a more comprehensive and more historical comparison which goes back to the origins of pragmatism and therefore compares Vico primarily with Peirce, and in relation to Descartes, on questions deriving chiefly from Aristotle's *Organon* and *Metaphysics*.[3]

---

[1] See, for examples, James K. Feibleman, "Toward the Recovery of Giambattista Vico," *Social Science*, 14 (1939): 31–40, esp. pp. 36–37, and *An Introduction to Peirce's Philosophy* (New York, 1946), pp. 69–70; Bertrand Russell, *Wisdom of the West*, ed. Paul Foulkes (London, 1959), pp. 207, 277, 296.

[2] Arthur Child, "Making and Knowing in Hobbes, Vico, and Dewey," *University of California Publications in Philosophy*, 16 (1953): 271–310; Descartes appears only on p. 301.

[3] Questions in large part, it might now be said, of the theory of knowledge; but this was not a separate discipline in Vico's time, and was not recognized as such by the pragmatists.

Organon

In the *Organon*, and particularly in the *Topics* and *Posterior Analytics*, Aristotle distinguished demonstrative from dialectical reasoning. The former was scientific; it started from first truths known by intuition, and its conclusions were necessarily true. The latter started from opinable or probable premises and drew opinable or probable conclusions. The former represented an ideal unapproached in antiquity except by Euclid's *Elements* and a few other mathematical works. The latter included the reasoning of the law court, the deliberative assembly, the philosophical dialogue, and, later, the interpretation of legal, classical, and biblical texts and the disputed question of medieval philosophy. The latter was problem-centered and social; the former was not. The latter called for an art of *finding* arguments (or middle terms), called *topic*, from the *topoi* or places in which to seek them, or, in Latin, *inventio*, for the skill of finding. Aristotle dealt with the *topoi* in his *Rhetoric* also, and topic or invention led an amphibious life thereafter, partly in logic, partly in rhetoric. Over against topic, the formal logic of Aristotle and of the Stoics and the medieval logicians came to be viewed as an art for *judging* arguments and to be called *critic* or, in Latin, *iudicium*.[4] Thus the division of logic into topic and critic, invention and judgment, overshadowed, if it did not displace, the earlier division of reasoning into probable and demonstrative. Bacon, while reserving the name of topic for the invention of arguments, and conceiving particular topics as "a kind of mixtures of logic with the proper matter of each science," extended the scope of the logic of invention to include the discovery of new arts and sciences by the aid of his *Novum organum*.

Descartes consigns the traditional logic—topic and critic alike—to rhetoric, and puts in its place the method of his *Rules* and *Discourse*; but he revives Aristotle's distinction in a Neo-Platonic and Augustinian form. There are, he says, but two "operations of our intellect by which we are able, without fear of deception, to arrive at knowledge of things," namely, intuition and deduction. Intuition requires clear and distinct ideas, like those of arithmetic and geometry. Deduction starts from intuition, involves intuition at every step, and is taken up into more complex intuitions. "Enumeration or induction" is not a distinct form of inference but a device for giving to long chains of deductions the certainty of intuition. No reasoning is demonstrative in Aristotle's sense, or deductive in Descartes's sense, which is not connected by a chain of uninterrupted and irreducible steps with intuited first truths, or which contains any premises not known to be true. All science is evident knowledge. There is no middle ground between knowledge and ignorance, and probability falls on the side of ignorance. In the

[4] Cicero, in his *Topics*, in a passage Vico liked to cite (1.2.6), said that the Stoics gave the name of "dialectic" to their logic that was only half a logic, all critic and no topic.

absence of knowledge we may have to act on probability, but it has no place in science. Experiments become necessary in advanced stages of a science, and Descartes performs many, but only to give direction to further deductions. A perfect science would be the work of a single scientist (adult from birth if that were possible) who should not rely on the experiments of others but perform his own. The aim of the method is to form the judgment of the single individual to separate truth from falsehood and to attain all the knowledge of which he is capable.

Metaphysics

From Aristotle's *Metaphysics* came the medieval conception of metaphysics or first philosophy as having two chief concerns: common or universal being and natural theology. Under the former the chief doctrine was that of the "transcendentals"—being, one, true, good—as standing above the distinction of categories, as applicable in every category (analogically or proportionally, at least), and as "convertible." That is, to be is to be true, and vice versa; and likewise with other pairs. *Verum*, true, as a transcendental, refers to the truth of things, not of propositions, and means intelligible. According to some Scholastics, including Duns Scotus, a thing may be said to be true by reason of its conformity to its maker as well as by reason of its conformity to an intellect that knows it. In Scotus, being is the first of the transcendentals; then follow one, true, and good, which are coextensive or convertible with being, and finally the disjunctive attributes (infinite-finite, substance-accident, necessary-contingent, actual-potential, etc.), each pair of which, taken in disjunction, is coextensive with being. Bacon separates first philosophy, metaphysics, and natural theology; makes metaphysics a part of natural philosophy, investigating formal and final causes; and puts under first philosophy a theory of disjunctive transcendentals, "handled as they have efficacy in nature, and not logically." [5]

There was no formal doctrine of transcendentals in which *factum*, made or done, was added to *ens, unum, verum, bonum*, and thus made convertible with *verum*, true; but there were hints from which such a doctrine might have been developed. In the Vulgate, God says "Let *x* be made" (*fiat*), and *x* is made so (*factum est ita*), and God sees that *x* is good (*bonum*). The Maker intends, He makes true, and He inspects and passes what He has made. Similarly, in Greek philosophy, craftsmanship is a standing paradigm both of creation and of knowledge. Socrates's mission takes him to the politicians, the poets, and

[5] *De augmentis* III. iv; Robert McRae, *The Problem of the Unity of the Sciences: Bacon to Kant* (Toronto, 1961), pp. 27–28, 114–15; James F. Anderson, *An Introduction to the Metaphysics of St. Thomas Aquinas* (Chicago, 1953); Allan B. Wolter, *The Transcendentals and Their Function in the Philosophy of Duns Scotus* (St. Bonaventure, N.Y., 1946).

the craftsmen, and it is only among the last, and only within their crafts, that he finds knowledge.   His talk, says Alcibiades, is of pack asses and blacksmiths, shoemakers and tanners.   Socrates in the *Phaedo* says that in his youth he devoted himself to those questions concerning the nature of things which the Ionian philosophers had pursued for a century and a half.   It turned out, however, that to every such question there were as many answers as philosophers and that there was no decision procedure.   Then one day he heard someone reading from a book of Anaxagoras that everything was arranged and caused by mind.   That seemed to promise a decision procedure, because mind does everything for the best and there cannot be more than one best.   Reading on for himself, however, Socrates found Anaxagoras making no use of his mind except to start the vortex.   After that curtain-raiser, material and mechanical causes stole the show as usual; and the many answers to each question were not reduced to one, but increased by one.   Finding the promise of Anaxagoras unfulfilled, and himself unable to fulfill it, Socrates worked up another way of inquiring into the causes of things, which involved hypotheses and "forms."   That is in the strictest sense true or intelligible, and therefore the proper object of science, which in the strictest sense *is*: namely, a form, which cannot seem other than it is or hide any part of itself.   Socrates in the *Republic* adumbrates a system of such forms, in which it is to the supreme form of The Good that the others owe both their being and their truth, and that the knower owes his power of knowing them.   There is no such science of the physical world itself, but only probable accounts; and none more probable, the *Timaeus* suggests, than that it is as if made by a good craftsman, a demiurge, after a perfect model given in the system of forms, but working on a given chaos in a given receptacle or space.   For Aristotle, physics is a science, not just a probable account; but, as both the *Republic* and the *Timaeus* had done, he not only admits final causes but subordinates material, efficient, and formal ones to them.   A science, then, of what kind?   Contemplating, doing, and making have each its mode of reasoning, and there are three corresponding kinds of truth or intelligibility, and of science: theoretical, practical, and "poetic"—that is, productive or creative.   In the *Metaphysics* Aristotle makes physics, along with metaphysics and mathematics, a theoretical science, but in the *Parts of Animals*, thinking of nature as craftsman, he makes physics productive rather than theoretical.   Natural things, that is, have the same kind of truth that works of craftsmanship have—which, an impetuous reader might think, is as much as to say that for physics, as for the crafts, the true is the made.   Later periods yield other hints, on down to Bacon's ringing equation of knowledge and power: "what in working is most useful, that in knowing is most true." [6]

[6] *Novum organum* I. iii; II. iv.   For a few other hints, see Rodolfo Mondolfo, "'Verum ipsum factum' dall' antichità a Galileo e Vico," *Il Ponte*, 22 (1966): 492–506.

Descartes in his *Meditations on First Philosophy* has no doctrine of transcendentals (as he has none of categories in his method), but he does have a
natural theology.   Universal doubt, the *cogito*, the proofs of God's existence
and veracity, bring him to a dualism of mind and body, of thinking and
extended substance, and to the exclusion of final causes from physics.
Leibniz reinstates the Aristotelian and Scholastic transcendentals, but still
without *factum*.[7]

Port-Royal Logic (*1662*)

The Port-Royal *Logic* of Arnauld and Nicole reduced to elementary textbook form not only the Cartesian method but the Cartesian metaphysics,
along with as much of the older logic as could be assimilated to it; more
critic, therefore, than topic.   There are two short chapters on topic: "Places;
or, the Method of Finding Arguments,—That This Method is of Little Use,"
and "Division of Places into Those of Grammar, of Logic, and of Metaphysics."   The latter ends: "It is nevertheless true, that we cannot attain, in
that way, any very valuable knowledge."   What is developed at greatest
length is the Cartesian doctrines of clear and distinct ideas and of demonstration.   The most original doctrine is that of the comprehension and
extension of ideas.   Because the aim throughout is to form the judgment
and render it as exact as possible in discriminating truth from error, the new
logic comes to be called the new critic.   Cartesianism in this textbook form
takes possession of higher education in the student's first year.   It is already
well established in Vico's time, and it remains so into Peirce's, when it is
still a standard textbook.   Peirce can say as late as 1903 that it is "a shameful
exhibit of what the two and a half centuries of man's greatest achievements
could consider as a good account of how to think" (5.84).[8]

Vico: Study Methods (*1709*)

At the University of Naples the academic year 1708–9 opens as usual with

[7] Gottfried Martin, *Leibniz: Logic and Metaphysics*, trans. K. J. Northcott and P. G.
Lucas (Manchester, 1964).

[8] References to Peirce are to the *Collected Papers of Charles Sanders Peirce*, 8 vols.
(Cambridge: Harvard University Press, 1931–58), by volume and paragraph.   References to Vico's *Study Methods* and *Ancient Wisdom* are to the pages of volume I of
Nicolini's edition of the *Opere* (Bari, 1914); and in the former case, after the semicolon,
to the pages of the translation by Elio Gianturco (Indianapolis, Ind., 1965).   References
to Vico's *New Science* are to the numbered paragraphs of volume IV of Nicolini's
edition of the *Opere* (Bari, 1928) and of the English translation by Thomas G. Bergin and
Max H. Fisch, new ed. (Ithaca, N.Y.: Cornell University Press, 1968).

a convocation addressed by the Professor of Eloquence, speaking not for his discipline but for the University. He considers the advantages and disadvantages of the methods of study of the Ancients and of the Moderns, and the possibility of such a conciliation as would unite the advantages of both and avoid their disadvantages. With a fine sense for the proprieties of the occasion, he nowhere names Descartes. Even the term "Cartesian" he uses only once, to remark that a student nowadays is likely to get his physics from an Epicurean, his metaphysics from a Cartesian (119; 77). Arnauld he does name four times in one short passage, but with respect and reserve (83–84; 17ff.). We gather quickly, however, that the Moderns are chiefly the exponents of the new critic (that is, Descartes, Arnauld, and their followers, including the Jansenists) and that the Ancients are chiefly the exponents of the old topic (that is, the Academics, Cicero, and their followers, including the Jesuits). The criticists of antiquity were the Stoics, who disdained topic, eschewed probability, and (like their modern follower Descartes) forged chains of deduction, and whose sage did not opine (83, 85, 118; 16ff., 23–24, 76). The fact that Latin *ingenium*, Italian *ingegno*, Spanish *ingenio*, are translated *esprit* in French—that is, that the faculty of invention is translated as the faculty of judging, what belongs to topic as belonging to critic—argues that only the French could have excogitated the new critic and analytic geometry (95; 40). It may nonetheless be that modern mechanics owes more to *ingenium* and to Euclidian geometry than to Cartesian analysis (87–88; 26ff.).

Vico begins with Bacon, and Bacon is the last author he names at the end. He associates his own criticism of the moderns for relying on chain arguments with Bacon's criticism of the Galenists for relying on syllogisms to the neglect of observation and induction (90; 32–33).

The great fault of modern methods is that college study begins with a logic that belittles topic and is dominated by the new critic, and it ends with a rhetoric in which, for the first time, topic is taken seriously. This inverts the natural order, in which invention comes before judgment, topic before critic. As a result, young minds are blighted at the start and rendered unfit for their subsequent studies; not only for languages, literature, art, history, ethics, politics, and for medicine, theology, and law, but for physics or natural science itself. Let formal logic, like formal rhetoric, be put at the end of college study. In the earlier years, let the place of critic be taken by geometry, taught not analytically but synthetically, in Euclidian fashion, to cultivate spatial imagination along with reason; and let the place of topic be taken by those studies in which memory and imagination generally, ingenuity and inventiveness, common sense, probability and induction, are cultivated (84; 19). Coming at the end rather than at the beginning, the new critic will be put to good uses—even in poetry, if the poetry is there first (96; 42).

But why does premature exposure to the new critic render the young unfit for natural science? Because, by applying the geometric method to physics, it causes to pass as true (*verum*) what is only true*like* (*verisimile*) or probable. What physics gets from geometry with Descartes's aid is expository method only, not demonstration. "We demonstrate geometricals because we make them. If we could demonstrate physicals, we should be making them." But the true forms of physical things, to which their nature is conformed, are in God, not in us (85; 23). And the geometric dress of Cartesian physics has not kept Leibniz from finding two of its laws of motion inexact (85; 21–22).

This is Vico's first approach to the *verum=factum* principle that he will develop in the *Ancient Wisdom* and the *New Science*. He does not connect it directly with the transcendentals, of which we hear only in another context: "The good [or appetible] is congruent with the true [or intelligible] and has the same force, the same properties" (91; 35).

Vico: Ancient Wisdom (*1710*)

Vico now set himself to expound and defend his system of philosophy in the form of a three-volume work *On the Oldest Wisdom of the Italians Recoverable from the Origins of the Latin Language*. Of the three intended volumes—Metaphysics, with an appendix on Logic; Physics; and Ethics— only the first was published, and that without the appendix.

The chief traditional themes of metaphysics, to repeat, were the transcendentals and natural theology. Vico's main innovation in the former was his *verum=factum* principle; in the latter, his metaphysical points. Both were directed against Descartes.

The first sentence of the first chapter pours the new wine of Vico's theory of knowledge into the old wineskin of the transcendentals. "In Latin *verum* and *factum* reciprocate, or, as the Schoolmen commonly put it, convert" (131). (As if to say: "Yes, to be is to be one, true, good—*ens=unum= verum=bonum*; but, since all but God that in any way is, is made—since *ens=factum*—it follows that the true is also the made, *verum=factum*; and, as I shall now argue, it is only as *factum* that it is *verum*, only as made that it is true or intelligible—and intelligible only to its maker.")

We must, of course, distinguish our making from God's. As Christians, we must further distinguish His outward making of the world in time from His inward begetting of the Word from eternity (132, 137, 208). We must correspondingly distinguish our *verum* from His, our *scientia* from His; and we must measure our trues by His true, and our sciences by His science (141, 191). And finally, among our sciences, we must observe a fundamental difference between mathematics and physics of which Descartes failed to take account.

(In the preceding paragraph and in some that follow, I depart from

English usage in the direction of Vico's Latin. English permits us to speak, somewhat stiltedly, of the good, the true, and the beautiful, but not of the trues and the beautifuls, and only in a debased sense of the goods. But Vico's *verum* means the true, not the truth, and its plural *vera* means not the truths but the trues or intelligibles; that is, the things, other than sentences or propositions, that are true in the transcendental sense of intelligible.)

Descartes confused two quite different things: (1) *verum*, the true, which is the object of *scientia*, scientific knowledge, and (2) *certum*, the certain, which is the object of *conscientia*, simple consciousness, awareness, or acquaintance. In the light of this difference, we see that *cogito ergo sum* cannot be the criterion of the true, because there are no trues in it. To be sure, even for the sceptic there is no doubt that he doubts, and no doubt that he exists, but what is not dubious is not therefore true but only certain; and the sceptic's certitude that he thinks and that he exists is that of simple consciousness, not of science (139, 147). Both the *cogito* and the *sum* (more exactly, *exsisto* [221]) are certain, but neither is true. And, as for the *ergo*, science is knowledge by causes, and my thinking is not the cause of my being mind but only a certain sign of it (140). So Descartes has erected a nest of mere certainties into a criterion of the true.

But if *cogito ergo sum* cannot be the criterion of the true, neither can clear and distinct ideas be its rule. (Not one of the three ideas—*cogito, ergo, sum*— is clear or distinct in the first place, but let that pass.) Arithmetic and geometry are models of clear and distinct ideas, but it is not for that reason that they are sciences of the true. "The criterion and rule of the true is to have made it" (136). In mathematics we make the elements by nominal definition, not out of any underlying thing but, as it were, out of nothing, as God makes the elements of the physical world; and we perform the operations and constructions not in or on or out of any physical thing but in that "world of forms and numbers" which man has built for himself (135) "and of which he is in a measure God" (156). The method of Descartes, the geometrical method, the method of intuition and deduction, is a method of exposition, not of discovery, and it cannot give demonstrative character to what would otherwise lack that character. What has the force of demonstration is not the formal proof of textbook expositions but operations and constructions. The reason why mathematics is science of the true is not that its ideas are clear and distinct but that, instead of being a theoretical science as Aristotle and Descartes held, it is wholly productive or constructive, "in its theorems as well as in its problems" (135). "Demonstration is the same as operation, true the same as made" (150).

It is generally acknowledged that arithmetic and geometry are more certain than mechanics, mechanics more than the rest of physics, and physics more than "morals" (psychology, ethics, politics, history, etc.) (136). Now, if clear and distinct ideas *were* the rule of the true, all the sciences might aspire to the condition of mathematics and eventually reach it by adopting the Cartesian method and persisting in it. But there is an ineradicable difference between mathematics and the other sciences, namely, that we make its elements and God makes theirs. A leveling of sciences is therefore not possible.

Nevertheless, whereas Vico in the *Study Methods* had said against Descartes that we cannot demonstrate physicals as we do mathematicals, in the *Ancient Wisdom* he finds something in physics that answers to demonstration in mathematics, namely, experiment. What is wanted in physics, he says, is not the deductive geometric method of Descartes but demonstration itself, which is inductive and which consists in "explaining particular effects in nature by particular experiments which are particular works of geometry" (184). (Vico's word is "peculiar," the opposite of common or general [147]; and I take him to mean that, to explain variations in natural phenomena, we vary our hypotheses and the experiments that are guided by them until we succeed in producing variations similar to those we are trying to explain.) Just as that which has the force of demonstration in mathematics is operation and construction, so, that which has the force of demonstration in physics is experiment, and what mathematics contributes to experiment, by way of mechanics, is definiteness of hypothesis and of experimental design and contrivance. This is the way to advance physics, and those who in modern times have thus advanced it have been Galileo and his followers in Italy (who explained numberless great natural phenomena before Descartes introduced the geometrical method into physics) and, more recently, the physicists of England (184-85).

But physics remains irreducibly different from mathematics in that, though we make the hypotheses and experiments, we do not make the elements of the physical things on which our experimental operations are performed, and our experimental effects are only like the natural effects we seek to explain and are not those effects themselves. In mathematics the causes are entirely within ourselves; we demonstrate by causes, we make the trues we know, and making is all one with knowing. In physics the elements of natural things are outside us; we cannot demonstrate by causes, what we make is not what we seek to know but only something like it, and making is not all one with knowing, nor the true all one with the made, but "we hold *for* true only that whose *like* we produce by experiments" (149-50, 191). That is, such quasi-truth or intelligibility as nature in part has for us, in spite of its being none of our making, lies in the control it exerts over our conjectures about it, as we assimilate our makings to it in successive approximations, and the tools of this assimilation are mathematics and experiment.

To sum up: Mathematics is wholly demonstrative in the sense of proving by causes; physics is partly demonstrative in a secondary and derivative sense; no science is demonstrative in Aristotle's or Descartes's sense. But there is progress in physics; agreement and consensus are reached; and this is brought about by experimental demonstration, not by the geometrical method. The logic of deduction is not the logic of science; experiment is central to the logic of physics, not just an adjunct; it is heuristic and inductive; it belongs to topic, not critic; and that is why the new critic of the Cartesians, who neglect topic as the Stoics did, cannot be the logic of science (180–85).

All of this is implicit, and much of it explicit, in the first two sections of chapter I. To round out his preliminary statement of it there, Vico sets it firmly in the framework of the transcendentals by a concluding paragraph on the convertibility of *verum* and *bonum* in God's making and ours (137).

We turn now from the transcendentals to the other chief theme of metaphysics: namely, natural theology, the relations between God and the world, and between mind and body. Here Vico is attacking Cartesian dualism, and his chief innovation is the doctrine of metaphysical points.

Descartes has clear and distinct ideas of thinking, extension, matter as identical with extension, and motion as a mode of extension. So, in effect, he takes extension and motion as given. But this is to substitute physics for metaphysics (158, 261) and to make all relation and transition between thinking and extension unintelligible. Without falling into Aristotle's opposite error of turning metaphysics directly into physics, we must start with God's making. On the hypothesis that our making in mathematics is as near as we can come to God's making, but that what we make are fictions and what God makes are realities, we reach the hypothesis that the elements made by God, out of which He makes the world of extension and motion, are metaphysical points. As in geometry we construct the extended line, plane, surface, and figure from the unextended geometrical point by postulation or hypothesis, and, as in rational mechanics we construct motion in the same way, so, in metaphysics, our hypothesis must be, first, that God produces extended bodies from points that are unextended and indivisible but endowed with infinite power of extension, and, second, that the conatus or power of motion ascribed by physicists to bodies must be ascribed instead to these metaphysical points. Thus, "as the metaphysical point is an infinite power of extension which equally underlies unequal extensions, so [its] conatus is an infinite power of moving which equally explains unequal motions" (157). By this hypothesis we can descend from metaphysics to physics, that is, from God and from the true Forms of things as they are in God, to the physical world (163, 259, 261); we escape dualism by taking the substance of bodies to be incorporeal, the causes of motion to be motionless; and thus, instead of taking the physical world as brute fact, we *explain* its existence. But of course our metaphysical hypothesis does not of itself explain particular bodies or particular motions. For that we must pursue particular experiments, and we can stretch our explanations only as far as we can carry our experiments.

The two main anti-Cartesian doctrines of Vico's metaphysics, *verum*= *factum* and metaphysical points, are related in this way. In mathematics, since the entire causes of the effects we produce are within ourselves, we demonstrate by causes; in physics, since the elements of natural things are outside us, we cannot demonstrate by causes. But in metaphysics we must propose a hypothesis as to what those elements are, and, guided by the *verum*=*factum* criterion, which only our mathematics can nearly satisfy, we are led to the metaphysical point as something we can "contemplate from the hypothesis of the geometrical point" (191).

In conclusion, Vico commends his metaphysics for the *kind* of physics we descend to from it. "By requiring us to hold for true in nature only that the like of which we can make by experiments, it serves the experimental physics which is now being cultivated to the great benefit of mankind" (191). Not the deductive physics, which turns to experiment when in doubt as to what to intuit or deduce next, but the inductive physics, which keeps its focus on experiments and whose demonstrations are the experiments themselves.

Vico: New Science (*1744*)

For lack of space, I pass over the *Universal Law* (1720–22), the first two editions of the *New Science* (1725, 1730), and the *Autobiography* (1729) and consider only the third and last edition of the *New Science* (1744). Here there is but one mention of Descartes by name (706), and it is incidental and unpolemic. I remark only that, as usual, Vico links him with the Stoics.

Some scholars see a positive influence of Descartes in the section entitled "Elements" (119–329), with its axioms, definitions (137–38, 142, 320–26), and postulates (192, 195, 248, 295, 306)—as if Vico were applying the geometrical method to history. But this is to forget that he has also a section on "Method" (338–60), as remote from the *Rules* and the *Discourse* as it could well be, and that he says he is applying to history the method Bacon in his *Cogitata et visa* proposed to apply to nature (163, 359).

Nearly all the nameless criticisms of Descartes and Cartesianism in the *Study Methods* were repeated in the *Ancient Wisdom* with the names; nearly all those in the *Ancient Wisdom* are repeated in the *New Science* without the names. What is both anti-Cartesian and new is the new science itself. It is anti-Vichian too, if we measure Vico by the *Study Methods* and *Ancient Wisdom*. In the latter, we have seen, there was a scale of diminishing certainty running from mathematics through mechanics and physics to morals. Only God's science fully satisfied the *verum*=*factum* criterion. Of man's sciences, mathematics came nearest to doing so; mechanics next; physics next, but only in small part and very imperfectly; morals, man's knowledge of himself, not at all.   Now, man's new science of himself heads the list.   It meets the *verum=factum* criterion better than mathematics (349).

No longer bound to the transcendentals, Vico has made the certain co-ordinate with the true and has elaborated the distinction between them. The true is still the intelligible; the certain is now the ascertainable.   The intelligible is that which may be understood by reason, in terms of causes, universals, laws.   The ascertainable is that which may be witnessed, or suffered, or known by the testimony of witnesses or from competent authority.   Science is knowledge of the true; *conscience*, the witnessing consciousness, is knowledge of the certain.   Philosophy *aims* at science; philology *aims* at conscience.

The philologians include "all the grammarians, historians, critics, who have occupied themselves with the study of the languages and deeds of peoples: both at home, as in their customs and laws, and abroad, as in their wars, peaces, alliances, travels, and commerce" (139)—more generally, "of all the institutions that depend on human choice" (7).   The philosophers include all the—scientists, Vico might have said if the word had existed, but Whewell did not coin it until a century later, in time for Peirce.

In these broad senses of the two terms, "philosophy has had almost a horror of treating philology, because of the deplored obscurity of the causes and almost infinite variety of the effects" (7).   Because of the estrangement of the two cultures in the Cartesian age, each has failed by half in its own aims (140).   The philologians, finding some help in the topic of the logicians, but none in their critic, have developed a philological or erudite critic of their own.   More recently this has been influenced by the new critic of the Cartesians, but with results almost wholly negative.

To "reduce to certainty human choice, which by its nature is most un-certain," and thereby "to reduce philology to the form of science" (7, 141, 390), a new critic was needed—new relative to the new critic of the Cartesians as well as to the merely erudite critic of the philologians (7, 143)—a critic which Vico now supplies and which he also calls metaphysical (348, 493, 662, 839) or philosophical (392).

Since Vico's new critic requires a complex interplay of philosophy and philology, science and conscience, moving back and forth between the true and the certain, it must have a criterion for the certain as well as one for the true.   Neither criterion bears any resemblance to "*I* think, therefore *I* am," or to the rule of clear and distinct ideas.   The criterion of the certain is "the common sense of makind" (145) "with respect to human needs or utilities" (141), "determined by the necessary harmony of human institutions" (348), "on which the consciences of all nations repose" (350).   The criterion of the true is the same as before, *verum=factum*, the true is the made.   If the new science is to satisfy that criterion, its "first undoubted principle" must then be that "the civil world has certainly been made by men.   Therefore its principles can, because they must, be found within the modifications of our own human mind. Whoever reflects on this cannot but marvel how all the philosophers studied seriously to attain the science of the natural world, of which, since God made it, He alone has the science; and neglected to meditate on the world of nations, or civil world, of which, since men had made it, men could attain the science" (331).

The new science is like mathematics in being constructive, but the way it satisfies the *verum=factum* criterion is different. Men *have* made the world of nations; it exists; it is real, as the world of nature is and that of mathematics is not. Moreover, in making it they have in a sense made themselves (367, 520, 692), which they can scarcely be said to do in the course of making the world of mathematics. But the science of the world of nations has not come *ipso facto* and *pari passu* with the making, as it does in the world of mathematics. The new science comes rather with a *re*making, a *re*constructing, which could not even begin until Vico had made a certain discovery, the master key of the new science (34), which had cost him the research of a good twenty years (338). Yet, after all, the new science takes place in the world of sciences, which is part of the world of nations, and so the remaking not only represents but continues and is part of the first making, and partakes of its reality. "When geometry is constructing the world of magnitudes from its very elements, or is contemplating it, it is at the same time making that world for itself. Exactly so does this science proceed, but with a reality greater by just so much as the institutions that order human affairs are more real than points, lines, surfaces, and figures are" (349).

That is, whereas Vico had been a nominalist in his constructive theory of mathematics, the new science of history, though also constructive, has made a realist of him, and has even modified the nominalism of his theory of mathematics. In the *Ancient Wisdom*, God made realities, and man in his most Godlike making made only fictions. In the *New Science*, man in his most Godlike making makes realities.

But science itself is true or intelligible only as made along with the making of the world of nations, and the history of science is therefore the science of it. This holds for the logic of science also, and the history of logic is a proper part of the new science. The priority of topic over critic is now justified by the new science of history. But the logic of the philosophers, topic and critic alike, was a late development, preceded by what Vico calls "sensory topic" (495), by autopsy or evidence of the senses (499), by Aesopian example, and, more importantly, by a vast development of a more strictly poetic logic (400–500), the terms of which were "poetic characters" (34, 412–27). After his long account of this poetic logic, Vico sketches the history of the logic of the philosophers, and once more contrasts the fruitful inductive method of the Pythagoreans and Hippocratics, of Socrates and Plato, with the barren deductive method of Aristotle with his syllogisms and the Stoics with their sorites, "to which corresponds the method of the modern philosophers" (that is, the Cartesians), and he concludes: "Hence with great reason Bacon . . . proposes, commends, and illustrates the inductive method in his [*Novum*] *Organum*, and is still followed by the English with great success in experimental philosophy" (499).

Two movements may be discerned in Vico's anti-Cartesianism. In the first he has put forward a new criterion of the true, opposed to Descartes's, as affording a better reason than Descartes's for the pre-eminence of mathematics among the sciences, a pre-eminence Vico does not yet challenge; and he has used the new criterion, along with his theory of metaphysical points, to sanction and serve a physics more inductive and experimental than Descartes's. In the second, out of the historical and philological studies that the Cartesians disdained, using anti-Cartesian criteria of both the true and the certain, and passing now from nominalism to realism, he has created a new science of history which supersedes mathematics as the exemplary science of the humanly true or intelligible. The stone the builders rejected has become the head of the corner.

Peirce: The Cognition Series (1868)

For the early Peirce, the chief business of logic was classifying arguments and determining their strength or validity by classes. There were three irreducible classes: deduction, induction, and hypothesis. The strength of an argument, as he put it in a paper of 1867, "is only the frequency with which *such* an argument will yield a true conclusion when its premises are true" (3.19). Realism, nominalism, and conceptualism were then understood as theories not only of universal terms but also of the import of propositions and of the validity of arguments, and this was the nominalistic theory of the validity of arguments. Hamilton, in his lecture on nominalism and conceptualism, had said: "In this discussion I avoid all mention of the ancient doctrine of Realism. This is curious only in an historical point of view; and is wholly irrelevant to the question at issue among modern philosophers." Mill in his *Examination of Hamilton* had agreed: "Realism being no longer extant, nor likely to be revived, the contest at present is between Nominalism and Conceptualism." [9] Peirce had declared for nominalism in a review of Venn's *Logic of Chance*. "The logic of the Middle Ages," he had said, "is almost coextensive with demonstrative logic; but our age of science opened with a discussion of probable argument (in the *Novum Organum*), and this part of the subject has given the chief interest to modern studies of logic." Conceptualism was plausible so

[9] Sir William Hamilton, *Lectures on Metaphysics*, lecture XXXV; John Stuart Mill, *An Examination of Sir William Hamilton's Philosophy* (London, 1865), chaps. XVII–XIX.

long as we focused on deduction, but now that the advance of science has pushed our focus to induction and hypothesis, the two classes of probable argument, we find that only nominalism will do as a general theory of validity. "[W]hat constitutes the validity of a genus of argument? The necessity of thinking the conclusion, say the conceptualists. But a madman may be under a necessity of thinking fallaciously, and (as Bacon suggests) all mankind may be mad after one uniform fashion. Hence the nominalist answers the question thus: A genus of argument is valid when from true premises it will yield a true conclusion—invariably if demonstrative, generally if probable" (8.1–2).

The editor of the *Journal of Speculative Philosophy* challenged Peirce to show how upon this nominalistic theory "the validity of the laws of logic can be other than inexplicable" (5.318). Peirce took up the challenge in a series of three articles on cognition (5.213–357). In the first, in the form of a medieval disputed question, attacking the intuitionism assumed by the conceptualistic theory, he argued that we have no power of intuition, but that every cognition is determined logically by previous cognitions and ultimately by probable inferences, that is, by inductions and hypotheses. This was as much as to say that there are no such first truths as Aristotle and Descartes supposed, and that neither science nor mathematics can have, or should desire, any such foundations.

Descartes is not named in the first paper, but Peirce begins the second with a four-point statement of "the spirit of Cartesianism" as opposed to scholasticism, continues with a four-point statement of the "spirit of opposition to Cartesianism" to which "modern science and modern logic" lead, and adds that the first paper has been written in this latter anti-Cartesian spirit. In all four respects "modern science and modern logic" are closer to scholasticism than to Descartes. (1) We cannot begin with universal doubt; if we could there is no absolute certainty which we could reach by it; if there were, it would be such a certainty as could not help, and might hinder, science. The doubts by which science is furthered are piecemeal doubts, for particular, not for general, reasons, in retail, not in wholesale, lots. (2) The test of certainty is to be found not in the individual consciousness, where the *cogito* sought it, but in the eventual agreement of competent investigators. "We individually cannot reasonably hope to attain the ultimate philosophy which we pursue; we can only seek it, therefore, for the *community* of philosophers." (3) The successful sciences trust rather to multitude and variety of arguments, like the "multiform argumentation of the middle ages," than to single chain arguments like Descartes's, which often depend on inconspicuous premises. A chain is no stronger than its weakest link, but a scientific conclusion supported by many reasons may be stronger than any one of them, and may even be made certain by them, though none of them is itself certain. (4) It is never admissible to suppose a fact to be absolutely inexplicable. "But there are many facts which Cartesianism not only does not explain but renders absolutely inexplicable, unless to say that 'God makes them so' is to be regarded as an explanation." All connection between mind and body, in perceiving, suffering, acting, and the laws of nature themselves, are thus rendered inexplicable by Descartes's dualism.

If, from this anti-Cartesian passage-at-arms in the opening pages of the second paper, we return to the first, we see that the *quaestio* form was not an antiquarian whimsy. It was intended to exemplify, as well as commend, "the multiform argumentation of the middle ages" and thereby to show that, though medieval logicians attended chiefly to deduction, the method practiced by medieval philosophers was inductive and hypothetical and thus closer than Descartes's to that of modern science. In the remainder of the second paper and in the third, Peirce takes the anti-Cartesian conclusions of the first as hypotheses and draws out their consequences, not so much to prove the consequences as to test the hypotheses further. It now transpires that the whole argument of the three papers is directed not only against Cartesian intuitionism but also against the incognizable thing-in-itself to which Descartes's dualism commits him, and that, in both directions, the argument turns on the medieval doctrine of the transcendentals, and more particularly on the convertibility of *ens* and *verum*. That doctrine was there in the first paper, but we had missed it, partly because, since the transcendental sense of *true* was no longer current in English, Peirce has substituted *cognizable*. In arguing that we have no conception of the absolutely incognizable, he had said: "In short, *cognizability* (in its widest sense) and *being* are not merely metaphysically the same, but are synonymous terms" (5.257).

Out of this transcendental equation, with the help of the other conclusions of the first paper, Peirce develops a sign theory of cognition, a semiotic idealism, a social theory of logic, and a minim of logical realism.[10] The principle of human individuation is ignorance and error. All thought is in signs. All our cognitions "have been logically derived by induction and hypothesis from previous cognitions." Along with the intuitions of Descartes we must reject the sense-data of British empiricism, which in this respect is only a species of Cartesianism (5.291–309). Cognitions "are of two kinds, the true [in the *non*-transcendental sense] and the untrue, or cognitions whose objects are *real* [= true in the transcendental sense] and those whose objects are *unreal*." The distinction between real and unreal, in turn, comes to that "between an *ens* relative to private inward determinations, to the negations belonging to idiosyncrasy, and an *ens* such as would stand in the long run." "The real, then, is that which, sooner or later, information and reasoning would finally result in, and which is therefore

[10] Max H. Fisch, "Peirce's Progress from Nominalism toward Realism," *The Monist*, 51 (1967): 159–78.

independent of the vagaries of me and you. Thus, the very origin of the conception of reality shows that this conception essentially involves the notion of a COMMUNITY, without definite limits, and capable of a definite increase of knowledge" (5.311).

From this theory of the real, with the help of the further premise that "no cognition of ours is wholly determinate," Peirce now infers that some generals or universals are real (5.312). Thus equipped, he proceeds in the third article to explain the validity of the laws of logic. His general theory of validity remains the same as that which he had called nominalistic in his opposition to conceptualism, but he no longer calls it nominalistic; and, though still adequate for deduction, it requires amendment for probable inference. We cannot say that inductions and hypotheses generally hold, or hold with any determinable frequency, but only that in an indefinitely long run of them "our errors balance one another" (5.350) and we approach those conclusions on which, if it reached them, the community of investigators would agree.

Peirce: The Pragmatism Series (1877–78)

The publisher, W. H. Appleton, informed of Peirce's views on the logic of science by shipboard conversations with him, invites him to write for the *Popular Science Monthly*, and Peirce contributes a series of six "Illustrations of the Logic of Science." [11]

The appeal to history, so slight in the cognition series as to have escaped our notice (5.215), is now emphatic. The logic of science is not spun out of the inner consciousness of a logical genius, once and for always, but is gradually learned from the practice of the successful sciences, "each chief step" of which "has been a lesson in logic" (5.363). As of the 1870's, the chief recent step has been the extension of statistical methods from economics to physics and biology. In the lesson taught by evolutionary biology, knowing becomes a species of believing; the opposite of believing is doubting; belief is primary; its essence is the habits of action by which alone one belief is distinguished from another; genuine doubt is breakdown of belief by surprise or frustration; inquiry is started by doubt and ended by the resettling of belief; and the scientific method is an emergent way of resettling

[11] *Popular Science Monthly*, 12 (1877–78): 1–15, 286–302, 604–15, 705–18; 13 (1878): 203–17, 470–82. A book under the same title was announced as in preparation for the International Scientific Series but never appeared. There is no accurate reprint of these papers. The only accurate account of them is in a master's thesis by Donald R. Koehn, "Charles S. Peirce's 'Illustrations of the Logic of Science'" (University of Illinois, Urbana, 1966). Mr. Koehn is writing a doctor's thesis on the same subject. His criticisms of a draft of the present essay have led to extensive revisions. See also Max H. Fisch, "A Chronicle of Pragmaticism, 1865–1879," *The Monist*, 48 (1964): 441–66.

belief, supervening upon such other ways as tenacity, authority, and the a priori. It is to the last that most philosophers, and Descartes above all others (5.391, 406), are committed. But it is only the scientific method that involves the conception of reality and that is such that the ultimate conclusion of every man shall be the same (5.384).

"The very first lesson that we have a right to demand that logic shall teach us is, how to make our ideas clear" (5.393). But the logic of science is a logic of discovery, and since "nothing new can ever be learned by analyzing definitions," Cartesian clarity and distinctness, even as amended by Leibniz, are insufficient. Heuristic science requires a "higher perspicuity" (5.392), the rule for which is, for each idea, to specify "sensible effects" and "habits of action" adjusted to them. Thus, in mineralogy, to make the idea of hardness clear, for the propositional function "x is harder than y" we may begin by specifying the sensible effect "x will scratch y and not be scratched by it" and the habits of using x when we want to scratch y (as when y is a sheet of glass to be divided) and of keeping x away from y when we do not want y scratched. (Peirce here for the first time in print explicitly connects meaning, and thereby truth and knowledge, with doing-and-making, and thus approaches the substance though not the language of Vico's *verum = factum*. This maxim or rule of logic he had for some years called "pragmatism," but he did not use that name in print until 1902. In a letter of 1912, he said he had derived the name "from πρᾶγμα, 'behavior'—in order that it should be understood that the doctrine is that the only real significance of a general term lies in the general behavior which it implies." [12] I shall return to this point in the Epilogue.)

The third degree of clarity is the decisive step that separates the method of science from those of tenacity, authority, and apriority. For them the first two degrees suffice, and if science were an affair of intuition and deduction, as Aristotle and Descartes had thought, the first two degrees would suffice for science also. But the logic of science is not that of proof or demonstration but that of hypothesis and induction; that is, of discovery. (This is the counterpart in Peirce of Vico's insistence that topic is prior to critic. The place of topic has been taken by the logic of science, the new organ of "invention" or discovery; and Peirce's identification and analysis of the third grade of clarity is the first American contribution to that organ.) It is "the prerogative of the method of science" to cause our opinions "to coincide with the fact" (5.387); its "fundamental hypothesis" is that of reality (5.384), and it submits particular hypotheses to that fundamental one by putting them through this third degree, so as to make them fully responsive to observation, experiment, and induction.

Between Vico and Peirce the doctrine of chances, or calculus of proba-

[12] MS L 321, draft of letter to Howes Norris, Jr., May 28, 1912.

bilities, had had a great development. The calculus itself is deductive, and belongs to mathematics rather than science, but the idea on which it rests has permeated science throughout, and changed the very conception of it. The probable, excluded from science by Aristotle and Descartes, is now seen to be of its essence. The data of science are probable, as being subject to probable errors of observation and measurement, if not also in a profounder sense; and the forms of inference proper to science, namely, hypothesis and induction, are probable only, not demonstrative. The idea which therefore, above every other, calls for the third degree of clarity, is that of probability—if indeed it is not rather a cluster of ideas all bearing the same name. This clarification is the principal task of the last four papers of the pragmatism series. We are brought to views similar to those of the cognition series, including the social theory of logic (2.652–55). What is new is the historical, the evolutionary, the pragmatic conception of science itself, in terms of which these views are now set forth and more fully developed.

Peirce: The Evolution Series (1891–93)

The fullest consecutive published statement of Peirce's mature metaphysics was made in a series of five articles in *The Monist*.[13] Like Vico's metaphysics, it is anti-Cartesian, idealistic, and commended as subserving experimental physics. "The old dualistic notion of mind and matter, so prominent in Cartesianism, as two radically different kinds of substance, will hardly find defenders today" (6.24). But, although we no longer have two substances, we still have two kinds of law, physical and psychical, and a problem as to the relation between them. Consider first the physical laws that were discovered first and are best understood, those of dynamics. "A modern physicist on examining Galileo's works is surprised to find how little experiment had to do with the establishment of the foundations of mechanics." That is not, as Vico says, because we make theoretical mechanics almost as we do mathematics, or because dynamics is the closest of all branches of physics to pure mathematics, but because, "our minds having been formed under the influence of phenomena governed by the laws of mechanics, certain conceptions entering into those laws become implanted in our minds, so that we readily guess at what the laws are." (Not *verum= factum*, we are tempted to say, but *verum=faciens*: it is not what our minds have made up, but what has made them up, that is intelligible to them.) "The further physical studies depart from phenomena which have directly influenced the growth of the mind, the less we can expect to find the laws

---

[13] 6.7–65, 102–63, 238–71, 287–317; see 5.436 for an intended sixth article that never appeared.

which govern them 'simple'" (6.10); and "When we come to atoms, the presumption in favor of a simple law seems very slender" (6.11). "To find out much more about molecules and atoms we must search out a natural history of laws of nature which may fulfill that function which the presumption in favor of simple laws fulfilled in the early days of dynamics, by showing us what kind of laws we have to expect" (6.12). What Peirce proposes, then, is a cosmogonic or second-order hypothesis of the evolution of the laws of nature, by which we may be guided in forming first-order hypotheses for experimental testing in the several branches of physics. The hypothesis is that the laws of nature are acquired habits, beginning in absolute chance, spreading, becoming continuous, and growing toward, but never reaching, absolute necessity; that is, the hypothesis that physical laws derive from the one psychical law, the law of association or habit-taking. "The one intelligible theory of the universe is that of objective idealism, that matter is effete mind, inveterate habits becoming physical laws" (6.24). So that, after all, there is a sense in which, for Peirce, as for Vico, *verum=factum*. "That which did all this was mind."

This, rather than Vico's metaphysical points, is Peirce's anti-Cartesian hypothesis for descending from metaphysics to physics; but in the detail of his argument he concludes that neither molecules nor atoms can be absolutely impenetrable and that "we are logically bound to adopt the Boscovichian idea that an atom is simply a distribution of component potential energy throughout space" (6.242)—an idea as close to Vico's as was possible for a working physicist in Peirce's time.[14]

Peirce: Other Writings (1890–1908)

What I promised at the beginning was not a comparison but the outline of an approach to a comparison—an outline which should bring into relief some of the features likely to lend themselves to fruitful comparison. For lack of space, I have omitted what is not deliberately anti-Cartesian; I have omitted pragmatists other than Peirce;[15] I have come only halfway with Peirce; and even within those limits I have omitted many relevant considerations. I conclude now with a few anti-Cartesian themes from Peirce's

[14] Peirce concerned himself with atomic theory until late in life. His first published professional paper, of 1863, was on "The Chemical Theory of Interpenetration." This aspect of his scientific work has not been studied.

[15] James, Dewey, Mead, and Lewis, for examples. Whitehead in his *Science and the Modern World* (New York, 1925) took James's "Does Consciousness Exist?" (1904) as marking the end of the Cartesian age in philosophy. For Dewey, see n. 2 above. Chapters I and XII of C. I. Lewis's *Analysis of Knowledge and Valuation* (La Salle, Ill., 1946) read like a pragmatic version of the transcendentals with Vico's *factum* firmly placed in the center: *verum=factum=bonum*.

later writings which have not appeared, or have not been prominent, in the three series of papers so far considered.

Mind as non-substantial, non-resident, and mostly non-conscious. In his Harvard Lectures on Pragmatism in 1903 Peirce said that the normative sciences—logic, ethics, aesthetics—are in the truest sense "sciences of mind." "Only, modern philosophy has never been able quite to shake off the Cartesian idea of the mind, as something that 'resides'—such is the term— in the pineal gland. Everybody laughs at this nowadays, and yet everybody continues to think of mind in this same general way, as something within this person or that, belonging to him and correlative to the real world. A whole course of lectures would be required to expose this error" (5.128).

As an experimental psychologist and one familiar with the literature, Peirce had written as early as 1890: "The doctrine of Descartes, that the mind consists solely of that which directly asserts itself in unitary consciousness, modern scientific psychologists altogether reject. Swarming facts positively leave no doubt that vivid consciousness, subject to attention and control, embraces at any one moment a mere scrap of our psychical activity." In part on the basis of his own experiments, he bluntly laid it down that: "(1) The obscure part of the mind is the principal part. (2) It acts with far more unerring accuracy than the rest. (3) It is almost infinitely more delicate in its sensibilities" (6.569).

Mathematics as constructive. Benjamin Peirce, the leading American mathematician of his day, defined mathematics as "the science which draws necessary conclusions." That made it coextensive with deduction. His two eldest sons, James and Charles, were also mathematicians. A two-volume edition of Charles's mathematical writings is in preparation. Charles's work on the logic of relations also influenced his conception of deduction as non-intuitive, regulated by choice and deliberate plan, yet reaching its conclusions, many of them surprising, by observation, and differing from induction mainly in that the objects it observes are of our own creation, whereas we have relatively little control over those of inductive science. No mathematical proofs are demonstrative in Aristotle's sense or deductive in Descartes's. "Mathematical reasoning . . . does not relate to any matter of fact, but merely to whether one supposition excludes another. Since we ourselves create these suppositions, we are competent to answer them. . . . Mathematical reasoning holds. Why should it not? It relates only to the creations of the mind, concerning which there is no obstacle to our learning whatever is true of them" (2.191f.). Mathematical knowledge "is to be classed along with knowledge of our own purposes" (5.166).

Science as a mode of life, social and historical. Descartes said that all science is certain and evident knowledge. The dictionaries called it systematized knowledge. But that, said Peirce, was shelved science (1.234), "the corpse

of science." "Science itself, the living process, is busied mainly with conjectures, which are either getting framed or getting tested" (1.234). "As
a living thing, animating men, it need not be free from error,—nor can it
be;—and it cannot be thoroughly systematized so long as it is in rapid
growth" (MS 965). "A" science is or implies "a social group of devotees"
(8.378). Science "as a living historic entity" (1.44) "is a mode of life . . .
and that which distinguishes the life of science . . . is not the *attainment* of
knowledge, but a single-minded absorption in the *search* for it for its own
sake." [16]

History as Science. The Greek name for science as knowledge was *episteme*
which Peirce anglicized as epistemy (1.232, 279). The Greek name for
science as inquiry was *historia*, which was already anglicized as history.
Though Peirce was less sure than Vico was of history's being science in the
former sense, he was perfectly sure of its being science in the latter sense. He
was himself a historian, more particularly of science, and several of the
quotations in the preceding paragraph are from drafts of his unfinished
"History of Science." He had given a course of twelve Lowell Institute
lectures in Boston in 1892–93 on "The History of Science from Copernicus
to Newton." One of the problems that concerned him was the logic of
Kepler's search for the orbit of Mars. Another was the shift from the moral
to the physical sense of "law of nature"—from its meaning something that
can but ought not to be broken, to its meaning something that cannot be
broken. He found the chief source of this scientific superstition in Descartes:
"Moreover, from this same immutability of God, certain rules, or laws of
nature, can be known, which are secondary and particular causes of the
different movements which we observe in bodies." [17] Peirce was even more
critical of German historical criticism, higher and lower, than Vico was of
the historical criticism more immediately influenced by Descartes. Peirce,
like Vico, gave much thought to the roles of hypothesis and induction in
historical inquiry as compared with their roles in natural science. It was no
accident that the last major revision of Peirce's general logic of science was to
take better account of history, and was presented to the National Academy
of Sciences in 1901 in a monograph "On the Logic of Drawing History from
Ancient Documents especially from Testimonies" (7.162–255). [18] So there
were two principal movements in Peirce's anti-Cartesianism as there were in
Vico's, the first in a broad sense metaphysical, the second historical. And, as

[16] *Selected Writings*, ed. Philip P. Wiener (New York: Dover Publications, 1966),
pp. 227–28. (For MS 965 and other unpublished papers see Richard S. Robin, *Annotated
Catalogue of the Papers of Charles S. Peirce* [Amherst: University of Massachusetts Press,
1967].)
[17] *Selected Writings*, p. 298.
[18] The fullest and best account of this is Willard Marshall Miller's master's thesis,
"History as Science in the Philosophy of Charles Sanders Peirce," University of Illinois,
Urbana, 1968. He is writing a doctor's thesis on the same subject.

it was by way of history that Vico moved from nominalism to realism, so it was by way of evolution and history that Peirce did so.

Epilogue

If we imagine that an approach like the one outlined above has been taken, and that the comparison has then been worked out in detail, and if we try to predict its conclusions, we may imagine them beginning somewhat as follows.

Vico and the pragmatists are among those philosophers who, for various reasons, have rejected the spectator theory of knowledge. Plato's "contemplation of all time and all existence" is a misconception of philosophy and science, of knowledge divine or human. The world is not given as an object for contemplation, a world we have not made, waiting to be known. If it may be said to be given at all, it is given as known and misknown from of old, with our past knowings and misknowings inextricably, unidentifiably ingrown, a world already construed and more or less misconstrued, a world in part constructed out of our doings and makings—our languages and other institutions, our domestications, our tools, machines, instruments, our experiments of all kinds—and the rest construed by imagined extensions of our doings and makings and by anticipations of their results. Our misconstruings are detected, explained, and rejected, for the most part one by one, with great difficulty, even painfully, in ways on which historians of science have begun to shed light; and the place of error is often taken by more ingenious error. The world is not cognitively innocent, any more than we are who desire its better acquaintance. A cognitively innocent world would be a world of incognizable things-in-themselves, such as Peirce discerned in Descartes. The mind is no more given for introspection than the world is for extrospection. Nor does it shine out through human faces, least of all from our own in the glass. It is known by hypothesis and induction from human doings and makings, in large part the same as those from which the world is known. The doings and makings by which world and mind are known enter into the making of both mind and world. If the human mind could be given at all, it would be in nothing short of the history of human institutions; but that history, like the history of the natural world, is a laborious, secular, incompletable construction.

The fact that Vico and the pragmatists should have held views approximating these is interesting enough. Much more interesting will be the conclusions precisely detailing the agreements and disagreements in these and other respects. For those conclusions we must await the actual comparison. I hope some reader may be moved to undertake it, and also, for good measure, to determine at what points, if at all, Vico and the pragmatists mistook Descartes, and how far he may be defended against their criticisms.[19]

A last suggestion. What if Peirce, toward the end of his life, had heard of Vico's *verum = factum*? He would have said: "The way to take that is to turn it first into Greek, the native language of philosophy, and then from Greek into English. The Greek for it is τὸ ἀληθές = τὸ πρᾶγμα. The English unpacking is that the true in the transcendental sense—the unconcealed, that which hides nothing, that which is intelligible without remainder—is the deed, action, behavior, practice, affair, pursuit, occupation, business, going concern. The Greek formula has several advantages over the Latin. The Latin *factum* emphasizes the completed actuality, the pastness, of the deed; the Greek πρᾶγμα covers also an action still in course or not yet begun, and even a line of conduct that *would* be adopted under circumstances that may never arise. The Latin is retrospective; the Greek is, or may be, prospective. The Latin is, on the face of it, individual, and it took Vico's genius and years of struggle to make it social in the *New Science*. The Greek would have offered no such resistance. The Greek leaves room for possibility and for generality, and so for Scholastic realism; the Latin, while perhaps not excluding realism, favors nominalism. Further, the transcendental sense of "true" is more obvious in the Greek ἀληθές than in the Latin *verum*. Now the doctrine of transcendentals, though metaphysical, includes a theory of knowledge, and the theory of knowledge includes, at least by implication, a theory of meaning. The Greek formula lends itself better than the Latin to the disengaging of the theory of knowledge from the metaphysics, and of the theory of meaning from the theory of knowledge. Vico disengaged the theory of knowledge but not that of meaning. He saw that the question of truth in the transcendental sense is logically prior to that of truth in the non-transcendental sense; he did not see that the question of meaning is also prior to that of truth in the non-transcendental sense. If he had thought in Greek instead of Latin, he might have taken that final step of disengaging the theory of meaning. If he had taken it, the result would have been pragmatism. Πρᾶγμα prompts us, as *factum* does not, to find the meaning of probability (for example) in (for example) the insurance business. And the meaning it prompts us to find is not so much how that business *has been, has come to be*, or *is* conducted, as how it *would be* conducted in a rational society."

---

[19] For an interpretation that finds in him some part of what his critics have failed to find, see Gerd Buchdahl, "The Relevance of Descartes's Philosophy for Modern Philosophy of Science," *British Journal for the History of Science*, 1 (1963) 227–49.

Antonio Corsano VICO AND MATHEMATICS

Of all aspects of Vico's thought, his views on the nature of mathematics has proved one of the most capable of achieving international recognition in recent years. It is extremely significant that Lord Russell, who failed to mention Vico in his brilliant *History of Western Philosophy*, instead pays particular attention to him in the later *Wisdom of the West*. In this book, Russell, the great mathematician and philosopher of science, accurately evaluates the seriousness and the critical significance of Vico's observations and points out their links with the most modern currents of the epistemology of mathematics.[1] Just as keen and accurate are Isaiah Berlin's remarks on the famous formula *verum ipsum factum*. Berlin scrutinizes the formula— from its earliest appearance vis-à-vis the problem of mathematical knowledge, down to the radical renovation that Vico expects from it—when he comes to grips with the far more complex problems arising from his search for the principles that govern "the development of nations," that is, the course of history.[2]

The task devolving upon this paper at present is that of tracing with precision the intellectual backdrop against which this Vichian doctrine should be projected. I shall have to point out the formative stages of the doctrine, its links with the speculative and cultural interests dominant in Vico's mind, and its connections with coeval European thought.

The image of himself which Vico gives us in the *Autobiography* should by no means be accepted as literally true. He portrays his position as that of an isolated thinker in a state of constant polemical tension with his contemporaries, whether fellow townsmen or citizens of other cultivated nations of Europe. Yet his works overflow with references to contemporary ideas. His most peculiar speculative attitude, of so genuinely Neo-Platonic a cast, not only should be linked with the Platonists of antiquity and of the Renaissance, that is, with such men as Plotinus, Proclus, Ficino, or Pico, but should be fitted within the coeval historical situation, where the major leaders were

[1] Bertrand Russell, *Wisdom of the West*, 2d ed. (London, 1960), pp. 206–7.
[2] Isaiah Berlin, "The Philosophical Ideas of G. B. Vico," in *Art and Ideas in Eighteenth Century Italy* (Rome: Edizioni di storia e letteratura, 1960).

convinced Neo-Platonists such as N. Malebranche, G. Berkeley, and A. Shaftesbury.

The same could be said in regard to the discussions concerning the epistemological and logical foundations of the exact sciences. Those discussions, engaged in by Hobbes and Pascal, Locke and Berkeley, and later by Hume, had by Vico's time reached an extreme degree of finesse and seriousness, so as to prepare the ground directly for Kant's discoveries. Kant himself was a theoretician and analyst of mathematical knowledge, both pure and applied.

In order to characterize Vico's position it will be necessary, in the first place, to ask what interests could have prompted this thinker, whose formation had been so authentically classical, humanistic, and juridical, to investigate the role, the capacity, and the limits of mathematical procedures, from the apparently simple and obviously elementary principles to the most elevated and complex problems; from the purest and most autonomous exactitude to the countless zones of application which the advance of scientific research was discovering and staking out.

It is too easy to assert that Vico was moved by a genuinely pedagogic and didactic interest; that he felt that it was a duty, connected with his position as *Regius professor* of rhetoric and inaugural speaker at the opening of the academic year of his university, to inquire into the educational value and the cultural impact of the teaching of mathematics. It is well known that in Vico's time a great infatuation with Descartes (and therefore with mathematics) existed in most cultural circles in Naples. These circles were made up of intellectuals hungry for novelties, of men who stood in sharp opposition to the *laudatores temporis acti*, to the hidebound conservatives whom Vico himself treated as devotees of "cloistral" philosophy.

As far back as 1699, when he had begun to deliver his *Inaugurals* (or academic "prolusions"), Vico had been faced with the embarrassing task of attempting to solve the conflict between the champions of the ancient methods and curricular organization of studies (based prevalently on the cult of the *bonae et humanae literae*, of *bonae artes* of the classico-humanistic tradition) and the new methods, whose most powerful tool of diffusion was the *Art de penser* (*Logique de Port Royal*) of Arnauld and Nicole. Although purporting to pay a sincere and unconditional homage to the classical world, the *Logique de Port Royal* did nevertheless introduce, in the realm of education, those requirements of clarity, distinctness, and order which Descartes had placed at the base of his philosophico-scientific reform.

For a long time Vico held the attitude of a mediator. He energetically advocated the humanistic heritage which in his first oration he epitomized as the Socratic maxim "know thyself," but which he envisaged also as being transposable into the Cartesian "I think, therefore I am." The Cartesian *cogito* might have appeared as a renewal of the Socratic message. On the other hand, Vico undoubtedly acknowledged, and felt respect for, the high cultural and social, pedagogic and practical, role of the new science, which so nobly and hopefully was directing its efforts toward the horizon of the future.

It is interesting to note that even in Vico's sixth oration this acknowledgment persists. It persists in terms that shortly afterward appear substantially reversed. The sixth oration is characterized by the strong pressure of a theological concern. Vico's conception of human nature, which particularly in the first oration had been characterized by a deep hopefulness (Vico extols the dignity of human nature almost to the threshold of godship), is dominated in the sixth oration by the pessimistic note of sinfulness, of original corruption. Vico, however, converts these negative features into stimuli for the restoration and cultural elevation of man:[3] it will be the task of good educational training and of wise instruction to remedy the effects of the Fall, thanks to a consistent, pertinacious, and unbending effort.

In contrast to Vico's future exaltation of imagination (*fantasia*), this faculty, in the sixth oration, is sharply set against reason as a symptom of the decline (from original perfection) that has taken place in man's nature: "Nothing is as antithetical to reason as the imaginative faculty. We can observe this antithesis in women. Since they are endowed with a strong imagination, reason, in them, is less active; consequently, they are more affected by potent and forceful passions than men."[4]

Perhaps we can attribute this antifeministic sally to some disappointment in love which Vico experienced in his youth.[5] But let us put gossip aside. In the sixth oration we find the assertion that the educator should act as a skillful physician, who knows how to cure a patient by means of expertly dosed poisons. The poison, in this case, is the Cartesian and Port-Royalist rigorousness of mathematical ratiocination, which is extremely apt to cure the intemperance of youthful and feminine imaginativeness. "Imagination must be cured, so that reason may be strengthened." It is therefore necessary to "administer mathematics to young people. It is often necessary to run over, mentally, an extremely long series of numbers and mathematical symbols, in order to achieve the truth of the demonstration which is the result of that procedure." Here Vico obviously refers to the Cartesian

---

[3] The synopsis of Vico's sixth oration is significant: "The knowledge of corrupt human nature invites us to range over the universal system of the liberal arts and sciences, and teaches us an easy and constant way to learn them." See *Le orazioni inaugurali, il de Italorum sapientia e le polemiche*, ed. G. Gentile e F. Nicolini (Bari, 1914), p. 57.

[4] *Ibid.*, p. 64.

[5] The reference is to Vico's youthful *canzone* entitled *Affetti d'un disperato*, written in 1693 at the beginning of his exile at Vatolla. The interpretation of this *canzone* is still debated. Some critics see in it the traces of an anti-Christian psychological and philosophical conception; others judge it to be the confession of an unhappy lover, coupled with the personal yearning of the author for his far-away hometown and with a lament for his isolation in a little village of the wooded and rock-ribbed Cilento. The *canzone* may be read in *L'autobiografia, il carteggio e le poesie varie*, ed. B. Croce (Bari, 1911).

longues chaînes de raisons utilized as a whip or as an unpalatable medicine, an image undoubtedly far from flattering to the Cartesians.

Immediately after this passage we encounter a more interesting statement:

And since mathematics takes into consideration points and lines, which are wholly devoid of thickness and volume, the human mind begins, as it were, to become less stiff, more flexible, and starts to get rid of its impurities. In a like fashion, young students become accustomed to extracting new truth from given truths, even in the realm of problems on which a general agreement has already been reached. And an equal result may also be attained in physics, where, instead, disagreement is often rife.[6]

Vico wishes it to be understood that, because of the arbitrary, *unreal* nature of basic geometrical concepts (such as dimensionless points and lines), such concepts would, by the unnatural forcefulness of their claims, have the power to loosen up and to "purge" (in a clinical sense) the gross, impure humors of the human mind. Furthermore, the procedure of geometrical deduction (deriving a new truth from a truth given: *ex dato vero, verum*), although starting from conventional data, generally and conventionally agreed upon, offers the advantage of training the mind to cope with research that, operating on uncertain data (such as research in physics), cannot lead to any solution unless it is kept within the bounds of the rigid coherence of the deductive process.

This, then, was the maximum credit which the Humanist and educationist Vico could grant to Cartesian–Port-Royalist mathematics. He was willing to accept its methodological and "pharmaceutic" role, on the condition that its "conventionalistic" foundations be recognized. Vico, then, has no objection to a Descartes construed through Hobbes and Pascal (the Pascal of *L'esprit de géometrie*). He settles for a Descartes "nominalistically" interpreted, conventionalized; for a geometry formalized into a science whose basic propositions are unnatural and unreal and, for that very reason, exact, and such as to constitute a firm support for the deductive *apodeixis*; for a geometry which shall be a model of coherence but not a pattern of truth. A little further on, summing up his argument, Vico lays it down that the young student's mind shall receive from mathematics the *data*, just as he shall receive from physics the *dubia*, but merely for the purpose of arriving finally at metaphysics. It is metaphysics "alone which discloses to us things true, certain, thoroughly pondered upon and scrutinized."[7]

Let us now look at the *De nostri temporis studiorum ratione*. Here the break with Cartesianism is final. The aim of the *De nostri* is a decided comparison of the pedagogico-didactic method of the ancients with that of Vico's contemporaries. The discussion broadens to a defense of what Vico considers to be the precious heritage of the classical and Renaissance world: rhetoric,

[6] *Le orazioni*, p. 65.
[7] *Ibid.*

baroque poetics, and politics, that is, the disciplines cast into disrepute by the fanatic cult of analytical reason of the Cartesian–Port-Royalist brand. The conflict is outlined with utmost clarity: "Shall we believe Arnauld, or Cicero?"[8]

Among the foundation stones of the Port-Royalist reform was the teaching of mathematics. But of what kind of mathematics? Obviously, the kind of mathematics which had been reformed by Descartes, both in its pure and in its applied form. The pure form consisted in the algebraization of geometry. Geometry ceased to be an intuitive and constructive science, and was to be treated by a rigorously analytical method, that is, by the systematic use of calculus notated by letters, such as had been definitely renewed by the path-breaking simplifications of Viète and Descartes. The applied form of mathematics consisted in the assimilation of physics to geometry through the employment of co-ordinates (orthogonical axes) which made it possible for the practical scientist to represent geometrically, to measure and calculate, any and every variation of physical phenomena, from the mechanical to the biological.

Starting from this latter aspect of what Descartes had called *mathesis universalis*, Vico thought that the radical assimilation of physics to mathematics was inadmissible. The reason for this is the fact that, by the very logical nature of the object, it is impossible for us to view the physical phenomenon, whose character is verisimilitude, as being susceptible of demonstration (that is, as something capable of becoming *necessarily true*). After all (Vico keenly remarks), Descartes himself aimed at performing a transferral of method from geometry to physics, and consequently at treating physics *as if* physics could be mathematically handled. However, no one can deny the substantial ontological divergence that separates the two fields of research. As Vico says: "We demonstrate geometrical propositions inasmuch as we can *create* them; if we could, therefore, demonstrate the phenomena of physics, we would have the capacity to create them. But the archetypes, the 'forms' of created things, with which their natures comply, exist only in the mind of God." It should be emphasized that for Vico, who is a confirmed Platonist, "form," the archetype, is the idea, or the intelligible essence, which should never be confused with the species, that is, with the signs or symbols employed by the human science of calculus and by mathematical reasoning in general. Those ideal "forms" are models and foundations of natural objects, and they are internal to the divine mind, which makes its own creative activity conform to them. This avowal of Platonic-Christian realism was a widespread conviction in Vico's times; it probably was handed over by Malebranche to Berkeley and, in some respects, also to Shaftesbury and Leibniz.

Vico does not at first dwell on the characteristic features of mathematical

[8] *On the Study Methods of Our Time*, trans. E. Gianturco (Indianapolis, Ind., 1965), p. 17.

knowledge.   The earliest formulation of the *verum-factum* is predominantly
negative.   It originates in controversy, and is theologically posited.   Vico
prefers to develop the methodological aspects, as well as the pedagogic
implications, of the *verum-factum*.   He advocates the genuinely experimental
character of physics and maintains that it would be impossible to treat
physical phenomena by means of the analytical procedure typical of Cartesian
mathematics.

Since the task of all research is the discovery of new principles, Vico continues, we should entrust such a task, not to analytical reason (which is a sheer
explication of what is already known), but to *ingegno*[9] (talent, ingeniousness,
that is, skill in devising or combining ideas or facts).   *Ingegno* is a synthetic
intuitive faculty, and is endowed with lightning-like speed in running
through the series of the elements of research so as to reach successfully the
solution sought for.   Vico gives historical evidence of this by mentioning
that the most important technico-scientific discoveries with which modern
civilization began—from clocks to great sailing ships to Brunelleschi's
architectural dome, so prodigiously suspended on a slim supporting structure
—were made before analytical geometry was devised.   Those discoveries,
therefore, were works of *ingegno*, achievements of artist-craftsmen endowed
with fresh talents for invention.   Hence, the pedagogic conclusion: "It may
be gathered from this that we need to train young minds to practice mechanics
by means of a close study of visual geometrical forms, and not by means of
abstract algebraic symbols."   In other words, what Vico is advocating here

[9] Chapter VII of Vico's *De antiquissima* gives the definition of *ingegno*: "It is the power
of conjoining and unifying things that are disparate and far asunder."   Vico envisages
ingegno as an eminently synthetic-intuitive faculty which is not subject to the laws of
analytical reason (that is, the gradual, constant, and impassive progression through each
link of the chain of arguments required by demonstration).   This *ingegno*, whose
fecundity and richness, particularly in the domain of applied physics (that is, mechanics),
Vico extols, is the same faculty ("wit") which the treatise-writers of the baroque era had
praised for being a powerful source of tropological and metaphorical inventions in the
fields of rhetoric and poetic imagery.   The most celebrated of those treatise-writers of
the baroque era was the Spanish Jesuit Baltasar Gracián (1601–58), author of a work
entitled *Agudeza y arte de ingenio*.   In the *De antiquissima*, as in the *De nostri*, Vico, always
ready to adopt suggestions of a linguistic-imaginative nature, maintains that our
attributing to *ingegno* the qualities of acuteness or obtuseness ("acute" and "obtuse"
being terms borrowed from geometry) is nothing but a reference to an intuitional
datum: the "acute" (or pointed) angle being more penetrating than the obtuse one, and
therefore more apt to bring about the inventive connection between "things different
and far apart."   However, by saying this, Vico did not mean to resort to an out-and-out
geometrical construction of the optical process, as Professor Gianturco seems to think,
following De Ruvo's opinion (see *Study Methods*, p. 24, n. 19).   Vico merely tries to
substitute a linguistic-geometrical image for that which was current in Italo-Hispanic
terminology.   In this terminology, *agudeza* was the chief ornamental device theorized
by baroque rhetoric.   Vico thus remained loyal to the linguistic association that is
embedded in the very title of Gracián's work.

is the classical geometry of Euclid and Archimedes, intuitive and constructive, the only geometry, according to him, which is capable both of
stimulating and of satisfying the demands of the active life peculiar to youth.

A singular insight into the depths of Vico's polemical reasoning is afforded
by his bringing out the similarities between intuitive geometry and poetry.
For him these similarities constitute an additional argument in favor of
Aristotelian-baroque poetics, which is vindicated from the attacks of the
new rationalistic criticism. Having reversed the opposition between fantasy
and critico-analytical reason, which we encountered in the sixth oration, in
total favor of fantasy, Vico pleads for the elimination of, or at least a limited
intervention of, criticism in the mental education of children. He maintains
that a too precocious and assiduous introduction of criticism cannot fail to
weaken their imagination and memory, "the offspring of which is poetry."

More apt to fecundate the adolescent mind's powers of invention and
combination is the geometrical method, provided, naturally, that such a
method is of the intuitive, visual, figural type, such as that practiced by
Euclid. This method is particularly apt to foster the invention of "poetical
figments" (*mendacia poetica*). The poet, by Aristotelically universalizing the
features of the figures or of the events that he portrays and narrates, fictitiously
invents with ingenious mendacity. The procedure of the geometrician is no
different: he invents imaginary symbols and teaches you how to contrive
them in your turn. "Starting from fictitious premises and data, led by their
method, geometrical and mathematical minds coherently fashion their own
truth." [10]

Vico might well have quailed at the eventually malevolent interpretation
of this bold assimilation of geometry to poetry. It would have been quite
easy for his Cartesian and Port-Royalist enemies to accuse him of having
invested poets and geometricians with the professional role of liars and
instructors in lying; whereas all that he meant to say was, at most, that the
poet is more closely akin to the philosopher (hence, to the geometrician) than
to the historian (according to the most orthodox pronouncement of Aristotle). The important thing is to hold fast to the view that the fictitious,
that is, the artificial and artful character of the primary geometrical concepts,
bears a kinship to the nature of poetical figments. Thus poeticized, the
initial artificiality loses some of the conventional arbitrariness that Hobbes
finds therein, and confirms that spiritual seriousness which, outside the range
of control by logic and metaphysics, Vico more and more intensely and
widely attaches to the world of poetry.

Let us now take up the *De antiquissima*. We know that Vico planned this
work in three sections—metaphysics, physics, and ethics—but that he wrote

[10] Gianturco, *Study Methods*, p. 42.

only the first part.   The second part corresponds, more or less, to what he must have written in his *On the Equilibrium of the Animal Body*, a work which is no longer extant.   In this work, Vico broadened the magnet theory to a general conception of nature very similar to that set forth by Robert Fludd. Vico's adoption of this viewpoint emphasizes still more strongly his opposition to the mechanistic theories that dominated the fields of Cartesian and post-Cartesian physics.

Starting again from the anti-Cartesian controversy, we notice in the *De antiquissima* that Vico's opposition takes another step (perhaps the last step) forward.   It is no longer a question of a pedagogic, hence methodological, interest.   Vico attacks the core of Descartes' reform: the *cogito ergo sum*. What Vico objects to (following in the footsteps of Malebranche) is that the *cogito* constitutes a basis, not of science, but of psychological awareness; not of *scientia*, but of *conscientia*.   Whereas *scientia* is "knowledge through causes" (*scire per causas*), psychological awareness (*conscientia*) is a simple mode of feeling, an inward way of perceiving, a psychological certitude devoid of any ontological confirmation.   In order to prove that "if I think, therefore I am," and in order thus to defeat the doubt of the skeptics, it is not enough to know that one is thinking (the skeptic does not deny this); it is necessary, instead, to prove that, if I think, God is thinking *in me*.   St. Augustine has warned us to "transcend ourselves" ("*Transcende te ipsum*").

Where the Cartesian criterion fails, the specifically Vichian one takes over: "Truth and fact are convertible."   Vico confirms the theological character of this principle by seeking for its prototype in the trinitarian doctrine.   St. Augustine had formerly interpreted this doctrine in terms propitious to a deduction of it from Platonic philosophy.

More precisely, in the formula *verum-factum* Vico discriminates between a relationship *ab intra*, that is, internal to the nature of God, in which nature the *verbum-son* proceeds inseparably from the *verbum-father* (in this case, rather than speaking of *verum-factum*, we should speak of *verum-genitum*), and a relationship *ad extra*, that is, the relationship between God and the world created by him.

This is a question, let it be clearly understood, of a negative theology which has no ontological claims.   Answering Descartes's and St. Anselm's ontological argument, Vico objects that, if it were possible for us to demonstrate God a priori, we would be able to *create* him.   The structure of the trinitarian dogma and that of the dogma of creation merely offer us a model to which we can refer in order to establish the foundations of a new theory of science. We are confronted with a case of epistemology directly connected with theology, which should not be a cause of wonder in the age of Malebranche and Berkeley.

Coming now to mathematical epistemology, we should warn against attributing to Vico a solidly consistent theory, such as, for instance, the modern ones of Poincaré, Mach, Meyerson, Whitehead, or Brouwer. Vico's thought vacillates between extreme tendencies that run the gamut from a nominalism of the Hobbesian type to a pluralistic metaphysical trend *à la Leibniz*, passing through the plastic-poetical suggestions that we have seen hinted at in the *De nostri*.

We start, then, from the still genuinely theological consideration of the basic difference between divine science and human knowledge. The feature common to all human sciences is for Vico the anatomic, dissecting, decompository procedure, which, in order to gain possession of any reality, is compelled to "cut it to pieces," as the anatomical knife cuts to pieces the organism to be studied. Thus, regardless of the subject matter of our research—whether it be an entity, a unity, a figure, a motion, a body, the intellect, the will—it is different in God. In God the subjects are a unity; in man they are sundered. "In God they live; in man they perish." Consequently, the mathematical sciences are not, strictly speaking, more "abstract" than any other science, from metaphysics, whose subject matter is the absolutely existent, to ethics, the object of which is will as distinguished from the activity of pure mind. The characteristic operation of mathematical abstraction is that of converting what is a disadvantage, a drawback, a defect, of human thought into helpful services, "*in utiles usus*," into conveniences and utilities.[11]

When man becomes aware of his inability to penetrate to the innermost nature of things (either because he does not possess in himself the primary and ultimate elements of those things, which are in God, or because his short life-span or his limited capacity does not permit him to embrace the total picture),

---

[11] According to *Le orazioni*, p. 135:

Therefore, when man starts inquiring into the nature of things, he becomes aware that it is utterly impossible for him to attain it. This impossibility is due to the fact that he does not possess in his mind the elements of which things are made, and, furthermore, to the fact that the powers of his intellect are limited. The totality of objects is external to his senses. Nevertheless, man succeeds in turning a shortcoming of his mind into an advantage. By means of that operation which goes by the name of abstraction, he fashions two terms: the point, which can be notated, and the unit, which is susceptible of multiplication. Both are fictitious entities, figments. If you note down the point, it is no longer a point, if you multiply the unit, it is no longer a unit. Furthermore, man took it upon himself to proceed from these two principles ad infinitum, so as to prolong the line unlimitedly and so as to repeat the unit innumerable times. And in this fashion (*hoc pacto*) he was able to construct a certain world of his own, such a world as he was able to contain, in its entirety, within himself. Thus, by prolonging, shortening, or combining lines, by adding up or substracting or calculating numbers, man was able to accomplish countless operations. It is evident that he had cognizance, within himself, of infinite truths.

Notice the expression "*hoc pacto*" (in this fashion, or, under this condition): it could be an indication that Vico fully accepts Hobbesian conventionalism. Nevertheless, such is not completely the case; some qualifications supervene to modify that impression, as we shall presently see. As for Vico's odd restraint with respect to the word "abstraction" (which he constantly couples with the words *quam dicunt* [which goes by the name of]), this usage may be accounted for by the insurmountable repugnance that he, with his humanistic taste, felt for the jargon of the Schoolmen.

his mind, working by abstraction or separation, creates two figments: one is the point, which can be represented graphically, and the other is the unit, which can be multiplied. Vico emphasizes the fictitious, artificial, that is, the unreal, character of these two elements. If the point is represented by a sign, he says, it will no longer be a point; likewise, if the unit is multiplied, it will no longer be a unit.

Having laid down, or postulated, the two terms, the mind deems itself entitled to develop ad infinitum the capacity with which it has vested itself. It proceeds to prolong ad infinitum the line and to multiply ad infinitum the calculations of arithmetics. Thus the mind fashions its own world of magnitudes, both spatial and numerical. It is a world which can be of infinite extension, variety, and complication because its constitutive elements are by now internal to the mind itself.

On the other hand, Vico does not hesitate to warn that, however vast and ambitious the task of the mathematical sciences, their foundation remains purely figmental; and with that warning he reaches the limit of a nominalistic formulation of his criterion. Having asserted that not only the solution of problems but also the demonstration of theorems is dependent upon an operational, that is, artificial, procedure, he precisely defines the characteristic features of such a procedure. Simply through the colligation of its own elements (point and unit) the mind irresistibly "bestows truth" on the objects it cognizes; namely, being unable to grasp objects in their existing truth (possession of this kind of truth is the exclusive prerogative of the Creator of all things, that is, of God), the mind resorts to the device of elaborating verbal definitions.

The only difference between this Vichian conception and the view held by the most orthodox Occamistic or Hobbesian nominalists is that the arbitrariness of the linguistic device is not attributed to the simple empirico-economic exigency of the *substitutio*, but is once again patterned on a theological premise. To fix the semantic content of words with absolute arbitrariness, independently of any ontological premise (*ex nulla re substrata*), is tantamount to acting according to the pattern of God, who creates *ex nihilo*. Thus it happens that the human mind fashions such nounal elements as point, line, surface. By the word "point" we understand something which has no parts, by the word *line*, the stretch traversed by the gliding of the point, that is, pure length, and so on. We could conclude by stating, in Leibnizian terms, that Vico does not admit any non-nominal definitions, but that he contends that the nominal definition can be carried into reality, can become actual, by means of the *fictio*. In this way, conventional arbitrariness is transformed into a productive (we might even say, creative) procedure. This procedure appears to be only metaphorically accounted for: it is something analogous to God's procedure, "*ad instar Dei*." The maximum effort made by Vico to explain this matter in non-metaphorical terms is his attempt at a utilitarian integration sufficiently congenial to the nominalistic origin of his argument. This fecundation, so highly inspired by a linguistic "dodge," corresponds in an immediate way to an exigency of pragmatic utility. It consists in turning a negative quality, a defect (the limited capacity of the human mind), into a positive value, into an authentic merit of original efficiency. What is denied to the physicist is secured for the mathematician. The latter, being capable of freely shaping the elements of his research and the laws of his procedures, succeeds in creating a veritable pattern of mental production. Such a pattern can be advantageously utilized by any other type of research.[12]

Vico takes a notably different position in regard to the theory of "metaphysical points," and this is one of the most perplexing aspects of his thought. The term "metaphysical points" is not in itself alarming: it represents merely an evident Leibnizian reminiscence. We know that initially Leibniz used that expression in order to denote what he later preferred to call by the more fortunate name of *monad*. Nor should we be worried about the fact that Vico rebaptizes the Leibnizian points as "Zenonian." We are acquainted with his typically humanistic propensity to retrodate and disguise modern concepts and terms under classical garb and features. The important point to establish is whether he (who insisted on being considered as a *laudator temporis acti*), as a convinced and self-taught conservative, did or did not grasp this speculative theme which was thoroughly new and original in his time and so pregnant with remote developments. It would be significant if he had grasped it (even if he had done so with the purpose of exploiting it as an additional argument in support of his anti-Cartesianism).[13]

[12] Typically pragmatico-utilitarian, in my opinion, is the transition from the relinquishment of the initial attempt to penetrate the essence of the primal factors to the active, dynamic impulse of production in the world of quantity. The agnostic renunciation patterned on negative theology (which is typical of agnosticism) turns into action, into the production of *utiles usus*. We should also consider that the transition referred to is not limited to mathematical and general epistemology. As Isaiah Berlin rightly observes ("The Philosophical Ideas of G. B. Vico," p. 173), Vico applied his argument to self-knowledge as well (once again in polemical thrust against the Cartesian *cogito*): I do not know my own essence, just as I do not know that of any other natural being. However, it is from this giving up of self-knowledge that there springs forth the impulse to range over the world of nations, attempting to reach an adequate adjustment of research, productive of historical knowledge, to the pragmatic creative energy of the *humanitas*, or civilization, through the entire spectrum of its degrees, from the darkest and most turbidly coarse, to the most elevated and enlightened. In the language of Lévi-Strauss's structural anthropology, we might say that for Vico the giving up of the ontological and gnoseological possession of one's own nature is compensated for by the discovery of a structural analogy between historical research and historical evolution. Both are rooted in the initial humanistic experience of "*humanitas ab humandis mortuis.*" Human civilization has sprung from the custom of burying the dead. This is precisely a datum of an anthropological-cultural experience.

[13] For the way in which Leibniz's thought and terminology effect a transition to the

It is interesting for us to find that Vico, after taking up the definition of the point as "that which has no parts," and after re-emphasizing its nature as a "nominal definition," thinks that he can validate the term by resorting to something other than the sheer similarity to the procedure of God (*ad instar Dei*). We find it noteworthy that Vico should resort to introducing into the geometrical datum a virtuality, or conation, originating in metaphysics. This virtuality or conation, in Vico's opinion, is supremely real, and is endowed with an infinite capacity of operation. Vico engages in open controversy with those "vulgar" philosophers who think that geometrical ideas derive, by abstraction, from physical, corporeal matter (Locke?). His preference is for those (hypothetical) ancient Zenonians who did not hesitate to introduce the concept of a "metaphysical matter" identifiable with the virtuality of extension.[14]

A more precise co-ordination of the two views supervenes when Vico, complicating his already confused historical reference, claims that the Stoic-Zenonians had already envisaged the geometric point as a symbol, a notational sign, of the metaphysical point. (*Sign* means a name; it is a verbal term.) The linguistic datum is thus rescued from the conventional arbitrariness of the Occamistic-Hobbesian position in order that it be validated by the pre-linguistic premise of Leibniz's metaphysics.[15]

---

final monadistic solution, and for Leibniz's youthful philo-Hobbesian attitude, see my study *Leibniz* (Naples, 1953), pp. 8off.

[14] Concerning this section see all of chap. V, sec. 4, of Vico's *De antiquissima*, entitled precisely "On Metaphysical Points, or Conations."

[15] A precise indication of the change in perspective is represented by the clear warning that, through the intervention of the Zenonian-Stoic-Leibnizian conception, the initial nominalistic position is modified. Vico states at first: "When the geometrician defines the point as 'that which has no parts,' this is a nominal definition, since it is not assumed that there exists some thing which has no parts, which yet may be taken down in notation by our mind or our pen. Likewise, the definition of the *unit*, given by arithmeticians, is purely nominal, since the arithmeticians present us with a *unit* which is not multipliable and therefore is no unit." This is the nominalistic position explicitly advocated by Leibniz in the Preface to the *De veris principiis* of Nizolio, and perhaps as late as Leibniz's titleless *Little Dialogue of 1677* (see my *Leibniz*, pp. 37ff.). But here we have the "realistic" position: "The Zenonians, instead, consider as real that definition of the point which is formulated after the pattern of what the human mind is capable of thinking in regard to the indivisible virtuality of extension and motion. The Zenonians, therefore, accuse of falsity that vulgar opinion which maintains that geometry, after having purified them, extracts its major concepts from matter; or, as the Schoolmen say, geometry *abstracts* its concepts." We are now confronted with a polemical reversal of the nominalism that Vico had previously advocated and that is now attributed *en bloc* to Hobbesian-Lockean empiricism, as well as to the Schoolmen in general. (Concretely, we may conjecture that Vico refers particularly to late Occamistic scholasticism, with which he was acquainted as far back as his years of study in the Jesuit school at the Gesù Vecchio, and as early as his personal perusal of the works of Suarez.) Medieval and contemporary empiricists are jumbled together by Vico because of that cult of abstraction, against which Berkeley was about to protest with an equal degree of energy,

But there is also a return to the aesthetically oriented considerations of the *De nostri*. This occurs when Vico, once again protesting the Cartesian attempt to geometrize physics through the external device of the co-ordinates, contends that it is more profitable for researchers to set up Euclidean geometry as a model of intuitional and constructive perfection. This is possible, thanks to the plastic-formal (that is, the almost poetic) nature of geometrical magnitudes. These figural magnitudes offer a precious tool to physics, not because they compel physics to deal with its objects through the obtuse mediocrity of deduction or through the sterile analytic precision of calculus ("neither through numbers nor through algebraic symbols"), but because the value of that tool consists in the evidence of those figural magnitudes which can be produced by the operatively brilliant action of inventive genius.

This is the major advantage, Vico observes, of Galilean research. Galileo treats geometry as a model of experimental exactitude, a pattern of formal perfection, to which the physicist can look in order to gain both inspiration and stimulation for his own research. Was this not the secret of the discredited poetics and rhetoric of the baroque era, of the *Agudeza y arte de ingenio* of Baltasar Gracián? Both poetico-rhetorical and scientific invention strive to teach us, through the use of our talents of invention and combination ("*ingegno*"), how to link together "things various, multiple, disparate, and remote."[16] And here is the conclusion, with its genuinely Kantian flavor: if you demand that physical truth be patterned upon truths such as "three and four make seven" or "the sum of two angles of a triangle is always greater than the third angle," you will not have analytically geometrized physics; you will have experimentalized geometry.

Mathematics as experimental science: this, perhaps, was Vico's major discovery.[17]

Translated by Elio Gianturco

---

although with a different orientation. If my interpretation is exact, it can be asserted that Vico must have gone through the same antinominalistic revolution experienced previously by Leibniz. Leibniz describes it perfectly in his essay *De veritate, cognitione et ideis*, dated 1684, in which the first precise formulation of the *definitio realis* is to be found.

[16] *Le orazioni*, p. 185.

[17] On the markedly experimentalist interest of the French cultural milieu in the Cartesian era, and on the subtle opposition to Descartes' mathematics, an opposition headed by his loyal friend and correspondent Mersenne, see Lenoble, *La révolution scientifique du XVIIe siècle* (Paris, 1958), esp. pp. 193–94.

H. A. Hodges   VICO AND DILTHEY

Everyone knows the type of philosopher who draws much of his inspiration from natural science. He has often appeared in the history of philosophy. There is another type, less frequently found but clearly recognizable, the philosopher who is deeply concerned with historical and social studies, with human life as it is seen in the social, political, and cultural records of the ages. Such a philosopher will dwell upon questions about historical knowledge, about the expression of human thought and experience in language and other media, about the understanding and interpretation of such expressions, about art and literature and the life of the imagination. R. G. Collingwood was a philosopher of this type; so was Croce. So was Vico, and so was Wilhelm Dilthey, with whom I am now to compare him.

In doing so I am paying homage to an old attachment. I was interested in Vico, and at one time thought of making a study of him, before I ever came into contact with Dilthey. I do not regret the change, however; the German philosopher has opened up wide fields for me. It is a pleasure now to bring the two men together.

Dilthey was not a disciple of Vico. He was not directly indebted to him through serious study of his works. If Vico influenced Dilthey in any discernible way, it was mainly through those of his ideas which were taken up by Herder and so were absorbed into the mainstream of German philosophical thought. If Dilthey arrives at conclusions which in some significant degree resemble Vico's, it is from a different starting point and by his own route that he reaches them. Nor can Vico really be said to have anticipated Dilthey's philosophy as a whole. He could not possibly have foreseen Kant and the post-Kantians or the wider intellectual scene as it was in the nineteenth century.

Yet, if we compare these two writers across the gulf of the years, while in detail everything is different, we find certain major points of likeness. I shall make the comparison under four headings.

The Human Studies (Geisteswissenschaften)

Dilthey has a great deal to say about historical study and historical writing, as also about the process of historical events; but he cannot be thrust into a

pigeonhole labeled philosophy of history and left there.   His concern is with
a much wider body of thought than that: with psychology and sociology,
moral and political theory and jurisprudence, the study of art and of religion,
in a word, with all those branches of study which together throw light on the
cultural and spiritual activities of mankind.   His name for this great field of
study is *die Geisteswissenschaften*.   It is hard to find an adequate rendering for
this in English, but in my two books on Dilthey I have used the phrase "the
human studies" and I shall use it here.   Dilthey insists on the unity of the
human studies, in spite of the great variety of methods which they employ;
they are one body of knowledge because their object is one object, namely,
man as an intelligent, self-conscious, self-expressing, value-realizing being.
   Vico similarly is misunderstood if he is treated simply as a philosopher of
history.   He puts forward the idea of a *scienza nuova* which is to be complementary to the natural science of which Galileo and Bacon and Descartes
were the exponents.   It is to be the science of humanity.   Undoubtedly,
history has a predominant place in it and provides the framework for the
whole.   But there is also jurisprudence, and what we should nowadays call
the sociology of law, as also of religion, with, on the other hand, the linguistic
and literary studies, philology and rhetoric and criticism and a kind of
aesthetics.   Vico gives us as good a hint as could be expected in his time of
the compass of the human studies.
   Both Dilthey and Vico had personal experience of work in more than one
field within the human studies.   Dilthey is known for his life of Schleiermacher and for his work on the history of ideas in the sixteenth, seventeenth,
and eighteenth centuries.   He was interested in biography and autobiography
as forms of historical writing.   Vico actually wrote an autobiography and
also a life of Count Antonio Caraffa, the Naples-born general who rose high
in the Austrian service and took part in the reconquest of Hungary from the
Turks.   Vico also studied Roman law, with special reference to its origins
and its social content.   Dilthey was a literary critic of some standing; in
particular, he was among the first to understand the significance of Hölderlin's
work.   Vico for most of his life was Professor of Rhetoric at the University
of Naples, and so was officially charged with the care of literary studies.
   Another point is that both found their work for the human studies leading
to an interest in the philosophy of education, though this is more manifest in
Vico than in Dilthey.

How is Knowledge Possible in the Human Studies?

   The human studies differ from the natural sciences, not only in their
subject matter, but in the methods by which they work and the assumptions
on which they proceed.   They have not the same epistemology, and one of

the things against which both our authors protest is the assumption so often made, that the epistemology of pure and applied mathematics or of experimental natural science is the theory of human knowledge as such. Vico and Dilthey are in similar, though not identical, situations.

For Dilthey the enemy is positivism, insofar as that means an attempt to apply natural-scientific methods and concepts to the human studies; and behind this again stands the Kantian philosophy with its theory of knowledge —mathematical, analytical, and abstract. Both positivism and Kantianism are right insofar as they declare the dependence of knowledge upon experience, but in Dilthey's view they misconceive the nature of experience and therefore also the way in which knowledge arises out of it. Experience in the human studies is not sense perception, but something quite different, and our approach to it is one not of detached observation but of understanding and interpretation, which is a wholly different procedure. It is true both for natural science and for the human studies that we are confronted with a series of events which can in some degree be explained and predicted because there are causal relations between them. But an event in natural science is merely a sensible phenomenon, observed or observable; and the laws by which we explain and predict are laws of time sequence which can be expressed in mathematical formulas and tested by deduction and experiment. An event in the field of the human studies is a human thought or action, ordinarily conscious and purposeful, and the causal relations between such events are relations that depend on purpose and judgment; we apprehend their working by a sympathetic understanding, not by drawing up formulas from which to deduce and so verify. The procedure is different at every point.

With Vico the enemy can be characterized by a single name: Cartesianism. Descartes and his disciples had held that mathematics is the model for human knowledge, and that every branch of study is genuine knowledge or "science" only insofar as it can be built up *more geometrico*. That is to make knowledge abstract and analytical, and the effect of such a view on education is to give a premature and excessive emphasis to logical analysis and criticism at the expense of the imaginative and intuitive side of the mind; yet, says Vico, it is on that side that our knowledge of human life and affairs particularly depends.

Both Vico and Dilthey say, in effect, that we are able to know the object of the human studies because we are ourselves that object. Human societies, laws and governments, cities and armies, arts and sciences and religions, are all the work of men, and we who study them are men. What one man has made, another man, if he uses proper care, can understand. This principle, however, emerges very differently in detail in our two authors.

Vico tries to make the principle "we know because we make" into the basis of a comprehensive theory of knowledge which will cover the human studies and the natural sciences and even Descartes's own special field of mathematics. Why have we such success in mathematics? Why can we reach demonstrative conclusions there as we cannot in most other fields? Because, says Descartes, our ideas here are clear and distinct. Yet, but why are they clear and distinct? Because, says Vico, the whole world of mathematics is our own creation, and of course we understand our own work. By an act of definition we create for ourselves the point, the line, the surface, and the solid. It is therefore not surprising that these, and all possible combinations of these, are transparent to us if only we think carefully. With the study of nature it is different, for nature is not our work; yet we understand it insofar as we can treat it as if it were our work. We understand natural processes when we can make a model of them, and this is genuine knowledge insofar as our model is true to the reality. In fact, of course, nature is God's work and not ours. He knows it with a maker's knowledge, in full. We know it with a quasi-maker's knowledge, in part. But the world of history and society is altogether our work. Not by an act of definition or an imaginative construction, but by purposing and planning and acting, we bring this world into existence and keep it in motion. Whoever knows in himself what it is to imagine, or think, or desire, or plan, or resolve, knows the way in which this world is made.

Dilthey's position is more complex. He inherits the Kantian theory of knowledge, according to which the human mind constructs the known world by a transcendental synthesis. From this starting point the post-Kantians had moved out to their sweeping idealistic constructions. Dilthey rejects that line of argument at once. Hard as it may be to know what nature is in itself, inevitable as it may be to say that we know it only in its appearances, it still remains clear that we do not make it, but find it. It acts upon us irresistibly and inexplicably, as an independent agent.

As regards the historical and social world, Dilthey of course agrees (for it is obvious) that it is made by human thoughts and actions, and that the historian or social scientist or Humanist is well placed to understand it because he is himself one who thinks and acts. He understands it because he is of one nature with that which makes it. But Dilthey adds to this Vichian point two others of his own.

For one thing, he shows that the formula can be turned about, and we can say that we understand history, not because we (that is, human beings like us) make history, but because history makes us. The forces that are at work in history, namely, men's thoughts and purposes, go on acting through their consequences and through their expressions and shape the mind and personality of us who study them. Suppose I am interested in the study of a great figure of the past—say, Luther, in whom Dilthey himself was much interested. Whether we today know it or not, Luther has influenced the institutional forms of our world, the thoughts we think, the questions we ask, the attitudes we take up; the substance of our lives and minds is different because he lived, and we can understand him very naturally, insofar as he has made us like himself.   And the influence becomes immediate and conscious when we read his writings and thus feel directly the impact of his thought.   In this way we can be said to understand historical reality, not because we make it, but because it makes us.

In the second place there is Dilthey's epistemological analysis of the process of understanding (*das Verstehen*), which is the work of his last years and one of the principal achievements of those years.   The fundamental conception is not peculiar to him, and is clearly present in Vico, but Dilthey's elaboration of it is especially full and painstaking.   To understand is to relive (*nacherleben*) the thoughts or experiences of another self.   This reliving is not, of course, an exact replica of what went on in him; it is patchy, in part conjectural, dependent upon our necessarily limited evidence, and needing always to be checked by re-examination of the evidence and amplified by the discovery of more.   Nevertheless, it is a reconstruction in our own imagination of what has already been enacted in the reality of someone else's experience.   And on this basis, by the labor of conceptual thinking, we build up historical narratives and the more abstract and generalized forms of study in this realm. It is significant that the title of Dilthey's last published work is *Der Aufbau der geschichtlichen Welt in den Geisteswissenschaften.*

The Model of Human Nature

Society is composed of human beings, and history is the record of the lives of human beings.   It seems obvious, therefore, that any systematic study of history and society presupposes a model of human nature.   Vico and Dilthey both hold that the human studies as an organized body of knowledge depend upon our having such a model.

Vico works from his educational studies, which give him a pattern of human development.   The mind in childhood and youth is not the same as the mind in maturity.   The imaginative and intuitive functions of the mind develop earlier than the analytic and critical ones; hence childhood is the age of story-telling and poetic fantasy, while the capacity for logical and mathematical thinking and for the sciences, which depend on these operations, comes later.   The educator must respect this pattern and give his pupil at each age what he is able to digest at that age.   Now, the same process of development is to be observed on a larger scale in human societies and civilizations.   They too have their childhood and youth and maturity; they too begin with poetry and come later to prose and to logical reasoning.

Dilthey in the middle years of his life worked out a detailed doctrine of "descriptive psychology" as the basic science of the human studies.   By this he means nothing recondite, nothing in principle new.   Historians, philosophers, critics, and others have always tended to have in their minds some working conception of human nature, in the light of which they interpret their facts or make their judgments. They do not always expound it systematically, as a doctrine by itself, though that too has sometimes been done. In the sixteenth and seventeenth centuries it was often known as anthropology, and Dilthey has written a study of the part which it played in the thought of that period. Dilthey himself works it out rather fully as a descriptive analysis of the principal functions of the human mind (cognitive, affective, volitional) and of the processes of personality-building, from which he finally derives a typology of human nature. All this he calls the structure (*Struktur*, *Strukturzusammenhang*) of the human mind. He applies his own very simple typology, as a key, to the study of the history of art, of religion, of philosophy itself. Dilthey's work here is in a halfway position between the relatively unsystematic ideas of Vico and the deep analyses made by twentieth-century psychologists. One might ask that it be amplified by a similar structural analysis of human relationships and interactions in the principal types of social grouping—the field of sociological study. But Dilthey's view is that the relationships and interaction patterns in social groups can be reduced to factors that lie within the individual human personality.

Interpretation and Interpretative Techniques

Past events cannot be observed. We know about them partly by inference from their present effects, but mainly through written testimony. Again, the object of inquiry in all the human studies is the thoughts and experiences and purposes of human beings, and these are in any case not observable as sensible objects are; they are known through expressions, among which verbal expressions are the most prominent. So any account of the methods and procedures of the human studies must include something about the inter-pretation of human expressions, especially verbal expressions and written records. There is an art or skill in this, for which some people seem better endowed than others; but there are also principles and methods that can be set forth as a doctrine. Such a doctrine of interpretation is called a herme-neutic. There is a tradition of hermeneutic doctrine which comes down from ancient times. It was called into existence primarily by problems of interpretation arising in connection with sacred texts, with ritual formulas and myths and legends, but also in connection with philological study and literary criticism. It was generalized and presented in a systematic form by Schleiermacher, on whose foundations Dilthey built.

Hermeneutic questions arise for Vico too, but in a less generalized form, coming up directly out of the work he was trying to do. He was trying to construct an over-all pattern of development of human societies and civilizations. To do this required a wide knowledge of how societies and civilizations have in fact developed; but Vico had to work without the aid of archaeology, which has thrown open to us such wide vistas of the remote past. He had to rely upon myths and legends, and he needed principles for the interpretation of these. He found these principles by appealing to his analogy between the development patterns of individuals and those of societies. As the individual child is a creature of imagination, not of logic, so societies in their early ages think and speak imaginatively, not logically. It is Vico's great achievement to have conceived a "logic" of imaginative thinking and to have worked it out, not merely as an aspect of aesthetics (though it is that too), but as an analysis of the way in which early civilizations talk about all their concerns. In ritual, in mythology, in legend, nay, even in the fabric of language itself, is stored a body of *sapienza poetica* which is the life-wisdom of youthful societies. We today, who have learned to think and speak analytically and abstractly, need to be able to translate this ancient wisdom into our own terms, to extract from myth and legend and from language itself the social history which is contained there; and principles can be laid down for doing this. Vico sets them forth in the list of *degnità* (a perverse translation of *axiomata*) which stands at the head of the *Scienza nuova*, and applies them systematically in the body of that work.

It is clear how much our modern interests in linguistic theory, in anthropology, in comparative mythology and comparative religion, are foreshadowed here in Vico, though we must not impute to him a prevision of all that has since arisen in these fields.

H. P. Rickman VICO AND DILTHEY'S
METHODOLOGY OF
THE HUMAN STUDIES

In the twelve massive volumes of Dilthey's collected works[1] there are about a dozen brief references to Vico; and though respectfully appreciative they are rather vague and perfunctory. The latest of them, in a fragment from the last years of Dilthey's life, consists of a single sentence, "Vico relates his research into the history of religion and law to the ultimate depths of human insight,"[2] and is characteristic of the others. Beside this sentence Dilthey scribbled on the margin of the manuscript, "Look up."

Nowhere does Dilthey acknowledge personal indebtedness to Vico's work or explicitly draw attention to the parallels in their approach. Expositors of the two authors have been equally reticent. Professor Hodges, though well acquainted with Vico's work, does not mention him when he discusses the sources of Dilthey's ideas in some detail.[3] Max H. Fisch and Thomas G. Bergin,[4] Benedetto Croce,[5] and Isaiah Berlin[6] all discuss the influence of Vico's work without referring to Dilthey.

Clearly Dilthey would not have referred to Vico several times if he had not had some knowledge of, and sympathy with, his work. After all, Weber's translation of Vico's New Science had been available in German since 1822, and a monograph on Vico by K. Werner appeared in 1881. But indirect influences were probably more important. We know that Dilthey was familiar with, and influenced by, such German writers as Hamann, Herder, Goethe, and Jacobi, philologists like Wolf, and historians of law like Savigny, all of whom knew Vico, were affected by him, or, at least, had affinities to him.

There are even less tangible connections, such as shared traditions and common problems producing similar lines of thought in the history of ideas,

[1] Wilhelm Dilthey, Gesammelte Werke, 2d ed. (Stuttgart, 1958).

[2] Ibid., vol. VII.

[3] H. A. Hodges, The Philosophy of Dilthey (London, 1952), chap. I.

[4] Max H. Fisch and Thomas G. Bergin, trans., The Autobiography of Giambattista Vico (New York, 1944), Introduction.

[5] Benedetto Croce, The Philosophy of G. Vico (London, 1913), app. on "The Later History of Vico's Thought."

[6] Isaiah Berlin, "The Philosophical Ideas of G. Vico," in Art and Ideas in Eighteenth Century Italy (Rome: Edizioni di storia e letteratura, 1960).

and it has been argued that Vico anticipated ideas developed by Kant and Hegel without, apparently, influencing them directly.   Once we accept this we need not be surprised that Dilthey, who was directly indebted to these two German thinkers, should also have affinities with the Italian.   This point was made forcibly by R. G. Collingwood when talking about history, though he did not mention Dilthey.

> The extraordinary merit of his (Vico's) work was not recognised until, two generations later, German thought had reached on its own account a point much akin to his own, through the great blossoming of historical studies which took place in Germany in the late eighteenth century.   When that happened German scholars rediscovered Vico and attached a great value to him, thus exemplifying his own doctrine that ideas are propagated not by diffusion like articles of commerce, but by the independent discovery by each nation of what it needs at any given stage in its own development.[7]

However, more important than the tracing of the labyrinthine ways in which ideas pass from person to person is the relation between the ideas themselves.   In commemorating a thinker of the past we want to assure ourselves, above all, of the continued vitality of his thought.   In the story of Vico's persisting importance Dilthey plays a crucial role, for he—probably more than any other single thinker—faithfully reflects the essential train of thought which makes the Italian's work relevant today.   But what in Vico were aphorisms, hints, and implications hidden in attempts to reconstruct the past (often factually inaccurate) became in Dilthey a coherent philosophy.

To gain a proper appreciation of Vico's ideas and of their development in Dilthey's hands we must consider the contemporary problems to which they offer solutions.   One of the major intellectual issues of our time, which is also of the most urgent practical importance, is the understanding of the human world.   In range and precision our knowledge of the physical world exceeds our knowledge of mental, social, and cultural phenomena, and, as a result, the predominant theories of knowledge today take physical science as the paradigm of the cognitive process and look askance at the elusive way in which we gain insight into mental processes.   Students of human nature, overawed by the fashionable philosophical models and dazzled by the triumphs of the physical sciences, have tried to imitate the methods of the latter by concentrating on how people behave and on problems that can be approached in terms of strict experiment and statistical analysis.   However, though they have achieved some positive results, the social sciences have suffered by comparison with physics or chemistry.   Precise observation and experiment are often impossible or morally objectionable.   (You can't look through bedroom keyholes or precipitate marital conflicts artificially.) Qualitative differences frequently defy quantification.   For example, classifying thefts in terms of the amount stolen may be meaningless if it submerges

[7] R. G. Collingwood, *The Idea of History* (Oxford, 1946).

the differences between theft for gain and theft for excitement or to gain attention. Sampling also may be misleading because of the variety of human manifestations. The results of an experiment in aerodynamics in Japan can be relevant in Britain, but a study of the attitudes of first-year students at M.I.T. may lack significance in Britain because it tells us something only about *those* students, without helping us to understand English students. Thus, social researchers who imitate the methods of the physical sciences instead of using lines of approach appropriate to their subject matter are pursuing a will-of-the-wisp. They could take advantage of the fact that it is possible to have a much clearer insight into how human beings work than they can ever have about how the physical world works. Instead, they ignore the methods this insight places at their disposal and produce results that fall short of those of their chosen models.

Behind these methodological inadequacies lie deficiencies in theoretical grasp which result, for example, in the absence of a grand strategy for inter-disciplinary co-operation. Behaviorist psychology, for instance, can neither receive help from, nor give help to, history. These weaknesses are of more than philosophical interest because they account for the failure of the social sciences to guide our social actions. History, sociology, psychology, economics, and criminology provide us with insufficient help for the solution of the moral, social, organizational, and political problems that confront us today.[8]

It is only against the background of these unsolved problems that we can appreciate Vico's and Dilthey's contributions to a conception of the social sciences. In their work they defined the nature of the human world and showed how it could form the empirical subject matter of the human studies. Rejecting a narrow and dogmatic definition which confines experience to sense impressions only, they developed an epistemology of the social sciences which showed the kind of knowledge revealed by them.

Vico's[9] subject matter is the "world of nations," or "civil world," which presents itself to us in terms of deeds, thoughts, ideas, languages, religions, customs, institutions, and myths. All these are manifestations and products of the human mind, though they may have originated in response to biological necessity and external circumstances. The civil world is the creation of men, and so we can understand and know it more intimately than we can understand physical nature. Indeed, these manifestations are more real than such abstractions as circles and lines.

[8] H. P. Rickman, *Understanding and the Human Studies* (London, 1967), contains a critical examination of approaches to the human studies which try to imitate the physical sciences.

[9] *The New Science of Giambattista Vico*, trans. Thomas G. Bergin and Max H. Fisch, Anchor Books ed. (Garden City, N.Y., 1961), pars. 31, 34, 138–40, 237, 314, 331, 332, 342, 345–47, 349, 368, 374, and *ibid.* (Ithaca, N.Y.: Cornell University Press, 1948), pars. 9 and 1108, contain the bulk of the arguments presented in my essay.

By looking into himself and observing the working of his mind the researcher gains invaluable clues about human nature, and they, in turn, help him to understand the world men have created. This, however, is not an effortless process. It may require a great intellectual and imaginative effort to grasp the purposes behind deeds or words (which are physical manifestations), particularly where people of a very different age are involved. However, we do not simply move from knowledge of human nature to an understanding of civil society. A kind of circle which deepens our knowledge is involved. We do not know human nature merely from introspection. As we study languages, religions, or social institutions, which are all products of human nature, our knowledge of human nature is enriched and we even come to understand *ourselves* better. This deeper insight in its turn leads us to a greater appreciation of the human world.

Here we must introduce the historical perspective so characteristic of Vico. We cannot treat the world of nations, religions, institutions, languages, and, for that matter, human nature itself, as timeless entities with fixed natures. (This was the mistake of the rationalists.) They are all involved in change and development and have quite specific characteristics at different times and in different places. Any explanation must therefore be genetic, that is, refer to origins and preceding causes. It must also make cross-references to the conditioning circumstances—physical or cultural—of a particular period. Vico applied these principles to his own autobiography; he said that he wrote "as a philosopher meditating causes both natural and moral as well as the occasions of fortune."

Vico called the empirical study of the history "of the languages, customs and deeds of peoples in war and peace"[10] philology. But he did not let matters rest there. In his work he claims that, "philosophy undertakes to examine philology . . . and reduces it to the form of a science by discovering in it the design of an ideal, eternal history traversed in time by the history of all nations."[11] This new science, he adds, studies "the common nature of nations in the light of divine providence, discovers the origins of institutions, religious and secular, among the gentile nations, and thereby establishes a system of the natural law of the gentes."[12] This idea of laws and ideal patterns underlying human affairs is profoundly ambiguous. On the one hand Vico seems to be propounding a scientific program, but on the other he appears to speak as a Christian convinced of divine providence, or even as a Platonist believing in an a priori order of things which manifests itself in time. I shall concentrate, however, on the interpretation that is relevant to the establishment of the social sciences.

For a discipline to achieve the status of a science it must be able to make

---

[10] Letter to Porcia, September, 1725, quoted in Fisch and Bergin's *Autobiography*.
[11] Bergin and Fisch, *New Science* (1961 ed.), par. 9.
[12] *Ibid.* (1948 ed.), par. 31.

successful generalizations and to establish laws about the way things follow each other and are causally connected.   In the case of the human studies it is not unreasonable to seek a starting point in certain constant features of human nature, for example, men have physical needs and sexual impulses, suffer from fear, and are capable of using symbols.   Vico made use of these facts and argued, for instance, that he was establishing his science of human affairs by analyzing "human thoughts about the human necessities or utilities of social life, which are the two perennial springs of the natural law of nations." [13] Common needs, then, give rise to universal institutions and, from these, universal principles can be derived.   In other words, human beings everywhere and at all times become aware of needing or wanting such things as food, shelter, security, and sexual satisfaction.   This gives rise to agriculture, the institution of marriage, and civil society.   On this basis we can make generalizations about social life.   But, of course, we cannot relate all that happens in history to the deliberate intentions of individuals.   Social interaction may have consequences—and serve ends—that none of the participants intended or even foresaw.   We may not wish to follow Vico in calling this Providence, but as social scientists we must certainly consider the occurrence of regular patterns.

Insofar as Vico believed that by means of the laws governing human life it was possible to trace the over-all pattern of universal history, he was undoubtedly mistaken.   (Indeed, it contradicts his own acute sense of the concrete differences produced by time and circumstances.)   Although many distinguished thinkers, such as Hegel, Comte, Marx, and, today, Toynbee, have followed him in this enterprise, most contemporary philosophers and historians would think that such schemes obscure historical research rather than illuminate it.   However, Vico's conviction that there are general laws and genetic patterns to be discovered in particular spheres of human life has proved immensely fruitful.   It has made him a pioneer of such disciplines as sociology, social anthropology, philology, comparative religion and jurisprudence, psychology, and the history of ideas, in all of which regularities can be established.   Although these do not provide a pattern for the whole of history, they can throw light on connections between particular historical events.

These views, elaborated with great philosophical acumen and stripped of any theological bias—and thus more unambiguously empiricist—are found again in Dilthey.[14]   He distinguished the human studies from the

---

[13] *Ibid.*, par. 347.

[14] H. P. Rickman, *Meaning in History: W. Dilthey's Thoughts on History and Society* (London, 1961), contains a selection of translated passages from vol. VII of Dilthey's collected works and a general introduction which explains his approach and places it in the context of modern discussions.   It also explains the translation of key terms.   All the material on which the present exposition of Dilthey is based can be found in this book.

physical sciences in terms of their subject matter, the former exploring humanity or human socio-historical reality, the latter dealing with physical nature. This means that they are concerned with human nature and its products, with individuals, families, nations, historical movements, social organizations, and cultural systems (the mind-affected world). As in Vico, this world is historical; it presents itself concretely as a process of changes and developments in which every manifestation is determined by its place in time.

Dilthey saw very clearly what Vico had already suggested (for example, in his reference to words), that every feature of this mind-affected world has a dual aspect. It is both a physical fact or event and the expression of thoughts, feelings, or aspirations. A sentence is a series of sounds or of marks on paper and, at the same time, a communication; an action is movement as well as the execution of a purpose. This dual nature gives meaning to these entities which Dilthey called "expressions." They form the concrete subject matter of the social studies which aim to extrapolate their meaning. The same idea must have been in Vico's mind when he used the term "philology"—usually confined to the study of language—for every kind of empirical study of human affairs.

Dilthey called the cognitive process by which we grasp the meaning of expressions understanding—to distinguish it from the quite different process of taking in the physical aspects of expressions or any other physical facts. In practice the two processes may often be hard to distinguish—as when we hear and understand a word simultaneously. They are, however, always *logically* distinguishable. We can hear a Chinese word as clearly as an English one and yet not understand it.

Understanding is a perfectly ordinary and familiar process which occurs constantly in everyday life. It is no more a matter of intuition, hunches, or flashes of insight than is the observation of objects. These forms of illumination can occur in any type of inquiry. Nor is understanding a mystical or mysterious process. We grasp what is in people's minds by watching their expressions and not by looking through their skulls, which would indeed be a peculiar achievement.

Basically we can understand expressions because we experience the connection between external manifestations and their content in ourselves. As we utter sounds we are aware of the thoughts we wish to convey; when we clench our teeth we also know that we are in pain; thus we can recognize what it means when someone else speaks or clenches his teeth. Basically Dilthey's fundamental epistemological point is the same as Vico's. Because we have a common human nature we can understand each other, and because the human world is the product of that human nature we can understand all its manifestations.

This does not mean that understanding is always a simple, immediate process. In most cases we must know or learn about the rules that govern the use of expressions (the linguistic conventions, for example, if the expressions are verbal) and the context in which they occur. When we deal with complex expressions or with those of a different age this can be an exacting business. It is the task to which Vico applied himself when he tried to recapture the mentality of early men, and he claimed that it took him many years of deep thought to reach his goal.

In pursuing this aim Vico was fully aware that he could not confine himself to the study of verbal expressions and their intended meanings. Actions speak louder than words, and the products of men bear the hallmark of the minds that created them. Even words can communicate a mental content, such as fear or prejudice, which the speaker did not intend to convey or of which he was unconscious. Vico, therefore, tried to recapture the spirit of nations from their deeds, language, religion, institutions, laws, mythologies, and literature. He saw clearly that both a language developed merely to serve practical needs and a poem written to celebrate some heroic action reveal the beliefs, conditions, and problems of a past age. In doing so he pioneered methods that enriched the study of history and prepared the ground for such disciplines as social anthropology and psychoanalysis.

Dilthey shared Vico's clear perception of the nature of the evidence with which the social sciences have to work. He carefully defined and distinguished different types of expressions and considered the value and limitations of each of them for an understanding of human nature.

However, we cannot rest content with the understanding of individual expressions. We want explanations, and in the human sphere, as well as in the physical, this means the discovery of general laws that govern the connections between events. Indeed, we cannot claim even to have properly understood an individual expression until we know why it came about, that is, how it follows from others in accordance with some established generalization. The social sciences are therefore committed to two different lines of inquiry which depend on each other. On the one hand they have to establish individual facts and the actual relations between them; on the other they must discover the laws that govern these relations.

We have already seen how Vico conceptualized this interdependence of approaches in terms of the co-operation between philology and philosophy. Dilthey, like the Neo-Kantians Windelband and Rickert, distinguished between history and the systematic human studies such as psychology or comparative religion. History he saw as the study of individual events occurring in time and thus providing *all* the evidence for our understanding of human nature. For example, the material of psychology consists of biographies, case histories, and accounts of particular experiments; that of economics is derived from economic history. Because, according to this definition, history is not a generalizing discipline, Dilthey concluded that there can be no historical laws as such. It is the systematic disciplines which establish laws and regularities and they repay their debt to history by throwing light on the connections between historical events in terms of these laws.

Here, once again, we must emphasize the difference, noted by Vico and carefully spelled out by Dilthey, between the physical sciences and the human studies. The former proceed from marshaling the facts—which is a kind of history—to explaining them, by means of hypothetical constructions, in terms of generalizations about their connections. In the human studies the connections that can form the basis for genetic explanations are themselves part of our experience. We see patterns in our lives which we recognize, more uncertainly, in history and which form the subject matter of the systematic disciplines.

Dilthey listed a number of typical relationships, such as that between means and ends, parts and wholes (for instance, the links between the constituents of a configuration or of a developmental process), outer and inner (that is, between overt expression and what it expresses), a situation and the value attributed to it, and that between an individual and his environment, which he affects and by which he is affected. We actually experience all these relationships and make judgments in terms of them, which is why life presents itself as meaningful.

He then analyzed our experience of time, for we certainly do not live only through a succession of moments. Every instant is enriched by recollection of the past and anticipation of the future. I could not appreciate a song if I simply concentrated on each sound as it occurred. Instead, each note takes its place in a context formed by my memory of preceding sounds and my expectation of others to come. I could not write this sentence if I did not remember what I had said before or had no idea of what I wanted to say next. Thus, because we look both backward and forward while experiencing the present, we are aware of continuity, and the movement through time becomes meaningful. This experience of time as something meaningful is the growing point of history. We are essentially historical creatures equipped not only to act in historical contexts but also to understand them.

Dilthey also showed how specific contexts are formed in a person's mental life. Seeing something may lead to our wanting it and resolving to get it. Thinking about how to do this will follow, and these various mental processes will produce an action. This need not be a continuous process. An abiding interest, feeling, or aspiration may link activities far apart in time although covering a man's lifetime (for instance, occasional visits to a museum, periodic meetings with a friend, or the step-by-step approach to a goal). In this way a person's life forms a pattern which becomes particularly obvious in retrospect. We see him—or he sees himself—gradually becoming what he ultimately was or achieving what he did.

From these converging insights Dilthey argued the importance of auto-biography and biography. In them we discover genetic patterns that we can apply to the more complex field of history. Here, too, Dilthey justified something Vico anticipated when he described his approach to his auto-biography. However, in Dilthey, as in Vico, the process is not all in one direction, from the study of the individual to that of humanity. The individual is himself a historical product. He is molded by historical forces and is affected by the conditions and prevailing opinions of his age. As a thinker, soldier, or politician he may contribute to the historical context. Thus there is a point at which every adequate autobiography or biography must expand into general history.

In setting out the striking parallels between Vico's and Dilthey's thoughts I have also, I believe, presented a viable theory of the human studies which is a relevant contribution to current discussions about the future of these disciplines. Their subject matter is socio-historical reality, which is mean-ingful because it consists of expressions of men's thoughts, intentions, feelings, and valuations. Because these are all produced by men their meaning can be understood by the human mind. In the social sciences understanding, which recurs in everyday life, is refined and combined with such intellectual processes as analysis, classification, and generalization to produce two types of knowledge. On the one hand it gives rise to history, that is, to the grasp of the rich variety of individual human manifestations and their relations to one another in time. On the other hand it leads to the development of systematic human studies that examine the causal and genetic laws behind the development of individuals as well as the patterns of interaction within and between social and cultural systems. The two main types of knowledge are interdependent and so are the different systematic disciplines.

This general view, based on a clearly articulated epistemology and worked out, as we have seen, in rich detail, provides the philosophical justification for a variety of theoretical concepts and research procedures that have proved, and are proving, their fruitfulness. Psychoanalysis has reached its conclusions by interpreting unconscious expressions; Gestalt psychology concentrated on configurations; sociology, social anthropology, and social psychology have used genetic and functional explanations; they have accounted for actions in terms of norms, rules, and purposes and have explored the connection between personality structure and social systems. Historicism, which rejects the application of non-historical criteria to historical phenomena and insists that each must be explained in terms of its own context, has greatly influenced the practice of historians. In all these fields we can see the impact of Vico's and Dilthey's thought on modern developments.

Over and above this influence on different spheres of research, such a philosophy of the human studies brings home to us the fact that each discipline acquires its subject matter by abstracting an aspect from concrete socio-historical reality, a fact which warns us not to regard the division into separate subjects as absolute and which should encourage constructive inter-disciplinary co-operation.[15]

---

[15] Rickman, *Understanding and the Human Studies*, presents a theory of knowledge and methodology of the social sciences along the lines developed by Dilthey.

Vico, as we all know, lived amidst incessant hardships while creating his great work. As he wrote in his *Autobiography*, "he lived in his native city not only as a stranger, but quite unknown."[1] Yet, despite the lack of recognition in his own time, Vico's problems are contemporary for us today, as contemporary as is the problem of the cycle that repeats itself, and as topical as the human will to overcome the repetition and to create a new epoch. In Vico the cycle seems in some way deterministic, fatal, naturalistic. At the conclusion of it there is a repetition of barbarism, a recurrence of the huge primitive forest, which constantly reappears like Cadmus' serpent or Hercules' hydra. The forest is nothing but the earth, unknown to man, similar to man's unconscious, to Freud's *libido*, to a radical invincible evil, an evil which can be destroyed, not by iron but by fire. The task of man, as the close of the *Scienza nuova* declares, is that of overcoming barbarism so that the direction of history may proceed from the rabble of Romulus to the commonwealth of Plato. Thus the content of history proceeds from chaos toward cosmos, and all aspects of human culture and activity find their forms, even though such forms are never final and the Platonic ideal of a just humanity in the world of nations appears as no more than a direction, an intuition, a symbol of perfection. We cannot, and must not, assert, however, that it is impossible to carry such an ideal, in an ever-improved and more concrete form, into the actual reality of the historical course. We must contend, instead, that such realization is possible, despite recurrence (*ricorso*), nay, in outright opposition to it. The actualization of that ideal is subordinated to the relationship between matter and form, between nature and culture. It is only by burning the forest that a well-defined space can be obtained, a dimension on which cities can be built and which is anti-

[1] See *The Autobiography of Giambattista Vico*, trans. Max H. Fisch and Thomas G. Bergin (Ithaca, N.Y.: Cornell University Press, 1944), p. 134. See in particular the Introduction, which contains a section on Vico's reputation in Europe and in the United States. This reputation still exists, but it is generic rather than precise and circumstantial. As for Vico's relationship with the trends of thought preceding his, and with the authors whom he influenced and who studied him, see B. Croce, *Bibliografia vichiana*, enlarged and recast by F. Nicolini, 2 vols. (Naples: Ricciardi, 1947–48). Very important is Nicolini's *Commento storico alla seconda Scienza nuova*, 2 vols. (Rome, 1949–50).

thetical to formless space.   And, while a "space for civil life" is thus carved
out of the forest, time, too, takes on form: time assumes a datable beginning,
a measure, a rhythm.   Time and place, set in order, render human communication possible.   Men and nations are able to meet in space and time,
in the mythical, artistic, functional, symbolic order of the spatio-temporal
process.   In Vico such terms as "function," "symbol," "form," are already
to be found.   We find in him phantasy, in the meaning of a mediation
between sensitivity and reason.   We find in the "recurrences" themselves
the characteristics of different civilizations, the various outlooks on life of
disparate cultures.   We find a panorama of the science of man who in the
present vitally re-experiences and, by intellection, grasps the past and transforms it according to a plan, to an image of the future.   Undoubtedly, the
terms "outlook on life" (*Weltanschauung*), "vital experience" (*Erlebnis*), and
"intellection" (*Verstehen*) are reminiscent of Dilthey: in this respect we may
say that Vico leads us to Dilthey's "critique of historical reason," and to its
problems.   Historical reason possesses a positive direction only insofar as
Vico's philosophy, as well as Dilthey's, is neither a science of nature nor a
science of the mind, but is both at the same time, that is, a philosophy of man.
I should furthermore like to remark that, when in Vico we come across such
terms as "function" and "symbol," when in him we find an analysis of
symbolic and mythical space and time, the present-day scholar is reminded
of Cassirer, just as, in connection with history's realization through a spatio-
temporal process, he is reminded of Whitehead.[2]

Probably, one of Vico's initial problems is that of nature, that is, the
problem of the relationship between nature and culture.   If nature is not
only good but also evil, if it is an object not only of knowledge but of force
and life as well, what could be the meaning of this vital force if it can also
become barbarism?   Vico grew up in a cultural milieu (it is enough to
mention Lionardo da Capua and Tommaso Cornelio, who took their
inspiration from Camillo Colonna) which Ferdinando Galiani characterized,

[2] See E. Paci, *Ingens sylva* (Milan: Mondadori, 1949); concerning Cassirer see p. 166.
For Whitehead the spatio-temporal process is the foundation not only of physics but also
of the sciences of man; see A. N. Whitehead, *Symbolism: Its Meaning and Effects* (New
York, 1927); idem, *Process and Reality* (New York, 1929); idem, *Adventures of Ideas* (New
York, 1933).   On Whitehead see E. Paci, *Relazioni e significati* (Milan, 1965), pp. 28–29.
A conjunction with the thought of Whitehead, as well as with that of Cassirer, is to be
found in the works of S. Langer: *Philosophy in a New Key* (Cambridge, Mass., 1942),
The Practice of Philosophy (New York, 1930), *Feeling and Form* (London, 1953); see, in the
last volume, pp. 7, 263 (on time's relation to symbolism), 307 (on the event's relation to
drama), and 404.   Cassirer does not speak of Whitehead's philosophical production but
mentions only the latter's *Principia Mathematica* (1910) and *An Enquiry Concerning the
Principles of Natural Knowledge* (1919).   References to Whitehead in relation to Cassirer
will be found in P. A. Schilpp, ed., *The Philosophy of E. Cassirer* (New York, 1949),
which also contains an essay by Mrs. Langer, in the essays of F. Leander (p. 357), W. M.
Urban (p. 437), D. Bidney, pp. 473 and 723, and W. M. Solmitz (p. 479).

with some exaggeration, as being akin to that of a "*risorgimento.*" It was a
milieu steeped in Galilean anti-Aristotelianism, influenced not only by Bacon
but by Descartes, by Gassendi's Epicureanism, and, consequently, by the *De
rerum natura* of Lucretius. It has rightly been remarked that the whole of
Vico's work[3] shows the impact of Lucretius, and that the youthful poem entitled *Affetti d'un disperato*, which reflects "Lucretian moods and studies in the
critical year 1692, . . . could not have been written by a devout Christian."[4]
Vico himself relates in his *Autobiography* (1725) that Epicurus, in Gassendi's
version, was fashionable in Naples and that he (Vico) was overtaken by a
desire to become acquainted with Epicurus by studying Lucretius.[5] That
reading of Lucretius led Vico to a negative judgment of Epicurus, of
sensationalism and empiricism, on the ground that Epicurus (and Vico's
judgment fits Lucretius equally well) explains quite adequately "the forms
of physical nature" (so that Vico felt much delight at this explanation) but
makes himself ridiculous when he proceeds to "explain the operations of the
human mind."[6] We find here a contraposition between "physical nature"
and "the operations of the human mind." It is the antithesis between *life*
and *mind*; and it is an antithesis because "physical nature," understood as
"corporeal life," may be either a good or an evil, either a positive or a
negative, form. In this sense, *life* and *mind* take on the meaning of a contrast
which in German appears as that between *Leben* and *Geist*. This is a theme
which dominates Ernst Cassirer's philosophy and the whole debate concerning the relationships between *Naturwissenschaften* and *Geisteswissenschaften*
(that is, *Kulturwissenschaften*), if we assume the term "*Leben*" to be equivalent to that of "*Natur.*" Vico's reading of Lucretius or Epicurus "served
only to confirm him still firmer in the doctrines of Plato, who from the
very form of our human mind, without any hypothesis, establishes the
eternal idea as the principle of all things, on the basis of the knowledge and
consciousness (*scienza e coscienza*) that we have of ourselves."[7] This Vichian
reference to Plato bears some analogy to the philosophical position held by
Cassirer in his *The Myth of the State*, a work in which the contrast between
nature and culture, between life and mind, becomes more pronounced, while
the whole problem of the relationships between *Naturwissenschaften* and
Geisteswissenschaften is again taken up for debate.[8]

[3] See F. Nicolini, *La giovinezza di G. B. Vico* (Bari, 1932), pp. 132ff.; see also the
Introduction to Fisch and Bergin's *Autobiography*, p. 32; N. Badaloni, *Introduzione a Vico*
(Milan, 1961); P. Rossi, Introduction to *Opere di Vico* (Milan: Rizzoli, 1959); *idem*,
F. Bacone (Bari, 1957), pp. 329–31 and 403–4 (on the relationship between Vico and Plato).
[4] Introduction to Fisch and Bergin's *Autobiography*, p. 36; Nicolini, *La giovinezza*,
p. 123; and Paci, *Ingens sylva*, pp. 15–33.
[5] Fisch and Bergin's *Autobiography*, p. 126.
[6] *Ibid.*, pp. 126–27.
[7] *Ibid.*
[8] See E. Cassirer, "Geist und Leben in der Philosophie der Gegenwart," *Die neue*

It is through a train of reasoning akin to that by which he criticizes Epicurus and Lucretius that Vico lays the basis for his criticism of Descartes. Essentially, Descartes contraposes *res cogitans* to *res extensa* and reduces physical nature, inclusive of the animals, to a mechanical construction. Vico sees in nature something living, even though barbaric, even though *giants* are associated with nature, are stupid and ferocious creatures frightened by the thunder of Jupiter, who is at the same time the god of maximal strength and of salvation because he dominates the giants and compels them to settle at a certain time, thus causing them to desist from their roaming, from their erratic wandering (as Toynbee would put it), in order to give inception to civilization. Inasmuch as Jupiter stops the nomadic roving of the giants, he is the "molder," the "stabilizer." "And for having put an end to the feral wandering of these few giants, so that they became the princes of the gentes, he received the epithet of *Stator*, stayer or establisher. The Latin philologists explain this epithet too narrowly from the fact that Jove, invoked by Romulus, had stopped the Romans in their flight from the battle with the Sabines." [9]

Rundschau, 41 (1930), 244–54; an English translation of this essay is contained in Schilpp's *Philosophy of E. Cassirer*. The contrast between *Geist* and *Leben* is characteristic of the work of Thomas Mann, for which Cassirer showed interest by writing an essay on Mann's novel *Lotte in Weimar* (Cassirer read this work in manuscript form in 1943). The essay was published, posthumously, in 1945; see E. Cassirer, "T. Manns Goethebild: Eine Studie über Lotte in Weimar," *Germanic Review*, 20, no. 3 (1945): 166–94. On this subject see R. S. Hartman, "Cassirer's Philosophy of Symbolic Forms," in Schilpp's *Philosophy of E. Cassirer*, pp. 291, 300, 323, 328, 331. Hartman refers to the problem of myth as it appears in Mann's novel *Joseph und seine Brüder*, and quotes K. Kerenyi, *Ein Briefwechsel mit Mann* (Zurich, 1945). In Cassirer's *Philosophy of Symbolic Forms*, myth is, above all, a mediation between life and spirit, in the sense that the two elements are inseparable. In his *An Essay on Man* (New Haven, Conn.: Yale University Press, 1944), Cassirer emphasizes the negative (or, at least, non-rational) element of myth considered as vital expressive function. In the *Essay on Man* Cassirer pursues a line which he had already traced in the *Zur Logik der Kulturwissenschaften* (Göteborg, 1942; English translation, *Logic of the Humanities* [New Haven, 1961]), where he again takes over the Vichian theme (pp. 11–14), and where he closes with an analysis of the tragedy of culture. In *The Myth of the State* (New Haven: Yale University Press, 1946), written in the period 1943–45, myth, in its relation to political history, is considered as the lowest level of life, and civilization is portrayed as a progressive liberation from the irrational elements that are present in myth. Cassirer criticizes Freud's theory of the unconscious and Durkheim's assumptions, as well as Hegel's absolute state, and speaks of the life-society that unites all living beings. The state, as myth and as absolute power, is set over against society; reason requires a fight against myth, whose mediating function dissolves, resulting in the contraposition between myth and reason, as if, in Vico's language, after the lapse of the ages of reason and of men, a new barbarism were to recur. Against barbarism, Cassirer champions a rational conception of the state, eulogizes the Platonic ideal, longs for artistic forms that are not mythical, and advocates ethics, science (understood not only as natural science but also as social science), and philosophy.

[9] See *The New Science of Giambattista Vico*, trans. Thomas G. Bergin and Max H. Fisch

This conception of God as Jupiter places Vico in a problematic situation. God, in fact, is not a force of nature, even though he created nature and, through divine providence, governs the "courses" and the recurrences of history: God alone, as Vico states in the *De nostri*, is "the path and the truth." God knows nature because he created it; man is unable to grasp it in cognition, but he may attain to a knowledge of history because history is his own work. This is the famous principle of the *verum*, which is carried into reality and fulfilled in the *factum*. According to Vico, we are able to demonstrate the principles of mathematics because we are the creators of it; were we capable, likewise, of demonstrating the principles of physics, we would be able to create physical nature as well. Physics (hence, nature) was not created by us, and therefore it remains unknown to men, whereas history by no means remains unknown to us. Consequently, we should not devote our efforts exclusively to the study of nature. Vico criticizes the method of study of his own time for cultivating predominantly the *Naturwissenschaften* instead of the *Geisteswissenschaften*. In his *On the Study Methods of Our Time* he says precisely: "But the greatest drawback of our educational method is that we pay an excessive amount of attention to the natural sciences, and not enough to ethics." [10]

With these words Vico seems to introduce himself as the founder of the moral sciences, the *Geisteswissenschaften*, and in particular (if we think of his theory of language, myth, and symbols) as the founder of the modern interpretation of myth. Cassirer sees him in exactly this light and emphasizes the fact that in this way we are brought back to man, to the "subject." Vico, however, criticizes Descartes in connection with this very point; he repudiates the subject as pure *cogito* and refutes the Cartesian doubt, which consists of the suspension of assent ("*per assensus suspensionem*"), or, as Husserl would say, is the same thing as an *epoché*. Man is made up of mind and body; thought is not the cause of the body, but is the cause only of the expression, of the *signum* (token). [11] We may note, incidentally, that Vico's

---

(Garden City, N.Y.: Doubleday, 1961), p. 77. "Wandering" is one of the technical terms used by Toynbee, *A Study of History* (London: Oxford University Press, 1934–54). According to Toynbee, peace is possible only after a long series of civil struggles such as took place in the time of Augustus; on the other hand, this very concept, while it establishes authority, prepares the recurrence of barbarism. Peace, therefore (exactly as in Vico), is a point of arrival, but, at the same time, by authoritarian imposition, it may prepare new wars. Tacitus says of the *pax romana* and of the Romans: *solitudinem faciunt, pacem appellant*. Since Toynbee fails to mention Vico, I have inscribed to him my abridged edition of the *Autobiography* and the *Scienza nuova* (Turin, 1949).

[10] See *On the Study Methods of Our Time*, trans. Elio Gianturco (Indianapolis: Bobbs-Merrill, 1965), p. 33.

[11] E. Cassirer, *Philosophie der symbolischen Formen*, I (Berlin, 1923), 90–91, II (Berlin, 1925), 6, where, among other things, Cassirer says that Vico reaches an authentic con-

viewpoint, in essence, does not differ greatly from that of Husserl.   For Husserl the *cogito* is not the cause of the world, and the *epoché* is a suspension of our prejudgments.   The *epoché* enables us (starting from the *cogito*, under-stood not only as the transcendental subject but also as living and concrete body—*Leib*) not to create but to establish a science of the *Lebenswelt*; it enables us to bring about the transformation of the "sign," and that of any activity or any science, into a *significance*.   This significance is shared equally by the function of the sciences and by that of history.[12]

Vico's God operates in nature as a spiritual *animus* which acts on the bodily soul.   "Just as God is in the world, so is the spiritual principle in our body. Perpetual is the activity of God: incessantly active is our soul.   Finally, God is the creator of physical nature, and, in the same way, the spiritual principle in us is (so to speak) the Creator, the Maker, of all the arts of man."[13]   In these sentences God is in the world and is operative in it.   *Animus* itself is godlike, inasmuch as God is *artifex naturae*, and the *animus* of man is the *artifex artium*.   If this viewpoint were stretched to the utmost limit, Vico would be saying, as Spinoza does, that nature itself is God.   Still more dangerous for Vico would it be to state that God not only has created the feral nature of the "age of the gods," but fuses into, and is confused with, this feral nature and with the gods.   These potential dangers of his thought led Vico to study the problem of war, that of the law of nations, of the *sapientia rei bellicae*, and that of the relationship of this *sapientia* to the science of human law (*humani juris prudentia*).   It is the world of Lucretius and Machiavelli which Vico presents as the world of Tacitus, just as he will see in Grotius the world of natural law and in Plato the idea of a perfect common-wealth toward which history should aim, just as he sees in Bacon a kind of synthesis of Tacitus with Plato.   God lives in the world as truth, but man has to face war, the worlds of law and politics.   It seems as if Providence were in want of error, human fallibility, and barbarism.   God himself (we

---

ception of the unity of mind which is articulated in the triad language, art, and myth. In modern philosophy, mythical hypostatizations are classified under *subjectivity*.   Cf. the English translation, *The Philosophy of Symbolic Forms*, I (New Haven, 1953), 148–49, and II (New Haven, 1955), 3.

[12] For this interpretation see E. Paci, *Funzione delle scienze e significato dell'uomo* (Milan, 1963).   The science of the *Lebenswelt*, achieved through the suspension of judgment, is construed here as a "new science" antecedent to all categories and therefore laying the foundations of all sciences.   This "new science" is not the confusion and indeterminate-ness of the subject-object, which Cassirer, in his *Philosophy of Symbolic Forms*, attributes to Schelling's *Philosophy of Mythology*, nor is it the mythology that Cassirer repudiates in the works of his late period.   It is, instead, the science of human operations, by which the groundwork of the sciences is established, conferring upon them a paramount role and significance in the formation of a new humanity.

[13] See Vico, *De antiquissima Italorum sapientia*, ed. G. Gentile and F. Nicolini (Bari, 1914), p. 8.

saw this when we spoke of Jupiter) seems to become a terrifying power, plying its own political policy, availing itself of the thunder-terror in order to cause civilization to be born.   Out of terror there arose the first Vichian figures, the first "plastic forms," the earliest formative ideas, the earliest living forms, or, as Cassirer would say, the first "symbolic forms," which are for Vico the giants.   The *Scienza nuova* depicts a continuing emergence of figures, not only in the age of the gods, but in the age of heroes, and in that of men as well.   These emerging figures are such in the same sense as are those of Hegel's *Phenomenology of the Spirit*, which Cassirer sees only as a "phenomenology of knowledge," even if it is true that Hegel's Absolute Spirit bears some analogy to Vico's God, and even though Vico's Providence has something predetermined and necessitarian about it which can be seen in Hegel's dialectics and in his philosophy of history.   For instance, the recurrence of barbarism in Vico's work seems to be something fatal, inevitable, pre-constituted.   In Vico a dialectic—that of the "courses" and recurrences—is present; and at times we seem to glimpse a dialectic even between ages and epochs, between kinds of natures, natural rights, governments, languages, written characters, legal systems, authorities, and reasons.[14]

In Vico we meet with dialectic in its political and social form as well, in the guise of a contrast between aristocratic and plebeian governments, a contrast which gives place to human governments.   The pattern of the relationship between servant and master (one of the most famous Hegelian patterns) is foreshadowed by Vico, at least in the sense that the early serfs or *socii* (associates, from whom society arises) are compelled by the heroes, their masters, to cultivate the latter's lands; they are fellowmen and understand one another.   This is an intuition of what Hegel calls "the servile consciousness."

The first *socii*, who are properly companions associated for mutual advantage, cannot be imagined or understood to have existed in the world previous to these fugitives, who sought to save their lives by taking refuge with the aforesaid first fathers, and who, having been received for their lives, were obliged to sustain them by cultivating the fields of the fathers.   These were the true *socii* of the "heroes."   Later, they were the plebeians of the heroic cities, and finally the provincials of sovereign peoples.[15]

The pattern of the "servant and master" may be considered as one of the main sources of Feuerbach and Marx.   Croce himself, in his *The Philosophy of G. B. Vico* (1911), mentions Marx's name in connection with Vico and remarks that, in the seventeenth century, jusnaturalism fulfilled for the bourgeoisie the same role as that discharged by Marxism "for the workers' class in the nineteenth century."[16]   But the above-quoted excerpt from

---

[14] Bergin and Fisch, *New Science*, pp. 285–300.
[15] *Ibid.*, p. 39.
[16] B. Croce, *La filosofia di Giambattista Vico* (Bari, 1965), p. 76.

Vico goes beyond this; it does not identify dialectic with a natural or naturalistic, preconstituted order. For Vico, consciousness is the act of becoming aware of the existence of servitude, an act which renders communication and the society of slaves (of plebeians) possible. Subsequently, these plebeians become the provincials and colonials of the dominant peoples. Here Vico stands up against the naturalistic materialism that Engels descries in evolutionism. Against evolutionism, Engels states that the dialectic of society *is not* that of naturalistic evolution, in spite of the fact that in his writing we find the expression "dialectic of nature."[17] This viewpoint is possible in an interpretation of Marx in which Marxism is linked with the *subject*, with *man* (in the sense given to this word by Husserl). It is interesting to note, on the other hand, that Marx himself contends that the dialectic, man's alienation, and the "*fetischization*" of wares all derive from a "metamorphosis of the subject into the object." Because of this metamorphosis wares become human, and men become things of physical nature, material things, and cease to be the creators of their own products.[18]

Now, Vico often falls into naturalism when he identifies ideas with things, a case in which the subject, and the relationship between subjects, is lost. He says, for instance, in Spinoza's fashion: "the order of ideas must follow the order of institutions";[19] and the "order of institutions" which he brings up, immediately afterward, is preordained and insurmountable. If such an order gives way to a dialectic, such a dialectic is impossible to modify and will always repeat itself: it is one of the aspects of the theory of the *corsi e ricorsi*. Thus, in every people, the same myths are repeated: every nation has its Jupiter and its Hercules,[20] and it is necessary that there should be "a mutual language common to all nations."[21] Things are born at certain times and in certain ways, and their dissolution and revival are repeated.[22] When men are ignorant of the truth, they cling to the certain, "so that, if

[17] Paci, *Funzione delle scienze*, p. 319.

[18] Karl Marx, *Manuscripts of the Years 1863–1865* (Russian text and translation, *Archiv Marxa i Engelsa*, ed. V. Adoratzski, II [VII] [Moscow, 1933], p. 34). In regard to the whole problem see Paci, *Funzione delle scienze*, pt. III; see also P. Gambazzi, "I fondamenti antropologici della storia in Marx," *Aut-Aut*, 1967, pp. 99–152. Marx's "subject" is not subjectivistic (in the sense of "private") or relativistic, but is concrete and, at the same time, transcendental and "*intentional*." This interpretation is connected with the characteristic of "need" which may be found in the *Lebenswelt* of Husserl, as well as with the dialectic between subjects or groups. Furthermore, it is connected with the establishment and structure of a society which does not transform man into a naturalistic object, into a brute animal, as Vico and Marx say. On this point see G. Piana, *Esistenza e storia negli inediti di Husserl* (Milan: Lampugnani-Nigri, 1965); *idem, I problemi della fenomenologia* (Milan: Mondadori, 1966); and G. D. Neri, *Prassi e conoscenza* (Milan: Feltrinelli, 1966).

[19] Bergin and Fisch, *New Science*, p. 38.

[20] *Ibid.*, p. 31.   [21] *Ibid.*, p. 25.   [22] *Ibid.*, p. 22.

they cannot satisfy their intellects by knowledge (*scienza*), their wills at least may rest on consciousness (*coscienza*)." [23]   For Vico, philology is the science of the *certum*, of factual events and phenomena, whereas philosophy is the science of truth (*verum*).   On the other hand, for him, philology and philosophy are one because *verum* and *factum* are mutually convertible.   The identification of truth with certainty, *verum* with *factum*, runs the danger of becoming that thing which, in Hegel, is the identification of the real with the rational.   In this Hegelian process the dialectic is lost because the "ideal" (that is, conceptual) categories coincide with the facts.   In Vico, however, when they are ignorant of truth, men cling to psychological certainty because they are unknowing, fallible, and incapable of achieving a total science.   This is why men endeavor to ground their will on their consciousness of the certainty of a particular fact, folkway, or habit.   It is a fact that certitude coincides with *authority*, and precisely with the authority of the will, we may say, with the prejudice accepted by human volition without being inquired into, without the consciousness of the *certum* becoming that of the *verum*.   Here philology and philosophy no longer coincide, and Vico falls into self-contradiction, into a conflict with "man fallen and weak," who (as Pico della Mirandola says) "stands at the center of the world, between good and evil."   "A great miracle is man," states Pico, "and God has created him so that he is neither heavenly nor earthly." [24]   He may move toward the heavenly, toward the truth of the "ideal" commonwealth of Plato, in the course of the history of his nation, but he may also (in the "recurrence") revert to barbarism.   In fact, man is confined within the circle of his qualities, as the authority of philology demonstrates.   But philosophy then dissents from philology.   "Philosophy contemplates reason, whence comes knowledge of the true; philology observes that of which human choice is the author, whence comes consciousness of the certain." [25]   Philosophy's truth fails to coincide with the certainty of facts due to the action of man fallen and weak; it is philosophy's duty, therefore, to consider man "as he should be." [26]   "To be useful to the human race, philosophy must raise and direct weak and fallen man, not rend his nature, or abandon him to corruption." [27]   Myth is to be found in the conflict between liberty

---

[23] *Ibid.*, p. 21.

[24] Pico della Mirandola, *De hominis dignitate*, ed. E. Garin (Florence, 1942), p. 102.

[25] Bergin and Fisch, *New Science*, p. 21.   The English word "choice" translates into *l'umano arbitrio* (literally, man's free will), which is correct; but Vico speaks of the "authority" of the *umano arbitrio*, of facts such as they are, not facts subject to criticism, in the name of the truth of philosophy.   As a matter of fact, Vico adds: "the philosophers failed by half in not giving certainty to their reasonings by appeal to the authority of the philologians, and likewise the latter failed by half in not taking care to give to their authority the sanction of truth by appeal to the reasonings of the philosophers."

[26] *Ibid.*, p. 20.   [27] *Ibid.*, pp. 19–20.

and authority, between corruption and perfection, between the brute natural fact, that is, force and violence, and the ideal truth, which should guide man and bestow meaning upon history. Undoubtedly, myth is a synthesis, a mediation between sense and reason, between Tacitus and Plato; this Vico asserts repeatedly, as does Cassirer in his *Philosophy of Symbolic Forms*. On the other hand, myth is faced with two possibilities: it may cause man to revert to barbarism, or it may help him, by means of the truth of philosophy, to lift himself to the level of reason. Thus Cassirer, who in his *Philosophy of Symbolic Forms* champions the autonomy of myth, in his *Logic of the Humanities* sees in Vico's philosophy of history a progressive liberation of reason from myth considered in its negative aspect, that is, from myth as it appears in Cassirer's *The Myth of the State*.

If the "courses" and recurrences (*corsi e ricorsi*) are not fatal, can the recurrence of barbarism be avoided? Philosophy itself is a struggle against that recurrence. Rather than speak of a return to barbarism, we should speak of a return to the "primitive" stage and should give to that word the meaning which Rousseau attaches to it: for him the primitive is the original and positive man who is reborn in us *in spite of* the corruptness of civilization. Undoubtedly, it is because of this ambiguity of myth that Cassirer finds such complexity in the apparently simple thought of Rousseau (see Cassirer's *Das Problem Jean-Jacques Rousseau*), whom he links with Kant and Goethe (see also Cassirer's *Rousseau, Kant, and Goethe*, trans. J. Gutmann, P. O. Kristeller, and J. H. Randall, Jr. [New York: Harper & Row, 1963]).

The ambiguity of myth in Vico is, then, bound up with the discrepancy between philology and philosophy, reality and truth. Men are capable of understanding history because history has been made by men: this is the basic principle of the *Scienza nuova*. It is the principle which Cassirer, in a Kantian sense, would call "Vico's Copernican revolution." Man is capable of understanding mathematics because he "makes" it. As Einstein used to say (and Cassirer remembers it) mathematics "is a free invention of the human mind." Vico thinks that man is ignorant of the physical nature to which mathematics is applied, because that nature is not man's work. Wherever mathematical knowledge is not applicable, a science of nature is impossible. But then Vico's *Scienza nuova*, to which mathematics is not applicable, is no longer a science in the usual sense. Thus Vico, the founder of the sciences of man, is also the thinker who posits the dualism between *Naturwissenschaften* and *Geisteswissenschaften*, and is therefore unable to discover the single foundation on which both sciences are based, that foundation which Husserl finds in the science of the *Lebenswelt*. In the *Lebenswelt* according to Husserl, a science is possible *qua* science of the operations of human subjects, common men, and scientists inasmuch as that science precedes all categories, both those of the sciences of nature and of the sciences of man. The *Lebenswelt*, finally, is the science of time and space, in which

the human subjects, the "monads" of the renovated Leibnizian monad-
ology of Husserl, meet and eventually clash. Vico himself thought of
a philosophy of nature while sketching his *De antiquissima*, which was
to include a *liber physicus*, followed by an appendix (no longer extant)
entitled "On the Equilibrium of the Animal Body" (*De aequilibrio corporis animantis*). It was a philosophy which spoke of points and of the
continuum in connection with Zeno of Elea; and these points, in many
respects, remind us of Leibniz.[28] We could thus say of Vico what Husserl says of Galileo in his *The Crisis of European Science*—that he was both
a great discoverer and a great "coverer." Vico was a discoverer because he was a founder of the human sciences; he was a "coverer" because
he failed to notice that even the sciences of physical nature are made by man,
are human operations, that they all depend on the liberation from prejudice,
on the assertion that men are not only thinking beings but also living beings
who possess their own bodies, bodies that are rooted in the inorganic body
of the planet Earth, in its precategorial, temporal, and spatial form. For
Husserl this conception of man is rendered possible by a non-Cartesian
method of *epoché* which finds in man a presence in *the first person*, a presence
capable of reconstructing the past and of moving toward the future, just as it
is capable, in the inwardness of time, of discovering the externality of space.
Husserl's "presence" is both a historical a priori and an animated and physical
a priori, which is to say that it is a certitude confirmed by reflection while, on
the other hand, it is "intentional" (in the sense that Husserl attaches to this
term).

Such a presence, though never exhausting truth, moves toward truth and
bestows a meaning on life and history insofar as, within the realm of the
finite and of determinedness, it tends toward a boundless and open horizon,
toward the continuous creation (in a constant struggle against throwbacks
and "recurrences") of a humanity in which all men are subjects and not
objects.[29] The *Scienza nuova* was meant to be—as in many respects it
is—an encyclopedia of the sciences, of culture, and of history. The whole
of Cassirer's work, for that matter, is intended to be precisely such an
encyclopedia.

It is therefore amazing that Cassirer never devoted a particular section of
his work to a thorough discussion of Vico's achievement, since Cassirer's
problems in contemporary philosophy are often the very ones brought up
by Vico.

---

[28] Croce speaks about the relationships between Leibniz and Vico on the last page of
his book *The Philosophy of Giambattista Vico*. In regard to the whole problem, and
particularly in regard to the fact that Vico was thinking precisely of Zeno of Elea, see
A. Corsano, *G. B. Vico* (Bari, 1956), pp. 122–27.

[29] May I refer, for this interpretation, to the first and second parts of my book *Funzione
delle scienze*.

Cassirer never speaks at length about Vico. In the first three volumes of his major work, for instance (*Das Erkenntnisproblem in der Philosophie und Wissenschaft der neueren Zeit*), there is no chapter devoted to Vico. In the fourth and last volume of this work, written in Sweden in 1940 and published in Germany in 1957 (*Von Hegels Tode bis zur Gegenwart, 1832–1932*), Cassirer refers to Vico's position in the development of historicism. Chapter V of the same volume (a chapter in which Cassirer describes the fundamental trends of historical research) is devoted to historicism. For Cassirer, historicism starts with Herder. As is his practice, Cassirer refers to Vico fleetingly, in order to deal at once with Herder, and, after Herder, with Niebuhr, Ranke, and W. von Humboldt. Subsequently, Cassirer treats Taine's positivism, analyzes the works of Mommsen, Burckhardt, and Lamprecht, and, finally, studies the relationship between the history of religion and historical knowledge in Strauss, Renan, and Fustel de Coulanges. Cassirer fails to speak of Hegel and of the Hegelian "left," and disregards Dilthey's great achievement. At the beginning of the chapter, Cassirer refers to his book *Philosophy of the Enlightenment* (German ed., 1932; English trans., 1951), in which Vico is mentioned, but in order to cast him in an isolated role. It is acknowledged, in 1940, that Vico has been the discoverer of myth, but it is observed that even Vico and Herder have not fully understood myth. This reference is a prelude to the strictures that, in *The Myth of the State*, Cassirer formulates against the conception of myth which he had expounded in the *Philosophy of Symbolic Forms*: myth thus appears in its negative aspect, in the light in which it occasionally appeared in Vico. *The Myth of the State* was written in the wake of *The Logic of the Humanities*, where the negativeness of myth represents the tragedy of culture and is its crisis. Beyond the contrast between *Leben* and *Geist*, the problem set forth is that of the necessity of passing from simple naturalistic change (which Cassirer calls *Umbildung*, transmutation) to the formation (*Bildung*) of a new humanity. At the end of his life Cassirer discovers the need for a natural change; and this is perhaps the most important topical feature of his thought. Having disregarded Hegel and the dialectic, Cassirer finds himself in the bosom of dialectic. Having criticized the absolutism and necessitarianism of Hegel's dialectic (and with some justification), Cassirer, before his death, calls for a new dialectic unburdened by the preconstituted, predetermined laws of the old dialectic, or, we might say, by the dialectic implicit in Vico's "recurrences." It is a question of a dialectic whose duty it is to fight against the recurrence of barbarism, on the one hand, and to give rise to a renovation, on the other.

In volume IV of *Das Erkenntnisproblem* the same problem surfaces in Cassirer's treatment of the science of nature *qua exact science* (chapter I): the problems of theoretical physics are no longer those of *Substanzbegriff und Funktionbegriff* (1910). The problem of function, on which Cassirer centered his interpretation of Kant, comes in contact, in the development of Cassirer's work, with the problem of the relationship between mathematics and myth, between mathematical logic and nature (Frege, Russell, Carnap), and, finally, with all the problems implicit in Einstein, problems whose enormous relevance to philosophy only Whitehead has been able to perceive.   In other words, science, too, must be a *Bildung*, must contribute to the "formation" of mankind, must have a teleological function and finality.   It must go back to the themes of Kant's *Critique of Judgment* and those of Vico, Herder, and Husserl.   The function of science is disclosed in the use that man makes of it.   Science may reduce humanity to a purely technical exercise and turn men into robots, just as it may avail itself of cybernetics and of atomic energy, not in man's behalf, but against him. Norbert Wiener, the founder of cybernetics, in the last book that he wrote, *God and Golem, Inc.*, warns mankind (as Einstein had done) of this impending tragedy.   Wiener says that the scientist believes in the human formativity of science and in scientific truth that is not reduced to automatic techniques and idolatry.   But this is precisely the reason why the modern scientist finds himself in the situation of the believer who, because he believes, celebrates a "black mass" against his God.   A new vision of humanity is necessary if we are to prevent this recurrence of barbarism.   We must bring about the transformation of the man of today into a new man, that man whom Rousseau saw at the beginning of civilization, although he emphasized the problematic character of this view.   It is a man, instead, whom we have not yet reached—as if we had not yet become men.   Such a man will have to feel (to feel, in the sense of precategorial life experience, *Erlebnis*) space, time, and all other categories.   Plunged into time, he will have to conquer an awareness of time and transform the unconscious and the dream into truth.   He will have to create an architecture and an art of town-planning which are non-technical and non-Cartesian (as Vico would say), but which are organic and alive, social and natural, without returning to barbarism: an architecture inspired by and continuing the work of Frank Lloyd Wright. Cassirer, in *The Problem of Knowledge*, is confronted with these problems in connection with biology and evolution.   There is a keener sense of the presence of Kant's *Critique of Judgment*; in connection with classification, teleology, and evolutionism, we come across Linnaeus and the famous controversy between Cuvier and Geoffroy Saint-Hilaire involving Buffon, Bonnet, and Lamarck; and, finally, in connection with the themes of formation (in the sense of *Gestaltung*, configuration, fashioning) and metamorphosis, we find the name dearest to Cassirer, Goethe.   Darwinism is examined in both a negative and a positive sense, that is, in Cassirer's language, as dogma and as the principle of cognition.   In biology the contrast between the sciences of nature and those of culture shapes up as one between mechanism and organicism.   The last author quoted by Cassirer is Ludwig von Bertalanffy, to whom, a propos of the relationship between cause and form, Cassirer refers also in *The Logic of the Humanities*.   Bertalanffy's name indicates that we are on the threshold of the transformation of the theory and phenomenology of knowledge into a new encyclopedia, into a new conception of science and history such as the one Goethe sketches in his *Doctrine of Colors* and in his *Metamorphosis of Plants*.[30]   Cassirer, as we know, devoted many essays to Goethe, and has given us a thorough study of Kant.   In his thought, the relationship

[30] See E. Cassirer, *Das Erkenntnisproblem . . .*, IV (Stuttgart, 1957), first published in English translation as *The Problem of Knowledge* by the Yale University Press in 1950; on Vico see pp. 217 and 296 of the English ed.   On cybernetics see N. Wiener, *God and Golem, Inc.* (Cambridge, Mass.: M.I.T. Press, 1964).   In regard to the "act of becoming aware" of time within the time process, it is in Husserl a question of the relationship between time and reflection (Cassirer tends to perceive the presence of this relationship in some hints to be found in Herder).   On this topic see Paci, *Funzione delle scienze*.

As for a possible connection between Vico and Frank Lloyd Wright, we must go back to the relations between Vico and Father Francesco Lodoli, who helped Vico in bringing about the plan for reprinting the *Scienza nuova* in Venice (an event which never materialized) and subsequently assisted him in publishing the *Autobiography*.   Lodoli did not write any works of his own, but his ideas stemming from the *Scienza nuova* are embodied in a book by Andrea Memmo, *Elementi dell'architettura lodoliana*, published by Paglierini in Rome in 1786.   So far as we know, Lodoli planned to write a *scienza nuova* of architecture, basing it mainly on "functionality" and on the relationships which architecture bears to places, epochs, and historical civilizations.   Vico's assumption is that man builds on the open space left free at the time of the clearing of the great forests, so that space, as well as time, is linked with the use of civilization among all peoples. Although space is functional, it is not functional in the mechanistic Cartesian sense, but in the sense, first mythical, then rational, that man transforms nature into culture. Function, here, is directly related to the life of man and to the manner in which man, in the various epochs and places, experiences "spatiality," has the *Erlebnis* of space.   In this sense, thinking of the way in which Frank Lloyd Wright experiences space and "renovates" the nature of social and natural building, it may be assumed that Vico's conception of space and time can be found again in Wright.   That conception would be likely to influence a new architecture, not only *qua* technical craft, but *qua* organic and "intentional" science, and would not be devoid of connections with some of Whitehead's and Husserl's ideas.   For Cassirer, architecture is an expression and incarnation of thought in its mythical aspects.   For us, instead of speaking of a myth, it would be more adequate to speak of a thought founded on the living experience of time and space in our bodies, of a thought based on the activities of building, as if physical nature and the operation of constructing were an integral part of our lives.   See Cassirer, *Philosophie der symbolischen Formen*, II, 107ff.   In a characteristic passage from this book, Cassirer, referring to Usener, reminds us that *templum* derives from the Greek root *tem*, which means "to cut": a perfectly Vichian example (although Cassirer might not have thought of Vico).   On the Vico-Lodoli-Memmo topic see E. Kaufmann, "Memmo's Lodoli," *Art Bulletin*, 46 (December 4, 1964).   As for Goethe, in his *Italian Travels* (entry dated March 5, 1787) he speaks of Vico, comparing him to Hamann.   Goethe's letter of January 31, 1797, accompanied the shipment of a copy of Vico's *Scienza nuova* to Jacobi. Yet Goethe did not know how close some of Vico's intentions were to his own.   For instance, Goethe's critical remarks on Newton resemble Vico's strictures against Descartes.   Had he taken his point of departure from Goethe, Cassirer might have reached a more intimate understanding of Vico's ideas.

between Kant and Goethe continuously passes over into that between Kant and Herder; and Herder, in his turn, is a stand-in for Vico. We should also mention that, after his *Inaugural Dissertation* of 1899, Cassirer wrote his first great book—on Leibniz—and that in this book we encounter a man who is not Russell's Leibniz, but the Leibniz of the encyclopedia of the sciences and culture, the philosopher of the individual, of the individual's conscience, and of the position of the monad in the *Geisteswissenschaften*. Cassirer never forgot either Leibniz or Goethe.[31] Let us point out that Vico also (in his "philosophy" of nature) is steeped in a Leibnizian atmosphere.

The philosophical and cultural lines that have been traced indicate, in the absence of a factual demonstration, Vico's presence in Cassirer. It is a presence which reminds us somewhat of that of a ghost, which acts without revealing its human story or its name. We could say that, in the case of Cassirer, Vico's presence or absence takes on symbolic meaning. In Goethe, in opposition to the formalism and legalism of Cohen and Natorp (that is, the Neo-Kantianism of Marburg), Cassirer seeks a broader and more concrete world of culture: a concreteness and a possibility not only of thinking but of *perceiving* the world. Opposing the interpretation of Plato offered by Natorp, in which an idea is reduced to a law, Cassirer searches for the *eidos*, a term which, in its original meaning, signified "vision" and "form." And this, too, was a cultural line of a Vichian, as well as of a Goethian or Herderian type, at least in the sense in which the idea of humanity is a *Gestaltung*, a molding, of the whole personality, considered almost in the way in which Gestalt psychology conceives it, in thorough plenitude and finality.[32] Goethe, however, in his universal encyclopedic morphology, is

---

[31] See E. Cassirer, *Leibniz' System in seine wissenschaftlischen Grundlägen* (Marburg, 1902).

[32] On Cassirer's progressive drawing away from Cohen and Natorp see L. Lugarini, "Criticismo e fondazione soggettiva . . . ," *Il pensiero*, nos. 1–3 (1966). Natorp's position with regard to Plato, set forth in his *Platos Ideenlehre* (Leipzig, 1930), was criticized in a work inscribed to Dilthey by J. Stenzel, *Studies on the Development of Plato's Dialectic* (Leipzig, 1917). Is Plato's "idea," the law of knowledge, or is it vision and form? Stenzel pleads for the latter position, but in conclusion blazes the path for our understanding the Platonic idea as *Bildung*, *Gestaltung* (formation, configuration). Finally, the "idea" may appear as an organic whole, as a totality whose parts are not modifiable unless the whole is modified too. We are confronted, in this case, with a structure interpreted in various ways (from Dilthey to structuralism); or we may be faced with the *Gestalt* of Gestalt psychology. Cassirer takes up *Gestalt*, in a psychological sense, in vol. III of his *Philosophy of Symbolic Forms*, but the most important text is to be found in an article of his entitled "Le concept du groupe et la théorie de la perception," which appeared in the July-December issue of the *Journal de Psychologie*. (There is an English translation in *Philosophy and Phenomenological Research*, 5 [1944].) See, in this connection, Felix Kaufmann, "Cassirer's Theory of Knowledge," in Schilpp's *Philosophy of E. Cassirer*, pp. 203ff., and, in the same volume, K. Lewin, "Cassirer's Philosophy of Science and the Social Sciences," p. 271; see also E. Cassirer, "Structuralism in Modern Linguistics," *Word*, August, 1945, pp. 99–120.

himself confronted not only by the transmutation of forms and their development but also by their possible deterioration.   The problem is naturally
present in contemporary evolutionism as well, and leads to the tragedy and
crisis of our culture.   Kafka, in whose mind Goethe was constantly present,
and who as a young man became interested in evolutionism, exhibits metamorphosis to us in two senses.   In his *Academic Report* we find a monkey
which has become a man, nay, a scientist; in the famous tale entitled *Metamorphosis* we find a man who has been transformed into an insect.   Kafka's
parabola is negative; but he, too, yearns (although this yearning is expressed
by an absurdity) for a new man, for a still unrealized human creature who
will sustain new relationships with others and with nature.[33]   In Joyce also,
particularly in *Finnegans Wake*, Vico is present.   Joyce's last work is a cycle;
in it the first sentence is to be found on the last page of the book, while the
continuation of the sentence appears on the first page.[34]   This is intended to
convey the idea that everything recurs, but, like the Irish ballad from which
Joyce drew inspiration, it means in reality that the mason fallen from the
scaffolding, whom his mates mourn for dead, may be reborn, and reborn as
a new man.   This is the *yes* opposed to the *no* of the *ricorso* and of the repetition, the *yes* with which, in the monologue of Molly Bloom, *Ulysses* ends.
Joyce's Homeric novel is not the novel of a single author, but is that of an
epoch, since (as Vico said apropos of Homer) Joyce represents a whole age,
an age in which mankind must *not* be reborn, in the sense of *recurring*,
but must be born as authentic humanity intentionally directed toward
truth.[35]

The situation just described is the contemporary one and is a situation of
crisis.   However, the crisis is a mask.   If we understand it, if we seek for the
reality and the truth of the things that are hidden behind it, if we free them
from their concealment, we become aware that a new man, a new science, a
new culture, are a-borning.

The attainment of consciousness by man, in order that he may truly
become a man, is not a recurrence of the great forest primeval of Earth.
Man will have to shoulder the burden of the present and future of this planet,

[33] See E. Paci, "Kafka e la sfida del teatro di Oklahoma," *Studi Germanici*, 5, no. 2
(June, 1967).

[34] When at the beginning of *Finnegans Wake* Joyce speaks of *commodus Vicus*, and on
the same page imitates in a long word the booming of thunder, he thinks of Vico, and
of the giants, scared by the thunder and lightning of Jupiter.

[35] Cassirer grasps the meaning of "intentionality" in Brentano but disregards the sense
that the word takes on in Husserl, even though he frequently quotes Husserl and criticizes
him for failing to establish a phenomenology of myth; see Cassirer's *Philosophie der
symbolischen Formen*, II, 16–17, III (Berlin, 1929), 227–29.   As for the dream and the ideal
of the waking state in Husserl, see E. Paci, "Toward a Phenomenological Analysis of
Sleep and the Dream," in *The Dream and Human Societies*, ed. Gustav von Grunebaum
and Roger Caillois (Berkeley: University of California Press, 1966), pp. 179–87.

will have to spiritualize the physical, arboreal, and animal nature surrounding him; he will have to transform his dwellings and cities into his own substance and future.

Translated by Elio Gianturco

Stuart Hampshire

VICO AND THE
CONTEMPORARY
PHILOSOPHY OF
LANGUAGE

For those contemporary philosophers in the English-speaking countries who have tried to develop the insights of G. E. Moore, Wittgenstein, and J. L. Austin, the study of language is the larger part of that whole inquiry which traditionally has been called philosophy; and for some it is even the whole of philosophy. But the study of language, as it is understood by philosophers today, is certainly not to be identified with that wide inquiry which Vico called philology. The study of language today is intended by philosophers to yield solutions to more or less precisely defined problems of epistemology and also to some traditional problems of ethics and aesthetics. Sometimes the study of language will show that nothing as definite as a solution can be found, because closer examination reveals that the conventions governing the correct use of language are much less determinate and exact than had been assumed in the original setting of the problem. In general, the closer and more detailed study of language shows that the traditional formulations of philosophical problems often presuppose a false picture of the functioning of language or depend upon a failure to notice distinctions that are in fact to be found within language as it is actually used. Then the problem disappears, or at least is transformed. Inquiries along these lines, which are characteristic of contemporary thought, are piecemeal inquiries and are not designed to sustain some larger theory of human nature, or of human history, and are not ancillary to a philosophical anthropology of the kind that Vico projected.

The second, and largely distinct, type of contemporary study of language is scientific in method, but its results may be of the utmost importance to philosophers. Linguists may in the foreseeable future be able to specify the principles that determine the grammatical structures common to many different languages: principles of word order and sentence construction. Theoretical linguists have suggested that there are innate principles which guide children toward certain preferred forms in learning a language, forms which are common to different languages. These theorists believe that they can show that the ability of children to learn to construct sentences in their native language cannot be explained except by postulating an innate readiness to use certain preferred syntactical structures. This hypothesis has great significance for philosophers: first, it suggests that empiricists have been mistaken in the account that they give of the formation of the categories of thought; second, it suggests that the ancient idea of a universal grammar may have some foundation in fact, and that the division of terms into types might be given some secure basis. There is the possibility that the intuitions upon which philosophical logicians previously have relied may be replaced by a theory of linguistic structures which is testable and capable of being confirmed by observation of speech habits, now made possible by new techniques.

The point of contact between Vico and the contemporary philosophy of language is to be found at a more general level. For Vico, as for many analytical philosophers of the present time, the study of the original metaphors and images from which the commonplace set of mental concepts has been formed is the province of the philosophy of mind. Vico's originality was to reject the possibility of a constructed language of clear and distinct ideas and to insist on the part that the imagination must always play in forming the vocabulary by which our experience is colored. It is the work of philosophy to engender a new self-consciousness about the imaginative sources of our thinking, and particularly of our thinking about our own mental states and functions. In setting these limits to the philosophical enterprise of "correcting" the understanding, Vico was anticipating the analytical philosophers of the present time, who have argued that philosophers must confine themselves to describing language as it is actually used, and that the project of a logically clear, or reformed, language can be given no substance. As some contemporary analytical philosophers reject the ambitions of Russell and of Carnap to discover the logical foundations and the adequate intellectual order of our claims to knowledge, so Vico rejected the similar ambitions of Descartes; and the nature of language was in both cases the point at issue.

Vico was born into a world dominated intellectually by Descartes, and he cannot be understood without some reference to this background. Descartes had prescribed a method, a method which was to be an infallible guide to all thinking about intellectual problems. The method, which may at first seem too simple and obvious, was that, in thinking about any problem, we should attend only to clear and distinct ideas; our arguments should move from one clear and distinct idea to another, tracing the connections between them in their proper order, the argument moving from the simple to the complex. If we proceed in this manner, we shall avoid all the confusions and uncertainties of Scholastic philosophy; every problem will be broken down into its simple elements, and our answers will involve only the most simple and self-evident propositions. The prototype and supreme instance of such a method was mathematics; the mathematician defines his terms precisely and in his deductions moves from the simple and self-evident to the more complex, setting out distinctly every step in his argument. So Descartes was in effect recommending that all thought, to be worthy of the name, must approximate to this mathematical ideal.

Within this program of so-called rationalism a firm distinction was implied between the intellect itself (the faculty of pure thought) and the imagination; and soon the point was made that the imagination is the prime source of all intellectual confusions. It is the weakness of the human mind, attached as it is to the body and dependent upon the senses, that it tends to rely on images in its thinking, images which must be derived ultimately from sense experience. We have the greatest difficulty in thinking in purely abstract terms; even mathematicians have recourse to diagrams and figures to illustrate their arguments. But their strength is that, in principle, their arguments do not depend on these illustrations, or indeed on any appeal to the senses and the imagination, for their validity. In philosophy we are systematically confused because its vocabulary is obviously imprecise and figurative, its terms not clearly defined and distinguished; our conception of God, for instance, is muddled and anthropomorphic because we try to understand the word "God" by forming an image of him; and so we are inevitably led to think of God in terms that are appropriate to human beings, although by definition such terms are inapplicable to God.

The rationalistic program involved eliminating from our thought, and therefore from our language, all figurative and metaphorical conceptions, all expressions that could be understood only by reference to images. These would be replaced by expressions that are abstractions. It is not difficult to see that this insistence on clear and distinct ideas naturally became a theory of language. The ideal of thinking only in terms that are abstract and clearly defined, of largely eliminating imagery and metaphors, became a doctrine of style—in fact, that of the classical style of seventeenth-century literature, both prose and poetry; it was a principle of style which required that even the most intensely expressive poetry should be entirely clear and logical and should employ a language of high abstraction, with a minimum of sensuous imagery and concrete illustration. In fact abstract concepts became the raw material not only of semiphilosophical prose, the reflections on abstract themes (such as old age, love, and vanity) which were the literary fashion of the period, but even of poetry; and from France this principle of style, of clear and distinct ideas logically arranged, spread throughout Europe. What distinguishes almost any typical page of eighteenth-century writing, whether poetry or prose, is the high proportion of abstract nouns and generalized conceptions and a use of words which pays strict attention to logical and literal meanings, and comparatively less attention to metaphorical meanings, that is, to the power, through association, to suggest images and analogies.

Against this background Vico anticipated the Romantic movement by declaring that it is only by the exercise of the imagination that the human mind can be genuinely creative. He develops this central doctrine both as a theory of history, that is, as a theory of the general order of development of human societies, and as a theory of language, of its origin and proper interpretation. He himself recognizes no essential distinction between a theory of history and a theory of language, because his second great principle is that the clue to understanding a civilization is the study of the forms of its language; each phase of the human mind, as it develops by stages in history, is reflected in the form of language, in the vocabulary, and in the type of word formation which is typical of that phase. Thus the name that he gives to the supreme science of the human mind is philology; for him the study of the evolution of the human mind is the study of the evolution of language, and vice versa. Philology is the supreme historical science.

Vico finds a parallel to the development of the human mind through stages in history in the development of an individual's mind from childhood to old age. He takes this analogy very seriously, finding the characteristics of the primitive mind, as revealed in primitive language, reproduced in the natural language of a child. The literal prose of his own time corresponded to humanity's later and declining years; it was staid, self-conscious, and unimaginative, with the quick life of the senses and imagination forgotten in middle age. In fact this analogy between the growing-up of humanity and the individual's growing-up became rather more than a mere analogy to Vico; for it enabled him to claim that his new science could achieve a certainty and self-evidence which could never be achieved in the natural sciences; for, in studying the history of the human mind as it is manifested in the successive states of society and civilization, we are only retracing the history of our own minds in macrocosm. By an effort of self-consciousness we can know intuitively what it was like to live in the heroic and barbarous ages, to be at the mercy of uncontrollable forces, without conscience or powers or reflection, because we have all lived through such a phase as children, when we were in fact absorbed in the sensations of the moment and in fantasies of the imagination, when we did not distinguish between fact and fable; we have all experienced the transition from the fantasy life of the child to the duller life of adult reason and reflection. Vico's case against rationalistic philosophies—and this means almost all philosophies of the mind previous to his own—is that they have cut themselves off from any adequate analysis of thought or language because they have been totally unhistorical in their outlook. So the new science, the science of man, anthropology in the widest sense, must be quite different in method, must be a different kind of science from the natural and mathematical sciences, which to Descartes were the exemplary forms of knowledge. Vico, unlike most philosophers before and since, was not overimpressed by the certainty of mathematics; precocious in this as in so many other respects, he remarked that the truths of mathematics seemed so certain to us simply because we had ourselves invented mathematics.

What we can discover, or rediscover, in the new science is the primitive poetry and the natural metaphysical imagery out of which our adult or civilized thought and language have developed stage by stage. Language is not created by an artificial convention among rational men, nor are the words of a language invented as mere labels for abstract ideas. Language begins in natural imagery, the words at first having little or no literal meaning. Primitive language appeals directly to the senses and the imagination, to what can be seen and touched; it is a thing language and contains very few expressions which directly represent psychological processes or states of mind; for primitive man, like a child, is un-self-conscious and is absorbed in the satisfaction of physical needs. To realize this is of the greatest importance in understanding the forms of civilized or adult language; when, in its adolescent phase, humanity gradually becomes self-conscious and intro-spective, we find (in Vico's words) that "to describe the operations of the pure mind, we must avail ourselves . . . of metaphors drawn from the senses," that is, we must extend the use of expressions which originally applied to material things and give them some wider, and therefore meta-phorical, meaning in describing the operations of our minds. Vico tried to uncover the original metaphors now concealed within some typical psycho-logical verbs of the Latin language; the metaphors, of course, are no longer felt as metaphors, because they have become familiar; it is only with an effort of self-consciousness that, for example, we can trace the English word "apprehend" back to its original concrete and physical meaning, and so discover in this instance that general movement from the concrete to the abstract which is characteristic of all words in their development.

If, as the philologists of the new science, we retrace the history of words like "law" or "liberty" or "the people" back to their first origins, within this word-history, in the successive extensions of the meanings of such words, we shall find a history of civilization. To trace the development of a word is to trace the history of an idea. To enter into the minds of the men of the Homeric age, or indeed of any of the other ages of man, is to uncover the similes and metaphors by means of which they interpreted their experience. The general beliefs and dominant ideas of a society at a particular stage—what Vico sometimes calls its "common sense"—are not to be found in explicit propositions that state the beliefs or define the ideas; they are implicit in the forms of the language itself. The great error of rationalists and philosophers is to assume that words like "liberty" or "justice" have some constant literal meaning as standing for some abstract idea, and so to consider any proposition in which they occur as eternally true or false, as they might consider some proposition in geometry. We cannot understand such words in any of their uses apart from the whole mythologies of which they were, or

are, a part.   In this principle of interpretation Vico anticipates, I believe, the
methods of modern anthropology, yet another science of which he can
reasonably be said to have written the first program.   We must not look for
literal meanings or for abstract statements at a stage in which the distinctions
between the literal and the metaphorical, between knowledge and myth,
do not exist.   Primitive language is all poetry; it is suggestion, not statement.   Science and philosophy begin as myth and fable, and myth and fable
are misconceived either when interpreted literally or when interpreted as
allegory.   The personified gods and forces of nature, the stories of strong
and wise men, are the beginnings of the speculation on abstract concepts, on
strength and wisdom, which later develop from them.

There is no doubt where Vico's own sympathies lie—with the childhood
of humanity, when the life of the mind was poetry, not prose, with the ages
of imagination, and not with the ages of reason and philosophy. (Like
W. B. Yeats, he hated a language of abstractions and loved poetry and
imagery, which philosophers call nonsense.)   He speaks magnificently of
philosophers as "these old men of the nations."   Although a philosopher
himself, he has the qualities of the primitive which he so admired—flashes of
insight alternating with wild absurdities, great imagination without any
powers of criticism, and an outrageous indifference to evidence and the literal
statement of fact.   It is easy, applying critical and scientific standards, to
point to absurdities in his philology and anthropology; in his poetical
description of the dark life of cave-dwellers, of the wild patriarchal world of
the first families, and of the first awakening of a sense of duty at the sound of
thunderclaps heard in the early world (Joyce makes great play with this
symbol of the thunderclap in *Finnegans Wake*).   In such passages he is often
absurd: it is poetry rather than literal statement.   But through all the
absurdities of detail the majestic conception of the history of the human mind
as reflected in the developing forms of its language emerges vividly.   The
metaphysics, the social philosophy and organization, the legal conceptions of
a people, reveal themselves, not in explicit propositions, but in the history
and derivation of words; we must dig the metaphysics and the social philosophy out of the language.

This leading idea of the new science makes Vico more than the precursor
of the Romantic movement or the prophet of historical method; it makes
him a figure of the twentieth, as well as of the nineteenth, century. It is
only in this century that philosophers have methodically turned back upon
the forms of language to discover the metaphors and models out of which
metaphysical theories develop, realizing that merely to study the explicit
propositions of philosophy is never to go to the root of metaphysical puzzles;
for the root of the puzzles is to be found in the ever-changing metaphors of
current language—for instance, in the transference of words originally
applied to things that we see and touch to apply to the operations of the

mind.   So the study of the development of language is not merely necessary for the historian of ideas; it is also the proper study for the pure philosopher. In Vico's own image, great rivers, when they enter the sea, preserve something of their own identity for a distance before they are merged in the ocean that is literal language, the ocean that is always being fed and gradually transformed by the influx of original metaphor.   We cannot fully understand, or analyze, the meaning of any now abstract word—say, the word "cause" or "substance"—without tracing it back through its various metaphorical extensions of meaning to its primitive root; only by so tracing its derivations can we find the image that will still cling to such an abstract word.

James M. Edie   VICO AND
                            EXISTENTIAL PHILOSOPHY

Writers on Vico, whether historians or philosophers, have spent an excessive amount of time in debate about whether, in the last analysis, Vico is to be credited with being the innovator he believed himself and claimed to be, or whether he is not best approached and understood as the summation and culmination of a period in intellectual history which he brought to an end. In one sense this argument is utterly otiose. Whatever the historical strength of the position of those who see Vico as the conclusion of a "classical" age of philosophical speculation rather than as the innovator of a new method and a new style, one *historical* fact is undeniable: that, through the three centuries that have elapsed since his death, and especially at the present time, Vico stands as one of those thinkers whom everyone can read with profit, in whom everyone finds some element of contemporary thought embodied or foreshadowed. In short, every philosophical ism since the eighteenth century, including the most recent—idealism, positivism, naturalism, pragmatism, existentialism—after proclaiming its own originality, has found itself *confronted* with Vico. As has been well pointed out, many of the philosophers who took the trouble to read Vico for themselves "did not so much learn from him as recognize in him what was already their own, and acknowledge him as the great forerunner of doctrines and causes to which they were already committed."[1]

Vico, it seems true to say, has been less of a *vis a tergo*, a historical force or cause at the origins of contemporary thought, than a thinker who is confronted, in spite of the difficulties of his language and style, as a contemporary, as one who faces us from ahead rather than as one who pushes us from behind. This is especially true when we read Vico through the eyes of contemporary existentialism, which, rightly or wrongly, is now beginning to find points of contact with nearly all of his major theories.[2] There is, to be sure, some danger in developing these points of convergence. We should remind ourselves that Vico has, after all, been found by overzealous interpreters to have been responsible, among many better things, even for fascism and

[1] Max H. Fisch, Introduction, *The Autobiography of Giambattista Vico*, trans. Max H. Fisch and Thomas G. Bergin (Ithaca, N.Y., 1944), p. 61.
[2] See Enzo Paci, *Ingens Sylva: Saggio sulla filosofia di G. B. Vico*, Milano, 1949.

nazism.[3]   If we look at some of the more extensive bibliographies consecrated to his historical influence, we sometimes wonder whether Vico has
not been responsible for the entire intellectual state of the contemporary
world in all its vagaries and contradictions as well as in its more progressive
and positive aspects.

Therefore, it is well to be on our guard, and to approach both the text and
the influence of this seminal and revolutionary thinker with caution.   I do
not intend, here, to write an exhaustive historical account of Vico's influence
on even a few contemporary philosophers, since such a work would go far
beyond what I can, at the present time, state with either assurance or
accuracy.   My intent is to call attention to two fundamental Vichian doctrines, one in the philosophy of language and the other in the philosophy of
history, in which I find such a striking convergence with contemporary
existentialist thought, and in which a common spirit is so evident, that no one
will be able to accuse me of excessive zeal in claiming that Vico's contributions are, and remain, of contemporary interest.

I think no one will deny that explicit references to Vico are very sparse in
contemporary existentialist literature and that he does not figure prominently
in the bibliographies of either the German or the French founders of
existential thought.   There is, however, at least one major writer in this
tradition who could have, and perhaps ought to have, recognized in Vico a
kindred spirit, a forerunner who had developed ideas similar to his own and
whose research he could profitably have extended in an organic and faithful
way.   I am referring to Merleau-Ponty.   If Merleau-Ponty himself had no
occasion to develop this aspect of his research, there is no reason why his
disciples should not do so in his place.[4]

I. *Philosophy of Language*

One of the reasons the philosophical tradition, prior to existentialism, has
found it difficult to assimilate Vico's insights completely is the fundamentally
rationalistic character of its theory of knowledge.   Vico stands out, particularly in modern Continental philosophy, for his rejection of two of the
most fundamental doctrines of Cartesian rationalism: (1) its notion of thinking, and (2) its notion of the subject of experience.

[3] Fisch, Introduction, *Autobiography*, pp. 67, 72.

[4] I am not claiming that these are the only points of interest for a comparison of Vico
and Merleau-Ponty, or of Vico and other existentialist philosophers, but am choosing
these two most salient points in order to develop them at some length rather than make
a quick *tour d'horizon* which would cover everything too rapidly.   A recent article in
the *Kenyon Review*, January, 1967, by Edward W. Said shows a just appreciation of the
relation between Vico's and Merleau-Ponty's views on the philosophy of history; see
"Labyrinth of Incarnations," p. 67.

According to the Rationalist tradition begun by Descartes, thought consists of the application of the laws of formally correct logical reasoning to fully discrete and perfectly clear and distinct mental elements called "ideas" (or "universals"). Such a view of the process of thinking both exalts the study of formal logic, putting it, as Descartes and Malebranche did, far above such substantive humanistic studies as history, etymology, philology, and literature, and at the same time denigrates the sciences, which consider the "material" meanings and essences that furnish us with the *content*, as opposed to the *forms*, of reasoning. Vico examines this state of affairs in his work *On the Study Methods of Our Time*, in which he shows that a truly valid epistemology cannot neglect the genetic and historical question of the origins of meaning and the origins of the forms of thought. Like Husserl and Merleau-Ponty, he seems to say that there is also a "material" or "transcendental" logic which underlies and preconditions the application of formal rules to the contents of knowledge.

The abstract and "analytical" method of Descartes and his followers, says Vico, reduces thinking to only one of its *rare* functions, namely, the manipulation of perfectly defined categorial concepts in fully reflexive judgments. Thinking, as it is experienced in individual life and as it is traced in the history of the human race, is vastly more complex than this and follows laws of meaning-contexture and relevance which have a prelogical, affective, pragmatic morphology that is completely missed by rationalism. Rather than restrict his epistemology to a formal analytic, Vico requires that it also be a "wisdom" or a "prudence" which will descend to the historical life-world arena to study ideas as they emerge from the vague and amorphous meaning-structures of preverbal experience. We need not only an epistemology which does justice to the fully reflexive acts of intellectual judgment but one which recognizes and analyzes the role of prereflexive awareness in human thought. Ideas are not first of all and primarily "clear and distinct" mental definitions; they are tools and weapons, instruments through which man gradually comes to himself and achieves his humanity, little by little, through a vast and difficult historical process. What Descartes neglected completely and what Vico was the first to discover is the manner in which ideas are embodied in our total affective interest in the world, as the focus of our intentions and the stimulus to human action.

Descartes had no philosophy of language; he produced only a philosophy of ideas. Vico takes the more modern route and establishes the "new science" at least in large part to show that there are no ideas apart from natural languages and that men neither can nor do think except through a gestural and verbal extension of their perceptual and existential embodiment in a cultural world. Vico therefore turns to the "poetic characters" and "fantastic universals" of primitive thought to illustrate the growth of the human mind and its gradual acquisition of the *power* to think through its

more primary and immediate experience of perceptual meaning.   Consciousness, as Merleau-Ponty said, is a power *to do* (*je peux*) before it becomes an
ability *to think* (*je pense que* . . .). Vico wants to go beyond a formal logic
to "a metaphysic of the human mind," [5] and he establishes this "metaphysic"
on a fundamentally new conception of *truth*.   Let us cite once more the
famous phrase from his work *On the Most Ancient Wisdom of the Italians*, in
which this anti-Cartesian doctrine is first clearly stated in its complete form:

> The rule and criterion of truth is to have made it.   Hence the clear and distinct idea
> of the mind not only cannot be the criterion of other truths, but it cannot be the
> criterion of that of the mind itself; for while the mind apprehends itself, it does not
> make itself, and because it does not make itself it is ignorant of the form or mode by
> which it apprehends itself.[6]

   Thus we see that Vico utterly rejects both the first methodological postulate
of rationalism and its notion of the subject as a pure *cogito* which can be fully
clarified and elucidated by a "turning within" to a realm of truth untarnished
by bodily sensations or unaffected by worldly and mundane projects.
Rather, truth is to be found through an examination of its incarnation in the
works, artifacts, institutions, myths, and religious practices that man has
created in order to understand himself.   We will come back to Vico's theory
of truth, *verum ipsum factum*, and its implications for contemporary philosophy, in the second part of this paper.   Here I wish to dwell on Vico the
philosopher of language, showing how this viewpoint both negatively, in its
critique of rationalism, and positively, in its conception of the experiencing
subject, converges with Merleau-Ponty's work in the phenomenology of
language.[7]
   From even a superficial reading one is struck by the number of theses Vico
and Merleau-Ponty hold in common, and it seems almost irrelevant to
determine with whom we will begin in listing them.   Certainly we cannot
recapitulate here all the work that has been done in the phenomenology of
language from Husserl to Merleau-Ponty, but we can recall briefly some of
the principal conclusions of this phenomenology.   First of all, there is the
fact that of all the French philosophers since Descartes, Merleau-Ponty is the
least Cartesian.   In this he distinguishes himself from both Husserl and
Sartre: the experiencing subject is not the purely contemplative activity of

---

[5] See Fisch, Introduction, *Autobiography*, p. 45.

[6] *De antiquissima Italorum sapientia*, in *Opere*, vol. I, ed. G. Gentile and F. Nicolini
(Bari, 1914), p. 136, as given in the English translation by Fisch in the Introduction to the
Autobiography, p. 38.

[7] I am relying on Merleau-Ponty's three major contributions to the phenomenology of
language, namely: "The Body as Expression, and Speech," chap. 6 of pt. I of *Phenomenology of Perception*, trans. Colin Smith (New York, 1962); "On the Phenomenology
of Language," in *Signs*, trans. Richard C. McCleary (Evanston, Ill.: Northwestern
University Press, 1964); and "La conscience et l'acquisition du langage," *Bulletin de
psychologie*, November, 1964, pp. 226–59.

cogito which can find truth and certitude in a non-worldly coincidence with itself. It is not purely an objectivating "transcendental ego" before whom all objects in the world and even its own body are spread out as objects of impersonal and disinterested awareness. It is rather a unitary, fully incarnate consciousness inhabiting a personal *place* in the universe which Merleau-Ponty designates with the term "my lived body." Against Husserl, Merleau-Ponty argues in chapter after chapter of his *Phenomenology of Perception* that the experiencing subject cannot be a disinterested "observer" or an innocent bystander in its perceptual and intellectual structuralization of the world, precisely because through its own body it is a presence to the world and to other beings in the world and lives within the lived space and the lived time projected by this incarnate consciousness.

More than any other phenomenologist Merleau-Ponty has concentrated on the phenomena of embodiment, that is, on the incarnation of meaning in gesture, the bodily expression of affectivity and emotion, the emergence of sense in behavior (in being, doing, and having), the impossibility of thinking except through the use of words whose ultimate foundation lies in the structures of perception. There is, to be sure, a "privilege of reason," but it does not consist in an already achieved rational consciousness which effortlessly constitutes its world; rather, it is founded in the existential and historical effort of the incarnate *logos*, which is man, to speak. And a man *speaks* in many ways that are more fundamental than his precarious use of already elaborated philosophical universals. He speaks primarily in the manner in which he organizes his perceptual world and gives to it a human meaning and value, in the institutions he founds and establishes prior to his being able to explain them to himself or even "name" them. The experience of *primary meaning* precedes the attempt to define and express it on the level of the concept, and this very attempt to define and express meaning is the human project of speaking.

With all of this Vico is in full agreement, and we can read him today not only as an anticipation, but as an illustration, of this theory of the expression of meaning. I would like to approach Vico as the first modern philosopher of language, and, since in contemporary philosophy *homo loquens* has become the focal point not only of existential philosophy but also of British analysis and French structuralism, this makes Vico "modern" indeed. We will turn primarily to Vico's lifelong concern with "poetic wisdom" and with establishing "a science of language" founded on his early insight that poetic expression is both historically and eidetically prior to logically ordered prose or syllogistic formulations.[8] His cardinal principle is similar to Heidegger's

---

[8] *The New Science of Giambattista Vico*, trans. Thomas G. Bergin and Max H. Fisch, rev. ed. (New York, 1961), par. 34: "We find that the principle of these origins both of languages and of letters lies in the fact that the early gentile peoples, by a demonstrated necessity of nature, were poets who spoke in poetic characters. This discovery, which

and Merleau-Ponty's: "minds" are formed by language, not language by "minds." "The human mind," he writes, "is naturally inclined by the senses *to see itself externally in the body*, and only with great difficulty does it come to understand itself by means of reflection."⁹ He descends into what at first appears to be the chaos of primitive myth to establish the basis for a philosophical "etymology" and a philosophical "philology" which will enable us to assist once again in the primeval emergence of sense from non-sense, that is, the vast and primary realm of prelogical human experience which does "not yet" have sense because we have not yet learned to "name" its aspects and express its articulations.

Vico states his "universal principle of etymology in all languages" as follows: "words are carried over from bodies and from the properties of bodies to signify the institutions of the mind and spirit. The order of ideas must follow the order of institutions."¹⁰ This principle is certainly the first formulation of a non-rationalistic theory of language which is today beginning to be adopted (whether or not in direct dependence upon Vico himself) by linguists; this principle underlies the work, for instance, of Professor Bruno Snell in his extremely important book *The Discovery of the Mind*, which I have previously analyzed in connection with Vico.¹¹ It is, above all, a principle which will guide the research of those who today wish to extend Merleau-Ponty's work on the phenomenology of language.

What Vico did, primarily, was to show the primordial importance of "the verisimilar" or "the metaphorical" in human thought, and to demonstrate, as a consequence, the impossibility of thinking without employing the mechanisms of metaphorical transposition. There are still some philosophers who believe that "category mistakes" are the chief enemy of clear thought and that whatever can be stated can be stated with mathematical clarity. Vico, however, like Merleau-Ponty, places the experience of the "ambiguous" in our mental life at the center of his investigations. He argues that metaphorical (or "poetic") thought is not an accidental weakness of human expression which could be overcome if only we were more astute or tried a little harder. He shows that metaphors are not the enemies of serious thinking, but that the "category mistakes" of metaphorical thought are the very source of all creative reflection.

His theory of metaphor could be developed as an illustration of Merleau-Ponty's thesis of the "primacy of perception" in our mental life. The in-

is the master key of this Science, has cost us the persistent research of almost all our literary life, because with our civilized natures we [moderns] cannot at all imagine and can understand only by great toil the poetic nature of these first men."

⁹ *Ibid.*, par. 236; see also James M. Edie, "Expression and Metaphor," *Philosophy and Phenomenological Research*, 23 (June, 1963): 548ff.

¹⁰ Bergin and Fisch, *New Science*, pars. 237–38.

¹¹ See Edie, "Expression and Metaphor" pp. 550ff.

escapability of metaphorical thought, says Vico, lies in the fact that (1) men are constrained in their attempt to "name" and thus understand the structures of the variegated chaos of preverbal experience by their deliberately associating (or "pairing") newly disclosed phenomena in experience with what has previously been discerned, and (2) we naturally discover the factor of relevance which justifies such analogies in those aspects of the phenomena which most directly call forth perceptual experience, or human needs, interests, and instruments that have already been named. "For that first language, spoken by the theological poets, was not a language in accord with the nature of the things it dealt with . . . but was a fantastic speech making use of physical substances endowed with life and most of them imagined to be divine." [12]

We think primarily "by examples" and "likenesses" [13] and only later are we able to examine the exact nature of the logical validity which justifies our using, for example, an agricultural vocabulary for sowing (*disserere*), gleaning (*intelligere*), gathering up (*recolligere*), and storing away (*observare*) to designate the psychological processes of cognition. The results of Vico's investigations led him to recognize that "metaphor makes up the great body of the language among all nations" [14] and that, therefore, we cannot hope or plan to purify human language of metaphor but rather must attempt to understand its essential functions in all the realms of human thought, from the most primitive to the most purified. The "privilege of reason" does not consist in some superhuman possibility of thinking clear and distinct ideas divorced from the words of any natural language whatsoever, but rather in the power to analogize itself, that is, to take the primary perceptual and emotive processes themselves as the symbols of the cultural, religious, legal, and other institutions that they enable us to construct.

The "vulgar wisdom" which is the object of study in Vico's *New Science* is rooted in man's perspective-perceptual insertion in nature, man, as always, having a bodily *place* within being and among beings to whom he is related through common interests and projects. The works of this "wisdom" are the historical institutions which man adds to nature and which he attempts to understand by singing "the world according to man" in poetic gesticulation and ejaculation. It is not my claim that Vico has provided us with a complete or exhaustive theory of language. He most clearly has not, nor has any other philosopher up to the present time. His importance lies rather in discerning one of the inescapable existential structures of human expression and thus of establishing a methodological principle which must be taken into account by any theory of language that would claim to give an adequate account of either the phenomena of speech or the experience of meaning.

[12] Bergin and Fisch, *New Science*, par. 401.
[13] *Ibid.*, par. 424.
[14] *Ibid.*, par. 444.

The fact that we have not yet progressed much beyond the bare statement of this principle only attests to the importance of Vico's work for the contemporary philosophy of language.

II. *Philosophy of History*

Verum ipsum factum. "The rule and criterion of truth is to have made it. . . . We can know nothing that we have not made." This formulation is the foundation of Vico's theory of truth and of his epistemology in general. It is also the basis of his philosophy of history and it states, in perhaps the most categorical manner possible, the hope and ideal, if not the method, of the philosopher in the face of history. Nothing seems more fraught with philosophical danger and difficulty than historical explanation, and nothing is more difficult to justify than the status of "truth" which we can ascribe to the historical hypotheses and explanatory concepts with which we systematize historical events *after the fact.* How are such hypotheses and concepts, which always emerge on the level of full cognitive awareness long after the events that they "explain" are dead and gone, to be justified as universally objective and valid truths? Plato and Aristotle did not know, like Schelling, that they held "mimetic" as opposed to "expressive" theories of art. Only someone viewing Greek culture from without, as a whole and after the fact, could know this. The inhabitants of Europe in the ninth century did not describe their social and economic systems in terms of an articulated concept of "feudalism." What is the precise reality of such historical force-concepts as "capitalism," "Calvinism," the "proletariat"? What is the nature of the bond that links the primary historical institutions to the concepts we now formulate to define them? Such questions as these confront any philosopher of history. It is in their approaches to these and similar problems of historical explanation that we find, for the second time, a unity of thought between Vico and Merleau-Ponty.

One of the most existentialist (as it is Marxist) themes in Vico is that "men make their own history" and that their history is their inescapable responsibility because they themselves have made it. In fact, for Vico that is what "history" means, namely, *what men have done,* and thus nothing human falls outside the scope of historical investigation. History is what man has added to nature; it is the realm of meaning and value, of intentions, goals, desires, aims, and drives that are specifically human; consequently we can blame our historical predicament neither on God nor on the impersonal forces of nature.

Vico's doctrine of *verum est factum* has a threefold application: first of all, and this is Vico's earliest concern, it enunciates an antirationalistic epistemological theory; second, it presents us with the concept that truth and meaning are inherent in individual human life; and, finally, it argues that truth and meaning are intrinsic to the intersubjective process of history itself.

Vico, unlike the Rationalists, does not believe that the mathematically enunciated "laws of nature" are a reading of the immutable mind of God; rather, they are a creative attempt by the human mind to impose an order of its own upon nature. We understand our mathematical sciences very well: "We demonstrate geometrical truths because we make them." [15] But we must understand also that this understanding is a precarious, gradually won, and still incomplete effort of human science. Vico stands out among his eighteenth-century contemporaries for his dynamic, historical notion of truth, which opposed the static concepts of his time. More than any previous philosophy, his is a conception of truth as process and becoming. The Greeks had defined *science (episteme)* as the knowledge of "what things are, why they are what they are, and why they cannot be otherwise than as they are" (in Aristotle's formula from the *Prior Analytics*)—that is, as knowledge of the necessary, eternal, unchanging forms or essences that transcend history and time and are objectively independent of the human mind as such. With the discovery of the foundations of higher mathematics and the application of mathematical forms of thought to physical phenomena, which was the great "discovery" of the seventeenth-century *physico-mathematici* led by Descartes, this Greek conception of truth was, if anything, reinforced rather than challenged. Vico was at first almost alone in rejecting this notion of truth as a skein of objective, impersonal ideas in favor of a notion of science (*scienza*) as an intersubjective human project whose principles are to be found not in the things themselves independent of human experience but rather "within the modifications of our own human mind." [16]

The "Copernican revolution" of Kant begins here, but so do the epistemologies of pragmatism and existentialism. Philosophy, Vico implies, must now gradually abandon the attempt to read the eternal mind of God and recognize that all its sciences are historical attempts to make sense out of experience; philosophy can no longer view truth *sub specie aeternitatis* from some non-historical, angelic standpoint, but must rather seek to discover and to know itself in its own works—the effort of understanding and expressing what it has already done without knowing it. In our effort to rationalize and understand the prereflexive conquests of human action we will perforce employ not fixed but dynamic concepts, which must be continually modified in terms of their present adequacy and usefulness. The validity of this project and its fruitfulness will be determined by the ability of the mind to come to see itself and know itself in what it has accomplished. *Verum et factum convertuntur.*

Vico's epistemology thus establishes a notion of "human truth" which the

[15] *Le orazioni*, in Gentile and Nicolini, *Opere*, I, 85.
[16] Bergin and Fisch, *New Science*, par. 331.

existentialists discuss in terms of "immanence." There are two levels of "immanence," by which I mean the incarnation of meaning and value in life, which Vico, like Merleau-Ponty, distinguishes. First of all, there is the more personal and individual level, which we have touched on in the first part of this paper. What distinguishes human life from all other forms of life is that it is the embodiment of meaning. This is not merely to define man as a "rational animal" or to identify him with his processes of logical thought, as we have seen. The phenomena of the incarnation of meaning in bodily behavior, in actions of possessing, making, doing, in gesture, gesticulation, dance, in posture and facial expressions, and, above all, in the animation of our organism by the intention "to speak"—all these bring us to the "immanence" (that is, to the experience of meaning) which is characteristic of human life. We live and act in the world in the company of other men without prior theoretical awareness of, or reflection upon, the human meanings we thus constitute.

I wish here, however, to concentrate on the second level of the immanence of meaning in behavior, namely, the intersubjective constitution of meaning which we call "history." We will be guided here by Merleau-Ponty's scattered and incipient reflections on the philosophy of history, all of which can be taken as meditations on Vico's dictum *verum ipsum factum*. The "vulgar wisdom" and the "judgments without reflection" to which Vico continuously returns, and which precede full awareness both in individuals and in institutions, are the latent "ideas" of historical development. Man acts in the world, makes it "human," and in so doing "humanizes" himself; it is only *after the fact* that he can *understand* what he has done. But this "understanding" is pre-contained and pre-scribed in the actions which incarnate it. Vico's *New Science* and his renewal of historical studies—after the depredations of Cartesian rationalism—consists in an attempt to go back beneath the sedimented constructions of civilization (its institutions, laws, myths, its *words*) to their origins in the lived experience of the human race.[17] Man, he is confident, can know his history because, most pre-eminently, it is *his*.

History has always presented rationalistic philosophy with its greatest conundrum, and there are many schools of philosophy—including, for instance, most contemporary analytical philosophy—which seek to escape from the dependence of human thought on its historical situation. Such philosophers seek to define the areas of philosophical research and philosophical concern as carefully as possible so as to exclude historicity. Philosophy then becomes the purely logical and formal analysis of discourse, a scholasticism directed toward the analysis of texts, to what other philosophers

[17] I am here repeating in modified form and in a new context a judgment first expressed in my review "Giambattista Vico: The New Science," *Italica*, 39 (June, 1962): 149.

have said up to now, rather than toward the analysis of experience as such, because, as soon as we turn toward experience rather than its sedimented verbalizations, we cannot escape the temporal and the historical. Merleau-Ponty is one of those who has most rigorously attempted to integrate the sinuosities of historical development into the elaboration of his philosophical concepts. "For my part," he writes, "I would not separate history from philosophy."[18] The reason for this is that here, above all, we have one of the most instructive, though it is the most complex, difficult, and unexplored, fields of research into the structures of immanence.

Vico was led to see history as the result of human intentionality, and we know what importance this conception has had for later Hegelianism and Marxism. It is of even greater importance for the non-absolutist, more rigorously dialectical conceptions of existential philosophy. "Men," Vico wrote, "have themselves made this world of nations . . . but this world has evidently issued from a mind often diverse, at times quite contrary, and always superior to the particular ends that men have proposed to themselves. . . . That which did all this was mind, because men did it with intelligence; it was not fate, because they did it by choice; not chance, because the results of their always so acting are perpetually the same."[19]

In his reflections on the modes of historical understanding Merleau-Ponty sees the problem of historical explanation as a special case of the relation between *fact* and *essence* in experience. In the *Ideas*, Husserl had established the strict correlativity of fact and essence (meaning) in experience as the basis of any phenomenological investigation. Whenever a fact is understood, he said, it is grasped as the typical instantiation of a meaning which, though it transcends any particular factual occurrence, is the meaning *of* that factual situation. The "essential" of the "meaningful" is the contribution of the human mind in any given organization of conscious experience. In applying this doctrine to historical experience, Merleau-Ponty discovered that "every *fact of consciousness* bears the transcendental within it."[20] When we move within the realm of historical facts, we necessarily discover within these facts meanings which we elaborate in concepts such as "feudalism," "capitalism," "Calvinism," etc.—concepts that may seem at first to have no substantial reality, that are no more than common nouns used to designate masses of facts that in their concrete historical existence have no internal relations. It is the task of the philosopher, then, to discover the reality of the *Gemeingeist* in history which "is ours as we are its."[21] History is a

[18] Maurice Merleau-Ponty, *The Primacy of Perception and Other Essays*, ed. James M. Edie (Evanston, Ill.: Northwestern University Press, 1964), p. 37.

[19] Bergin and Fisch, *New Science*, par. 1108.

[20] Maurice Merleau-Ponty, "The Philosopher and Sociology," *Signs*, p. 106.

[21] Maurice Merleau-Ponty, "The Crisis of the Understanding," *The Primacy of Perception*, p. 202.

"strange object," says Merleau-Ponty, unlike others because our relation to it can never be that merely of a spectator; it is an "object which is ourselves."[22]

To say that history teaches the philosopher what the *Gemeingeist* is, is to say that it gives him the problem of intersubjective communication to think about. It makes it necessary for him to understand how there are not only individual minds (each incumbent in a perspective on the world) which the philosopher can inspect by turns without being allowed (and even less required) to think of them *together*, but also a community of minds coexisting for one another and as a consequence invested individually with an exterior through which they become visible. As a result, the philosopher may no longer speak of mind in general, deal with each and every mind under a single name, or flatter himself that he constitutes them. Instead he must see himself within the dialogue of minds, situated as they all are, and grant them the dignity of self-constituting beings at the very moment that he claims that dignity for himself. We are on the verge of the enigmatic formulation Husserl will arrive at in the texts of the *Krisis der europäischen Wissenschaften*, when he writes that "transcendental subjectivity is intersubjectivity."[23]

The "universal essences" that we employ in discourse about historical events require us to reshape our conception of what the "relationships of mind to its object" are. To take historical consciousness and the meanings it disengages through a reflection on historical events and processes as belonging to an "ideal order" independent of the internal relations of historical happenings themselves, is to fail to see that mind does not operate *only* on the level of the ideal and the abstract but that it was mind itself which first of all and primarily (even when in ignorance of its own works) articulated the historical relations we now attempt to understand.

Because of the fact that the order of knowledge is not the only order, because it is not enclosed in itself, and because it contains at least the gaping chasm of the present, the whole of history is still action and action is already history. History is the same whether we contemplate it as a spectacle or assume it as a responsibility.[24]

History, because it is human action, and because human action is never completed, can never exist completely without taking into account what "comes after," the incarnate, operating intentionality which is at work in the open field of the temporal, and whose future is always "in suspense." Historical reality, like historical knowledge, contains within itself an appeal to the judgment of the future generations toward which it is groping. The "essences" of historical knowledge can never be fully closed and fixed systems of clear and distinct ideas defined according to genus and specific difference, but must always be enunciated as "probable" and "ambiguous"

[22] *Ibid.*, p. 195.
[23] Merleau-Ponty, "The Philosopher and Sociology," *Signs*, pp. 106–7.
[24] Merleau-Ponty, "The Crisis of the Understanding," *The Primacy of Perception*, p. 194.

essences which overflow their formulations because the actions they express are not yet complete.

The meaning of historical events and institutions, writes Merleau-Ponty,

> can be compared to the meaning of a spoken language, which is not transmitted in conceptual terms in the minds of those who speak, or in some ideal model of language, but which is, rather, the focal point of a series of verbal operations which converge almost by chance. Historians come to talk of "rationalism" or "capitalism" when the affinity of these products of the historical imagination becomes clear. But history does not work according to a model; it is in fact the very advent of meaning.[25]

It is this conception of history as the "advent of meaning" which leads us most forcibly to list Merleau-Ponty among the descendants of Vico. On the level both of the individual consciousness and of the intersubjective community of history, Merleau-Ponty employs a conception of the emergence of sense and meaning in behavior which can be rendered justly by the Vichian formula *verum ipsum factum*.

Again, as in our discussion of Vico's contributions to the philosophy of language, we conclude not with a completed theory but with a program, with the establishment of a heuristic principle which can and must guide contemporary and future research. The fact that it can guide us is a demonstration of Vico's importance to us; the fact that it must guide us is a vindication of his own theory of historical meaning, for the understanding of the human project which is "philosophical knowledge" requires that we face the future in the past.

[25] *Ibid.*, p. 200.

Enzo Paci   VICO, STRUCTURALISM,
AND THE PHENOMENOLOGICAL
ENCYCLOPEDIA OF THE SCIENCES

In the second book of the *New Science* Vico offers us a definition of wisdom:

Wisdom is the faculty which commands all the disciplines by which we acquire all the sciences and arts that make up humanity. . . . Man, in his proper being as man, consists of mind and spirit, or, if we prefer, of intellect and will. It is the function of wisdom to fulfill both these parts in man, the second by way of the first, to the end that by a mind illuminated by knowledge of the highest institutions (*cose altissime*), the spirit may be led to choose the best (*si induca all'elezione delle cose ottime*).[1]

Vico is thinking of a wisdom which would contain all the disciplines. From these disciplines we learn all the sciences and all the arts. He poses therefore, unequivocally, the problem of an encyclopedia. We must note that Vico distinguishes disciplines, sciences, and arts. If there are *Naturwissenschaften* and *Geisteswissenschaften*, both come after the disciplines because they are learned on the basis of the disciplines. The encyclopedia is thus the ensemble of the disciplines from which the sciences and the arts are derived.

Furthermore, Vico defines man in his *proper* being. His proper being is what he is in the first person, and not what we can know of him indirectly; his proper being is *what he does*, as *mind* and *spirit* (or, we could say, *soul*). And Vico adds the clarification that the *mind* corresponds to the intellect, the *spirit* to the will. The will is animated by the intellect, by consciousness, and thus becomes an operating will, the *animus artium*, as Vico put it in the first of his inaugural orations. Wisdom must unify, fulfill, and overcome the initial distinctions; on this level there is no opposition between praxis and theory. The sciences and the arts are operations to be accomplished; they are constituted by conscious actions and are directed toward a "perfect" end. In this sense wisdom rules the encyclopedia of sciences and arts in all their operations. But all their operations are those of the disciplines. It is, therefore, a question of an encyclopedia of the disciplines, and Vico calls this encyclopedia *poetic wisdom*. It is the wisdom of the theological poets, a primitive metaphysics (*una metafisica rozza*), from which are derived, as branches from the trunk of a

[1] *The New Science of Giambattista Vico*, trans. Thomas G. Bergin and Max H. Fisch (Garden City, N.Y., 1961), p. 70.

497

tree, sciences and arts in the making, that is, in their *poetry*, in the Greek sense of *poiesis*. "From this, as from a trunk, there branch out from one limb logic, morals, economics, and politics, all poetic; and from another, physics, the mother of cosmography and astronomy, the latter of which gives their certainty to its two daughters, chronography and geography—all likewise poetic." [2]

Vico speaks of a rough metaphysics (*metafisica rozza*). *Rozzo* means primitive, confused, violent, barbaric. This is the *negative aspect* of metaphysics, and it must be negated. But metaphysics also has a *positive aspect*,

[2] *Ibid.*, p. 72. This is the ancient notion of science which is found in alchemy and in the hermetic tradition and which reappears in Lull, Bacon, Descartes, Leibniz, and Goethe. As an encyclopedia it evolves from the great French *Encyclopédie* to that of Comte and of Hegel. In our epoch there is the noted *International Encyclopedia of Unified Science* of Chicago which has raised so many hopes and posed so many problems. This is tied to logical positivism and in part shares its fate. The problems raised concern, above all, the attempt to reduce all the sciences to physics, to physicalism in the sense of Neurath and Carnap. Carnap's own work demonstrates all the difficulties of the relationship between logic and experience, between logical and empirical structures. Logical positivism is today in a critical situation, especially because of the work of C. G. Hempel, among whose writings we limit ourselves to citing *Fundamentals of Concept Formation in Empirical Science* (Chicago, 1952) and *The Theoretician's Dilemma* (Minneapolis: Minnesota University Press, 1958). While Hempel represents the problem of the theories—and ultimately of the philosophy—from which the sciences cannot escape, W. V. O. Quine, in *From a Logical Point of View* (Cambridge, Mass., 1953) and especially in his later works, restates the problem of ontology, taking this term in a very special sense, and tends toward a unitary and holistic conception of science. Cf. S. Veca, "Note su Quine," *Aut-Aut*, no. 95 (1966); the same author relates these problems to a reinterpretation of Kant in "Fenomenologia delle scienze nei 'Principi di Kant,'" *Aut-Aut*, no. 94 (1965). The problem of the encyclopedia actually seems to come down to the problem of the *foundation* of the sciences as we find it particularly in the early Carnap; see R. Carnap, *Der logische Aufbau der Welt*, 2d ed. (Hamburg, 1961). On the whole problem in relation to Husserl see E. Paci, "Sul problema della fondazione delle scienze," *Il pensiero*, 10, no. 1–2 (1965); *idem*, "Informazione e significato," *Archivio di filosofia*, Istituto di studi filosofici, no. 1 (Rome, 1967); "Sulla struttura della scienza," *Aut-Aut*, no. 86 (1965). The problems of foundation also involve English thought after Russell, Wittgenstein, and Ryle, as well as the neopositivism of Ayer. In this regard see E. Paci, "Ayer e il concetto di persona," *Aut-Aut*, no. 93 (1966). P. F. Strawson represents a special case; see his *Introduction to Logical Theory* (London, 1952) and *Individuals* (London, 1959). On the relations between Strawson and phenomenology see C. Sini, "Logica formale e discorso comune in Strawson," *Aut-Aut*, no. 94 (1966). For the problem as seen by a theoretical biologist see L. von Bertalanffy, "General Systems Theory: A New Approach to Unity of Science," *Human Biology*, December, 1951, and "General Systems Theory," *Main Currents*, March, 1955. For a point of view closer to Vico's and for a return to the "tree of the sciences," see G. Tagliacozzo, "The Tree of Knowledge," *American Behavioral Scientist*, October, 1960; *idem*, "The Literature of Integrated Knowledge," *ibid.*, October, 1962; see also "General Systems Theory as a Taxonomy of Culture and as a Curriculum of General Education," paper presented at a Symposium organized by the Society of General Systems Research, Cleveland, December, 1963.

namely, the fact that, understood as *poiesis*, it is not abstracted from, nor reduced to, unfounded formal categories but rather to the operations that give birth to categories, operations which are those of the disciplines as a whole. These operations are the *poiein* from which all science, all technology, all art, derive. Thus the encyclopedia will have to fight on two fronts: On one side it will have to prevent civilization and culture from returning to metaphysics understood as violence and barbarism; on the other it will have to keep civilization, science, and art from becoming categorial abstractions, for as such they would deny their foundations in the present, past, future, and therefore *historical* operations of the human subject. More precisely, in the second case the encyclopedia will have to keep abstractions from being considered as reality, or from appearing to be concrete realities. It will have to remove the abstractions that are a cloak of ideas (recall the technical term used by phenomenology and repeated in a new sense by Italian phenomenology, *Ideenkleid*) covering human reality, human will, and the truth which acts in such reality. We can call this cloak of ideas *ideology*, which, understood in a negative sense, hides the real and its value of truth—the *verum* that Vico identifies with the *bonum* and that acts, even when unrecognized, even in human mistakes and errors, within every man who is conscious of himself as a man in the first person. All men who free themselves from prejudices, from false cloaks of ideas, from isolated and objectified categorial abstractions taken in themselves, can find within their lives and experience a positive and certain original self, a primary nucleus. This positive nucleus is the concrete human subject of which Husserl speaks. The operation necessary to reach it is the negation of the mundane, of mundane violence, an operation which is called *epoché*. The fundamental characteristic of phenomenology is *intentionality*, the tending toward a truth and a good for all humanity.

Poetic wisdom thus has two aspects: the first is barbaric; the second is original and foundational and can be discovered only through overcoming the barbaric. The first victories are language and speech, which, while remaining *physical*, carry a value of *truth* and are operations of the will, are themselves the will. If they do not fall back into evil and violence, these operations can, as the intentional operations of all the sciences and arts, *form* a new humanity and prevent the recourse (*ricorso*) of barbarism. As a whole, to the extent that the *epoché* is accomplished, they give rise to the *disciplines*, to the encyclopedia of the disciplines. For Vico the encyclopedia has its own *logic*, which he calls *poetic logic*, and is, in a new sense, a *science*—not an abstract and categorial science, but rather a concrete and precategorial science, similar to what Husserl called the science of the *Lebenswelt*. Vico considers abstract categorial science, which ignores the operations through which the categories are derived, to be a new barbarism, and he calls it the *logic of the learned*. The learned forget the origin and aim of the sciences; they forget the function of the sciences, technology, and the arts. They lose the sense of life and history because they do not recognize that truth is an end, that truth acts in the world, in the mundane, without giving in to or falling back on the mundane, without becoming identified with the mundane. The learned think that linguistic and logical categories are the whole of knowledge, the whole encyclopedia. They forget the sensible, the imagination, the *type*, the idea, the structure as form, as *Gestalt*. In short, they forget the social and historical formation of man, the *Gestaltung* of humanity. They forget human *fallibility*,[3] which we must understand if we are to comprehend the struggle between truth and barbarism. They forget the "vow of poverty," which is necessary to every operation, to every science, to every art, to every *institution*. They forget that every culture contains a universal value, that every religion has a positive nucleus within its literal expression. Iran has donated to the United Nations a marvelous tapestry which was made, deliberately, with a flaw. All cultures and all men can recognize their errors. This is necessary in order to initiate any radically new path, in order to bury the past and the diabolical events of the past. It is from this act of *burying* the past that a new humanity, the true humanity, can be born. "Oliver Cromwell's cry echoes down the ages, 'My brethren by the bowels of Christ I beseech you, bethink you that you may be mistaken.'"[4]

These are the words of Whitehead, to which we should perhaps add the following: "Peace is the understanding of tragedy, and at the same time its preservation."[5] Preservation, but not return or repetition, or, as Freud

[3] For an understanding of the concept of fallibility in connection with Kierkegaard and Husserl, in a context in which philosophy is presented as the struggle for the emancipation of man, see E. Paci, *Funzione delle scienze e significato dell'uomo* (Milan, 1963), pp. 284–85, 355–61; *idem*, "Die positive Bedeutung des Menschen in Kierkegaard," *Schweizer Monatshefte*, no. 2 (1963): 177–88; *idem*, "Kierkegaard et le sens de l'histoire," a paper given at the symposium held under the auspices of UNESCO in Paris in April, 1964, and published in *Kierkegaard vivant* (Paris, 1966). For an analysis of fallibility see P. Ricoeur, *Philosophie de la volonté*, vol. II: *L'homme fallible* (Paris, 1950). For the notion of the *Lebenswelt* see E. Paci's paper for the symposium held in Mexico City in September, 1963, "Die Lebensweltwissenschaft," published in *Symposium sobre la noción husserliana de la Lebenswelt* (Mexico City: University of Mexico, Center of Philosophical Studies, 1963), pp. 51–75.

[4] See A. N. Whitehead, *Science and the Modern World* (New York, 1926), p. 21.

[5] See A. N. Whitehead, *Adventures of Ideas* (London, 1948), p. 328. The mention of the word "tragedy" is important. In fact the struggle of religion, myth, poetry, logic, science, and ethics against the negative is a tragedy and always constitutes precategorial operations that are victories. These operations are its very expression (also in Kierkegaard) and in poetry its katharsis. In psychoanalysis it is the struggle against unconscious repression. The process of the operations thus indicated is found in all cultural and social forms, including myth. Thus we pass from the *epoché* to forms, that is, to the type of *epoché* which acts in every form, for which, in this sense, every form is dialectical and is a tragic struggle against recourse and barbarism. These and other modalities bring Whitehead close to Husserl. In this respect see E. Paci, "Ueber

would say, the compulsion to repeat. Preservation in the sense of under-standing the errors of the past and of opening the way to a new dialectic, which will be neither deterministic nor preconstituted, but conscious of the fact that it must guard against falling back into the errors of the past and that it must guarantee the recognition of what is positive in opposite points of view. It must, finally, comprehend the struggle of those who, deprived of the rights of man, are fighting to gain them. Vico knew all this when he spoke of burials, which, in his *Idea dell'opera*, are related to all the themes of the *New Science*. The word "humanity," he said, is derived from *humando*, to bury.[6] Words are founded on operations and give them a meaning: they are, in fact, a type of operation. This is how the meaning of language arises, which, insofar as it is culture and civilization, is not merely sound, but sound that expresses, signifies, and gives meaning to social and historical life. Language is poetry because it is the expression and meaningful form of *poiesis*, because it is a *poiein* which makes possible not only communication but civilization, and the continual rediscovery and rebirth of civilization. Language is a "poetic character" which operates with "fantastic universals." It is in this sense that the nature of the first men was poetic, a poetic wisdom. This discovery, says Vico, "is the master key of this Science."[7]

This is a discovery which contains many others, some of which even today are perhaps only potential and which in Vico himself are confused with one another. We will limit ourselves here to stressing two points. First of all, poetic wisdom is not merely poetry in the way we moderns understand it; it

einige Verwandschaften zwischen der Philosophie Whiteheads und der Phänomeno-logie Husserls," *Revue internationale de philosophie*, no. 56–57 (1961): 237–50. See also the papers devoted to Whitehead in *Aut-Aut*, among which the following are related to our theme: P. A. Rovatti, "L'atteggiamento etico nella filosofia del processo," no. 90 (1965): 43–57; *idem*, "Logica e filosofia in Whitehead," no. 94 (1966): 76–100. For the notion of the abstract and the concrete see P. Gambazzi, "Note sulla dialettica tra astratto e concreto," *Aut-Aut*, no. 90 (1965): 68–78. The problem of the dialectic between forms and within forms in relation to what Croce called the form of the useful and what later became the form of the vital, even in a negative sense, is defined in terms of a discussion between Paci and Croce, the bibliography of which we cannot give here for want of space. Thus we limit ourselves to citing the following: E. Paci, "Il significato storico dell'esistenzialismo," *Studi filosofici*, no. 2 (1941): 113–220 (republished in *Esistenzialismo e storicismo* [Milan, 1950]), and Croce's reply in *Critica*, I (1942), 48–49 (republished in *Pagine sparse*, III, 415–17). Other writings of Croce's on this question are cited in *Esistenzialismo e storicismo*. For a short résumé of the question see E. Paci, *La filosofia contemporanea*, 3d ed. (Milan, 1961), pp. 65–67. In this connection cf. R. Franchini, *Esperienza dello storicismo* (Naples, 1953), pp. 124–33, 294–99; *idem*, *Metafisica e storia* (Naples, 1953), pp. 108–13; E. Garin, *Cronache di filosofia italiana* (Bari, 1955), pp. 279–80; and, for a more ample treatment, A. Santucci, *Esistenzialismo e filosofia italiana* (Bologna, 1967).

[6] This reference is to a passage of the *Idea dell'opera* which is not translated in the *New Science*; see G. B. Vico, *La scienza nuova*, ed. F. Nicolini, 4th ed. (Bari, 1953), p. 12.

[7] *New Science*, p. 5.

cannot be reduced to poetry as it was understood, for example, by Benedetto Croce.   Nor is it merely myth, though it is more myth than poetry.   For Vico, poetic wisdom includes all the disciplines.   It is precisely in this sense that it is a making, a *poiein*, a praxis; and everything, for Vico, is a praxis. But praxis can be more or less conscious; it can have degrees of negativity and positiveness.   Insofar as the *epoché* operates within it, it is a fight against the negative, beginning from the subject and from human subjectivity.   It is a fight against the recourse (*ricorso*); it is a struggle which is greater, the more it is animated (in various gradated modalities) by the life of truth, a life which is non-mundane, non-naturalistic, and non-vitalistic.   In the intentional *poiesis*, oriented toward truth and goodness, nature continues itself, but it performs *a qualitative leap*.   The point, the place and time, of this trans- formation and of this decisive turning point of evolution is man.   It is man as he transcends his naturalistic self and becomes the subject of a positive *poiesis*.   The science of this *poiesis*, which for Vico is a primitive metaphysics, must become the science of the *Lebenswelt*, the precategorial encyclopedia of all the disciplines.

Second, let us recall that Vico criticizes the logic of the learned.   Poetic wisdom is the *sensory topics* of the first authors of *humanitas*.   These first authors, to clarify Vico, are we ourselves, even today, in our concrete existence, reflection, and intentionality.   The first stage of the world is within us, in the present and in our genetic past.   But in us it must undergo a qualitative mutation; it must recommence from the life of truth implicit in the subject and uncovered by the *epoché*.   With these observations we can accept what Vico says of the precedence of *topics* over *judgment*.   The topical is the *typical*, the poetic genus, the concretely intended idea, the *eidetic*, the precategorial operation, the science of the *Lebenswelt*, phenomenology. Criticism is the *predication of things*.   But, for us, this judging must be founded precategorially and must be freed from presuppositions.   Topics without presuppositions is an exercise and a *discipline*.   The disciplines from which civilization arises are thus disciplines founded in the human subject and rendered possible by the *epoché*.   Here we must clarify our terms: Vico defends the operations that precede the "judging of things."   This judging he calls *criticism*.   But, because criticism makes possible a freedom from pre- suppositions, it is, in reality, implied in topics and renders topics itself possible. It is a judgment, then, which does not forget or hide topics, does not conceal the topicality and the typicality of history; it is a *founded judgment*.   It is a *critical topics*, or, if you wish, a critique of pure reason, which becomes a critique of all the disciplines and a *critique of historical reason*.   Criticism founded on topics is the true criticism.   Critical judgment, detached from topics, is non-founded judgment; it is logic separated from its foundation; it is the *logic of the learned*.

The dilemma of the logic of the learned consists in distinguishing the

Naturwissenschaften from the *Geisteswissenschaften*—the learned do not know how to trace them back to the precategorial *Lebenswelt*, to poetic science, to one and the same tree, to the same roots.   The dilemma of neopositivism is its refuting theories while being unable to free itself from them and while being unable to *reduce* theoretical discourse to its foundation (Hempel).   The dilemma of pure logic is the impossibility of finding a complete system of postulates in which every proposition is expressed (Gödel).   The dilemma of moral life is the problem of living in the world according to an end without returning to barbarism.   The dilemma of physics and biology is the possibility of a future in spite of irreversibility, in spite of the loss of energy and the correlative augmentation of entropy.   The dilemma of psychoanalysis is that every psychoanalyst must himself by psychoanalyzed, that he cannot recover, once and for all, the autopsychoanalysis of Freud, but must achieve his own *epoché* and his own autoanalysis in order that the autoanalysis of his patient be possible.[8]

The preceding considerations enable us to grasp, to correct, and to bring up to date the thought of Vico.   Poetic logic deals with languages, and languages form a part of topics.   Languages are not separated from the operations of speaking, from the subjects who speak.   The subject speaks with gestures, marks, sounds, which become meaningful and typical *characters*.   Speaking is an art, a *poiesis*, a discipline:

But the difficulty as to the manner of their origin was created by the scholars themselves, all of whom regarded the origin of letters as a separate question from that of the origin of languages, whereas the two were by nature conjoined.   And they should have made out as much from the words "grammar" and "characters."   From the former, because grammar is defined as the art of speaking, yet *grammata* are letters, so that grammar should have been defined as the art of writing.   So, indeed, it was defined by Aristotle, and so in fact it originally was; for all nations began to speak by writing, since all were originally mute.   "Character," on the other hand, means idea, form, model; and certainly poetic characters came before those of articulate sounds. . . .[9]

The scholars of whom Vico is speaking here are the learned.

Let us dwell for a moment on the discourse which Vico directed to the learned who do not recognize topics.   He writes: "The first founders of humanity applied themselves to a sensory topics, by which they brought together those properties or qualities or relations of individuals and species

[8] Cf. E. Paci, "Il ritorno a Freud," *Aut-Aut*, no. 98 (1966): 62–73, and *idem*, "Autoanalisi e intersoggettività," *ibid.*, pp. 104–5, where the problem is studied with reference to Lacan and Ricoeur.   On Ricoeur's interpretation of Freud see E. Renzi, "Freud e Ricoeur," *ibid.*, pp. 7–51.   This last study is an important analysis of P. Ricoeur's *De l'interpretation: Essai sur Freud* (Paris, 1965).   For the other problems consult the issues of *Aut-Aut*, especially those from 1959 to the present.

[9] *New Science*, p. 97.

which were, so to speak, concrete, and from these created their poetic *genera*." [10]   This is a fundamental passage.   Vico takes into account the speaker and the listener, the subjects who speak and those who listen and in their turn speak.   Communication, the "constitution of the other," takes place when individuals are caught in their concrete existence—this is the problem of Husserl's *Cartesianische Meditationen*. [11]

The operation of speaking, says Vico, is "the primary operation of the human mind." [12]   In the passages that follow we will recall the observations made above, particularly with regard to the terms "criticism" and "judgment."   Criticism appears here as "exactitude," but exactitude is abstract and unfounded, and it is necessary to see by what precategorial operations it is reached—a point of view analogous to that adopted by Husserl in the *Krisis der europäischen Wissenschaften*:

Providence gave good guidance to human affairs when it aroused human minds first to topics rather than to criticism, for acquaintance with things must come before judgment of them.   Topics has the function of making minds inventive, as criticism has that of making them exact.   And in those first times all things necessary to human life had to be invented, and invention is the property of genius.   In fact, whoever gives the matter some thought will observe that not only the necessaries of life but the useful, comfortable, pleasing, and even luxurious and superfluous had already been invented in Greece before the advent of the philosophers.   On this point we have set forth the axiom above: namely, that "children are extraordinarily gifted in imitation," that "poetry is nothing but imitation," and the "arts are only imitations of nature and consequently in a certain sense real poetry."   Thus the first peoples, who were the children of the human race, founded the first world of the arts; then the philosophers, who came a long time afterward and so may be regarded as the old men of the nations, founded the world of the sciences, thereby making humanity complete.

And just below this passage Vico has recourse to the evidence of the senses as the foundation of the categorial: "This history of human ideas is strikingly confirmed by the history of philosophy itself.   For the first kind of crude philosophy used by men was *autopsia*, or the evidence of the senses." [13]

[10] *Ibid.*, p. 123.

[11] See the English translation by D. Cairns (The Hague, 1960).   This problem is present in the whole of contemporary English philosophy (Ayer, Wisdom, Strawson).   Cf. C. Downes, "Husserl and the Coherence of the Other Minds Problem," *Philosophy and Phenomenological Research*, 2 (1965).

[12] *New Science*, p. 123.

[13] *Ibid.*, p. 124.   For Husserlian parallels to this passage which permit a deeper understanding of Vico and bring out the presence of his problems in contemporary philosophy, see E. Husserl, *Die Krisis der europäischen Wissenschaften und die transzendentale Phänomenologie* (The Hague, 1954); in particular, for an argument related to our text, see vol. III, appendix, pp. 365–68.   See also E. Paci, "Struttura temporale e orizzonte storico," *Aut-Aut*, no. 87 (1965): 7–19.   An understanding of Husserl's "evidence," with all its variations, requires a study of the whole of his work, which is being published by the Husserl Archives, directed by H.-L. van Breda, under the auspices of UNESCO.

These passages call forth several observations. We note the opposition between genius or the ingenious and exactitude. The ingenious indicates a *poiein* which is not simply analytical, which is not a deduction but a constitution. Although this *poiein* is not science, a science of it is possible; this is precisely Vico's *New Science*. It is the science Dilthey will look for on the basis of a new way of understanding psychology; it is the science that structuralism will present as a science of structures and that phenomenology will describe as a science of the operations of the *Lebenswelt*, a science which must become, in a new sense, a *phenomenological encyclopedia*.

Vico then refers to the useful and the pleasurable; we are here on the level of economic activities and of operations that tend toward satisfaction. The *poiein* is, therefore, a world which lacks something, a *world of needs*—in fact, a world of work and production. The science of these activities is a discipline: it studies productive work and the mode of the exchange of products.

To date, ten volumes have appeared, *Husserliana*, I–X (The Hague, 1950–66). The rebirth of phenomenological studies throughout the world is attributed to Van Breda. For the relation of phenomenology to the sciences, and especially to Gestalt psychology, see M. Merleau-Ponty, *La structure du comportement* (Paris, 1942), *La phénoménologie de la perception* (Paris, 1945), and *Signes* (Paris, 1960); in this last work, with reference to our argument, see especially "Sur la phénoménologie du langage," pp. 105–22, and "De Mauss à Lévi-Strauss," pp. 145–57. The latest and very important work on Merleau-Ponty is A. Bonomi's *Esistenza e strutturalismo: Saggio su Merleau-Ponty* (Milan, 1967). With respect to phenomenology we should also mention the name of Aron Gurwitsch (now living in the United States), who gave phenomenology to France at a time when it was unknown, thus fulfilling the role in France which Antonio Banfi performed in Italy. For American phenomenology there is the important work of Alfred Schutz. The journal *Philosophy and Phenomenological Research*, edited by M. Farber, is well known; among Farber's writings we could cite: *Philosophical Essays in Memory of Husserl* (Cambridge, Mass., 1940); *The Foundation of Phenomenology*, 2d ed. (New York, 1959); *The Aims of Phenomenology* (New York, 1966); *Phenomenology and Existence* (New York, 1967). See also James M. Edie, ed., *An Invitation to Phenomenology* (Chicago, 1965). J. Wild and James M. Edie are editing the important collection *Northwestern University Studies in Phenomenology and Existential Philosophy*. The development of phenomenology in Germany is tied to the important and decisive contributions of L. Landgrebe and E. Fink; since the bibliography on this movement is too large to be given here, we refer the reader to H. Spiegelberg, *The Phenomenological Movement* (The Hague, 1960). For the rebirth of phenomenology in Italy see E. Paci, ed., *Omaggio a Husserl* (Milan, 1960); idem, *Tempo e verità nella fenomenologia di Husserl* (Bari, 1961); idem, *Funzione delle scienze e significato dell' uomo* (Bari, 1961); idem, "Attualità di Husserl," *Revue internationale de philosophie*, no. 71–72 (1965) (dedicated to Husserl); in the same issue of the *Revue* see the special bibliography of Italian studies; see also C. Sini, *La fenomenologia* (Milan, 1963). There are several bibliographies of studies on Husserl; see, especially, J. Patocka in *Revue internationale de philosophie*, no. 2 (1939) (dedicated to Husserl), and the bibliographies established by G. Maschke and I. Kern in the same issue. For a first introduction to Husserl see the book by D. Christoff, *Husserl* (Paris, 1966), or that by L. Kelkel and R. Scherer, *Husserl* (Paris, 1964). For an introduction to Husserl's principal theoretical doctrines see C. Sini, *Introduzione alla fenomenologia come scienza* (Milan, 1965).

To forget real work and to see only products and merchandise would be to run the risk of reducing man himself to a mercantile value and of forgetting the historical situation of living work.   This would be to forget the *discipline* that gives rise to political economy; it would be to forget the *structure* of concrete human relationships and reduce them to an abstract science.[14]   This is to say that political economy can become oblivious to the living *poiein* and begin to think that only its own operations are real.   In such an event economics would need to return to the forgotten concrete subjects by means of a "Copernican revolution" similar, in certain respects, to Kant's critique of pure reason and to Dilthey's critique of historical reason.   In this respect it is most significant that Marx's *Kapital* bears a subtitle which the Marxists frequently forget: *Critique of Political Economy*.

We note also that Vico speaks of poetry as imitation.   Here, too, we risk missing his meaning if we think of poetry as poetic works and not as *poiein*. It is not a question of poetry as it would be understood by a poet.   It is a question of *learning*; children learn by operations and from examples and not from exact results.   To teach, we must work out the primary operations ourselves and not simply exhibit conclusions.   Poetry becomes a concrete, or, as Vico would say, a "real," poietic art.   We can say the same thing of the "imitation of nature."   If Vico had examined this point of view more closely, he would have modified his theory of the incomprehensibility of nature.   Science, in fact, is not knowledge in which the human subject is absent.   And the "imitations" of which Vico speaks are essentially the *experiments* in which the logic of science—mathematics—is not separated from its concrete contents.   It is precisely because nature is a book written in mathematical characters, as Galileo said, and precisely because it is we who create mathematics, as Vico himself said, that science is possible.   And science is possible because, while remaining subjects, we are also natural bodies and must take account, in physics itself, of the observer and of the experimenter. The first fact was demonstrated by Einstein, the second by Heisenberg.[15]

With respect to *learning* and children we must observe that we are not children once and for all, as if there were one kind of thought reserved for the primitives and another kind of thought belonging exclusively to the civilized.   The whole development of French anthropology, from Durkheim to Lévy-Bruhl, from Mauss to Lévi-Strauss, is implied in this problem. In the context of our preceding argument on economics, on the body, and on living work, the important studies of Mauss on the forms of exchange and giving, as well as on the "techniques of the body," are particularly relevant.[16]

[14] See E. Paci, "Struttura e lavoro vivente," in *Relazioni e significati* (Milan, 1965), pp. 215–20.

[15] See E. Paci, *Tempo e relazione*, 2d ed., with an appendix on cybernetics (Milan, 1965).

[16] See M. Mauss, "Essai sur le don: Forme et raison de l'échange dans les sociétés archaïques," *L'Année sociologique*, I (1923–24): 30–186; *idem*, "Les techniques du corps," *Journal de Psychologie*, 32: 271–93.

The problem of the children must be related to psychology, and particularly to the studies of J. Piaget on the formation of judgment and reasoning in the child—on which depend the formation of the notions of physical causality, of symbols, of numbers, of movement and velocity, of space and "spontaneous geometry."[17] The problem of psychology must be taken here in a very wide sense which would include Dilthey and all the works of Husserl, from his criticisms of "psychologism" in the *Logische Untersuchungen* up to the problem of the foundation of psychology, which is treated in the third part of the *Krisis* and which was interrupted by the author's death. Here, once again, the problem of the *epoché* enters the picture.

As for the "complete humanity" of which Vico speaks, we must recall that this is true for Vico because the disciplines are always concerned with the whole man, but we must also remember that the "complete" does not exclude the *telos* of history, which Vico sees in the ideal Platonic republic.

Vico observes that the history of philosophy confirms his point of view. This would be most doubtful if the history of philosophy were separated from the disciplines and if it were presented according to a logical order independent of nature and civilization. We know in fact that Vico is looking for just the opposite and that he is looking, at one and the same time, for the point of departure of every science and every art. For him the point of departure in its original and actual form is *evidence*, an evidence which is self-consciousness and sensitivity. This is a very difficult point; actually, only Husserl resolved this problem, through the unity of the concrete and the transcendental subject. If this unity is possible, it is possible only with the *epoché* and in the analysis of the structures of time and space. For example, in present time-consciousness evidence is retained, as the present moment passes, in the modality of *retention*. When I reflect on the past present I am in a new present which retains the past present. The other temporal modalities render a genetic phenomenology possible and, at the same time, allow for the constitution of the past as history. The past is in me even if I am unaware of it. It functions in the present of all men and in the present of the world in such a way that phenomenology can become a science, not only with respect to the future, but also with respect to the past, which is sedimented in us and *reactivated* by us. These phenomenological investigations are among the most difficult and they are strictly tied to space-time structures and to the structures of living beings and of the organic and inorganic worlds. It is important to note that these and other structures are present in all the disciplines, all the arts, all the operations, in the whole cosmos. They are present and thus "founding," even if we are not aware of it. It is of extreme importance, however, to remember that we can begin

[17] Over and above the well-known works of Piaget see *Etudes d'épistémologie génétique*, beginning with the first volume, W. E. Beth, W. Mays, and J. Piaget, *Epistémologie génétique et recherches psychologiques* (Paris, 1957). The relations between Vico and Piaget have been noted by G. Tagliacozzo (see n. 2 above).

only from present evidence; it is consciousness which understands the unconscious, not the inverse. It is by rediscovering in ourselves the "total"
and concrete man, who contains not only the planet earth but the whole
universe, that we can uncover and study what there is of the universe in
ourselves and what we represent in the universe. This is the theme of the
macrocosm and the microcosm, which is but another and different expression
of "phylogeny recapitulates ontogeny," a theme so warmly and fantastically
defended by E. Haeckel. It is a theme tied to repetition, recapitulation, to
course and recourse, to evolution, to involution, to progress. The fundamental thing is not the repetition and recapitulation but the presence of a
past which, as pure permanence, does not repeat the dialectical modalities of
its own development. When the past is reactivated in the present, in the
modalities of time and space which Husserl describes, reflection, in nature
and in the subject itself, passes on to something that has never before existed
and that is not the repetition of the laws of evolution which led to human
experience. Sensory self-awareness is implicit in the evolutionary leap, just
as reflection is implicit in evidence and in intentional self-consciousness.[18]
At this point, which is central for the phenomenological encyclopedia, we
meet spatial structures and temporal structures, along with all the other
structures. The concrete and total man, that is, non-abstract man, the true
and inevitable point of departure *for us*, is complete—there is no paradox
here—only when he discovers in himself, and thus in the universe, a new
horizon within the totality. There is in the finite an actual infinite, according
to the important discoveries realized in the mathematics of Georg Cantor,
discoveries which had been indicated by Einstein and which were required
for the development and transformation of the theory of relativity in relation
to the quantum theory. Only a completely determined science, based on
old prejudices or following outmoded myths, can deny *teleology*. We can
express this in the words of Julian Huxley, remembering that what Huxley
calls *mind* is, for Husserl, evidence, reflection, and intentionality, and, for
Vico, the fight, in all the disciplines, against the return of barbarism:

Each step in evolutionary progress has brought new problems, which have had to be
solved on their own merits; and with the new predominance of mind that has come
with man, life finds its new problems even more unfamiliar than usual. The future
of progressive evolution is the future of man; if it is to be progress and not merely a

---

[18] The complete works of Husserl connect evidence in the first person (the subject)
with time, space, and the history of man and of the cosmos. Nevertheless, in spite of
the precise use Husserl makes of ontogeny-phylogeny, as a phenomenological method
this theme must be developed and rendered more precise in a phenomenological encyclopedia. The Husserlian manuscript "Universale Teleologie," published in an appendix
to E. Paci's book *Tempo e verità* (Bari, 1961), is only a beginning; but see also L.
von Bertalanffy, *Das biologische Weltbild*, I (Bern, 1949), 81 and 108. With reference to
Kafka see the end of E. Paci's "Vico and Cassirer," pp. 457–73 of the present volume.

standstill or a degeneration, it must be guided by a deliberated purpose.   And this human purpose can only be formulated in terms of the new attributes achieved by life in becoming man.

Huxley negates "naturalistic" man by means of the *epoché* and in such a way that this negation implicates all the disciplines.   Husserl would say that at the moment when the separated categories are reintegrated in the complete man, and man rediscovers himself with the world in a plenum, at that very moment, in our present experience, a new dialectic is born in which—and in which alone—man discovers that he must still become an authentic man. This is the sense of the verse that Huxley cites from the *Eve future* of Villiers-de-l'Isle-Adam: "L'Homme ... seul dans l'univers n'est pas fini." [19]

Today we see all this as the ultimate development of Vico's suggestions concerning poetic wisdom.   Retrospectively, then, we are no longer surprised to see that in Vico poetic wisdom contains all the disciplines and, with these, sensible evidence, *autopsia*, the *telos* of human history.   We thereby understand better how Vico could look for a structure in all the disciplines, a science of the *Lebenswelt* which would comprise both the *Naturwissenschaften* and the *Geisteswissenschaften*.   And, in fact, poetic wisdom comprises logic, ethics, economics, politics, physics, cosmography, astronomy, chronology, geography, and, as we know, linguistics and mythology. [20]

This investigation has enabled us to bring out the concept of *structure*. We must expect such a term to be valid not only for linguistic structuralism but for all the disciplines.   In Dilthey it indicates the attempt to base the sciences of the mind and the Copernican revolution of history on the foundation of the *Erlebnis*.   In linguistic structuralism it is the effort to discover, in various ways, a general system of structures and an object of study for linguistics which is not, as Saussure says, the *parole*, but the *langue*.   Thus the collective object is not the individual subject; this kind of investigation is presented as an objective science, independent of the psychological and other variations of the man who speaks.   In Lévi-Strauss, finally, it is the attempt to apply the method of structuralism to anthropology and, by hypothesis, to all the human sciences.   Dilthey attempts to discover a new psychology; linguistic structuralism searches for a method which would utilize precise connections and significant oppositions; structural anthropology is directed toward a universal history based on exact models.   All of these attempts lead back to Vico and to Husserl and, finally, to a phenomenological encyclopedia.

Dilthey was the key figure in the discussions about the *Naturwissenschaften* and the *Geisteswissenschaften* in Germany at the end of the nineteenth century

[19] J. Huxley, *Evolution: The Modern Synthesis*, 2d ed. (London, 1963), pp. 577 and 572
[20] *New Science*, pp. 85ff., 127ff., 135ff., 166ff., 212ff., 218ff., 227ff., 230ff., and 234ff., respectively.

and the beginning of the twentieth. Linguistic structuralism, which was born at Kazan, in the easternmost university of Europe, is now circling the globe and is being diversified in several directions. Structural anthropology, which originated in the French current of anthropological studies and in Mauss, in the cultural anthropology of the Anglo-Saxons, and in the early Brazilian studies of Lévi-Strauss, now faces fundamental problems of the greatest interest, particularly in its attempt to utilize the unconscious and to elaborate what could be called, in a Vichian manner, a poetic logic, that is, a logic of myth and a theory of models. Moreover, Lévi-Strauss attempts to find a bridge between linguistic structures and those of reality, thus taking up a theme of logical positivism, even if he does not mention it or even recognize it. This is the theme of the relationship between logical language and real facts, which is also the ancient theme of accounting for the application of mathematics to nature.

All these movements provide valuable results, but they misfire if they are not based on phenomenology and on the developments of the Husserlian tradition in the sense of a phenomenological encyclopedia, which would be not a sum of the sciences and scientific knowledge, but rather the reflexive activity and the functional operation of present humanity—humanity as constituted of a plenum which is open and intentionally oriented toward the social constitution of man and toward man's authentic individual and social humanity.[21]

The problem of structure in Dilthey is tied to the whole development and

---

[21] Cf. E. Paci, *Fenomenologia e antropologia: Corso di filosofia, 1961–62* (Milan, 1962), pp. 159–90; E. Renzi, "Per una antropologia fenomenologica," *Aut-Aut*, no. 67 (1962); E. Paci, "Il senso delle parole: Struttura," *ibid.*, no. 73 (1963); *idem*, "Strutturalismo, fenomenologia e antropologia," *ibid.*, no. 77 (1963); *idem*, "Fenomenologia e antropologia culturale," *ibid.*; *idem*, *La filosofia di Whitehead e i problemi del tempo e della struttura: Corso di filosofia, 1964–65* (Milan, 1965), pp. 150–200; *idem*, "Sul concetto di struttura in Lévi-Strauss," *Giornale critico della filosofia italiana*, 4 (1965); *idem*, "Il senso delle strutture in Lévi-Strauss," *Revue internationale de philosophie*, no. 73–74 (1965) (dedicated to the concept of structure). See also C. Lévi-Strauss, "Elogio dell' antropologia," *Aut-Aut*, no. 88 (1965); this issue, dedicated completely to Lévi-Strauss, contains, besides the integral text of his inaugural address at the Collège de France, January 5, 1960 (presented by P. Caruso), the following: E. Paci, "Antropologia culturale e fenomenologia"; *idem*, "Antropologia e entropologia"; *idem*, "Pensiero concreto"; E. Renzi, "Sulla nozione di inconscio in Lévi-Strauss"; P. Caruso, "Il crudo e il cotto"; *idem*, "Bibliografia generale degli scritti di e su Lévi-Strauss." From P. Caruso see also "Intervista a C. Lévi-Strauss," *Aut-Aut*, no. 77 (1963). In another issue of *Aut-Aut*, no. 95–97, we find: E. Paci, "Fondazione fenomenologica dell'antropologia ed enciclopedia delle scienze"; A. Bonomi, "Implicazioni filosofiche nella antropologia di Lévi-Strauss"; G. Daghini, "La funzione dell'immagine nella praxis"; P. Gambazzi, "I fondamenti antropologici della storia in Marx." For the works of Lévi-Strauss himself we refer the reader to the above-mentioned "Bibliografia generale" by Caruso, and for the Anglo-Saxon sources to the bibliography given in the appendix to C. Lévi-Strauss, *Anthropologie structurale* (Paris, 1958). Among the works by Lévi-Strauss not included in Caruso's bibliography, we refer to *Du miel aux cendres* (Paris, 1967).

to all the problems of contemporary German historicism. We must add to Dilthey the names of W. Windelband and H. Rickert, of G. Simmel and M. Weber, and, finally, those of O. Spengler, E. Troeltsch, and F. Meinecke. The development of the themes in question involves Marxism, Mannheim's sociology of knowledge, Heidegger's existentialism, Croce's "absolute" historicism, Dewey's historicity of the human world, and Popper's neo-positivistic critique of historicism.[22] Present studies in sociology, anthropology, and ethnology rediscover the whole problem that binds them to

[22] Cf. Pietro Rossi, *Lo storicismo tedesco contemporaneo* (Turin, 1956); *idem*, *Storia e storicismo nella filosofia contemporanea* (Milan, 1960); W. Kluback and M. Weinbaum, *Dilthey's Philosophy of Existence* (New York, 1957). For the problem of the primitives in relation to the human sciences cf. R. Cantoni's *Il pensiero dei primitivi* (Milan, 1941), 2d ed. rev., *Il pensiero dei primitivi: Preludio a un'antropologia* (Milan, 1963), and, most recently, *Illusione e pregiudizio* (Milan, 1967). For the relationship of the problem of the primitives to cultural anthropology and the human sciences we refer the reader to the bibliography given in this last volume. In this context the work of E. de Martino is of great importance, particularly his first work, *Naturalismo e storicismo nell'etnologia* (Bari, 1940), and his last two works, in which the fundamental lines and problems of ethnology and anthropology are treated with clarity and singular insight: *La terra del rimorso* (Milan, 1961), and *Furore simbolo valore* (Milan, 1962). For sociological studies, with special reference to those of the Anglo-Saxons, we refer to *Quaderni di sociologia*, ed. N. Abbagnano and F. Ferrarotti, now in its second series. For a first approach to the work of Abbagnano (whose *La struttura dell'esistenza* [Turin, 1939] we recall), see N. Abbagnano, *Scritti scelti* (Turin, 1967), where we find the basic lines that link positive existentialism with sociology. An appendix to this volume contains a bibliography of the writings by and on Abbagnano. For the influence of American sociology and its problems (we are thinking, for example, of Merton, Parsons, but also of C. Wright Mills and of the theme placed in relief by J. K. Galbraith, *The Affluent Society* [Boston, 1958]) in relation to structuralism, we limit ourselves to J. Viet's *Les méthodes structuralistes dans les Sciences Sociales* (Paris and The Hague, 1967), which contains a relatively rich bibliography. For the influence of the work of Galbraith on economics cf. C. Napoleoni, *Il pensiero economico del Novecento* (Turin, 1963), pp. 184–85, and the *Rivista trimestrale*, from no. 1 (1962) to the present; see also C. Napoleoni, ed., *Dizionario di economia politica* (Milan, 1956). We also refer to the Italian works of F. Ferrarotti: *La sociologia, storia, concetti, metodi* (Turin, 1961); *La sociologia come partecipazione* (Turin, 1961). On this last-named work see E. Renzi, "Sociologia e fenomenologia," *Aut-Aut*, nos. 68 and 72. On R. Dahrendorf's *Soziale Klassen und Klassenkonflikt in der industriellen Gesellschaft* (Stuttgart, 1957) (improved and enlarged English edition, *Class and Class Conflict in Industrial Society* [London, 1959], translated into Italian, with an introduction by A. Pizzorno, *Le organizzazioni, il potere e i conflitti di classe* [Bari, 1963]), see G. Piana, "Una critica sociologica a Marx," *Aut-Aut*, no. 86 (1965). With respect to the work of Pizzorno, and as an example of his activity, we recall the special issue of *Quaderni di sociologia*, no. 3–4 (1966), dedicated to the social and political sciences as well as to political activity. We would also like to recall the work of N. Bobbio, *Politica e cultura* (Turin, 1955); in relation to our theme see his contribution to *Rivista di filosofia* (Turin, 1957), and, finally, the work and activity of R. Treves, president of the Italian Association of Social Sciences. See also the *Bollettino delle ricerche sociali*, from no. 1 (1961) to the present, and, in general, the works of sociology published by *Il Mulino* in Bologna. For a general bibliography see R. Koenig, *Soziologie* (Frankfurt, 1958), and the translation of this work by L. Gallino (Milan, 1964).

Dilthey, not to mention that which derives from Kant, Herder, and Hegel, or, one could say, from the "age of Goethe."[23]

We can note certain historical threads. Dilthey exercised a critical role with respect to Neo-Kantianism and also with respect to Windelband and Rickert. The problems that Dilthey brought into play were problems of phenomenological foundation in the sense of a "poetic wisdom" and a "psychology" which, on the one hand, opened up the way to Husserl, but which, on the other hand, impeded the development of a "rigorous" phenomenology, in terms of the Husserlian *Erlebnis*, which follows the *epoché*. The result was a meeting and a collision with Husserl, who nevertheless ended by recognizing the great importance of Dilthey. At the time of their meeting Husserl was engaged in his critique of "psychologism" and "naturalism," insofar as he was searching for a foundation of logic in the direction of Brentano's theory of intentionality and in the sense of a discipline which would account for both formal and transcendental logic. From the very beginning Husserl tended toward a science of the *Lebenswelt*, but such a science was neither Dilthey's vital course or *Lebensverlauf* nor "life" in Simmel's sense. In Husserl's eyes *Erleben* as *Selbstbiographie* remained on the naturalistic and, therefore, on the mundane, level, prior to the *epoché*. In this sense it was impossible for Dilthey to arrive at an encyclopedia of the precategorial *disciplines* and hence at a founded, precategorial science in the Husserlian sense.[24] Nevertheless, Dilthey saw very well that "structure" cannot occur without subjectivity. The structural complex (*Strukturzusam-*

---

[23] For Italian and foreign studies in this direction we refer the reader to V. Verra's "Vent'anni di studi sul pensiero dell'età di Goethe," *Cultura e scuola*, no. 16 (1965).

[24] See W. Dilthey, *Gesammelte Schriften*, 12 vols. (Leipzig-Berlin, 1914–36). For the *Selbstbiographie* and for the term "*Lebensverlauf*" see VII, 191–92; the former is treated exclusively on pp. 199–202. The theme of understanding others is also Husserlian; see pp. 205ff. For the polemic between Husserl and Dilthey cf. E. Husserl, "Philosophie als strenge Wissenschaft," *Logos*, 1911, pp. 239–41, and W. Biemel, "Correspondencia entre Dilthey y Husserl," *Rivista de filosofia de la Universidad de Costa Rica*, 2 (1959). In 1925 Husserl speaks of the reform of psychology undertaken by Dilthey, in *Husserliana*, vol. IX: *Phänomenologische Psychologie* (Haag, 1962), pp. 5–6; in relation to Brentano, see pp. 33–35. Moreover, the problem is taken up again in the *Krisis*, in the third uncompleted part, and requires the completion of Husserl's point of view in a phenomenological encyclopedia. The criticism of Dilthey from a phenomenological point of view was undertaken by L. Landgrebe, "W. Dilthey's Theorie der Geisteswissenschaften," *Jahrbuch für Philosophie und phänomenologische Forschung*, 9 (1928); see also idem, *Phänomenologie und Metaphysik* (Hamburg, 1949), pp. 32–42. Landgrebe's criticism differs from our point of view. In any event it was essential for Husserl that phenomenology not be confused with naturalistic psychology, and that the *Lebenswelt* not be confused with "life," which should be put in parentheses insofar as the *Lebenswelt* contains the operations of all the sciences, on the one hand, and, on the other, is not a metaphysics in the traditional sense. This does not free Husserl from the serious problem of founding psychology, of founding logic in its various modalities, or even of founding, in the sense we have indicated, history.

menhang), according to Dilthey, cannot occur without the subject and inter-subjective relationships, which are necessary to historical understanding and any other type of understanding; and this is so precisely because the subject itself is structured, and "psychic structures" characterize groups, communities, institutions, cultures, "world views." If all this is founded on a psychology, what psychology is it? How can psychology be at the same time both analysis and description? Analysis has to understand relations, the concreteness and organic nature of forms, of *Gestalten*, of structures; it must not separate them to break them up into a logic of the learned. Its method will be that of *Erleben* and therefore will be founded on "experienced" evidence. The important point is whether this experience, purely as such, permits *a science of experience*, which is what phenomenology is. The *Erlebnis* must explain nature itself, "world views" themselves, poetry itself, dreams and myths, and at the same time it must be the instrument of a science, a science of logic, a science of nature and mind.

Just as Husserl was related to, but opposed to, Dilthey, so was he in opposition to neocriticism. Here it should be easier—on the basis of the Kantian notion of idea as law—to comprehend the sense of phenomenological investigations. Nevertheless, Natorp and Husserl found themselves in opposition. Husserl saw that he needed to give a new meaning to Kantian critical philosophy and to transcendental operations. This required a critique of psychology, a concretization of man, the possibility of a descriptive approach, intentionality, and finality. It required the *epoché* and the science of the precategorial. Husserl perceived this very early, in 1904 and in 1906–7, when he proposed to himself the task of elaborating a complete critique of practical, theoretical, logical, and historical reason.[25] If Natorp did not understand this direction of Husserl's thought, Cassirer, in his own reaction to Natorp, did understand Husserl's critique of psychologism. Thus he wrote, in his last work, that Husserl had cleared the whole atmosphere of the period, like a hurricane, and he had done this by demonstrating that logic could not base itself on psychology. From this it followed that linguistics could no longer base itself on psychology. And Cassirer resolved for linguistic structuralism all the problems raised by such a tie, even if, at least at first, he did not realize that he was doing so. These are the problems of Goethe's *Gestaltung*, the problems of a basic structure which would be at one and the same time permanent and historical, that is to say, in the language of structuralism, the problems of *synchrony* and *diachrony*. Cassirer cites the work accomplished by Dilthey and Rickert and refers to the problem of the symbol and signification, a problem which Husserl had

---

[25] These observations presuppose an understanding of the manner in which Husserl undertook his topics of research and an awareness of the development of his thought. See E. Paci, "*Tema e svolgimento in Husserl,*" *Aut-Aut*, no. 95 (1966), and, in reference to this study, *idem*, "Per lo studio della logica in Husserl," *ibid.*, no. 94 (1966).

confronted from the very beginning in an intentional direction and which, in *Krisis*, appears as being clearly teleological.[26]

The situation presented by Cassirer is paradoxical. It is a matter of fact that structuralism, from its beginnings in Russia, was tied to Husserl and especially to the *Prolegomena* (that is, the Introduction to *Logische Unter-suchungen*, which was translated into Russian in 1909) and to the *Philosophie als strenge Wissenschaft* (translated in the Russian edition of *Logos* in 1911). In Russia, Husserl was known precisely for his critique of psychologism, and so structuralism was presented as a formalism. Thus, from its very begin-nings, structuralism ignored the precategorial linguistic operations that are rooted in time and history, and that W. von Humboldt had called the living body, or *Sprachleib*, of language. Roman Jakobson himself is closely tied to Husserl, even though he does not speak of the subject in the first person, which Husserl established through the *epoché* and through a non-psychologistic, phenomenological science of the genesis of language. Structuralism is now finding itself faced with the problems of a new phenomenological science and with those of the encyclopedia. It is for this reason that I have always held, as, in fact, did Merleau-Ponty, that structuralism cannot but be based on phenomenology. With this we return, in a roundabout way, through Dilthey to Vico and to the problems analyzed at the beginning of this paper. In any event, Dilthey himself named Vico before Lessing and Herder; he listed him in connection with the attempt by Sebastian Franck to establish a "universal theory." In fact, he traced his Vichian ideas back to Plato, Aristotle, Polybius, Cicero, Machiavelli, and Grotius, and emphasized the connection between law and religion in Vico.

Lévi-Strauss, in the field of structural anthropology, frequently makes us think of Vico. When he wrote at the end of *Tristes tropiques* that anthro-pology should be called *entropology*, he meant that, with the augmentation of entropy, evolution is necessarily bringing about the end of the world, and humanity itself is implicated in this end. In *La pensée sauvage* the relations between diachrony and synchrony, between event and form, between history and system, between the individual and the class, between personal names and predicates, become profoundly problematical. And the problem of *Le cru et le cuit* is presented as the problem not only of the relation between logical structures and the structures of reality but also as the relation between culture and nature. The mediation is entrusted to music: structures are connected according to musical "rhythms." The purely formal relationship, in the logical sense, is devoid of content. Lévi-Strauss has, like phenomenology, to speak of real operations; the intelligibility of syntactical chains requires a "Kantian" critique; myths end up by acquiring an intentional meaning.[27]

[26] See E. Cassirer, "Structuralism in Modern Linguistics," *Word*, 1 (1945): 99–120.

[27] For structuralism and Russian formalism see V. Erlich, *Russian Formalism* (The Hague, 1954). For the *Sprachleib* of W. von Humboldt see Paci, *Funzione delle scienze*,

The contributions of linguistic structuralism and of the encyclopedic universalism of cultural anthropology are reviving Vico and are sending us back to Husserl.[28] They require, finally, a new encyclopedia *in progress* and modalities on which the sciences, the arts, and history are to be founded. These are the modalities of the precategorial and intentional *poiein*, of a *poiein* which is coming to awareness, emerging from the shadows and from forgetfulness, acquiring a meaning and a finality.

Translated by James M. Edie

---

pp. 219–26.   The bibliography on structuralism and linguistics is enormous; thus we refer to the one which is contained in G. A. Lepschy, *La linguistica strutturale* (Turin, 1966).   Lepschy lists the essential works of Saussure, of the school of Prague, of the school of Copenhagen, of the beginnings of American structuralism (Sapir, Bloomfeld), of functional linguistics (Jacobson, Martinet, and others), and of the structural linguistics typical of American structuralism.   To Lepschy's bibliography we add the one mentioned in the special issue of *Verri*, no. 24 (1966).   For the relationship between Jakobson and Husserl, see R. Jakobson, *Selected Writings*, I (The Hague, 1962).   Jakobson spoke to me of Husserl in a private conversation, telling me that in all his travels he carried the *Logische Untersuchungen* with him, and he observed that structuralism would have to take account of the *Cartesianische Meditationen* and the later development of phenomenology. For Dilthey's references to Vico mentioned in the text see, respectively, W. Dilthey, *Gesammelte Schriften*, I, 90; II, 87; III, 233; IV, 160; V, 269; VII, 314.   For what is said of Lévi-Strauss in the text see C. Lévi-Strauss, *Tristes tropiques* (Paris, 1955), *La pensée sauvage* (Paris, 1962), and esp. *Le cru et le cuit* (Paris, 1964), pp. 246, 315, 345.

[28] Apart from what has been said in this study we can note that the concept of structure is found in all the sciences and is also related to the notion of logico-mathematical structure as it occurs in Russell and Wittgenstein.   In this regard see E. Paci's article on the word "*struttura*" in the *Enciclopedia della Scienza e della Tecnica* (in preparation in Milan).

A. William Salomone   PLURALISM
AND UNIVERSALITY
IN VICO'S
SCIENZA NUOVA

The explosive multiplicity of the modern mind's cultural experience seems at the moment utterly irreducible to any unified system of values. At the same time, a fulfillment of recurring dreams of the real unity of mankind appears to have become a chimera. And yet, it is exactly lest that multiplicity be translated into a total "anarchy of values" and lest those dreams be too easily transformed into phantasmagorical nightmares of human destiny that old quests must be revisited and new ones undertaken toward the gaining of a novel understanding of, or at least of fresh perspectives upon, the human mind and human values in history. Those who refuse to be self-victimized either by illusions of intellectual grandeur or by delusions of cultural despair know that varieties of human experience in history all bear witness to recurring heroic efforts—those efforts of mind and spirit grappling with the meaning of life and the nature of truth in the world of men, however elusive they may be and however antinomic their reflections in the "mirrors" of modern visions of the world and of man's fate may appear. For it may be that, after all, those varieties of cultural and spiritual experience can, must, and ought to be again subsumed under a novel dialectic of reason and liberty, of historical reason and human freedom, operating as creative forces against those dark Dioscuri of our times, unreason and nihilism. It is because we believe that there are in Giambattista Vico's *Scienza nuova* fertile suggestions for a vital revaluation of the vortex of uncertainties stirring at the pit of the profound crisis of values of our time that we shall seek to revisit the structure and to reinterpret the meaning of Vico's work, less as a philosophy of history than as a guide to a philosophy of life.[1]

---

[1] The distinction between the two "types" of philosophy may not seem important, but it is, in fact, crucial. An explicit clarification of the difference would require a discussion ranging far beyond the scope of this essay. The essay itself, it is hoped, will suggest the difference by its very character, procedure, and emphases. Underlying these is the hypothesis that, to paraphrase a well-known dictum from another "discipline," a philosophy of life is too important to be left exclusively to professional philosophers of history! As will be suggested in the text and notes, Vico's *Scienza nuova* itself had one of its fundamental premises in the acceptance of such a distinction. The indispensable bibliographic, exegetic, and critical labors of Benedetto Croce and Fausto Nicolini on Vico, particularly on those parts of his work which deal with his influence,

I. *The New Science of the Human World*

Giambattista Vico's *Scienza nuova* is at once a methodology of knowledge, a philosophy of history, and a vision of life. It may perhaps be argued that in its final form, the *Scienza nuova seconda* of 1744, which, in a technical sense, constituted a "third" version of his original work, may still appear to contain the fundamental constituents of a sketch of a structure and not a full-fledged system of philosophy, since, unlike the "finished" works of the systematizers of Western thought, Vico's book is richer in the implications of its ideas than in any explicit, definitive formulation of doctrines.[2]   I shall suggest later why such a view of the *Scienza nuova* may be correct, but for reasons other than those commonly adduced.   Be it sufficient for the moment to call attention to the fact that Vico's work, when it is closely and carefully analyzed, does approximate as complete an organization of his "formal" thought, through both its orderly procedure and its rigorous exposition, as any really novel organic vision of life and history can hope to attain.[3]   In a real sense, the very richness of Vico's thought—the concentrated suggestiveness of its discoveries, the power of its images, the sharpness of its intuitions, the clarity of its fundamental ideas, if not always of its language—has frequently tended to distract attention from that organic inner structure which is one of its most revolutionary novelties.   Unless, therefore, the methodological, philosophical, and historical foundations of Vichian thought are kept in view within their "revolutionary" context, the whole of the *Scienza nuova* can be, as it has occasionally been, turned into an obscure construct of a "genial but erratic" mind.[4]

---

rediscovery, "fortune," and, one is tempted to say, with the uses and abuses suffered by the *Scienza nuova* from the era of romanticism to the age of existentialism, amply illustrate some of the ways in which the distinction between philosophies of life and philosophies of history has not always been honored.   See, in particular, the implicit treatment of this problem in Benedetto Croce and Fausto Nicolini, *Bibliografia vichiana*, 2 vols. (Naples, 1947–48), I, *passim*; Benedetto Croce, *La filosofia di Giambattista Vico*, 4th ed. rev. (Bari, 1947), pp. 319–32; Giambattista Vico, *Opere*, ed. Fausto Nicolini (Milan-Naples, 1953), pp. xvi–xlii; and the masterly Introduction by Max H. Fisch to *The Autobiography of Giambattista Vico*, trans. Max H. Fisch and Thomas G. Bergin (Ithaca, N.Y., 1963), pp. 61–107.

[2] Croce, *La filosofia di Giambattista Vico*, pp. 43–44.

[3] Vico's *magnum opus* is its own best illustration of the order and rigor of his methodology and of the "revolutionary" novelty of his vision of life and of history.   The best critical edition of the original is Giambattista Vico, *La scienza nuova seconda*, ed. Fausto Nicolini, 2 vols. (Bari, 1942); in English see *The New Science of Giambattista Vico*, trans. Thomas G. Bergin and Max H. Fisch (Ithaca, N.Y., 1948), of which an excellent abridgment (Garden City, N.Y.: Anchor Books, 1961) is available.   References and citations will be made to the Nicolini edition of *La scienza nuova seconda* and to the Bergin and Fisch abridged edition of the *New Science*.

[4] See Vico's self-characterization of personal and intellectual temper in Fisch and Bergin's *Autobiography*, pp. 199–200.

As a "covering" substantive, Vichianism may well serve to subsume almost the whole of the mature thought of Vico under the concept of a new "universal" philosophy of life and history. Obviously, its very richness precludes also any brief synthesis of that thought. The bibliographic and exegetic labors of Benedetto Croce and Fausto Nicolini on the *Scienza nuova* testify, among other things, to the recurring dilemma of the Vichian student.[5] Moreover, in Vico's thought, all that preceded the self-disciplined elaboration which is characteristic of the economy of his masterpiece—even those parts of it which at some moments he repudiated—amounted to a philosophical and philological, intellectual and spiritual, preparation for the final form of his ideas. Difficult as it sometimes may be to establish a direct relationship between them and of all of them to the *Scienza nuova seconda* of 1744, there is hardly any question that all of Vico's lectures and essays, his poetry and polemical works, the first *Scienza nuova*, of 1725, and the tantalizing and hermetic *Autobiografia* of 1731, constituted irreversible stages in Vico's intellectual and spiritual itinerary and that, therefore, they were all, in varying degrees, "integral" to the definitive formulation of his thought.[6] Obviously, however important and revealing it might be, the genetic approach to Vichian thought amounts to a task of such gigantic proportions as to involve not only all the details of his biography but also a review of the major stages of Western philosophy from Plato to Vico himself. Since the scope and purpose of this reinterpretative essay is infinitely more modest than that, a brief word will have to suffice concerning the genesis and premises of Vichian thought.[7]

[5] See especially the superb hermeneutic-exegetic work by Fausto Nicolini, *Commento storico alla seconda scienza nuova*, 2 vols. (Rome, 1949), without whose aid no critical reading of Vico seems complete. In this context, see also the pithy, itself almost hermetic, but uniquely illuminating Introduction by Fisch to the *New Science*, pp. xxi–lii.

[6] See Croce and Nicolini, *Bibliografia vichiana*, I, 9–131, for a systematic "catalogue" and critical analysis of the corpus of Vico's works of the period of his maturity and old age. On the personal and intellectual vicissitudes of Vico's youth see Fausto Nicolini, *La giovinezza di Giambattista Vico* (Bari, 1932). See Croce, *La filosofia di Giambattista Vico*, pp. 239–48, for an intellectual portrait of Vico as a "rebel" against his times and "culture." On the social, religious, and philosophical aspects of Neapolitan culture during Vico's youth see Salvo Mastellone, *Pensiero politico e vita culturale a Napoli nella seconda metà del Seicento* (Messina-Florence, 1965), pp. 208–35; Raffaele Colapietra, *Vita pubblica e classi politiche del Viceregno napoletano, 1656–1734* (Rome, 1961), pp. 85–118, 131–32, deals with the milieu of politics, juridical science, and culture. For three almost mutually exclusive reinterpretations of Vico's philosophical and spiritual "itinerary" to the eve of the *Scienza nuova* see Antonio Corsano, *G. B. Vico* (Bari, 1956), whose emphases are Neo-Cartesian and Catholic; Nicola Badaloni, *Introduzione a G. B. Vico* (Milan, 1961), whose tone is Neo-Marxian; and Enzo Paci, *Ingens sylva: Saggio su G. B. Vico* (Milan, 1949), whose philosophical attitude is existentialist.

[7] In their works, Croce, Nicolini, Corsano, Badaloni, and Paci are, each in different fashion, concerned with the problem of the genesis of, and connections between, the three "versions" or editions of the *Scienza nuova* (1725, 1730, 1744). In English the

Historically, the *Scienza nuova* represented one of the first truly novel, original, and "total" alternatives to that cluster of intellectual, cultural, and spiritual values which had become predominant for the European mind on the eve of the Enlightenment.   Since, by their very *raison d'être*, humanism, rationalism, and the new mathematico-physical science of the post-Renaissance period had themselves had to grapple, from the fifteenth to the seventeenth century, with a multiplicity of ancient and contemporary systems of thought, Vico found himself engaged, so to speak, in a kind of "total" war of ideas in which the tactics employed against immediate "antagonists" had to be correlated with the strategy necessary for a successful encounter with the more distant, and often more formidable, "adversaries" of the classical and medieval eras.   Thus Vico's fundamental "alternative" in the *Scienza nuova* consisted, essentially, of no less demiurgic a task than that of seeking new roads to truth.   Ultimately, through the dialectic of critique and construction, he pitted his vision against a vast and complex variety of other heuristic approaches, whether philosophical or historical, to the reality of the human world.   In some cases those "approaches" had become apparently unshakable parts of the fabric of the Western mind dating from the dawn of the Christian era, and their resistance was tenacious.[8]

Philosophically, therefore, the Vichian "alternative" was first of all aimed against the reduction of *all* reality—social and historical as well as mathematical and physical—to mere objects of Cartesian epistemology and of Galilean-Newtonian physics.[9]   Beyond these, the "attack" was more subtly aimed against a whole variety of ancient and new philosophies, whether of transcendence (Augustinian and Thomistic) or of immanence (Averroistic or Gassendist, Brunian or Spinozan).[10]   Furthermore, whether directly or implicitly, the Vichian "alternative" likewise rose against those visions of life which tended to predicate either absolute contingency or progress, either

---

best (clearest and most suggestive) critico-historical discussion of the problem is in the Introduction to Fisch and Bergin's *Autobiography*, pp. 31–46.   For the Italian original of the autobiography, see Giambattista Vico, *L'autobiografia, il carteggio e le poesie varie*, ed. B. Croce and F. Nicolini (Bari, 1929), pp. 3–102.

[8] See Fisch and Bergin's *Autobiography*, pp. 120–30, *passim*, for the strange, incisive manner in which Vico appraises his studies of classical, scholastic, and Renaissance thinkers and "contemporary" philosophers, particularly, of course, his encounter with Descartes.   See Croce, *La filosofia di Giambattista Vico*, pp. 310–11, and Paci, *Ingens sylva*, pp. 14–15, for two related yet opposing views on the potentialities and limits of using the *Autobiografia* as a biographical function of the *Scienza nuova*, as Vico's "history of his own life" subsumed under the principles of his major work.

[9] Mario Fubini, *Stile e umanità di Giambattista Vico* (Bari, 1946), p. 209, incisively summarizes the Vico-Descartes relationship in these words: ". . . quel Cartesio di cui egli [Vico] come è il piu grande avversario, è anche il più grande continuatore. . . ."; see also Corsano, *G. B. Vico*, pp. 52–62, *passim*, for similar views.

[10] For a brief critical summary of most of these philosophies and of Vico's "reaction" to them see the Introduction to Fisch and Bergin's *Autobiography*, pp. 20–31.

the dominion of chance or the myth of human perfectibility. Thus Vico had had to place in different dimensions the ancient iron dilemma of freedom and necessity in the human world, even as he had "removed" human destiny in history from the grip of all "outside" elements, be they identified with providence or with fate.[11] For, if the atmosphere of the Counterreformation which still lingered in the Naples of his youth had either directly or by subtler pressures tended to inhibit Vico from too open, and therefore very dangerous, a profession of his new idea of "providence" in history, exposure to the cultural revolution of his age, on the other hand, had led him to discontent with, and then attack against, the prevailing alternatives of a Machiavellian and Hobbesian concept of chance and the Spinozan idea of fate.[12] In the final form of his work, therefore, Vico sought—more directly, more openly, than he had been able or willing to do with the concept of Christian providence—to dethrone fate from its position as arbiter over a ferocious, unalterable, and inescapable Manichean conflict ever raging in the human world. For Vico knew that Machiavelli, Hobbes, and Spinoza had, in a sense, merely substituted chance and fate for providence, only to give some sense to an otherwise universal and nihilistic domination by cosmic chaos.[13] It was when he had fully understood the hopelessness of the sterile philosophical dialectic between Providence and Fate that Vico fully envisioned his own "revolutionary" alternative. In both their places Vico put mind, intelligence, ever at grips with the self-engendering mystery and antinomy of human history. Noteworthy is the fact that he reiterated his great "discovery" in no uncertain terms toward the very end of the *Scienza nuova seconda*: "It is true that men have themselves made this world of nations, . . . but this world without doubt has issued from a mind often diverse, at times quite contrary, and always superior to the particular ends that men have proposed to themselves; which narrow ends, made means to serve wider ends, it has always employed to preserve the human race upon this earth.

[11] Cf. *ibid.*, pp. 166–73, 192–99.

[12] *La scienza nuova seconda*, I, 85–86, II, 164–65; *New Science*, pp. 28, 383: ". . . Hence Epicurus, who believed in chance, is refuted by the facts, along with his followers Hobbes and Machiavelli; and so are Zeno and Spinoza, who believe in fate."

[13] Nicolini, *La giovinezza di Giambattista Vico*, pp. 95–129, clarifies the eclecticism of Vico's study of both ancient and modern philosophies and emphasizes how, during the period of "preparation" preceding the writing of the first, "negative" version of the *Scienza nuova* (1725), Vico passed from a dark personal-philosophical vision of life as seen in his quasi-Leopardian poem *Affetti di un disperato* to the view of the "providentiality or the internal logic of history." If the moment—and the character—of Vico's great spiritual crisis as reconstructed by Nicolini is correct, Vico broke through the "darkness" of his philosophical despair by rejecting, among other alternatives, both a Lucretian and an Augustinian philosophy of life, of history, and of nature. The poem *Affetti di un disperato* is contained in Croce and Nicolini's edition of Vico's *Autobiografia*, pp. 313–17; an English translation by Thomas G. Bergin is now available in *Forum Italicum*, 2, no. 4 (December, 1968): 305ff.

. . . That which did all this was mind, for men did it with intelligence; it was not fate, for they did it by choice; not chance, for the results of their always so acting are perpetually the same."[14]

The Vichian "alternative" to some of the major "idols" of the European mind was thus fully revealed. But, before arriving at that "conclusion," Vico had had to retrace, revisit, and reconstruct some of the very foundations of the dominant philosophies of his day. And he had had, first of all, to grapple with the sway of Cartesian rationalism and Galilean-Newtonian science.[15] Related and connected as these seemed to be, for Vico, Cartesian reason and Galilean-Newtonian mathematical physics belonged to different separate realms of the operations of "mind" at grips with the nature of reality. In essence, he saw Cartesian reason merely as one mode, one procedure, one instrument, in the mind's own search for self-understanding of a limited sphere of its own operation. If Cartesian reason was a new "logic" of understanding, its validity was proportionate only to the rigor with which that "logic" was applied to a limited sector of the human mind's own creations, to the "fictions," that is, which it occasionally found useful in order to give meaning to its vision of the world. Taken from and applied out of its proper sphere, as had indeed occurred by Vico's day, Cartesian reason was a "logic" tampered with, misdirected, and therefore invalidated. Reimmersed within the context of the historical moments of its assertion and claim to primacy as an absolute method of understanding, reason became a function not of the logical but of the psychological springs of mind, of intelligence, at grips with the world of men and of nature.[16] The Neo-Cartesian inclinations that some of his students have espied in the last phase of Vico's thought can be accepted only in the perspective of the crucial Vichian conversion of "reason" from the sphere of logic to the realm of psychology in human history.

On an even higher level Vico did homage to the Galilean-Newtonian "reading" of the book of the universe and of nature.[17] He regarded that

[14] Cf. La scienza nuova seconda, II, 164; New Science, pp. 382–83.

[15] Concerning the "sway" of Cartesianism and the new Galilean-Newtonian science on both the European and the Italian levels during the period of Vico's youth and maturity, cf. Paul Hazard, The European Mind, 1680–1715, trans. J. Lewis May (Cleveland–New York, 1963), pp. 119–54; Peter Gay, The Enlightenment. An Interpretation: The Rise of Modern Paganism (New York, 1966), pp. 308–19.

[16] Corsano, G. B. Vico, pp. 234–36, calls emphatic attention to Vico's return to Descartes during the period between the publication of the 1730 edition and the completion of the final version of the Scienza nuova seconda of 1744. Corsano seems to emphasize a "logical" rather than a "psychological" revisiting of Cartesian reason by Vico.

[17] The homage that Vico pays to Galileo and Newton is almost unique and is in a sense less conditional than that which he pays to his four master authors, Plato, Tacitus, Grotius, and Bacon. In his Della mente eroica (1732), which is included in the Nicolini's Opere, p. 925, Vico refers to the "sublime Galileo"; in La scienza nuova seconda, I, 128,

"reading" as perhaps the most intelligent, orderly, and awesome that the mind of man had as yet come upon.   While the certainties that the Galilean-Newtonian laws of the world of nature offered might seem absolute, for Vico the "truth" concerning the physical universe was still relative and elusive.   If for Galileo and Newton the world of nature was stupendously written in the decipherable script of mathematical laws, it had been "read" before and therefore would continue to be "read" in other times, by other men, in other languages—scientific, philosophical, and "poetical"—that would claim the possession of its "ultimate truth" with no less certainty, if with different "justification."   Methodologically, therefore, Vico proceeded in analogous manner in dealing with Cartesian reason and Galilean-Newtonian science as he had done with Machiavellian chance and Spinozan fate.   It is only by understanding this complex procedure as the methodology of Vichianism that it is possible to isolate the fundamental significance of its substantive finality.   Through that methodology Vico had grappled with and had separated the epistemological, psychological, and philosophical elements that bound together varieties of alternative systems of human life and mind in history.   The exquisite revelation distilled as the heart of Vico's message of a unique discovery of a new "truth beyond all question" represented at the same time the fulfillment of an arduous intellectual process and the explosion of an intuitive illumination:

In the night of thick darkness which envelops the earliest antiquity, so remote from ourselves, there shines the eternal and never-failing light of a truth beyond all question: that the world of human society has certainly been made by men, and its principles are, therefore, to be found within the modifications of our own human mind.   Whoever reflects on this cannot but marvel that the philosophers should have bent all their energies to the study of the world of nature which, since God made it, He alone truly knows; and that they should have neglected the study of the world of nations, which, since men made it, men can truly know.   This aberration was a consequence of that infirmity of the human mind, by which, immersed and buried in the body, it naturally inclines to take notice of bodily things, and finds the effort to attend to itself too laborious.[18]

Men can know their own history because history is subject to "laws" that neither God nor Nature, but men alone, create and that the human mind can understand.   Vico's *verum-factum* is thus the statement of a truly novel identity, the sole one which human understanding can—indeed, must—posit,

---

Vico speaks of Newton and Leibniz as "the two major geniuses [minds] of our time": ".... i primi due ingegni di questa età."   Strangely, the Bergin and Fisch edition of the *New Science*, 62, makes an elision at the point where the parentheses containing that reference to Newton and Leibniz occur.

[18] *La scienza nuova seconda*, I, 117–18; *New Science*, pp. 52–53.   In the quotation given in the text we have left out the concluding simile: ". . . just as the bodily eye sees all objects outside itself but needs a mirror to see itself."

not merely as an epistemological, but as a psychological and moral, dictate of a new historical reason.   Now, that dictate alone can rescue, indeed, redeem, the integrity, autonomy, and dignity of a "logic" of life vaster than Cartesian reason and different from Galilean-Newtonian science.   In the *Scienza nuova* a new philosophy of life constitutes the foundation of a new logic of mind; a new vision of the human world underlies a new philosophy of history and anticipates a metaphysical revolution.   Vico's new historical reason does not detract from the grandeur of mind grappling with the "unknown God" and with the "laws of Nature"; rather, it reasserts the potentialities and reinsures the responsibilities of "intelligence" in the world that men themselves "make."   In this sense, therefore, for Vico it was as if the ancient riddle of freedom and necessity had been implicitly resolved by men's making their own history, insofar as "the world of human society" is at the same time responsive and responsible to their "mind," and their destiny is identical with their doings.   Destiny-as-history is civilization.   Neither Providence nor Necessity, neither Chaos nor Chance, neither Fate nor Accident rules over or dominates the world of human society.   Freedom alone seems to have become a function of the "historic logic" that human life—as action, intelligence, and conscience at the same time—creates through the course and recourse of civilization, of humanity in history.[19]

The fundamental distinction between the world of nature and the world of human society, which Vico regarded as a first, incontestable principle of his "new science," is thus suggestive in its affirmation and implications. The world of nature had by Vico's time been studied, and has continued to be studied, by the mind of man.   Indeed, we now know that it has been "pierced" and "manipulated" in awesome fashion.   But we also know that, despite the stupendous systems and techniques for its "mastery," nature's ultimate principles of being, if not all its modes of operation, have tended to become ever more elusive with practically every stride toward its ultimate conquest.[20]   Ancient and modern cosmological formulations, mathematical theories, astronomical hypotheses, and biophysical systems have all in different ways reflected different, frequently contradictory mental paths to a reality whose mystery has deepened with every giant step taken toward the plucking of its secrets.[21]   Human processes of knowledge of the world of nature,

[19] Guido De Ruggiero, *The History of European Liberalism*, trans. R. G. Collingwood (Boston: Beacon Press, 1959), p. 280.

[20] Cf. J. W. Sullivan, *The Limitations of Science* (New York: Mentor Books, 1949), pp. 125–50.

[21] For vast-ranging and frequently profound discussions of the large scientifico-philosophical problems which I have sought to synthesize through a single sentence in the text, see the contributions of Walter Heitler, Hans Margenau, Hans Reichenbach, F. S. C. Northrop, Leopold Infeld, Herbert Dingle, Kurt Gödel, Aloys Wenzl, and Andrew Paul Ushenko, and Einstein's "Reply to Criticisms" in *Albert Einstein: Philosopher and Scientist*, ed. Paul Arthur Schilpp, 2 vols. (New York: Harper Torchbooks,

however profound the theoretical principles sustaining them and however "verifiable" their practical achievements, have tended to be islands of certainty within the uncharted ocean of truth. Induction and deduction, analysis and synthesis, empiricism and idealism, nominalism and conceptualism, rationalism and mysticism, were, for Vico, genuine but ineffectual instruments or modes of understanding, and, however refined or blunt, they were equally impotent in leading the human mind to "truth" concerning the world of nature and the universe. These diverse labyrinthine itineraries of the human mind in its quest for the "truth" of the realm of nature all met, sooner or later, at a philosophical dead-end which they often mistook for the gate of truth beyond which lay the Absolute or Nothingness. For Vico, the "real" truth of the world of nature is only in the mind of God, for whom "knowing and doing are the same thing." [22]

The human world, on the other hand, has been made, and is continually being made, by men through autonomous acts of creation. Human society and culture, the world of nations and civil orders, systems of thought, scientific doctrines, and mathematical theories, artistic expression, varieties of religious experience, and formulations of secular faiths, principles of justice, spiritual ideals, and images of truth—all these and more are the works of man himself. And, since men have done and do these things in their journey through time, and then, through mind, seek to give them structures of meaning, "men can truly know" the world of human history. *Verum-factum*: this alone was for Vico the indestructible theoretical foundation for men's apprehension of the truth of their human condition as a function of their own historic "doing." [23]

1959), I, 181–98, 245–68, 289–311; II, 387–408, 477–99, 537–54, 557–62, 583–606, 609–45, 665–88.

[22] In *La scienza nuova seconda*, I, 131, Vico's original phrase reads: ".... perocchè in Dio il conoscere e 'l fare è una medesima cosa"; in the Bergin and Fisch's *New Science*, p. 63, the translation reads: ". . . since in God knowledge and creation are one and the same thing."

[23] On the fundamental Vichian principle of *verum factum convertuntur* see Vico's own "anticipated" explanation in his *Della'ntichissima sapienza italica* (1710) in Nicolini's *Opere*, pp. 248-50. The famous *degnità* in *La scienza nuova seconda*, I, 78, which Nicolini believes crystallizes Vico's concept of *verum-factum*, reads as follows in the original: "Natura di cose altro non è che nascimento di esse in certi tempi e con certe guise, le quali sempre che sono tali, indi tali e non altre nascon le cose." The English version by Bergin and Fisch, *New Science*, p. 22, reads: "The nature of institutions is nothing but their coming into being (*nascimento*) at certain times and in certain guises. Whenever the time and guise are thus and so, such and not otherwise are the institutions that come into being." I wanted to call attention to the wider implications of the Italian word *cose* used by Vico, as against the restrictive term "institutions" used in the translation, in order to suggest the larger sphere of application of the Vichian *verum-factum* concept. See Croce, *La filosofia di Giambattista Vico*, pp. 21–35, for an authoritative discussion of Vico's theory of knowledge.

Nothing would perhaps do greater violence to the significance of the Vichian postulate on the convertibility of historic *doing* into human *knowing* than its loose translation into the terms of immediate, and therefore crude or petty, pragmatism.[24] Furthermore, the Vichian formula of *verum-factum* cannot be turned upon its head, as Marx turned Hegel's "idea," without somehow tearing the unique message of the *Scienza nuova* from its truly innovating context. Whatever rapprochement may be discovered between some aspects of the last phase of Vichian thought and the early stages of Descartes' philosophy of reason, Vico cannot thereby be turned into a mere post-Cartesian "rationalist." Whatever "anticipations" of Hegel's system of philosophy may be espied in parts of the Vichian interpretation of history, Vico cannot thereby be converted into a mere proto-Kantian or proto-Hegelian idealist. *Knowing*, for Vico, is more than reason historicized; *doing* is less than history idealized. All these things, and perhaps even others that are similar, should be reiterated lest—as has sometimes occurred even on the part of some of the best-intentioned among students of Vichian thought—Vico be almost totally turned against himself.[25]

Retained, on the other hand, within its proper context of meaning, the Vichian formula of *verum-factum* constitutes, in novel, almost revolutionary form, an alternative, if not a full resolution, of the ancient, ceaseless quest for the "truth" of the human world. For not even his four master guides—Plato, Tacitus, Bacon, and Grotius—had fully charted, Vico felt, all the arduous paths toward the fulfillment of that quest. Despite the stupendous depths of their insights and the sweep of their magnificent glimpses, for none of them had "the eternal and never-failing light of a truth beyond all question" fully broken upon them when they had turned their gaze, as Vico himself was to do, upon "the night of thick darkness" which envelops the origins and development of the world of human society.[26] For Vico that "light" had become a dazzling illumination. And it was then that, Machiavelli-like, if in different spirit and purpose, that "light" had led Vico to his own perilous and wondrous resolve "to open a new route which has

---

[24] The word "pragmatism" is used here as a generalizing concept of varieties of immediate conversions of theoretical thought into types of practical action. On the ways in which such conversions of Vichian thought have been made historically see Croce and Nicolini, *Bibliografia vichiana*, II, 673–78; Nicolini's Introduction to *Opere*, pp. xxx–xxxv; Fisch's Introduction to the *Autobiography*, pp. 99–107.

[25] See Badaloni, *Introduzione a G. B. Vico*, pp. 405–6, for one of the most recent attempts to "convert" Vico into a sort of demiurge who had sketched the general "lines of the historical movement and the theorization of the popular participation" in the social struggles of the age of the Enlightenment in Italy, since it was from Vico that the *illuministi* "abstracted the general scheme of the antifeudal struggle."

[26] See Fisch and Bergin's *Autobiography*, pp. 138–39, 154–55, for Vico's reconstruction and characterization of his ideal encounters with his four master authors, Plato, Tacitus, Bacon, and Grotius.

not yet been followed by anyone," and he, too, had plunged upon the discovery of a new world of human society through the "exploration of unknown seas and continents" of human history.[27]   With the guidance of that "light" Vico had at long last espied the limits, but also the potentialities, of the dialectic of human consciousness and the reality of the world of history. Thus, in an idiom that was as strange as it was audacious, with a certainty that was as wise as it was prophetic, the *Scienza nuova* reasserted in new guise the equilibrium between consciousness and human society, between mind and reality, between life and history—an equilibrium between what men do and what men can know and must understand.   For this reason, above all, the Vichian principles of his "new science" concerning the world of human society may be validly subsumed under the concept of a humanistic science, of an ideal type of a new historical humanism.

II. *Antinomy and Providence in History*

The view here advanced that Vico's *Scienza nuova* contained—in fact, constituted—the first modern revolutionary formulation of a new humanistic science and of historical humanism requires further elaboration from other points of view.   A full-fledged critical textual exegesis is obviously precluded here.   It may, therefore, be desirable to tackle the problem of minimal elucidation through a brief discussion of two major, and at the same time contrasting and related, "attacks" that can be, and have occasionally been, brought against the reduction of Vico's "new science" to historical humanism. Both of these "attacks" have sprung from within rather than from outside the concentric contexts of Vichian thought and modern philosophies of history.   One of these "attacks" raises fundamental questions concerning the idea of providence in Vico's thought; the other poses significant problems related to the Vichian idea of recurrence in history and, therefore, at least by implication, questions the "humanistic" function of Vichian historicism. Both touch upon the very heart of the meaning and structure of Vico's thought in the *Scienza nuova* and are therefore worthy of serious consideration and appraisal.

Not since the Renaissance revival and the Machiavellian revision of the classical function of *Fortuna* had a European philosopher found himself grappling as strenuously as did Vico throughout his mature life in dealing with the double problem of fate and antinomy in human history.[28]   Again

[27] The phrases used in the text are not Vico's but Machiavelli's; see the Introduction to the First Book of *The Discourses* in Niccolò Machiavelli's *The Prince and the Discourses* (New York: Modern Library, 1940), p. 103.

[28] See Paci, *Ingens sylva*, pp. 58–84, 177–78, for an "existentialist" interpretation of "existence and image" in Vichian thought.

and again Vico had keenly seen and reiterated throughout his work that there is recurrently apparent in the world of human society a great contrast, a patent disparity, between actuality and visions of reality. He knew, of course, that, in part, this contrast resulted from the diffraction undergone by reality as it passed through the prism of appearances. But there was more than that at the heart of human history—there was the secret of antinomy, the mystery of the irony of history. These seemed to be perennially pitting ends against means, motives against goals, events against consciousness, result against purpose, necessity against will, fulfillment against desire, consequences against expectations, change against permanence, "providence" against "fate." [29] Now, therefore, for the first time since Augustine had reduced the contrast between the City of God and the earthly city to a providential process pursuing an eschatological finality, Vico confronted the antinomy of history on its own immanent terms, as an inextricable function of the autonomy of the world of human society itself, of the self-determining destiny that men themselves forge for their civilizations. In a word, for Vico the great "contrast" had become the resultant of the ceaseless clash between the expectant rationality of human vicissitude and the freedom of history, between reason and liberty in history. [30]

What Hegel a century later was to call the "cunning of reason," Vico tended to subsume under a novel concept of "providence." [31] When Vico insisted that "this world without doubt has issued from a mind often diverse, at times quite contrary, and always superior to the particular ends that men have proposed to themselves," the meaning of "superior" in that phrase could hardly have been intended to imply a mind beyond, higher, or outside that of humanity itself—unless, of course, the larger context of the logic and

[29] La scienza nuova seconda, II, 164; New Science, pp. 382–83; cf. Nicolini, Commento storico, I, 119 (no. 344), on the Vichian idea of the "heterogony of ends."

[30] For some of the most significant, concordant or contrasting, variants of the new dialectic between "reason and liberty" which I seek to suggest in the text, see De Ruggiero, History of European Liberalism; Paci, Ingens sylva, pp. 217–20; Corsano, G. B. Vico, p. 236; Fubini, Stile e umanità, pp. 221–30, passim. Noteworthy also are the different approaches to this problem in Friedrich Meinecke's Die Entstehung des Historismus, Italian translation by M. Biscione, G. Gundolf, and G. Zamboni, Le origini dello storicismo (Florence, 1954), p. 50; Benedetto Croce, La storia come pensiero e come azione (Bari, 1938), pp. 244–45; Carlo Antoni, La restaurazione del diritto di natura (Venice, 1959), pp. 33–34.

[31] The Vichian concept of "providence" is, of course, one of the most crucial and debated in interpretations of the Scienza nuova; references will be given here to only a few of the most significant contrasting or concordant views among modern Vichian students: Croce, La filosofia di Giambattista Vico, pp. 115–25; Meinecke, Le origini dello storicismo, pp. 41–43; Karl Löwith, Meaning in History (Chicago, 1949), pp. 122–24; Badaloni, Introduzione a G. B. Vico, pp. 289–307, passim; Fausto Nicolini, La religiosità di Giambattista Vico (Bari, 1949), pp. 84–88, 209–13; Paci, Ingens sylva, p. 207; Frederick Copleston, A History of Philosophy, vol. VI: Modern Philosophy (Garden City, N.Y.: Image Books, 1964), pt. I, p. 188.

intention inherent in that assertion were to be almost completely shattered.[32]
Not merely the phrase that precedes that assertion, "It is true that men themselves have made this world of nations," but the vast base of the Vichian
discourse in the *Scienza nuova* upon which that well-nigh concluding maxim
rests, seem to suggest no other fundamental reading than that not the direct
"will of God" but the mind of men, however diverse, contrary, and
superior to "the particular ends" that men propose and envisage, is immanent in history itself.   Seen in this light, in his fashion and for his own
special philosophical purposes, Vico "banished" a transcendent divinity
directly operating in the human-historical world in a manner which only in
this sense seemed analogous to the Galilean-Newtonian vision of the autonomy of the world of nature.   This he did, not because (again like Galileo
and Newton in their sphere) he did not believe that God was in some manner
still in his new world of human history—in some unfathomable way somehow "behind" its "origins"—but rather because, if, as the classic prov-
identialists claimed, God still directly ruled that world, he could hardly be
distinguished, as the monists and pantheists asserted, from a finite world—
however multiple its forms and expressions of civilization might be—in
which he would have to be infinite being.   If the opposing claims were true,
Vico would have had to envision men sharing divinity, not merely through
the chrism of piety and of sacramental bonds, through faith and grace, but
directly, as identity with God, as the fact of human history's always being
"made" in the presence of God.   This, of course, would amount to a
reductio ad absurdum of human self-delusion and folly and would deprive the
world of human history of the very autonomy, "integrity," and responsibility which the *Scienza nuova* had so arduously discovered in that world.
Thus it becomes clear that to have reintroduced *at that point*, toward the very
end of the *Scienza nuova*, the purely Christian idea of providence as the
ultimate arbiter of the antinomy of history would only have signified that
Vico, having let Cartesian reason out the front door of his philosophical
structure, was now, practically in the last moment, willing to re-admit
theological providentialism through the back door.   Some old and new
interpreters of Vichian thought have indeed insisted upon translating Vico's
protestations of personal piety, of religious orthodoxy, of Catholic faith and
Christian devotion, into expressions of theologico-philosophical "consistency."[33]   After the exegetic work of so careful, dedicated, and acute a

[32] Cf. Nicolini, *Commento storico*, I, 138 (no. 385).   There is an interesting reference to
"eminent Catholic writers" who had made efforts "to reduce Vico into an orthodox
thinker" in the Preface to the 1921 edition of Croce's *La filosofia di Giambattista Vico*,
p. x.

[33] Nicolini, *La religiosità*, pp. 19–50, makes a critique of Catholic critics, particularly
Antonio Corsano, who, in the "first" edition of *G. B. Vico*, entitled *Umanesimo e
religione in G. B. Vico* (Bari, 1935), had protested against the reduction of Vico to an
essentially "humanistic" and therefore "immanentist" dimension.   Interesting changes

Vichian scholar as Fausto Nicolini such an interpretation seems at best erroneous and at worst tendentious.   We believe that, however plausible and perhaps "charitable" such translations of the biography of Vico into the philosophy of the *Scienza nuova* may be, they are much too easy, too literal and simplistic, to be really faithful to either the structure or the spirit that informs the Vichian vision, the "new science," of the world of history.

Reduced to its simplest terms, Vico's "providence" was perhaps but another name for the very operation of the complexities of human history which has often been subsumed under the concept of the "irony of history." The proposition that in Vico's view of this there may linger apparently contradictory elements of a Lucretian world vision and, even more problematically, perhaps of a Hermetic image of contrast and concord in the universe of human civilization, is a tantalizing but unsolvable question.[34]   It seems certain that, at its most mysterious, Vico's new "providence" acts as a function of that obscure, unfathomable element, variously consecrated in the traditions of both Occidental and Oriental philosophies, which is by Vico himself fully transmuted and transposed as an immanent force within the most intimate yet elusive and inaccessible recesses of human history.[35]

---

of approach and emphasis are evident when one compares the first and second editions of Corsano's work on Vico.

[34] The great impression made on Vico by the revival of Lucretian and Epicurean doctrines in the Naples of his youth is attested to by practically all those scholars who have written on the Italian aspects of "the crisis of the European conscience" familiarized by the work of Paul Hazard, *The European Mind*.   Whether, and, if so, to what extent, Vico may have felt the influence of other currents of Western and Oriental thought is a more difficult problem.   In connection with the Hermetic tradition in Italy after the execution of Bruno and the death of Campanella, there is no book comparable to that by Frances A. Yates, *Giordano Bruno and the Hermetic Tradition* (Chicago, 1964), on Vico or his contemporaries, nor is there any study of some possible relation between Brunian philosophy and Vichian thought.   One wonders whether, by some chance, Vico may have been "exposed" to Bruno's dialogue *De l'infinito universo et mondi*.   Some fruitful analogies, we believe, could be drawn between Bruno's cosmologic ideas in that work and Vico's historical conceptualizations.   In his *Commento storico*, II, 24–25 (no. 807), Nicolini touches upon the question of a possible exposure of Vico to Bruno's work, particularly to the *Eroici furori* and the *Theses de magia*, and concludes his investigations with the tantalizing comment that it should not be forgotten that Vico was the son of a bookseller and that during his youth he was an eager, if somewhat disorderly, reader of whatever books fell under his eyes in his father's little book-shop: "…. *tra i quali non si può escludere a priori fosse, magari celato in qualche ripostiglio, qualche esemplare di questa o quell'opera bruniana*" (italics added).

[35] See Nicolini, *Commento storico*, I, 193 (no. 473), for a reference to Vico's "anticipations" of the later studies by European students of comparative philology and the history of religions, with the *Avesta* and the *Vedas* as Oriental sources.   Interesting, if hardly documented, references are made by Paci, *Ingens sylva*, p. 176, to "distant worlds mysteriously connected by subterranean currents" of Oriental thought, the Hermetic tradition, and Italian Neo-Platonism in Vico's philosophy of myth and language; but Paci is merely impressionistic.   On the other hand, in impressively more severe style and

Whatever its terminological or conceptual derivation, Vico's new "providence" acts as the principle immanent in the "ultimate" sense and meaning of human history.   As such, therefore, it at the same time encompasses and, paradoxically, truly "transcends" the very dialectic of necessity and freedom in history.   Benevolently creative as it is for the "higher ends" of preserving "the human race upon this earth," Vico's "providence" appears also as a sort of benign "revenge" which time and vicissitude conspire to take upon their restless pursuers—mind, idea, intelligence.   For time and human vicissitude are strange lovers whose secret or open embraces tend to strew a unique progeny of historic realities and purposes and meanings upon the world of human society, and they often defy even the keenest powers of rational analysis and metaphysical divination.

III. *The New Science as Method*

In method, no less than in the substance of principles, the *Scienza nuova* emphasized the connections as well as the distinctions that must be maintained between the "whole" and the "parts" of human doing and knowing. For Vico the method of understanding the "parts" of historic doing—and this, fundamentally, involved the creation of civilization—must be kept distinct but cannot and must not be separated from the vision of the "whole." Difficult as this dualistic procedure may be, it alone safeguards the mind from the pursuit of both transcending abstractions and fragments of reality.   The *real* multiplicity manifested by human history must challenge and be challenged, but it must not be permitted to overwhelm the *ideal* unity required by the coherence of human consciousness.[36]   The "whole" of universal history cannot be apprehended through a single act of the human mind.   If this were possible, the totality of so "cosmic" an operation would indeed make man's mind almost literally capable of a Godlike act of comprehension.   In such a case, history for men would become what nature is for God—the changing but unmoving continuum of an eternal present in which would be destroyed all distinction between existence and being, permanence and mutability, time, vicissitude, and idea.   But the absurdity of such a possibility was, for Vico, implicit in the very nature of man's

---

through almost lapidary phrases, Ernst Cassirer, *The Philosophy of Symbolic Forms*, trans. Ralph Manheim, 3 vols. (New Haven–London, 1965), in I, 149, speaks of Vico as having "posed the problem of language within the sphere of a general metaphysic of the spirit," and in II, 3, refers to Vico as the "founder of the modern philosophy of language" and of "a completely new philosophy of mythology."   In Cassirer there is no mention of the "sources" cited by Paci.

[36] Some eminent students of Vico have, in this and in other connections, more than intimated at a Vichian typology of history—even Croce in *La storia come pensiero e come azione*, p. 66, and, more understandably, Meinecke, in *Le origini dello storicismo*, p. 47.

consciousness, in the very stages intrinsic to the mind's development. For "mind," not only as Cartesian reason, but also as Vichian intelligence, is self-limited in both the modalities and the objects of its apprehension of truth. It is, therefore, exactly the interplay between time and mind that requires and may thus facilitate the operation of modes of understanding of particular historical realities. The dialectic of consciousness and reality reduces historic multiplicity to "objects" comprehensible within the framework of the larger historic process. Thus men must study the nature and meaning of the "parts," but only as a function of their search for the truth of the "whole." Vico was only too acutely aware that the expressions of the historic "whole" may be almost infinitely varied and complex. He knew, moreover, that their investigation and comprehension must proceed according to autonomous principles immanent in their nature. But those principles must not and ought not to be removed from the organic consciousness of the inter-related "modifications" of the human mind. None of the principles governing the pursuit of the "part," of the particular, must by itself be allowed to arrogate to itself the prerogative of absolute primacy among the disciplines of understanding of the human world.

Such a prerogative of absolute primacy had been traditionally claimed, at least in the secular world, by philosophy. By its very nature, philosophy had sought to act as the translator of the "languages" of particular human sciences into the discourse of universal knowledge. Philosophy had asserted the function and role of mediator and interpreter between the "parts" and the "whole" not only of mind in history but of the nature of truth in the cosmic and natural order as well.[37] As self-reflective reason in search of meaning, philosophy had acted as the sustained effort of mind in the search for its own "modes of operation." As a ceaseless endeavor of the human spirit in quest of the boundaries between knowledge and wisdom, philosophy had made men conscious of the limits of necessity and the freedom of the mind. It, too, had been a function of wisdom in the human world as long as it had not confused its limitations with its potentialities in its quest for absolute truth in both the human and the cosmic realms of reality. But now, in Vico's time, in a variety of ways, of which Cartesian rationalism and scientific naturalism were the most significant, philosophy had sought to

[37] For a direct, internal reconstruction of the development of Vico's views on the function of philosophy as they appear distilled in the sections on the elements, the principles, and the method of the *Scienza nuova seconda*, I, 72–131 (*New Science*, pp. 18–65), a systematic study of Vico's analytical works, written during the period of "preparation," particularly his *Il metodo degli studi del nostro tempo* (1708) and *Dell' antichissima sapienza italica* (1710), is indispensable; these works are now easily accessible in Nicolini's *Opere*, pt. II, pp. 169–364. They reveal a sense of depth behind the Vichian maxims which takes them out of the realm of "intuition" and "geniality" to which they have all too often been relegated by hasty and superficial readers of the *Scienza nuova*.

impose a spurious hegemony over the sciences of life. By so doing, for Vico, philosophy had forfeited its prerogative of primacy among avenues to truth. The conversion it had attempted of "parts" of its epistemology and logic into the whole of the human mind's quest for truth in the world of men seemed to testify to a dangerous delusion of grandeur which Vico viewed with increasing impatience. He stood against such a *boria*, such a conceit, with the passionate resistance of a fearless wayfarer who, having espied a new "light" in the "night of thick darkness" which envelops the road to wisdom, sees that "light" put out or dimmed by clouds of philosophical error and intellectual arrogance. It was for this reason that in the *Scienza nuova* Vico had to make a *tabula rasa* of his own in the guise of an almost unique antiphilosophical act of violence (the like of which was not to recur again in the history of Western thought until Marx's rejection of idealism and Nietzsche's defiance of metaphysics) in order to undertake a new quest for the truth of the world of human society.[38] In the making of such an "antiphilosophical" *tabula rasa* lay the true sense of Vico's wondrous and awe-inspiring pristine assumption and hypothesis of labor as it is stated in the *Scienza nuova*: "For purposes of this inquiry," he boldly asserted, "we must reckon as if there were no books in the world."[39] The books of the philosophers had become misleading or irrelevant to the pursuit of a new science of life and of history; they had to be closed or ignored. The burden of philosophy had become unbearably obstructive; it had to be overthrown.

The reconstruction of a new philosophy of life was predicated upon the work of demolition achieved in the beginning of Vico's new science of history. Now new paths had to be broken, fresh methodologies had to be worked out toward the re-analysis of each of the important "parts" in order to better understand the "whole" of the world of human society. Thus, in terms that had not yet been consecrated by taxonomic nomenclature, ethnography and anthropology, psychology and sociology, cultural history and the history of ideas, no less than philology and textual criticism, had to be separately adopted, utilized, and correlated as functions of the larger new science of man.[40] Significant as the innovations in method and substance

[38] That by his own historico-existential *tabula rasa* Vico was, so to speak, turning the Cartesian "model" of the *Discourse on Method* upon its head seems to be quite clear and is agreed upon by all serious students; see, as an example, the opening pages in Croce, *La filosofia di Giambattista Vico*, pp. 1–3.

[39] *New Science*, p. 52; *La scienza nuova seconda*, I, 117: "…. quindi, per questa ricerca, si dee far conto come se non vi fussero lidri nel mondo."

[40] The key point that I wish to make here concerns the "mode of operation" which, for methodological purposes, finds the dialectic of the human sciences constantly moving between separation and correlation, isolation and integration, specificity and universality, in dealing with the understanding of aspects, expressions, and forms of the "world of human society." It is in this context that Vico's axiom, as formulated in *La scienza nuova seconda*, I, 113 (*New Science*, p. 49), "doctrines must take their beginning from that of the matters of which they treat . . . ," must be viewed.

were in these fields, in Vico they were always made to transcend the particularity of their meaning through the universality of their relevance, the unity of their significance. Vico never lost sight of the real unity that binds all historic phenomena and their separate "sciences" to the totality of human experience.

The rediscovery of, and influence exerted by, the *Scienza nuova* during the era of romanticism and historicism lie beyond the scope of this essay. But there is no question that the core of its rich suggestiveness lay exactly in the multiform variety of new approaches to the study of all the fundamental expressions of the world of human society that the "new science" contained.[41] For our purposes a mere descriptive summary of its most significant innovations will have to suffice. The *Scienza nuova* descried the crystallization of custom into systems of law; it sought out the connections between hieratic functions and hierarchical organization; it delved into the origins of social stratification and the rise and decline of institutions; it uncovered the foundations of political regimes in the wake of class struggles and civil conflicts. Cycles of forms of domination—sacerdotal and kingly, oligarchic and democratic, Caesarean and Augustan—the relations between authority and liberty in the rule of the state, the "revolt of the masses" as a phenomenon of moral rebellion, stages in the corrupting influence of power, the metamorphoses of faiths into religions and of religions into creeds, the decay of philosophy into sterile intellectualism, the search for justice and its perversions into official cruelties, the yearning for peace and its abuses for the ends of war, the decline of spiritual values and their transformation into secular passions, the fearful succession of the "barbarism of reflection" to the "barbarism of sense"—all these and more, under different names perhaps, but with similar meaning, were seen by Vico as aspects and functions of historic vicissitude in the world of human society.[42] And he traced also cycles of splendor and heroic action, of achievement and victory, of poetic beauty and spiritual triumph, and of tragedy and death in the courses of the rise and decline of civilizations. This almost infinite variety of expressions of the historic "whole," however, does not fully circumscribe the potentialities that the freedom of history can encompass. There are no iron laws governing human destiny-as-history. Above all, neither the multiplicity nor the antinomy revealed by the manifestation of all the separate "parts" of the "whole" should allow the consciousness of men to lose sight of the essential unity that binds their *historicity* to their *humanity*. It is exactly such

---

[41] Cf. the references in Croce and Nicolini, *Bibliografia vichiana*, II, 525–672, 741–824, on the "fortune" of Vico during the eras of romanticism and historicism. See also the clear, fine synthesis by Erich Auerbach, "Vico and Aesthetic Historism," in his *Scenes from the Drama of European Literature* (New York: Meridian Books, 1959), pp. 183–98. Cf. Fubini, *Stile e umanità*, pp. 211–12, and Paci, *Ingens sylva*, pp. 176–77.

[42] Cf. *La scienza nuova seconda*, II, 157–66, and *New Science*, pp. 375–84, for the "Conclusion of the Work," from which most of generalizations in the text are derived.

a bond that some modern philosophies of history have tended to forsake, thereby contributing to the profound crisis of values which has gripped the human conscience in our time.

IV. *The Idea of Recurrence:* Corsi-Ricorsi

The Vichian concept of the *corsi-ricorsi* of civilization has frequently been seen, even by otherwise sympathetic students of the *Scienza nuova*, as involving a denial of real historic change through its suggestion of an eternal recurrence in the human world.[43] That Vichian concept has been viewed as self-contradictory within the very terms of the Vichian dialectic between the dynamic autonomy, the freedom, of the human mind, which Vico posits, and the static necessity implied by the circularity of historic vicissitudes, with which he appears to delimit it. Needless to say, the modern cyclicalist historicist "philosophers," particularly Spengler and Toynbee, have, with their works, seemed to corroborate, in different but related ways, the anticipated misgivings of even so faithful a Vichian "disciple" as Benedetto Croce.[44] In other quarters, logical critiques have been compounded with analogical judgments to spell an almost full-fledged misinterpretation of the Vichian theory of *corsi-ricorsi*. In the light of the fundamental purport of this essay, an effort on our part toward a restoration of meaning of one of the most crucial aspects of Vico's "new science" must be undertaken. A brief revaluation of the problem and, hopefully, a critical contribution to its proper resolution may at least help to clarify a master idea *implicit* in Vichian thought which I have *explicitly* elaborated upon in different terms and context elsewhere: the idea of the freedom of history.[45]

The modern cyclicalists, whatever the plausibility of their quasi-Vichian

[43] See Löwith, *Meaning in History*, pp. 132–34, for variations on his view that Vico's "typical course of humanity" is "a progression without end and fulfillment," that "history has no fulfillment and solution but is ruled by recurrences," and that it is concerned with "origins" and "foundations" but "not with hope and faith in future fulfillment."

[44] See Croce, *La filosofia di Giambattista Vico*, pp. 127–37, for an attempt at a systematic critique of Vico's theory of *ricorsi* from the point of view of Croce's idealistic philosophy of history. For an almost "final" summation of his critique on the Vichian *corsi-ricorsi* see Croce, *La storia come pensiero e come azione*, p. 70, as rendered in translation by Sylvia Sprigge, *History as the Story of Liberty* (London, 1962), p. 82: "The Italian Vico, it is true, had allowed himself to be oppressed by the idea of 'course' and 'recourse' *as a law of nature imposed upon history*, which only within the limits of that law could move dynamically and dialectically; and thereby he shut off from himself the idea of progress" [italics added]. Croce's phrase "as a law of nature imposed upon history" seems to me at best gratuitous and at worst questionable.

[45] See the summary of my ideas in the brief version of my article on "The Freedom of History," *Colloquium*, 3 (April, 1965): 1–10.

procedure, have utterly shattered the unity of historic structure as well as the potentialities of historic movement which sustain the Vichian dialectic of consciousness and reality.[46] By their reduction of "recurrence" to a series of self-enclosed historical cycles, Spengler and Toynbee deny not only the freedom of history but also the universality of civilization. For them, the disjointed plurality of cultures is only too tenuously held together by the bonds of biological analogy and morphological similarity. The modern cyclicalists have thus done for the world of human society what Vico never granted could or should be done with separate aspects of a single culture. The nine cultures of the Spenglerian pattern and the twenty-odd civilizations of Toynbee's charts are essentially new phenomena of "nature," biophysical cycles of human life and decline and death under the semblance of "historic" stars and suns and cold moons that momentarily appear, shine, flicker, and vanish into a Lucretian universe of silence and meaninglessness.[47] For Spengler and Toynbee, civilizations live and die *alone*, as complete strangers to one another despite their brief encounters and contacts and conflicts, as if hopelessly "alienated" from one another, exactly because they possess no immanent principle of unity to bind them to some common meaning. There is no possibility of self-recognition among them beyond the narcissistic reflections of themselves in their separate dark historic mirrors. In the civilizations of Spengler and Toynbee, morphological similitude and analogical destiny cannot but be quasi-naturalistic fictions imposed upon them by their historians. In Spengler and Toynbee the plurality of historical cycles tends to constitute only a sort of purely nominalistic inscription upon a non-existent membership list of an anarchic society of civilizations. The societies and cultures, the nations and peoples, the arts and sciences, the philosophies and the faiths, that together go under the name of "civilization" seem to assume the guise of historical Pirandellian "characters in search of an author" of a play that never finds a common theme. The Spenglerian-Toynbeean cycles of "civilizations" will never find an "author" nor will they recognize a common bond and theme, exactly because they are only,

---

[46] See the interesting summation on philosophers of cyclical history by Frank E. Manuel, *The Shapes of Philosophical History* (Stanford, 1965), pp. 153–58. H. Stuart Hughes, *Oswald Spengler: A Critical Estimate* (New York, 1962), pp. 37–40, mentions, briefly, Joachim of Floris and, more extensively, Vico as the two "precursors" whom the cyclical historians "might have regarded with reverence."

[47] For sustained critical analyses of Spengler and Toynbee conducted from very different points of view, see Alfredo Galletti, *Natura e finalità della storia nel moderno pensiero europeo: Dalla storia filosofica allo storicismo idealistico* (Milan, 1953), pp. 365–417, on Vico, briefly, then on Spengler and Toynbee; Pietro Rossi, *Lo storicismo contemporaneo tedesco* (Turin, 1953), pp. 389–437, on Spengler; Pietro Rossi, *Storia e storicismo nella filosofia contemporanea* (Milan, 1960), pp. 69–89, 333–60, on Toynbee and Spengler; Pieter Geyl, *Debates with Historians* (New York, 1956), pp. 91–178, on Toynbee and Sorokin.

inescapably, prisoners of their own self-images. Indeed, since those "civilizations" are endowed with absolutely no universal principle of the historic drama of which they are "actors," they would not even know in what "idiom" they should recite their parts. For the modern cyclicalists, "civilizations" are single and self-contained, as if mere "existential" islands unto themselves, lonely reefs of time upon which human history briefly lives and then dies numerous deaths as again and again *that* history becomes submerged into a sea of nothingness.[48]

The Vichian concept of *corsi-ricorsi* has only the vaguest and most superficial resemblance to contemporary cyclical-historicist theories. No less than Dante and Galileo, whose language he uses in a different quest, Vico would first of all have abhorred the aesthetic disorder and then the ethical confusion implicit in Spengler's and Toynbee's cyclical systems. Further, it is as if Vico anticipated and obviated a whole series of philosophical "dangers" that these philosophers of history have not avoided. For Vico, the greatest of these "dangers" had by his time consisted of eschatological mysticism, metaphysical providentialism, naturalistic immanentism, and their varieties.[49] Now, contrary to those interpreters—and, as we have previously suggested, among them must be counted even so uniquely faithful a Vichian student as Benedetto Croce—who for different reasons have tended to regard the Vichian idea of *corsi-ricorsi* as at best mistaken, at worst contradictory, and at least superfluous, we view that idea as indispensably, irremovably central to the substantive and methodological *raison d'être* of the *Scienza nuova*. Seen, as it must be, in the perspective of Vico's concept of "ideal eternal history" (*storia ideale eterna*), which provides the larger contextual "logic" of civilization, the Vichian idea of *corsi-ricorsi* in human history serves a decisive philosophical function.[50] Together, the idea of *corsi-ricorsi* and the concept of *storia ideale eterna* constitute at most the real binding principle and at least the ideal framework of the "new science" of history. For, if with the idea of

[48] Most of the students and critics of Spengler and Toynbee cited in notes 46 and 47 above have, it seems to me, isolated and appraised the more evident historicist, naturalistic, or typological aspects of modern cyclical history. A critical re-reading of parts of Spengler's *The Decline of the West* and of portions of Toynbee's *A Study of History*, with Vico's *Scienza nuova* as a major, and philosophically active, point of reference, has led me to adopt the quasi-"existentialist" interpretation and critique that I have suggested in the text of this essay.

[49] Cf. the Introduction to Fisch and Bergin's *Autobiography*, pp. 38–45, *passim*. Having been "through" them in his youth and during the period of "preparation" for the writing of the *Scienza nuova*, even in its "negative" form (the *first* 1725 version), Vico could not, it seems to me, "return" to Augustinian and Joachimite eschatology, Thomistic providentialism, and Lucretian naturalism any more than, even after the "second" version (of 1730), he could "return" to and accept in its pristine form Cartesian "reason."

[50] See *La scienza nuova seconda*, I, 97, 128, 152–59, and *New Science*, pp. 37, 62, 79–84, for Vico's recurrent, insistent variations on the theme of *storia ideale eterna* as both the foundation and the capstone of his vision of human history.

corsi-ricorsi Vico wants to account for movement, change, and development in human history, through the concept of *storia ideale eterna* he seeks to relate mutability to a "fixed point," to a principle of permanence, of continuity, and of universality. The relationship between *corsi-ricorsi* and *storia ideale eterna* spells the highest, the most intimate, "universe of discourse" in the Vichian philosophy of history.

A closer look, from a different angle of vision, at this novel Vichian dialectic between movement and permanence in history may perhaps help to clarify its revolutionary import. If it be firmly, clearly, unequivocally understood that the Vichian principle of the universality of human history cannot by any stretch of the imagination be *really* identified with a basic postulate of physico-mathematical science, then *storia ideale eterna* may be hypothesized as the *constant* "space"—the realm of "permanence"—struck by, so to speak, the *variable* constituted by the "time" of history (*corsi-ricorsi*). Given the basic principles of the "new science," it becomes evident that the "space-constant" without the "time-variable," and vice versa, cannot but imply a return either to a metaphysics of eternalism or to a doctrine of naturalism. As a matter of fact, if properly understood in the context of Vico's thought, the juxtaposition of the two terms "constant" and "variable" amount to the suggestion of a uniquely Vichian "space-time continuum."[51] Within that "continuum" human history has persisted in ceaseless change. "Space" (*storia ideale eterna*) as the postulate of permanence and "time" (*corsi-ricorsi*) as the principle of mutability make no "sense" except as functions of each other. For "space-permanence" insures the idea of an immanent "absolute" within the structure of the universality of the human mind while "time-mutability" safeguards the idea of the temporal "relativity" of human history. In the interplay of permanence and change, of universality and plurality, of continuity and movement, may be said to

---

[51] The brief section on Vico in Stephen Toulmin and Jane Goodfield's *The Discovery of Time* (New York: Harper Torchbooks, 1966), pp. 125–29, deals with the problem of time in the *Scienza nuova* as a function of *Kronos* rather than as a human-historical reflection of "cosmos." From the point of view of methodology at least, George Kubler, *The Shapes of Time: Remarks on the History of Things* (New Haven, Conn., 1965), pp. 12–14, 16–24, 96–122, offers approaches to time in history which are potentially more creative than those found in more complicated works; although there is no mention of Vico in Kubler's book, he seems to be much closer to the Vichian concept of time than is apparent on a first reading. On Kubler's ideas see the perceptive comments by Siegfried Kracauer, "Time and History," *History and Theory*, 6 (1966): 67–69. In R. Klibansky and H. J. Paton's *Philosophy and History: Essays Presented to Ernst Cassirer* (Oxford, 1936), pp. 35–52, 91–105, 107–23, Guido Calogero, Giovanni Gentile, and L. Susan Stebbing deal differently with the problem of time in history. One of the most stirring pieces of contemporary writing on the related problems of time and terror, freedom and faith, in human history, as that history appears from both the linear and the cyclical angles of vision, is contained in Mircea Eliade's *Cosmos and History: The Myth of the Eternal Return* (New York: Harper Torchbooks, 1959), pp. 141–62.

lie the outermost sphere of the postulates of Vico's "new science." The modes of human thought, the "modifications" of the human mind, as Vico calls them, grappling with the works, with the manifestations, of historic doing, represent the inner concentric circles within that "higher" sphere. The poetic metamorphosis of human history in Dante's *Divine Comedy* finds an exquisite counterpart in the historical metamorphosis of poetic intelligence in Vico's *Scienza nuova*.[52]   The very structure, real and symbolic, of Vichian thought satisfies some of the most legitimate requirements of the human mind in its quest for wisdom, without sacrificing some of the most irrepressible demands of the human spirit in its search for intellectual beauty.   Vico's "new science" succeeded in attaining, in its highest reaches, that conceptual and aesthetic balance, that historical and vital equilibrium between reality and a vision of the world which again and again has been strenuously sought by other men, through other paths, in other fields of human endeavor and creativity.[53]

The mind's search for truth at some moment requires at least the hypothesis of an essential order and unity, if not *outside*, in the elusive "substance" of reality, then *within*, in the very structure of its vision of the world.   The *Scienza nuova* transmuted substance and structure but without recourse to such rigid and formalized alternatives as are to be found in Platonic and Hegelian idealism, on the one hand, or in Cartesian rationalism and Marxist materialism, on the other.   Viewed in terms of method, the Vichian idea of *corsi-ricorsi* fused with the concept of *storia ideale eterna* to offer a vision of the unifying threads that bind, in fact and in theory, the otherwise senselessly atomistic cycles of the Spenglerian-Toynbeean patterns of "civilizations." Unlike those cycles, Vico's *corsi-ricorsi* are bound by a common yet immanent participation in a drama of *civilization*, of universal history, that gives ideal meaning to their separate and particular destinies.   In the words of a perceptive student of Vico: ". . . The *ricorsi* describes the path which history traverses between the pluralism of the world of nations and the absolute ideal unity of universal history."[54]   This "ideal unity of universal history" may

---

[52] By the very title of his "essay" on Vico, Paci, in his *Ingens sylva*, seeks to make explicit his idea that the intellectual "journey" undertaken by Vico through the historical world of the "human comedy" was analogous to Dante's quest through the spiritual world of the *Divine Comedy*: at the start of Vico's journey Dante's "*selva oscura*" has become "*ingens sylva*." In Paci's work (pp. 14–15) it is more than suggested that metamorphosis and fulfillment occur, almost without any "mediations," from the personal-existential needs and desires expressed in Vico's *Autobiografia* to the historico-universal world of the *Scienza nuova*.

[53] For an exploration of some of the other "paths" I am seeking to suggest see especially Susanne K. Langer, *Philosophy in a New Key* (New York: New American Library [Mentor Books], 1962).

[54] A. Robert Caponigri, *Time and Idea: The Theory of History in Giambattista Vico* (London, 1953). In the *New Science*, p. 62, Vico's own reiterated concept reads: "Our

perhaps seem to constitute and set the limits of the "outermost" forms that historic reality can attain and that the "modifications" of the human mind can encompass. On the contrary, as we now know, even beyond the highest reach of Vico's imaginative configurations, the concept of the "ideal unity of universal history" extends practically to the boundaries of the Absolute the relativity of the freedom of history.

Conclusion: The Humanity of History

The possibility of a stupendous metamorphosis of historic fatality into human liberty had been implicit in Vico's vision of the world of history. The circles of the relative wherein freedom and necessity grappled over man's fate had been transformed into functions of a new absolute that was Godlike but not divine: the "providence" immanent in history which secured the ends of "the human race upon this earth." The bonds between the pluralism in the world of human society and the ideal unity of mankind, the universality of civilization, had been keenly perceived and subtly descried in the universe of discourse of Vico's "new science." Thus, in the form of a new science of history, Vico had re-created a new philosophy of life. In this philosophy of life, historicity and humanism fused to suggest new paths toward an equilibrium between the freedom of the mind and the burden of history which had been repeatedly glimpsed in the great, long Socratic quest that characterized the spiritual history of the West and which was revitalized through the Renaissance "philosophy of man." It is true that successive waves of other spiritual or vitalistic and activistic alternatives continued to vie, before and after Vico, for mastery over the human mind and the world of human society. Again and again those alternatives have read contrasting or contradictory meaning into human vicissitudes and man's fate in history. Their force is not yet spent. Indeed, their varieties have multiplied and the conflict among them has become fiercer. The great issues at stake in their struggles for supremacy will perhaps never be fully resolved, at least not so long as the human mind retains its birthright and continues to pursue truth by the light of its humanity, under the guidance of some forms of reason and liberty. One thing we know: the "ideal unity of universal history" has been questioned and denied, attacked and violated, but it has not yet been utterly shattered by even the most savage blows of unreason and nihilism.

In his unique spiritual quest, Giambattista Vico sketched and in large part filled in the grand outlines of a new historical humanism which, bound as it was to the tradition of the Renaissance philosophy of man, reasserted in novel

---

Science therefore comes to describe at the same time an ideal eternal history traversed in time by the history of every nation in its rise, development, maturity, decline, and fall."

guise Pico della Mirandola's vision of man standing "at the center of the world" and Leonardo's view that "man is the model of the world." In the *Scienza nuova* Vico discovered and lighted "the never-failing light of a truth beyond all question": that, in "the night of thick darkness" which might, which can, re-engulf mankind in this our own historic epoch, we, who believe ourselves spectators, but are in fact the true actors, who consider ourselves contemplators, but are the sole protagonists of a drama that concerns the fate of humanity in history, must not, dare not, lose sight of the quintessence of the Vichian message—man makes his own history. The fullest meaning of this truth has perhaps not yet been actively understood, and its implications have therefore been blurred or repudiated by those who have corrupted its imperative demands by turning that truth upon its head in order to claim History as the maker of their "fate." Thus, that truth has been killed again and again, every time and in each place where "the terror of history" has been allowed to persist or to run amok in the world of human society. For that truth cannot live except through the fusion of the spheres of individual and collective historic action and through the bond that renders man's creative autonomy and his direct responsibility in history functions of each other. Through that fusion and that bond alone can faith re-enter history and *help to lighten, but not to lift*, the burden of the tragedy and the guilt for the "terror" in history. Perhaps only in this manner can men help to transform the bondage of time and vicissitude into the truly redemptive mission of human freedom.

Raffaello Franchini   VICO, HISTORICAL
METHODOLOGY, AND
THE FUTURE OF PHILOSOPHY

To those familiar with the themes and problems of historicism in its most
mature form, a discourse on Vico may seem almost superfluous since his
majestic meditation has penetrated so deeply into the body of the most
advanced philosophy of our own day that even to "think" seriously without
considering him would be truly difficult.   This does not mean that the most
advanced areas of thought, like those of civilization, exactly because they are
such, necessarily constitute if not a common, at least an easily and widely
accessible, patrimony.   Vichian ideas are difficult, even if they seem familiar
and "catchy," and it is not by chance that three centuries after the birth of
the great thinker they retain intact their fascination and their capacity to
stimulate and to act as tests of verification for some of the most diverse
methodological and hermeneutic experiences.   And it is not rash to prophesy,
or at least to suppose, that even in the future the texts of the Neapolitan
philosopher will continue to be accompanied by incomprehension and
misunderstanding, since their very notoriety, as indeed is the case with all
classics, will always run ahead of a genuine and sympathetic knowledge of
them.

Of all this, which is testimony to the value, that is, to the rarity, of the
works of human genius, Vico himself was conscious.   On the morrow of the
publication of the *Scienza nuova*, he not only declared that he had intended
to address himself to the wise, "who always and everywhere have been very
few: not [to] men who crib from others' books . . . but [to] men of the
loftiest intellect, of a learning all their own, generous and great-hearted,
whose only labor is to enrich with deathless works the commonwealth of
letters," [1] but he also added that "the book has been issued in an age in which,
in the expression of Tacitus where he reflects upon his times so similar to our
own, '*corrumpere et corrumpi "saeculum" vocatur*,' and therefore, as a book
which either repels or disturbs a great many people, it cannot gain universal
applause," because "the only books that are liked are those which, like
dresses, follow the styles." [2]   In thus speaking with Stoic contempt for

[1] See the letter to Bernardo Maria Giacco, October 25, 1725, in Vico, *Opere*, ed.
F. Nicolini (Milan-Naples, 1953), pp. 118–19.
[2] See the letter to G. L. Esperti, 1726, in *ibid.*, pp. 127–28.

immediate success, in the proud certainty of his "deathless" destiny as a
thinker, Vico quietly singled out the attitude of those authors "who love to
enjoy their fame while still alive and [seek] to unite a seasonable glory with
utility and [to] gain money through their books" by "turning their pens to
the taste of the times so that they might fly more rapidly according to the
times." [3]

Who could claim that, beyond the obvious changes which have occurred
in three centuries, the situation is substantially changed? Have conformism
and canonical obedience to literary and philosophical styles perchance been
forever overcome? However different and varied the conditions and possibilities of life which a thinker faces in our day, the dangers to which the
very nature of his mission exposes him have remained substantially the same;
and yet, when all is taken into consideration, those dangers are worth facing,
because a closer look will reveal that they constitute the thinker's very title
of honor if not altogether his very *raison d'être*. For, the philosophy which,
as Hegel observes, expresses its own time in the form of the concept, that is,
in the highest and most accomplished manifestation of concrete speculative
needs, is one thing, while that *Mockphilosophie* of which Shaftesbury spoke
when he contraposed it to *Homephilosophie*—as an eternal moment of that
philosophy which retires upon itself, refuses all vulgar clamor and applause,
and ideally links itself with its great historical past in projecting itself toward
the future—is another.

Vico is modern; he is a necessary component of whatever speculative effort
might today be undertaken with any hope of success. And since for men—
to paraphrase a saying of the young Goethe—it is impossible to detach the
past from a vision of the present, in our opinion it is impossible to "rethink"
Vico by transcending those interpretative categories which we are wont to
utilize. Vico is present, alive, and active in anyone who feels himself engaged
in the perennial labor of reconstruction which, through its very nature, is the
task of philosophizing. For, in an age of abstract rationalism and extreme
scientism, Vico dared to return to the humanistic tradition in order to deepen
it and vivify it through contact with history, and thus to discover and
rediscover—as always happens with true thinkers who never throw away
tradition (of which they feel themselves children)—the purity and autonomy
of the philosophical method. And, because the demonstration of such an
autonomy was not pursued by him through a dialogic and ethical process, as
Socrates had done, but rather through a renewal and application of the
Baconian *cogitare et videre* to history,[4] Vico could at last and with good right
cry out his *eureka* and proudly call *new* his science, a philosophy which
redressed a long-standing error into which past speculation had fallen. Vico
was able to achieve such a "correction" through a grandiose rethinking of

[3] *Ibid.*, p. 128.
[4] Vico, *Scienza nuova*, par. 359, in Nicolini's *Opere*, p. 106.

man as a historical being whose very obscure origins were at last to be illuminated by his new methodology:

But in the night of thick darkness enveloping the earliest antiquity, so remote from ourselves, there shines the eternal and never failing light of a truth beyond all question: that the world of civil society has certainly been made by men, and that its principles are therefore to be found within the modifications of our own human mind. Whoever reflects on this cannot but marvel that the philosophers should have bent all their energies to the study of the world of nature, which, since God made it, He alone knows; and that they should have neglected the study of the world of nations, or civil world, which, since men had made it, men could come to know. This aberration was a consequence of that infirmity of the human mind by which, immersed and buried in the body, it naturally inclines to take notice of bodily things, and finds the effort to attend to itself too laborious; just as the bodily eye sees all objects outside itself but needs a mirror to see itself.[5]

The new method was at the same time—as has often been remarked by the best students of Vico—both anti-Cartesian and Cartesian: it challenged abstract naturalistic rationalism by calling the attention of the philosopher to the matter that was humanly closest to him, history; but it did not, in its turn, commit the error of placing itself outside Cartesian experience, for it pointed out a new dimension of self-consciousness when it insisted upon the necessity of the mind's learning the art of seeing itself with an eye which was no longer bodily but spiritual. Now, this was exactly what Descartes himself had insisted should be done—the Descartes, that is, whose figure was much more complex and profound than was suspected by the Cartesians, who were too easily inclined to ignore the lessons of the classics and to be satisfied with immediate evidence, victims of the pleasant illusion of "learning much in brief" ("*d'apparar molto in brieve*"). The master himself, however, as Vico saw, "despite the fact that he dissembles it with great art in words, was most proficient in every sort of philosophy; a most celebrated mathematician as the world knew him, he lived a very retired life and, what is more important, [possessed] a mind whose like not every century can offer."[6]

In this manner the new methodology constructed and proposed by Vico was the precise contrary of what it is too often judged to be. For it was not part of a philosophy of history[7] but rather of a philosophy of the spirit; better still, that methodology was *an organ of historical knowledge* such as to

---

[5] *Ibid.*, par. 331; Bergin and Fisch translation, p. 479.

[6] Vico, "Seconda risposta al 'Giornale dei letterati,'" in Nicolini's *Opere*, p. 362.

[7] This is the traditional view, reflected recently in J. Thyssen, who, in his *Geschichte der Geschichtsphilosophie* (Bonn, 1954), p. 43, writes: "the word 'philosophy of history' (*Geschichtsphilosophie*) comes from Voltaire, but the discipline from Vico." Thus Thyssen obscures the distinction that both language and usage require between *Geschichtsphilosophie* in a modern and methodological sense and *Philosophie der Weltgeschichte* in the Hegelian, metaphysical sense.

satisfy through anticipation the typical exigency of the most mature historiographic thought of the nineteenth century.   For Vico was that "Bacon of
the historical sciences" whose advent Droysen invoked in 1857 and whose
prefiguration he perceived only in Wilhelm von Humboldt.[8]   Vico had
indeed been that "Bacon," since it was he who had drawn inspiration for his
masterpiece from the first of his "four authors" and had given his own work
a title which can be considered almost an ideal anagram of the *Novum
organum*; and it was Vico who had conducted in the field of history the same
battles against the *idola*, that is, against the prejudices and false beliefs of
traditionalism and dogmatism, which Bacon had waged in the sphere of the
natural sciences.   These historical *idola*—as Collingwood, guided by Croce,
summarizes them[9]—were the conceits (*borie*) of the ancients, of nations, and
of scholars, that is to say, the tendency to attribute illustrious and rational
origins to things and to the sciences, whereas the beginnings of mankind
were uncertain and dramatically barbaric; the idea that nations succeed one
another with almost scholastic rhythm, learning from one another the principles of law and of the arts, whereas every nation is a historical formation
all its own which derives from the universal nature of man; and, lastly, the
prejudice that the ancients were better informed than the moderns in
reference to their own times (in the refutation of this prejudice lies a principle
of historical methodology ever more widespread in our own day, for, being
under the impression that, on the contrary, knowledge of the past depends in
ever greater measure on what the future will be in a position to discover
concerning the genesis of events, we tend to place historiographic activity in
larger perspective).[10]

Vico, therefore, is the anti-Descartes and the new Bacon.   There is enough
here to grant Vico full membership in the inner circles of the history of
modern philosophy, and to recognize his non-anachronism, on the one hand,
and his capacity to anticipate future developments, on the other.   For,
toward both "fathers" of modern thought Vico adopted an attitude of
severe criticism, not one of passive acceptance, conscious as he was (as we
have pointed out above) that those who lead knowledge forward are not
mere erudites or weary repeaters of others' doctrines, but rather are those who
innovate through "hard and continual meditation" ("*aspra e continova
meditazione*") on truth, without ever artificially deviating from the progressive line of history or of tradition itself.   And, for Vico, the discoverer
of philosophy as an organ of historical knowledge (witness his celebrated

8 Cf. J. G. Droysen, *Historik . . .*, ed. R. Hübner (Munich, 1960), p. 324.

9 R. G. Collingwood, *The Idea of History* (Oxford, 1949), pp. 68–69, and B. Croce,
La filosofia di Giambattista Vico, 6th ed. (Bari, 1962), pp. 162–65.

10 Droysen, *Historik*, pp. 265–68, and E. H. Carr, *What is History?* (New York, 1962),
p. 173; cf. my own *Teoria della previsione* (Naples, 1964), and my review of Carr's book
in *La logica della filosofia* (Naples, 1967), pp. 242–48.

formula on the unity of philosophy and philology, *geminae o*
is something more profound than the discovery of the auto
therefore historical—character of the philosophical method, so
important than the necessity, upon which he insisted, of utilizi
in its more congenial field of history. For Vico, philosop
abstract methodology which can, even successfully, be applied to an object,
even to a "sympathetic" object; on the contrary, it is conceivable only as a
historical relationship, as a concrete inquiry into concrete matter. And,
despite the apparent suggestions in certain famous Vichian maxims, neither
is that methodology a metaphysical key capable of opening all doors. It is
true that Vico speaks of "universal history," that he theorizes upon an ideal
eternal history (*"storia ideale eterna"*), upon which (and not within which) the
particular histories of nations run their course, and, finally, that he is convinced that he is giving us a "reasoned civil theology of divine providence."
Nevertheless, how difficult would be a comparison between his "monstrous"
masterpiece (which is "monstrous" in the way that the *Divine Comedy* and
the *Phenomenology of the Spirit* are "monstrous") and the lucid universal
histories and the well-ordered philosophies of history of the age of the
Enlightenment!

Vico's true aim was not, and could not be, the narration of the universal
history of mankind; rather, it was the discovery of the universality of history,
of the supreme laws that govern it and that are immanent in its very process,
just as the reconstructive activity of the historian-philosopher is immanent
within the process. For the Vichian formulation of a theory of history,
despite the frequent and inevitable mixture in it of historical metaphysics and
an empirical science of society—as Croce in due time pointed out[11]—
develops as concrete historical inquiry, not only in the two best-known
historical passages of the *Scienza nuova* (that is, in the pages on Homer
and on the Law of the Twelve Tables), but also in the recurring inquiries
(philological, juridical, political, aesthetic, mythological) that are found
on practically every page of Vico's work. For his is a history not simply
of ideas but also of the customs and facts of the human race; that is, it
is indeed a history of ideas, but one that sets them within terms of "times
and places," of "when and where these human thoughts were born."
Thus, through the aid of a—so to speak—metaphysical or ideal geography
and chronology, Vico makes use of a continually critical and hermeneutic
procedure, which is itself a moment of the very history he is describing:

Now, as geometry, when it constructs the world of quantity out of its elements, or
contemplates that world, is creating it for itself, just so does our Science [create for
itself the world of nations], but with a reality greater by just so much as the institutions
having to do with human affairs are more real than points, lines, surfaces, and figures
are. And this very fact is an argument, O reader, that these proofs are of a kind

[11] Croce, *La filosofia di Giambattista Vico*, pp. 34 and 149ff.

divine and should give thee a divine pleasure, since in God knowledge and creation are one and the same thing.[12]

The "new science" is, therefore, nothing but philosophy understood in its modern sense, a philosophy which definitely has burned the bridges that lead back to naturalism and abstract rationalism. For the metaphysics of nature the new science has substituted a metaphysics of mind which, strictly speaking, is not metaphysics but the history of human ideas concretely conditioned in time and space. *Avant la lettre* of Kant and Hegel, it has unified the truth of reason and the truth of fact in a synthesis of philosophy and philology. While on the one hand it has reasserted the sentimental and fantastic character of poetry and the economic character of bonds of dependence, it has, on the other, rejected with no less vigor the rationalistic interpretation and the abstract overcoming of the religious factor in history by placing it at the beginning of the moral and civil life of mankind.

If all this is true—as it has been amply demonstrated to be true by the best interpreters and continuers of Vichian thought during the last half-century and in a singular way by the study of Benedetto Croce—and granting the possibility that many of the numerous suggestions contained in Vico's thought (which, many-sided as it is, is furthermore frequently, almost proverbially, agitated and even confused in its exposition) may be further developed in diverse directions, the path to pursue is sufficiently clear. In fact, that path has already been beaten and widened in the attempt to join the highest points of Vico's meditation to contemporary philosophy and even to that of the future. For the famous definition of Kant is still valid insofar as it justly claims that the real task lies not in philosophy but in philosophizing. Even apart from those many and often unsuspected cases in which Vichian thought has constituted an efficacious stimulus of primary importance within the body of fundamental or significant developments of contemporary European and world thought—from Gadamer[13] to Löwith,[14] from Thyssen[15] to Jaspers,[16] from Widgery[17] to Gardiner[18]—there is still enough to indicate how varied and impressive the vital presence of Vichian thought has been and in what directions of philosophical inquiry it can still further prove fruitful.

[12] *Scienza nuova*, in Nicolini's *Opere*, par. 349; Bergin and Fisch translation, p. 489.

[13] Cf. H. G. Gadamer, *Wahrheit und Methode: Grundzüge einer philosophischen Hermeneutik* (Tübingen, 1960), pp. 16ff.

[14] Cf. K. Löwith, *Weltgeschichte und Heilsgeschehen* (Stuttgart, 1961), chap. VI.

[15] Cf. Thyssen, *Geschichte der Geschichtsphilosophie*, p. 43, and by the same author, *Der philosophische Relativismus* (Bonn, 1946), p. 47.

[16] Cf. K. Jaspers, *Vom Ursprung und Ziel der Geschichte* (Zurich, 1949).

[17] A. G. Widgery, *Interpretations of History from Confucius to Toynbee* (London, 1961), pp. 152–57.

[18] P. Gardiner, ed., *Theories of History* (Glencoe, Ill., 1960), which opens with a long extract from bk. I of the *Scienza nuova*.

First of all, any speculative inquiry which is truly conscious of its ends and duties cannot, under pain of becoming alienated from the concreteness and reality which constitute history, transcend the Vichian discovery of the unity of philosophy and philology.   This is the original and yet unsurpassed definition of the unity of philosophical thought not with its own history (which is a position typically and orthodoxically Hegelian), but only with history in general.   Thought as a metaphysical or empiricist abstraction cannot but remain confined in the inevitably practical field of finite intellect: the latter may claim to break its necessary bonds with the infinite, that is, with the All, but it forsakes how *this* consists always of the part dialectically conjoined with the individually specified but infinite manifestations of the whole.   Vico's insistence on the double deficiency of his own times, which found, on the one hand, philosophers neglecting to verify their affirmations through the authority of the philologists and, on the other, the latter refusing to validate their findings through the truths discovered by the former, is today no less valid; indeed, it is even more relevant, and it could constitute a bridge between the Kantian-Hegelian-Crocean conception of the concept, in its modern form as judgment, and certain a-dialectical tendencies of contemporary philosophy, such as Husserl's phenomenology and logical empiricism.   Insofar as other tendencies are concerned, whether of idealistic or of Marxist origin, a reappraisal of the relation established by Vico between philosophy and the "real" could, if it is opportunely filtered through a more modern and sharper experience, prove of great aid in clearing the mind of prejudices that have been handed down and passively followed according to set traditions.

Within a context of reappraisal, another essential point which, if it was not coherently theorized by Vico, is nevertheless deducible from his tortured but always illuminating pages, could be pursued: it is that which concerns the peculiarity of historico-philosophical knowledge and its absolute autonomy vis-à-vis the abstracting operations that the intellect conducts for practical ends in the field of nature.   And here, of course, the discourse should be deepened and widened since, on one side, it would require a further explanation of how Vico, while he attributed a greater reality to history than to mathematics, certainly had no intention of holding the latter field in contempt.   For mathematics, as well as for science in general and for scientific progress, as his admirable oration *De mente heroica* demonstrates, Vico nourished an admiration and trust without bounds, undoubtedly not inferior to those of the most convinced representatives of the age of the Enlightenment.   On another side, it would be equally necessary to clarify how the revival of interest in our day in the autonomy of historico-philosophical knowledge and of the distinction it implies between cognitive and practical activity can no longer signify a resumption *sic et simpliciter* of Dilthey's thematic analysis that separated the fields and objects of *Natur-* and *Geistes-wissenschaften*.   For, on the contrary, the two fields are not rigidly divisible and pertinent only to their respective realms as such, that is, to the sciences and to philosophy-history, but rather adhere to their gnoseological and practical forms, which do not cease operating *within* that somewhat extrinsic, if in its own time and manner beneficent and praiseworthy, partition. Anyone who wishes to see the Vichian conception become revivified through contact with new problems of contemporary speculation must be aware that that conception is not, and does not wish to be, characterized as a proud but sterile refusal of science in the name of a recourse to a rhetorical humanism which, as such, would certainly be no less abstract than the world of the empirical sciences to which it would be opposed. Instead, what that conception entails is a view of a harmonious coexistence of all branches of knowledge in the great tree of the civil progress of mankind [19]—a coexistence which implies, therefore, not a contraposition but rather a distinction of methods, of aims, and of interests in the unity of critical, that is, of methodological-philosophical consciousness.

Another fundamental point the further elaboration of which contemporary philosophy can with certain profit take up again from the texts of the great Neapolitan thinker is the sentimental—fantastic, creative, and therefore cognitive—conception of poetry and language. The wonder-filled Vichian pages that deny Homer a hidden wisdom and indirectly also deny Dante the greatness of a poet for whatever the *Comedy* retains of an intellectualistic structure, are nothing but concrete expressions of a new aesthetics. As such they are part of a barely sketched but coherent and, even in its rough form, grandiose philosophy of spirit which, in its own state, cannot be transferred naturally into the world of contemporary thought, at least not before it is purified of much that is formless and confused, as, for instance, the not-too-clear distinction between poetry and myth and, even more so, the continual oscillation between a diachronic and a synchronic definition of the world of poetry. In this respect it may be opportune to go back, even in connection with Vichian philosophy, to a distinction which has demonstrated its efficacy in the hermeneutics of a thought in many ways akin to Vico's—Hegelian thought. This is the distinction between methodology and metaphysics, made because the two exigencies, the one of which is legitimate and the other illegitimate (the second not being rigorously justified), overlap and are continually superimposed on each other in the pages of the Neapolitan thinker, thus often giving rise to ambiguities which have greatly harmed and continue to harm the comprehension and the development of the solid and fecund core of so many truths that still live in the *Scienza nuova* (as they do in all the works of Vico). For poetry, that is, aesthetic activity, which is language and expression, is not—as the systematic propositions of Vico

[19] Cf. G. Tagliacozzo, "General Systems Theory as a Taxonomy of Culture and as a Curriculum of General Education," paper presented at the AAAS, Society for General Systems Research Section, meeting at Cleveland, December, 1963, an explication of his *Tree of Knowledge* (1958), pp. 14ff.

would all too frequently lead one to believe—to be identified with only one epoch in the historical development of mankind. Poetry is internal to all epochs, essential and necessary in all of them, as an ideal and eternal moment of the human spirit, even if, or rather because, it unfolds and takes shape in time and in the concreteness of single works. Neither can reason completely unfolded ("*la ragione tutta spiegata*") ever dissolve poetry or, worse, "surpass" it rationally, since between the two there is no relationship of negative opposition in a dialectical sense but rather one of ideal succession between positives. If this ideal relationship, which at any rate lives only in the concrete and in the individual, becomes rigidified into a repetitive scheme and into a formula and constant law, it becomes a false relationship of a metaphysical, and no longer methodological, type.

Nevertheless, the very acceptance, perhaps the exaltation, of the methodological character of Vichian thought must, in our opinion, involve the implicit acceptance of a modern conception of methodology which, in turn, through its persistent contact with history, whence it has its source, has the capacity to prevent self-rigidification into an adiaphorous formula valid for all times and for all cases. In fact, Vico, quite beyond certain traditionalistic forms of expression and the love for symmetry (which, at any rate, negatively affected other philosophers, as readers of Kant and Hegel know), continually immersed his principles of method in the concrete and supreme reality of history. Thus he again and again renovated those principles, not only through further researches, such as those we have referred to, but also in the course of other minor inquiries, so that it becomes almost impossible to tell to what point the principles have been inductively derived from the particular research or the research deduced from the principles. It is, however, important to underscore that, while Vico has not left us an explicit theory concerning those processes, he placed himself beyond or, perhaps still better, at the dialectical center between induction and deduction exactly because of his adoption of the philological-topological-critical method. The Vichian methodology of history thus escapes—and for this reason is, in our opinion, strictly connected with the most promising prospects of contemporary thought—the danger of rigidifying into an abstract systematization and, therefore, through this and other ways, into a metaphysics. This, after all, is what tends to happen to the adiaphorous methodologies of our time which, despite their not always vain efforts, testify to the urgent need for new instruments of inquiry in our contemporary philosophizing. The Vichian methodology escapes that danger, not because it precludes uncertainty, that is, the problematical character of every inquiry, but because, rather than to criticism or reason (which is a necessary moment inseparable from inquiry), it gives a prior place to *topica*, that is, to the art of invention, the no less necessary geniality and unpredictability of the inquiry, which no systematic planner can be assured of a priori. In this sense, therefore, in Dewey's fashion, the logic of Vico's inquiry recommends itself to the future of philosophy as inquiry in action, as a great moment, but still only a moment, of man's perpetual inquiring.

Translated by A. William Salomone

Maria Goretti VICO'S PEDAGOGIC
THOUGHT AND
THAT OF TODAY

I. *Vico's Pedagogic Work*

Giambattista Vico was appointed professor of rhetoric at the University of Naples on January 31, 1699, and held this position until almost the end of his life.[1]

The opening lectures[2] that he delivered might be considered as a mere discharge of academic duties, all the more so since the subject matter treated by the lecturer naturally lent itself to didactic and methodological discussions.[3] Vico's lectures, instead, are considerably more. Those inaugural orations which were delivered between 1699 and 1707[4] can be viewed as

[1] Vico left his professorship in 1742. He was succeeded by his son, Gennaro, who at that time was already his academic assistant.

[2] The opening lecture, or *prolusione*, is an inaugural speech given by a recently appointed professor.

[3] Rhetoric is the art of speaking and writing in an appropriate and efficient manner, so as to induce persuasion in the listeners. In other words, rhetoric teaches one how to present ideas in the most convincing form. The whole of classical antiquity attached prominent importance to this discipline, placing it at the basis of the education of youth. Italian humanism links up with this tradition. In rhetoric, three parts may be distinguished: (1) *invention*, or the search for the arguments and the proofs to be developed; (2) *disposition*, or the search for the order in which such arguments and proofs should be arranged; and (3) *elocution*, that is, the skill with which to set forth in the clearest and most intense way those arguments and proofs considered in isolation. Usually, the theorists of rhetoric add to these three parts *action*, that is, voice intonation, the mimic play of physiognomy, and gesturing, which accompany the utterance of words, and, finally, *memory*. Obviously, an education which attaches great importance to rhetoric must emphasize the exercise of memory as well as that of scholarly, philological research, on the strength of the conviction that maturity of expression (language, writing) is the counterpart of maturity of personality, and that such maturity can be achieved only through linguistic exercise. The main feature of such education is the concept of the disinterested character of culture.

[4] Vico's inaugurals were held on October 18 of the years 1699, 1700, 1701, 1704, 1705, 1707, and 1708 (the last being the *De nostri*). They were almost certainly recast in 1709 in order to bring them into stricter line with the seventh inaugural, which Vico reelaborated with particular care. They were not, however, published. In his *Autobiography* Vico, speaking about himself in the third person, points out: "He was . . . glad that he had not published these Orations, for he thought the republic of letters, bending under so great a pile of books, should not be burdened with more, but should only be offered books of important discoveries and useful inventions" (*The Autobiography of Giambattista Vico*, trans. Max H. Fisch and Thomas G. Bergin [Ithaca,

the premise of his original pedagogic thought, which found expression, in systematic form, in the inaugural discourse of 1708.[5]   This work, entitled *De nostri temporis studiorum ratione* (*On the Study Methods of Our Time*), is not only the most significant of his educational writings (inasmuch as Vico voices therein, in organic form, his basic ideas concerning pedagogic problems) but also constitutes the transition point, the bridge, leading to all those works in which Vico's historicism takes its characteristic configuration. The *De nostri*, therefore, has a twofold significance.   It represents, on the one hand, a systematization of Vico's educational thought (and we find confirmation of this in a passage of the *Autobiography*); on the other hand, this oration marks that important moment in a thinker's life when the basic principles that henceforth will determine and guide his thought are delineated.[6]   We may therefore consider *On the Study Methods of Our Time* as the written document to which one should refer in order to obtain a knowledge of Vico's educational thought: it is the work that secures for Vico, in the history of pedagogic theories, a place not inferior in rank to those occupied by Locke and Rousseau.[7]

N.Y.: Cornell University Press, 1963], p. 146).   The first six orations were not published until 1869, by Antonio Galasso (Naples: Morano).

[5] Apropos of this, Vico writes: "But in the year 1708 the Royal University resolved to have a solemn public inauguration of studies and to dedicate it to the king with an oration to be delivered in the presence of Cardinal Grimani, viceroy of Naples.   The oration for this occasion was therefore to be published . . ." (*ibid.*).   It was, in fact, published by the author under the title *De nostri temporis studiorum ratione* (Naples: Mosca, 1709).

[6] Vico himself writes that "the dissertation appeared the same year in duodecimo from the press of Felice Mosca.   Its argument is in fact a first draft of what he later worked out in his *The Principle of Universal Law*, with its appendix *The Consistency of the Jurisprudent*" (*Autobiography*, p. 146).   The *De uno universi iuris principio et fine uno* and the *De constantia jurisprudentis*, are considered the immediate antecedents of his major work, the *Scienza nuova*, and in them the Vichian fusion of philology (*certum*) and philosophy (*verum*) is carried out in the domain of law.   In these works Vico reduces the traditional distinction between natural law and positive law to a distinction between two directive principles of jural thought, that is, between the rational element (the form of truth, *verum*), and *authority* (the form of positive enactments, *certum*).   Such principles, Vico shows, are intimately connected; and it is precisely this intimate connection which demonstrates that history (the realm of the *certum*) proceeds through philosophy (the sphere of *verum*).

[7] Locke, Vico, and Rousseau make up the triad of the great educational thinkers of the Enlightenment.   Being connected by a deeper link than is usually, at first sight, surmised, they laid the groundwork for modern pedagogic problems.

It would be futile to remark that Vico was not thoroughly acquainted with Locke, whom he constantly scorns, and that he obviously could not have known Rousseau.   However, his, Locke's, and Rousseau's are three voices which, despite the inevitable contrast, are at one in determining and emphasizing the productivity, so to speak, of the human mind.   Locke, who asserts that man is able to attain freedom only if, as a child, he acquires the capacity of "doing," is not as remote from Rousseau as he appears to be, since Rousseau also requires from the child the "invention" of knowledge.   But that

II. *The Evolution of Vico's Educational Thought*

Vico himself tells us (see note 4) that he thought best not to publish the six inaugural orations which precede the one of 1708. This might lead us to

---

"doing" and this "invention," which in a way unite the intellectualistic exigencies of Cartesian rationalism (Descartes demanded the personal conquest of knowledge) with the experimental requirements of Baconian empiricism (Bacon insisted on the "production" of knowledge), achieve a synthesis and mediation in Vico's concept of the *verum ipsum factum.* In such an identification a solution is found for the same problem as it particularly drew the attention of the "new" education, that is, the psycho-pedagogic problem of the way in which man apprehends, gains cognizance of, and establishes learning. Moreover, we should not forget to mention the revaluation of the so-called irrational forces (feeling, emotion, instinct) which Vico started, a revaluation which bears its most conspicuous, if not most important, fruit in Rousseau's praise of feeling. It behooves us to emphasize that Vico is connected with the pedagogy of the Enlightenment, not only through his problematic judgments, but by stronger bonds than it is usually thought. He has in common with Locke, who precedes him, and with Rousseau, who follows him, the following points: (1) the critical position in regard to traditional education; (2) the awareness that the educational problem is, above all, a philosophical problem, that of an outlook on life; (3) the belief that the thorough solution of this problem is bound up with the concept of the *productivity* of the human mind. Concerning this topic, and Vico's position in the history of educational theories, see particularly R. Fornaca, *Il pensiero educativo di G. B. Vico* (Turin: Giappichelli, 1957), and F. Nicolini, *Vico e Rousseau* (Naples: Giannini, 1949).

Let us remark in passing that the bibliography on Vico as an educator is very scanty, a non-Italian bibliography on this subject practically non-existent. In this connection we should like to quote a remark by Elio Gianturco, to whom credit should be given for having translated into English for the first time Vico's *De nostri.* As far as we know, what Gianturco says is equally valid for the bibliographies in French and German. "The *De nostri* is conspicuously absent (as far I know) from all histories of education and educational thought (many of them otherwise excellent) written by English and American scholars" (Elio Gianturco, trans. *On the Study Methods of Our Time* [Indianapolis, Ind.: Bobbs-Merrill, 1965], p. xi). The high rating given to the *De nostri* by one of the most outstanding Vichian scholars obviously has not been taken into account as it should have been. Quoting Gianturco again: "Fausto Nicolini, the *doyen* of Vico studies, aptly underlines its significance by pointing out that 'it is the most important pedagogic essay between Locke's *Thoughts on Education* (1693) and the *Emile* (1762) of Rousseau'" (*ibid.*, p. x).

Other writings in which Vico particularly discusses the pedagogic problem (exclusive of the school pieces, collected in vol. VIII of the *Opere di Vico*, ed. F. Nicolini [Bari: Laterza, 1941]), are the following: "La lettera a Francesco Saverio Estevan" (Naples, January 12, 1729), in which Vico re-emphasizes his Cartesian position, and his *De mente heroica*, the last of his inaugurals (1725), which, as Gianturco writes, "may be considered the logical prolongation of the *De nostri.* It is one of the most inspired 'invitations to learning' ever penned, a scintillating paean in praise of what Goethe would have called the Faustian impulse toward encyclopedic knowledge. The eros of learning has seldom been expressed in more electrifying terms" (*Study Methods*, p. x). At any rate, such writings do not add anything substantial to Vico's educational thought, as it is outlined in the *De nostri.*

think that such orations are not particularly contributive to the illustration of Vico's educational thought. In fact, Antonio Corsano considers them as mere rhetorical exercises, devoid of any philosophical value.[8] In the Introduction to his edition of the *De nostri* (for school use) Corsano again attaches but slight importance to the orations. Gentile, instead, views them as "the first phase" of Vico's philosophy.[9] It may be that (as Fausto Nicolini, one of the most outstanding Vico scholars, observes) truth lies between these two statements.[10]

Meanwhile, it is important to observe that Vico himself (who was glad of the fact that they had not been published) gives a rather extensive account of them in his *Autobiography*. Since we know that in the latter work he set out to portray the evolution of his thought, this is an indication that he attached some value to those writings. Moreover, if their originality appears to be slight (since, in them, Vico still moves within the orbit of the educational conceptions of the tradition of humanism), nevertheless, in spite of their eclecticism, in which well-known themes of Ficino, Pico della Mirandola, Cardano, Bruno, and Campanella stand out, those orations do not fail to arrest our attention, because of the energetic resoluteness with which the professor of rhetoric vindicates the worth and dignity of those rhetorical studies whose prestige had been considerably downgraded in scientific circles. We are informed, in this connection, that the Chair of Rhetoric at the University of Naples was considered *minor*; but it is exactly from this chair— vis-à-vis an audience firmly convinced that the value of the teaching of a subject matter depends primarily on its practical usefulness—that the young professor had the courage to throw into full relief the basic value of literary studies. Thus, Vico's orations symbolize that "defense" of humanism which he subsequently develops with such signal originality in the *De nostri*.

It is therefore worthwhile to say a few words about those six orations.

In the first, Vico "proposes that we cultivate the force of our divine mind in all its faculties . . . [and] proves that the human mind is by analogy the god of man, just as God is the mind of the whole [of things]."[11] This idea, especially, epitomizes the Renaissance conception of man as a *mortal god*;[12] but the application that Vico makes of this conception deserves our notice.

[8] See A. Corsano, *G. B. Vico* (Bari: Laterza, 1956), pp. 52–83, where the *De nostri* is discussed, and *passim*.

[9] See G. Gentile, *Studi vichiani* (Florence: Le Monnier, 1915).

[10] See F. Nicolini's article on Vico's inaugural orations in Bompiani's *Dizionario letterario Bompiani delle opere e dei personaggi di tutti i tempi e di tutte le letterature* (Milan, 1947–63), V, 269.

[11] Fisch and Bergin, *Autobiography*, p. 140.

[12] The expressive simile of man as an "earthly and mortal god" is found in Bovillus (Charles de Bouelles) who, as Garin says, "grasped the deepest intuition of Pico," that is "the ideal of Man, as the Renaissance had idolized him"; see E. Garin, Preface to Bovillus' *De sapiente*, Italian translation [Turin: Einaudi, 1943]).

He finds confirmation of that human "Godlikeness" in the psychology of children. Such Godlikeness is evinced, he writes, in the fact that "children, who are free of evil affections and vices, at the end of three or four years of idle play are found to have learned the entire vocabulary of their native tongues."[13]

The second and third orations, which are perhaps less significant for the development of Vico's educational thought, are, however, of interest because they emphasize the constructively moral role of teaching and repudiate the purely technological concept of school instruction. Vico says not only that must we "inform the spirit with the virtues by following the truths of the mind," but also that intellectual intercourse between scholars "must be rid of every deceit" through the cultivation of "true not feigned, solid not empty, erudition."[14]

The fourth and fifth orations are very important. They eulogize the basic principles of humanistic educational thought, that is, (1) the conception of the essentially "disinterested" character of culture (humanism conceives of culture as autonomous value, not as instrumentality) and (2) the concept of the coincidence of civilization and culture (the degree and the character of civilization depending on the degree and character of culture). As a matter of fact, Vico declares that his fourth oration "is directed against the false scholars who study for advantage alone and therefore take more pains to seem learned, than to be so."[15]

The theme of the fifth oration is that the "commonwealths most famous for military glory and most powerful politically" have been those distinguished by the greatest flowering of intellectual culture.[16]

The sixth oration, finally, is of the greatest interest because of its perspicacious remarks on children's psychology; in a way, these remarks foreshadow Vico's thought in the phase of its maturity.

[13] This psychological remark is reminiscent of what Montessori said about the child's "absorbing brain," in reference to the extraordinary power of the child's mind to "absorb" the resources of language and the qualities of the environment. Because Vico is interested in tracing the nature of the mind in its genesis ("The nature of institutions is nothing but their coming into being . . . "), we find in the *Scienza nuova* many interesting observations on child psychology. Consider, for instance, the following: ". . . it is characteristic of children to take inanimate things in their hands and talk to them in play as if they were living persons." "Children excel in imitation; we observe that they generally amuse themselves by imitating whatever they are able to apprehend." "Languages must have begun with monosyllables, since in the present abundance of articulated words into which children are now born they begin with monosyllables, in spite of the fact that in them the fibers of the organ necessary to articulate speech are very flexible." (*The New Science of Giambattista Vico*, trans. Thomas G. Bergin and Max H. Fisch [Garden City, N.Y., 1961], p. 29, axiom XXXVII; p. 33, axiom LII; p. 35, axiom LX.)

[14] Fisch and Bergin, *Autobiography*, pp. 141–42.

[15] *Ibid.*, p. 142.

[16] *Ibid.*

First and foremost, Vico exactly determines the importance of language, to which he attaches a significance of a moral-pedagogic nature, showing that, "as languages were the most powerful means for setting up of human society, so the studies should begin with them, since they [i.e., languages] depend altogether on memory which in childhood is marvellously strong." [17]

In the second place, the sixth oration defines, in a manner which is already quite explicit, the role of human phantasy as a premise and prelude to a logical structuralization. In other words, Vico makes us feel distinctly that he has advanced beyond the intellectualistic antithesis between the rational and the irrational and that he has already glimpsed the essential role of the imagination in the educational process. In fact, he declares: "The age of childhood is reasonable but it has no material on which to reason; let children then be prepared for the art of good reasoning through a study of quantitative sciences, which call for memory and imagination." [18] Therefore, for Vico, the sequence of the subject matters to be taught is as follows: (1) infancy— letters (of the alphabet), prevalence of memory; (2) adolescence—math- ematical sciences (The predominance of fantasy in adolescence helps the student to understand the "science of measurements," but, on the other hand, reflection on abstract matters deprives fantasy of concrete corporeality and tames its passionateness. "Thus by the vast and corpulent physical images and by the delicate ideas of lines and numbers, let them be prepared to grasp the abstract metaphysical infinite by the science of being and the one." [19]); (3) youth—theology, ethics, legal studies.

At this point, what profitable suggestions do we derive from Vico's pedagogic thought? Let us hypothetically assume that nothing by Vico was extant except these six orations (mentally adding to them, perhaps, the *Scienza nuova*). They would not tell us much. Apart from the "clues," the "hints" that we have underlined, the first six orations do nothing but delineate for us the essential values of humanistic education, that is, the values elaborated through the Neo-Platonic tradition of the Renaissance. Those values were crystallized in the practice of a school which was felt to be more and more remote from the demands of an epoch in which the ferments of two revolutions, the American and the French, were already stirring.

Nevertheless, just as a word or a sentence takes on its specific value only from the context in which it is embedded, so these orations are thrown into

---

[17] *Ibid.*, p. 144.

[18] *Ibid.*, p. 145. This concept, according to which the study of quantitative sciences requires, not merely ratiocination, but memory and imagination as well, is not only an anticipation of Vico's most original thought, but also an intuition confirmed by modern psychological studies concerning the function of fantasy in abstract ideation. In the *De nostri*, Vico writes: "the Ancients required their youths to learn the science of geometry, which cannot be grasped without a vivid capacity to form images" (Gianturco, *Study Methods*, p. 14).

[19] Fisch and Bergin, *Autobiography*, p. 145.

outstanding relief when we view them as the intellectual landing point which Vico reaches after the voyage of his meditative youth. They constitute the prelude to that defense of humanism which Vico undertakes in the seventh oration. If we envisage the six orations in this light, it becomes clear that Vico's pedagogic position is already on the way to appearing as an alternative to the educational practice of his time. That time was under the spell of abstract Cartesian ideas, whereas Vico conceived of education as a historical process, in the course of which, man, through language and imagination, builds his own logical structures. By means of these structures, he creates a world of his own. It would be too lengthy (even though interesting) to follow Vico in his autobiographical account of the evolution of his thought. We should like, however, to refer to what he says in regard to "two pernicious practices in use today."

"The first," he writes, "is in introducing philosophy to children barely out of grammar school with the so-called logic of 'Arnauld,'[20] full of rigorous judgments concerning recondite matters of the higher sciences, remote from vulgar common sense . . . ; the other practice consists in teaching young students the elements of the science of magnitudes by algebraic methods. . . ." "The result," he continues, "is a blasting of those youthful mental gifts which should be regulated and developed each by a separate art, as for example memory by the study of languages, imagination by the reading of poets, historians and orators, perception by plane geometry."[21] Moreover, "such practice obscures their imagination, enfeebles their memory, renders their perception sluggish, and slackens their understanding." He states finally: "And these four things are all most necessary for the culture of the best humanity."[22]

This seems to me enough to allow us to assert that Vico's eulogy of the educational values of humanistic culture is not to be considered a rhetorical exercise, much less a conformist compliance with scholastic rules. Vico's plea for humanistic culture is the affirmation of a deep-rooted conviction,

[20] Antoine Arnauld (Arnaut or Arnault), called *the Great* in order to distinguish him from his brother, the Bishop of Toul (1612, Paris–1694, Brussels), was one of the most efficient propagandists of Jansenism in France and the soul itself of Port Royal. His controversial writings against Jesuits and Protestants are very numerous. Vico's reference is to the *Port-Royal Logic* (1662), which Arnauld wrote in collaboration with Nicole, and which is an attempt at reconciling Aristotle's logic with that of Descartes. However as G. de Ruggiero points out in his *Storia della filosofia* (Bari, 1948), IV, it is the Cartesian spirit which is most in evidence in the *Port-Royal Logic*: "This work evinces a decided taste for clear ideas, a trend toward simplification, and a typically Cartesian intolerance for scholastic subtleties." Vico criticizes the *Port-Royal Logic* for its cold "geometric" spirit; he contraposes to it the passionate eloquence of Cicero, which, although full of frequent contradictions, is vibrant with life. Vico, as we know, constantly maintains that life is not a theorem.

[21] Fisch and Bergin, *Autobiography*, p. 124.

[22] *Ibid.*

achieved through personal experience, in which humanism is perceived as a *new* value. This new value is posited as a constructive alternative to Cartesian mathematics. And this is, in fact, the thesis advocated in the *De nostri*.

III. *The Problem of the* De nostri temporis studiorum ratione[23]

The central problem of the *De nostri* is a didactic-methodological one. It is articulated in a set of other problems which, in their multiple irradiation, touch the very issue of the value of life itself.

These problems can be listed, in schematic fashion, thus:

1. *Methodological problem*: Which is, or should be, the method of study suited to our time?

2. *Historical problem*: Who is right, the ancients, who prize literary scholarship, or the moderns, who prize scientific culture?

3. *Cognitive-psychological problem*: What is the role of phantasy and that of reason (conceptualization) in the process of learning?

4. *Moral problem*: In the texture of life, what is the weight and value of the rational and of the irrational?

5. *Educational problem*: Does the value of schooling consist in the fact that the school preserves forms which have attained the fullness of spiritual life in an outward perfection of their own? Or does the value of schooling consist in the fact that it is capable of destroying the static forms of the past, and has the strength of building up new modes of expression suited to the continuously changing times?

The bare enunciation of these problems is enough to make us aware of the

---

[23] Vico's *De nostri* begins with a panoramic survey of the culture of his age, which was torn between traditional-humanistic education and the new education, which advocated the analytical method (*ratio geometrica*). After having emphasized the one-sidedness of both positions, Vico asserts that: (1) Man is a unity; hence, fantasy, the irrational, although obscure, should not be identified with the false, but probably conveys, in "corporeal," vividly impressive, forms, that truth which the single individual, and mankind as well, achieves in the period of maturity. (2) Moreover, the analytical method, because of its abstractness and generality, cannot be of any help to us in our effort to understand concrete and polyhedric experience. (3) Every teaching, therefore, although tending toward ideal truth, must always take into account specific circumstances. Accordingly, the starting point of all instruction should be the sense of concreteness: teaching should begin by strengthening, in the young student, imagination, memory, and the feeling for tangible reality. (4) The manual, the textbook, can only have the role of a "street sign," that is, can merely serve to indicate the direction in which the pupil has to move. Vico applies these principles to the study of legal science. Finally, he refers to the invention of printing and the creation of higher seats of learning as basic "helps" of modern culture, underlining their advantages as well as their eventual drawbacks.

fact that, in Vico's time, the methodological controversy about schooling had taken on the meaning of a struggle between a traditionalistic position (humanism) and an anti-traditionalistic one (scientism).

The humanistic school placed the emphasis on a past which made up the cultural substratum of the present and therefore constituted an essential part of its structure [24] (so it was alleged); but it was easy to answer that humanism leaned upon principles which could be condemned as passive (such as the mnemonic principle and that of authority). The new school, by opposing the vacuous world of poetical invention with the rigorousness of mathematics and the fecundity of experimental research, transformed the quest for truth into a battle for freedom. That battle shaped itself as a liberation from those preconceptions which Bacon had stigmatized as *idola*, and it was fought for an enfranchisement from any authority which claims recognition on the merely external ground of acquired rights. [25]

On the logical plane, however, the contradictory positions of the contenders are identical, that is, abstract and static. Humanism had become stiffened into formalism; it set up history as a dogma and thus negated history, which obviously is against any dogmatism.

Antihumanism (under either the guise of scientific experimentalism or that of rationalistic analysis) likewise negated history, putting forth a claim to explaining and promoting history through unchangeable laws. Yet both humanism and scientism are the products of man and history. The former is the expression of "the human" as an exigency to institute order and to understand and modify the mutability of experience through structures of a universal character. The problem is this: since expression and truth are the two basic aspects summing up man's activity, can they be so sharply distinguished as to repudiate each other? Or shouldn't we instead find a way to achieve an understanding of both, in a mutual integration, so that they may concretely weave themselves into the world of man?

IV. *The Defense of Humanism*

This is Vico's pedagogic problem. In the *De nostri* he states the issue itself in the polemical terms of his epoch: "Which study method is better, ours, or

[24] No one, not even Locke, doubted the instrumental value of the *humanae literae*.

[25] Bacon's theory of the *idola* (the *pars destruens* of the method) is one of those essential themes which run through the whole of seventeenth- and eighteenth-century thought. It animates the most revolutionary and subversive part of the Enlightenment. Bacon distinguishes four kinds of errors (*idola mentis*) stemming, respectively, from our sensory apparatus, from a subjective turn of thought, from social relationships, and, finally, from philosophical or scientific doctrines handed down by tradition. It is hardly necessary to mention that the French *Encyclopaedia* was conceived, edited, and written under Baconian inspiration.

the Ancients'?"[26]   This was the alternative choice as far back as the time of the *Querelle des anciens et des modernes*.[27]   It has rightly been observed that Vico posits the problem in the spirit of the *Querelle* itself.   "Of this discussion," writes Elio Gianturco, "a most important fruit was G. B. Vico's *De nostri temporis studiorum ratione*."[28]   The "modern" method, Vico states, is the analytical one, which boils down to the application of the *ratio geometrica*.   In other words, this method revolves around the quest for a *certitude* (*certum*) which can be translated into a mathematical truth (*verum*). If, however, we follow this method, it is evident that imagination becomes,

[26] The discourse, however, begins by paying dubious homage to Bacon, inasmuch as Vico, although emphasizing the importance of Bacon's reform of the sciences, underscores its abstractness: ". . . while he discovers a new cosmos of sciences . . . he proves to be rather a pioneer of a completely new universe than a prospector of this world of ours.   His vast demands so exceed the utmost extent of man's effort, that he seems to have indicated how we fall short of achieving an absolutely complete system of sciences rather than how we may remedy our cultural gaps" (Gianturco, *Study Methods*, p. 4). Vico's deep indebtedness to Bacon's philosophical thought has been pointed out by modern scholarship (see, in the present symposium, Enrico De Mas's article "Vico's Four Authors"); it is, however, impossible to ignore the fact that Vico is far from being in complete agreement with our modern admiration for that so eulogized experimental method.   It is somewhat astonishing that Vico, after having extolled Bacon's scientific pioneering, should compare him to a despot: "Thus, Bacon acted, in the intellectual field, like potentates of mighty empires, who, having gained supremacy in human affairs, squander immense wealth in attempts against the order of Nature herself, by paving the seas with stones, and other vain exploits forbidden by Nature" (Gianturco, *Study Methods*, p. 4).   In these words we can already recognize that Vichian idea which tends to restore the value of worldly reality, imperfect and relative as such reality may be.   It is precisely in this imperfection and relativity that Vico discovers not only the positiveness of history, the "human" science, but also its very richness, the unmistakable sign of its spirituality, a spirituality which gains self-awareness in a continuous process of self-discovery, self-loss, and renewed discovery of self.   Vico, by tracing at the very inception of the *De nostri* the limits of the Baconian reform, seems to tell us, in my view, that both empiricism and rationalism are likely to lead us to abstract and intellectualistic positions by setting in opposition to the dogmatism of tradition the dogmatism of antitradition; by setting up literary dogmatism (humanism) against scientific dogmatism (scientism). Thus, contact with experience is lost, and a despotic violence is exerted upon nature. To conclude: This is one of those not-too-rare passages in which Vico (I am borrowing De Mas's striking formula) "baconizes against Bacon."

[27] The *Querelles des anciens et des modernes* was a literary debate which split the French cultural world in the seventeenth century.   The party of the moderns was headed by Pierre Charles Perrault (1628–1703, Paris), the party of the ancients by Boileau (Paris, 1636–1711).   The controversy, though appearing to be purely literary, involved deeper and more complex meanings.   It was, at bottom, a struggle between an old and a new world, between tradition and innovating science.   Bernard Fontenelle (1657, Rouen–1757, Paris), who in a certain sense recapitulates the *querelle*, pleading the defense of the moderns, shows that the Cartesian method has already become a corrosive agent. Scientific belief in progress, and in reason, which constructs it, is by now a revolutionary force.

[28] Gianturco, *Study Methods*, p. ix.

according to an old French saying (which Lamy applies to school method-ology),[29] *la folle du logis* (the crazy maid of the house). Vico writes: "Our modern advocates of advanced criticism rank the unadulterated essence of 'pure' primary truth before, outside, and above the gross semblances of physical bodies."[30] But, Vico wonders, is mathematical truth the *only* truth in existence? And is whatever does not appear clear and distinct to the *ratio geometrica*, by the same token, false? If there is no doubt whatever that what is clear and distinct is true, it is by no means proven that the unclear and non-distinct is, on account of this blurredness, false. Between truth and error stands a *tertium quid* which is represented by the verisimilar. Vico remarks: "It is a positive fact that, just as knowledge originates in truth and error in falsity, so common sense arises from perceptions based on veri-similitude. Probabilities stand, so to speak, midway between truth and falsity, since things which most of the time are true can only very seldom be false."[31] Now, the verisimilar, which dominates the field of topics,[32] is totally banned by the critico-analytical method, which admits solely a truth ascertained through the Cartesian standard of clarity and distinctness. Hence, a spontaneous query arises in our mind. Who is right, Arnauld or Cicero? Arnauld, the champion of the new logic built upon the *ratio geometrica*, or Cicero, who, availing himself of eloquence, seeks the often tortuous and contradictory, but nevertheless reliable, path of the persuasion of the human heart?

In his reply to this dramatic query Vico's peculiar educational position, as

[29] Bernard Lamy (1640, Mans–1715, Rouen), an Oratorian, with his *Entretiens sur les sciences* (1633) supplies us with the pedagogic systematization of the Cartesian method. The influence of the *Entretiens* on the eighteenth century was most notable. Especially remarkable was Lamy's impact on Rousseau, who mentions him in his *Confessions* as "one of my favorite authors." Lamy, like Rousseau, deems it dangerous "to nurture the mind of youth with fabulous tales," which he terms "lying oddities." The Enlightenment thus heralds its own arrival, taking a position diametrically opposed to that of Vico, who sees the truth of history shining through the obscurity of myth. (*See* B. Lamy, *Entretiens sur les sciences* [Paris: Presses Universitaires, 1966], pp. 110 and *passim*.) In order to clarify Vico's position and to emphasize its antagonism to that of Lamy, I shall quote Lamy's definition of imagination: "C'est une faculté ou pouvoir que l'âme a de se représenter dans la substance du cerveau les images des choses sensibles; ainsi ceux qui ne font usage que de cette seule faculté sont toujours hors d'eux mêmes; et ne voient point ce qui est dans leur âme . . . une vie pleine de désordre et des discours malsenséz en représentent les égarements" (*ibid.*, p. 132).

[30] Gianturco, *Study Methods*, p. 13.

[31] *Ibid.*

[32] *Topics* (from Greek *topos*, place) was, in ancient logic, the search for, and the exposition of, the arguments that were brought forth concerning any subject whatsoever. Vico contraposes to the "critical" method of Descartes the "topical" method, which consists of the search for ideas. The *Topics* are those Aristotelian books on logic in which hypothetical or verisimilar syllogisms are expounded. See the article by E. Grassi in this volume, pp. 39–50.

well as its modernity, is revealed.   According to Vico, both the traditionalists
and the anti-traditionalists are wrong; the traditionalists because they often
mistake the false (the imagined object) for the true, and fall into verbalism,
into passive and mnemonic formalism, substituting words (that is, euphonious
sounds) for facts; the anti-traditionalists because, between true and false, they
leave no place for the verisimilar, and therefore dogmatically reject all that is
obscure as if it were false, and shut themselves off from an understanding of
life, which, in its passionate and emotional texture, in its polyhedric experimentalism, is obviously obscure, but not, therefore, inevitably false [33]

Now, traditionalistic education threatened to transform the pupil into a
mere "listener."   The chief role of a student of philosophy was to listen.
Most appropriately students were called "auditors."[34]   Anti-traditionalistic
education, on the other hand, may turn a human being into an abstract
theoretician whose heart is cold, indifferent, and incapable of grasping those
"reasons of the heart" which Pascal sets in opposition to the reasons of the
intellect.   Vico says: "Doctrinaires judge human actions as they ought to be,
not as they actually are. . . . Satisfied with abstract truth alone, and not being
endowed with common sense, unused to following probability, those doctrinaires do not bother to find out whether the things that are truths to them
are also such to other people." [35]

As a consequence, there is a need for a mediation and integration of the
principles of the two educations.   "To avoid both defects, in my opinion,
young men should be taught the totality of sciences and arts, and their
intellectual powers should be developed to the full. . . . Let their imagination
and memory be fortified so that they may be effective in those arts in which

[33] Soon, when the Enlightenment principle of the "clear and distinct" idea has
been left behind, such obscurity of the deeper life of man will be the object of the
meditations of Leibniz on the "*petites perceptions*," as well as of those of Rousseau.   The
latter will again bestow full value upon the emotional and complex life of "feeling"
in the determination of man as a moral person.   As is known, Vico, starting from a
meditation upon that primitive obscurity, outlines a pattern of development of the
history of mankind parallel to that of the development of man.   In the *Scienza nuova*,
for instance, we find this: "In children, memory is most vigorous, and imagination is
therefore excessively vivid.   This axiom is the principle of the expressiveness of the
poetic images that the world formed in its first childhood" (Bergin and Fisch, *New
Science*, p. 33, axiom L).   "Men at first feel without perceiving, then they perceive with
a troubled and agitated spirit, finally they reflect with a clear mind" (*ibid.*, axiom LIII).
"Whatever appertains to men but is doubtful or obscure, they naturally interpret
according to their own natures and the passions and customs springing from them. . . .
According to it, the fables originating among the first savage and crude men were very
severe, as suited the founding of nations emerging from a bestial freedom.   Then, with
the long passage of years and change of customs, they lost their original meanings and
were altered and obscured in the dissolute and corrupt times [beginning] even before
Homer. . . ." (*ibid.*, axiom LIV).

[34] Gianturco, *Study Methods*, p. 20.

[35] *Ibid.*, p. 35.

fantasy and the mnemonic faculty are predominant. At a later stage, let them learn criticism so that they can apply the fullness of their personal judgment to what they have been taught."[36]

This thesis is maintained on two fronts: in the first place, by showing the abstractness of the geometric method, which leads to an a priori dogmatism[37] and to a basic lack of understanding of human life;[38] in the second place, by pointing out that "eloquence" (that is, all that which, through intuition, calls upon the concrete reality of life, upon the nature of man, who feels first and then reasons) constitutes the path which man must travel in order to reach the persuasion of truth, nay, the discovery of truth, and, consequently, the generosity of a commitment to action.[39] Vico underscores that "the rational part in us may be taken captive by a net woven of purely intellectual reasonings, but the passionate side of our nature can never be swayed and overcome unless this is done by more sensuous and corporeal means. . . . the soul must be enticed by physical images and impelled to love; for, once it loves it is easily taught to believe; once it believes and loves, the fire of

[36] *Ibid.*, p. 19.

[37] It is a dogmatic apriorism because the acceptance of certain principles excludes any contact with experience, which is the real guide to truth, and, moreover, because it leads to the immobility that is inherent in any dogmatic position, since the deductive procedure debars the possibility of progress. Therefore, Cartesian deduction, commended as the conquest of a liberating truth, is, on the plane of logic, like Aristotelian deduction. Both get their living "from inherited wealth" (as Vico says); both dwell in their palaces "appointed" once and for all, in which only some item of furniture or some trimming or knickknack can be moved around. The most important achievements of modern thought—induction, the sense of progress, enfranchisement from despotic authorities—are thus nullified. Pointedly, Vico alludes (without giving specific details) to certain laws of mechanics set forth by Descartes which have turned out to be erroneous. He probably refers to the second and third rules, concerning the clash of physical bodies, stated in the *Principia philosophiae*.

[38] In regard to medicine, Vico contraposes modern trends of medical practice and thinking to the practice and science of the ancients, which was based entirely on verisimilitude, hence on the unprejudiced and flexible observation of indicia and symptoms, as well as on the belief that each sick person is different from every other. It is therefore dangerous to categorize and treat all patients in the same way. Still less justified is the analytical method in practical life, where imponderable factors have such great importance and where the complexity of human actions, in their intricate interplay, very often leads to unforeseeable results.

[39] This is why Vico has such importance in the thought of the Italian *Risorgimento*, from Vincenzo Cuoco to Foscolo and Mazzini. His influence in the educational field is particularly evident in Gino Capponi, the Florentine historian who, in his famous *Fragment on Education*, obviously draws his inspiration from Vico. Especially when Capponi refers to the "synthetic" nature of the child's mind, and when he connects the mythical fantasy of primitive peoples with the child's imagination, the Vichian impact is undeniable. Besides, Capponi's whole essay is directed against the analytical method, against the Cartesian *reason* of the Enlightenment. (See G. Capponi, *Il pensiero educativo*, ed. Maria Goretti [Florence: Le Monnier, 1967].)

passion must be infused into it so as to break its inertia and force it to will." [40]

Vico closes the *De nostri*, after giving a sharp outline of his thought with reference particularly to the teaching of Roman law, with a peroration in defense of humanism. But this peroration is not (as one might be inclined to think) a defense of "tradition." It is, instead, the presentation of a new humanism, of a new concept of education. It is a concept which takes into account the "nature" of man concretely unfolding in its psychological articulations, and thus considers, above all, the growth of the human mind, which, starting from the gross corporeality of images, attains the bodilessness of concepts. Thus the child, as Vico assumes him to be, is a man in the process of becoming, of being realized in a development which mirrors the development of humanity. [41] The nature of man, like that of institutions, is a *nascence*, a genesis; human life is not a contraposition of the rational to the irrational [42] but a *truthification*, the transformation of the irrational into the rational. Hence fantasy, the imaginative power, is not a prius to be overcome, to be left behind, but a prius as a starting point, as an anticipation of that which will later be an organic, rational systematization. The products of the imagination do not belong to a prehuman stage; they are, instead,

[40] Gianturco, *Study Methods*, p. 38.

[41] Gianturco (*ibid.*, p. xxvii) writes in this connection: "Vico believes in the existence of a psychogenetic law by which the individual develops through a certain series of phases, the sequential order of which is immutably fixed by nature. . . . In other words, the single individual recapitulates the entire process of development of the species." On this point, we beg to differ with Gianturco. The psychogenetic law originates from a scientifico-analytical mentality and from evolutionistic doctrines. Vico's notion of a parallelism between the history of the individual and the history of mankind (*storia ideale*) is a historicist and synthetic conception. In other words, progress is determined through the action of the biogenetic law and runs in phases, stages, whose "sequential order is immutably fixed by nature." For Vico such progress is not "evolution" but *storia ideale*, continuous development ceaselessly reverting to itself, with a higher degree of determinate reality and of knowledge: it is an eternal "unfolding." History, for Vico, has this meaning: it is the study of the forms through which the *spirit* creates itself. Attention should be drawn to Vico's discrimination between nature and *nascence* (genesis). It is true, as Gianturco states, that "Vico believes that education should be founded on this natural order of stages," that is, it is a fact that Vico pleads for an education which would "conform with nature." But we should not forget that nature, for Vico, is not an inertly physical concept; it is a dynamic *nascimento* (genesis). "The nature of things is nothing . . . but their coming into being."

[42] This was the contraposition in which Locke's concept of education had bogged down. Locke, in spite of his wide awareness of the child's problems, ended by theorizing an education of the disciplinary Puritan type. Somehow, Rousseau also found himself caught in the coils of the same contraposition, in spite of his efforts to reconstitute the unity of the human spirit. In fact, Rousseau, striving to confer a positive value on the irrational, does not avoid the danger of delineating a scheme of education impaired by a sentimental subjective background. He either endorses anarchic positions or accepts dogmas of the Enlightenment, such as that of the danger of fantasy set forth by Father Lamy.

things human which, passing through corporeally sensuous forms, will one day shape themselves into logical guises. In the same way, a logical structure presupposes imagination, and in imagination only does it become concrete, alive, and active. Consequently, the world of the child is a man's world which, painfully and laboriously, taking its point of departure in the obscurity of sense perception, discovers, after passing through the stage of the corporeality of images, the effulgence of a *verity* which is also a *certainty*. Education, therefore, should be viewed as the process of man's becoming civilized, in the same way that the civilization of man is but a process of education. Hence, as Vico shows in the *Scienza nuova*, philology and philosophy merge, the former being the awareness of the *certum*, the latter the awareness of the *verum*. In educational terms this means that there is no such thing as a duality of cultures, unless we wish to assume, hypothetically, the existence of "two cultures" (and this would be a purely abstract scheme or a "deviation"). There does not exist, on one side, a humanistic culture, and, on the other, in opposition to it, a scientific one. A single culture exists, which determines mankind's progress by forging the technical means either for a better physico-economic life or for giving precise form to moral values, so as to bestow significance and substantial worth on man himself. Hence the antithesis between traditional and non-traditional education is fruitless and abstract also. Such an antithesis is only a recurrent mirage created by the intellect in the hope of coursing through the harsh path of civilization by "scorching" its stages, through miracles of technique, and by considering as "superstructures" all that does not coincide with technical or economic factors.[43]

[43] In his *Autobiography* Vico points out the psychological process in the formation of the antithesis that injuriously affects the study methods of his time; he tells us how he reached the conviction that, essentially, the *geometrica methodus* should be withdrawn. Mathematics, he says, abstractly deduces concepts with a thorough disregard for the actual existence of the figures and numbers studied, whereas philosophy cannot do as much. In other words, Vico realizes, at a very early stage, that the principle of contradiction (that is, the logic of Aristotle) is powerless to explain the causal relationships of reality; but this cannot be done by the Cartesian method either. In reality the opposition between action and reaction leads to a phenomenon which has actual existence. Hence, mathematics has nothing to do with existence, whereas life, thought, and, consequently, philosophy cannot afford not to take account of reality. (In the last analysis, this was Kant's problem also.) In his *Autobiography* Vico states:

He decided to apply himself to geometry and to penetrate as far as the fifth proposition of Euclid. And reflecting that its demonstration turned on a congruence of triangles, the sides and angles of one triangle being shown one by one to be equal to the corresponding sides and angles of the other, he found in himself that it was an easier matter to grasp all those minute truths together, as in metaphysical genus, than to understand those particular geometrical quantities. . . . So he gave up this study as one which chained and confined his mind . . . and in the constant reading of orators, historians and poets his intellect took increasing delight in observing between the remotest matters ties which bound them together in some common relation (Fisch and Bergin, *Autobiography*, p. 123).

V. *Vico's Educational Thought and That of Our Time*

It is always risky to set up relationships of similarity or contrast between thoughts far apart in time, since this may lead to false analogies. Nevertheless, for a better comprehension of Vico, in order to determine his importance in the educational field (an importance which is often unjustly disregarded), we shall draw attention to two particular points.

1. Vico's educational thought, both in regard to its problematic judgments and to its way of positing some specific problems, shows similarities to modern educational thought. It would be interesting to investigate those similarities in depth.[44]

2. Does Vico's defense of humanism possess a constructive topicality today, in the civilization of technique and machines? An exhaustive reply to these two points would require a treatment which obviously would overstep the bounds of this essay; we will, however, jot down some brief remarks.

In the first place, Vico's pedagogic problematic judgments should be underlined. They fit emblematically within the framework of the *Querelle des anciens et des modernes* and bear an undeniable kinship to the educational problems of our time. Vico asked himself: "Arnauld or Cicero?" No less dramatically, we ask ourselves: "Scientific or literary culture?"[45] Vico

[44] In addition to what was discussed in note 7 above, it is characteristic that Serge Hessen, in emphasizing the relationships between culture and education, while perceiving in mankind's history the affirmation of what he calls "ideal goals," never mentions Vico. Yet his thought borrows many aspects of Lombardo-Radice's educational position, aspects which, through Croce's and Gentile's mediation, hark back to Vico. To quote an example, Hessen fears the excessive specialization of university research. (See Hessen, *Fondamenti della pedagogia come filosofia applicata*, Italian translation, published by Sandron, esp. chapter XII, "Theory of the University," pp. 407–29.) Vico expresses exactly the same fear in the *De nostri*: "Students' education is so warped and perverted as a consequence, that, although they may become extremely learned in some respects, their culture on the whole (and the whole is really the flower of wisdom) is incoherent" (Gianturco, *Study Methods*, p. 77).

[45] Resonances perhaps disproportionate to the intrinsic value of the piece, but significant insofar as they are symptomatic of universally felt exigencies, have been aroused by C. P. Snow's essay *The Two Cultures and the Scientific Revolution* (Cambridge: At the University Press, 1959). The slogan "the two cultures" has acquired wide currency in our day. Snow writes: "Two polar groups, at one pole we have literary intellectuals . . . at the other scientists. . . . Between the two a gulf of mutual incomprehension, hostility and dislike, but most of all a lack of understanding" (*ibid.*). He concludes: "Education isn't the total solution to this problem but without education the West can't even begin to cope. . . . Closing the gap between our cultures is a necessity in the most abstract intellectual sense, as well in the most particular. When those two senses have grown apart, then no society is going to be able to think with wisdom" (*ibid.*, p. 48). Just as in Vico's times the *querelle* between the ancients and the moderns contained and concealed the political premise of the conflict between authority and liberty, so in our age the distinction and battle between literary and scientific culture shapes up in the same terms. It may be configured as the ideological contrast between the culture of the

queried: "Topics or *ratio geometrica*?" Today we wonder whether the text-book, the school manual (and the school manual, at bottom, represents the *Topic* of traditional education), is not superannuated, and should be replaced by something else (by work, for instance).[46]

Vico alerted his contemporaries to the fact that their epoch, the Cartesian epoch, had already decided that study methods and the value of life were to be found in the *ratio geometrica*, in scientific rigorousness; but he simultaneously criticized the formalism into which literary studies had fallen. Today, the methods that attract the most attention and find the widest application are those which are offered to us in the name of science and technique, strengthened by the support lent to them by experimental psychology, sociology, and mathematical logic. In contrast, the traditional school, centered upon the "textbook," seems to draw farther and farther away from modern life, to prove more and more inadequate for the demands of modernity. In other words, we of today still discuss "the study methods of our time"; we are torn between the ideal of culture as the "all-round formation of a personality," oriented toward synthesis, and the ideal of a culture of the technico-vocational type, based on the notion of specialization.

In the second place, I wish to refer briefly to the fundamental positions of Vico that show, if not an exact parallelism (this would be uninteresting), a kind of interrelationship with some thought positions of our time. Today great interest is aroused among scholars by genetic epistemology, by which we are enabled to pass from the ideal of a logical language characterized by universally valid structures (Russell) to the historicization of analysis. Thus we reach the conclusion that the cultural history of a certain environment is written up entirely in the structures of language. As a consequence of the illuminating theories of Wittgenstein, there has been a realization that logical forms in their purity do not, at bottom, denote anything at all if we disregard the activity of the subject. In other words, the desideratum is a meeting between logico-semantic analysis and genetic epistemology. Now, it is impossible not to see that, at bottom, the point of perspective of analysis is the *verum* (pure logical truth), while the point of perspective of genetic

---

West, which in the ultimate analysis goes back to the presuppositions of classical antiquity, and the culture of the Soviet world, which, having programmatically broken contacts with that culture (from which its language and its civilization stemmed), relies mostly on the conceptions of a rigidly scientific education, with the systematic and integral application of mathematical and cybernetic methods and with didactic techniques where the mathematization of reality finds its counterpart in the utilization of electronic universal computers. See, for instance, L. B. L. Itelson, *Matematiceskie i Kiberneticeskie metody v pedagoghiki* (Moscow, 1964) (Italian translation by Andrea Daziano [Milan: Feltrinelli, 1966]).

[46] See, for instance, C. Freinet, *Plus de manuels scolaires* (Saint Paul, Switzerland: Alpes Maritimes, 1930), not to mention all the methods that revolve around "learn by doing," productive plans, Dalton and Kerschensteiner Plans, etc.

epistemology (Piaget)[47] is Vico's *certum*.   Vico stated: "Philosophy con-templates reason, whence comes knowledge of the true; philology observes that of which human choice is author, whence comes consciousness of the certain. . . . the philosophers failed by half in not giving certainty to their reasonings by appeal to the authority of the philologians, and likewise the latter failed by half in not taking care to give their authority the sanction of truth by appeal to the reasoning of the philosophers."[48]   The Vichian demand for clarifying logical structures through man's *doing* appears to be revived (or so it seems to me) in the studies made by Bruner and his team concerning the manner in which man grasps and determines the attributes of things.[49]

On the other hand, the Vichian identification of philology (apprehension of the *certum*) and philosophy (apprehension of truth) leads to the "unitary" conception of the life of man and the life of the child.   Man is *intuition* (passion, feeling, fantasy) which becomes *pure mind* (faculty of reasoning), in the sense that not only does reasoning articulate with intuition, but, while intuition is a foreshadowing of ratiocination (just as primitive myths and fables foreshadow philosophico-scientific reflections), reasoning, concretized, becomes "human" when it is incarnated in facts and history.   Thus, reason-ing utilizes mathematical schemes as structures, not in order to understand the essence of things (the essence being unintelligible to man), but in order to confer on them a logical structure.   But this brings us back to the central role of language in the formation of man and of the various national cultures.   According to Vico, it is in language that the typical expression of man manifests itself, disclosing the complementarity of intuitive and analytical thought.   Giving a new twist to Aristotle's thought, Vico writes: "The mind uses the intellect when, from something it senses, it gathers something which does not fall under the senses; and this is the proper meaning of the Latin verb 'intelligere.' "[50]

And, speaking of "poetic logic," he says: "Thus . . . the first language in the first mute times of the nations must have begun with signs, whether gestures or physical objects, which had natural relations to the ideas. . . . For this reason *logos* or word meant also 'deed' to the Hebrews and 'thing' to the Greeks. . . ."[51]   Professor Bruner has developed his psychological researches, applied to educational practice, by emphasizing the complementarity of intuitive and analytical thought.   He writes: "The child is able to give structure to the things he encounters, but he is not yet really able to deal with

[47] See E. Riverso, *Analisi dell'esperienza estetica* (Naples, 1967), and J. S. Bruner, *A Study of Thinking* (New York, 1956).

[48] Bergin and Fisch, *New Science*, p. 21, pars. 138 and 140.

[49] J. S. Bruner *et al.*, *Studies in Cognitive Growth* (New York, 1966).

[50] Bergin and Fisch, *New Science*, p. 70.

[51] *Ibid.*, p. 85.

possibilities not directly before him or not already experienced. . . . It is at this point that the child is able to give formal or axiomatic expression to the concrete ideas that before guided his problem-solving but could not be described or formally understood."[52] Bruner therefore speaks of the "sequence of learning" by which we pass from "active representation" (based on action) to "iconic representation" (that is, the possibility of recognizing visual schemata) to "linguistic representation" (the child succeeds in dealing with things by utilizing their translation into language). Vico writes: "The human mind is naturally inclined by the senses to see itself externally in the body, and only with great difficulty does it come to understand itself by means of reflections. This axiom gives us the universal principle of etymology in all languages: words are carried over from bodies, and from the properties of bodies, to signify the institutions of the mind and spirit."[53]

Essentially, Vico was impelled by the exigency of reconciling the experimentalistic (synthetic) desiderata of his beloved Bacon with the analytical principles of the *ratio geometrica* which, in his age, had been responsible for some of the most exciting discoveries in the realm of physical nature. Modern thought is impelled by the same exigency, particularly in its pedagogic applications. Its aim is dual: to prevent pragmatic experimentalism from being sterilized into an education of pure instrumentality, while prohibiting the analytical approach from luring future generations into doctrinaire abstractions.

VI. *Conclusion*

Today the debate revolves not only around the worth of the two cultures but, above all, around the value of methodological processes. In our time, as in that of Vico, the danger lies in the monism of method, in a new mathematization of reality. This, in our opinion, conceals baleful omens of authoritarianism. Hence we are interested in Bruner's position. He sets forth the need for complementing intuitive with analytical thought. "The complementary nature of intuitive and analytic thinking should, we think, be recognized. . . . Once solutions . . . are achieved by intuitive methods, they should if possible be checked by analytic methods. . . . Indeed, the intuitive thinker may even invent or discover problems that the analyst would not. But it may possibly be the analyst who gives these problems the proper formalism."[54]

[52] J. S. Bruner, *The Process of Education* (Cambridge: Harvard University Press, 1965), pp. 37–38.
[53] Bergin and Fisch, *New Science*, p. 36.
[54] Bruner, *The Process of Education*, p. 58. I wish to quote from an interesting *Dialogue* on school reform as it is envisaged by American educators (Voice of America,

We have centered our discussion on Bruner and on the trend initiated prior to the Woods Hole Conference, since it is our belief that this trend represents the "new phase" of educational problematic judgments being made in America and other countries. The trend aims at going beyond both the purely scientific methods (of the Pestalozzian, Herbartian, and Spencerian type) and the experimental ones (of the pragmatistic, Deweyan type, the learn-by-doing schools).[55] Actually, the "new" education, which centered on the movement of the "active school," found its emblem in Dewey's credo. But such a credo was, in a way, parallel to the conception of the

---

Marconi University of the Air, no. 588; participants, Giorgio Tagliacozzo, Aida Mastrangelo, and Jerome Bruner).   In this dialogue some problems concerning the possibility of teaching mathematical theories (functions, concept of probability) in non-abstract form are debated.   In my opinion, because of a certain affinity to the Vichian position, particular importance attaches to what is affirmed in the following statements: "In literature, we may have the child reach spontaneously the concept of "literary kind," without introducing, into teaching, notions like 'epic, lyric, tragic poetry,' and so forth."   We may notice, here, an affinity with Vico, inasmuch as the abstract notion (*verum*) emerges from the concrete one (*factum*), and the attainment of the awareness of their identity as "internal genesis," as "historical creation," is conceived of as the real goal of teaching.   Teaching is viewed by the participants in this *Dialogue* as the formation of a culture which is not a mnemonic passivity but a construction.   I think that Bruner's concept of "structure" could also be illuminated by Vico's position, insofar as Bruner's principles, although harking back to "general concepts," hence to a deductive-analytical method, take on validity because of the fact that they are presented as vehicles enabling us to descend to the particular and to determine the "intelligibility" of that particular. In fact, in the *Dialogue*, Professor Tagliacozzo remarks: "This is why it is said that classical education enriches man's personality more than the technical or narrowly vocational one."   This is Vico's fundamental concept, the "structure," so to speak, of his defense of humanistic values.   The reader is invited to peruse the following passage: "Arts and Sciences, all of which, in the past, were embraced by philosophy, and animated by it with a unitary spirit, are, in our day, unnaturally separated and disjointed . . ." (Gianturco, *Study Methods*, p. 77).   Equally interesting, it seems to me, was the two-week meeting held in June, 1966, at M.I.T.'s Endicott House in Dedham, Mass.   The meeting was important because it highlighted the necessity of determining a possibility of communication between social scientists, historians, and humanists.   In such a meeting there emerged also the need for new methods, toward the realization of which a specially appointed planning committee directed its efforts.   The basic point, it seems to me, is the decision that "the textbookish question-and-memorized-answer approach would be abandoned; substituted for it would be an attempt to engage children in the real problems of human society and of its history."   (See *A Short History of the Social Studies Program* [Cambridge, Mass.: Educational Services Incorporated, 1966].)

    [55] Although Bruner acknowledges the value of the famous credo of Dewey, he opposes it with a different pedagogic conception, emphasizing his own structural principle, on the strength of which "everything can be taught to everybody," inasmuch as "the task of teaching a particular subject-matter to a child of a certain age consists in finding a way to represent the structure of that subject-matter in the way of perceiving things peculiar to the child."   (See J. S. Bruner, *Educational Reconstruction after Dewey*, Voice of America, Marconi University of the Air, no. 613.)

American apparatus of production, which is consumer oriented, dominated by the goal of maximum immediate profit. The logical consequences of this conception were the "instrumentalist" viewpoint and the concept of meliorism. Once these directives had been set up, the realization grew, not only that schooling had been demoted to a technique (in spite of good verbal intentions), but that education was a failure even on the productive economic plane, since it was unable to bring forth a class of specialists capable of coping with the prodigious technological progress of our time. Today, therefore, the American production system is controlled by the urge to exploit the discoveries of science and to forge ahead toward new discoveries; it is science oriented.[56] This demands a radical change in teaching and methods, because we have become aware that the "disinterest" of the purely scientific dis-

---

[56] It has been noted that, up to twenty years ago, Detroit and Pittsburgh were prestigious symbols of power, but that these symbols today have shifted to Harvard University and to M.I.T., as well as to the New York–New Jersey zone, where Columbia and Princeton and the scientific laboratories of Bell and General Electric are located; to the Washington-Baltimore area, around The Johns Hopkins University, and to California (University of California at Berkeley, Stanford University at Palo Alto, and California Institute of Technology at Pasadena).

Something analogous is occurring in Europe, and precisely in Germany, where the Uni-Bochum, the new University of the Ruhr, is coupled with the colossal industrial complexes of the Ruhr, and where the new universities of Konstanz, Bremen, Bielefield, Düsseldorf, and Ratisbon, which are being planned, are tied up, directly or indirectly, with the great economic and political centers of Europe and to those overseas. Out of this, very precise demands are emerging in regard to the orientations of pedagogy. These demands may be summarized as follows:

1. Assessment of culture as absolute and primary value. That does not mean that scholarship should, as something abstract, be disjoined from concrete reality. It means, instead, that it is exactly such disinterested cultural activity or "primality" which has the power to descend into, and permeate with its spirit, the particularities of life, bestowing on them not only intelligibility but also its own ability to stimulate and increase progress in an economic sense.

2. Value of scholarship, not in view of the services that it can render, but in view of its being what it *is*. If we view scholarship as a tool, it becomes technique tied up with the particular and conditioned by it. The particular is specific and subject to change; a day comes when it is no longer serviceable. If, instead, scholarship is viewed in its essence, *qua* value, if we consider the universal (Bruner would say the structure), then scholarship is serviceable, and it may be adjusted to all circumstances, to all particulars, because it is not conditioned by a single particularity. Culture is all the more instrumental, the more non-instrumental it is.

At bottom, the pragmatist position repeated the Spencerian mistake of asking pedagogy this question first: "For what purpose?" Thus scholarship, research, and the humanistic element were considered as luxury items. It is far from my intention to belittle Dewey's merits, which are great, especially that of having emphasized the relationships which must obtain between the world of education and that of labor. The wrong point, in my opinion, was his subordinating the former to the latter; it should be the other way around, or, rather, we should aim at a position of integration and synthesis (*verum–factum*).

covery becomes, in the last analysis, of the highest and most durable economic interest, and that, therefore, not only is a cultural investment the most profitable, but culture must be restored to its typical role of research, discovery, value—in other words, to its essential unity.   Hence we have also become aware of the necessity to develop humanistic culture.   Without humanistic culture, not only would the progress of science be blind, but it would risk promoting a lame education in which technico-scientific knowledge would forge ahead while humanistic scholarship would remain, in the best of cases, in a state of corpselike rigidity.   Bruner writes: "If . . . the risks of an overemphasis on science and technology, and the devaluation of humanistic learning, are to be dealt with, we shall have to maintain and nurture a vigorous pluralism. . . . The theatre, the arts, music, and the humanities . . . will need the fullest support." [57]

In presenting the Italian translation of Vico's *De nostri temporis studiorum ratione*, I wrote:

Vico, the opponent of the geometric spirit, who is not, however, deaf to the powerful voices of the modern achievements of science and technique, appears to us not so much the adversary of the Cartesian spirit as, rather, the enemy of the intellectualistic schema: a schema which forces tumultuous, contradictory human nature into the strait jacket of an absolute truth. . . . On the other hand, he . . . the estimator of that verisimilitude which makes up the warp and woof of vital human communication, appears to us . . . not only as the vindicator of "worldly" reality but also as the master of modern humanism.   Vico established precisely humanism's most authentic and durable values.   These values are not to be found in traditional conservatism . . . but are expressed by the emphasis which Vico places on the reality of man.   This reality is unitary and complex, made up not only of intelligence, but of passion and sensuousness as well. . . . consequently, the school, as well as science, if they wish to be human, that is, if they wish to be instruments of education, to be tools for shaping

---

[57] Bruner, *The Process of Education*, p. 80.   Vico organized his pedagogic discourse around three principal points:

1. Nature of the child.   This nature "ideally" follows the same development as that of mankind.   Thus Vico makes it clear that imagination is not an irrational, antirational, or rational element, but is prerational.   This element therefore precedes and presupposes rational activity.

2. Education cannot rely on analytical methods, which impoverish the polyhedric reality of life, reducing to bloodless *scheme* that which is its substance.   The scheme, the "conceptual" and universal structure (pattern), cannot concretize itself except by becoming a factual, historical reality.

3. Since factuality and truth, concrete and abstract, are identified in the historical process, educational methods should orient themselves toward an *operational* conception in which the child becomes aware of himself and of culture as processes in the way of becoming (*in fieri*).

It seems to me that such orientations, even today, could hold valid stimulations toward constructive methodological reflections, since they are in tune with requirements that are being evolved by the needs of our own time.

the minds of young men, should also address themselves to their hearts; in enlightening their intellects, they should also kindle their wills and spark their enthusiasm.[58]

May I be allowed to close my article with these words, which still seem to me a fitting conclusion.

Translated by Elio Gianturco

[58] *Il metodo degli studi del tempo nostro*, trans. Maria Goretti (Florence, 1957), Introduction, pp. 20–21.

Gillo Dorfles   MYTH AND METAPHOR
IN VICO AND IN
CONTEMPORARY AESTHETICS

"Aesthetics must truly be considered as one of Vico's discoveries."[1]   This
statement, which is to be found in one of Croce's finest books, may still be
fully endorsed, especially if we take aesthetics to be, exactly in the Vichian
sense, something more than a limited and sophisticated "philosophy of art,"
namely, if we view it as that branch of the sciences of man which, through
the study of the various artistic forms, aims at investigating the development
and the anthropological, psychological, and linguistic stages of mankind.

It is only in this sense, and after having thus broadened the term "aesthetics," that we will be able to realize Vico's *topical* significance, not only
by reassessing some principles which he advocates, but by endeavoring to
reach a world-view which assigns a prominent place, a foreground position,
to the study of the imaginative symbolic, mythical, and metaphorical factors,
even in those sectors of human thought which seem to be at the most remote
distance from those factors.

I advance this premise at the very outset in order to justify my contention
that Vico should be considered as the real "father of modern aesthetics," and
not only as the pioneer or harbinger of an idealistic aesthetics (to view him
only as such would be to do him an injustice).   And, as a matter of fact,
although I have but now referred to Croce's authoritative statement, I should
like to make it absolutely clear that my interest, in the present essay, does not
focus on Vico the progenitor of idealism, even if I have to run counter to
Croce's express warning.   It was he who remarked, in a fit of sarcastic
peevishness: "The great idealist of the *New Science* was not even spared
the opprobrium of being paid homage to by the adherents of positivism."[2]

I am interested, instead, in one of Vico's aspects which has been studied only
to a slight extent.   The Vico who attracts me is the thinker who analyzes
with sufficient rigor (although often with inadequate critical and scientific

[1] See B. Croce, *La filosofia di Giambattista Vico* (Bari, 1911), p. 50: "Aesthetics must
truly be considered as one of Vico's discoveries, with the reservations, however, by which
all attributions of discoveries are usually hedged about, and in spite of the fact that Vico
did not deal with it in a special book, and forgot to bestow upon it the fortunate name by
which Baumgarten, some decades later, baptized it."

[2] *Ibid.*, p. 292.

equipment), with notable acumen (even though, at times, with excessive lack of sophistication), certain surprising linguistic concatenations, certain strange etymological derivations, certain previously unthought-of correlations between language and custom, myth and word, poetry and history.

After the broad treatment to which the symbolic forms of myth have been subjected by Cassirer,[3] there is no need to emphasize the philosophico-anthropological importance of Vico's discoveries in this sphere. I shall, instead, limit myself to throwing into relief (as far as the brevity of this essay allows) the significance which the most recent aesthetics, particularly Anglo-American aesthetics, attaches to the symbolico-metaphorical, or mythico-metaphorical, element. I shall also examine the question of the extent to which these researches can be deemed to hark back to Vico's theories (although this connection may be altogether unrecognized and often not even articulated in hypothetical form).

Vico's case is not the first, nor is it the only one, in which surprisingly anticipatory ferments have been shelved and wholly ignored for decades and even centuries.

Does this fact perhaps mean that, in the final analysis, an authentic influence by certain thinkers never had a chance to exert itself ?   Does this mean that "man's thought" has traveled its course in utter disregard of those thinkers? Or does it mean that their ideas have germinated, and engendered subsequent developments, in ways which were completely mysterious and hidden ?   In Vico's case this circumstance is particularly noticeable.   It is not, therefore, an act of nationalistic vanity on my part to attempt to connect some "discoveries" featured in intellectual trends peculiar to our epoch with the work of a philosophical genius who was born no less than three centuries ago.

Many Anglo-American authors, who certainly have had no contact or familiarity with Vico's work, evince to an astonishing degree what we may call a "Vichian mentality," and reach, in the field of aesthetics, conclusions that would seem possible and obvious only on the basis of a study of Vico. I shall let others engage in more minute comparisons and verifications and shall confine myself to the examination of a precisely circumscribed field concerning symbolism and the metaphorical nature of the language of art and myth.   It is a field which, in the last two or three decades, Anglo-American aesthetics has abundantly cultivated.   I had the opportunity, some years ago, to devote a short study to the symbolic-metaphorical element in

[3] See Ernst Cassirer, *The Philosophy of Symbolic Forms*, trans. Ralph Mannheim (New Haven: Yale University Press, 1953–57), II, 3: "Anyone aiming at a comprehensive system of human culture has, of necessity, turned back to myth. In this sense, Giambattista Vico, founder of the philosophy of language, also founded a completely new philosophy of mythology. For Vico the true unity of human culture is represented by the triad of language, art, and myth."

modern Anglo-American aesthetics,[4] and some of my observations, viewed in the light of an analysis of Vico's work, may still, I think, be of interest, because they disclose many curious coincidences.   I noted, for instance, that in the work of Richards, of Susanne Langer (partly in the wake of Cassirer's investigations), we find obvious attempts to identify, in the symbolic element, one of the most significant "constants" of art.   When, for instance, Susanne Langer[5] asserts that symbol should permit us to conceive the idea which it presents ("presentational symbol"), regardless of any more or less conceptualized meaning, any discursive "truth," she refers to "symbols of our feeling," which are akin to those of myth, of ritual, and hence to that "imaginative" thought to which Vico addresses himself.

Likewise, when E. Empson[6] affirms that "the machinations of ambiguity are among the primal roots of poetry," he takes "ambiguity" to mean the metaphorical quality of artistic language, or, to phrase it as Wimsatt[7] does, he tends to admit the presence of an illogical and irrational element in artistic language.   And does not Philip Wheelwright's[8] distinction between "literal" and "expressive" language in his *Semantic of Poetry* bear a kinship to the analogous Vichian conception of a poetic, hence artistic, thought?

The discrimination made by Richards[9] between "statements" and "pseudostatements" (the latter being unverifiable and peculiar to literary expression, in contrast to the verifiable and exact assertions of science) falls within an acceptance of artistic language which postulates a cleavage between emotional and referential meaning.   However, what neither Richards nor

[4] See my essay "Simbolo e metafora come strumenti di comunicazione in estetica," in *Il pensiero americano contemporaneo*, ed. F. Rossi-Landi (Milan: Comunità, 1958).

[5] Susanne K. Langer, *Philosophy in a New Key* (Cambridge: Harvard University Press, 1942); and my essay "L'estetica 'simbolistica,' e l'opera di Susanne Langer," *Rivista critica di storia della filosofia*, 14 (1956).

[6] William Empson, *Seven Types of Ambiguity* (New York, 1947); and, in regard to the problem of metaphor, see mainly the chapter on "Metaphor" in *idem*, *The Structure of Complex Words* (New York: New Directions, 1951), where, among other things, Empson says (p. 331): "Language is full of sleeping metaphors, and the words for mental processes are all derived from older words for physical processes."   This is a statement singularly concordant with Vico's assertion: "It is noteworthy that in all languages the greater part of the expressions relating to inanimate things are formed by metaphors from the human body and its parts" (*The New Science of Giambattista Vico*, trans. Thomas G. Bergin and Max H. Fisch [Garden City, N.Y.: Doubleday, 1961], par. 405).

[7] W. K. Wimsatt, "Symbol and Metaphor," *Review of Metaphysics*, 4 (December, 1950).   On the same topic see also Kenneth Burke, *A Rhetoric of Motives* (Englewood Cliffs, N.J.: Prentice-Hall, 1950).

[8] Philip Wheelwright, "On the Semantics of Poetry," *Kenyon Review*, 1940.   On this subject see the basic volume by the same author, *The Burning Fountain: A Study in the Language of Symbolism* (Bloomington: Indiana University Press, 1954), as well as *Metaphor and Reality* (Bloomington: Indiana University Press, 1962).

[9] See I. A. Richards, *Principles of Literary Criticism* (London, 1926) and *The Philosophy of Rhetoric* (New York–London, 1936).

his disciples and followers seem to have understood correctly is the fact that even in artistic "pseudostatements" there may be hidden a datum of the scientific kind, even though that datum may be formulated through a type of discourse quite different from the exclusively denotative language of science. "It is not the poet's business to make scientific statements," says Richards in his *Science and Poetry*,[10] "yet poetry has constantly the air of making statements." It is here, it seems to me, that we can glimpse an intuition which may degenerate into an excessively constricting conception of literary and poetic values in general, because of the failure to take into account a possible conceptual value of verse, regardless of any actual denotative validity that verse may possess. The error—in the words of another outstanding American critic, Cleanth Brooks[11]—is that of thinking that "poetry communicates an idea of ours to the reader, rather than that it is poetry itself which is being communicated." Poetical experience is at least partially communicable; the poet, however, should be referred to as *poietès*, and not as an expositor or communicator.[12]

Here, perhaps, is the point of greatest discrepancy between an aesthetics such as could be derived or drawn directly from the Vichian source, and an aesthetics like that which was formulated in the writings of some of the major "new critics" of America, or that which has dominated some of the most recent trends of Europe's critical thought concerning poetry. The art of our day, especially that of literature and poetry, has taken shelter, to an even greater extent than heretofore, in a symbolic-metaphorical limbo, shunning, with set purpose, mere denotative validity, in order to turn its yearning toward the absolute prevalence of the connotative quotient. Modern art, in the final analysis, has lost most of its conceptual and rational values, and emphasizes, instead, the acoustic, phonetic elements, or at least those values of a semanticism stemming from the contextual positions of the words or, conversely, from their *de-contextualization*, as we can see in the case of what the poetic doctrine of the Russian formalists, for instance, Sklovsky,[13] calls

[10] I. A. Richards, *Science and Poetry*, 2d ed. (London, 1935).

[11] Cleanth Brooks, *Modern Poetry and the Tradition* (New York, 1939); *idem*, *The Well-Wrought Urn* (New York, 1947).

[12] *Ibid.*

[13] In regard to the problem of the *ostranenie*, that is, of the "estranging" (or, more exactly, of the "becoming strange") of a certain word within a given context, see Viktor Sklovsky's essay "Iskusstvo kak priëm" (Art as Artifice), *Poetika*, 1919. There is an extensive account of the theories of the Russian formalists in Victor Erlich's book *Russian Formalism* (The Hague: Mouton, 1954), where on p. 190 we read: "While, in informational prose, the aim of metaphor is that of rendering more convincing or more accessible to the audience a particular speech, in poetry, metaphor becomes a means to reinforce the aesthetic effect envisaged [by the writer]. Rather than translating into familiar terms what is unfamiliar, the poetic image bestows strangeness upon what is ordinary and usual by presenting it in a new light and within a context different from the one where we would expect to find it."

ostranenie. *Ostranenie* is the process whereby a certain word is forced to "become strange," that is, to assume an unfamiliar, strange meaning, by being divorced from its context.

In the case of primitive poetry (written in that language of the heroic times to which Vico refers) the symbolism and metaphoricalness, hence the non-rationality of the poetic element, were not attributable to a dislike for syntactic-semantic values, to a disinclination toward denotative elements; this poetry was symbolic-irrational by nature, that is, because of that necessary mode of being of a poetry which had *not yet* deteriorated to the level of prose. In other words, primitive poetry of the Vichian type (unlike modern poetry) was *not* animated by the purposeful desire to be prose no longer.

The same viewpoint applies to the whole realm of metaphor; but, in this case, modern authors have become fully aware that in this rhetorical trope (that is, metaphor) there still remains some residue of that ancient faculty of linking-up, by sudden illumination, rational and irrational, conceptual and imaginative, aspects.

According to Mrs. Langer,[14] for instance, metaphor is an example of our ability to employ "presentational symbols." Hence, primitive language originates in metaphor, which subsequently fades away and dies. According to Owen Barfield,[15] metaphor is a throwback to the mythical potentiality of the primitives; according to Brooks,[16] we should distinguish between functional and illustrative metaphors, while, according to Wimsatt,[17] "metaphor could be a vicious circle to express concepts"; and, finally, according to Richards,[18] metaphor consists of an interaction of "tenor" and *vehicle* (where *vehicle* indicates the "subject," the image contained in the metaphor, and *tenor* refers to the ideas that are signified through the metaphorical process). Consequently, according to this view, metaphor (as Kaplan maintains[19]), is to be understood as a "composite referential term," that is, as a form of discourse where one of the terms is constantly denotative. John Middleton Murry[20] had already stated that metaphor should not be

[14] *Philosophy in a New Key*, p. 141.
[15] Owen Barfield, *Poetic Diction: A Study in Meaning* (London, 1952).
[16] *Modern Poetry* and *The Well-Wrought Urn*.
[17] "Symbol and Metaphor"; Wimsatt discriminates, moreover, between a logical form of stylistic meaning and a "counterlogical," or poetical, form. He analyzes, besides, the metaphorical value of pun, which, according to him, underscores an extra-rational aspect of metaphor by concentrating, through an analogy of sound, on the symbolic value of the metaphor itself.
[18] See *The Philosophy of Rhetoric*, p. 96.
[19] The reader is referred to A. Kaplan's article, "Referential Meaning in the Arts," *Journal of Aesthetics and Art Criticism*, 12, no. 4 (1954), where *metaphor* is defined as a "compound reference, referring to its tenor by way of its vehicle" (p. 469).
[20] J. Middleton Murry, *The Problem of Style* (London, 1925).

considered as a simple comparison between two terms, but rather as "almost a mode of apprehension." This would do away with the ancient debate between those who admit and those who reject the priority of the "abstract" meaning of the word. As we know, Vico is among the latter.

Finally, in order to wind up this swift review of divergent opinions, I may mention that Ezra Pound himself (in an old essay)[21] observed that it is essential for us to keep in mind the distinction between simply "ornamental metaphor," which is false metaphor, and "interpretative metaphor," which may be identified with the creative image present in all poetry.

These few hints, jotted down in telegraphic style (and which obviously could be greatly expanded), are enough to indicate the importance attached by a whole sector of Anglo-American thought to the mythico-metaphorical element. The debates between "cognitivists" and "emotivists" have not died down, and have even been blazing up again with the recent revival of interest in more decidedly linguistic problems, that is, in problems akin to those which were once discussed by such scholars as Sapir, Bloomfield, Whorf, Carnap, and Morris. On the other hand, it is not hard to detect an equal concern for the problem of metaphor (rather than for the problem of myth), and for the relationship that metaphor bears to the half-logical dimensions of language, in most of the major linguistic currents of Western Europe (or of Europe in general) as represented by such leaders as Roman Jakobson, André Martinet, Roland Barthes, and others.

For these recent researchers (who have given a more scientific slant to their investigations, and who are completely free from any, even casual, tieup with Vichian philosophy), the symbolic-metaphorical element of language is basic not only to literary, but to philologic and glottologic, inquiry. Most frequently, obscure meanings are embedded in metaphors, and it is only through a study of metaphors that we are able to decipher some etymological and mythopoeic symbols otherwise destined to remain utterly inoperative and dead.

To re-evaluate myths, to re-evaluate them in the sense of bestowing on them that which, in the view of many people, had been only fable and figment—the value of events that had actually occurred—meant also to bring about a positive reassessment of the *raison d'être* of art. Art was envisaged as being much more than the "spiritual activity" cherished by the adherents of idealism.

When Vico asserts: "It has been demonstrated that myths are true and strictly serious histories of the folkways of the primitive peoples of Greece,"[22]

[21] His introduction to Ernest Fenollosa's article, "The Chinese Written Characters," *The Little Review Anthology*, 1953.

[22] While most of the other quotations from Vico in this article are taken from Bergin

or when he states that "heroic fables were veritable histories of the heroes and of their customs, such as are found to have been practiced in all nations at the time of their barbarism," he obviously means that they are narratives based on facts, not on fictions.   If the "hero" is something more than a man, this is no reason for viewing him as a fictitious being, non-existent in reality. A considerable part of what is seen as "aesthetic" may for that matter be made to fall under the Vichian category of the "heroic."   Of the three kinds of language enumerated by Vico, the first is wordless: it consists of mimical gestures.[23]   The second, the "heroic language," is made up of similitudes, comparisons, images, metaphors.   The third, the "human" language, is made up of "conventional," agreed upon, expressions.   Of these three languages it is the second, the *heroic*, which is of the greatest interest to us.   This vehicle of expression demands a closer and longer investigation, since it is in that language (from the very outset, and not at the end) that we find the rich imaginative texture with which our speech (in the "age of men") is still saturated and pregnant, especially when, from being a "common speech," it is transformed into the language of poetry.

In the case of the third language, the language of men, we are faced with "conventional, agreed-upon, terms," that is, we are confronted with "*institutionalized* elements" (as we would phrase it today).   In this conventionalized language, as De Saussure states, the link between the sign and the object or idea denoted is ankylosed and irremovable, unless resort is had to violent strainings and to experimental, asyntactical turns of speech.   This third language, therefore, which is ours here and now, does not interest us, and we can leave it to the minute analyses of linguists.   It has, for that matter, already been catalogued adequately by Vico's label "language consisting of conventional terms."[24]   The second language is that which engages our interest.   In this language, discourse is made up of metaphors, similitudes, metonymies, synecdoches, of any kind of trope capable of transposing into an image that which otherwise would be a bare concept.   It would, however, be absurd to think of a previous conceptualization of imaginative elements.   As Vico emphasizes, it is a question of a *successive* conceptualization of data and events that were present in the minds of the men of the

---

and Fisch's translation of the *New Science*, 1961 edition, I am taking these two sentences, instead, from the Italian edition, *La scienza nuova di G. B. Vico*, published by Rizzoli in Milan in 1963, pp. 28–29.   These sentences have been left out in the American edition, which is an abridgment.   Concerning the "truthfulness" of fables, and, consequently, the Vichian interpretation of myth, see Schelling's basic work *Einleitung in die Philosophie der Mythologie* (An Introduction to the Philosophy of Mythology) (Munich: Beck, 1927), vol. VI; see also Cassirer, "The Philosophy of Symbolic Forms."

[23] Bergin and Fisch, *New Science*, p. 3.

[24] *Ibid.*, pp. 3–4.

heroic period *only* in the form of images (as they can be present in the minds of the artists of any period).

Metaphors and similitudes therefore constitute the sole mode of communication possible for the "heroic" period; but we may further assume that they are the real and authentic mode of aesthetic communication in all epochs.

Today we naturally tend to confer on the communicative-metaphorical element a value different and less "cosmic" than the Vichian one. We are also inclined to hypothesize in the two operations, metaphorical and metonymic, different developments of discourse. For Jakobson, for instance, discursive development may take place along two different semantic lines,[25] depending upon whether it is a metaphorical process (a process by similarity), or a metonymic process (a process by contiguity) which is being instituted. Hence, the metaphorical process will have priority in poetical creations which have a romantic or symbolistic tendency, whereas the metonymic process will predominate in literary currents of a "realistic" nature. For the same reason we will find a prevalence of metaphor in poetry, and of metonymy in prose. For Vico, no sharp, clear-cut distinction exists between these two poles. But we should not forget that, very often, one trope encroaches upon another, and that it is not always possible to draw a definite line between the two forms of image transfer.

"The early gentile peoples, by a demonstrated necessity of nature, were poets, who spoke in poetic characters."[26] How many idle speculations have been spun, deplorably, around this statement of Vico's! Such speculations were the result of assigning to verbal terms meanings acquired in the course of centuries, meanings that no longer correspond to the original import. In saying that the first nations were made up of poets, Vico does nothing but re-emphasize his persuasion that human thought, in the first stage of its development (a stage which today we would call "precategorial"), was not of the rational, but of the predominantly imaginative type. This is tantamount to admitting the existence, in primitive mankind, of that

---

[25] Roman Jakobson, *Essais de linguistique générale* (Paris: Editions de Minuit, 1963), p. 61. Jakobson, starting with the study of aphasia, analyzes the differences between metaphor and metonymy. He shows the disappearance of one or the other trope according to the "verbal" disturbance which may take place, that is, according to "*le trouble de la contiguité.*" It may be interesting, in this connection, to remark that Vico did not fail to perceive the importance of aphasia as a method for the study of some linguistic features. He mentions the case of a man suffering from aphasia, as the result of apoplexy, whose lexical patrimony was grievously impaired; the man was able to use nouns, but had completely forgotten verbs. See *Scienza nuova*, Rizzoli ed., p. 237.

[26] Bergin and Fisch, *New Science*, p. 5.

"visual thinking," of that thought through images, which scholars (H. Read and others) only recently have identified and re-evaluated.[27]

When Vico goes so far as to claim that the discovery that primitive peoples were made up of poets and spoke in poetical characters is "the master key" of the *New Science* and had cost him "the persistent research" of almost all of his literary life,[28] he evidently realizes the importance of that discovery and its undeniable value. Therefore, to assume in a primitive mankind a priority of the imaginative element, of "visual thinking," is tantamount to positing that "men at first feel without perceiving, then they perceive with a troubled and agitated spirit, finally they reflect with a clear mind."[29] Vico means that men, who originally were "stupid, insensate and horrible beasts,"[30] achieved at a later time a primitive kind of wisdom which was "poetical." If we transpose this sentence phylogenetically, it may be tantamount to saying: "At first the artist has a perception of reality as yet non-rationalized and mainly emotional, this perception later being replaced by a rationalized and conscious awareness."

Metaphorical language, for Vico, is the most typical example of the primitive (hence, poetical) mentality. That is why we must pay utmost attention to the manner in which he conceives of metaphor: a trope which for that matter has been most attentively described by ancient rhetoricians. But what Vico's thought brings out with greater clarity than that of other scholars has done, is the fact that metaphor "gives sense and passion to insensate things,"[31] that is, that metaphor is not merely an embellishment of poetic discourse, or a means of enriching language, but is an authentic epistemological factor. It is obvious that this position is very close to that taken by Aristotle in his *Poetics* and *Rhetoric*, when he states: "to know how to invent fine metaphors means to know how to grasp the resemblances that objects bear to one another" (*Poetics* 1459a); and "in philosophy, too, the ability to perceive similarities between objects which are far apart is evidence of an acute mind" (*Rhetoric* III. II.1414a.9).

Hence, metaphor possesses a singular gnoseological importance. Metaphorical expression is helpful in conveying in precise fashion a meaning which otherwise would not be so exactly rendered or would not strike our mind with an equal vividness. Consequently, metaphor is a strange example of "extension of the semantic area" achieved, not through scientific or

[27] See chiefly Herbert Read's statement in *Icon and Idea* (London, 1955), a volume wholly predicated upon the assumption of the priority of the imaginative element over the conceptual. Read's trend of discourse follows the path blazed by Vico: "I believe," he writes, "that art . . . is, even historically, prior to language as a system of communication. . . . It follows that a non-necessary verbal equivalent exists for the visual work of art. . . . The design has meaning, but not a verbal meaning, logical or rational."

[28] Bergin and Fisch, *New Science*, p. 5.

[29] *Ibid.*, p. 33, axiom LIII.   [30] *Ibid.*, p. 74, par. 374.   [31] *Ibid.*, p. 87, par. 404.

philosophical, learned, or denotative language, but rather through a type of language which is connotative and tropological. This is why, in my opinion, the "case of metaphor" seems to be among those which enable us to prove, almost scientifically, how much of our cognitive power still remains entangled in the coils of a form of discourse which is predominantly irrational. In connection with this, I should like to remark that I am not inclined to accept the idea of those theorists (and they are perhaps the majority) who consider the "case of the metaphor" as evidence of the prevalently rational and cognitive value of poetry. Even if it is true that poetry—that art in general—may and should be a vehicle of knowledge, that it should be allowed to avail itself of any psychological or scientific reference, this does not prevent us from asserting that the type of knowledge represented by metaphor (as well as by other aspects of art) should be viewed as having a prerational, metarational, or often a preconscious character. It is precisely this character which allows art to achieve a kind of intersubjective communication unlike that of scientific discourse.

At this point, however, metaphor (besides evincing the semantic value just referred to) is envisaged as the equivalent to, and partly as the linguistic counterpart of, myth.

"Thus every metaphor so formed is a fable in brief," [32] says Vico. It is a "brief fable," that is, a myth: a myth considered, from its inception, as a tale. The tale is not "euhemeristically" realistic, but is endowed with those epochal and existential values which cause it to be the most authentic "correlative" of any archaic age.

Because myth survives, and is to be found at distances in time which are very remote from the moment of its origin, and because it is the testimony of a long-ago epoch, whose consequences and influences are still felt, it is closely tied to metaphor. Metaphor first arises, like myth, in the archaic atmosphere where everything is still immersed in the "synchronic," but it keeps on manifesting itself—germinating anew in subsequent times, even today—as the only attestation to the continuity of man's creative and ideational thought. This faith in myth and metaphor as elements not only agreeably imaginative but actually and factually formative and constitutive of our world, of our life, is endorsed by Vico's well-known phrase: "So that, as rational metaphysics teaches that man becomes all things by understanding them (*homo intelligendo fit omnia*), this imaginative metaphysics shows that man becomes all things by not understanding them (*homo non intelligendo fit omnia*). . . ." [33] The fact that man sets himself up as the "rule of

[32] *Ibid.*

[33] *Ibid.*, p. 88, par. 405. I don't believe that several of the examples adduced by Vico for the purpose of explaining the rise of metonymy and synecdoche are wholly reliable. The fact that *caput* (head) replaced *man* because primitive beings saw in the woods, in the faraway distance, barely the head of a man (p. 89), or that the word "roof" replaced

the universe," that "man makes a whole world of himself," is identified
with the creative construction of this world by the process of non-intellec-
tion. Through this process, through his non-rational apprehension, man
creates reality, and, by transforming himself into it, becomes the world.

This is tantamount to affirming that man identifies himself with the world
and its objects exactly because of the fact that he does not understand them
cogitatively; he grasps reality by an imaginative process, which is a kind of
empathy, of *Einfühlung*.

As a matter of fact, as Vico explains, when man understands, he reaches
out to things with his thought, whereas, when he does *not* understand, he
becomes one with the objects, and transforms or transposes himself into
them: "for when man understands, he extends his mind and takes in the
things; but when he does not understand, he makes the things out of himself,
and becomes them by transforming himself into them."[34]

One instance of Vico's thought (or, more exactly, of a perhaps unconscious
Vichian conception of the relationships between language and thought)
appears today in the very provocative remarks made by Benjamin LeeWhorf
on the basic effect of our way of speaking on our way of thinking.[35] When,
for instance, Whorf quotes some typical expressions of the Hopi language
referring to time and space and to certain definitions of colors and plants,
and compares them with what he calls the "standard European language"
(that standardized and fossilized language which the average West European
uses, and which by now precludes him from any chance of getting nearer to
modalities of perception and thought more imaginative, more closely bound
up with the rhythms of nature and creation), he shows us, with irrefutable
data, to what extent our thought, our phantasy, is slavishly dependent upon
the language we speak: "The structure of the language one habitually uses
influences the manner in which one understands his environment."[36]
For example, Whorf finds that one of the characteristic features of our
culture is "our binominalism of form plus formless item, or 'substance,' our
metaphoricalness, our imaginary space, our objectified time."[37]

---

the word "house" because, "in primeval times, a roof was enough to offer the same
protection as an entire house," does not seem at all convincing. It is more probable
that the cause of metonymy and synecdoche was the desire not to mention objects or
persons by their own names. This was attributable to a kind of apotropaic prohibition,
to a sort of *taboo* of the name, not to a tendency to replace the whole by its parts, as Vico
would have us believe, or because of the fact that "particulars were elevated into
universals" (p. 89).

[34] *Ibid.*, p. 88.
[35] See Benjamin Lee Whorf, *Language, Thought, and Reality* (Cambridge, Mass., 1956).
[36] Benjamin Lee Whorf, *Four Articles on Metalinguistics* (Washington, D.C., 1949).
[37] *Ibid.*, p. 187. As for the differences between the spatio-temporal conception in

Obviously, I cannot discuss Whorf's complex statements at length; but none of my readers, I hope, will fail to notice the similarity which the thought of the American scholar (who is more scientifically equipped and more abreast of modern research) bears to Vico's remarks on the relationship between human civilizations and their respective languages.

I have elsewhere [38] hinted at this problem, which is still of burning interest to me, and have dwelt on the fact that today, more than ever, we should not fail to take into account the relativity and the corelatedness of our conscious thought, which is almost always conditioned by the presence of a parti-cular patrimony of ideas tied with a double knot to our linguistic heritage.

What import, then, does the train of thought expounded above have, from the viewpoint of aesthetics? Precisely that of showing that our linguistic expressions (our literary and artistic creations) are intimately bound up with our cogitative, perceptive, and "hedonic" attitudes and habits. Owing not so much to an altered or insufficient decoding, but principally to a failing, to a wearing out, to a process of entropy undergone by our linguistic code, some ideational and expressive possibilities die out, or are transformed, and can therefore account for the analogous or homologous transformation of all other artistic phenomena. The wealth or poverty of our thought (hence of our art, of our outlook on life) is strictly dependent on such factors. We can escape their influence only up to a certain extent, because those factors, in turn, depend on deeper causes that are not amendable by human skill, because they involve the whole socio-psychological makeup of a nation, of an epoch.

To identify myth with metaphor is dangerous; it is still more dangerous to identify myth and metaphor with art *tout court*. However, if we decide to focus our attention exactly on that aspect of Vico's thought which most closely concerns aesthetics, we must take into account, first of all, those irrational, imaginative, and even illogical elements which play such a momentous role in Vico's description of "heroic" languages. If we do this, our reference to *myth* as *historical metaphor* and to *metaphor* as *linguistic myth* will not seem altogether impertinent or dangerous. Exactly these two elements, the mythical and the metaphorical, lend themselves to being drawn close together and mutually compared. Myth, in fact, is one of the rare links between today and the past, for it enables us, with due inter-pretative reservations, to reconstruct some tracts of human history which

Western thought and that of the Hopis: "The experience of time and phasing tends to be objectified in S.A.E. as a sequence of separable units. In Hopi, phases of cycles are linguistically distinct from norms, or other form-classes."

[38] See my volume *Nuovi riti nuovi miti*, particularly the chapter on "Objectified Time and Imaginary Space" (Turin: Einaudi, 1965).

have disappeared from sight but which are determinant for the rise and development of any civilization. Moreover, myth is exactly that vehicle of conceptual, but at the same time transrational, communication which supplies us with a "truth of the image" often no less reliable than historical truth. (In this, the truth of the image is no different from the truth of art.) That is why art, by necessity, is one of the primary instruments of any mythical language, just as metaphor is the linguistic instrument which most easily partakes of the mythopoeic quality at the very moment of its genesis. Myth and metaphor are the conscious or unconscious tools of all those creative clues, of those expressive incitements, which art has always conveyed, and which make up the most original and autonomous patrimony of every human culture. Vico clearly understood and affirmed all this at a time when these ideas were most remote from the main highway of coeval thought; his was an epoch which was soon to be carried by a violent groundswell of impetuous rationalism to the point of refusing to grant any credence to the apparently fanciful and irrational assumptions (still tinged with Gnostic-Hermetic tradition) brought forward by the Neapolitan philosopher. But the influence of myth and metaphor often extends beyond what is usually considered to be their field of natural action, and it seeps through into quite remote and as yet unexplored domains—a fact which constitutes additional evidence of the vitality of the symbolic-metaphorical element in modern life.

It is only in recent times that we have witnessed the extension of studies in metaphor to more modern and even "futuristic" phraseology such as the language of commercial advertising and graphics. In an interesting essay published a short while ago, Gui Bonsiepe minutely lists many cases of elements of advertising, relative to both copywriting and "figural" pub-licity, whose persuasive efficacy depends mostly on the use of metaphors, metonymics, and synecdoches, or on "tropological" metaphors bound up with "literary" ones so as to form a persuasive set of idioms whose "double meaning" may turn out to be at times immediately manifest, while at other times half-concealed, so as to be endowed with that particular interpretative ambiguity which is an extremely effective factor of coercive persuasion.[39]

I cannot expatiate on the aesthetic as well as the "promotional" importance of the use of this metaphorical material, but I have referred to this example for the express purpose of indicating the still unexplored possibilities of this field. What constitutes the most singular aspect of such a phenomenon is the fact that, most of the time, the awareness of the tropological employment of a term, an image, a phrase, exists not in the person who uses it, and not even in his addressee, but in the individual who observes the poetical, literary "quote," or the figurative image, from the outside, and, occasionally even from a historical point of view. The assumption could even be posited that

[39] Gui Bonsiepe, "Visual/Verbal Rhetoric," *Dot Zero*, 2 (New York, 1967).

a veritable and authentic metaphor, such as constitutes a model of synchronic activity, becomes manifest in its essential function as a tool of communication exactly because of, and in the process of, its *diachronization*.   This tells us that the figurative use of a term takes place in an almost instinctive way, that we are led by a spontaneous sensitivity adherent to the ways of an epoch.   That figurative use definitely does not occur on the basis of a linguistic "recipe," artificially contrived and neatly dished up.

Vico was among the first to enlighten us concerning the historical, anthropological, and aesthetic value of myth and metaphor *qua* main elements of interpersonal communication in the "heroic" epoch of mankind.   The fact that in our day the role of myth and metaphor has again become of topical interest, in the manipulation of the language of art (and of advertising as well), should cause no wonderment in those who realize the basic importance of such tropes.   I should like, however, to underline the desirability that today, on the occasion of the third centennial of Vico's birth, wider circles be alerted to the intense modernity and determinant vigor of Vico's analysis of the symbolic factors of human thought and human creativity.   Without those factors, man would not be that *animal symbolicum* which is capable of understanding and construing the world in terms of a continuous process of tropological transposition.   Such a process leads from myth to history, from the metaphorical to the concrete word, from the synchronic to the diachronic.

Translated by Elio Gianturco

Herbert Read   VICO AND THE
                                      GENETIC THEORY
                                      OF POETRY

One of the clearest exponents of Vico's thought has warned us against the
danger of seeking in this philosopher a justification of romanticism.   This,
according to Professor Caponigri,

is the fallacy that Vico conceived the reflective moment as a moment of instability, of
moral malice, even of essential perversion and of the moment of spontaneity, by
contrast, as possessing a monolithic integrity; in a word, that Vico is at once anti-
intellectual and romantic.   It is true, indeed, that Vico is a relentless critic of abstract
intellectualism; his critique is not advanced, however, in the name of a romantic faith
in the veridical quality of spontaneity or in its moral integrity; it is advanced wholly
in the interests of the integrity of the life of the spirit.   He is entirely innocent of the
romanticism which certain critics and interpreters impute to him, for the most part
on the basis of the distinction between the barbarism of sense and the barbarism of
reflection.[1]

I shall take this warning to heart in the pages that follow, but I would first
observe that romanticism (a post-Vichian phenomenon) is not necessarily
inconsistent with the integrity of the life of the spirit, nor is it necessarily
dependent upon a belief in the veridical quality of spontaneity.   In my
earliest essay in literary criticism,[2] written long before I had any direct
acquaintance with Vico, my declared purpose was to reconcile the concepts
of "reason" and "romanticism," and to maintain an integrity of spirit whose
total presence, as demanded by Vico (and interpreted by Caponigri), "must
embrace sense and intellect, image and idea at once."   To that ideal, however
incoherently, I have been faithful in all my criticism.

Nevertheless, Vico's criticism of the "barbarism of reflection" is relevant
to the Romantic philosophy of art, and his conception of poetry is identical

[Perhaps the most striking example of Herbert Read's Vichianism is his *Icon and Idea:
The Function of Art in the Development of Human Consciousness* (Cambridge: Harvard
University Press, 1955), now available also in paperback (New York: Schocken Books,
1965).   I had the pleasure of discussing a possible analogy between the thesis of this book
and Vichian ideas with Sir Herbert in 1960 and found him in general agreement with
my remarks.   On Read and Vico see p. 585 of this volume.—Editor.]

[1] Robert Caponigri, *Time and Idea: The Theory of History in Giambattista Vico*
(London: Routledge & Kegan Paul, 1953), p. 135.

[2] Herbert Read, *Reason and Romanticism* (London: Faber & Gwyer, 1926).

with the Romantic conception of poetry as formulated by Wordsworth, Coleridge, Shelley, and Keats (not to bring German philosophers of the same period into the discussion). My purpose in this brief essay is to establish certain essential similarities between Vico and what I conceive to be the Romantic theory of poetry.

These similarities spring from Vico's principle of the priority of the poetic moment in the life of the human spirit, and from the implication that such a "moment" is spontaneous. What Vico means by *spontaneous* is not in doubt, and, although we are again warned by Caponigri that as a concept spontaneity cannot be divorced from those further stages of the life of the human spirit which proceed from spontaneity to rational reflection, nevertheless, spontaneity is distinctly associated with poetic creation, with the origins of language and myth, and that is all that matters from the point of view of a philosopher of art.

Vico's basic axiom must be examined literally, for he meant it to be precise. It may be that the original words lose some of their precision in the process of translation; the meaning of the word *avvertenza*, for example, which we translate as "advertence," is obscure. What is implied is that the primary act of apprehension is sensational or reflexive. We are not even conscious of it until we put a stop to the reflexive process, until we "stop to consider," which means, "allow to enter the field of consciousness." When it enters this field it causes a commotion, as Vico says; it sets into action our feelings and emotions. Then follow those stages of comparison and coordination which enable the mind to grasp the experience "with clarity and serenity."

Nothing in this process need be intellectual, for what is implied by the stage of clarification and serenity is a process which in our time has been described by the Gestalt theory of perception, according to which the elements of sensation achieve in the act of perception a balance or structure that gives them coherence and "meaning." We may, with Croce, call this final stage in the process of perception an *intuition* of form, but the word is not essential. Nor need we insist on the logical sense of "meaning"; it is sufficient if the coherence is "manifested" (in Wittgenstein's sense), that is to say, if it is present in the consciousness as significant form.

I shall leave to other contributors to this volume the difficult task of tracing Vico's direct impact on the Romantic movement in general. My purpose is more limited: to estimate the debt of the modern movement in English poetry to Vico's philosophy, insofar as this debt is not accounted for by the Romantic theory of poetry in general, which we know was directly inspired by Vico. How direct this inspiration was must remain an estimate rather than a scientific demonstration, as the significant example of Coleridge indicates. Coleridge typifies the manner in which ideas are absorbed by a process of mental osmosis. The fact that Coleridge was well acquainted with the *Scienza nuova* is not in doubt, and the paucity of the evidence in his case is no measure of the extent of the debt. A direct acquaintance with Vico's work cannot be documented before the year 1825, some ten years after Coleridge's essential ideas on the nature of poetry had been formulated in the writing of *Biographia literaria*. But as Fisch has shown in his Introduction to the Fisch and Bergin translation of the *Autobiography*,[3] Vico's *New Science* had been absorbed by Jacobi (thanks to Goethe) as early as 1792, and in 1814, at the very period of the gestation of the *Biographia literaria*, Coleridge had "lifted" a quotation from Jacobi "and adapted its context in his *Theory of Life*." The passage in question includes Vico's statement that "the clarity of metaphysical truth is like that of light, which we know only by means of things that are opaque; for we see not light but light-reflecting objects. Physical things are opaque; they have form and boundary, and in them we see the light of metaphysical truth"—a distinction which has direct bearing on Vico's theory of poetry and on Coleridge's.

Fisch has traced Vico's influence in England from Coleridge to Thomas Arnold to various Broad-Church leaders (Hare, Thirwall, Maurice, and others), then on to John Stuart Mill and other positivists and to historians such as Grote and Buckle, but in these theological or rationalistic debates Vico's theory of the nature and origin of poetry has no place. Any effect it might have had on poetic theory or practice in nineteenth-century England was lost in the general confusion of the Romantic tradition.

That tradition was to be restored in our own time by the imagist movement, using this term to include the prose writer James Joyce, perhaps permissible if one remembers his close association with Pound, and the fact that his writings were appearing in the same periodicals (*The Egoist, Poetry*) as *imagist poems*. The name "imagist" was given to the movement by Pound and, like most labels of its kind in the history of literature and art, was a misnomer. What Hulme and the poets who followed him (Aldington, Flint, H.D.) were striving for was the *concreteness* of the image in poetry— precision, definite outlines, visual acuity, and physical mimesis. Joyce's prose style, from *A Portrait of the Artist as a Young Man* onward, exhibits these same qualities, and there is at least the possibility that they were inspired by Vico's theory of poetry. The fact that by 1905 Pound had already "read and digested Vico" has been pointed out by Fisch.

The more general influence of Vico was re-established in England by the publication of R. G. Collingwood's translation of Croce's book *The Philosophy of Giambattista Vico*, which appeared in 1913, published by Howard Latimer. At the end of this volume there is an announcement of the "authorized translation" by T. E. Hulme of Georges Sorel's *Reflections on*

---

[3] Max H. Fisch and Thomas G. Bergin, trans., *The Autobiography of Giambattista Vico* (Ithaca, N.Y., 1944), pp. 68–69.

Violence. For some reason (perhaps because Howard Latimer went out of business) this volume was transferred to George Allen and Unwin, and did not appear until 1916. It is produced in the same type and format as *The Philosophy of Giambattista Vico*, from which we might conclude that the sheets had been transferred from Howard Latimer to Allen and Unwin some time between 1913 and 1916 (we must remember the outbreak of World War I in 1914).

The significance of this typographical association of the two volumes is that Hulme's Introduction to Sorel's book contains a reference to Vico (footnote, page xi), and that Hulme was the originator of the imagist movement in English poetry. The footnote merely says that Hulme "would have liked to have noted his [Sorel's] relations to Marx, Proudhon, and to Vico, and also to have said something of his conception of history, of which Croce has written in the preface to the Italian translation [of *Reflections on Violence*]."

Hulme was thoroughly familiar with Croce's work, but there is no evidence of his *direct* knowledge of Vico's original writings. If one examines Hulme's formulation of the principles of poetry, however, a distinct resemblance to Vico is evident. For example, Vico writes:

> Modern physics, too, I would be inclined to think, is conducive to poetic craft. Poets, today, employ expressions describing the natural causes of physical phenomena, either because they wish to arouse our admiration for the brilliance of their diction, or because they intend to vindicate their ancient claim, the earliest poets having been singers of physical phenomena. Notice such expressions as "blood-sprung" for "begotten", "to vanish into air" for "to die", "breast-burning fire" for "fever", "air-condensed vapour" for "cloud", "cloud-flung fire" for "thunderbolt", "earth-shadows" for "night". In ancient times, all the subdivisions of time were expressed in terms of the astronomers; poetic diction abounded in metonymy, in which the cause, instead of the effect, is stated. In conclusion, inasmuch as modern physics borrows its most sensuous images, expressive of natural causes, from mechanics, which it uses as its instrument, it endows poets with a treasure of new expressions both striking and novel.[4]

Now, turning to Hulme:

> All emotion depends on real solid vision or sound. It is physical.
> Each word must be an image *seen*, not a counter.
> With perfect style, the solid leather for reading, each sentence must be a lump, a piece of clay, a vision seen; rather, a wall touched with soft fingers.
> Solidity a pleasure.
> Always seek the hard, definite, personal word.
> All poetry is an affair of the body—that is, to be real it must affect body.[5]

---

[4] Elio Gianturco, trans., *On the Study Methods of Our Time* (Indianapolis, Ind., 1965), pp. 43–44.

[5] "Notes on Language and Style," reprinted as an appendix to Michael Roberts' *T. E. Hulme* (London, 1938).

This new verse resembles sculpture rather than music; it appeals to the eye rather than to the ear.   It has to mould images, a kind of spiritual clay, into definite shapes. . . . It builds up a plastic image which it hands over to the reader, whereas the old art endeavoured to influence him physically by the hypnotic effect of rhythm.[6]
   Vico's theory of poetry is part of his wider cosmic philosophy in which "poetic wisdom" is seen as a first stage in the evolution of all the arts and sciences—as "a poetic or creative metaphysics, out of which there developed in one direction logic, morals, economics and politics, all poetic; and in another direction physics, cosmography, astronomy, chronology, geography, all likewise poetic."[7]   From his point of view, "The most sublime labor of poetry is to give sense and passion to insensate things; and it is characteristic of children to take inanimate things in their hands and talk to them in play as if they were living persons" (New Science, paragraph 186).   Poetic sentences "are formed by feelings of passion and emotion, whereas philosophic sentences are formed by reflection and reasoning" (New Science, paragraph 219).   This reasoning relegates poetry, and indeed all the arts, to a pre-reflective stage of human development, a point of view that Hegel was to take up and develop systematically.   There is a certain sense in which this evolutionary hypothesis must be accepted, but its stultifying effect was over-come in Vico's philosophy by his difficult concept of ricorsi, usually inter-preted as a recurrence theory of history.   Caponigri has given the clearest interpretation of what Vico meant by this process, of which the essential point, so far as it affects the continuity of poetic creation, is that

"ricorso" in universal history and as the principle of universal history is the act by which the human spirit renders present and contemporaneous to itself the life of all the individual nations in their eternal and ideal principles.   This act of "ricorso" is the supreme and constitutive act of humanity in its own ideas and presence.   By this act, the human spirit reaches, so to say, back through all time, that is the time of the life of the individual nations, and down into the depths of consciousness to bring the entire content of history before itself in a single and total act of presence.[8]

This interpretation would bring Vico's concept into line, not only with the familiar Greek association of memory with inspiration (the Muses) but with recent theories of poetry as recollection (not only Wordsworth's general concept, but also Ernest Schachtel's modern theory of inspiration as a

[6] Ibid., pp. 269–70 (from an early lecture on modern poetry given in about 1912–13).
[7] Max H. Fisch, Introduction, to The New Science of Giambattista Vico, trans. Thomas G. Bergin and Max H. Fisch (Garden City, N.Y., 1961), pp. xlvii–xlviii.
[8] Caponigri, Time and Idea, p. 141; cf. Gianturco, Study Methods, p. 42: "I have stated that the type of abstract philosophical criticism prevalent in our day is detrimental to poetry, but only if imparted as a school subject to adolescents.   That type of criticism benumbs their imagination and stupifies their memory, whereas poets are endowed with surpassing imagination, and their immanent spirit is Memory, with her children, the Muses."

momentary lifting of the veil of childhood amnesia,[9] and Jung's hypothesis of the collective unconscious as a depository of archetypal forms available to the creative artist).[10]

Vico's theory of poetry is essentially *genetic*, and that is its real significance for a modern theory of poetry. From an ethnographical or philological point of view modern scientists may have found it necessary to revise Vico's hypothesis, but as a psychology of the creative process I do not think we have improved on his axiom that "men at first feel without perceiving, then they perceive with a troubled and agitated spirit, finally they reflect with a clear mind" (*New Science*, paragraph 218). Vico allows us to interpret this either in the evolutionary sense, "that in the world's childhood men were by nature sublime poets," or in the psychological sense, that poetry is essentially an act of perception or, as Heidegger calls it, an establishment of being by means of the word: "The poet names the gods and names all things as what they are. The naming does not consist of merely in something already known being supplied with a name, it is rather that when the poet speaks the essential word, the existent is by this naming nominated as what it is. So it becomes known as existent."[11] This is exactly what Vico was saying.

It is because Vico's theory of poetry is genetic that it is still relevant to poetic practice; human consciousness cannot be conceived of as something static. Historically it expands, with the aid of new inventions such as the telescope and the microscope; and subjectively it is modified by human experience, not only by historical events, but also by intense dimensions of personal experience (tragedy or joy). The consciousness of Shakespeare is wider, if not deeper, than the consciousness of Homer; the consciousness of Proust or Joyce may be narrower than that of Shakespeare, but it is, within its chosen area, more intense. For these reasons the poet is still relevant, still essential "to give sense and passion to insensate things."

For these same reasons Vico reached the surprising conclusion that if the world is to continue to have great artists, the great masterpieces of the art of the past should be destroyed. At least, they should be kept apart, "for the benefit of lesser minds. Those, instead, who are endowed with surpassing genius, should put the masterpieces of their art out of their sight, and strive with the greatest minds to appropriate the secret of nature's grandest creation."[12] Vico's theory of education is an anticipation of those modern theories of education (including my own) which stress the innate creativeness

---

[9] "Memory and Childhood Amnesia," *Metamorphosis* (New York, 1959), pp. 279–322.

[10] There is no doubt that Vico was a precursor of this theory of archetypes; cf. Gianturco, *Study Methods*, p. 23: "The archetypal *forms*, the ideal patterns of reality, exist in God alone. The physical nature of things, the phenomenal world, is modified after those archetypes."

[11] Douglas Scott, trans., *Existence and Being* (London: Vision Press, 1949), p. 304.

[12] Gianturco, *Study Methods*, p. 72.

of the child—in the words of Elio Gianturco, theories that have as common features

the defense of the child's world against the oppression of the adult; the conscious certitude that the positive results of any educational method are dependent upon the recognition of the functional autonomy of childhood; the thesis of the predominantly nonrational nature of the child; the incongruity of a type of education that proposes the turning out of "erudite adolescents and senile children." [13]

I conclude with a personal statement which may have some general significance. If I look back on my own writings extending over more than forty years, I am conscious of a prevailing Vichian spirit. From the beginning I called for a "genetic" method of criticism and perhaps incautiously advanced a theory of "organic form." These ideas were derived, in the main, directly from Coleridge and were supported collaterally by my reading of Croce and Bergson. But wherever I searched, from Goethe and the whole range of the Romantic poets and philosophers to contemporary philosophers such as Whitehead and contemporary psychologists such as Freud and Jung, the ideas that came to me, like filings to a magnet, I now recognize as ideas prefigured and often explicitly stated by Vico in works that I had never, at the time of the adoption of these ideas, read at first hand. This I take to be evidence, not of my own perspicacity or even of a Vichian temperament, but of the universal penetration, in the Romantic philosophy of our time (as distinct from what Vico himself would have called a logical barbarism), of Vico's ideas. Vico is probably the most unacknowledged source of ideas in the history of philosophy; as Croce pointed out in his book, in itself a great but belated act of revelation and restitution, Vico has never had justice done to him in works devoted to the history of modern philosophy. That period of neglect is now ended, and Vico takes his place among the few seminal minds of the modern epoch, the peer of Descartes (whom he so effectively opposed), of Kant, Schelling, Hegel, Nietzsche, Bergson, Cassirer, and Heidegger. Vico was inspired by an English philosopher, Francis Bacon; Vico in his turn inspired Coleridge. Vico has been completely neglected by contemporary British philosophers (Collingwood apart), but I have tried to show that, nevertheless, his influence has been most fertile in our creative literature, where I imagine Vico himself would have been most content to find it.

[13] *Ibid.*, p. xxviii.

Giorgio Tagliacozzo   EPILOGUE

1. Having reached the end of this symposium, some readers must wonder what type or scheme of over-all reinterpretation of Vico's thought these studies presage. A precise answer to that question would be premature; nevertheless, some speculation might not be entirely out of place. As indicated in the Preface,[1] the future reinterpretation of Vico's thought will hinge—in my opinion—on the problem of the unity of knowledge. In this Epilogue I shall briefly explain the bases for this opinion and then summarize those which seem to constitute the main reasons for the extraordinary importance of Vico's thought in our time.

2. In my view the future reinterpretation of Vico's thought must be based mainly on his conception of the unity of knowledge, the very quintessence of his thought. Vico's conception of the unity of knowledge has already been discussed by Professor Paci in this volume, in terms with which I basically agree.[2] Nevertheless, it might be useful to present Vico's ideas on this subject in yet another way, in the image of the *arbor scientiae* or "tree of knowledge," an image which has a long and noble tradition[3] and which

[1] See p. xi.
[2] "Vico, Structuralism and the Phenomenological Encyclopedia of the Sciences" (see pp. 497–515).
[3] See Paolo Rossi, *Clavis universalis* (Milan-Naples, 1960), *passim*, and Frances Yates, *The Art of Memory* (Chicago, 1966), *passim*. Vico's *New Science*, in spite of its unsurpassed originality, seems to have some roots in common with the tradition of the "art of memory" (and hence of the "*arbores scientiarum*"), particularly in its seventeenth-century stage, when Bacon, Descartes, Leibniz, and other thinkers turned it "from a method of memorizing the encyclopaedia of knowledge, of reflecting the world in memory, to an aid for investigating the encyclopaedia of the world with the object of discovering new knowledge" (Yates, *The Art of Memory*, pp. 368, 369). Such a remote connection is confirmed by Antonio Corsano ("Vico e la tradizione ermetica," in the symposium *Omaggio a Vico* [Naples, 1968]) and by the picture placed by Vico in the *New Science* as a frontispiece in the hope that "it may serve to give the reader some conception of this work before he reads it, and, with such aid as imagination may afford, to call it back to mind after he has read it" (quoted by Rossi, *Clavis universalis*, p. 39). According to Professor Paci, "The *Scienza nuova* was meant to be—as in many respects

Vico himself used.[4]   I do this because the image of the tree: (*a*) makes
Vico's viewpoint visualizable; (*b*) allows a schematic assessment of its merits
as compared to other viewpoints; and (*c*) indirectly helps detect its corollaries and applicability to the problems of our time.

3. Vico compared his "poetic wisdom" to a "trunk" (that is, "a crude
metaphysics"), "from one limb of which there branch out. . . . logic, morals,
economics, and politics, all poetic, from another physics, the mother of
cosmography and astronomy, the latter of which gives their certainty to two
daughters, chronology and geography—all likewise poetic."[5]   From this
description of Vico's "poetic wisdom" it is not difficult to reconstruct his
conception of an over-all "tree of knowledge."   His distinction of "three
kinds of natures," divine, heroic, and human;[6] his giving the "poetic"
sciences the same names as those of the corresponding "human" ones and
considering them "poetic" precursors of the latter;[7] his conviction that his
approach "discovers the ancient world of the sciences, how rough they had
to be at birth, and how gradually refined, until they reached the form in
which we received them";[8] his statement that "just as poetic metaphysics
was above divided into all its subordinate sciences, each sharing the poetic
nature of their mother, so this history of ideas [the *New Science*] will present

---

it is—an encyclopedia of the sciences, of culture, and of history" (see Paci, "Vico and
Cassirer," p. 467 of this volume).   Vico's use of the image of a tree to outline the
"division of poetic wisdom" (*New Science*, par. 367) is a specific confirmation of
his acquaintance with the tradition of the "*arbores scientiarum*" or, in any case, with
the use of the tree image by Bacon in his *De dignitate et augmentis scientiarum* (see Robert
McRae. *The Problem of the Unity of Sciences—Bacon to Kant* [Toronto, 1961], p. 26;
Rossi, *Clavis universalis*, p. xii and *passim*) and by Descartes in his letter to Mersenne
(see McRae, *Unity of the Sciences*, p. 57; Rossi, *Clavis universalis*, p. 12 and *passim*).
It is, I believe, uncertain whether, and to what extent, Vico was acquainted with
the trees of the universe of knowledge proposed by Alsted and by Comenius as a
basis for a reform of education.   On Alsted and Comenius see Rossi, *Clavis universalis*,
chap. VI, pp. 179–200, and Eugenio Garin, *L'educazione in Europa* (Bari, 1957), esp.
chap. VII.   The image of a tree of science has been used frequently in recent times by
George Sarton; see, for instance, his essay "History of Science" (1956) in *Sarton on the
History of Science*, ed. Dorothy Stimson (Cambridge, Mass., 1962), pp. 1–14.

[4] See section 3 of this Epilogue; see also Paci, "Vico, Structuralism and the Phenomenological Encyclopedia of the Sciences," pp. 497–98 of this volume.

[5] Thomas G. Bergin and Max H. Fisch, trans., *The New Science of Giambattista Vico*
(Garden City, N.Y., 1961), par. 367.

[6] *Ibid.*, pars. 916–18 and par. 218.

[7] *Ibid.*, par. 779.

[8] Quoted by Max H. Fisch in the Introduction to the *New Science*, par. K6, from the
second edition of Vico's *New Science* (1730), par. 37.   Vico also states: "As much as the
poets had first sensed in the way of vulgar wisdom, the philosophers later understood in
the way of esoteric wisdom" (Bergin and Fisch, *New Science*, par. 363).

the rough origins both of the practical sciences in use among the nations and the speculative sciences which are now cultivated by the learned"[9]—all this clearly reveals that, had he cared to describe his "Tree of Knowledge" in full, he would have presented it as a trunk (the "human mind," the maker of the "world of civil society"[10]) subdivided according to the "modifications of our own human mind"[11] into three main branches—"religious wisdom," "poetic wisdom," "human wisdom"—all equally made up of equally named sciences, so that the name of each science would appear in the Tree three times, once in each of those branches, the three appearances symbolically representing the three main stages of the history of each science and the three different natures it passed through during the course of time. The three main branches probably would have been represented by Vico as occupying, or quickly reaching, the same level on the Tree, thus symbolizing their co-existence. This because, according to him, although the types of thought respectively represented by those branches might have been born at different times or, if born simultaneously, might have had a comparatively different relevance at the time of their birth, they coexist for an indefinite time. In other words the Tree is both diachronic and synchronic. That this was basically Vico's conception of the "Tree of Knowledge" is confirmed not only by the whole context of the *New Science* but also by such specific statements as "these three languages began at the same time,"[12] "poetic style arose before prose style,"[13] and by Vico's explanation of how "the poetic speech . . . continued for a long time into the historical period,"[14] and of how "that religious way of thinking . . . persisted . . . within these human governments,"[15] by comparing "poetic speech" to "great and rapid rivers" . . . which "continue far into the sea, keeping sweet the waters borne on by force of their flow" and by pointing out the resemblance of "that religious way of thinking" to "the kingly river" which "re-tains far out to sea the momentum of its flow and the sweetness of its waters."[16]

4. It must be acknowledged that the above reconstruction of Vico's "Tree of Knowledge" is somewhat arbitrary. Furthermore, like any

---

[9] *Ibid.*, par. 391.   [10] *Ibid.*, par. 331.   [11] *Ibid.*

[12] *Ibid.*, par. 446.   [13] *Ibid.*, par. 460.   [14] *Ibid.*, par. 412.

[15] *Ibid.*, par. 629.

[16] Antonino Pagliaro ("La dottrina linguistica di G. B. Vico," in *Memorie: Classe di scienze morali, storiche e filologiche*, Accademia Nazionale dei Lincei, ser. VIII, vol. VIII, fasc. 6 [Rome, 1959], p. 486) points out that, after giving a diachronic image of the three stages of language—divine, heroic, and human—Vico realized, and explicitly declared, that the different factors are present in each of them and are operating synchronically.

graphic representation, it emphasizes some features of what it aims to portray while disregarding, minimizing, or distorting others. For instance, it fails to indicate that for Vico the metaphysics of human times grows out of the metaphysics of heroic times, and the latter grows out of that of divine times (and likewise for all the sciences). In fact, the Tree that I would have Vico draw, with its discontinuous main branches and the repeated appearance of the sciences in different branches, might at first appear to deny that continuity. Of course, it is not intended to do so: the discontinuity is only a practical necessity of the graphic representation, similar to the apparent discontinuity of the verbal expressions "divine," "heroic," and "human" times. In other words, my reconstruction of the Vichian Tree should be taken as only approximate. But it can probably be held to convey Vico's conception faithfully enough. This would accord, I believe, with Professor Paci's opinion, because he has pointed out the Vichian nature of an enlarged and updated "Tree of Knowledge" which I developed in 1958 on the principles of, and analogous in structure to, the one described above.[17]

The discontinuity among the branches of the reconstructed Vichian Tree could be reduced to some extent by subdividing the Tree's main branches into subbranches representing the successive historico-genetic stages of their development—with each subbranch in turn subdivided into all the sciences. This amounts to saying that perhaps, had Vico undertaken to draw his Tree in full, the three main branches of the latter—"religious wisdom," "poetic wisdom," "human wisdom"—would not necessarily have been identical in the sense that Vico would have drawn them in equal detail. For instance, while remaining faithful to the scheme indicated, he might have enriched the "Human Wisdom" branch by subdividing it into stages, each of which would have been equally or similarly subdivided by him into the same number of equally or similarly named sciences. (He might have done the same also with the other main branches, but in that case his effort would have

[17] See Paci, "Vico, Structuralism and the Phenomenological Encyclopedia of the Sciences, p. 498, n. 2, of this volume. My "Tree of Knowledge" was originally developed and published as a chart bearing that name, and was designed by Hildegarde Bergheim under my direction to serve as a visual aid for a course, also bearing that title, which I delivered at the New School for Social Research in New York for the first time in 1959. The "Tree" has since been reproduced in smaller format on the cover of the *American Behavioral Scientist*, 4 (October, 1960), and is briefly described in that issue of the magazine. The broadest description and explanation of the "Tree" is the one contained in Giorgio Tagliacozzo, "General Systems Theory as a Taxonomy of Culture and as a Curriculum of General Education" (paper presented at the symposium "General Systems and the Two Cultures," AAAS, Society for General Systems Research Section, Cleveland, December, 1963), which has been circulating privately. See, however, my forthcoming article, "Une 'unité du savoir' de type vichien," in a special issue of *Etudes philosophiques*, no. 3-4 (1968), dedicated to Vico and edited by Alain Pons.

been far more speculative.) Furthermore, if Vico had lived in our time—
and hence had been aware of the fundamental differences existing between
the "Euclidean world view," which started in Greece and still dominated the
scene in his time, the "non-Euclidean world view," which began to emerge
with Boole, Gauss, and Riemann around the mid-nineteenth century, and
the "organismic-transactional (or 'phenomenological') world view," which
characterizes so many aspects of contemporary thought—he might have
divided the "human wisdom" branch into three subbranches ("Euclidean
world view," "non-Euclidean world view," "organismic-transactional
world view,") all equally or similarly made up of equally or similarly named
sciences.[18]   Of course, this type of subdivision could have been carried much
further.

The above remarks will give the reader an idea of the route, based on
analogy and extrapolation, that I followed in 1958 in order to develop a
contemporary "tree of knowledge" along the lines of the Vichian one.
My Tree, being far more detailed and modern in technique than that reconstructed from Vico's scanty remarks, magnifies, sharpens, and brings
into relief certain features and corollaries of the latter which otherwise it
would be almost impossible to detect.   For this reason I believe that some
familiarity with my Tree[19] would be useful for a fuller understanding of
sections 5–9 of this Epilogue.

5. If we compare Vico's conception of the "Tree of Knowledge," as
described above, with any of the best known *arbores scientiarum* or other
attempted solutions to the problem of the "unity of knowledge" which
have preceded or followed it, we immediately discover its revolutionary
originality.   Let us think, for instance, of (*a*) Bacon's ordering the "sciences
of nature" (his "natural history," "physics," "metaphysics") in relation to
one another in such a way as to reflect, as in a pyramid, the ascent from the
multiplicity of individual things to their ultimate unity in the summary law
of nature;[20] (*b*) Descartes' idea of distinguishing sciences within the one
comprehensive deductive system and of comparing philosophy as a whole to
a tree "whose roots are metaphysics, whose trunk is physics, and whose
branches, issuing from the trunk, are all other sciences" (reduced to three

[18] Vico has pointed out that "every epoch is dominated by a 'spirit,' a genius, of its
own" (see Elio Gianturco, trans., *On the Study Methods of Our Time* [Indianapolis, Ind.,
1965], p. 73).
[19] See n. 17 above.   In addition, because my 1960 *American Behavioral Scientist* article
gives an incomplete picture of my more recent views and my 1963 Cleveland paper is
not readily available, I have summarized, schematically, the main features and implications of my "Tree of Knowledge" below (see pp. 610–13).
[20] See McRae, *Unity of the Sciences*, p. 34.

principal ones: medicine, mechanics, and morals);[21] (c) Leibniz' idea that, when the catalogue of human thought has been achieved, and each concept has been given its characteristic number and sign, we shall have secured a complete demonstrative encyclopedia of all knowledge;[22] (d) the Encyclopedists' view that the unity of human knowledge is not a unity in diversity, nor the unity of a whole in relation to its parts, but unity of continuity among parts wherever such continuity may be found;[23] (e) Kant's insistence on the need to isolate the various modes of knowledge according to kind and origin, complemented by his equal insistence that all the sciences taken together have the unity of a single organized whole and that the unity of science has its foundation in the nature of reason itself, which demands that knowledge be brought into systematic unity;[24] (f) Comte's classification of the sciences, which is based on the idea of placing them in such a way that each science is dependent on those preceding it and independent of those which follow;[25] (g) the logico-empiricist philosophers' view of the unification of science as the reduction of all sciences to physics—that is, the reduction of all phenomena to physical events—through the unification of the vocabulary of the sciences.[26] The radical novelty of Vico's Tree becomes apparent immediately in a study of its key features: (a) three main branches issuing from the trunk (instead of the trunk merely being extended), the result of Vico's discovery of two aspects of "wisdom" which had been overlooked by philosophers up to his time—"religious wisdom" and "poetic wisdom;" (b) identical names and an identical number and organization of the key sciences in the three coexisting branches, which indicate the "religious" and "poetic" origins of each science and, more generally, the idea that any science (as well as any of its "daughters," "granddaughters," and so on) traverses an unlimited series of stages; (c) the fact that, once born, the older stages of any science (known today as the "outdated theories") survive indefinitely beside the newer ones. Obviously, the above features are corollaries to the "master key" of the *New Science*: Vico's "discovery" that "the early peoples, by a demonstrated necessity of nature, were poets who spoke in poetic characters."[27] In other words, as "within the picture of the

---

[21] *Ibid.*, p. 57.   [22] *Ibid.*, p. 81.   [23] *Ibid.*, p. 119.

[24] *Ibid.*, pp. 125, 128, 130, 133.

[25] Auguste Comte, *Cours de philosophie positive* (Paris, 1949), vol. I, second lesson, esp. sec. VI, p. 138.

[26] A recent authoritative presentation of the logico-empiricist approach to the unity of science may be found in Paul Oppenheim and Hilary Putnam, "Unity of Science as a Working Hypothesis," in *Minnesota Studies in the Philosophy of Science*, vol. II, ed. H. Feigl *et al.* (Minneapolis, 1958); see also Paul Oppenheim, "A Natural Order of Scientific Disciplines," *Revue Internationale de Philosophie*, fasc. 3 (1959), and "Dimensions of Knowledge," *ibid.*, fasc. 2 (1957).

[27] Bergin and Fisch, *New Science*, par. 34.

New Science the theory of language occupies a central place, or rather is the nucleus around which . . . the edifice of Vico's thought . . . has . . . developed,"[28] so within the picture of Vico's "Tree of Knowledge" the historical-genetic-semantic factor is the most essential. Or, to put it more straightforwardly, the Vichian "Tree of Knowledge" is revolutionary precisely because it is historical-genetic-semantic.[29] Conversely, what has just been said indicates that the failure to produce convincing and durable results of all the attempts hitherto made to solve the problem of the unity of knowledge may probably be attributed to the following causes: (1) all those attempts (except three to which I shall refer in sections 6–9) have overlooked two aspects of "wisdom": "religious wisdom" and "poetic wisdom"; (2) they have ignored the fact that each science goes through different stages, that is (to extrapolate within the "human wisdom" branch), each science is characterized by different trends and currents, all bearing its name, which have followed one another and have intertwined with one another in the process of time and which are surviving today, either individually or in combination; (3) all the above-mentioned attempts (I refer especially to the modern ones) have paid exclusive attention to a given scientific trend or current, generally the most recent, which they have considered the ultimate one, in spite of the fact that theories born at different times often coexist, that science is continually developing new theories, and that at times it combines several viewpoints or awakens dormant ones;[30] (4) as a consequence of the above, the name of each science has appeared in any tree or scheme only once; (5) in other words, each science has been considered *in abstracto*, like a monolith— that is, independently of its origin, history, stages, strains, and so on—rather than in its historical-genetic-semantic reality, that is, as something similar to a mosaic of strains of thought born at different times, variously combined, and often having very little in common except name and a certain analogy of subject matter; (6) sciences *in abstracto*, having lost their historical-genetic-semantic roots, lend themselves to unification only within narrow limits, if they are unifiable at all.

6. As we have seen, Vico, with his historical-genetic-semantic conception of the unity of knowledge, transcended all the above shortcomings. In so doing he laid the foundations for a solution to the problem of the unity of knowledge that outstrips even the theory formulated in our time by Cassirer.

[28] Antonino Pagliaro, "La dottrina linguistica," p. 379.
[29] Let us recall here these words of Vico's: "Doctrines must take their beginning from the matters of which they treat. . . . This axiom . . . is universally used in all the matters which are herein discussed" (Bergin and Fisch, *New Science*, pars. 314–15).
[30] See Gianturco, *Study Methods*, p. 73; Thomas S. Kuhn's *The Structure of Scientific Revolutions* (Chicago, 1962) might also be consulted in this connection.

If, in fact, it is true that Cassirer's theory of symbolic forms—which could be represented graphically as a tree whose trunk (the symbolizing activity of the mind) is divided into as many branches as are the "symbolic forms"—is, to a certain extent, more elaborate and certainly far more modern than Vico's analogous theory of the "modifications of the human mind," represented by his Tree, nevertheless, Cassirer's Tree lacks any indication of the criteria guiding the subdivision of the main branches into sciences and does not organize those branches identically with sciences bearing the same names. In other words, Cassirer's Tree cannot be called historical-genetic-semantic, like the Vichian Tree; it can only be compared to an unfinished though well-founded and imposing building that does not rise above the second floor. Above that floor Cassirer's treatment of the problem of the unity of knowledge offers only—as he explicitly recognizes—a "systematic review" of "the individual developments of knowledge."[31]

7. After schematically outlining the unique merits of Vico's viewpoint on the unity of knowledge on the basis of his reconstructed Tree, I must add a few words on: (*a*) Vico's Tree and the phenomenological "encyclopedia" of the sciences; (*b*) Vico's Tree and Professor Garin's "Philosophy as historical knowledge."

Professor Paci has demonstrated in this symposium[32] the fundamental analogy which exists between the Vichian and the phenomenological "encyclopedias." He has not, however, offered a specific explanation for the actual arrangement of the "sciences" within the phenomenological or the Vichian encyclopedias. Thus the following questions arise. (*a*) To what extent does the phenomenological viewpoint agree, or overlap, with the historical-genetic-semantic one on which Vico's Tree, according to my reconstruction of it, is based? (*b*) Would the phenomenological viewpoint permit a detailed presentation of the "sciences" analogous, *mutatis mutandis*, to a contemporary version of that Tree, one that presents similar features and corollaries? I cannot venture a definite answer to these questions, but I might express my belief (supported, I think, by Paci's

[31] Ernst Cassirer, *The Problem of Knowledge* (New Haven, 1950), p. 19.

[32] "Vico, Structuralism and the Phenomenological Encyclopedia of the Sciences" (see pp. 497–515 above). Paci's demonstration is fully supported and further strengthened by the following works of his in which the phenomenological viewpoint is strongly interspersed with allusions to Vico: *Diario fenomenologico* (Milan, 1961); *Funzione delle scienze e significato dell'uomo* (Milan, 1963); "Problemi di unificazione del sapere," in *L'unificazione del sapere*, a symposium volume (Florence, 1964), pp. 63–76. For an analogous viewpoint, but without reference to Vico, see Robert Welsh Jordan, "Husserl's Phenomenology as an 'historical' Science," *Social Research*, 35, no. 2 (Summer, 1968): 245–59.

acknowledgement of the Vichian nature of my Tree)[33] that the two approaches are not irreconcilable and might be complementary to each other.

8. Professor Garin's conception of "philosophy as historical knowledge"[34] also contains, in a sense, a viewpoint on the unity of knowledge. Garin believes that "the over-all vision, which is perhaps the only constant aim of philosophizing. . . . can only live as an effort to achieve a history which tries to understand and to portray the changing articulations of human experience. . . . in its various manifestations."[35] He pleads against "the partial 'philosophies' and their partial 'histories,' presented as having a total value," and pleads for "a history which, by connecting the various perspectives and their meanings, avoiding any generalizing tendency, and using functional connections and deep genetic probings, reaches out from the mere temporal relationships (contemporaneity-succession) typical of immediate experience to the 'rational' construction of a real and true 'historicity,' which for that very reason will amount to an 'appraisal' based not on extrinsic standards but on rational ones internal to the very process of understanding the real connections among the various classes of components of human development in the world."[36] This is a history—he points out—which "for the very reason that it wants to be an integral historicization, proffers itself as 'philosophy,' that is, as a legitimate way of philosophizing which recognizes the value of logical, methodological, linguistic inquiries, and so on, while proclaiming the necessity for clarifying their genesis, their relationships with a real situation, and their historical 'reasons' in all the complexity of the human horizon within which they arise." [37] Such a history, according to Garin, "far from recognizing itself as 'philosophia inferior' . . . very frankly proffers itself as a direction in which, today, a unitary consideration of reality as afforded by our experience can still be seriously attempted."[38] "Because"—he explains—"there is no history if not in a perspective which considers *ideas* and their vicissitudes, the articulation of systems, and the urgency and the changing nature of problems against their human background, in their rhythms within the consciences of men, in the concreteness of their real life. . . . History is the retrieving of the genesis of ideas in the lived time, their way of converging, and their behavior among men. History of thought is the retrieving of the unity of thought, the focusing on the unity of thought, the human *flesh* without which those thoughts would not be in the world, and the revealing of the relationships of those thoughts

---

[33] See n. 17 above.
[34] *La filosofia come sapere storico* (Bari, 1959).
[35] *Ibid.*, pp. 50–51.   [36] *Ibid.*, p. 93.   [37] *Ibid.*, p. 32.   [38] *Ibid.*

with *human flesh*."[39]   All of this brings to mind what Max H. Fisch[40] has called "the controlling methodological postulate of Vico's new science," that is, that "doctrines must take their beginning from that of the matters of which they treat."[41]

Although these few quotations do not represent Garin's viewpoint adequately, nevertheless, their strong Vichian (hence the name "neo-Vichianism," often applied to Garin's "philosophy as historical knowledge"[42]) and phenomenological[43] flavor, together with a notable affinity with Marc Bloch's and Lucien Febvre's pleas, "in the tradition of Vico,"[44] for a "broader and more human history,"[45] give us a pretty good idea of it. Garin, like Paci, has not offered a specific explanation of the relationships among the various "sciences" within the "over-all vision" he contemplates. It is my impression, however, that his "philosophy as historical knowledge" resembles the historical-genetic-semantic viewpoint on the unity of knowledge on which the Vichian Tree is based—that is, the meaning of "philosophy as historical knowledge" resembles that of "philosophy as historical-genetic-semantic knowledge." Thus Garin's "philosophy as historical knowledge" might perhaps permit a detailed presentation of the "sciences" analogous, *mutatis mutandis*, to a contemporary version of Vico's Tree more easily than does the strict phenomenological approach.

9. To sum up: there are two related and complementary aspects of Vico's viewpoint on the unity of knowledge.   One is broader, more imposing, more profound, more general, and is represented by the *New Science* as a whole.   The other is narrower, more modest, less profound, but is more specific and yields more easily to visualization and application; it is represented (incompletely) by Vico's allusion to a "Tree of Knowledge" through his comparison of "poetic wisdom" to the trunk of a tree.   Paci's conception of Vico's "encyclopedia" deals mainly with the first aspect; Garin's viewpoint on the unity of knowledge also shows specific affinity only with the first aspect.   In other words, neither the phenomenological nor the "neo-Vichian" position on the problem of the "unity of knowledge" embodies a conception that is fully comparable to Vico's idea of a Tree of

[39] *Ibid.*, pp. 136–37.
[40] See Fisch, Introduction to the *New Science*, p. xxii, A4.
[41] Bergin and Fisch, *New Science*, pars. 314–15.
[42] See Enrico De Mas, "Vico and Italian thought," p. 164 of this symposium.
[43] Garin's viewpoint does not seem very different to me from Paci's as to basic concepts, but it is obviously quite different in approach.   In his *Diario fenomenologico*, p. 90, Paci speaks of "important discussions with Garin, who has presented the problem of phenomenology from a historical viewpoint."   Garin's *La filosofia come sapere storico* contains some remarks by Paci on Garin's viewpoint (pp. 33–43).
[44] See H. Stuart Hughes, *History as Art and as Science* (New York, 1964), p. 27.
[45] *Ibid.*; see also Garin, *La filosofia come sapere storico*, pp. 100 and 134–36.

Knowledge actually portraying the concrete historical-genetic-semantic development of all ways of thought and "sciences." The two aspects of Vico's viewpoint on the unity of knowledge are, however, complementary; so, in my opinion, any future reinterpretation of Vico's thought as a whole should be complemented—and would be aided in its application to contemporary problems (for instance, to those of education)—by the far more modest, but useful, study and modern interpretation of Vico's "Tree of Knowledge."

10. I hope that the panorama of Vichian studies offered by this symposium may give the reader an idea of the main reasons for the renewed international interest in this great Italian thinker. Vico had the unique ability to encompass, absorb, and transform into parts of an organism governed by few fundamental principles all the expressions of human thought, past and present. His thought is like a common denominator of the culture of all times and provides a common anchorage for contemporary philosophers belonging to almost every school and for scholars in almost every field. There is no other thinker, living or dead, of whom the same can be said. To originate one or another important idea is one thing, but to be the forerunner of an immense array of key ideas (and this thanks to the discovery of a set of philosophical principles capable of unifying those ideas) is an entirely different, infinitely more rare—indeed a unique—achievement. To put it another way, Vico achieved a synthesis of a type and solidity which probably still remains unequaled in our time. While it is easy to think of the relativism, iconoclasm, and decline of ideologies which tend to dominate today's thought—and have, to an increasing extent, permeated social and political life—there is also an increasing tendency to look squarely at reality, at facts, and to put aside tradition, commonplaces, pious illusions. No thinker proclaimed more firmly than did Vico the necessity of taking into account the "nature" of things (that is, the facts) as a guide to the actions of men. Furthermore, there has probably been no thinker who has built more or better on the famous maxim of Terence: "*Homo sum: nihil humani a me alienum puto.*" This, perhaps, explains why the *New Science* represents probably the widest philosophical viewpoint devised, until very recently, to encompass in a unique diachronic and synchronic synthesis man's history and his culture. Finally, it should be pointed out that Vico absorbed, enriched, and developed the Roman and Renaissance rhetorical-juridical tradition in such a way as to make of it almost a new philosophical strain, as against the long idealist-rationalist tradition inherited from Greece.[46] Such a strain presents striking

[46] This view seems to be confirmed by the conclusions Professor Fisch reaches in his essay in the present volume (see p. 423).

analogies to contemporary trends,[47] thus making Vico a forerunner of certain basic aspects of modern thought and shedding further light on the reasons for the return to him today.

Tree of Knowledge [48]

The following are some of the features and implications of my "Tree of Knowledge":

a. It encompasses past and present culture within the boundaries of "general culture" (see *r*).

b. It is "diachronic" and "synchronic" (see below, especially *l*, *n*, and *o*).

c. Its ramifications represent philosophical and scientific concepts, including names of sciences which appear repeatedly (at the top of different branches). These concepts simultaneously perform a historical, a historico-genetic, and a taxonomic-integrative task, as will be explained below. They are, in fact, arranged by kingdoms, phyla, classes, orders, families, genera, species, and subspecies, rising from the bottom to the top of the chart, according to a plan resembling the basic taxonomic scheme of modern biology.

d. From the genetic-historical viewpoint (that is, as a "taxonomy of culture") the "Tree" shares the general logical character of the basic taxonomic scheme (see Morton Berkner, *The Biological Way of Thought* [New York, 1954], chapter IV), that is, it resembles the "New Systematics" (*ibid.*), in which taxonomy and evolution (that is, history) are intertwined, and rests on postulates which, *mutatis mutandis* (that is, substituting concepts of the type indicated for "organic systems" or "organisms"), are analogous to some characteristic doctrines of "Organismic Biology" (*ibid.*, chapter I and *passim*). I allude in particular to the doctrine of *historicity*, according to which organisms and other organic systems possess a historical character, that is: (1) they have histories, and it is part of the duty of the biologist to give a descriptive account of those histories; (2) the past of an organic system determines, or helps to determine, its present structure and behavior; (3) many types of organic change—for example, regeneration and evolution—are irreversible; (4) many organic changes are properly described by the term "development," which includes growth, elaboration, and differentiation; (5) the course of development from germ to adult organism is determined in part by the past history of the ancestors of the organism. It is interesting to point out in this connection that the taxonomic viewpoint on which the "Tree" is based is in full harmony with Vico's equating the "nature" of "institutions" with "their coming into being at certain times and in certain guises" so that "whenever the time and guise are thus and so, such and not otherwise are the institutions that come into being" (*New Science*, paragraph 147).

e. The trunk of the "Tree" ("symbolism") is subdivided into two "kingdoms": "presentational symbolism" and "discursive symbolism" (two concepts borrowed from Susanne Langer's *Philosophy in a New Key*). Presentational symbolism (the right branch issuing from the trunk) in turn subdivides into four "phyla": "magic," "myth," "religion," "art." These follow one another from right to left, as four parallel vertical branches of the "Tree," symbolizing the corresponding "modifications of our human mind" (see note 11). Discursive symbolism (the left branch issuing from the trunk), not being subdivided, is identical with the fifth phylum, "science," whose subdivisions

---

[47] On such trends see Enzo Paci, "Attualità di Husserl," *Revue Internationale de Philosophie*, no. 71–72, fasc. 1–2 (1965).

[48] See above, nn. 17 and 19, pp. 602 and 603.

at all levels follow one another from left to right. This change of direction is intended to symbolize: (1) the continuous intercourse taking place between presentational symbolism, a source of incandescent bundles of thoughts, and discursive symbolism, a selection and rational development of some of those thoughts; (2) the history of science in its various stages; (3) the trend of successive world views (see *g*) toward an ever fuller grasp of reality.

f. All the phyla of the "Tree" are, in theory, analogously structured. For practical reasons, however, the "Tree" presents only a fully developed taxonomy of "science" and a less developed taxonomy of "art." The former will be described briefly in *g*.

g. "Science" subdivides into three "classes": "Euclidean world view," "non-Euclidean world view," and "organismic-transactional world view." These symbolize the three different modes of "scientific" thought, born at different times from antiquity to the present day, and based on different conceptions of space, time, and causality, which coexist in our time. A few remarks on the taxonomy of the first of these classes, the "Euclidean world view," will be added here in order better to clarify the way in which the "Tree" is constructed. The "Euclidean world view" class has three "orders": "rationalist philosophy" (which originated with Plato and is still alive today); "scientific empiricism" (the scientific trend, based on the hypothetico-deductive method, which originated with Galileo); and "philosophical empiricism" (born with Bacon and based on the inductive method). "Rationalist philosophy" is in turn subdivided—at taxonomic levels ranging from "family" to "species"—into logic, metaphysics, physics, ethics, education, economics, politics, aesthetics. "Scientific empiricism" has two "families": "physics" and "chemistry." "Philosophical empiricism" has two "families": "epistemology" and "utilitarian ethics." The former includes among its "genera" the mathematical "theory of probability" and, among its "species," statistics. "Utilitarian ethics" has three "genera": ethics (in turn subdivided into four "species": ethics proper, education, economics, politics); psychology (born, as will be remembered, of a combination of utilitarian ethics and physiology); and (Darwinian) biology (whose principle of "natural selection" is related to Malthus' population theory and to the theory of competition of economic science).

h. All the branches of the "Tree" reach the top at the same level, as names of sciences, through a varying number of ramifications. The uppermost level portrays: (1) the latest genetic developments that have occurred in each branch; (2) the coexistence of various strains of thought within each "science"; and (3) the history, including semantic history, of each basic science. Thus the top level of the "Tree" has a genetic as well as a taxonomic-historical-semantic connotation.

i. The "sciences" repeatedly appearing at the top of the "Tree"—each time, of course, in a different sector of it—happen to be basically those of Vico's tree: logic, ethics, economics, politics, physics. Some names, however, are modified, and there are several additions.

j. A typical example of a science repeatedly appearing at the top of the "Tree" is economics. Within the "Euclidean world view" class alone, it recurs once in the "rationalist philosophy" order, as a species of its "ethics" family, and once in the "philosophical empiricism" order, as a species of the latter's "ethics" family. To be more precise, in its first appearance economics is subdivided into two subspecies, Platonic economics and Aristotelian economics—two quite different strains of economic thinking which have made their influence felt in very different ways throughout the centuries. The first has been the springboard of a long series of utopian ideas for the socio-economic reform of society; the second, reinforced by the thought of Thomas Aquinas, is still the basis of the Catholic-corporative trend of economic thinking (see Ralph H. Bowen, *German Theories of the Corporative State* [New York, 1947]). In its second appearance economics represents the economics (born from utilitarian ethics) of Adam

Smith and his followers. (Economics is further encountered in the "non-Euclidean world view" and "organismic-transactional world view" branches of the "Tree"; but those appearances will not be discussed here.)

k. The above implies that, for instance, any reference to economics in the sense to be attributed to this term when it appears at the top of the philosophical empiricism branch of the "Tree" also embodies a reference to the following genetic ladder: symbolism—discursive symbolism (kingdom)—science (phylum)—Euclidean world view (class)—philosophical empiricism (order)—utilitarian ethics (family)—ethics (genus)—economics (species). Similarly, any reference to economics in the sense to be attributed to this term when it appears at the top of any other branch also embodies a reference to an analogous genetic ladder. Furthermore, the above description of the "Tree" implies that, for instance, economics as a "species" of the ethics "genus" belonging to the utilitarian ethics "family" of the philosophical empiricism "order": (1) is far closer genetically to the politics "species" of that "genus," "family," and "order" than it is to the politics "species" of the ethics "genus" and "family" of the rationalist philosophy "order"; (2) is also far closer genetically to the physics "family" of the scientific empiricism "order" than, for instance, to the physics "family" of the rationalist philosophy "order" or to the physics "family" of an "order" belonging to a "phylum" different from "science."

l. The general conclusion to be drawn from the above example is that the name of any science or philosophical or scientific concept appearing at any level within the framework of the "Tree" (1) embodies its own genetic history, and (2) is linked to all others in various genetic-taxonomic ways.

m. This "Tree" further suggests the existence of some analogies between culture as a whole (of mankind, of a society, of a single individual) and an organism such as a plant. It has been demonstrated that substances required in the metabolism of plant cells not only travel up from the roots but also move about in other directions (on this phenomenon, called "translocation," see Susanne and Orlin Biddulph, "The Circulatory System of Plants," *Scientific American*, February, 1959, and J. W. Mitchell *et al.*, "Translocation of Particles within Plants," *Science*, June 24, 1960). Phenomena analogous to translocation also probably occur within culture.

n. The fact, mentioned in *h*, that all the branches of the "Tree" reach the top (through a varying number of ramifications) indicates that the leading trends of thought, once born, tend to survive indefinitely—although they may, of course, change their outer appearances as fashions change, or blend with other trends until they are hardly recognizable. The idea of such a survival, which has been expressed clearly by Vico (see section 3 of this Epilogue and notes 13 and 14), is found again in Dilthey (see Pietro Rossi, Preface to Wilhelm Dilthey's *Il secolo XVIII e il mondo storico* [Milan, 1967], p. 14).

o. The above implies that the different strains coexisting within any science have, in a sense, a different age, irrespective of the apparent modernity of their latest presentation, and that what is generally called a "science" (for example, philosophy, ethics, economics, physics, and so on) is in fact a mosaic of parts of varying age, derived from different strains of thought, and at times having little in common except their name and a certain analogy of subject matter. (For this viewpoint in Vico see section 5 of this Epilogue.)

p. It may also be inferred from the above that to speak of a "science," without specifying which strain or strains of that science, is semantically confusing.

q. Obviously the organic "unity of knowledge" portrayed by the "Tree" is at the same time "pluralistic," in the sense that it justifies different viewpoints "historically." Because of this the "Tree" tends to dispel exclusivisms and stimulates comparisons among various trends of thought. (It might be recalled here that "Vico blessed his good fortune in having no teacher whose words he had sworn by, and he felt most grateful for . . . [having] followed the main course of his studies untroubled by sectarian prejudice." See his *Autobiography*, trans. Max H. Fisch and Thomas G. Bergin [Ithaca, N.Y., 1944], p. 133.)

r. As indicated in *a*, the "Tree" encompasses the whole of culture within the boundaries of general culture. These boundaries are taxonomically represented by the "sub-species" level at the top of the "Tree." The above schematic description of the "Tree" indicates, and a full explanation would demonstrate, that the taxonomically organized concepts composing the "Tree" (of which there are about 225, about 130 of which reach the top) are sufficient to encompass the essential minimum and the attainable maximum for the purposes of general culture. In this sense the "Tree" can be said to succeed in precisely defining general culture for practical purposes. The definition achieved is a genetic one, that is, a definition simultaneously specifying the basic *contents* of general culture and its genetic *nature* and taxonomic *organization*.

s. General culture and general education are, ideally, like the two faces of a coin (see Giorgio Tagliacozzo, "General Education: The Mirror of Culture," *American Behavioral Scientist*, 6 [October, 1962], 22–25; *idem*, "Culture and Education—The Origins," *ibid.*, 6 [April, 1963]; and *idem*, "Culture and Education: The founding of the Classical Tradition," *ibid.*, 7 [January, 1964]). Thus a Vichian "Tree of Knowledge," while defining general culture, also provides basic suggestions for a curriculum of general education. Because of the genetic nature of the definition of general culture achieved by the "Tree," the nature of that curriculum is also genetic. Furthermore, because of its genetic nature, such a curriculum suggests a way of fulfilling the basic requirements of a modern theory of education. (I refer principally to Jerome Bruner's theories embodied in his *The Process of Education* [Cambridge, Mass., 1960], *On Knowing* [Cambridge, Mass., 1962], *Toward a Theory of Instruction* [1966], and *Studies in Cognitive Growth* [1967].) In fact, owing to the genetic nature, organization, and presentation of its elements, such a curriculum would be: (1) *necessary* (that is, exclusively made up of elements of general culture); (2) *sufficient* or "complete" (that is, inclusive of all the essential elements of general culture); (3) *balanced* (that is, giving each of its elements the relevance it deserves according to objective taxonomic criteria); (4) *unitary* (because of its genetic-taxonomic organization); (5) *economical* (because it would make it possible to deal once, rather than repeatedly, with basic concepts common to several disciplines); (6) *psycho-genetic* (on Vico's belief in the existence of a psycho-genetic law, whereby the individual develops through a certain series of necessary phases parallel to a set of "culture stages" traversed by the whole of mankind, see Elio Gianturco, trans., Introduction to *On the Study Methods of Our Time*, p. xxvii); (7) *integrative*, and hence *most favorable to the transfer of training* (because of the integrative task performed by the concepts of which it is made up); (8) *teachable to anybody in some form*—a "*spiral curriculum*" (because it lends itself to being taught repeatedly at increasingly higher levels). While fulfilling the basic requirements of a modern theory of education, this curriculum—a corollary of the Vichian "Tree"—would also help in the present-day fulfillment of Vico's educational aim: "that all divine and human wisdom should everywhere reign with one spirit and cohere in all its parts, so that the sciences lend each other a helping hand and none is a hindrance to any other" (Fisch and Bergin, *Autobiography*, p. 146). It might also be said that such a curriculum would promote the adoption in our time of the advice Vico gave to students in 1732: "Devote yourselves, during your study time, to nothing but a continuous comparison among all the things you are learning, so as to create such a connection among them as will enable them all to harmonize with each of the disciplines you study. . . . Once the habit of comparing has settled in you, you will also have acquired the ability to compare the sciences, which, like celestial limbs, compose the divine body of knowledge in all its fullness" (Giambattista Vico, *Della mente eroica* (1732), trans. F. Nicolini in his *Opere* [Milan-Naples, 1953], p. 920).

BIBLIOGRAPHY

*Works Published in English during the Past Fifty Years
Dealing Wholly or Partly with Vico*

Adams, H. P. *The Life and Writings of Giambattista Vico.* London: George
Allen & Unwin, Ltd., 1935.

Albini Grimaldi, Alfonsina. *The Universal Humanity of Giambattista Vico.*
New York: S. F. Vanni, 1958.

Arendt, Hannah. "History and Immortality." *Partisan Review,* Winter,
1957: 11–35.

————. *Between Past and Future.* New York: Viking Press, 1961. See
especially "The Concept of History."

Arieti, Silvano. *Interpretations of Schizophrenia.* New York: Brunner, 1955.

————. *The Intrapsychic Self.* New York: Basic Books, 1967.

Auerbach, Eric. *Scenes from the Drama of European Literature.* New York:
Meridian Books, 1959. See especially "Vico and Aesthetic Historism."

Beckett, Samuel. "Dante . . . Bruno . . . Vico . . . Joyce." In *Our Exagmination Round His Factification for Incamination of Work in Progress,* edited
by Samuel Beckett *et al.* Paris: Shakespeare and Company, 1929.

Berlin, Isaiah. "The Philosophical Ideas of Giambattista Vico." In *Art and
Ideas in Eighteenth-Century Italy.* Rome: Edizioni di Storia e Letteratura,
1960.

Berry, T. M. *The Historical Theory of G. B. Vico.* Washington, D.C.:
Catholic University of America, 1949.

Cairns, Grace. *Philosophies of History—A Study of the Greek Cyclical Theories
of History in Oriental and Western Thought.* New York: The Citadel
Press, 1962. Pp. 337–52 *passim.*

Caponigri, Robert. *Time and Idea: The Theory of History in Giambattista
Vico.* London: Routledge & Kegan Paul, 1953.

Child, Arthur. *Making and Knowing in Hobbes, Vico, and Dewey.* University of California Publications in Philosophy, XVI:13. Berkeley–Los
Angeles: University of California Press, 1953.

NOTE: The most accurate source of information on publications in English dealing
with Vico (up to 1944) is Max H. Fisch's Introduction to *The Autobiography of Giambattista
Vico,* included in this list.   The standard work in English on Vico is, of course, Robert
Flint's *Vico* (Edinburgh, 1884).   See also by Flint, *Philosophy as Scientia Scientiarum* and
A History of the Classification of the Sciences (Edinburgh, 1904), pp. 127–29.

Clark, Robert T. "Herder, Cesarotti and Vico." *Studies in Philology* 44 (1947): 645–71.

Collingwood, R. G. *The Idea of History.* Oxford: The Clarendon Press, 1946. Pp. 67–71 and *passim.*

Danto, Arthur C. *Analytical Philosophy of History.* Cambridge: At the University Press, 1965.

De Santillana, George. "Vico and Descartes." *Osiris* 21, no. 3 (Autumn, 1950): 565–80.

Donagan, Alan, and Donagan, Barbara. *Philosophy of History.* New York: Sources in Philosophy series, Macmillan Company, 1965. See especially "Giambattista Vico: A New Conception in Historiography."

Edie, James M. "Giambattista Vico: The New Science." *Italica,* June, 1962.

———. "Expression and Metaphor." *Philosophy and Phenomenological Research* 23 (September, 1962–June, 1963): 548 and *passim.*

Feibleman, James. "Toward the Recovery of Giambattista Vico." *Social Science* 14 (1939): 31–40.

Fisch, Max H. "The Coleridges, Dr. Prati, and Vico." *Modern Philology* 41 (1943–44): 111–22.

———. Introduction to *The Autobiography of Giambattista Vico,* translated from the Italian by Max H. Fisch and Thomas G. Bergin. Ithaca, N.Y.: Cornell University Press, 1944. Reprinted in Great Seal Books series, Cornell University Press, 1963.

———. "Vico on Roman Law." In *Essays in Political Theory Presented to George H. Sabine,* edited by M. R. Konwitz and A. E. Murphy. Ithaca, N.Y.–London, 1948.

———. "The Academy of the Investigators." In *Science, Medicine, and History: Essays in Honour of Charles Singer,* edited by E. A. Underwood. Vol. I. London–Toronto, 1953.

———. Review of A. Robert Caponigri's "Time and Idea: The Theory of History in Giambattista Vico." *Journal of Philosophy* 54 (1957): 648–52.

———. Introduction to *The New Science of Giambattista Vico,* translated by Thomas G. Bergin and Max H. Fisch. Garden City, N.Y.: Anchor Books, Doubleday & Co., Inc., 1961. The same introduction has been reprinted in the revised edition of their unabridged 1948 translation of the *New Science.* Ithaca, N.Y.: Cornell University Press, 1968.

Forbes, Duncan. " 'Scientific' Whiggism: Adam Smith and John Millar." *The Cambridge Journal* 7 (1954): 658.

Forum Italicum. Special Issue: A Homage to G. B. Vico in the Tercentenary of his Birth 2, no. 4 (December, 1968). A volume of studies, notes, translations, and reviews of books dealing with Vico and Vico studies.

Gardiner, Patrick. *Theories of History.* Glencoe, Ill.: The Free Press, 1959. Pp. 12–21.

————. "Vico." In *Encyclopedia of Philosophy*. New York: Macmillan Company, 1967.

Gianturco, Elio. "Suarez and Vico." *Harvard Theological Review*, 1934: 207–10.

————. *Joseph De Maistre and Giambattista Vico: Italian Roots of De Maistre's Political Culture*. New York: Columbia University Press, 1937.

————. "Bodin and Vico." *Review of Comparative Literature*, 1948: 272–90.

————. *A Selective Bibliography of Vico Scholarship (1948–1968)*. In *Forum Italicum, Supplement* 1968. Florence: Grafica Toscana, 1968.

————, trans. Introduction to *On the Study Methods of Our Time*. Indianapolis, Ind.: The Library of Liberal Arts, Bobbs-Merrill Company Inc., 1965.

Gilbert, Stuart. "Prolegomena to Work in Progress." In *Our Exagmination Round His Factification for Incamination of Work in Progress*, edited by Samuel Beckett *et al.* Paris: Shakespeare and Company, 1929.

Gorman, Herbert. *James Joyce*. New York, 1939. Pp. 332–35.

Hall, R. A., Jr. "G. B. Vico and Linguistic Theory." *Italica*, 1941: 145ff.

Hampshire, Stuart. "Vico and his 'New Science.'" *The Listener*, April 7, 1949: 569–71.

Harris, H. S. "Vico." In *Encyclopedia Americana*. New York: Americana Corporation, 1967.

Harris, Marvin. *The Rise of Anthropological Theory*. New York: Columbia University Press, 1968.

Hughes, H. Stuart. *Oswald Spengler: A Critical Estimate*. New York: Charles Scribner's Sons, 1952.

————. *History as Art and as Science*. New York: Harper Torchbooks, Harper & Row, 1964. See especially "History, the Humanities and Anthropological Change."

Kaufmann, Edgar J., Jr. "Memmo's Lodoli." *Art Bulletin* 46, no. 4 (December, 1964): 159–76.

Levin, Harry. *James Joyce: A Critical Introduction*. Norfolk, 1941.

Lifshitz, M. "Giambattista Vico." *Philosophy and Phenomenological Research* 8, no. 3 (1948): 391–414.

Löwith, Karl. *Meaning in History*. Chicago: The University of Chicago Press, 1949. See especially "Vico."

Manuel, Frank. *The Eighteenth Century Confronts the Gods*. Cambridge: Harvard University Press, 1959. See especially "Vico: The 'Giganti' and their Joves."

————. "In Defense of Philosophical History." *Antioch Review*, Fall, 1960: 331–43.

————. *The Prophets of Paris*. Cambridge: Harvard University Press, 1962. Also New York: Harper Torchbooks, Harper & Row, 1965.

————. *Shapes of Philosophical History.* Stanford: Stanford University Press, 1965.

Mazlich, Bruce. *The Riddle of History: The Great Speculators from Vico to Freud.* New York: Harper & Row, 1966. See especially "Vico."

Momigliano, Arnaldo. "Vico's 'Scienza Nuova': Roman 'Bestioni' and Roman 'Eroi.'" *History and Theory* 5, no. 1 (1966).

Neff, Emery. *The Poetry of History.* New York: Columbia University Press, 1947.

Noether, Emiliana P. *Seeds of Italian Nationalism, 1700–1815.* New York: Columbia University Press, 1951. Chapter II, pp. 48–62.

Rand, Calvin. "Two Meanings of Historicism in the Writings of Dilthey, Troeltsch and Meinecke." *Journal of the History of Ideas,* October, 1964: 503–18.

Randall, John Herman, Jr. *The Career of Philosophy.* 2 vols. New York: Columbia University Press, 1962, 1965. See I, 955–61.

Read, Herbert. *Form in Modern Poetry.* New York, 1933. Pp. 36–38.

————. *In Defense of Shelley and Other Essays.* London, 1936. Pp. 150–56.

————. *The Forms of Things Unknown.* New York: Horizon Press, 1960.

Robertson, J. C. *Studies in the Genesis of the Romantic Theory in the Eighteenth Century.* Cambridge: At the University Press, 1923.

Russell, Bertrand. *Wisdom of the West.* New York: Doubleday and Co., 1959. Pp. 206–9 and *passim.*

Said, Edward W. "Labyrinth of Incarnations: The Essays of Maurice Merleau-Ponty." *Kenyon Review* 29, no. 1 (January, 1967): 67.

Sewell, Elizabeth. *The Orphic Voice: Poetry and Natural History.* London: Routledge, and New Haven, Conn.: Yale University Press, 1960. Pp. 181–84 and *passim.*

Stark, Werner. *The Fundamental Forms of Social Thought.* London: Routledge & Kegan Paul, 1963, and New York: Fordham University Press, 1964. Pp. 8, 11, 12, 219–22.

Tagliacozzo, Giorgio. "Economic Vichism." *Quarterly Review of the Banca Nazionale del Lavoro* 85 (June, 1968): 95–119.

Thompson, John Hinsdale. "Finnegans Wake." In *Modern Poetry: American and British,* edited by Kimon Friar and Malcolm J. Brinnin. New York: Appleton-Century-Crofts, 1951, pp. 88–97.

Tindall, W. Y. *James Joyce.* New York: Charles Scribner's Sons, 1950.

————. *A Reader's Guide to Finnegans Wake.* New York: Farrar, Straus & Giroux, 1969.

Toulmin, Stephen, and Goodfield, June. *The Discovery of Time.* London: Hutchinson and Co., Ltd., 1965. See especially "Vico: The Mendel of History."

Ullmann, Stephen. "Semantic Universals." In *Universals of Language,* edited by Joseph H. Greenberg. Cambridge: The M.I.T. Press, 1963.

Vaughan, C. F. "G. B. Vico, An Eighteenth-Century Pioneer." *John Ryland's Library's Bulletin* (Manchester, England) 6 (1921): 266–88.

————. *Studies in the History of Political Philosophy Before and After Rousseau.* Manchester, 1925. I, 207–53.

Vittorini, D. "G. B. Vico and Reality: An Evaluation of the De Nostri Temporis Studiorum Ratione." *Modern Language Quarterly* 13 (1952): 90–98.

Wellek, René. Review of *The Autobiography of Giambattista Vico,* translated by Max H. Fisch and Thomas G. Bergin. *Philological Quarterly* 25, no. II (April, 1945).

White, Hayden V. "Vico, Giovanni Battista." In *International Encyclopedia of the Social Sciences.* New York: Macmillan and the Free Press, 1968. XVI, 313–16.

Whyte, Lancelot Law. *Essay on Atomism: From Democritus to 1960.* Middletown, Conn.: Wesleyan University Press, 1961. P. 53.

————. Essay on Boscovich's atomism. In *Roger Joseph Boscovich: Studies of his Life and Work on the 250th Anniversary of his Birth,* edited by Lancelot Law Whyte. London: George Allen & Unwin, Ltd., 1961.

————. *The Unconscious before Freud.* Garden City, N.Y.: Doubleday & Co., 1962.

Wilson, Edmund. *To the Finland Station.* Garden City, N.Y.: Doubleday & Co., 1940. See especially pp. 1–7, 62, 141, 193, 467.

Wittaker, Thomas. "Vico's New Science of Humanity." *Mind* 35 (1926). Reprinted in *Reasons and Other Essays,* Cambridge, 1934, pp. 133–89.

In making up the Index, the editors were forced to choose between a complete listing of every proper name and an adequate topical handling of the themes of the book. We opted for the latter, with the result that the listing of names has been selective. We trust, however, that the principal historical figures of Vichian studies are adequately indexed herein. Regarding the listing of references to Vico's major works, found under his name, we have cited passages which deal primarily with the history of the texts involved, not every mention of the various works, since they are, of course, mentioned repeatedly throughout.